THE
VOGUE
SEWING
BOOK

THE VOGUE SEWING BOOK

PUBLISHED BY
VOGUE PATTERNS
NEW YORK, NEW YORK

Library of Congress Catalog Card Number 73-78329

Revised Edition

Copyright © 1975 by

Butterick Publishing—Div. of American Can Company

161 Sixth Avenue, New York, N.Y. 10013

Printed in the U.S.A.
by the Butterick Plant, Altoona, Pa.

First Edition, September 1970
Second Edition: First Printing, April 1973
Third Edition: First Printing, January 1975
Second Printing, April 1975
Third Printing, May 1975
Fourth Printing, October 1975

Preface

The contemporary woman has learned to appreciate more than just the visual impression of fashion by turning her interests toward the technical aspect—sewing. Her thirst for sewing information has become insatiable, whether motivated by economy, the rapid decline in quality workmanship available in ready-to-wear, the desire to be creative and original, or simply for the sheer fun of it. What greater manner of self expression! The added dimension of sewing makes fashion not only an aesthetic pleasure, but a fulfilling experience to be enjoyed over and over again as well.

This book is dedicated to you, the woman who sews. No longer will you be content to be a mere by-stander, for now you can realize the enjoyment of complete involvement in what is a fascinating and interesting avocation. What pleasures you derive by being a beautiful, well-groomed, impeccably attired woman are enhanced a thousandfold by the knowledge and inward pride of having created the fashion yourself.

Your interest in sewing as an integral part of fashion made this book possible. Its goal is to communicate to you the technical expertise necessary to develop your sewing craftsmanship to the point of professionalism that you demand. The editorial approach throughout was designed to enlighten, not only by showing you how to do certain things but also by telling you why. It was meant to stimulate and lead you into an enjoyable learning experience.

With this larger scheme in mind, it will guide you through a comprehensive understanding and appreciation of fashion and how it relates to you. It will explain the Vogue Pattern products that enable you to achieve your goal; and, finally, it will introduce you to the techniques applicable to most every conceivable sewing situation. The techniques illustrated are by no means the only methods suitable. However, after careful testing and evaluating they are, in my opinion, those which will prove most versatile in their application to your many sewing projects. For ease in interpretation, the instructions were done from the perspective of you as a participant rather than an observer. And for those of you who are willing to tackle a more formidable task, such as tailoring, you will surely gain a special reward of self satisfaction.

The Editors

Acknowledgments

Adventurous home sewers have been confronted with the problems of working with modern fabrics—knits, furs, suedes, metallics, and new fashion trends—sewing and tailoring for men. Vogue Patterns has responded with answers and direction, by providing the latest sewing information for handling these new materials and techniques. Our findings are within—a challenge and an inspiration for the creative individual.

Elizabeth J. Musheno: *Editor, Revised Edition*

Tony Serino: *Art Director*

Barbara Trujillo: *Technical Editor*

Janet Lombardo: *Technical Illustrator*

Caroline Dill: *Copy Editor*, Marian Bartholomew: *Writer*

Alfred Raphael and Leopoldo A. Hinds: *Menswear Consultants*

Paul Milbauer: *Production*

Patricia Perry: *Editor, First Edition*

The creation of *The Vogue Sewing Book: First Edition* involved many talented people throughout our organization, and their efforts are greatly appreciated.

Patricia Perry, editor of the first edition, was instrumental in creating this sewing treasury. Her past experience in designer workrooms, her vast technical knowledge, and her understanding of the creative individual enabled her to tailor the contents of this book to the special needs of all serious home sewers. She was ably assisted by Janet DuBane, Betty Faden, Ellen Kochansky, Jeanne Johnson, and Sheila DiBona. Other staff members were Gisela Sachs, Susan Frye, Doreen Williams, and Grace Guerrera. Dorothy Martin, Elaine Poprosky and Lynne Perrella for technical and fashion illustration. Joe Molko and Helen Nemeth for technical reviews. Our own Fashion Information Center.

The use of products and materials from the following companies aided the editors in testing and developing new sewing techniques:

Pellon Apparel Research Center, Viking Husqvarna, The Singer Company, David Traum, Inc., Dritz-Oakville Division, Wm. E. Wright Company, J. Wiss and Sons Company, Unique Zipper Distributing Service, Elégance International, Inc.

Vogue Patterns

Contents

BOOK I

The
Fashion
Game

Fashion Sewing as an Art Form

Fashion sewing can be compared, in some ways, to the classic art of sculpture. The sculptor involves himself in his medium—manipulating clay or carving stone into a form. Sewing demands the same involvement with a medium—touching, appraising, and working with fabric that will be molded and shaped into a three-dimensional design.

The creative forces necessary to make flat, two-dimensional fabrics take on strong, structural three-dimensional shapes are no less important than those required to chip marble or mold clay. Just as a sculptor expresses his dynamic ideas with plaster, bronze, or stone, the seamstress uses fabric to manifest her ideas about fashion.

Inspiration, as both artists know, comes only after attaining a good working knowledge of one's craft, and after a period of deliberation on the specific project. The end result must be firmly in mind before you begin. A sculptor wouldn't tap idly on a piece of marble with his chisel until inspiration came to him, and it makes no more sense for you to unwrap a length of fabric with your scissors poised until you've considered the relationship between the style and the fabric.

First, the sculptor carefully selects his basic material; it must be just right for his planned creation. No less consideration should be given to the selection of fabric. The silhouette you desire, the mood to be created, the type of body being covered—all are important to the proper fabric selection.

If ten seamstresses were given the same fabric and pattern, probably none of the finished garments would be exactly identical. With an eye to her own pluses and minuses, each would select, adapt, and embellish. The result would be what looks best on her. *A person who sews is a creative artist because she individualizes fashion to her own special preferences and requirements.*

The same principles that make a sculpture visually pleasing apply as well to clothing for the human body. A fashionable woman is aware that she is a three-dimensional form that can be seen from all angles. She must create a pleasing total visual impact by discriminating among colors, textures, and lines to discover the combination that is best suited to her own individual features. She is more than just a seamstress—she is an artisan, too. She draws upon her talents as artist, decorator, and designer to make unique creations which far surpass average ready-to-wear standards. She has, in other words, a good fashion sense.

Like creativity, good fashion sense is not limited only to designers and editors, but is a quality most women have in some degree or another. If you possess a strong sense of professionalism; if fine workmanship, good lines, and quality impress you; if you find shopping for patterns, fabrics, and trims irresistible; if the world of fashion intrigues and excites you; if you have good personal taste—then you are already on your way to attaining good fashion sense.

One of those qualities, personal taste, is especially important. It is, most broadly, the ability to relate fashion to yourself—your needs, figure, and preferences. Basic to that ability is being able to recognize which clothes and accessories will best accentuate natural good features. Any woman who truly cares about her appearance is very much aware of her figure's limitations, as well as those of her coloring. She analyzes her feelings about clothes—why she never wears pink and loves red; why she feels comfortable in Empire styles and never in a lowered waistline. She forces herself to be open to change, simply for the sake of improving the way she looks and feels.

Just as a sculpture communicates a certain mood or message, a woman's clothes convey much about her. What's your fashion image? Do you picture yourself as a certain type? If not, what image would you like to convey: elegant sophisticate, sweet romantic, perky gamin, tailored classicist, avant garde dazzler? Since there is more than one side to every woman, your wardrobe will undoubtedly reflect the many facets of your personality, with all its feelings and moods. But a woman with strong fashion sense and personal taste relates her various looks to form a unified image, which conveys the confident air of a woman who knows who she is and enjoys being herself. How does one achieve this? Pick up ideas from your pattern catalogue, magazines, advertising, window displays, and other well-dressed women. Even though styles and colors shift seasonally, an awareness of your personal fashion identity will enable you to discriminately choose and select among them to organize your particular look.

The Fundamentals of Your Art

Every artist has had to absorb and apply the basic principles of design to achieve his desired artistic effect. You should do the same; once firmly grounded in them, you may confidently choose to follow them with a strict interpretation or with artistic license to achieve your exact fashion effect.

- ☐ HARMONY is achieved when all elements are working together in a pleasing manner. It refers to elements of likeness, but not necessarily sameness; the key here is appropriateness and relativity.
- ☐ PROPORTION requires all parts to be related to one another in size, length, and bulk.
- ☐ BALANCE is achieved by maintaining equal amounts of interest in either direction from the natural center of interest.
- ☐ RHYTHM is created by the eye moving smoothly and easily, connecting points of interest without jerking from point to point.
- ☐ EMPHASIS means attracting the eye to one feature and subordinating all others.

Every fashion idea you have should be backed not only with an understanding of these principles, but also of the artistic components of color, texture, print, proportion, and balance. Just as the sculptor must understand the qualities of his raw material, whether it be rock, clay, or metal, you must understand the qualities of your fabric—color, print, and texture. Then you transform it into a design with the same components the sculptor uses to transform his material into a sculpture—line, proportion, and balance. Our aim in the next few pages is to provide guidelines in hopes that you'll find inspiration there to create a prettier, newer, and more fashionable you.

Color

What is the first thing noticed about a garment? Invariably the answer is its color. We talk about "the woman in the blue dress" or "my brown suit"; only a designer would refer to "the slim low-waisted dress with inverted pleats and bateau neckline." This fact alone makes color quite worthy of consideration and a power to be placed at your disposal. Thus a fashion-conscious woman must be aware of the language and principles of color, immersing herself in all the thrilling effects that color can produce. Color know-how combined with a comprehension of her own needs and requirements can make the difference between being "sensational" or just "well-dressed."

Elements of Color

This is the technical language commonly used to describe color; learn it well, referring to the diagram and the color wheel following page 16.

HUE, a term often used interchangeably with color, is the quality or characteristic by which we distinguish one color from another. The *primary* hues—red, yellow, and blue—are the basic building blocks of color from which all others are blended. The *secondary* hues, produced by mixing two primaries, are orange, green, and violet (purple). The *tertiary* hues (often called intermediates) stem from various combinations of the basic six; they are the "double-name" colors, such as yellow-green and blue-violet.

VALUE is the lightness or darkness of a color. Hues with white added are called *tints* and are higher in value than the original colors. To produce lower values, black is added to hues to create *shades.* Hues differ in their inherent value as well; yellow, for example, is higher in value than blue.

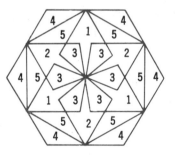

1—PRIMARIES
2—SECONDARIES
3—TERTIARIES
4—TINTS
5—SHADES

INTENSITY refers to the brightness or dullness of color. Again, certain hues have a higher intensity than others—orange is higher than violet, for example. *Tones* are hues with their complementary color or gray added, which reduces their intensity.

COLOR SCHEMES are many in number, but three of them are most common. A *monochromatic* color scheme uses various values and intensities of one color, or one color with black and white. These are sure and easy schemes to achieve, but the danger of monotony lurks if the variations are too similar. Use both ends of the spectrum to add contrast, such as beige to chocolate brown. An *analogous* color scheme utilizes hues which are closely related on the color wheel, or in other words, that contain similar components, such as blue, blue-green, and green. These are the real "mood-makers" and are often the most pleasing and restful combinations. A *complementary* color scheme is one which involves direct opposites on the color wheel, such as red and green or blue and orange. These are exceedingly strong, bold combinations. To truly enhance each other, judgment must be used with variations in value and intensity, as complementaries used in combinations make each other look stronger. Remember that colors should never be seen as isolated entities, but in relation to each other.

Now, armed with an understanding of the basic concepts of color, turn your attention to what color can do for you. As every artist and advertising expert knows, color has profound psychological effects on all of us, as evidenced by such expressions as "seeing red," "green with envy," "black mood," "yellow streak," and "feeling blue." Some colors are cheering, compelling, vivacious, frivolous, active, and just plain fun, while others are restful, serene, relaxed, subtle, and dignified. Some lift the spirits, others subdue them; they can be soft and fresh or brassy and bold. It is not merely by chance, therefore, that we may reach into the closet for our brightest dress on a rainy day, or slip into a pastel gown to relax after a hectic day.

But color can do far more for you than reflect or influence your multitude of moods and images. The skillful use of color can help present you at your loveliest. Too often women are led merely by whim, pure preference, or simple prejudice in their color selection, and not enough by what looks best on them. Always take your personal coloring into consideration. Before you buy any fabric, hold it up to your face and take a long, thoughtful look into the mirror. How does it relate to the color of your hair, eyes, and complexion? (Remember that sometimes a different shade of lipstick or a touch of rouge will make a so-so or even unacceptable color smashing. Don't, however, use this as an excuse to buy a color that clashes outright with your natural coloring.) And don't mistakenly think that just because that jade green dress looks so good on you, kelly green will be just as becoming; often even a slight variation in value or intensity can make all the difference in the world. Because of this fact, many of the oft-quoted dictums about wearing colors in the final analysis mean only that certain shades of some colors are not flattering to persons of a particular coloring. These rules—sallow skins should avoid yellow, redheads look awful in pink, etc.—should be taken as warnings, but the vast number of variations in colors and personal coloring belie a down-the-line interpretation. Always let your eye—or the helpful eye of a reliable friend—be the final judge.

Play tricks with color by discovering the optical illusions they can create. They can create impressions of size; cool colors of blue, green, and violet make the figure appear smaller, warm colors of red, yellow, and orange increase the apparent size of the figure. The degree of brightness or dullness can also affect size appearance—brighter colors make you look larger, duller colors make you look smaller. Boldly contrasting colors will create an impression of greater size; a more subtle color scheme will appear more compact. Another thing to note is that the eye will be attracted first to the brightest of contrasting colors; use this principle to draw your viewer's eye to or from particular areas.

Accessories can be the answer to many of your color quandaries. Use a gaily colored scarf or belt to add new spark to a dull dress, or dark shoes and bag to bring a boldly colored dress a bit closer to earth. If your figure demands subtle coloring, don't say goodbye to bright colors forever—use them in a scarf, bracelets, or necklace. Let a bright sash riding on the hipline of your dress distract from bulk above the waist, or use a bright necklace to coax the eye away from excess width through the hipline. And that dress—we all have one—that you bought because you loved it even though it does awful things to your coloring can be put back on a wear-often basis by adding a shawl or scarf in a better color next to your face.

The manipulation of color is not only one of the most artistic elements of fashion sewing but one of the most exciting. Experiment with it—contrast, complement, combine, or go solid. Don't be afraid of new colors or let yourself be boxed into a one-color wardrobe. Go on a creative fling to create a more colorful you.

Print

From plaids to paisleys, stripes to florals, dots to borders, prints are fashion's fun, and often its beauty as well. To create a truly harmonious effect, however, they must be carefully related to all the other design elements of your garment.

Prints are first and foremost combinations of colors, and the same rules apply to them as to solids. Vividly contrasting colors or bright shades will appear larger than subtle combinations or calmer shades. Prints can give you an advantage you may miss with solids; if you love a color which is unflattering on you, you may be able to wear it combined in a print with a more suitable color. Most prints will have a dominant color, and that is the one to consider in relation to your coloring; it will usually be either the brightest shade or the one that occupies the largest area (such as the background). Another thing to keep in mind is that colors used in combination may affect each other's apparent hue—red and blue used together, for example, may appear purple.

Also consider garment lines when selecting a print. While a solid color may require intricate lines for interest, they may be overwhelmed or appear cluttered in a print. Be aware that plaids, stripes, and many other prints have lines of their own, and make sure they are flattering to your build. Also relate the direction and shape of the various lines; a curved bodice seam would only work against an angular print and be lost.

Lastly and most importantly, relate the print to your own figure. A print that is greatly out of scale with the wearer and the garment will emphasize the contrast, making their size only more obvious. Use the placement of your print to attract or distract attention to your pluses and minuses. A border print placed at the hemline will distract from the bodice or hips and draw attention to your legs. A dominant plaid or stripe will attract the eye, so place it only at attractive locations. And placing a dominant large-scale motif at the bust or derrière is definitely to be avoided.

Texture

The texture of your fabric is created by the characteristics of its fiber (wool, silk, etc.) and the manner of its construction (knitted, woven, etc.). All too often overlooked or taken for granted, it can be a special asset in the business of illusion-making.

The object is to create fluid eye movements in which the eye stops to rest at attractive, predetermined points of emphasis. Stiff textures hang straight without draping and thus will slide the eye smoothly up and down the lines of a sleek silhouette. One figure problem can be concealed this way, but over-all roundness cannot. On the other hand, clingy fabrics rendered in straight or very simple designs do just one thing—reveal. If your figure is less-than-perfect, use them only in softly draped styles. And, of course, gauzy transparency should never reveal an unattractive body area.

Textural effects also contribute to an impression of size. Rough, thick textures always seem more bulky than they really are. If you adore chunky tweeds but wish to avoid their bulk, use them just at a slender section of your body, perhaps in a vest or skirt. Shiny, lustrous fabrics reflect more light and thus make you appear larger; just the opposite is true of rougher, duller textures. In other words, velvet, which absorbs light, may be a better choice in an evening dress than glittering sequins for a heavier woman.

Color is...

Texture & Weave

Prints

Knits

Tweed & Plaid

Dots & Stripes

Glitter & Lace

Color Scheming

The primaries . . . red, yellow, and blue . . . the basic building blocks from which all colors come. Use them in combination to make a bright, bold color statement.

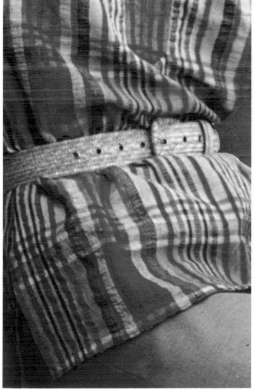

Opposites attract . . . and complementary color schemes are exceedingly strong, bold combinations . . . sure show-stoppers that enhance each other and you.

Analogous schemes have a
color in common . . . violet,
blue-violet and blue . . . or
orange, red-orange and red.
Closely related color
clusters are real mood-makers.

The quick change artistry of value
and intensity make monochromatic
color schemes sure and easy ways
to let your best color be your
best asset.

Blues

The icy cool blues—
azure, indigo, October-
sky blue—imperturbable
colors with a marvelous
soothing influence . . .
Delicate pastel blues—
periwinkle, robin's
egg, forget-me-not—
from barely-there pales
through the soft,
ceramic Delft blue
and copen . . . Rich royal
may be what is meant by
"true blue". . . Mesmer-
izing—a blue that
matches your eyes . . .
Vibrant, assertive
blues—peacock and
sapphire steal the spot-
light nicely for those
with less-than-lively
coloring . . . Perennial
neutral, navy—spruce
and snappy as the click
of an officer's heels . . .
Match blues in daylight—
they're easily affected
by artificial lights . . .

top to bottom:
printed cotton sateen
wool crepe
pleated polyester-cotton voile
paisley cotton broadcloth
cotton velvet
diamond pattern wool twill
petit-point double-knit
acrylic twill
silk and wool lamé
polyester herringbone knit

Reds

The cheery spirit-lifters—cerise, fire-engine, lacquer red—indispensable for perking up a gray day . . . Moody, rich wine reds—crimson, burgundy, Persian, maroon . . . Clear ruby reds—party dazzlers, and sheer drama for brunettes . . . Luscious berry tones—strawberry, currant, pomegranate . . . Just a dash of red's a lively note with neutrals—a perennial accessory favorite. . .Warm reds just naturally express an extrovert, but they do marvelous things to bring out the hidden glow of a shy type, too . . .

top to bottom:
polyester double-knit
cotton velvet
printed cotton knit
double woven wool houndstooth
wool gabardine
wool and suede novelty weave
printed wool challis
wool felt
polyester novelty knit
acrylic double-knit

Purples

The dusty tapestry
purples—misty mauve,
soft lilac, heliotrope—
dewy-eyed romantics with
a grandmother's parlor
air...The natural aris-
tocrat—Tyrian purple,
granted only to royalty
and high priests for
centuries. The most
expensive color in the
world—its formula was
a state secret ... Plum,
aubergine, the deep
black-purples—in their
element in velvet, by
candlelight ... Another
mood is purple in the
soul-color brights—
jaunty magenta, parma
violet—a knockout,
if you're careful
not to let the color
wear you!...

top to bottom:
silk and worsted
knit nylon ciré
wool tweed
silk surah
silk ribbed cloqué
plaid wool gabardine
wool bouclé
wool melton
polka-dot silk surah
herringbone pressed velvet

Oranges

High-spirited and happy—
the oranges abound with
personality... Soft yellow
oranges echo Spring
with gorgeous fruity
tints—apricot, tangerine,
peach, mango ... Orange
gives zesty flavor to the
red range—bittersweet,
flamingo, salmon, coral—
easier with auburn hair
than the true reds ...
Flaming, devil-may-care
brights—poppy, pumpkin,
marigold—these bold
strokes of sunshine
bring summer to the
gloomy seasons ... Orange
and brown are affectionate
cousins—they provide
each other with striking
accessories... Burnt orange,
rust, terra-cotta—lower
key colors that swing
into fall with vigor,
and play beautiful har-
mony with the season ...

top to bottom:
wool crepe
gingham check wool gabardine
petit-point double knit
silk cloqué
laminated wool jersey
cotton piqué
tucked cotton
shadow plaid wool fleece
wool tweed
synthetic brocade
rayon acetate moss crepe

Yellows

Happy memories of sunny
kitchens and wandering
among the buttercups;
yellow can't help feeling
warm and comfortable . . .
The vibrant ones—taxi-
cab yellow, sunflower,
canary, lemon—demand
attention, and earn it
in high style . . . Softer
yellows—just a little
to the butter side of
cream . . . Rich saffron
glows with a fascinating
Eastern savor . . . A touch
of the brown-green spec-
trum adds excitement to
amber, mustard, and
bronze . . . Beware of
the mustard shades if
your complexion tends
toward sallow—they're
usually best on bru-
nettes . . . The honey
tones are kinder to
fair coloring . . .

top to bottom:
synthetic moss crepe
slubbed fibranne
cut velvet on satin
basket weave wool
double woven wool crepe
silk gabardine
acetate shantung
silk broadcloth
wool fleece
lattice weave wool tweed

Greens

Capture the image of budding Spring in yellow greens—lime, apple—vibrant accents for yellow and brown tones . . . Sail off into the blue-greens— cool, limpid, reminiscent of the sea . . . Smashing on redheads—the clear kelly and emerald greens, or the elegant pastel of the dusty sage and pale celery greens . . . Look to the brown-greens—khaki, olive, loden—for an imaginative neutral that's perfect for the fair types . . . Use greens to bring a cool forest glen into a sunny room . . .

top to bottom:
acetate rayon crepe
knitted cotton terrycloth
wool houndstooth check
satin brocade
synthetic brocade
printed cotton sateen
lattice-weave wool
wool melton
polished cotton
petit-point wool

Neutrals

These are the indis-
pensable subtleties of
fashion, and the founda-
tion of a handsome
wardrobe . . . Don't stop at
charcoal and navy—
look for neutrals in the
down-beat tones of any
color you like . . . Use
them not just as rest
space between brights,
but for their own
character. . .Try combining
camel and pewter, or
smoky brown and platinum
for understated chic . . .
Never trust your memory
to match a beige—there
are hundreds! . . . Warm and
cool ones, gray, green,
or pink ones . . . Play the
many variations against
each other and in harmony
with your own coloring—
use them like makeup to
give zip to skin tones . . .
Make them work for you.
Let the knowing use of
neutrals write your
fashion story . . .

top to bottom:
rayon tissue faille
camel's hair
covert
wool linen
wool and synthetic brocade
striped wool flannel
cotton bengaline
wool tweed
natural slubbed linen
petit point gabardine

Browns

Teak, mahogany, chestnut, hickory—the mellow wood tones with a strong, sporty character that fashion loves . . . Deep, chocolate brown—a stunning way to highlight blondeness, and an elegant accessory tale to tell with oranges or greens. . .Buttery caramel— the neutral made for redheads . . .Tortoiseshell, cinnamon, auburn— the rich orange-browns— grand for lifting tired complexions . . . Make brown an evening color— nothing sets off gold jewelry to greater advantage, and it moves with aplomb wherever the "little black dress" is at home . . .

top to bottom:
wide wale corduroy
crushed patent vinyl
baby houndstooth check
cut velvet on silk chiffon
wool tweed
suede
checked wool
camel's hair
wool gabardine
silk foulard

Blacks

Eternal sophisticate—
reserved, refined,
serene, and just a
little sexy . . . Watch it
sparking prints and
tweeds to life . . . Don't
be without that savvy
little black "nothing
dress" that does every-
thing with perfect
composure . . . Dare yourself to test the
legendary effect of
lavish black lace . . .
Or play black against
black in several
textures—wool bouclé
with leather with silk . . .
The mysterious almost-
blacks—infused
with a cast of blue,
or brown, or green—
as definitive as black-
black, but somehow
softer . . . Be emphatic
with makeup, since lots
of black can be hard
on a pale face . . .

top to bottom:
point d'esprit
cut velvet on silk chiffon
pin dot silk surah
double woven cotton
all-over sequinned faille
rayon velvet
wool broadcloth
cut velvet on silk satin
ruffle-tucked taffeta
glen plaid bonded wool
sheared lamb cloth

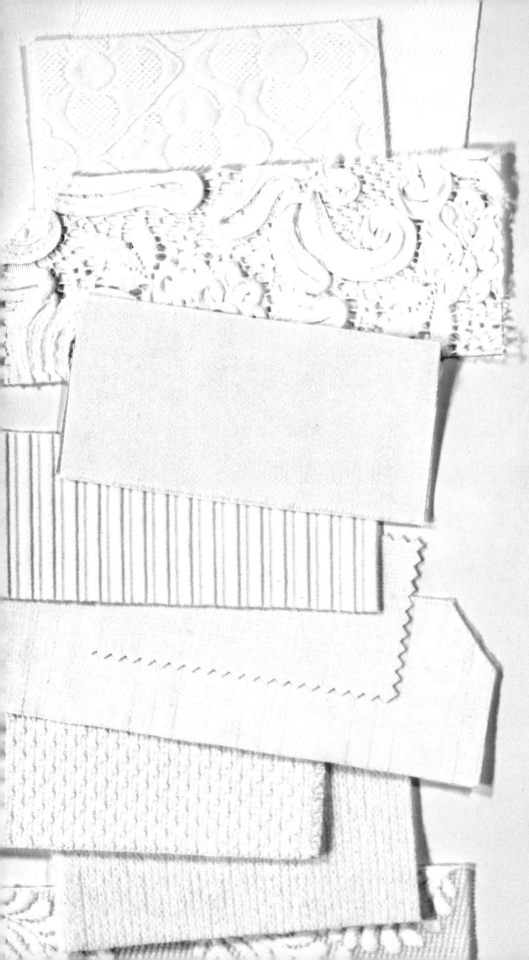

Whites

The many moods of white. Antique whites— ivory, cream—have a well-bred Victorian elegance . . . Innocent chalk-white's an old favorite—knock-them- over-with-a-feather flattery for a summer tan . . . But don't limit white to a season— warm whites, with a hint of yellow or pink, can be the best thing that's happened to winter . . . The easy- care fabrics give it a new practical dimen- sion . . . Bring out the true personality of a neutral shade with the immaculate lady-look of white accessories . . .

top to bottom:
cotton twill
cotton jacquard
milan lace
rayon crepe
ribbed polyester knit
silk gauze
wool plaid damask
petit point wool
wool sweater knit
embroidered wool

Line

Line, as it applies to fashion, is often used synonymously with style. Every design is a carefully conceived structure of lines and shapes. The final garment will present three major sets of lines to the viewer's eye: body lines, silhouette lines, and detail lines. The ability to relate them to one another and to you in a pleasing and flattering manner will require, therefore, a basic understanding of the visual element of line. Set out to discover what line can do for you. Realize that lines influence eye movements, establish shape, and form moods, just as color can. Direction and placement of line will be your main concern.

The first thing you should realize about line is that our eyes are conditioned to move naturally in the direction we read—left to right, top to bottom. While there is a certain "pull" between the two directions, if given two equal intersecting lines, the eye will follow the horizontal more readily than the vertical. This leads us to another important concept—lines rarely are equal, as there are several factors which tend to make certain lines dominant. If a line is longer, wider, brighter, or more often repeated than another, it will be more dominant. A final point to keep in mind is that the eye follows a straight line directly and rapidly, making it the most severe and architectural line, while the eye moves more slowly along a curved line, making it a softer, relaxed line often used as a transitional to lead gracefully from one point to another.

Thus lines often play tricks with our eyes and create illusions, and you want all those illusions to work for and not against you. Your primary target: to be a master of illusion and camouflage by knowing the rules of the fashion game. First, be your own best inspiration by taking a realistic look at yourself. What has nature given you that is worth emphasizing or concealing? Then follow the suggestions below to put line to work to make a more appealing you. After all, beauty is in the eye of the beholder and the clever use of line can subtly coax his eye just where you want it.

Never forget the relationship of your design to your raw material. Remember that fabric patterns often have line and direction of their own. For example, horizontal stripes will be dominant even if the dress is vertically seamed, and even a less obviously directional fabric could possibly distract from your intentions. And when buying a plaid, check first to see if the plaid lines are dominant in a particular direction.

Verticals

Choose the strong classical effect of a vertical line to appear taller and thinner by leading the eye in an up and down direction. Single verticals give the strongest impression of height; when they are repeated at even intervals across the garment, the illusion of length is blunted because our eyes tend to move sideways from line to line as well. A straight or long unbroken silhouette also creates a vertical impression (1).

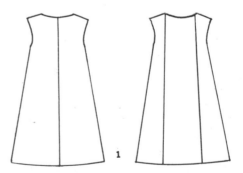

Horizontals

It is common knowledge that horizontal lines emphasize width, especially when two are used together. Placing a single horizontal line above or below the median of the body can, however, create an illusion of length throughout the longer area. Since horizontals are the strongest lines, avoid placing them at unflattering locations on the body. You can distract from a horizontal by using an opposing vertical, by placing it at other than the center, or by modifying it in the form of a diagonal or curve (2).

Diagonals

The modifying effect of diagonals depends primarily upon the angle and length of the line. As shown, the shorter diagonal line will lead the eye from side to side, giving an impression of width, while the longer line leads the eye equally downward and sideways for a longer, narrower look. And remember that the line should always move in the same direction as our eyes, from left to right, for the most pleasing effect. Diagonals possess both the discipline of straight lines and the softness of curves (3).

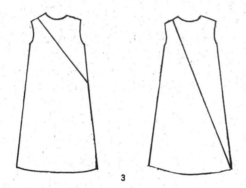

Curves

Whether they are created by shaped seaming or edges or soft draping, curved lines perform the same function of illusion as straight lines but in a less obvious manner. Curved lines also emphasize the curves of the feminine form by repetition, making them more defined. Many times a line which would be unflattering if straight can be nicely worn if modified by a curve. A curved bodice seam or front closing will be softer visually than a horizontal or vertical (4).

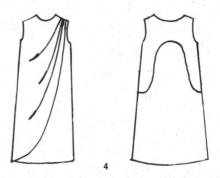

These are the basic "rules" for using line, but don't be misled into thinking they are necessarily hard and fast. The relationship of several lines is invariably greater than the direction of one of them. You need not do without unflattering lines entirely; simply do not use them as *dominant* lines. And don't forget that any woman, regardless of her figure or the direction of the line, should always be sure that the garment lines do not draw attention to an unattractive portion of her body; a horizontal across too-large hips will not look any better on a tall woman than on a short one.

Proportion and Balance

Have you ever changed the hem on the skirt of a suit, and suddenly the jacket and skirt no longer seemed to go together quite the way they did before? Or seen a woman in a top and skirt which seemed to coordinate in almost every visible way but somehow didn't look quite right together? Perhaps you've stood before a mirror wondering why that style which looked so great on your best friend looks so odd on you. All of these problems may very likely be caused by an error in proportion and balance. The skillful use of the color, print, and texture of your fabric and the lines of your garment will all be for naught unless they are artfully related by these two elements. That beautifully coordinated, "well put together" look that accompanies a truly well-dressed woman is in large part due to an eye well-trained in the subtleties of proportion and balance.

Proportion

This applies to the space relationships within a design, and involves relating such measurements as size and bulk. The most visually pleasing division of an area is one that creates the two aesthetic qualities of unity and variety—in other words, one that creates areas that are similar but not so alike as to be dull. Areas of identical size or exact divisions of space like halves, fourths, or thirds used together, while not displeasing, are often less interesting than divisions which are just far enough away from basic dimensions that the eye does not catch them immediately. Thus the most pleasing relationships, in mathematical terms, are two to three, three to five, five to eight, and so on, rather than two to two, two to four, two to six, etc. *Scale* is a term which also refers to size relationships; similar sizes are in scale with each other, widely disparate sizes are not and are visually jarring (1).

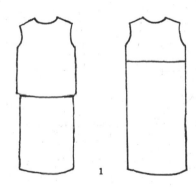

1

2

Balance

A design is balanced when an equal amount of interest is maintained in either direction from the natural center of interest. There are two kinds of balance: formal and informal. Formal balance is achieved when two halves of a design are exactly the same. If two halves are visually balanced but are not identical, it is called informal or asymmetrical balance. This is accomplished by shifting the center of interest with emphasis. *Emphasis* attracts the eye to one feature or area and subordinates the others (2).

Don't be misled into thinking that all that is involved in creating a perfectly proportioned and balanced fashion look is counting the number of buttons on each side of a jacket or measuring the length of a bodice and skirt. As important as it is to relate the various parts or areas of your garment to one another, several other elements need to be considered in order to establish a total, "put together" look.

Of course, the most important thing is to relate everything to you. Don't forget that you have proportions of your own as well, and thus a garment which is beautifully balanced and proportioned on the hanger may not be once you try it on. If you are large-busted but have small hips, the bodice is already heavier visually than the skirt, and you may need to make the skirt longer, fuller, bolder, or more intricate to balance the impression of weight. Conversely, ruffles or a bold print in the bodice may help distract from the additional width of large hips in a skirt. If you are very long-legged, an Empire style will simply accentuate the lack of natural proportion, in the same way that it will distract from it if you are short-legged. And don't forget to relate the size of a print or fabric pattern to your body proportions as well. Be sure that it is always in scale with both your build and garment dimensions, as a too-large or too-small design will only emphasize your size by contrast.

As has been implied, other design elements besides size and regularity can contribute or distract from a pleasing sense of relativity. You can shift emphasis and give an illusion of weight or size by using a print in opposition to a solid, intricacy to simplicity, a bright color to a duller one, a heavily textured fabric to a flat fabric, a shiny finish to a dull one. For example, a print skirt may help to balance a solid blouse for a top-heavy woman, but could overwhelm the blouse for a large-hipped woman. Even a woman with ideal measurements may need intricate seaming, long full sleeves, a shiny fabric, or a bright scarf on the solid blouse if the print skirt is very bright or very full; on the other hand, if the print is quite conservative, she may need a simpler or quieter blouse to balance it properly. In other words, each design element does not work by itself but interacts and relates to the others to create the whole.

And don't forget accessories. How many times have you seen a woman with a look beautifully and creatively planned, except for a handbag that is too small or shoes that are too heavy-looking? The whole effect is spoiled because her sense of scale and relativity is off. Accessories are meant to complement, not distract.

But, of course, all the theories and warnings in the world won't do you any good until you train your eye to perceive what is perfect balance and proportion and what isn't. How can you gain this type of artistic sensitivity? By learning to look, honestly and objectively. Analyze the composition of various fashion approaches you see in magazines, illustrations, store windows, and on women you see on the street. But most importantly, *look at yourself.* Learn to "practice" in front of a mirror. Try different combinations, lengths, and accessories, all the time asking yourself questions and answering them objectively. Are your accessories too large or small, delicate or massive, bright or dull? Are your lengths, colors, details, widths, and textures related? Are the design of your fabric and the lines in your garment in proportion to your size and build? Be as honest as possible; if in doubt, ask someone whose judgment you respect. When you have analyzed your present wardrobe, continue to do so with every new outfit you make. It is not an indication of vanity, but just of a desire to always look your very best. After awhile, putting together a well-balanced and proportioned look will seem as second nature as straightening a crooked picture on a wall.

Your Figure Analysis

On the previous pages we have discussed the basics of artistic theory. As you know, these elements take a very active part in the over-all visual impact of clothing. The next step is to learn how to use them in relation to the individual needs of your figure. To help you learn more about your figure, we, as a pattern company, have done extensive surveys of the possible figure variations which may occur. The results of these studies indicate that *height* is the single most important factor when trying to camouflage a figure problem or trying to emphasize a particularly positive feature.

Automatically, three basic height divisions come to mind: short, average, and tall. But we believe there are really only two true groupings—*Short* and *Tall*. Even though a woman's height in inches may seem to make her average, this designation is misleading. Actually, average is a statistic, not necessarily the ideal. Due to their bone structure, build, and individual features, most women appear to be either short or tall. Described on the following pages are the important principles which the short woman, 5'4" and under, and the tall woman, 5'7" and over, should follow when selecting garments. If you fall somewhere in between, study yourself to determine the category into which your bone structure places you and the impression of height you wish to convey—delightfully small or gracefully tall. You will find that once you have established yourself as either one or the other you will have a fresh approach toward the clothes that are right for you.

Short

Don't consider being short a figure problem. Your attitude toward yourself is crucial; you must consider your height an advantage and boldly proceed with that very important outlook. Of course, there are some practical tips to follow before you can fool the observer into thinking that you are actually more petite or slimmer or perhaps taller than you really are. Above all, dress to your own scale. At this point, if you have not done so already, read Proportion and Balance, on pages 19 and 20, as small women should be particularly concerned with these principles. For example, a short woman, especially if she is not model-slim, will do well to avoid very large prints; they will be greatly out of scale with her build and the size of her garment, making her seem even shorter and wider. You should concentrate on an uncluttered appearance with everything in proportion to your height. Begin by avoiding the unnecessary bulk of billowing skirts or very heavy fabrics. Short, fitted jackets, gently flared silhouettes, and delicate detailing are your best choices. The scale of accessories should be appropriate as well. They can help pull an outfit together into a neat, fashionable picture or completely destroy all your devoted efforts. Don't let yourself look overwhelmed by massive jewelry or overpowered by a tremendous handbag.

Line, in both fabric and garment design, will be one of your most valuable tools. If you want to add inches to your height, no matter what your weight, depend upon the illusions vertical lines will provide. One-piece dresses with shoulder to hemline seaming will give the strongest, most immediate impression of height. Lengthening details such as long sleeves, V-necklines, pleats, or raised or lowered waistlines will all tend to heighten your appearance. Stay away from anything which may cut your figure by interrupting the up and down movement of the eye, such as wide belts, tight waists, very short skirts or repeated horizontal construction.

Should you not be as slim as you would like, a little extra thought is required. On the whole, vertical lines are perfect slenderizers, but the appropriate ones for you should be chosen with discretion. Avoid gathers or pleats unless they are stitched down to the hip. Wear simple lines. Use a single vertical line or the repeated vertical seaming of a princess silhouette to whittle away the inches while adding to your height.

Color should be a very influential factor when dressing. In general, one color outfits or monochromatic costumes will contribute to elongating your appearance. Color coordinated accessories, such as belts or shoes, can be most helpful to your illusion. Warm colors and bright colors will tend to increase your stature visibly. Subtle colors may seem to diminish your size, but be sure they do so in a beguiling feminine fashion rather then making you blend unnoticed into the background.

If you are slim, your color range is almost unlimited, although you will find that solid colors, neat textures, and small prints are best for your body build. The same is true for the slightly heavy woman, but the use of vivid colors or shiny fabrics should be restricted to well-placed splashes for accent.

Tall

If you are tall, you have an immediate fashion edge. You are the fortunate woman who can carry the exotic prints or dramatic designs which can only be draped over a taller frame. Even though you have this head start, you must be as concerned with proportion and balance as short women. You will need to make an effort to wear clothes that are right for your size. Very tiny prints on a tall, large woman will emphasize the contrast between their delicacy and the size of the woman wearing them. You should take advantage of your size; select colorful prints, nubby fabrics, and bold stripes. Balance your height with horizontal divisions to present an impression of equality to the observer's eye. Wide belts, medium-long jackets, and crosswise stripes will contribute toward your goal of optical equilibrium.

Accessories should also warrant your concern when trying to maintain proper proportion and balance. Work with your height and lean toward large-ish jewelry and handbags, and do indulge in some of the more daring fashion accents.

Line, in both garment and fabric design, should be consistently utilized to your advantage. Should you have a full figure, lean toward easy fitting, unfussy silhouettes, and curved or diagonal vertical lines. Gently lowered necklines with ties or collars will emphasize a pretty face while balancing a heavier figure. Orderly prints will be better looking than splashy plaids or repeated horizontal stripes. If you are extremely tall and you wish to appear shorter, cut your height dramatically with wide colorful cummerbunds, crosswise yokes and other horizontal construction lines. Of course, if you are tall and willowy, the world of fashion is open to you. Be feminine with frills to fill out your curves or be dramatic with yards of drapey, clinging fabric in unusual patterns. Appreciate your capacity to follow the whims of fashion or to branch out on your own.

Color can also be cleverly used to your advantage. Remember that cool colors as well as the duller hues make the figure appear smaller. Make your color selections according to your weight and width. As always, to appear more slender, wear medium to dark color values in your solids and soft shades for prints, plaids, and textures. To add bulk and roundness to the slim figure, select bright colors with shiny or chunky textures. Contrasting separates are always recommended for the tall gal. They will cut your height no matter what your girth and successfully balance your appearance. The degree of contrast and the division of the areas will influence the final effect. A note of caution before you get carried away with your use of color: make a conscientious effort to keep your total silhouette in mind and avoid a busy look.

A Personal Interpretation

Described above are the basic concepts related to height, but your individual physical characteristics also deserve special consideration. Any figure extremes must be dealt with first. Bosom size, width of hips, length of waist, etc., are all prime problem areas for many women, and the solution for these problems is closely related to height. Harmony and emphasis now come into play. Place a ruffled jabot on a blouse to fill out a shallow bodice or to distract the eye from width below the waist. Well placed lines in the form of trim or accessories can draw the viewer's attention away from negative features and to figure pluses. For example, rows of beading at the hemline will help you flaunt well shaped legs. Camouflage can also be accomplished with the carefully applied use of color, print, or texture. Should you have very slender hips, increase their width with a heavy tweed skirt. This treatment will make the areas of your body above and below your waist visually equal and immediately prevent an unbalanced impression.

Frequently, the tides of fashion change so rapidly that it is difficult to discover the styles that are right for your figure. To tell you what is best for your body build, Vogue Patterns has prepared a visual dictionary illustrating the eighty-two fundamental components that comprise most garment designs, accompanied by a chart which covers these design components and fourteen of the most familiar figure variations. Turn to the following pages to see the most important elements of fashion. Use them as a handy reference when selecting patterns, reading pattern descriptions, or planning a new wardrobe. The entire chart is divided into Short and Tall sections to maintain proper scale. On the left hand pages, you will find the figure variations in a vertical column. Across the very top of the pages, all the components or Fashion Templates are listed. Working from the left, slide your finger across a figure problem line related to you to discover what skirts, pants, silhouettes, etc. are recommended for the shortcoming. The blank squares indicate suitable styles, checks represent the most attractive garment lines for your figure, while X's mark styles inappropriate for you. Do the same for the remaining areas of your body and you will realize that there are a vast number of styles which you can mix or match to create consistently flattering garments. With this knowledge, you can purchase patterns which combine these elements and will help you achieve your goal of appearing perfectly proportioned and attractively groomed at all times.

Your Fashion Templates

Silhouettes

A-line

Shift

Empire

Blouson

Asymmetrical Closing

Yoke

Princess

Sheath

Shirtwaist

Tunic

Raised Waist

Low Waist

Tent

Jackets

Cardigan

Bolero

Short Fitted

Blazer

Tailored

Vest

Cape

Pants

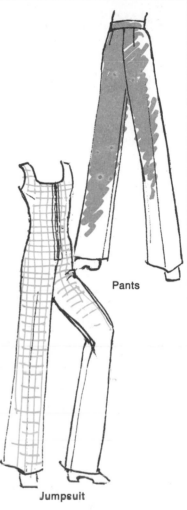

Bermuda Shorts   Shorts

Pants

Jumpsuit

Culottes

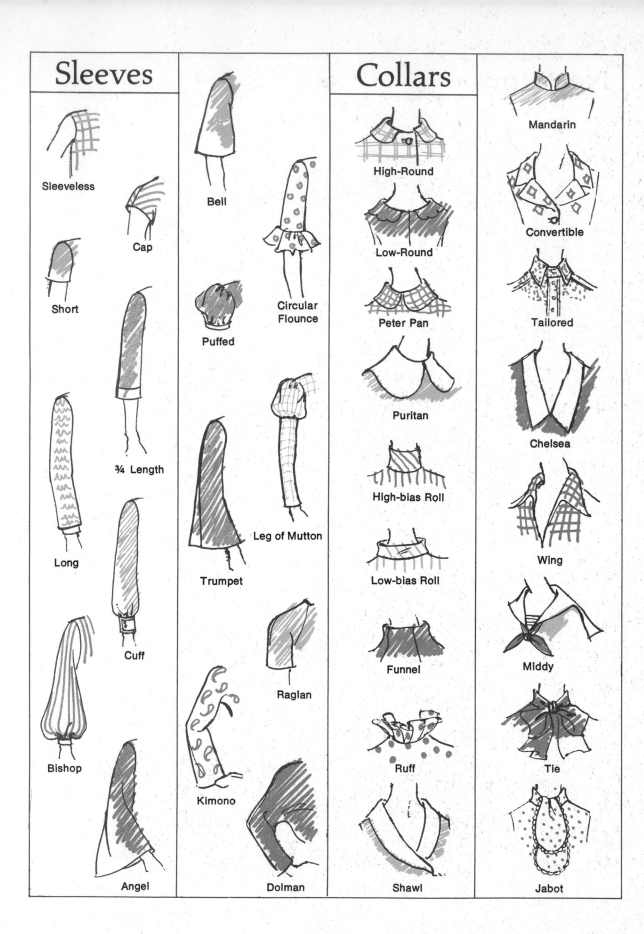

Sleeves

Sleeveless

Cap

Short

Bell

Circular Flounce

¾ Length

Puffed

Long

Leg of Mutton

Cuff

Trumpet

Bishop

Raglan

Kimono

Angel

Dolman

Collars

High-Round

Low-Round

Peter Pan

Puritan

High-bias Roll

Low-bias Roll

Funnel

Ruff

Shawl

Mandarin

Convertible

Tailored

Chelsea

Wing

Middy

Tie

Jabot

Necklines

Round

Scoop

U-neck

V-neck

Square

Bateau

Draped Cowl

Yoke

Cardigan

Keyhole

Halter

Skirts

Straight

A-line (without waistband)

A-line (with waistband)

Gathered

Panel

Gored

Flared

Wrap

Single Front Pleat

Double Front Pleat

Pleated

Hip Stitched Pleats

Yoke

SILHOUETTES / PANTS

Legend:
- ✓ Very Flattering
- ☐ Suitable
- ✗ Not Appropriate

SHORT

	A-line	Shift	Princess	Sheath	Raised Waist	Empire	Asymmetrical Closing	Shirtwaist	Low Waist	Blouson	Yoke	Tunic	Tent	Bermuda Shorts	Shorts	Pants	Jumpsuit	Culottes
Short Neck																		
Long Neck																		
Narrow Shoulders							✗						✗					
Broad Shoulders						✗												
Thin Arms																		
Heavy Arms																		
Small Bosom					✓	✓		✓		✗	✓							
Large Bosom	✓	✓		✓	✗	✗	✓	✓		✓	✗							
Short Waisted	✓	✓	✓		✓	✓			✓	✗							✓	
Long Waisted	✓	✓			✓	✓			✓								✓	
Small Hips														✓	✓	✓	✓	✓
Large Hips				✗						✓					✗			✓
Skinny Frame		✗			✓			✓		✓	✓	✓	✓	✓	✓	✓	✓	✓
Large Frame	✓		✓			✗	✓	✓	✗		✗				✗		✗	✓

TALL

	A-line	Shift	Princess	Sheath	Raised Waist	Empire	Asymmetrical Closing	Shirtwaist	Low Waist	Blouson	Yoke	Tunic	Tent	Bermuda Shorts	Shorts	Pants	Jumpsuit	Culottes
Short Neck																		
Long Neck																		
Narrow Shoulders							✗						✗					
Broad Shoulders						✗												
Thin Arms																		
Heavy Arms																		
Small Bosom					✓			✓		✓		✓						
Large Bosom	✓	✓			✓	✗	✓	✓	✓		✗							
Short Waisted	✓	✓	✓		✓				✓			✓					✓	
Long Waisted	✓	✓			✓				✓	✓		✓					✓	
Small Hips														✓	✓	✓	✓	✓
Large Hips				✗											✗			✓
Skinny Frame		✗			✓			✓		✓	✓			✓	✓	✓	✓	✓
Large Frame	✓		✓			✗	✓	✓							✗		✗	✓

| | JACKETS | | | | | | | SLEEVES | | | | | | | | | | | | | | |
Cardigan	Bolero	Short Fitted	Blazer	Tailored	Vest	Cape	Sleeveless	Cap	Short	¾ Length	Long	Cuff	Bishop	Angel	Bell	Circular Flounce	Puffed	Leg of Mutton	Trumpet	Raglan	Kimono	Dolman
✓																						
			✓	✓																		
					✗			✓									✓	✓		✓		✗
	✗																✗	✗			✓	✓
							✗	✗				✓							✓		✓	
							✗	✗	✗			✓					✗	✗	✓		✓	
	✓	✓			✓	✓																
✓	✗					✓																✗
	✗	✗														✗						✗
✓	✓	✓		✓																		
	✗	✗		✓																		
✓			✓		✓	✓																
✓	✗	✗		✓																		
✓																						
			✓	✓																		
					✗			✓									✓	✓		✓		✗
																	✗	✗		✓	✓	
							✗	✗					✓	✓	✓			✓				✓
													✓	✓	✓		✗	✗				✓
				✓	✓	✓																
✓	✗					✓																
	✗	✗		✓																		
✓	✓	✓	✓	✓	✓																	
✓	✗	✗		✓												✗	✗	✗				

NECKLINES and COLLARS

Legend:
- ✓ Very Flattering
- ☐ Suitable
- ✗ Not Appropriate

		Round	Scoop	U-neck	V-neck	Square	Bateau	Draped Cowl	Yoke	Cardigan	Keyhole	Halter	High-Round	Low-Round	Peter Pan	Puritan	High-bias Roll	Low-bias Roll	Funnel
SHORT	Short Neck		✓	✓	✓	✓				✓		✗		✓		✗	✗		✗
	Long Neck							✓			✓	✓					✓		✓
	Narrow Shoulders					✓	✓		✓							✗			
	Broad Shoulders	✓	✓	✓	✓	✗			✗										
	Thin Arms																		
	Heavy Arms																		
	Small Bosom	✓	✓					✓	✓			✓				✗			
	Large Bosom								✗							✗			
	Short Waisted															✗			
	Long Waisted																		
	Small Hips																		
	Large Hips																		
	Skinny Frame																		
	Large Frame															✗			
TALL	Short Neck		✓	✓		✓				✓		✗		✓		✗	✗		✗
	Long Neck							✓			✓	✓	✓			✓	✓		✓
	Narrow Shoulders					✓	✓		✓				✓						
	Broad Shoulders	✓	✓	✓	✓	✗			✗										
	Thin Arms																		
	Heavy Arms																		
	Small Bosom	✓	✓					✓	✓			✓							
	Large Bosom								✗										
	Short Waisted																		
	Long Waisted																		
	Small Hips																		
	Large Hips																		
	Skinny Frame																		
	Large Frame					✗									✗				

	COLLARS										SKIRTS												
	Ruff	Shawl	Mandarin	Convertible	Tailored	Chelsea	Wing	Middy	Tie	Jabot	Straight	A-line (w/o waistband)	A-line (with waistband)	Gathered	Panel	Gored	Flared	Wrap	Single Front Pleat	Double Front Pleat	Pleated	Hip Stitched Pleats	Yoke
	X		X	✓					X	X													
	✓		✓						✓	✓													
		X			✓																		
		✓		✓			✓		✓	✓													
		X							✓	✓													
		✓		✓				X	X	X													
														X				✓					
														✓									
														✓	✓						✓	✓	
														X	✓	✓	✓	✓					X
														X									
	X		X	✓					X	X													
	✓		✓						✓	✓													
		X			✓																		
		✓			✓	✓			✓	✓													
		✓							✓	✓													
		✓		✓				X	X	X													
														X									✓
														✓									
														✓	✓						✓	✓	
														X	✓	✓	✓	✓			X		
											X												
	X																						

31

The
Wonderful World
of Fabrics

Fabrics are a delight to the senses. The artist in fashion finds the material she uses a thrill and an inspiration, for she is aware that every aspect of a fabric will influence her finished garment, and she knows how to use it with her own personal flair. Her most valuable asset is that elusive sixth sense that can successfully match style line with fabric texture, color, and character to form a harmonious, pleasing, and flattering whole. While this sense is to some extent instinctive, it can benefit by experience and an understanding of the structure and origin of textiles. They are not made by magic, though some of the procedures they undergo may seem mysterious.

Every aspect of a fabric's history influences its character and hand—the things which have most to do with its success or failure as the medium for your sewing endeavors. Fluid, stiff, crisp, rough, soft, thick, or shaggy, it will lend its personality to the design. From fiber to yarn to cloth, from the loom to the finishing mill to the fabric shop, each detail of its past is a fascinating clue to the way it ultimately looks, acts, and feels. But its characteristics are not limited to tactile and visual ones; among the considerations most important in your busy contemporary world are those of care and performance. New developments in fibers and finishes have placed at your disposal fabrics which lighten your laundry chores and keep you looking your most impeccable self. Ask for the information on fiber content and finishing treatments which will help you choose and care for the fabric on which you will spend so much effort and time. Learn to distinguish quality fabric not by prices, but by a thorough understanding of the components which lend durability and the unmistakable touch of luxury. Fiber content, the tightness of the weave, the amount of twist and the structure of an individual yarn, and the permanence of finishes and color treatment all have a bearing on its quality. These factors determine the amount of wear a fabric can withstand, how it will drape and fold, and whether it is worthy to serve as your fashion signature.

Fibers

Where does fashion begin? The realization of a concept of silhouette, texture, and color depends on the basic stuff of fabric—the fiber of which it is made. Especially since the advent of synthetic fibers, textile classification has developed into a bewildering maze of technical subtleties and chemical terms. Few consumers will need to be familiar with the quirks of the anhydroglucose molecule, but a basic understanding of the general fiber categories is an invaluable aid in the practical business of buying and caring for fabrics. Although its properties may be altered by yarn and fabric structure and by finishing treatments, ultimately a fabric's origin and chemistry are its soul. The primary distinction in fiber types is a very simple one—a fiber is either natural or man-made.

Natural Fibers

Fibers exist in nature in many guises. Animal, vegetable, and mineral substances all provide the raw material for cloth. The wool of the sheep, the hair and fur of other creatures, and the fine filament from which the silk worm spins his cocoon are animal fibers composed of *protein*. Dozens of plants produce usable fiber in *cellulose* form. For example, linen is made from the fibrous stalk of the flax plants. The familiar cotton fiber grows as a puff protecting the seeds of the cotton plant, and grasses and leaves provide many other textile fibers. Minerals yield asbestos, which occurs naturally in fiber form and is used for fireproof fabrics, and metals that can be pounded into foils and cut into strips for luxury fabrics.

The unmistakable characteristics of the natural fibers are born in their structure. The familiar warmth of wool, the downy softness of cotton, the rich, dry texture of silk, and the crisp sheen of linen originate in the plant or animal that made them, and from the fact that natural things can never be quite uniform. The irregularities in their formation give them their distinction and explain many of their peculiar properties, such as the ability of wool to lock into felted constructions, the generally high absorbency of natural fibers, and the wide variation in quality among fibers of the same type.

WOOL is among nature's masterpieces. The fuzzy coat of the sheep possesses several remarkable and unique properties which make it especially adaptable to textile use. The wool fiber, which varies in length from 1½″ to 15″, has a natural crimp which facilitates the spinning of yarns and increases elasticity. The fiber itself is covered with minute scales. When wool is subjected to heat and pressure, these scales interlock, holding the fibers together and creating wool's unique felting capacity. The protein molecule of which wool is composed is spiral or spring-shaped, contributing great resiliency, "loft," and shape keeping ability. The fabric is highly absorbent and consequently very receptive to dyes but, in contrast, the surface tends to shed water. The hair and fur of other animals contribute fibers which are also classed as wool, and possess these properties in varying degrees.

SILK has a romantic history shrouded in regal legend, and the silk worm's life cycle is itself an exciting drama. A moth lays eggs which, after an incubation period, hatch into tiny, hungry silk worms. In about a month, each worm eats thousands of times its weight in mulberry leaves, growing rapidly and shedding its skin several times. Then it spins its cocoon. If allowed to continue the cycle, the worm transforms itself into a moth, which emerges from the cocoon to mate and lay more eggs. If the cocoon is to be used for silk, however, the worm is baked and dried in its blanket, and the fine protein fiber is unreeled in a continuous filament, which may be from 1500 to 4000 feet long. A stiff natural gum called sericin is boiled away, and silk filaments are combined to form very fine threads. Silk is extremely strong, absorbent, warm, resilient, and highly elastic.

COTTON is a vastly popular, versatile, and relatively inexpensive fiber that produces durable, comfortable fabrics. Magnified cotton has a ribbon-like appearance and is of fairly uniform thickness. The many types of cotton fibers range in length from ½″ to 2½″. It is naturally soft and easily spun into a variety of textures. The cellulose of which cotton is composed is an inert substance, and as a result untreated cotton may have little resiliency and wrinkle easily. However, its normally high strength increases when wet, making it exceptionally easy to launder, and its natural absorbency makes it receptive to a variety of treatments, such as mercerization, color application, and wrinkle-resistant and easy-care finishes, which add to its desirability.

FLAX is the plant from whose stems linen is made. By a process developed at the dawn of civilization, the outer woody portion of the stalk is rotted away, leaving long, soft, strong fibers composed of cellulose. The magnified fiber has a jointed structure similar to that of bamboo, and the thickness may vary widely. Length ranges from 5 to 20 inches. Because of their similar composition, linen resembles cotton in many ways, including its ability to withstand high temperatures and its easy launderability and low resistance to wrinkling. In addition, it is extremely durable and, if stored properly, will withstand years of use. However, the flax fiber tends to be stiffer than cotton, and linen fabrics are subject to abrasion and wear along edges and creases.

Man-made Fibers

For thousands of years, natural fibers were the only materials available for the creation of fabric. Then, in the middle of the nineteenth century, scientists began to experiment with the production of "artificial silk" from regenerated cellulose. The resulting fiber, rayon, heralded a new era for the textile industry. Rapid developments have greatly increased the number and refined the properties of man-made fibers, which have made themselves indispensable in the contemporary world.

The chemical complexities of man-made fibers are endless, but one of the distinctions among them is the fact that some fibers are derived from **natural** materials such as cellulose or protein, while others are completely **synthesized** or developed from basic chemical sources. In either case, the production involves similar steps. A chemical solution is formed which contains the basic components of the fiber. The solution is forced through the tiny holes of a *spinneret* into a chemical-coagulating bath or air chamber which hardens the substance into filament form. A continuous "rope" of unlimited length is produced, and goes on to be textured and processed. The same solution can produce filaments with varying properties, depending on the size and shape of the holes in the spinneret and the nature of the hardening procedure.

Great advances have been made in the development of man-made fibers since their relatively recent inception. New formulas and techniques are constantly improving their properties and increasing their advantages for the woman who sews (see pages 47-49).

Yarns

Yarn is the medium of fabric construction. However the fabric is formed, its character is determined to a great degree by the manner of yarn from which it is made.

Before they are formed into yarn, fibers are referred to as either staple or filament. Silk and all the man-made fibers originally exist as long continuous strands, or *filaments*, which simply require a small amount of twist to form yarn. All the natural fibers except silk occur in short lengths, or *staple* form; man-made fibers may also be cut into short staple lengths to imitate them. These require more complex yarn-making techniques. A mat of random fibers is first sorted, cleaned, and blended into a uniform mixture and then subjected to several procedures which align the fibers and impart twist. *Carding* produces a loose strand of more or less parallel fibers about an inch in diameter. Further *combing* eliminates shorter fibers and produces a strand of higher quality. (*Woolen* and *worsted* yarns are, respectively, the wool counterparts of carded and combed yarns in other fibers.) The strand is then further stretched, twisted, and finally spun.

2 PLY YARN

Yarn as it comes from the original spinning frame is called a *single*. Twisting several singles together produces a *ply yarn* and improves uniformity and strength. The character of a yarn is also influenced by the degree of twist. Low-twist yarns, soft and relatively weak, are used for napped fabrics. Tighter twist increases strength and crispness. Very high twist is used for crepe effects, as the tension causes puckering.

COMPLEX OR NOVELTY YARNS include several types, most of which are produced primarily for appearance value since they are seldom strong. They may be single or ply, and often contain components of several colors or fiber types for visual variations. Novelty single yarns, called *slub* yarns, vary along their length in thickness and amount of twist. The typical novelty ply yarn illustrated here is composed of a strong base yarn which forms the support and determines the length, combined with an effect yarn which is held in place by a binder. Examples of this type are *bouclé*, *ratiné*, *spiral*, and *knot* yarns.

3 PLY NOVELTY YARN

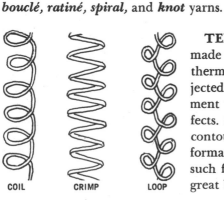

COIL   **CRIMP**   **LOOP**

TEXTURED YARNS are produced from man-made fibers which possess the useful characteristic of thermoplasticity, which means they will melt when subjected to heat. Through the use of this property, filament yarns can be heat-set in interesting textured effects. Several manufacturing methods can change the contour of the filament to a *coiled, crimped,* or *looped* formation from its original rod-like shape. Yarns from such filaments may have the qualities of light weight, great bulk, or a high degree of stretch.

Fabric Structure

The thread of textiles weaves through history, touching each civilization since the dawn of man and creating a tapestry of variety and excitement. Each culture has made its unique contribution, and the panorama of fabric designs and types provides deep insight into the development of artistic achievement. Despite these subtle cultural distinctions and mechanical developments which have vastly increased the speed at which textiles can be produced, the basic principles involved in textile construction have remained essentially the same for centuries. Weaving, knitting, knotting, felting, and a recent innovation called Malimo are the techniques by which fabric is formed.

Weaving

A woven fabric is easy to recognize by the fact that it is composed of two sets of yarns at right angles to each other. The loom which produces it, while it may be an extremely complex device, works on a fairly simple principle. A frame holds a series of yarns called the *warp* taut between two rollers, one each at the front and back of the loom. Arranged in a specific order and extending the width of the projected fabric, these yarns are each drawn first through a *heddle*, which has an eye like that of a needle and may be raised to alter the position of its yarn, and then through a space in the *reed*, which is a comb-like device at right angles to the warp yarns, serving to keep each thread straight and in its proper place. The heddles are raised in a specific sequence as the design dictates, and a single crosswise or *filling* yarn or *pick* is drawn between the warp yarns with a *shuttle* and beaten into place against the previous filling threads by the reed. Then the warp yarns are lowered, a different series is raised, and another filling yarn is drawn through and packed in place. This series of crosswise threads forms the *weft* or *woof*. As the fabric is completed, more yarn is released from the back *warp beam* and the fabric is rolled toward the front of the loom and wound on the *cloth beam*.

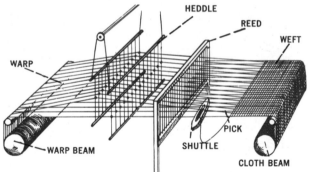

The warp must withstand considerable strain in weaving. It undergoes tension as it is held between the front and back beams and considerable abrasion as the reed slides back and forth through it. Its threads must be strong, tightly twisted, and uniform in structure. Consequently, the lengthwise grain (warp direction) will stretch less, may wear better, and because of its stronger yarn, will drape differently than the crosswise grain (filling direction). The *selvage* is formed along the edges of the warp where the filling thread changes direction. It is likely to be a tighter weave, since the warp edges must support the greatest strain. One indication of durability is in the "balance" of the cloth, or the proportion of warp to filling yarns. Fabric with nearly an equal thread count in both directions often gives longer wear.

BASIC WEAVES

There are several fundamental weaving structures which account for a vast majority of the fabrics we use. All the basic weaves can be produced on a simple loom, requiring no special attachments.

PLAIN WEAVE, true to its name, is the simplest and most common of weaves. Also called **tabby**, it is the prototype of woven structure: each yarn in both the warp and filling directions runs alternately over one and under one of the yarns it crosses. Though basically sturdy, this weave may vary in strength according to the weight of the yarn and the compactness of the weave. Cotton (percale, voile, calico, and gingham), linen (crash), silk (organza and chiffon), synthetic (organdy and taffeta), and wool (challis) are familiar fabrics in plain weave.

The **rib** variation occurs when the yarns in one direction of a plain weave are heavier or closer together than those in the other. Examples of ribbed fabrics, in order of fine to heavy rib, are broadcloth, poplin, faille, grosgrain, bengaline, and ottoman.

When the same alternating construction employs paired or multiple threads, it is called a **basket** weave. Such fabrics tend to be softer and less stable than fabrics of similar weight in single thread plain weave, and may pose the problem of seam slippage. Examples you may be familiar with are oxford cloth, monk's cloth, and hopsacking.

PLAIN WEAVE   RIB WEAVE   BASKET WEAVE

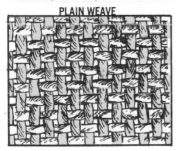 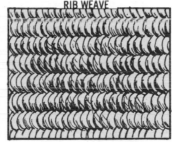 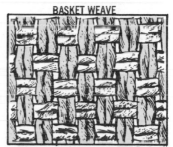

TWILL WEAVE is often used to produce strong, durable fabrics such as denim and gabardine. A handsome weave characterized by a diagonal ridge usually running from lower left to upper right, its appearance depends to a large extent on the yarn weight and specific twill construction. A frequent variation in the twill weave is the **herringbone**, in which the diagonal ridge switches direction back and forth, creating a zigzag design.

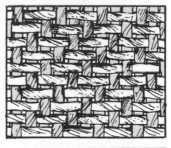

SATIN WEAVE has a characteristic luxurious shine. The surface is composed of **floats**, or warp yarns which pass over many filling yarns before being caught under one. The surface yarns, usually of filament fibers, intersect cross threads at points randomly spaced so the smooth texture appears unbroken. A variation called **sateen** has similar surface floats, but they run in the filling direction and are usually of a spun staple yarn.

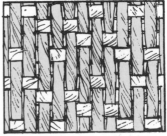

DECORATIVE WEAVES

There are two basic types of fabric designs—those which are a product of the fabric's woven construction, and those which are applied to the fabric by such processes as printing or embossing. To create woven designs, the basic weaves may be varied and combined, surface floats may form involved designs, and complex mutations of the age-old loom may produce elaborate fabrics whose beauty wins constant attention.

PILE WEAVES provide soft, thick, textured fabrics for many purposes. Several different constructions may be employed to emphasize specific characteristics such as absorbency in terry, density and durability in carpeting, or texture in velvet. Extra warp yarn may be woven over wires, which cut the loops as they are withdrawn. In terry cloth, some of the warp yarns are woven with slack tension and forced up into loops as the filling is beaten back. Corduroy is woven with long filling floats which are cut after weaving to produce wales or cords. Some velvets are woven face to face, sharing warp yarns between two layers which are slashed apart when completed.

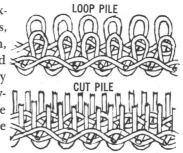

LOOP PILE

CUT PILE

PATTERN WEAVES are the glory of the weaver's art. Delicate traditional coverlet designs can be created on a simple loom by an intricate order of threading. Other pattern weaves, such as crisp piqués, filmy curtain gauze, and patterns of flowers and scrolls in rich, deep brocades owe their existence to more complex variations of the loom.

Leno weaves are used most effectively in lacy, open fabrics. A special attachment twists the warp yarns around each other in a figure eight as the filling passes through, imparting stability to fabrics with widely spaced yarns. The leno construction is often combined with other weaves in a decorative effect for casement fabrics and may be especially attractive when designed with novelty yarns. Small figured and textured designs such as birdseye piqué are *dobby weaves,* produced on a more complicated loom. Usually a geometric pattern in a small repeat, these designs frequently employ heavy "stuffer" yarns in the filling to float on the back of the fabric and add texture to the weave. Further elaborations on the basic weaving process produce *jacquard weaves,* some of the most complex and beautiful fabrics available. These include huge repeats, detailed brocades, damasks, and tapestry effects. The jacquard loom controls each warp yarn individually with a series of punched cards like a computer deck. Since one card determines one filling pick, the repeat in the design can include as many threads as there are cards in the deck, permitting an unlimited range of design possibilities.

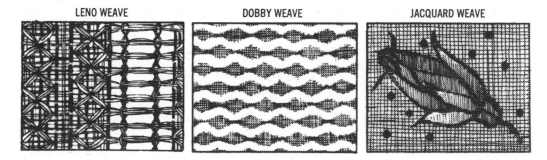

LENO WEAVE   DOBBY WEAVE   JACQUARD WEAVE

Knitting

A relatively recent development in the history of cloth, knitting has grown through technical advancements from a tedious hand construction to a fast, economical means of producing comfortable, packable, and beautiful fabrics. The knit industry has developed to such an extent that there are now as many weights, textures, and structures in knit fabrics as there are in woven ones. Knits owe their many advantages to their structure. While the yarn in a woven fabric is in a straight position, the knit construction arranges a continuous yarn into interlocking loops. Since these loops can straighten out under tension without straining the yarn, knit fabrics are inherently stretchy and flexible.

Several terms are used to describe knit goods. The *gauge* of a knit refers to the number of stitches in 1½ inches of fabric. *Denier* is a term dating from Roman times, when the weight of a coin by that name was used as a standard for buying and selling silk. It describes the weight of the yarn per unit length. A *wale* is a column of loops running parallel to the long measurement of a knit fabric, corresponding to the lengthwise grain of a weave, and a *course* is a crosswise row.

WEFT KNITTING

The first knitting machines were designed to reproduce the type of knitting done by hand. Called weft or filling knit, this construction uses a continuous single thread to form a crosswise row of loops which links into the previous row and is in turn linked into the row that follows it. Two stitches, *knit* and *purl,* are the basis for all knitting constructions. The knit stitch is a loop drawn through the front of the previous one, the purl is drawn through the back. Simple weft knits are uniquely fragile, since all the loops in a vertical row are dependent on each other. A broken loop will release all the others in the row, marring the fabric with a run. Wool knits tend to have greater resistance to runs because of the capacity of the wool fibers to cling together, locking the stitches. Weft knitting produces fabric in both tubular and flat form.

KNIT

PURL

PLAIN KNITS, found in the familiar fabric known as jersey, have a flat surface and a back characterized by short, horizontal loops. The right side exhibits the appearance of the knit stitch, and the loops on the back are the purl stitch. This structure is a common feature of hand knitting, where it is called stockinette.

RIB KNITS are made by alternating sets of knit and purl stitches in the same row, forming pronounced vertical ridges. The purl stitch tends to recede while the knit stitch advances, creating a fabric with a wavy cross-section and superior crosswise stretch. Rib knits have good insulation properties, and provide a snug fit.

PURL KNITS also have pronounced ridges, but in a horizontal direction. Entire rows are formed alternately of knit and purl stitches, yielding a fabric which has considerable crosswise stretch. It is completely reversible, since the appearance of the face is identical to that of the back, and similar to the reverse side of the flat knit.

PATTERN KNITS are produced from the two basic weft knit stitches by re-arranging, dropping, adding, alternating, and crossing them. The beautiful "fisherman knits" are prime examples of the vast variety of patterns which owe their depth of texture to the fact that the knit stitch tends to advance and the purl stitch to recede. The machines which produce these fabrics, while they are not very economical to operate, can recreate hand-knitted structures with great fidelity.

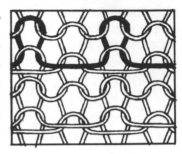

DOUBLE KNITS, a versatile form of weft knitting, resist runs and have great stability. Produced by the interlock stitch, a variation of the rib stitch which can only be done by machine, double knitting employs two yarns and two sets of needles which draw loops through from both directions. It yields a heavy, firm, easily handled fabric which has the same rib-like appearance on both sides. Jacquard-type machinery has been adapted to produce highly decorative double knits.

WARP KNITTING

The technique of warp knitting, unlike that of simpler weft knitting, employs many yarns. Wound parallel to each other on a warp beam, the yarns are fed into the knitting machine and form loops in a lengthwise direction. Each yarn is controlled by its own needle and follows a zigzag course, interlocking with its neighbors along the length of the fabric. Warp knitting produces several varieties of durable and relatively run-proof fabrics whose low cost and vast design potential have won them enthusiastic consumer acceptance and a secure place in the future of the textile industry.

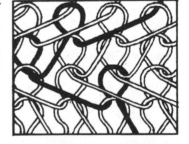

TRICOT is the prevalent choice of manufacturers for the backing of laminated fabrics and it is frequently used for lingerie because of its good permeability and comfort. This strong, drapable fabric can be recognized by a fine crosswise rib which appears on the wrong side, and by the fact that it will stretch much more in the crosswise direction than in length. It is resistant to both running and fraying. The name tricot is taken from the French "tricoter," meaning "to knit."

RASCHEL knits are becoming increasingly familiar as they are being produced in a wide variety of fabrics. While tricots and many weft knits are best suited to fine, uniform yarns, raschel knits can take advantage of every conceivable texture and fiber type because of a specially designed latch needle. Raschel knits range from fragile tulles to coarse fur cloths. They may often be identified by a chain of fine yarn which restrains and stabilizes a heavier textured yarn in a lacy, open construction.

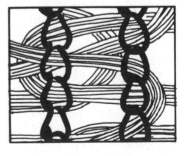

Other Fabric Constructions

Beautiful fabrics are produced by many methods other than weaving and knitting. Some have been developed from old hand processes, while others are strictly a product of modern technology. They may be limited to specific uses by their character or cost.

NETTING is the fabric construction which encompasses both the strong, simple, burly texture of fish-net and the delicate and complicated tracery of lace. Knots may secure sets of threads together where they cross each other, or continuous coils of thread may loop through each other, forming the hexagonal mesh which can create a background for further embroidery. The most elaborate machines in the textile industry can reproduce laces in many styles and weights.

CROCHETING is also adapted from a hand process which involves the use of a hook to form a chain of loops from a single continuous yarn.

BRAIDING forms fabric whose yarns lie at acute angles to the edges in a bias woven structure, usually a narrow strip. All the yarns originate from the same direction.

FELTING is a time-honored method for producing warm, versatile, though not very durable fabrics of wool or fur fibers by the application of heat, moisture, friction, and pressure. This economical construction doesn't require spun yarn or weaving, but depends on the natural ability of wool fibers to shrink, coil, and lock together to form a mat. As there are no yarns to unravel, edges of felt fabrics require no finishing techniques. Since they do not depend on looped yarns, however, they have little or no elastic recovery. When stretched, they will not return to their original shape. Felt exists in many weights and qualities, from fine garment fabric to heavy industrial padding. Wool may be mixed with a certain proportion of cheaper non-felting fiber and still retain its felting capacity.

BONDING produces non-woven fabrics by fusing together a mat of textile fibers other than wool with the aid of an adhesive or bonding agent. The fibers are distributed on a belt and made into fabric by one of two methods. An adhesive may be applied directly to the web, or the mixture of fibers may contain some which melt at a very low temperature, fusing the fabric together when heat is applied. Many different characters of fabric may be produced by this method, depending on the length, concentration, and orientation of the fibers. Non-woven fabrics have the advantage of equal flexibility in all directions, since they have no grain.

The term bonded has come to include those textiles which are technically called *laminated* fabrics. These are composed of two separate layers of knitted or woven cloth which are fused together for improved stability, opacity, or handling ease. Sometimes a thin sheet of plastic foam is fused between the face and backing fabrics to add texture and insulation. This process may change the "hand" or draping qualities of the face fabric, and off-grain or impermanent bonding may cause dissatisfaction.

Plastic film may be given greater durability and made suitable for apparel use by fusing it to a base of woven or knitted fabric. Simulated leather and patent vinyl fabrics are produced this way.

MALIMO is a new textile process which produces extremely stable fabrics at great speed. Many filling yarns are laid across the warp series simultaneously, forming an acute angle, and both sets are stitched together with a chain stitch by a third set of yarns.

Finishes

Fabrics as they come off the loom bear little resemblance to those that reach your sewing machine. Before they are sold they may have been washed in chemical solutions, brushed, pressed, beaten, and polished. Substances and treatments may alter their texture and appearance and improve their resistance to moths, static electricity, spotting, staining, shrinking, sagging, wrinkling, and burning. All the processes undergone by the fabric after its initial transformation from yarn to cloth are called *finishes*. The fuzzy surface of a wool fleece, the shine of a polished cotton, and the elusive pattern of an acetate moiré are all visible results of specialized finishing. These are some of the common finishing procedures.

BEETLING, applied to linen or cotton, involves prolonged pounding with wooden blocks to flatten the yarns, fill out the weave, and impart an elegant luster to the cloth.

CALENDERING is a process in which the fabric is passed between heated rollers under pressure. Like a large iron, a calender may simply press the fabric flat. However, there are several variations. Smooth, high-speed metal rollers and a resin application produce a finish called *glazing.* When two layers of a ribbed fabric are calendered slightly off grain, a *moiré* effect results. Thermoplastic fibers, or those which melt in sufficient heat, can be permanently textured by *embossing* with rollers engraved with a raised design.

FULLING takes advantage of the natural shrinkage capacity of wool. Subjecting the cloth to moisture, heat, and pressure compacts the yarns, strengthens the weave, and imparts warmth, body, and stability. It is similar to the *felting* of non-woven fibers.

MERCERIZATION has improved the beauty and durability of cotton and linen for over 50 years. Immersing cotton under tension in a solution of caustic soda greatly increases its strength, luster, and affinity for dyes by swelling the fibers. If the fabric is not held taut, mercerizing will shrink it considerably, a factor which can be used for crepe and stretch effects. Printing the caustic soda solution in a selected pattern on untreated cotton fabric results in a puckered effect called *plissé*.

NAPPING is a common finish by which short fiber ends of spun yarn are raised to the surface of a fabric by a series of revolving wire brushes. When the brushes are of a stiff vegetable burr called a teasel, the process is called *gigging*.

TENTERING straightens the fabric, setting the width and grain, and dries it in the set position. The conveyor-like frame is lined with "tenter-hooks," which hold the fabric's selvages and stretch it into shape. An electronic or hand-operated mechanism controls the two belts of hooks, keeping filling yarns at right angles to the warp. Off-grain fabric is a result of improper tentering. If it has been heat-set off grain during tentering, it cannot be straightened.

Temporary Finishes

Several finishes may be added which improve the fabric's hand and appearance, but which are quickly removed by normal wear and care. Some substances may temporarily alter the character of a fabric in such a way that poor quality is disguised.

SIZING, or *dressing,* provides body, weight, and luster. Fabrics are stiffened with glue, clay, or wax which is not fast to laundering. Starch may restore this finish, but if fabric is of poor basic quality (low thread count) it will wear out quickly.

WEIGHTING is a process applied to silk to restore the weight which is lost when the natural gum is removed. Metallic salts are absorbed, which allows heavier fabrics to be produced but weakens the fiber. Weighted silk water-spots easily.

FLOCKING is used to make a firmer, more compact cloth by steaming short wool fibers into the back of a wool fabric. The practice may be used to conceal a loose weave, but since the treatment is not durable, such fabric will wear thin more quickly.

Performance Finishes

In recent years, manufacturers have been increasingly conscious of the consumer demand for fabrics with improved and specialized characteristics. Special finishes have been developed to enable natural fibers to compete in care and performance with the rapidly growing number and quality of synthetics. Finishes can counteract the inherent disadvantages of certain untreated fibers, and give them texture and aesthetic appeal as well as safety, durability, and adaptability to special purposes.

As you weigh a potential fabric purchase, anticipate the kind of life your garment will lead. The vast array of terms and trademarks may seem bewildering, but if you can read their language, they will help you choose the fabric that best suits your needs.

Keep in mind the fact that "permanent," as used in the textile industry, is only a relative term. So called "permanent" finishes would more accurately be called durable, since they are only designed to withstand normal wear, and must be treated and laundered as the manufacturer recommends. Here is a list of terms which will help you in your search for the perfect fabric. Look for them on hangtags, bolt ends, and labels.

COLORFAST Color in fabrics so labeled will not fade with normal use if laundered as recommended.

CREASE RESISTANT A term applied to fabrics which have been treated to resist and recover from wrinkling caused by normal wear.

DURABLE PRESS A standard of garment performance indicating fabric will wash and dry by machine, shed wrinkles, and retain shape without ironing. Pleats and creases can be set only temporarily in garments so treated. They must be re-set after laundering.

FIRE RESISTANT Fabrics which have been treated to prevent the spread of flame.

OIL REPELLENT Fabrics so labeled are non-absorbent to oil-based stains.

PERMANENT PRESS Another term for *durable press;* see above.

PRE-SHRUNK Fabric which has undergone a preliminary shrinking process. *Residual shrinkage,* or the percentage of possible shrinkage remaining in a fabric, must be declared.

SANFORIZED Ensures that fabric will not shrink more than one percent in washing. *Sanforized Plus* means fabric has also passed standardized tests for wash-and-wear performance.

SHRINKAGE CONTROLLED Fabric which has undergone compressive shrinkage in manufacturing. Increases durability by compacting the weave.

SOIL RELEASE Treatment which makes possible the removal of oil stains from permanent press fabrics. It makes water resistant fibers absorbent so the washing solution can penetrate the fiber and remove soil.

STAIN AND SPOT RESISTANT Fabric finished to repel water and oil-based stains.

WASH AND WEAR Fabrics which can be washed and re-worn with little or no ironing. This property may be produced by heat-setting or resin treatment and varies in permanence. Also termed *easy care* and *minimum care.*

WATER REPELLENT Fabrics which have been treated to reduce their affinity for water yet still remain porous.

Color and Fabric Pattern

We can be sure that when cave men first began painting hunting scenes on walls of caves, the first textile designer was also painting the animal skins he wore. Though the content, construction, and finishing of a fabric provide all of its essential properties, richness of color and pattern have always held the most primary appeal. For centuries, special formulas for color and fabric have been jealously guarded secrets. Vast industries have developed on the basis of changing tastes and new technical developments in color and applied textile design in order to satisfy man's unquenchable decorative instinct.

Dyeing

The complex science of dye chemistry has developed in response to demand for fast, vivid color which will withstand wear, sunlight, and the rigors of modern laundering.

Natural fibers, which frequently have distinct colors of their own, often require bleaching before they can be dyed. Many fibers naturally resist color, and among the chief advantages of such innovations as mercerizing is the improvement of a fabric's affinity for dyes. With the advent of synthetic fabrics and the increased importance of the chemical industry in textiles, the number and quality of synthetic dyes has grown by leaps and bounds since their inception in 1856.

Dyes are classified in several ways, including chemical category and fibers to which they can be applied, hue produced, and method of application. The appearance of a fabric is often determined by the stage in manufacturing at which the dye is applied.

FIBER DYEING is used to produce color in a mat of fibers before they are spun into yarn. Colors penetrate the fibers thoroughly, and are likely to be fast. This method is commonly used on wool; hence the expression "dyed in the wool." It permits the spinning of tweed and mottled yarns from several batches of variously colored fibers.

SOLUTION DYEING is a procedure for coloring man-made fibers by introducing pigment into the chemical spinning solution before it is formed into filaments. Since the color is an inherent part of the fiber, it is extremely permanent.

YARN DYEING is one of the oldest methods of coloring textiles. The spun yarn is dyed in a skein, or it may be wound on a cylinder known as a *package,* which is then dyed from the inside out in a machine similar to a pressure-cooker. Typical yarn dyed fabrics are ginghams, plaids, checks, stripes, and those with iridescent effects.

PIECE DYEING is the most common and economical means of coloring fabric. It involves immersing the woven goods in a dye bath. The procedure is practical because it permits manufacturers to store a volume of undyed goods and dye to order as preferences in color change. Piece dyed fabrics are usually a solid color, but an exception to this rule occurs with *cross dyeing*. Fabrics to be so treated are woven of a combination of fiber types, each with a different affinity for certain dyes. Those dyes which are accepted by one fiber are rejected by others, resulting in fabrics which can resemble either yarn dyed or fiber dyed fabrics. Difficulties may be encountered in attempting to dye fiber blends a solid color, and many must be dyed twice to impart the same color to both fibers.

Applied Design

The surface of a fabric provides enticing stimulus to an artist's creative imagination. An infinity of surface patterns can be reproduced in many ways.

SCREEN PRINTING is really a sophisticated version of the stencil process. The design to be printed is cut out of a thin sheet of film, which is then adhered to a frame covered with a fine, strong mesh fabric such as organdy. The fabric to be printed is stretched out on a table, the screen laid on top, and the pigment or dye is forced through the screen in the areas where the non-porous film does not act as a barrier. Adapting photographic processes to cutting the film has allowed screen printing to produce fine gradation of tone and delicate detail. Though it is slower than roller printing, it is a more economical means of producing limited quantities of a print. Very large repeats can be accommodated, and exclusive, high-quality dress goods are often printed in this manner.

ROLLER PRINTING, or direct printing, is a simple procedure used to produce large quantities of a design inexpensively. The design, whose repeat size must be the exact circumference of the roller, is engraved on a series of rollers, one for each color to be used. These print rollers are arranged around a large drum in exact positions, and color is applied to them by another roller resting in a trough of pigment or dye. When the fabric feeds between the rollers and the drum, the areas of color coincide to form the complete design. Usually the fabric is bleached before printing. Occasionally, where there is to be a white design on a fabric with a colored ground, a variation of roller printing called *discharge printing* is employed. In this process, fabric which has been piece dyed a solid color is printed with a bleaching paste, removing the color from the printed areas. Fibers in the bleached areas may be weakened by this treatment. *Flocking* is another variation which adds textural interest. It involves printing a design on the cloth with a wet resin or glue and then dusting the surface with short fibers which adhere to the glued areas.

TIE DYEING is an ancient craft which produces interesting and varied textile designs. Puffs of fabric are wrapped in waxed thread or sewn and tightly gathered, then dipped in dye, creating intriguing sunburst effects as the dye penetrates the fabric unevenly. The blending of several colors and the combining of techniques contribute to the unique effect. Developed to a fine degree in Japan and practiced widely in India, the technique has been copied effectively by a machine process.

BATIK is a process which can be used to create striking and delicate designs. It is a method of resist dyeing in which wax is applied to the cloth in areas which are not to receive color. After dyeing, the wax is boiled off, and the process repeated for several colors. Originally developed in Java, batik is a hand process in which wax is applied with an instrument called a *tjanting*. It has now been adapted to machine printing.

EMBROIDERY was developed from a tedious hand process into a lucrative industry by the invention of the Schiffli machine. Hundreds of needles embellish the pre-woven base fabric with an infinite variety of lace and eyelet designs which are programed into the machine on punched cards. Holes for eyelet fabrics are punched or cut automatically as the edges are finished by machine stitching. Same varieties of lace are produced by chemically dissolving the base fabric, leaving just the stitched lace design.

Fiber and Fabric Facts

Natural Fibers

	Fabrics	Properties	Care
Cotton	Extremely versatile in weight, texture, and construction. Found in fabric types such as organdy, broadcloth, poplin, terry, corduroy, seersucker, denim, tweed. Used widely for summer wear, work clothes, and in heavier weights, for warm transitional garments.	Quite strong, even stronger when wet. Not susceptible to pilling or seam slippage. Comfortable, absorbent; carries heat from body. Free from static electricity. Good affinity for dyes. Will deteriorate from mildew; weakened by sunlight. Tendency to wrinkle. Fabrics may shrink badly unless treated.	Wash 10 minutes in hot water at regular speed with heavy-duty detergent. Can use chlorine bleach on white cottons; however, some finishes react to chlorine bleach and turn yellow (see label). Fabric softener will reduce wrinkling. Tumble dry on regular heat setting but don't over-dry. Press with hot iron while damp until completely dry or use a steam iron with a slightly dampened press cloth.
Linen	Beautiful, durable, and elegant, has a natural luster. Can be made into sheer, medium, or heavyweight fabrics. Used for summer dresses, blouses, and suiting.	Tendency to wrinkle unless treated. Exceptionally strong, but stiff; may show wear at the edges and folds. Comfortable; excellent absorbency, carries heat away from the body. Poor affinity for dyes; bright colors may bleed when laundered. Fabric will shrink unless treated. Will deteriorate from mildew but not from moths. Does not lint.	Usually dry cleaned, but launders well if pre-shrunk. Wash 5-8 minutes in hot water at regular speed with heavy-duty detergent. Can use chlorine bleach but over-bleaching may weaken the fiber. Tumble dry on regular heat setting, but remove and iron while still very damp. Iron at high setting (unless treated with special finishes; see label). For maximum durability, creases should be finger pressed, not ironed into the garment.
Silk	Beautiful, luxurious to touch, has a deep luster. Available in a variety of weaves and weights from sheer drapable chiffon to stiff rich brocades in brilliant colors and beautiful prints for dresses, suits, blouses, linings, lingerie. Fabrics such as crepe, brocade, satin, jersey, tweed.	Good wrinkle resistance. Builds up static electricity and may cling. Exceptionally strong for its fineness. Very absorbent; will hold in body heat. Excellent affinity for dyes, but may bleed. May yellow and fade with age or the use of strong soap or high iron setting. Weakened by sunlight and perspiration; excellent resistance to mildew and moths.	Usually dry cleaned. If marked washable, use mild suds in lukewarm water; can also machine wash for 3 minutes at gentle speed. Avoid using chlorine bleach. Tumble dry at low setting for short time or hang up to dry, but avoid prolonged exposure to light. Iron on wrong side while damp with a low heat setting or use a steam iron; however silk is easily water spotted, so you may need to protect the fabric with a thin cloth.

| Wool | Versatile in weight, texture, weave, color.
Unique properties of wool permit constructions not possible in any other fiber.
Tailors well because of ability to be molded into shape.
Used for coatings, suitings, crepe, tweeds, knits, gabardine, flannel, jersey. | Excellent wrinkle resistance and elasticity.
Limited abrasion resistance.
Weakens and stretches when wet.
Exceptional absorbency; holds a large amount of moisture before it feels damp.
Traps air in fibers, providing great natural warmth.
Good affinity for dye.
Weakened by sunlight.
Requires moth proofing; may be attacked by mildew if damp or soiled.
Susceptible to shrinking and pilling if not treated.
Tailors well; can be molded. | Should be brushed between cleanings. Usually dry cleaned. For hand washables, use mild suds in cool water; can also machine wash for two minutes at gentle speed, interrupting the agitation time for 10 minutes to let the fabric soak, and then completing the cycle. Do not tumble dry; block to shape on a flat surface away from heat. If labeled "machine wash-and-dry," wash 3-8 minutes in warm water at gentle speed with mild suds. Tumble dry at regular heat setting but remove while slightly damp. Do not use chlorine bleach; it will weaken and yellow the fibers. To avoid stretching, press gently at low heat setting on the wrong side using a damp press cloth or steam iron. |

Man-made Fibers

| Acetate

□□ ACELE
△△ AVICOLOR
△△ AVISCO
★★ CELANESE
★★ CELAPERM
★★ CELARA
◆◆ CHROMSPUN
◆◆ ESTRON | Silk-like appearance, luxurious soft feel, deep luster, excellent draping qualities. Found in fabrics such as satin, jersey, taffeta, lace, faille, brocade, tricot, and crepe, and often in blends with other man-made fibers.
Used for dresses, foundation garments, lingerie, linings, and blouses. | Tendency to wrinkle.
Accumulates static electricity.
Takes colors well, but some dyes are subject to atmospheric fading.
Relatively low strength.
Resistant to mildew and moths.
Weakened by light.
Moderately absorbent; holds in body heat.
Resistant to stretch and shrinkage. | Usually dry cleaned. If washable, use mild suds in warm or cold water at gentle speed for three minutes. Tumble dry at cool setting for short time or hang up to dry away from heat. Or hand wash, gently squeezing suds through fabric and rinsing in lukewarm water. Iron while damp with light pressure on the wrong side at lowest temperature; a hot iron may melt the fabric. Can also iron on the right side, using a press cloth and steam iron. Always place a strip of brown paper between the garment and seam allowances or darts. Do not use acetone (as in nail polish remover) or other organic solvents. |
| Acrylic

●●● ACRILAN
● CRESLAN
□□ ORLON
●● ZEFKROME
●● ZEFRAN | Commonly soft, light, fluffy fabric construction.
Available in sheer fabrics, knits, fleece, furlike, and pile fabrics, and blends with natural and man-made fibers.
Used for sweaters, dresses, suits, sports, and work clothes. | Good wrinkle resistance.
Lightweight.
May accumulate static electricity.
Low absorbency; quick drying.
Good affinity for dyes; colorfast.
Quite strong.
Excellent resistance to mildew, moths, chemicals and sunlight.
Heat sensitive.
May pill.
Holds shape well, good pleat retention. | Remove oily stains before cleaning. May be dry cleaned or laundered. Wash for 3-5 minutes. For sturdy fabrics use regular agitation with heavy duty detergent. For delicate fabrics use gentle agitation with mild suds or hand wash. For bright colors use cool water; otherwise, warm water. Rinse in warm water, using a fabric softener. Gently squeeze out water. Chlorine bleach may be used for white fabrics. Dries quickly; may be tumble dried at low heat setting or hung up to dry. (Sweaters, however, must be dried flat.) Seldom requires ironing if removed from dryer as soon as the cycle is completed; otherwise use low heat setting, never hot, on wrong side. |

Man-made Fibers

	Fabrics	Properties	Care
Metallic •• LUREX	Fibers glitter in gold, silver, and other colors. Provides decorative yarns to be used in blended fabrics and trims for apparel and bathing suits.	Non-tarnishing if plastic coated. Not affected by salt water, chlorinated water, or climatic conditions.	Can be laundered or dry cleaned if plastic coated. Iron at low setting. Mylar polyester covering withstands heat better than acetate covering.
Modacrylic ♦♦♦ DYNEL ♦♦ VEREL	Available in deep-pile, fleece, and fur-like fabrics; used chiefly in blends and no-iron fabrics for deep-pile coats, trims, and linings.	Good wrinkle resistance. May accumulate static electricity. Non-allergenic. Quick drying. Retains shape well, excellent elasticity. Resistant to moths, mildew, chemicals, and sunlight. Very heat sensitive, softens at low temperatures. Flame resistant.	Fur-like deep-pile garments are most safely cleaned by a furrier; other fabrics may be dry cleaned or laundered. If washable, follow same directions as for acrylic. If ironing is absolutely necessary, iron at lowest temperature to prevent stiffening or glazing. Finger press fur-like deep-pile fabrics. Do not use acetone.
Nylon ▢▢ ANTRON ••• BLUE C ★ CAPROLAN ★★ .CEDILLA ★★ CELANESE ▢ ENKALURE ▢▢ QIANA ★ TOUCH	Several types of nylon produce a wide variety of fabric textures, from smooth and crisp to soft and bulky. Often found in blends. Used for lingerie, dresses, suits, stretch fabrics, and thread.	Very good wrinkle resistance. Exceptional strength. Washes easily. Low absorbency; holds in body heat. Good affinity for dyes but may fade in sunlight. Can be heat-set to hold shape, pleats, and embossed effects. High resistance to moths, mildew. Very elastic. Does not soil easily, may pill. Will melt under high heat. Resistant to non-oily stains.	Remove oily stains before cleaning. Machine wash for 3-5 minutes with regular agitation for sturdy fabrics and gentle agitation for delicate fabrics, using warm water. For bright colors use cool water. Wash whites separately to avoid graying. Fabrics may yellow; bleach frequently with sodium perborate bleaches. A fabric softener in the rinse water will reduce static electricity. Tumble dry on wash and wear setting or drip dry; dries quickly. Wash delicate items by hand in warm water with soap or detergent; rinse well. If removed from dryer immediately, may not require ironing, otherwise use low temperature on the wrong side. Never use a hot iron.
Olefin ★★★ HERCULON ▢▢▢ MARVESS	Wool-like hand, slightly waxy feel. Adaptable to textured, bulky yarn types for suit, dress, and coat fabrics. Light weight makes it especially good for deep pile and fake fur constructions.	Excellent elasticity and resiliency. Lightest of textile fibers, will float on water. Virtually non-absorbent; quick drying. Will not shrink unless overheated. Very sensitive to heat, melts easily. Non-allergenic. Resists pilling, staining, and insects. Difficult to dye.	Machine wash in lukewarm water; add a fabric softener to final rinse. Machine dry only on very low setting, and remove immediately after cycle has stopped. Preferably drip dry. Iron on lowest possible temperature setting, or not at all. Stains may often be blotted away with absorbent tissue. Olefins should not be dry cleaned if perchlorethylene is the solvent used.

Polyester	Available in many weights, textures, and weaves; often used in blends and minimum care fabrics. Used for durable press (permanent press) and knit fabrics in suits, shirts, slacks, dresses, blouses, lingerie, and thread.	Excellent wrinkle and abrasion resistance. Accumulates electricity. Wash/wear, quick drying. High strength. Resistant to stretching and shrinking. Low absorbency; may hold in body heat. May yellow, but otherwise colorfast. Retains heat-set pleats and creases. Exceptional resistance to mildew and moths. Occasional seam slippage. May pill and pick up lint.	Remove oily stains before cleaning. Machine wash for 3-5 minutes with regular agitation for sturdy fabrics, and gentle agitation for delicate fabrics, using warm water. For bright colors use cool water. A fabric softener in the rinse water will reduce static electricity, rinse well. Chlorine bleach can be used for whites before the spin cycle; others can be tumble dried at wash and wear or low setting. If removed from dryer immediately, may not require ironing; otherwise use a medium warm setting or steam iron.
Polyester △△ AVLIN ••• BLUE C □□ DACRON □ ENCRON ★★ FORTREL ◆◆ KODEL □□□ QUINTESS ○○○ TREVIRA △ VYCRON			
Rayon ◆ AVICOLOR △△ AVRIL ○ BEMBERG ○○ COLORAY △ CUPIONI □ ENGLO □ ENKROME □ ZANTREL	Comes in wide range of qualities; can be made to resemble natural fibers; can be lightweight or heavy constructions. May have smooth surfaces or bulky napped textures. Soft hand, drapes well. Used for dresses, suits, blouses, coats, lingerie, slacks, linings, non-woven fabrics, and blends.	Soft and comfortable. Absorbent; holds in body heat. Good affinity for dyes, generally colorfast. Low resistance to mildew. Relatively low strength; weaker when wet. Wrinkles unless specially finished. May shrink or stretch if not treated. Weakened in prolonged exposure to light.	Usually dry cleaned; if wet may weaken, ravel, or shrink. If washable, use mild detergent in warm water at gentle speed for 3-5 minutes. When hand washing use mild lukewarm suds, gently squeeze them through fabric, rinse in lukewarm water. Do not wring or twist. Do not soak colored fabrics. Chlorine bleaches or the peroxygen type can be used; some finishes may be sensitive to chlorine bleach. Tumble dry; if hung to dry avoid direct sunlight. Iron while damp at a moderate setting, on wrong side to prevent shine.
Spandex □□ LYCRA	Found in stretchable, flexible, supple fabrics for foundation garments, swimwear, ski pants, and other sportswear; elastic banding.	Lightweight; great elasticity. High strength, durability. Non-absorbent so repels body oils. May yellow with exposure to light.	Hand or machine wash in warm water for 3 minutes with gentle agitation. Do not use chlorine bleach, which will cause permanent yellowing. Use oxygen or sodium perborate bleach. Rinse well. Drip dry or tumble dry at cool setting, being careful not to over-dry. Can be ironed at a low temperature.
Triacetate ★★ ARNEL	Often found in blends, fabrics such as tricot, sharkskin, flannel, and taffeta. Used for garments which require pleat retention, sportswear.	Good wrinkle and shrink resistance. Antistatic finish can be built in. Low strength. Good affinity for dyes; colorfast. Can be permanently pleated; holds heat-set shape and texture. Easily washed.	Machine wash; tumble dry, except permanently pleated garments which should be hand washed and hung to dry. Usually requires ironing; can withstand higher temperature than acetate. Do not use acetone, as in nail polish remover, or any other organic solvent.

TRADEMARKS	★ Allied Chemical	★★ Celanese	★★★ Hercules
	○ American Bemberg	○○ Courtaulds	○○○ Hystron
	• American Cyanamid	•• Dow Badische	••• Monsanto
	□ American Enka	□□ DuPont	□□□ Phillips
	◆ American Mfg. Co.	◆◆ Eastman Chemical	◆◆◆ Union Carbide
	△ Beaunit	△△ FMC Corp., Amer. Viscose Div.	

How to Choose the Correct Fabric

Perhaps the most critical phase of any sewing project is that moment in the fabric store when, pattern in hand, you make your fabric decision. Be careful not to make it lightly, for the success of each sewing venture hinges on the quality and the suitability of the fabric you use. Quality is an elusive factor which does not depend on high price. Learn to recognize it by touch, not necessarily by cost, and don't skimp. Sleazy fabric never justifies the time and effort you spend on it. The best judgment is based on experience, but these guidelines will also help prevent disasters due to a poor fabric choice.

- ☐ Feel the fabric's weight, bulk, and texture. Does it lend itself to your pattern's lines? Will it drape or gather effectively?
- ☐ Test it for wearability and performance. Crush it. Is it wrinkle resistant? Stretch it. Does it give? Does it spring back? Read the label for fiber content and finishes pertinent to sewing and care.
- ☐ How will it look on you? Unfold some fabric and hold it up to your face before a mirror. Do the color and scale suit you? Carry snips or color swatches of other wardrobe items which must coordinate. Will the fabric be appropriate for the garment's intended use and care?
- ☐ Hold it up to the light. How strong and close is the weave? (Loose weaves ravel easily and require more finishing details.) Is the grain correct? Does the print correspond to the grain? Is the fashion fabric on straight grain with bonding and anchored permanently?
- ☐ Check the back of the pattern envelope. If it is a diagonal, plaid, or striped fabric, your pattern may not be suited to it.

Fabric Width Conversion Chart

We have provided this guide to help solve those quandaries that occur when the width of the fabric you've chosen is not included on the pattern envelope. It is strictly an *estimate,* and does not include changes in your fabric requirements caused by pattern alterations, large-scale fabric designs, directional fabrics, and garment designs with unusually shaped or large pieces. In these instances, it's best to exercise your own judgment about how much fabric you'll need.

Fabric Width	32"	35"-36"	39"	41"	44"-45"	50"	52"-54"	58"-60"
Yardage	1⅞	1¾	1½	1½	1⅜	1¼	1⅛	1
	2¼	2	1¾	1¾	1⅝	1½	1⅜	1¼
	2½	2¼	2	2	1¾	1⅝	1½	1⅜
	2¾	2½	2¼	2¼	2⅛	1¾	1¾	1⅝
	3⅛	2⅞	2½	2½	2¼	2	1⅞	1¾
	3⅜	3⅛	2¾	2¾	2½	2¼	2	1⅞
	3¾	3⅜	3	2⅞	2¾	2⅜	2¼	2
	4	3¾	3¼	3⅛	2⅞	2⅝	2⅜	2¼
	4⅜	4¼	3½	3⅜	3⅛	2¾	2⅝	2⅜
	4⅝	4½	3¾	3⅝	3⅜	3	2¾	2⅝
	5	4¾	4	3⅞	3⅝	3¼	2⅞	2¾
	5¼	5	4¼	4⅛	3⅞	3⅜	3⅛	2⅞

Reprinted courtesy of New Jersey Cooperative Extension Service, Rutgers, The State University

The Art of Stain Removal

Stains seem to materialize at the most inopportune times, but a thorough background in the science of stain removal can help you keep your equilibrium during these moments of stress. The first rule is **prompt treatment.** Spots set by heat or age are almost impossible to remove. Always keep in mind the nature of both the stain and the fabric.

THIN OR LOOSELY WOVEN FABRICS: Place the stained section inside out over a small bowl. Pour appropriate solvent into the bowl through the cloth. Repeat if necessary. Rinse in the same manner and let dry before laundering or dry cleaning.

THICK OR FIRMLY WOVEN FABRICS: Place stained section inside out on a dry sponge or pad. Dampen the stain with another sponge moistened in solvent. Several applications with a small amount of remover solvent are best. ❖ Always work from the center to the outer edge of the stain, feathering the stain to prevent formation of a ring.

HARDENED STAIN: Place a solvent-dampened pad on the stain and one underneath it until it is softened and can be removed. Remember: before tackling any spot, be sure to test your fabric in an obscure area with the solution you intend to use.

GREASY STAINS: For *washable* articles, regular laundering by hand or machine may remove a mild stain. For others, rub detergent directly into the stain, rinse with hot water, and then launder. However, a grease solvent may be needed even after the garment has been washed. If so, sponge thoroughly with the solvent, dry, and repeat if necessary. Use a chlorine or peroxygen bleach if a yellow stain remains after treatment.

For *non-washable* articles, treat thoroughly with a grease solvent as described above, as soon as you can after the stain occurs. Dry and repeat if necessary. Have patience because greasy stains are among the most difficult to remove. Extra time and care may be needed to restore your garment's fresh appearance.

NON-GREASY STAINS: For *washable* articles, sponge stain with cool water or soak for 30 minutes or longer. Some stains might require soaking overnight. If the stain remains, rub in a detergent and rinse. If necessary, use a chlorine or peroxygen bleach.

For *non-washable* articles, sponge first with cool water, using a sponge underneath the fabric to absorb water. If needed, work in a small amount of detergent and rinse. Sponging with alcohol will help remove the detergent and dry the fabric more quickly.

Spot Removal

Stain	Washable	Dry Cleanable
Alcoholic Beverage	Soak in cold water, wash in warm sudsy water, rinse. If stain remains, soak silk, wool, or colored items in 2 tablespoons hydrogen peroxide to 1 gallon water for ½ hour and rinse twice. Soak white linen, rayon, and cotton 15 minutes in 1 tablespoon household bleach to 1 quart water. Rinse twice. Caution: alcohol may remove the dye.	Sponge with water or hydrogen absorbent such as cornstarch.
Ball-Point Pen	Place blotter under fabric. Drip home dry-cleaning solvent through spot. Soak in solution of detergent and warm water. Rinse in cold water. Use mild bleach, but test fabric first.	At dry cleaners, specify stain was made by ball-point pen.
Blood	Soak in lukewarm water and detergent. If yellow stain remains, apply laundry bleach. For stubborn stains, apply a few drops of ammonia.	Treat with cold water to which table salt has been added (1 ounce per quart of water). Salt helps prevent color bleeding. Rinse and blot with towel. Try warm water and hydrogen peroxide to remove final traces.
Candy	Regular laundering.	Sponge with warm water.
Chewing Gum	Apply ice and remove gum from surface with dull knife. Soak affected areas in cleaning fluid.	Same as washable fabrics.
Chocolate	Rinse in lukewarm water. If brown stain remains, apply laundry bleach. For sturdy fabrics, pour boiling water through fabric over a bowl.	If colorfast, sponge with lukewarm water.
Coffee or Tea	If safe, pour boiling water through spot from a height of 1-3 feet or soak with a safe bleach.	Follow directions for a non-greasy stain, page 51.
Cosmetics	Pretreat with detergent, rubbing into spot. Launder.	Use greasy stain solvent. Dry clean.
Fruit and Berry	Launder. If stain remains, apply white vinegar. Rinse. If necessary, bleach with hydrogen peroxide.	If safe, apply small amount of detergent locally. Rinse. Or, apply white vinegar; rinse.
Grass, Flowers, Foliage	Work detergent into stain, then rinse. Or, if safe for fabric, sponge stain with alcohol. Dilute alcohol with 2 parts water for use on acetate. If stain remains, use chlorine or peroxygen bleach.	Same as washable, but try alcohol first, to see if it is safe for the dye.
Grease	Place towel under stain. Scrape off as much grease as possible, and pour cleaning fluid through stained area.	Sponge wools with trichlorocthane.

Ink	Pour water through stained area; repeat if bleeding of ink continues. If stain does not bleed, dry the treated area. Wet again with water and apply detergent and white vinegar. Rinse. A patented rust remover is also useful on ink stains and may be tried either alone or in combination with above treatment. Rinse thoroughly. Apply household ammonia. Rinse. Bleach remaining traces with laundry bleach.	Same as washable fabrics.
Mildew	Pretreat fabric as soon as possible with detergent and launder. Expose to sunlight; if any stain remains, sponge with rubbing alcohol.	Have dry cleaned or try a 4 to 1 solution of water and hydrochloric acid.
Milk and Cream	Immediately soak in cool water and detergent. Rinse and launder.	Sponge with cleaning fluid. If colorsafe and stain still remains, sponge with water.
Nail Polish	Do not use polish remover. Sponge with amyl acetate. Launder. If necessary sponge with alcohol mixed with a few drops of ammonia.	Do not use polish remover. Sponge with amyl acetate or mixture of alcohol plus a few drops of ammonia.
Paint, Varnish	Rub detergent into stain and wash. If stain is only partially removed, sponge with turpentine. For aluminum paints, try trichlorethylene; however, do not use on triacetate or polyester. Soak overnight in detergent.	Sponge with turpentine. If necessary, loosen more of the paint by covering the stain for 30 minutes with a pad of cotton dampened with a solvent. If stain remains, apply one drop liquid detergent and work in with bowl of a spoon.
Pencil	Erase with soft eraser. If mark remains work detergent into stain. Rinse. If necessary, put ammonia on stain, then repeat detergent treatment.	Erase or, if colorsafe, follow directions for washable fabrics.
Perfume	Follow directions for alcoholic beverages.	Follow directions for alcoholic beverages.
Perspiration	If garment color has been affected, sponge a fresh stain with ammonia, an old stain with white vinegar. Rinse and launder.	Same as washable fabrics.
Salad Dressing	Treat as a combination of greasy and non-greasy stains, page 51.	Sponge with warm water if possible. Dry clean.
Scorch	Alternate applications of detergent, water, and ammonia. Rinse well.	Dampen with hydrogen peroxide until stain is removed. If necessary mix a few drops of ammonia with 1 tbsp. peroxide and moisten stain. Sandpaper scorch from heavy wools.
Shine	Steam or sponge with hot vinegar or ammonia and water.	Steam or sponge with hot vinegar or ammonia and water.
Smoke and Soot	See cosmetic treatments.	For wools, raise nap with brush. See cosmetic treatments for other fabrics.

The Language of Fabrics

A

acetate Generic term for relatively inexpensive man-made fiber with a luxurious hand, good draping qualities, and low tensile strength; often used in blends with silk, cotton, rayon, and other man-made fibers.

acrylic Generic term for light but bulky man-made fiber with soft, woolly hand; often used with natural and other man-made fibers to make wool-like fabrics and knitted goods.

ajour Lacy, openwork embroidery.

alencon Needlepoint lace, usually worked in floral designs, outlined with heavy thread on sheer net ground.

alpaca Soft, lustrous, strong fiber made from the hair of the South American alpaca; classified for labeling as wool. Term also applies to lightweight fabric made from cotton and alpaca or rayon.

angora Smooth, soft hair of angora goat, often known as mohair; also, the fine, silky hair of the angora rabbit. Angora is classified for labeling as wool.

antique lace Handmade bobbin lace of heavy linen thread with large, irregular square-knotted mesh on which designs are darned.

antique satin Heavy, dull-face satin.

antique taffeta Crisp taffeta made of uneven or slubbed yarn.

appenzell Fine Swiss hand embroidery worked in a buttonhole stitch.

appliqué A separate motif or design sewn or otherwise affixed to fabric or garment.

argyle plaid Plaid design composed of large, solid color diamonds, with contrasting diagonal overstripes.

armure Stiff, rich looking fabric woven of silk, cotton, wool, rayon, or mixtures, plain, striped, or ribbed with small fancy designs suggesting chain armor.

astrakhan cloth Heavy knitted or woven fabric with a deep-pile surface of loops or curls resembling the pelt of an astrakhan lamb.

azlon The generic term for a man-made fiber composed of regenerated protein derived from natural substances such as peanuts, corn, and milk.

B

bagheera Fine woven or knitted velvet with uncut pile, used for evening gowns and capes.

bainin Handwoven woolen homespun fabric from Ireland.

barathea Closely-woven fabric with broken granular twill weave producing smooth satin-like surface.

Made from silk, rayon, cotton, wool, or combined fibers.

bark cloth Nonwoven fabric made in the tropics of inner tree bark, soaked and beaten thin, dyed and/or ornamented with printed patterns. Also, a modern fabric imitating the rough appearance of the above.

bark crepe Rough crepe made of twisted yarns woven to imitate tree bark. Usually used for evening wear.

barré Stripe, bar, or rib effect running crosswise on fabric from selvage to selvage.

basket weave Plain weave variation achieved with two or more warp and filling yarns. Fabric woven this way has a flat look, porosity, and give; can be heavy or lightweight. Any fiber can be woven by this method.

batik Method of resist dyeing originating in Java. Parts of the cloth are covered with wax, leaving uncoated parts to take the dye. This produces characteristically multi-colored patterns and designs, often with streaked effects where the dye penetrates cracks in the wax. Batik is often simulated in modern roller or screen printing. Term also applies to fabric so dyed.

batiste Soft, sheer cotton, linen, or synthetic fabric of plain weave, usually in white or pastel colors. Fine batiste is used for handkerchiefs, lingerie, blouses, and children's wear. Coarser weave often

used for linings. Wool batiste is a lightweight fabric with an even weave, usually thinner than challis and used for dresses, negligees. Also silk called *batiste de soie*.

battenberg Coarse form of renaissance lace, made by hand or machine, with linen braid or tape and linen thread worked to form various designs.

bayadere Multicolor crosswise stripes, either woven or printed.

beading Lace, embroidery, or open-work trimming through which a ribbon may be interlaced.

beaver cloth Woolen fabric with a soft finish and thick nap, made to resemble beaver fur. Also, a plushy pile fabric used in millinery.

bedford cloth Sturdy ribbed fabric of wool, silk, cotton, synthetics, or blends with raised lengthwise cords, similar in appearance to plain piqué. Often used for dresses, suits, sportswear, children's wear.

Belgian lace Pillow lace with machine-made grounds from Belgium, including Antwerp, Brussels, Mechlin, and Valencienne.

benares Silk and metal tissue fabric made in India.

bengaline Finely-woven fabric with pronounced crosswise ribs similar in appearance to poplin or faille, but heavier; usually used for coats, suits, dresses, trimmings.

binche Firm, durable lace with cloth-like texture worked in simple, snowflake-shaped motifs.

birdseye Over-all pattern of small diamond shapes, each having a center dot resembling a bird's eye, woven into cotton, linen, or synthetic fabrics. Also a type of piqué with this design.

blanket cloth Heavy, reversible fabric characterized by two-color jacquard weave with soft, thick filling. Also, a heavy, napped overcoating fabric.

blazer cloth Striped flannel.

bleeding Loss or change of color after washing or dry cleaning.

blend Combination of two or more fibers and/or colors in one yarn, resulting in new fabric and performance characteristics, or a tweed effect.

block printing Process of printing fabric by hand, using carved wooden or linoleum blocks to apply design.

bobbinet Fine machine-made net with hexagonal mesh used for dresses, foundations, and gowns, and as a base for embroidered and appliquéd laces.

bombazine Fine English fabric, usually twill weave, of silk and worsted.

bonding Joining of two fabrics by an adhesive process, making knits, sheers, laces, and other fragile fabrics easier to handle through added body and stability.

botany Generic term for finest grade of wool. worsted yarns, and fabrics. Used interchangeably with *merino*.

bouclé Woven or knitted fabric with a loopy, knotted surface and usually, a springy, spongy hand.

bourdon lace Net lace with corded edges.

bourrette Yarn spun from carded short fibers of lower quality waste silk.

braid Narrow fabric for binding or trimming, usually woven or plaited flat, but sometimes round or tubular. Includes rick rack, soutache, military, etc.

bretenne (breton) lace Net designs embroidered with heavy thread, often colored.

broadcloth Closely-woven fabric with very small crosswise ribs, made in many weights, fibers and blends, and often resembling fine poplin. Worsted and woolen broadcloths have a glossy finish and velvet-like texture with the nap running in one direction.

brocade Jacquard woven fabric with raised, over-all interwoven designs giving an embossed effect, often emphasized by contrasting surfaces and colors and gold or silver threads. Ground may be satin, twill, or a combination of weaves.

brocatelle Heavy, cross-ribbed jacquard-woven fabric for furnishings and draperies with raised figures or designs more pronounced than in brocade.

brussels lace Net lace with heavily outlined designs made separately and appliquéd.

burlap Coarse and heavy plain weave fabric made of jute, hemp, or cotton. Used mainly for wrapping, bagging, wall covering, drapery, and sometimes for clothing.

butcher linen Coarse homespun linen originally used for French butchers' aprons. Now widely imitated in many man-made fiber fabrics.

C

calendering A mechanical finishing process producing a flat, glossy surface by pressing the fabric between a series of heated cylinders.

calico Plain-woven cotton fabric, lightweight and similar to percale, printed with small figured pattern.

cambric Fine, closely-woven white or solid color cotton, with glazed or glossy looking right side; inexpensive.

camel's hair Lustrous, extremely soft underhair of the camel, used either alone or combined with wool and spun or knitted into textiles for coats, sweaters, blankets, etc. Classified for labeling as wool. Also, lightweight coating fabric, thick and warm usually in twill weave with a high glossy finish, made entirely or partly of camel's hair, mohair, or, in cheaper grades, of cow hair. Usually light tan.

canton crepe Soft crepe-woven fabric with small crosswise ribs, originally made of silk in Canton, China. Similar to crepe de chine but heavier.

canvas Heavy, strong, firmly-woven cotton, linen, or synthetic fabric, either soft-finished or highly sized. *Ada* or *Java* canvas is stiff, open weave fabric used for needlework. *Awning stripe canvas* has printed or woven stripes.

carrickmacross lace Irish lace having appliquéd motifs connected by knotted hexagonal mesh.

casha Fabric woven of wool and Cashmere goat hair. Similar to flannel.

cashmere Soft, flossy hair of the Cashmere goat, spun and knitted or woven into very soft fine fabrics. Often combined with silk, cotton or wool. *Kashmir, cassimere,* and *cashmere* also often refer to the pattern or design known as paisley, or Persian.

carding Process by which fibers of cotton are separated and brought into line as a thin web, then compacted into a continuous strand or *sliver*. Removes most impurities.

cellulose acetate Chemical compound from which acetate yarns are produced. Related to rayon.

challis Soft, supple, light-weight fabric usually printed with delicate floral, Persian, or cravat effects. May be wool, rayon, cotton, or blends.

chambray Fine quality plain weave fabric with a linen-like finish, combining colored warp and white filling yarns. Comes in stripes and checks.

chantilly Bobbin lace with fine hexagonal mesh ground and a pattern, usually elaborate floral and/or scroll designs, outlined in heavy, silky thread. Used for dresses, draperies, etc.

charvet Soft tie fabric of silk or rayon with crosswise stripes, dull finish, and satin-like texture.

check Pattern of small woven or printed squares, similar to a checkerboard.

chenille Fabric containing tufted, velvety pile yarns similar in appearance to fuzzy caterpillars.

cheviot Wool fabric in twill weave, with short, close nap and rough surface, similar to serge but heavier and less smooth. Also, heavy cotton shirting, either striped or checked, of coarse yarns.

cheviot tweed Tweed fabric, usually diagonally twilled or woven in a chevron pattern, available in a wide range of colors and grades. Differs from other tweeds in that warp and filling yarns are the same color.

chiffon Delicate, transparent fabric in plain weave, of silk, rayon, etc., usually soft, but sometimes with a stiff finish. Often used double. The word also connotes lightness and softness, as in *chiffon wool* or *chiffon velvet*.

china silk Plain weave silk of various weights. Lighter weights are used primarily for lining, heavier for blouses and custom shirts.

chinchilla cloth Heavy fabric, usually wool, with a spongy texture and tufted, nubby surface achieved by a special finishing process.

chino Cotton fabric in twill weave, of combed yarns, mercerized and Sanforized. Used for sportswear.

chintz Glazed, plain-woven cotton fabric, brightly printed with figures, birds, flowers, etc. Often used for slipcovers, draperies, etc.

circular knit Fabric knitted in tubular form on circular machinery, as jersey, hosiery, tubular belts, etc.

ciré Shiny, patent leather effect produced on fabrics, ribbons, laces, etc., by the application of wax, heat, and pressure.

ciselé Velvet with contrasting cut and uncut loop pile, forming a pattern.

cloqué Fabric with irregularly raised or "blistered" surface; similar to matelassé.

cluny lace Bobbin lace made with heavy linen thread in large open designs; *wheat ear* and *wheel* designs are characteristic.

coated fabric Woven fabric whose surface has been impregnated with substances such as lacquer, varnish, plastic, paraffin, rubber, etc. for water- or heat-proofing.

coating Fabric suitable for making coats.

coin dots Dime-size or larger dots.

combed cotton Cotton yarn that has been cleaned with wire brushes and roller cards to remove all short fibers and impurities. More expensive than cotton that has been merely carded.

corduroy Cut pile fabric of either plain or twill weave, with wide or narrow wales, cords, or ribs.

cotton Fibrous substance, soft and downy, obtained from seed pods of the cotton plant, which is spun into yarn and then woven into textiles. Also, fabric made of cotton.

covert Durable, hard- or soft-finished fabric of medium to heavy weight, in diagonal twill weave. Made of tightly twisted two-ply yarns, one woolen or worsted, the other, contrasting wool, cotton, silk, or synthetic, giving cloth a finely speckled surface.

crash Coarsely-woven, rough-textured fabric, made of thick uneven yarns. Includes plain-weave linen or cotton, used for dresses, blouses, etc.; plain weave linen mixed with jute, used for curtains; an absorbent, linen-cotton mixture, used for towels. Also, a rough-textured novelty wool fabric.

cravat patterns Small prints and weaves typical of those used for neckties or cravats.

crepe Fabric with a pebbly, crinkled or puckered surface, which is achieved by embossing, weaving, chemical treatment, or the use of hard twisted yarns. Crepes may be of silk, cotton, wool, synthetics, or combinations of fibers in weights that range from light and sheer to heavy and opaque.

crepe-back satin Fabric with satin face and crepe back.

crepe de chine Lustrous, plain weave crepe, usually made of silk. Can be light, medium, or heavy in weight.

crepon Fabric with lengthwise crinkles or "treebark" texture, resembling crepe, but thicker and firmer in texture and sometimes patterned with jacquard designs.

cretonne Medium-weight unglazed fabric usually made of cotton or linen in a variety of weaves and finishes, printed with large floral designs. Used chiefly for curtains, slipcovers, etc.

crimp Natural or manufactured wrinkles or waviness in fibers. Lends bulk and resilience.

crinoline Open, stiff weave fabric, usually of hair or stiffened silk, cotton, or synthetic fiber. Often used as a foundation or supporting fabric. Also, fabric with a stiff starched or permanent resin finish, such as cheesecloth or sheeting.

crochet Interlocking loops or stitches worked with a hook in plain or fancy designs forming a fabric, article, trimming, or lace. Also, fabric, article, trimming, or lace made in such a way.

cuprammonium The generic name for a type of rayon, or the chemical process by which it is produced. Commonly known by the trademark *Bemberg*.

D

damask A reversible, firm, glossy, jacquard weave fabric woven in patterns. Similar to brocade, but flatter.

damassin Damask or brocade fabric with floral patterns woven in gold or silver threads.

delhi work Rich-looking Indian embroidery worked in metal and silk on satin and other fabrics.

denier Unit of weight indicating the fineness or coarseness of a fiber filament; the higher the denier number, the coarser the yarn. Also, term denoting the weight and thickness of individual threads in nylon stockings.

denim Strong, coarse, washable twill weave cotton fabric, usually inexpensive. Made with colored warp and white filling, or woven in plaids, stripes, etc.

diagonal weave A pronounced twill weave.

diaper cloth White cotton fabric, absorbent and soft, which may be dobby, plain, or twill weave.

dimity Sheer fabric, usually made of combed cotton, with fine lengthwise cords, stripes, or checks.

discharge prints Designs printed by partially extracting the color of a previously dyed fabric. A design in a different color may be imprinted at the same time. Also called *extract printing*.

dobby A mechanical loom attachment which permits the weaving of small geometric patterns beyond the range of simple looms. Also, fabric woven on such a loom. Piqué is a dobby weave.

doeskin Properly, leather made from the skin of the doe. Term also describes a heavy satin weave cotton fabric napped on one side; or a heavy, short-napped woolen fabric used for menswear.

donegal Originally a thick, homespun woolen tweed handwoven in the county of Donegal, Ireland; characterized by colorful thick spots or slubs woven irregularly into the fabric. Now, any tweed with these characteristics.

double cloth Fabric made of two layers woven at once on the same loom and held together by binding threads. Face and backing may contrast in weave and color.

double-faced Term applied to fabric that can be used on either side; includes double cloth and some of the bonded fabrics.

double knit Fabric knitted on a special machine that uses a double set of needles to produce a double thickness of fabric. It has excellent body and stability.

doupion Uneven, irregular double silk thread produced when two cocoons have nested together.

drill Strong twilled cotton fabric similar to denim. Called *khaki* when dyed that color.

duchesse satin Lustrous, smooth, satin weave fabric with plain back.

duck Heavy, tightly-woven fabric usually of cotton or linen, made in various weights in plain or rib weaves. One of the most durable of all fabrics.

duvetyn Smooth, close-napped twill weave fabric that has been sheared and brushed for a velvety or suede-like appearance.

E

écossais Two-color fabric, woven in lengthwise satin stripes which stand out on the surface of the fabric, alternating with plain weave stripes, often barred or checked, of another color.

écru Light tan or beige; the color of unbleached cotton, wool or silk fabrics and laces.

eiderdown Warm, lightweight fabric, either knitted or woven, napped on one or both sides; used for infant's wear, negligees, etc.

embossing Raised figures or designs on the surface of a fabric usually obtained by passing the fabric through heated engraved rollers.

embroidery Ornamental needlework done on fabric with either silk, cotton, metal, or other threads by machine or by hand.

end An individual warp yarn, thread, or cord.

end-and-end Fine check effect woven with warp threads of alternating colors, one of which is usually white. Often used in cotton chambray; used less frequently in broadcloths and oxfords.

éponge Fabric with a soft, spongy weave made with uneven, nubby twisted yarn.

etamine Lightweight fabric with open plain weave made in many different weights, different fibers, or blends.

even-sided twill A twill weave in which the warp threads run above the filling for the same number of threads they run below.

eyelash Fabric with fringed oblongs resembling eyelashes on the surface, usually metallic for evening.

eyelet embroidery A lightweight fabric characterized by cutout areas with decorative stitching around them.

F

fabric Any cloth knitted, woven, braided, felted, bonded, or laminated, of fibers or yarns.

face The side of a fabric which looks better because of weave or finish.

faille Fabric with light, flat crosswise ribs or cords, usually soft and slightly glossy. Often of silk, synthetics, or cotton, faille belongs to the grosgrain family of cross-rib materials.

fake fur Fabric which simulates animal fur.

fall-on print Fabric design in which colors are applied on top of one another to get several different colors.

feather cloth Fabric, usually wool or a blend, to which feathers have been added for softness or decoration.

felt Non-woven fabric produced by processing a mat of fibers with heat, moisture, and pressure. Usually wool, fur, or mohair, as these fibers possess natural felting properties, but may contain cotton or rayon.

fiber The fundamental unit used in the production of textile yarns and fabrics. A small strand of matter, either naturally formed or produced by man, whose length is many times its diameter. Usually refers to *staple,* or short, spinnable lengths, but may also include continuous *filament.*

fiber dyed Yarns or fabrics, the component fibers of which have been dyed before spinning. Usually indicates a tweedy effect.

fibranne Generic French term for viscose rayon staple.

filament Continuous single strand of silk, rayon, acetate, or synthetic fiber.

filet lace Lace with square knotted mesh ground on which square patterns are darned or woven. Used for dresses, tablecloths.

filling Crosswise yarn in a weave, sometimes called *weft* or *woof.* Also, a term for sizing substances which give body or weight to a fabric.

finishing Term used for any of the processes that convert gray goods, or fabrics as they come off the loom, into finished cloth.

fisheye Large, diamond-shaped woven pattern resembling the eye of a fish; similar to, but larger than birds eye.

flake Novelty fabric with tufts or "flakes," often in contrasting colors, woven or glued on the surface.

flannel Soft fabric, either plain or twill weave, usually of cotton or wool, with slight nap on one or both sides. Also called *outing flannel.*

flannelette Soft, plain weave cotton fabric with a nap on one side.

flax Soft, silky fiber of the flax plant, which is processed and used to make linen.

fleece Woolly coat of the sheep, usually shorn from the animal in one piece. May also be used to describe the woolly coat of any animal (such as the goat or camel) whose hair is used to make fabric. Also, any heavy-napped or pile fabric with a deep, fleece-like surface.

float In weaving or knitting, a portion of yarn which extends for some length over the surface of the fabric before being bound back in by adjacent yarns. The surface of satin fabric is produced by floats.

flocking The application of short, fibrous particles or short hairs to form dots or other designs on a fabric. A common method is to print the motif on the cloth with an adhesive substance, then to dust with the flocks, which adhere to the printed areas.

foulard Lightweight twill or plain-weave fabric, often of rayon or silk; usually printed with cravat figures.

french crepe Very light-weight crepe used most often for linings and lingerie. Now known as *lingerie crepe.*

frieze Thick, heavy fabric with a rough, raised surface usually made of uncut loops. Often used as upholstery fabric.

fringe Short lengths of thread; loose, twisted, plaited,

or tasseled, and used as a border or trimming. Also, raveled fabric edge.

frisé Fabric with a curly, looped, or knotted surface.

fulling Finishing process used on woolens whereby the fabric is dampened, then beaten under heat. This causes shrinkage and an increase in weight, and obscures the weave of the cloth.

G

gabardine Firm, tightly-woven, twilled fabric often finished with a high sheen. Can be made of many different fibers and blends. Excellent for tailoring.

galatea Strong, sturdy, twilled cotton fabric.

galloon A narrow tape or braid of cotton, wool, or silk. Also a double-edged lace.

gaufré Term used to indicate any of various embossed fabric patterns.

gauge Unit of measurement for knit goods and hosiery signifying the number of needles per inch of width. The greater the gauge number, the closer and finer the knit it describes.

gauze Thin, sheer, woven fabric similar to cheesecloth.

georgette Sheer, dull-textured crepe fabric, with a

pebbled or crinkly surface. Heavier than chiffon.

gimp Trimming composed of flat, narrow open-work strips of twisted strands of silk, wool, cotton, etc., run through with metallic wire or coarse cord for body. Also, in lacemaking, coarse thread or cord used to outline or emphasize the design.

gingham Firm, light to medium weight cotton fabric, yarn dyed and woven in checks, plaids, or stripes of two or more colors.

glass Federal Trade Commission's generic term for manmade mineral fiber of glass.

glazing Finishing process that imparts luster and sheen to a fabric, such as chintz.

glen checks Any of a wide variety of small, even check designs originating in Scotland. Often used in tweeds.

gossamer Soft, filmy gauze-like fabric often used as veiling and for bouffant gowns. May also describe a sheer, thin fabric.

granite cloth Durable, hard finished but lightweight fabric with a pebbly, figured weave, the surface of which suggests the grainy surface of unfinished granite. Often made of worsted or linen.

gray (or greige) goods Used to describe fabric in an unbleached, undyed, or unfinished state. *Greige* is also a color between gray and beige.

grenadine Fine, loosely woven leno fabric similar to marquisette with a clipped dobby design or spaced warp.

grisaille French fabric usually of cotton or wool, with a black and white printed warp effect.

gros de londres Crisp, shiny, lightweight fabric, usually of silk, with alternating narrow and wide flat ribs. Sometimes incorrectly referred to as *faille taffeta*.

grosgrain Firm, closely woven fabric or ribbon with pronounced crosswise cords or ribs, heavier and rounder than those of poplin.

guanaco Fine, silky-soft fur of the guanaco, an animal related to the llama and alpaca. Fleece ranges from reddish brown to white and is considered rare.

guipure French word for machine-made laces with heavy gimp designs connected by bars; has no mesh ground.

H

habutai Soft, lightweight silk dress fabric originally woven in Japan.

haircloth Stiff, wiry fabric, with a warp of cotton, linen or, worsted, with horsehair filling. Used for interfacing or stiffening garments and upholstery.

haircord English dress muslin constructed with thick warp cords. Also bleached English cotton fabric with colored warp cords. Similar to dimity, but heavier.

hair fibers Textile fibers which include the hair of alpaca, angora goats, camels, llama, etc., often used in combination with wool. Classed as specialty fibers; lower grades may be used for felt.

hand Feel, drape, or handling qualities of a fabric; refers to texture and quality.

harlequin plaid Fabric with diamond shapes in contrasting colors creating a vivid plaid design.

harris tweed This name refers only to woolens hand-woven on the islands of the Outer Hebrides off the Northern coast of Scotland.

heather mixture Combination of fibers or colors that suggest the color of Scottish heather fields.

hemp A lustrous, coarse, and durable textured fiber from the hemp plant. Used for weaving into coarse fabrics like sailcloth; also for cordage, twine. Fibers are steel gray to creamy white.

henequen Coarse, hard fiber, white to reddish yellow in color. Obtained from the leaves of the henequen plant. Used primarily for cordage.

herringbone Broken, irregular twill weave, giving zigzag effect, like the backbone of a herring.

hessian Rough, coarse fabric of hemp or mixed jute combined with hemp. Often used for sacking.

high-count fabrics Closely-woven fabrics.

high-pile A long pile, as in plush; distinguished from *low-pile*, as in velvets and velveteens.

homespun Loosely-spun woolen fabric in plain or twill weave, usually of coarse yarn, having rough hand. Woven by hand, can be imitated by machine. Also, coarse fabric of jute, linen, cotton, or mixtures.

honan Fine grade of Chinese wild silk in pongee class; first made in the province of Honan. Has occasional lustrous thick-thin thread

honeycomb Heavily textured fabric woven to resemble the cells of honeycomb. Sometimes called *waffle cloth*.

hopsacking Rough-surfaced cotton, linen, or rayon fabric, of plain weave; usually coarse.

houndstooth check Four-pointed star check, in a broken twill weave.

I, J

ikat Any one of various chiné silk fabrics made in Java.

illusion A term for very fine, sheer tulle, net, or maline fabric used for veils, dresses.

jacquard A complex loom with a versatile pattern-mak-ing mechanism which permits the weaving of very elaborate designs. Damask and brocade are jacquard-woven.

jaspé A heavy fabric for draperies and upholstery, woven with a warp stripe of differing shades of the same color.

jersey A knitted fabric which originated on the Isle of Jersey; usually in tubular form, and in the stockinette stitch.

jig dyed Fabrics dyed in open width, moving between two rollers in a deep solution of dye, in a "jig" machine.

jute A glossy fiber from India used for sacking, burlap, and twine, and for rug and carpet backing.

K

kapok A filling for mattresses, pillows, life preservers, etc. made of the silky fiber from seed pods of the kapok tree of Malaya.

kasha A fine, wool-and-hair twilled fabric, softly napped, with a crosswise streak.

kemp Coarse, wavy fibers of wool or mohair. Used in mixed wools for special novelty effect.

keratin Fibrous proteins in wool and hair that produce elastic properties in fibers.

kersey A cloth of coarse wool, or wool and cotton, in a plain or twill weave. Used especially for work clothes and uniforms, usually in blue, black, or brown.

khaki A sturdy cloth of cotton or wool, often used in military uniforms and sportswear. Also, a light yellowish-brown color.

knitting Method of constructing fabric by interlocking a series of loops of one or more yarns. The three classes of knits are *warp knit* (which includes *tricot, milanese,* and *raschel*), *circular knit,* and *flat knit*.

L

lace fabric A fine open-work fabric with patterns of twisted, knotted, or looped threads on a ground of mesh or net. Usually made of cotton, rayon, or nylon.

laine French word for woolen or worsted cloth.

lambsdown A heavy knitted fabric, napped on one side, in all wool, or with cotton backing and woolen face.

lambskin fabric A cotton or wool cloth made to resemble woolly, unsheared lambskin.

lamb's wool The soft and elastic fleece obtained from a seven- or eight-month-old lamb's first shearing. Can be woven into a superior fabric. Used in padding, underlinings, etc.

lamé A fabric made of metallic threads, sometimes combined with silk or other fibers, in plain or fancy weaves.

laminated Two or more layers of fabric joined together by means of glue, resin, or other adhesives, or by heat. Also, a face fabric backed with synthetic foam.

lampas A fabric with jacquard-like, ornamental design, woven in two or more colors—often in silk, sometimes in rayon or cotton.

lansdowne A light-weight dress fabric in twill weave, with rayon or silk warp and cotton or worsted filling.

lappet A weaving process for small-figured cloth such as dotted Swiss, in which the pattern is embroidered into the body of the fabric as the cloth is woven.

lawn A sheer, thin cloth of combed or carded cotton. Has a crisp finish. Sometimes woven with satin stripes or a crinkled plissé effect.

leatherette An imitation leather, made of paper, cloth, or plastic material, and embossed to copy the grain and texture of real leathers.

leno A weaving process in which the warp yarns are paired and twisted, giving the fabric strength and stability, as in *marquisette*.

levantine Formerly a rich, twill-woven silk cloth, usually black, made in the eastern Mediterranean. Now a glossy finished twilled cotton fabric used for linings.

linen Fabric made from nat-

ural flax fibers, outstanding for its luster and strength. Usually in a plain weave, but also appears in damask and other patterns.

linsey-woolsey A coarse fabric of wool combined with flax or cotton; originally made in Lindsey, England.

lisle A tightly twisted, smooth cotton yarn. Used mainly in knitted hosiery, gloves, and underwear.

lisse A filmy silk gauze used for trimmings, frills, dresses.

llama Textile woven from the long hair of the South American llama. The natural color of the fleece is black, brown, or white. Often blended with wool.

lockram A coarse-woven linen cloth.

lock-stitch A machine stitch in which the top threads and bobbin threads lock together with each stitch.

loden A thick, coarse woolen cloth of Tyrolean origin, in a characteristic color called *loden green*. Wind and water resistant.

longcloth A fine, plain weave cotton cloth with a soft finish, bleached white, and often used for underwear and infants' clothes. It was one of the first fabrics to be woven into long pieces.

loom The machine or frame for weaving cloth by interlacing warp and filling yarns.

luster The quality of shine or sheen of a fiber or fabric.

lyons velvet A stiff velvet with short thick pile, usually silk, used in hats, clothing.

M

mackinaw cloth A heavy, durable cloth for outerwear, usually all-wool or wool blended with other fibers. Often double-faced and napped; usually front and back are different colors, or one side is plaid.

mackintosh A waterproof, lightweight cloth, originally of rubber-coated cotton.

madagascar lace Lace made by natives of Madagascar with thread twisted into loops and scallops.

madras Fine, hand loomed cotton fabric from India in natural color, or dyed with bleeding vegetable dyes and woven in plaids or stripes. Also, *curtain madras,* a leno-weave fabric with a dobby-figure effect formed of heavier filling yarns.

malimo Fabric constructed on a recently developed machine from East Germany which produces fabric very rapidly from three sets of yarns — warp yarns, filling yarns laid across the warp, and a third set of yarns which stitches them together. Such fabrics are technically neither woven nor knitted, but are said to be more stable than either.

malines Hexagonal open mesh or net, usually stiffened with sizing, to be used for veiling, millinery, neckwear, etc. Usually made of silk, cotton, or rayon.

man-made fibers Filaments or fibers produced by man from mineral substances such as glass, chemically produced synthetics, or transformed cellulose base fibers.

manta A plain-woven, coarse fabric of cotton of South American origin.

marabout A delicate, thin silk fabric made from twisted raw silk.

marl Yarns of two different colors or lusters twisted together for novelty effect.

marocain crepe A dress crepe with cross-ribbed texture, of wool, cotton, or silk.

marquisette A lightweight, open leno weave fabric. For use in sheer curtains, dresses, veiling, etc.

marseilles A firmly-woven cotton fabric, reversible, with raised design such as in piqué. Used for trimmings, vests, etc. and in its heavier weights for bedspreads.

matelassé A double fabric with raised woven designs, often jacquard, having a surface that looks puckered or quilted. In lighter weights of silk, synthetics, etc, and often combined with metallics; used for evening wear.

matte finish A fabric with a dull surface.

matte jersey Tricot with a dull surface made of fine crepe yarns.

mechlin lace Bobbin lace with design outlined by a lustrous thread.

meisen A plain Japanese silk weave with fancy pattern of blurry crosses achieved by hand coloring yarns before weaving them.

mélange A fabric of mixed fibers, such as cotton warp and woolen weft, or a fabric woven with yarn spun from fibers of differing colors.

melton A short-napped, non-lustrous, heavy, and thick material finished without glossing or pressing. Usually in all-wool or with cotton warp and woolen weft.

mercerize To treat cotton yarn or cloth in a caustic soda solution, usually under tension. Increases strength, luster, and affinity for dyes.

merino A soft, luxurious fabric resembling cashmere, originally made from the fleece of merino sheep. Now refers also to a superior, fine woolen or wool and cotton blend fabric, and to wool and cotton yarns used in knitwear and hosiery.

mesh An open-textured fabric with even spaces between the yarns. Can be knitted, knotted, or woven, in fine or coarse threads or yarns.

messaline A high-luster satin fabric of closely woven silk; light and soft.

metallic cloth A tinsel-like, shiny fabric incorporating metallic threads. Often combined with silk or other nonmetallic fibers. Metallic threads may be all metal, plastic coated metal, or a core fiber surrounded by metal.

middy twill A firm, compact twill-woven cotton cloth, used for middy blouses, shirts, uniforms, slipcovers, etc.

milan lace Bobbin lace with net ground and tape or braid scroll or floral motifs.

milanese A warp-knit fabric made with two sets of yarn knitted in diagonal directions, creating a diamond effect. Stretchable, wrinkle and run resistant, absorbent.

mirror velvet A pressed-pile, lustrous and shimmering velvet, used mainly for hats and trimming.

mixture A blend of two or more fibers of different colors or types, as in homespuns and heathers.

modacrylic A synthetic textile fiber formed by a long-chain polymer. Wrinkle resistant, resilient, with a pleasing hand, but sensitive to heat.

mogador A plain weave fabric resembling faille, in silk or man-made fibers, usually in colorful stripes. Used for neckties and sportswear.

mohair Long, silky, lightweight, resilient hair of the Angora goat.

moiré An irregular, wavy finish on corded or ribbed fabrics of silk, cotton, and many of the man-made fibers. It is produced by engraved rollers, steam, heat, or chemicals.

moleskin A strong, solid-surfaced cotton fabric, lightly napped and sheared to produce a suede-like finish.

momie cloth A sheer, crepe-like, pebble-textured cloth; usually a blend of rayon, cotton, or silk, with wool. Used for dresses, and as a foundation for embroidery. Also called *mummy cloth,* after a loosely-woven fabric the Egyptians used for wrapping mummies.

momie weave A weave in which the yarn is twisted, giving it a granite or pebble effect, as in crash toweling.

monk's cloth A coarse, heavy, basket-weave fabric, usually made of cotton or linen, with identical warp and filling threads. Can be difficult to sew because yarns have a tendency to slide.

monofilament A single, untwisted synthetic filament, such as nylon, in any diameter or strength which can be used in the normal weaving process.

monotone tweed A tweed fabric produced by combining yarns in varying shades or tones of the same color.

mordant A chemical substance—a metallic salt—used on yarns or fabrics to improve their capacity for accepting a dye.

moreen A strong, stout upholstery and curtain fabric, cross-ribbed with coarse warp yarns and fine filling yarns, sometimes with embossed or watered finish. Made in cotton and/or wool.

mossy crepe A crepe woven with a fine, mossy texture.

motley An English fabric used for clothing from the 14th to 17th Centuries; made of woolen yarns in variegated colors.

mousseline A muslin-like, fine, sheer cloth with a crisp finish, closely woven of highly twisted yarns.

muga Silk from the cocoon of the muga, an Indian moth.

mule A complex spinning frame used mainly for spinning wool.

mull A soft, sheer, plain-weave cloth of cotton, silk, or man-made fibers; used for bookbinding and clothing.

multifilament Man-made yarns composed of many fine filaments, (usually 60 or more) twisted together.

mungo A cheap, low quality, short-staple wool cloth made from mill wastes.

muslin A wide variety of plain-woven cotton fabrics ranging from sheer to coarse. It can be bleached or unbleached, dyed in solid colors, or printed. The finer grades are used for undergarments, shirts, pillowcases, etc.

multiple fabric Fabric composed of two, three, or even four layers bound together by the structure of the weave.

N

nacré velvet An iridescent, changeable velvet produced by weaving the back from one color and the pile from another.

nainsook A lightweight, soft, mercerized cotton cloth, plain woven, with a lustrous finish. Used mostly for children's clothing, lingerie, and curtains.

nankeen A durable cotton cloth, at first hand-loomed in Nanking, China, using a native yellowish cotton. Term now refers to a twilled cotton fabric dyed to imitate the original.

nap A soft, fuzzy finish raised on various fabrics, usually by brushing cloth against a cylinder covered with short protruding wires. Gives fabric a soft hand and downy appearance, and makes it warmer and more durable.

natural A yarn or fabric in its original unbleached or undyed state.

natural fibers Animal, vegetable, or mineral materials which occur naturally in fibrous form.

needle-finished A fine fabric such as nainsook, handkerchief linen, or light muslin, finished without sizing or with the sizing removed to prepare it for sewing.

needlepoint canvas A stiff canvas with clearly defined

meshes, used as a base for needlepoint embroidery. Finer mesh size is *petit point* and larger is *gros point*.

needlepoint fabric A soft-surfaced novelty wool coating fabric made of curled or nubby yarns.

needle loop In knitted goods, a loop drawn by needle through a loop in the fabric.

neps Little knots or clusters in cotton or wool fibers, formed either naturally or during processing.

net An open-work fabric that may be sheer and fine, such as tulle, or coarse and open, such as fish net. Constructed in three basic types—*bobbinet, tricot,* and *raschel*—and in various fibers.

ninon A good quality, sheer, smooth fabric of hard-twisted yarns, in plain or novelty open weaves, with a clear, transparent surface. Sometimes called *triple voile*.

noil The short fibers removed in the carding and combing process. Can be combined with longer fibers and spun into novelty yarns. It may be of low quality (especially noil silk, which is often waste), or of high quality (as in camel's hair, when the noil is the choicest part of the fleece).

non-woven fabrics Sheets or mats of fibers held together by interlocking or by a bonding agent. Often used for linings, interfacings, and where disposable fabrics are needed. Term does not include fabrics made by the felting process, or to paper products.

novelty weave Any weave which varies or combines the three basic weaves; *plain, satin,* or *twill*.

novelty yarns Yarns of irregular or unusual textures. Used for creating special effects in weaving or knitting.

nub yarn A novelty yarn spun intentionally with slubs, knots, etc.

nun's veiling A plain-weave, sheer, soft cloth of good quality, usually made of worsted, silk, or cotton. Used for dresses, nun's veiling, etc.

nylon Generic name for man-made polyamide yarns or fibers. It is very strong and resilient, with high wet strength. It blends well with other fibers, and washes easily, dries quickly.

nytril A synthetic fiber related to acrylics, which is soft, resilient, easy to care for, and wrinkle-resistant.

oatmeal cloth A soft and durable pebble-surfaced fabric made of wool, cotton, linen, etc., with fine warp and coarse filling yarns.

oilcloth A waterproof, coated fabric consisting of heavy cotton muslin, coated on one side with a glossy finish of oil, clay, and pigments.

oiled silk Silk fabric that has been treated with an oil preparation to make it waterproof. Has a transparent look.

oilskin A cloth such as cotton, linen, synthetics or silk, treated with oil to make it waterproof. Used for raincoats.

olefin The generic name for a paraffin-based manufactured fiber. It has a luster and holds dyes easily, is strong and tough, and wears well.

ombré A rainbow colored effect in fabrics, either dyed or woven in, with colors graduated usually from light to dark. Effect can be in varying shades of the same color, or a mixture of different colors.

ondule A wavy, rippling pattern produced in fabrics by alternately spreading and converging a small group of warp threads. Used for decorative fabrics such as curtains and draperies.

organdy, organdie A very fine, thin, transparent cotton cloth with a crisp finish, woven of tightly twisted yarns.

organza A fine transparent fabric similar to organdy, using highly twisted yarns. Made in silk and synthetics.

organzine Silk yarn of high quality, formed of several strands of raw silk twisted together in the opposite direction to the way the component filaments are twisted.

oriental crepe A handwoven crepe from China or Japan.

Also, another name for *Canton crepe*, which is soft and heavy, and has a slight cross-ribbed effect caused by weaving tightly twisted filling yarns and loosely twisted warp yarns.

osnaburg A rough, coarse fabric originally made of flax, and named after a town in Germany. Now, a plain-woven, coarse cotton of loose, but durable construction. Can be medium to heavy in weight. In its unbleached state, it is often used to make heavy bags for cement, grains, etc. Also used for sportswear, draperies, and slipcovers.

ottoman A heavy cross-corded fabric with larger and more rounded ribs than bengaline or faille; a variation of the plain weave. Made in wool for coats, dresses, suits, etc. Also made in silk or synthetics for evening wear, trimmings, etc.

outing flannel A soft, lightweight, plain, or twill woven fabric with nap on one or both sides. Made from cotton or rayon, and used for infants' wear, sleepwear, diapers, etc.

overcheck A textile or design with two superimposed check patterns in different sizes or colors.

overplaid A textile or design with two superimposed plaid patterns in different sizes or colors.

oxford cloth A cotton shirting fabric in plain or basket weave, with two fine warp yarns and a heavier filling yarn. Has a lustrous, soft finish. Also, a dark gray woolen cloth made of yarns that are mixtures of black and white fibers.

P

package dyeing A method by which the dye solution is circulated through yarns wound around perforated tubes.

padding Soft, bulky materials like wool or cotton wadding, used to stuff or pad such things as quilted coat linings, shoulder pads, etc.

paduasoy A rich, strong, slightly corded silk fabric, originally woven in Padua, Italy, and used for clothing and upholstery. Also called *peau de soie*.

paisley An intricate, all-over design incorporating abstract, curving figures. The term also applies to a fine, soft, woolen cloth printed with a paisley design.

panama cloth A fabric suggesting the texture of Panama hats. Sometimes lightweight and made from hand-twisted worsted yarns; other times, coarser, as in a basket weave, and made from cotton or other fibers or blends.

panne A finish for velvet or satin produced by pressure. It flattens the pile of velvet, giving it a lustrous sheen. Satin is made smoother and more lustrous.

parachute fabric Plain-weave fabric of silk, cotton, nylon, or rayon, used especially for making parachutes, but sometimes for clothing. It is lightweight, compact, closely-woven, and has a silky sheen.

paragon A closely-woven, nearly waterproof fabric made of wool or silk, sometimes combined with hair.

paramatta A lightweight fabric for dresses. Originally made with weft of combed merino wool and warp of silk. Now often made with cotton warp.

parti-colored In variegated or mottled colors.

passementerie A general French term referring to edgings and trimmings usually made from gimp, cord, beads, etc.

patchwork Small pieces or patches of fabric of different colors and patterns sewn together at the edges. Used for quilts, counterpanes, pillow covers, etc. Also used in dresses and sportswear.

patole A richly decorated Indian silk sari woven in the chiné technique. A pattern is printed, dyed, or painted on either the stretched warp or filling threads before weaving.

pattern In fabrics, this applies to the decorative design or motif, and to the repetition of any design or weave.

pearl (or perle) cotton A mercerized cotton thread or yarn in various colors and sizes, used for embroidery and other needlework, as well as for knitting and crocheting.

peau de soie A French term meaning "skin of silk." Originally a satin weave made from silk, but can now be made from synthetic fibers. Either single- or double-face.

pebble weave A fabric with a rough pebbly surface produced by a special weave or by highly twisted yarns, as in pebble crepe.

pekin A fabric originally made in China of silk; characterized by figures or vertical stripes in alternating weaves or colors. Often made in luxurious combinations of satin and velvet.

pepper-and-salt A fabric made of black and white yarns mixed and woven together, giving a flecked look.

percale A fine, lightweight, plain-weave cotton fabric with a firm-balanced construction (i.e., an equal number of threads per inch in warp and weft.)

percaline A plain-woven, lightweight cotton that is sized and calendered to give it a glossy or moiré finish.

permanent press Term describing fabrics which uphold certain standards of performance in shape retention, wrinkle resistance, and washability. There are two basic manufacturing techniques: *deferred-* or *post-cure,* and *flat-* or *pre-cure.*

persian lawn A plain-weave, sheer, fine cotton fabric; usu-ally white with a high luster. Used for neckwear, dresses, etc.

persienne A cotton or silk fabric with fanciful printed or painted-on designs.

peruvian cotton A rough, hairy, long-fibered cotton grown from a Peruvian plant.

petersham A rough woolen cloth used mainly for men's trousers or heavy coats. Usually in navy blue.

photographic prints The result of a process by which photographs are transferred to cloth by the use of photo-engraved rollers. One of several processes adapted from color printing.

phulkari Cloth of East Indian origin decorated with floral patterned embroidery.

pick In weaving cloth, term refers to one throw of the shuttle across the loom, interlacing filled with warp threads. Also, an individual filling thread.

pick-and-pick Pick threads of one type alternating with those of another type, such as nylon and elastic threads alternating in fabrics for bathing suits or foundation garments.

picot A decorative woven edge consisting of tiny loops on the selvages of ribbon, lace, etc. Effect may also be achieved by cutting machine hemstitching through center.

piece dyed Fabrics which are dyed after being woven or knitted. Such fabrics are a solid color unless they are resist- or discharge-printed, or cross dyed.

pigment An insoluble coloring substance in finely ground powder form which imparts its color to other materials. In the case of synthetic yarns, pigments are usually added to the solution before the filaments are formed.

pile fabric A fabric woven with an extra set of warp or filling threads which stand up to form a soft, thick, deep surface. The standing loops can be left uncut or cut. Also made by a knit process.

pilling Forming small tangles of fibers on the surface of a fabric as a result of abrasion. Considered a defect.

pilot cloth A coarse, thick twilled woolen cloth in indigo blue, heavily napped on one side. Often used for seamen's blue uniforms.

pima A strong, high-quality cotton developed from certain Egyptian cottons.

piña cloth A soft and lustrous transparent fabric woven from the silky fibers of the pineapple plant.

pin check A very small check made from yarns of different colors; smaller than the shepherd's check.

pinstripe A fine, narrow stripe, approximately the width of a straight pin, on a fabric. Term also refers to fabric with such a stripe.

pinwale A very narrow edge or rib that is found in fabrics such as corduroy.

piqué A term referring to a fabric that has raised, lengthwise cords, welts, or wales in various plain or patterned effects. A dobby weave.

plaid Refers to a pattern of colored stripes or bars crossing each other. From the Scottish term for a shawl-like garment woven in a traditional *tartan,* or clan plaid pattern.

plain weave The most fundamental type of weave in which each filling yarn passes alternately over and under each warp yarn, alternating each pick. Also, *tabby.*

plaiting The arrangement of cloth in plaits or folds (synonymous with pleating). Also, braiding, or interlacing strands of rope, straw, etc.

plated A knit fabric having one yarn forming the front and another the back. Can have a different color yarn on each side.

plissé Term refers to puckered stripes or pattern on cotton fabric. Effect is achieved either by weaving with yarns of different degrees of shrinkage or by chemical treatment.

plush A warp-pile fabric having silk or wool pile longer than that of velvet, but not as densely woven.

ply yarn Yarn composed of two or more strands or filaments twisted together.

point d'angleterre A type of bobbin lace made with either bobbin or needlepoint patterns. Of Flemish origin.

point de paris A type of bobbin lace that has a six-sided mesh ground design in a cloth-like texture, usually outlined with a heavy cord.

point d'espagne Spanish needlepoint lace that has gold or silver threads, or heavy designs on its fine ground.

point d'esprit A type of cotton bobbin net that has square dots scattered on the surface.

pointed twill Used mainly for woolen cloths, this is a weave in which threads of the right hand twill and the left hand twill come to a point, producing a zigzag effect.

polished cotton A cotton fabric with a shiny face achieved either by satin weave or by waxed finish.

polyester Generic term for a synthetic fiber with superior properties of wrinkle resistance and ease of care. Often used in blends with cotton.

polyurethane fiber First made in Germany during World War II, a strong, manmade fiber that has a low melting point. Commonly used in elastic fabrics.

pongee A plain-weave silk fabric that is thin, naturally tan-colored, and has a rough-weave effect. Term also refers to a finely combed cotton used in underwear.

poodle cloth Fabric resembling the coat of a French poodle. Usually woven of a loopy bouclé yarn.

poplin Plain-weave fabric that has a fine rib running from selvage to selvage. Similar to cotton or rayon broadcloth, but with a slightly heavier rib.

popline Refers to a fabric that resembles poplin. Usually has silk or rayon warp, and wool filling.

post-cure A durable press finish that is applied to the fabric by the garment manufacturer after the garment has been made and pressed.

poult de sole A plain weave silk fabric having heavy filling strands that form cross ribs. Can be made from manufactured fibers and is sometimes referred to as *faille taffeta.*

pre-cure Durable press process in which the finish is applied at the mill before the fabric is manufactured into garments.

pre-shrunk Fabrics or garments which have been treated by a chemical or other shrinking process.

press cloth A strong fabric used for filtering or other industrial purposes. Also, a cloth used between an iron and a garment being pressed, to protect the garment fabric.

pressure dyeing A method of coloring textiles quickly by holding the fabric and dye liquor under steam pressure.

protein fibers Textile fibers derived from protein sources. Wool and silk are protein fibers, as is the man-made fiber azlon. Differentiated from cellulosic fibers such as cotton, linen, and rayon.

puckered cloth A term referring to nylon cloth that has a pebbled, crimped plissé or cockled finish.

pulled wool Wool taken from pelts of dead animals. Usually used for lower quality fabrics, since using the entire wool fiber, including the root, results in yarn of coarse texture.

pure silk Refers to silk fabric that does not contain metallic weighting or finishing materials exceeding ten per cent. For black silk, fifteen per cent is allowed.

pyroxylin A coating applied to cotton or rayon fabrics to make them waterproof and stain resistant.

Q

quilting Fine hand or machine stitches running through two thicknesses of material with a third layer of padding between. Traditionally in a design such as diamonds, scrolls, etc. Also, material used for quilts.

quintin A sheer fabric, from the town of the same name in Brittany, France.

R

rabanna A coarse matting handwoven from raffia fibers in Madagascar and used for draperies and curtains.

rabbit hair This natural hair is normally of a pale brown hue and soft texture. It is often combined with other fibers in weaves or knits for a softening or special effect.

radium A supple, pliable lingerie fabric made of synthetic yarn with a natural sheen and a dull finish.

radzimir (or rhadzimir) Modified term for the French "ras de Saint Maur," a short-napped cloth of that region. Traditionally a silk fabric, used for mourning clothes. Also the name for a fine silk or rayon fabric having lengthwise ribs or a broken twill weave.

raffia Natural or colored straw taken from the raffia palm of Madagascar and used for tying plants or making articles such as baskets.

rajah A silk fabric with a rough surface, similar to pongee and used in clothing.

ramie A strong, inexpensive bast fiber taken from an East Asian plant which can be spun or woven into a fabric similar to linen or silk. Used chiefly for household goods.

raschel A versatile type of warp knitting, raschel is coarser than other warp knits and is used in open-work patterns like lace and net.

ratiné A textured yarn made by twisting a thick and a thin fiber under uneven tension. Also a rough, nubby fabric of ratiné yarn, loosely woven in plain weave.

ratiné lace A bulky machine-made lace with heavy loops, similar to turkish toweling.

rattail Narrow and rounded soutache braid, ideal for sewing on fabrics for decorative designs or effects.

ravel To pull away the yarns, making a fringe on the fabric edge. Also, to unwind.

raw silk Silk fibers as they are taken from the cocoon, before the natural gum has been removed.

rayon Generic term for filaments made of certain solutions of modified cellulose (i.e., wood pulp). The solutions are pressed or drawn through an opening and then solidified in filament form. Term usually refers to viscose rayon, but also includes cuprammonium.

red cross (nurse's) gingham Heavy cotton fabric having alternate blue and white yarn dyed stripes.

reeling The process by which single silk filaments are wound from unbroken cocoons into skeins which are called *raw silk*. When the filament is twisted during reeling it becomes *thrown silk*. Highest quality silk is obtained through reeling.

renaissance lace A lace having woven tape motifs joined by various flat stitches.

rep (reps or repp) Term referring to cotton, wool, or silk fabrics distinguished by a well-defined weft woven in crosswise ribbed effect.

residual shrinkage This term refers to the percentage of shrinkage one can expect of a fabric or garment that has been preshrunk. Residual shrinkage occurs gradually each time the garment is washed.

resist printing Applying dye-resistant substances to portions of the fabric in order to obtain a design when the fabric is piece-dyed. *Batik* is a resist process.

ret To soak or expose cellulosic fibers to moisture in order to loosen the fiber from the woody tissue by bacterial or chemical action. Used in processing flax and hemp.

reticella lace Form of needlepoint lace having geometric designs connected by picoted bars. Used for table linens and trimming.

reversible fabric A fabric that is finished and usable on both sides.

rib A straight raised cord running horizontally, vertically, or diagonally in a woven fabric; usually in a close regular pattern created by using a coarser yarn in the warp or weft, or by a twill weave. In knitting, a vertical ridge formed by alternating knit and purl stitches in a regular pattern.

ribbon A relatively narrow piece of woven fabric such as silk, satin, or velvet, usually with a cord finish along both edges instead of selvages.

rickrack Flat, woven braid in wavy, zigzag pattern.

right-and-left plaid A plaid with the stripes placed so that the design is one-sided, making it necessary to place all the pattern pieces running in the same direction in the cutting layout.

ripple cloth A woolen dress fabric with a long nap on the right side. Like *zibeline*.

roller prints Printing on fabric using engraved copper rollers, one roller for each color in the pattern.

roman stripes Brilliant contrasting stripes usually running in the warp direction.

rose point Venetian needlepoint lace, worked in relief, which has designs of flora and scrolls delicately connected by small bars. Also, *gros point* and *Venetian rose point*.

rope-silk A heavy, silk embroidery thread.

roughers Woolen cloth as it comes off the loom, before fulling or finishing.

round-thread linen A soft, plain linen woven of hard-twisted yarn and popularly used for embroidery and fancy work because its threads are easily separated and fringed.

rubber The generic name for a fiber made from a substance composed of either natural or synthetic rubber. Natural rubber is the substance made from latex, the sticky sap of the rubber tree.

rubberized fabric Fabric with a rubber coating on one or both sides which renders it waterproof.

rumswizzle A material made in Ireland of imported, natural-colored wool.

run-proof A particular knitted construction whose locked loops prevent the occurrence of runs.

run-of-the-mill Textile products that are often sub-standard and can be referred to as *seconds*.

rygia A breed of coarse-wooled Norwegian sheep.

S

sack cloth Coarse fabric of cotton, linen, or goat's hair used in making sacks or bags. Worn traditionally as a symbol of penance or mourning.

sailcloth A very heavy, strong, plain-weave fabric made of cotton, linen, or jute.

saran A synthetic fiber, weather-resistant, flame-, moth-, and mildew-proof. Used for screening, floor coverings, outdoor furniture.

sateen Cotton fabric characterized by satin weave.

satin Smooth fabric of silk or man-made fibers whose face is dominated by long floats, usually of warp threads. Often combined with other weaves, such as brocade, velvet, and jacquard.

schiffli A form of shuttle embroidery done on a ground of sheer fabric by a machine which is guided by hand. Open areas are burned out.

scrim Lightweight, loosely woven open cotton or linen cloth, used for curtains, needlework and theatrical stage drops.

seersucker Lightweight cotton blend with crinkled stripes woven in the warp direction by setting some of the warp yarns tight and others slack.

selvage A narrow woven edge portion of fabric parallel to the warp, often made with stronger yarns and a tighter weave construction than the body of the fabric to prevent raveling and support tension in weaving.

serge A crisp flat fabric with an even right hand twill, woven in several weights from natural fibers. Commonly used for suitings.

shading Effect produced on some fabrics such as satin by the finishing process, causing the fabric to give a different impression in color or texture when its direction is reversed.

shantung Originally a name for a hand-loomed, plain-weave fabric with an irregular surface, made in China of wild silk. Today, the term refers to a plain weave fabric with heavier, rougher filling yarns, which may be cotton, silk, or man-made fibers.

sharkskin An even twill weave wool fabric whose warp and filling yarns are alternated, white with a color, usually black, brown, or blue. Also, a sleek, hard-finished, pebbly-surfaced fabric made of tightly-twisted yarns of cotton, linen, silk, or man-made fibers woven in either a plain or basket weave construction.

shepherd check A distinctive fabric pattern of small uniform checks of white and another color (usually black) woven in an even twill weave.

shetland Soft, lightweight, warm fabric made from the wool of the Shetland sheep. Also knitted fabric made of this wool.

silk Continuous protein filament produced by the larvae of the silkworm (Bombyx mori) when constructing their cocoons. The filament is reeled off and boiled to remove a stiff natural glue, and woven into fabrics noted for their soft luster, luxurious hand, and strength.

sizing General term for compounds applied to yarn or fabrics to impart smoothness, abrasion resistance, luster, or improved body.

spandex Generic term for a synthetic fiber with superior elastic qualities. Used for foundation garments, swimwear, and hosiery.

spun silk Silk yarn made of short lengths of silk fiber obtained from silk waste or pierced cocoons rather than the long continuous silk filament. Also, fabric woven from such yarns, of nubby texture, often incorrectly termed *raw silk*.

suede cloth Woven or knitted fabric of cotton, man-made fibers, wool or blends, finished to resemble suede leather.

surah Soft, fine twilled fabric, often of silk or man-made fibers, available in plaids, stripes, or prints.

Swiss Fine, sheer cotton fabric that may be plain, dotted, or figured. Usually is crisp and stiff. Also *dotted Swiss*.

synthetic fibers Trade group of man-made fibers made by chemical synthesis or "building up" of one or more simple chemical compounds. Does not include rayon or cellulose acetate.

T

taffeta Basic group of fine, plain-weave fabrics, smooth, crisp, usually lustrous. Called *faille taffeta* when woven with a fine rib, or *changeable taffeta* when warp and weft are different colors, causing iridescent effect.

tapa cloth A non-woven cloth made in the South Seas of the beaten fibers of the paper mulberry tree.

tapestry A heavy, decorative handwoven fabric whose design is formed by the filling threads, which completely cover the warp. Also, a machine-made imitation whose pattern is woven in by means of colored weft threads.

tartan The twilled woolen or worsted plaid design associated with a specific Scottish clan; i.e., dress Campbell.

tattersall A simple over-check pattern in two colors on a white or contrasting ground.

terry cloth Woven or knitted fabric with loop pile on one or both sides. Usually of cotton, and very absorbent.

textured yarns Continuous filament man-made yarns which have been treated to give them lofty hand and/or stretchy qualities.

ticking Strong, durable, closely woven fabric, usually in a twill weave. A distinctive red or blue yarn-dyed warp stripe is traditional.

tie silk Wide range of silk fabrics suitable for men's ties. Often confused with *Thai silk*, a plain-weave fabric woven in Thailand, often in a large, brightly-colored, yarn-dyed plaid design.

toile de jouy An elaborate floral or scenic design on cotton, linen, or silk, finely colored and printed from an engraved copper plate.

triacetate Generic name for cellulose triacetate, which is similar to acetate, but has higher heat-resistance and improved ease-of-care characteristics.

tricot Most important warp knit fabric, made from two sets of threads and recognizable by vertical wales on the face and crosswise ribs on the back. Highly run-resistant. Has very little lengthwise stretch. Used as backing on nearly all bonded knits.

tropical suiting Lightweight summer suiting made in several fibers and weaves.

tulle Machine-made net with hexagonal mesh made from fine silk, cotton, or synthetic fibers. Used for veils.

tweed A wide range of rough-textured, sturdy fabrics characterized by fiber dyed, mottled color effects.

twill A basic weave characterized by a diagonal rib, or twill line, usually running upward from left to right. Used to produce strong, durable, firm fabrics.

U, V

uncut velvet A type of velvet made with terry pile, the loops of which are left uncut.

valenciennes A flat bobbin lace worked in one piece, with the same thread forming the ground and pattern. Commonly known as *val lace*, it may be hand- or machine-made.

vellum A fine, glazed, very transparent cotton fabric used as a tracing cloth.

velour (velours) A soft, closely-woven, smooth fabric with a short, thick pile. Usually of cotton, wool, or mohair, it can be knitted or woven in several structures.

velours frappé A velvet with raised patterns produced by pressing the pile with heated cylinders.

velvet A warp pile fabric with short, closely-woven cut pile, usually silk. Can be woven two ways: 1) Double cloth, woven face to face with the pile ends interchanging between layers, and cut to produce two layers of velvet. 2) Single layer, the pile of which is cut by wires inserted with the filling and withdrawn.

velveteen An all-cotton fabric with a short, close filling pile cut to resemble velvet.

venetian A strong, warp-faced sateen.

venetian point lace A heavy, needlepoint lace with a floral design in relief.

venise A fine, damask table linen with large floral patterns; made in the Netherlands and France.

vichy A stiffly-finished, yarn-dyed cotton fabric woven in checks. Similar to *gingham*.

vicuña A wild relative of the llama, yielding the finest of all animal fibers.

vinyl Includes several thermoplastic fibers of varying chemical composition. Made in monofilament, yarn, staple, and film form. Also, *vinal*.

virgin wool Wool which has never previously undergone any manufacturing process.

viscose One of the three types of rayon, and that which is produced in the greatest quantity. Also, the process by which cellulose is transformed into rayon filament.

viyella A lightweight British twill fabric in a 50-50 wool and cotton blend.

voile A lightweight, sheer fabric with a crisp, wiry hand. Made from hard twist yarns in a plain weave.

W

wale In woven fabric, one of a series of ribs, cords, or raised portions. In knitting, a series of loops lying lengthwise in the fabric, formed by the action of a single needle.

warp The set of threads running lengthwise in a woven fabric, parallel to the selvage.

warp knit A type of knit constructed of several yarns, generally running lengthwise. Tricot, milanese, and raschel are examples.

warp print Fabric whose warp has been arranged in order and printed before weaving. Results in a pattern of indistinct outline and subdued colors. Also called a *shadow print*.

weft In weaving, the yarns which are laid perpendicular to the warp. Also known as *woof* or *filling*.

weighting Imparting weight or body to a fabric, either chemically or mechanically. Usually refers to silk, to which tin salts are added. Amount of weighting is now controlled by law.

whipcord A rugged fabric with a sharply defined upright warp twill, usually of cotton or worsted.

wild silk Silk obtained from the cocoons of silkworms which feed on other than mulberry leaves.

woad A natural blue dye similar to indigo, used in Britain and Europe from ancient times, chiefly on wool.

wool The fine, soft, fiber covering of the sheep. Also includes the hair of the angora or Cashmere goat, and may refer to the *specialty fibers* from the hair of the camel, alpaca, and vicuña. Distinguished from *hair* by its covering of minute scales, which give it its unique felting and insulation properties. *Reused wool* must be so labeled, and is taken from cloth which has been used or worn. *Reprocessed wool* is reclaimed from manufacturing scraps of cloth.

woolen A method of yarn-making in which the fibers are carded and then spun directly without combing. The nature of the fibers used is less critical than in any other system, and yarns are more bulky and randomly oriented and less tightly twisted than those produced by the worsted process. Also, fabrics made of such yarns, as are most bulky, heavily fulled or napped wools.

worsted Fabric woven from yarn spun from combed wool. Also, a yarn spinning system. Yarn is fine and strong; fabrics are usually smooth, tightly woven, and have a crisp hand.

Y, Z

yarn A continuous strand of textile fibers. May be spun of short fibers or composed of continuous filaments.

yarn dyeing Coloring the yarn before it is woven or knitted. Yarn dyeing is used to produce woven check and plaid patterns, and is a common form of dyeing.

zante lace A form of reticella lace made on the Ionian Islands of Greece.

zephyr Any of several sheer, lightweight fabrics, often containing silk. Used for shirting, shawls, embroidery.

zibeline A woolen over-coating with a long, hairy, lustrous nap pressed in one direction, hiding the basic satin weave.

zigzag twill A broad term applied to weaves in the broken twill class.

The Undercover Story

Designers' styles require fabrics to take many different shapes. They depend on either the fabric's natural ability to flare into a silhouette or hidden inner components that support the fabric in its desired shape. Underlining and interfacing, when chosen and used correctly, will help achieve the designer's intended effect with relative ease. They are the concealed elements that help garments retain their shape and wear longer. In lining a garment, the designer uses only fabrics that will comply with the drape of the style and will be attractive, comfortable, and smooth. The use of these hidden components, correctly executed, is one of the hallmarks of fine couture.

When choosing underlining, interfacing, and lining, consider the type of care required by the fashion fabric. A washable fashion fabric necessitates a washable inner fabric. Use as much care in shrinking it, when necessary, as you do in shrinking the fashion fabric. Remember that even a steam iron can have different effects on the inner and outer fabrics, causing one to shrink more than the other or in a different direction. A residual shrinkage of less than 1% in the underlining, interfacing, lining, or outer fabric will not require pre-shrinking. When in doubt, however, pre-shrink the fabric by using a suitable method (pages 168 and 169).

The durability of the inner fabric should be as great as that of the fashion fabric so that it will last the life of the garment. There is nothing more annoying than having to replace a lining that has weakened and torn from normal use, pulled away from the seams at points of stress, and crumbled at the armholes from moisture and wear. Think about the dress left hanging in the closet because the body imparted by the underlining was washed away after the third or fourth wearing. And what about the dress with the once beautiful funnel collar? The interfacing lost its stiffness and now the collar does nothing more than wrinkle around the neck.

Although virtually all your sewing will require the shaping influence of underlining and interfacing, there are several instances when they are unnecessary and may even hamper the desired effect. For example, a sheer overdress that is meant to reveal an underdress of heavier fabric should not be underlined. Tie collars on many blouses and dresses are made without underlining or interfacing in the tie section for ease in tying the bow. A chiffon cowl collar is often self-underlined to ensure a perfect drape without resistance from an underlining that might have slightly different draping qualities. Underlining certain knits, such as wool double knits, might inhibit the comfort inherent in the stretchability of the fabric. When permanent pleats are desired, pressing sharp creases will be more difficult with the added layer of underlining, and the normal addition of edgestitching will result in rippling and puckering of the underlining, preventing the pleats from lying flat and sharp.

Underlining

Use underlining to impart a sculptured look to your garment. It is cut from the same pattern pieces as the garment fabric. Then the underlining and fashion fabric are basted and sewn together to act as one layer. When used for shaping, underlining gives the outer fabric the support necessary to hold a silhouette that otherwise could not have been maintained. It adds body, reduces wrinkling, and lengthens the life of your garment by protecting the outer fabric from abrasion.

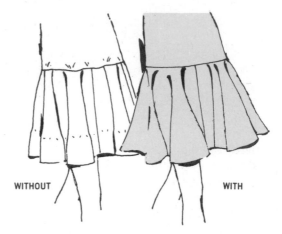

WITHOUT   WITH

An underlining is also used to facilitate marking and stitching your garment. First mark your underlining, pin to wrong side of your fashion fabric, and transfer necessary markings to the fabric. Slight changes or adjustments can be recorded on the clearly marked underlining without overhandling the garment.

The underlining further acts as a hanger for the garment so that facings, interfacings, and hems can be sewn without stitches or ridges appearing on the right side of the garment. To accomplish this, the underlining should be lighter in weight and as soft or softer than the outer fabric so as not to affect the outside of the garment, except in cases where subtle shaping is desired.

When selecting underlining, test it with the fashion fabric by draping both together over your hand to make sure they relate well to each other. A tightly-woven fabric is best for preventing stretching and preserving the shape of your garment. Test the tightness of the weave by scratching the fabric with your thumbnail. If the yarns spread apart or slide, the fabric generally will not wear well.

To achieve different effects in different areas of the same garment, more than one kind of underlining is often necessary. A lightweight wool dress with a draped yoke neckline and an A-line silhouette will need a soft, lightweight underlining for the yoke and a crisp underlining for the rest of the dress.

Batiste, china silk, and marquisette are lightweight and perfect for underlining crepe, voile, dress weight cottons and blends, and lightweight wools. For wool coating and suiting or heavy brocade, use medium to heavyweight underlinings such as taffeta, muslin, organdy, or organza. Many commercial products are especially manufactured as underlinings. They come in a wide selection of colors and fiber blends and are usually labeled for softness or crispness. The softer commercial underlinings are perfect for even the lightest fabrics, while the very crisp ones have enough body to give shape to heavyweight wools. Refer to the chart on underlinings, pages 84 and 85, to aid you in your selection.

You may wish to stabilize a loosely-woven fabric by bonding underlining to it. This can be done either by fusing the two layers with iron-on bonding net or by replacing underlining with featherweight iron-on interfacing. Test first to be sure finished product is not too stiff and that the bonding agent will not show on the outside of garment.

Interfacing

Areas such as collars and lapels, cuffs, belts, buttonholes, and opening edges should be interfaced to maintain their shape and firmness. The interfacing provides strength and stability, prevents stretching, adds body, and gives added crispness without bulk. When cut and inserted on the bias, it maintains the gentle roll desirable in many collars and hems. It may also be used on heavy or flat fabrics to prevent bumps or ridges of seam allowances from showing through to the outside of the garment.

The appropriate interfacing varies with the weight of the fashion fabric, the area in which it is used, and the amount of stiffness and shape desired. In any one garment you may need to use as many as three different weights of interfacing to create the desired effects. You may interface the body of a lightweight garment with lightweight interfacing for body, the buttonhole area with medium weight interfacing for stability, and the pockets and facings with iron-on interfacing for ensured body and immobility. The interfacing should generally be lighter in weight than the garment fabric.

WITHOUT   WITH

When a pattern calls for interfacing to support the shape of the entire garment or a large portion of it, pattern pieces are usually provided for that purpose. Whether you choose a light, medium, or heavyweight interfacing depends upon how much extra firmness is necessary to maintain the garment contours. Seam allowances are generally trimmed away and the interfacing is applied with catchstitches and long running stitches. You will find methods of application throughout Book III, where the individual garment areas are discussed. Tailoring a garment will require special handling of the interfacing; see the tailoring section. Do be sure to choose an interfacing fabric that will allow your garment enough pliability to be wearable.

Interfacing may be either woven or non-woven. Both types are available in light, medium, and heavy weights, usually only in black, white, and neutral colors. Non-woven interfacing, made by fusing fibers with heat, has no grain. They can be cut in any direction and won't ravel or lose their shape. Some non-wovens have an "all-bias" construction with stretchability in every direction for more flexible shaping and support. Other varieties can be purchased with durable press finishes for use with durable press fabrics. See the adjoining chart, pages 82 and 83, for an accurate listing of interfacings.

Iron-on interfacing, available in both woven and non-woven fabrics, adheres to fabric under the heat and pressure of an iron and holds the threads of the fabric in a stable position. If used in areas other than patch pockets or belts, it should be applied to the facing rather than to the outer garment fabric. Test first to make sure that the result is not too rigid for your purposes and the fixative does not show through to the outside of the garment. Since the iron temperature required is quite high, a pressing cloth may have to be used.

Lining

Lining gives your garments a smooth, luxurious feeling for added comfort as well as a quality finished, custom-made look. It is either cut from the same pattern pieces as the garment or from separate lining pieces, if provided; it is assembled separately, then sewn into your garment by hand or machine. A lining prolongs the life of the garment by covering the inner construction details and protecting the fashion fabric from abrasion during wear. It prevents stretching, helps preserve the shape, reduces wrinkling, and adds body to limp fabrics when desired.

The lining fabric should not affect the fit or characteristics of the outer fabric. Generally it should be softer and lighter in weight than the outer fabric, but not so lightweight as to reveal ridges and bumps from construction details. A lining fabric that is too firm for your fashion fabric may distort the silhouette of your garment. Use fabric that is not affected by weather changes. Some fabrics become sticky in the heat and stiff in the cold; because of their weave, they do not absorb moisture very readily. A lining should also be static-free; otherwise it might cling to the wrong side of the garment or to your undergarments, creating wrinkles and unattractive clinging in your garment. It should also be smooth and slippery to help your garment slide easily over your other apparel, especially in a jacket or coat.

WITHOUT

WITH

When selecting a lining fabric, consider how often you plan to wear and clean the garment. China silk is lovely for a velvet dress you may be wearing occasionally for elegant evenings, but it will not last in a garment worn or dry-cleaned often. Lining fabrics, like interfacings and underlining, must be able to receive the same care as your outer fabric. Do not choose a lining that is only dry cleanable if your fabric can be washed by hand or machine. Lining fabrics should also have corresponding performance qualities, such as those imparted by special finishes. There is no sense in inserting a cotton lining which would require ironing into a garment made of durable press fabric. When shopping for a lining, note the special characteristics of the fabric listed on the bolt in addition to its fiber content. The majority of trade-name linings are colorfast, perspiration-proof, wrinkle-resistant, and have non-cling finishes, as well as other desirable attributes.

INTERLINING: Some coats must have linings that serve the additional function of providing warmth. Durable satin linings backed with wool, a metallic reflective finish, or a laminated foam-type insulation are available. Since the wool or foam types add more bulk than lining alone, you must make an allowance for this added thickness when cutting the pattern. Interlining, a separate layer of wool or fuzzy cotton placed between the lining and underlining, may also be used for warmth. For application, see page 373.

Fashion Inside and Out

Color is important in choosing a lining fabric, especially in a jacket or coat where the lining may show when the garment is opened. Matched linings and fabrics are best if the jacket will be worn over different colored blouses and sweaters. The lining itself can be a perfect costume accessory for jackets that will be worn over matching dresses or tops. Fancy foulards or snappy stripes may be just the personal touch needed to finish your garment with verve.

If the lining fabric is darker in color than the fashion fabric, make sure it does not show through to the outside of the garment as shown in sketch. Use an opaque underlining that matches the fashion fabric, then insert lining.

Camisoles, Foundation Supports, and Fabric Stays

These design features are used to support many garment areas; choose a fabric from either the lining or underlining category to coincide with the fashion fabric.

Camisoles support skirts or portions of skirts to allow free swing to the design of the garment bodice. Use underlining or a lightweight taffeta for a camisole in order to keep fabric thickness to a minimum.

Make your foundation supports requiring feather boning from medium weight taffeta or underlining fabric. The support takes the place of your

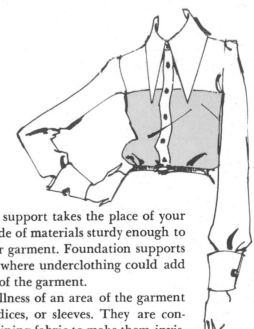

undergarment and must, therefore, be made of materials sturdy enough to shape your body and to hold up the outer garment. Foundation supports are found most often in evening clothes, where underclothing could add bulk or detract from the sleek, smooth fit of the garment.

Fabric stays are made to control the fullness of an area of the garment and can be used effectively in skirts, bodices, or sleeves. They are constructed from lightweight lining or underlining fabric to make them invisible from the right side of the garment, but they must be firmly woven to retain the shape and drape as a stay is intended to do.

Guide to Linings

Fabric Name	Type	Weight	Color	Use	Points to Note
* **Armo-Wool**	woven	medium	white	interlining in tailored dry cleanable garments, padding under topstitching	dry cleanable
⊡⊡ **Bisque**	woven	light	all colors	crisp hand for shape, ideal for permanent press fabrics	machine washable
brocade	woven	heavy	all colors	fur coats and evening coats	dry cleanable
□ **Butterfly**	woven	light	all colors	very lightweight garments, lace dresses, and fabric for slips	machine washable, dry cleanable, crease resistant, static free
○ **Casino Plus**	woven	light	all colors	sheath, jacket, lightweight upper linings	machine washable, dry cleanable
china silk	woven	light	all colors	soft silks, lightweight rayons, wools, all weights for soft supple silhouette	dry cleaning recommended
* **Ciao Polyester** anti-static	woven	medium	all colors	lining or underlining all weights for soft silhouette	machine wash warm, tumble dry, remove promptly
cotton	woven	light to heavy	all colors	all weights, washable cotton fabrics	pre-shrink, machine washable
crepe	woven	light	all colors	lining or underlining jerseys, knits when softness and "give" is desired	hand and machine washable, dry cleanable
		heavy		heavyweight coats, suits, and jackets	dry cleanable
⊡⊡ **Earl-Glo** Acetate Sheath Crepe de Chine Permanent Press	woven	light	all colors	lining and underlining all weights but sheers	hand and machine washable
Woven Nylon				stretch lining, ideal for knit fabrics	machine washable, dry cleanable
Acetate Faille Acetate Prints		medium		medium weight jackets, coats, and vests	hand wash
Acetate Milium Satin Acetate Satin Crepe Back Satin Crepe Back Milium Satin				lining for coats, jackets, and vests	
Quilted Satin					dry clean only
Quilted Polyester					machine washable

fake fur	pile	heavy	all colors	wool coats and suits	dry cleanable
* **Gingerbread** anti-static	knit	light	all colors	line and underline knits	machine wash warm delicate cycle, tumble dry low, use cool iron
○○ **Keynote Plus**	woven	light	all colors	especially for use with perma-nent press fabrics	machine washable
lawn	woven	light	all colors	very lightweight garments	machine washable, pre-shrink
○ **Loomgold**	woven	medium	all colors	milium insulated lining for heavy coats and suits	dry clean only
□□ **Marvelaire** anti-static	woven	light	all colors	all weights, wash 'n wear	machine washable
◇◇ **Milium**	woven	heavy	all colors	combination lining and inter-lining for wool coats and suits	dry cleanable
□□ **Nylon Sheath**	woven	light	all colors	lining and underlining all weights but sheers	machine washable
organza	woven	medium	all colors	medium weight dress and skirt fabrics	dry cleanable
percale	woven	light	all colors	light and medium weight dress and skirt fabrics	hand and machine washable
† **Pet N' Pur**	knit back fake fur face	medium	all colors	lining for jackets and coats	machine washable, tumble dry
◇ **Saja**	woven	medium soft, crisp	all colors	all weight dress fabrics	anti-static, machine washable, dry cleanable
silk	woven	medium	all colors	medium weight dress and skirt fabrics	dry cleanable
○ **Sunback Satin**	woven	heavy	all colors	combination lining and inter-lining in one fabric for coats and suits	dry cleanable
□ **Thermolan** Polyester Fleece	non-woven	light	white	interlining fabric, always used with a lining for coats and jackets	dry cleanable, machine washable
★★ **Tritessa**	woven	light	all colors	lightweight garments	machine washable, dry cleanable
□ **UnderCurrent**	woven	medium soft, crisp	all colors	all weight dress and skirt fabrics	dry cleanable, static free
○○ **Ultressa**	woven	light	all colors	lining and underlining all weights, soft silhouette	machine washable
voile	woven	soft	all colors	for lining sheers and light-weight dresses	dry cleanable, machine washable, pre-shrink
△ **Wistful**	woven	light	all colors	lining and underlining light-weight garments	machine washable, dry cleanable, permanent press

NOTE: See trademark identification on page 85.

Guide to Interfacings

Fabric Name	Type	Weight	Color	Use	Points to Note
◇ **About Face Basic Liner**	woven	medium	black, white natural	shaping material for light and medium weight fabrics	machine washable
* **Acro** Hair canvas	woven	light	ecru	washable garments	machine washable and dry cleanable
* **Armo** Hair canvas P 17, P 26 P 20, P 27	woven	medium	natural	shaping and underlining medium weight wools and blends	dry cleanable
		heavy		shaping heavyweight wools, support in hats and bags	
* **Armo Press**	woven	light	white, black	light, medium weight polyester	permanent press
* **Armo Tie** Interfacing	woven	heavy	ecru, natural	for silk and woolen ties, coats, suits (professional)	dry cleanable
		medium		for silk and woolen ties, coats, suits (economical)	
		light	white	for coats, suits	washable
▢ **Bravo Canvas**	woven	light	nat., white	all tailoring in suits and coats	preshrunk, drycleanable
▢ **Bravo Set**	woven	light	eggshell	light and medium weight wools and blends	machine washable, dry cleanable
▢ **Durable Press**	woven	light	white, black	underlining for easycare fashion	machine washable, dry cleanable; no preshrinking needed
▢ **Earlaire of Reemay**	non-woven	light	white, black	light, soft shapes	machine washable, dry cleanable
		medium	white, black	light, firm shapes	
◇ **Face Flex**	iron-on non-woven	medium	black, white	detail-reinforce small areas such as welts, cuffs, buttonholes	machine washable, dry cleanable; no preshrinking needed
	iron-on woven		natural black, white	all purpose	
◇ **Face Form**	iron-on non-woven	light	black, white	reinforce small garment areas such as openings for gussets	machine washable, dry cleanable
	woven	medium	natural, black, white	suits and coats	
◇ **Facelon**	non-woven	light	black, white	light soft shapes	machine washable, dry cleaning, no pre-shrinking necessary, crease and wrinkle resistant
		medium		light firm shapes	
		heavy		well-molded silhouettes	
	non-woven bias	light	black, white	when "give" of bias is needed; knits, durable press	
* **Fino** Hair canvas	woven	medium	natural, white	shaping/underlining light, medium weight suits, coats, hems	dry cleanable
* **Finolight** Hair Canvas	woven	light	natural	medium weight coats, suits	dry cleanable
* **Fusible Acro**	iron-on woven	medium	natural	interfacing for jacket and coat fronts, collars	machine wash warm, delicate cycle, tumble dry low, use cool iron dry cleanable

★ **Fusible Formite**	iron-on woven	light	natural	interfacing jacket and coat front cuffs, hems	dry clean only
▢▢ **Fusible Reemay**	iron-on non-woven	light	black, white	interfacing, light firm shape	machine washable
▢ **Hair Canvas**	#77 woven	light	natural	for lightweight suits and coats	dry cleanable preshrunk
	#88 woven	medium	natural	for medium weight suits and coats	
	#99 woven	heavy	natural	for medium to heavyweight suits and coats	
★ **Instant Armo**	iron-on woven	light	white, black	interfacing shaping small detailed areas, mending	machine washable
▢ **Interlon**	non-woven	bias feather-weight	white	lightweight fluid shapes	machine washable, dry cleanable
		light	white, black	lightweight shaping for light and medium weight fabrics	
† **Kyron**	non-woven	light	all colors	light, soft shapes	machine washable, dry cleanable
		medium		light, firm shapes	
		heavy		well molded shapes	
†† **Pellon**	non-woven all-bias	feather-weight	white, grey	interfacing or underlining for soft, light to medium weight fabrics	machine washable, dry cleanable
		lightweight		interfacing or underlining, firm shape and body, for medium to heavy weight fabrics	
		fleece white		provides full and lofty shapes, for all fabrics, lingerie, swimwear, shoulder pads	
†† **Pelomite Detail**	non-woven iron-on	medium	black, white	reinforce small garment areas such as openings for gussets	machine washable, dry cleanable
◇ **Prima Canvas**	woven	medium	natural	medium, heavyweight coats, suits	dry cleanable
▢ **Shape-Flex Iron-on**	all purpose woven	light	black, white	for supple hand in small or large areas	pre-shrunk, washable, dry cleanable
	non-woven	medium		reinforcement in small areas	washable, dry cleanable
▢ **Sta-Shape** Hair Canvas	woven	light	natural	medium and heavyweight suits and coats	dry cleanable
		medium	black, white		
▢ **Suit-Shape**	woven	light	natural, white	for easy tailoring, compatible with polyester, wool, and blends	washable, dry cleanable, pre-shrunk
▢ **Thermolan**	non-woven	light	white	soft shaping, slightly padded look to cuffs, hems	machine washable, dry cleanable
▢ **Worsted Canvas**	woven	fine	natural, white	especially for use with medium weight luxury fabrics	pre-shrunk, dry cleanable, crease resistant
		light	natural	lightweight luxury fabrics	

Fusing Agents
Used to attach interfacing; substitute for hand-sewn hems, facings, etc.

†† **Fusible Web**	non-woven	light	clear	works with most fabrics, pretest, fused areas retain "give."	machine washable, dry cleanable
△△ **Polyweb**	non-woven	light	clear	works with most fabrics, pretest, fused areas retain "give."	machine washable, dry cleanable
▢ **Stitch Witchery**	non-woven	light	clear	works with most fabrics, pretest, fused areas retain "give."	machine washable, dry cleanable

NOTE: See trademark identification on page 85.

Guide to Underlinings

Fabric Name	Type	Weight	Color	Use	Points to Note
◇ **About Face**	woven	medium soft	all colors	underline all weight garments for soft hand	machine washable, dry cleanable, residual shrinkage controlled
		crisp		underline all weight garments for firmer hand	
◇ **About Face Basic Liner**	woven	light	natural, black, white,	shaping material for light and medium weight fabric	machine washable, dry cleanable, crease and wrinkle resistant
* **Acro**	woven	medium	natural	medium, heavyweight cotton, silks; defined look for medium weight wools, heavyweight knits	machine washable, dry cleanable
* **Armo-Wool**	woven	medium	white	interlining in tailored dry cleanable garments, padding under topstitching	dry cleanable
batiste	woven	light	all colors	all weights for soft fluid garments	shrink before using
▯ **Bisque**	woven	light	all colors	crisp hand for shape, ideal for permanent press fabrics	machine washable
○ **Casino Plus**	woven	light	all colors	underline all weight garments, line lightweight garments, use for camisole and stays	machine washable, dry cleanable
china silk	woven	light	all colors	all weights for soft, supple silhouette	dry cleaning recommended
Ciao	woven	medium	all colors	underline and line all weights for soft sihouette	machine wash warm tumble dry remove promptly, dry cleanable
▭▭ **Earl Glo** Acetate sheath	woven	light	all colors	lining and underlining all weights but sheers	hand and machine washable
* **Gingerbread** Anti-static	knit	light	all colors	underline and line knits	machine wash warm delicate cycle, tumble dry low, use warm iron
▯ **Interlon Bias**	non-woven	light	black, white	soft supple shape and drape for lightweight construction	machine washable, dry cleanable
marquisette	woven	light	all colors	mesh, adds body to chiffons and sheers	dry cleanable, shrink for washable garments
▯ **Marvelaire**	woven	light	all colors	all weights of dresses, suits, and coats	machine washable
muslin	woven	light	natural, white	dresses, suits	shrink before using
▭▭ **Nylon Sheath**	woven	light	all colors	lining and underlining all weights but sheers	machine washable
organdy	woven	light	all colors	delicate, stiff finish for lightweight definition of silhouette	shrink before using if cotton, dry clean if silk

84

organza	woven	light	all colors	all weight garments	shrink before using if cotton, dry clean if silk
†† **Pellon All Bias**	non-woven	light	black, white	softly molds entire garment, used as underlining	machine washable, dry cleanable
* **Poly-SiBonne** Anti-static	woven	medium	all colors	underline and line all weight garments; interfacing for light-weight garments	machine wash warm tumble dry remove promptly, dry cleanable
◇ **Saja**	woven	medium soft	all colors	all weight garments for soft hand	machine washable, dry cleanable
		crisp		all weight garments for firmer hand	
* **Siri**	woven	soft	black, white	underline all weight garments for a soft hand	machine wash warm tumble dry remove promptly, dry cleanable
		firm		underline all weight garments for a firmer silhouette, interfacing for lightweight garments	
taffeta	woven	light	all colors	crisp, lightweight definition of shape	dry cleanable
** **Tritessa**	woven	light, soft finish	bone, black, white	medium weight, soft finish for dresses, suits	machine washable, dry cleanable
		crisp finish	all colors	medium weight, firmer finish for skirts, dresses	
○○ **Ultressa**	woven	light, soft finish	all colors	lining and underlining all weights, silhouettes	machine washable
□ **UnderCurrent**	woven	light, soft finish	all colors	underline all weight garments for soft hand	machine washable, dry cleanable
		light, med. soft finish		underline all weight garments for firmer finish	
□ **Veriform** Static free	woven	light, soft finish	black, white	easily molded silhouettes, and interfacing	machine washable, dry cleanable
		light, crisp finish		all-purpose underlining, bouffant silhouettes, and interfacing	
△ **Wistful**	woven	light	all colors	lining and underlining light-weight garments	machine washable, dry cleanable, permanent press

Notions
Indispensable
Sewing Accessories

Having chosen your fabric, you must now remember to stop at the notions counter and pick up those little necessities that might otherwise entail a later trip to the store. Generally, it is a good idea to keep on hand a supply of the more standard notions—needles, hooks and eyes, etc.—to save yourself the frustration of having to continually interrupt your sewing to purchase some small item you have forgotten. There are some notions, however, that you will have to buy each time you purchase fabric to ensure that they will match and be appropriate to your particular fabric and style; buttons, thread, zippers, and bindings or tapes are perfect examples. Still other notions are so specialized that you will need to purchase them only as they are called for by a specific garment, such as horsehair braid for the hem of an evening gown or boning for a swimming suit.

Completing the inside of your garment in an aesthetic manner will result in a finished garment that is a delight to wear. Tapes, laces, and bindings in matching colors will give the inside of your garment a custom-made look—not to mention perfectly finished edges! Couture finishing requires the proper sizes and types of notions. Since the notions counter contains a seemingly endless array of gadgets, use the back of your pattern envelope and the following descriptions to guide your selection.

Belting ranges in width from ½″ to 3″ and comes in black or white. Both regular and iron-on types are available by the yard or in pre-packaged lengths.

Bias Tape is made of cotton in ¼″, ½″, and 1″ widths. The 1″ width has edges folded ¼″ to the wrong side. It may be either single-fold (with the edges folded to the wrong side to meet at the center) or double-fold (with an additional fold just slightly off center.)

Boning is made of nylon for flexibility and is usually covered with fabric. Available by the yard or in short pre-packaged strips, it is used where stiffness is required to maintain and mold shape.

Buckles are available in a wide variety of styles and widths (from ½″ to 3″). They come in gold or silver or may be covered for a custom finish. They can be found singly or in kits with belting.

Cording, ⅛″ to 1″ in diameter, may be made of cotton, cellulose, or synthetic fibers. Used as filler for piping, tubing, or buttonholes, it is sold by the yard.

Drawstring Elastic is cord-like round elastic for making casings.

Elastic comes in white, black, or pink in widths from ¼″ to 1¼″. It is sold by the yard or in pre-packaged lengths.

Eyelets come in kits for belts and other uses, such as lacing.

Fur Tacks act as studs to hold collars and fur pieces to coats and suits.

Grosgrain Ribbon ranges in width from ³⁄₁₆″ to 3⅛″ and is used for a multitude of sewing tasks, such as staying waistlines or for belting, as well as decorative purposes.

Hammer-On Snaps are strong enough to withstand hard usage, making them ideal for children's clothes, sportswear, pajamas, and work clothes.

Heat Fusable Adhesive adheres two layers of fabric by pressing rather than sewing. It comes in the form of a fiber mesh in ¾", 1½", and 5" widths. It is to be used as a sewing aid, not as an interfacing.

Hem Facing is a cotton or rayon bias strip with ¼" folded in at the edges. 2" wide, it is used for facing and binding.

Horsehair Braid is the ideal hem facing for soft flare, available in widths from ½" to 6".

Labels are a must for personalizing your workmanship—the ultimate touch.

Lace Seam Binding gives your seams and hems a pretty finish. It may be cotton or elasticized in ½" or ¾" widths. Pre-shrink to prevent puckers.

Lingerie Strapholders are available in black, white, and pink. They are attached to the garment at shoulder seams to keep your lingerie straps from wandering.

Nylon Closure Tape consists of two strips, one faced with minute hooks and one with pile, that intermesh when pressed together. It can be an indispensable aid for lightweight, jam-proof fastening.

Piping is a ⅛" corded bias strip with a ¼" seam allowance. It comes in many colors of cotton in pre-packaged lengths and is used for decoration.

Seam Binding, a truly indispensable sewing notion, comes in wash and wear, rayon, iron-on, and bias versions. It is sold in pre-packaged lengths in ½" and 1" widths.

Shoulder Pads serve as a garment foundation and provide camouflage for sloping or too narrow shoulders. They are available in dress or coat styles, covered or uncovered, with round or squared ends, and are used for dressmaking and tailoring.

Stays, made from metal spirals or plastic, are used for shaping, molding, and vertical reinforcement. They come in 4", 6", and 8" lengths. The plastic ones are most commonly used for staying collar points.

Trims are available in a multitudinous variety; refer to the trims section.

Twill Tape, used in tailoring and for waistline stays, comes in black and white in ¼" to 1" widths.

Weights help control the drape of your fabric. Lead weights range in size from ¾" to 1⅛" and are covered and sewn inside garment. Lead weight strips consist of lead pellets encased in a fabric and are sold by the yard. Gold chain weights come in different widths and weights and provide decorative weighting.

Zipper Adhesive is a double-stick tape to use in place of pins for easy application of zippers. It is applied to zipper tape, pressed to fabric, and then zipper is sewn.

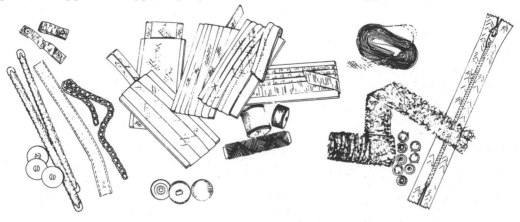

Buttons

Make your buttons work as an accent to your garment. Buy them to enhance your creation, not merely to finish it. See pages 303 through 305 for a detailed discussion of types and how they may be used. Cover your own buttons with sophisticated fabrics, fur, or leather. To determine button size, use the button gauge below. Technically, buttons are sized in "lines"—40 lines equal one inch. When the size is known in inches, refer to the chart to convert the size into lines.

1. Line 20 or 24—general size for shirts and shirtwaist dresses.
2. Line 30—size of a dime.
3. Line 36—size of a nickel.
4. Line 40—size of a quarter.
5. Line 60—size of a silver dollar.

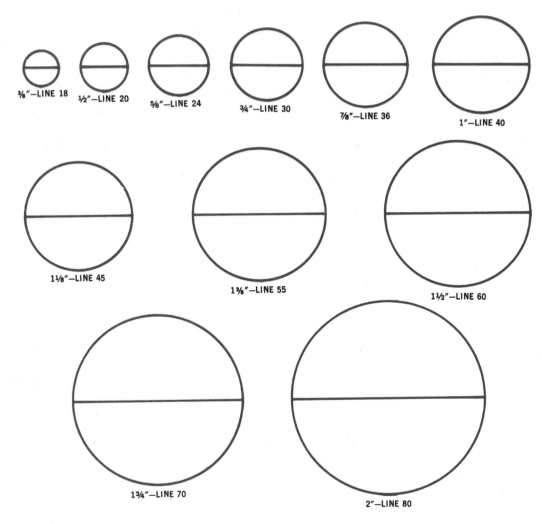

⅜"—LINE 18 ½"—LINE 20 ⅝"—LINE 24 ¾"—LINE 30 ⅞"—LINE 36 1"—LINE 40

1⅛"—LINE 45 1⅜"—LINE 55 1½"—LINE 60

1¾"—LINE 70 2"—LINE 80

Fastenings

SNAPS, used for closing and anchoring garments, are available in many sizes and types. Dress fasteners come in nickel or black enamel-coated metal, from sizes 4/0 to 1 (small), the most popular sizes, and 2 to 4 (large). Silk covered snaps, ideal for suits and coats, come in large sizes suitable for heavy-duty use. You may cover your own for special color combinations (see page 382) or purchase see-through nylon snaps in black or clear to blend with the color of your garment.

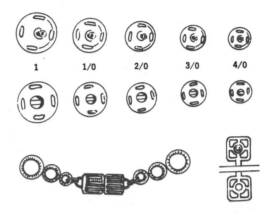

Fur snaps are perfect for attaching fur collars and other accessories to your garment.

HOOKS AND EYES come in a variety of designs for special holding purposes. The standard type is made of brass, nickel, or black enamel-coated metal, and comes in sizes 00 to 5. Coat sizes for heavyweight fabrics come in nickel or black.

Silk covered hooks and eyes make sturdy fastenings for coats or other items, especially fur. Specially shaped adjustable or skirt hook and eye closures make practical fasteners for waistbands, as shown on page 301.

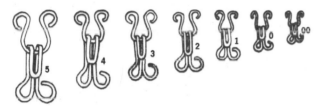

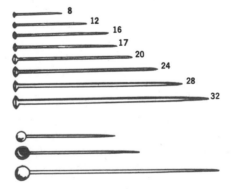

Pins

PIN sizes and types vary, too. Pin size is stated in sixteenths of an inch according to length; a size 16 is $^{16}/_{16}$" or 1" long, a size 8 is ½" long. Bank pins are heavy-duty household pins. For general sewing, #17 dressmaker pins are most commonly used. These are slender pins of medium diameter. For fine sewing and delicate fabrics, #17 silk pins —very slender with very fine points—are recommended. Larger, coarser pins are advisable only on heavy, coarse, or very loosely knitted fabrics. All pins must be rustproof; brass, nickel-plated steel, or stainless steel pins are all good. Plastic or glass headed pins, available in various sizes, are easy to see because they contrast with the fabric.

Needles

Choose a needle according to type for the job it will be doing and to size for the thread it will be pulling through the fabric. Generally, the finer or sheerer the fabric, the sharper and more slender the needle should be. SHARPS are medium length needles with small, rounded eyes used for general sewing. BETWEENS, shorter needles with small, rounded eyes, are for fine, detailed handwork that requires short, fine stitches. EMBROIDERY needles are medium length with long, larger eyes; generally used for embroidery and crewel work, they can also be substituted for Sharps. For long basting stitches and millinery work, long needles with small, rounded eyes such as MILLINER'S are best. A CALYX EYE needle has an eye with an open top for easy threading.

Needles come in sizes ranging from 1 to 24. The smaller the number of the needle, the longer and coarser it is. Sizes 7 through 10 are best for most dressmaking, while the other sizes are for heavier or specialized sewing.

For specialized sewing, such as tapestry or needlepoint, use TAPESTRY needles, which are short and heavy with large eyes and blunt points. DARNERS come in two types. COTTON DARNERS are long with long eyes, and may also be used for basting; YARN DARNERS, the longest needles, have large eyes and are used for darning with heavy or multiple yarns. There are also special needles for home repair sewing, including the GLOVER'S needle, handy for leather and fur, and the TOY and YARN needle. Another specialty needle is the BEADING needle, which is fine and flexible.

Sewing machine needles should be selected first by the brand and model of your machine and secondly by the weight of fabric to be sewn. Size numbers or names can vary quite a bit, so be sure to buy the needles recommended on the package for your machine.

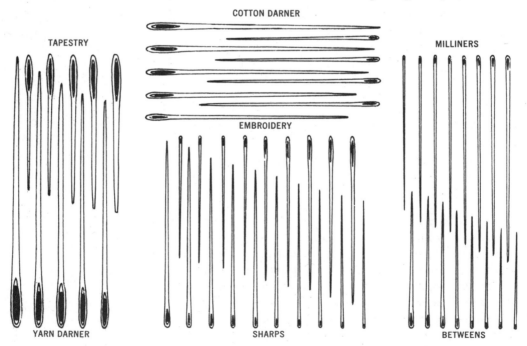

Thread

A quality thread is strong, smooth, elastic, consistent in thickness, and resists tangling. Select the proper thread according to fabric weight, purpose, and color. Thread should be the same color or slightly darker than the fabric. For multi-colored prints and plaids, select thread colors according to the predominant hue in the fabric.

MERCERIZED COTTON thread is strong, smooth, lustrous, and resists shrinkage. Size 50, a medium diameter thread, is suitable for all hand and machine sewing on light and medium weight fabrics. For sewing on heavier suits, coats, slipcovers, and draperies, use a heavy duty mercerized thread. Heavier threads are indicated by smaller numbers on the spool and some have additional plys (four and eight ply). These are indicated by the word "cord" on the spool. Glazing, waxing, and silicone finishes impart extra strength and optimum slickness to threads for the hand sewing of buttons and quilting. For specific thread weights to use with various weights of fabric, see pages 92 and 93.

SYNTHETIC THREADS, alone or in combination with cotton, provide strength and elasticity needed for sewing on knit, stretch, bonded, synthetic, and permanent press fabrics. Polyester/cotton thread combinations consist of cotton-wrapped polyester strands as shown. The cotton sheath provides resistance to heat and makes the thread sew and look like cotton, while the polyester core gives strength and elasticity. A spool of nylon thread is one continuous filament, or several continuous filaments bonded or twisted together, thus it gains its great elasticity and durability from its inherent continuity. It is much stronger than any of the natural fibers and is best used on synthetic fabrics or where very heavy duty treatment is required, such as canvas. These synthetic threads require machine adjustments and new needles for best results. To achieve the loose tension necessary to prevent puckering, you may have to adjust both the bobbin and the needle tension.

SILK THREAD is a good selection for basting and stitching fabrics containing animal fibers. With properties congenial to both silk and wool, it combines durability with elasticity, and leaves no lint, fuzz, or imprints—even under the hottest iron. Because of its "give," you must test the pressure and tension of the machine before you use silk thread. Therefore, stitch first on a scrap of your garment fabric as directed on pages 451 and 452.

Needle and Thread Chart

Uses	Threads		Needles	
FABRIC WEIGHT AND TYPE	**NATURAL FABRICS**	**MAN MADE FABRICS**	**HAND**	**MACHINE**
Very light: Net, chiffon, fine lace, georgette, ninon, marquisette, silk organdy, organza	**Cotton:** Mercerized Sewing Mercerized Best Cord #70, 100 Bel-waxed Sewing Cotton #70 Top Cord #60 **Silk A**	**Dacron/Cotton:** Dual Duty Polyspun **Polyester:** Poly-Bond **Nylon:** Nymo	Sharps, Betweens, Embroidery: 12, 11, 10, 9	Finest: 9, 11 Stitches per inch: 18-20
Light: Lawn, dimity, pure silks, batiste, voile, paper taffeta, chambray, sheer crepe, organdy, dotted Swiss, handkerchief linen, silk jersey, ciré	**Cotton:** Mercerized Sewing Mercerized Best Cord #60, 70 Bel-waxed Sewing Cotton #60, 70 Top Cord #60 **Silk A**	**Dacron/Cotton:** Dual Duty Polyspun **Polyester:** Poly-Bond **Nylon:** Nymo	Sharps, Betweens, Embroidery: 8	Fine: 11 Stitches per inch: 12-16
Medium light: Gingham, challis, surah, taffeta, satin, sheer wool crepe, peau de soie, cut velvet on chiffon, pongee, silk surah	**Cotton:** Mercerized Sewing Mercerized Best Cord #60, 70 Top Cord #60 Bel-waxed Sewing Cotton #60 **Silk A**	**Dacron/Cotton:** Dual Duty Polyspun **Polyester:** Poly-Bond **Nylon:** Nymo	Sharps, Betweens, Embroidery: 8, 7	Fine: 11, 14 Stitches per inch: 12-14
Medium: Flannel, velvet, shantung, piqué, corduroy, broadcloth, linen, satin worsted, wool double knits, bonded fabrics, poplin, faille, muslin, ottoman, moiré, wool jersey, sharkskin, serge, bouclé, lamé, silk and worsted, satin-backed crepe, cut velvet on satin	**Cotton:** Mercerized Sewing Mercerized Best Cord #50, 60 Top Cord #50, 60 Bel-waxed Sewing Cotton #50, 60 **Silk A**	**Dacron/Cotton:** Dual Duty Polyspun **Polyester:** Poly-Bond **Nylon:** Nymo	Sharps, Betweens, Embroidery: 7, 6	Medium: 14 Stitches per inch: 12
Medium heavy: Terry, burlap, quilted fabric, denim, tweed, gabardine, felt, fleece, vinyl coated cloth, twill, brocade, fake fur, imitation leather, crash, bengaline, rep, plastic sheeting	**Cotton:** Mercerized Sewing Mercerized Best Cord #40 Bel-waxed Sewing Cotton #40 Top Cord #40 **Silk A**	**Dacron/Cotton:** Dual Duty Polyspun **Polyester:** Poly-Bond **Nylon:** Nymo	Sharps, Betweens, Embroidery: 6	Medium Coarse: 14, 16 Stitches per inch: 10-12

Heavy: Covered plastics, sailcloth, drapery fabrics, ticking, heavy backed vinyl, corduroy, double-faced wools	Cotton: Mercerized Best Cord #24, 30, 40 Top Cord #40 Heavy Duty Mercerized Button and Carpet Silk A	Dacron/Cotton: Dual Duty Polyspun Polyester: Poly-Bond Nylon: Nymo	Sharps, Betweens, Embroidery: 5, 4	Coarse: 16 Stitches per inch: 8-10
Very heavy: Canvas, duck, work denim, upholstery fabrics, wide wale corduroy, leather and suede	Cotton: Mercerized Best Cord #8, 16, 20 Top Cord #8 Button and Carpet	Nylon: Nymo	Sharps: 3, 2, 1 Betweens: 3 Embroidery: 5, 4, 3	Coarse: 16, 18 Stitches per inch: 6-8

Miscellaneous

Uses	Threads	Needles
Basting	Cotton in size and type according to fabric weight preferably with glazed finish, Silk A	Cotton Darner, Milliners, and Sharps
Beading	Blends, Cotton (coat with beeswax), Nylon, or Polyester	Beading, Sharps
Buttons, buttonholes	Blends, Cotton (coat with beeswax), Nylon, Polyester Silk D	Use largest type appropriate to fabric weight
Darning and mending (light)	Blends, Cotton (coat with beeswax), Nylon, Polyester, and Silk A	Sharps, Embroidery
(heavy)	Mending and Darning Cotton, Mending Yarn	
Embroidery, and other decorative features	Embroidery Floss, Metallic, Silk D, and Yarn	Toy and Yarn, Yarn Darner Embroidery, Sharps
Fastenings (light)	Blends, Cotton (coat with beeswax), Nylon, Polyester, and Silk D	Embroidery, Sharps
(heavy)	Blends, Button and Carpet, Nylon, Polyester, and Silk D	Embroidery, Betweens
Fur and leather	Blends, Button and Carpet, Cotton (coat with beeswax), Nylon, Polyester, and Silk A	Glover's
Gathering and shirring	Blends, Cotton, Elastic, Nylon, Polyester, and Silk A	Betweens, Embroidery, Sharps
Quilting	Quilting or other thread, depending upon desired effect	Betweens
Topstitching (light)	Blends, Cotton, and Silk A	Betweens, Sharps
(heavy)	Cotton, Silk D	
Trapunto	Yarn; size depends on space to be filled	Embroidery, Sharps, Toy and Yarn, Yarn Darner

TRADEMARKS	★○□ Button and Carpet, Heavy Duty Mercerized, Mercerized Sewing, Silk
★ Belding Corticelli ○ Coats and Clark □ Talon	★ Bel-waxed Sewing Cotton, Nymo, Poly-Bond ○ Dual Duty, Mercerized Best Cord □ Polyspun, Top Cord

Zippers

At last there is a zipper for every woman and every conceivable fastening problem. To select a zipper, first base your choice on performance. Which of three types will be suitable for the job to be done? The oldest and most common type, the regular zipper with teeth visible on both sides of the zipper tape, is the usual choice for most standard zipper applications on most garments. There are also special regular zippers made for heavy duty uses. Think about using the second type, the zipper with covered teeth, if your fabric might have a tendency to catch in the teeth of a regular zipper or if you prefer the aesthetics of covered teeth. For an inconspicuous, seam-like appearance from the right side of your garment and a truly quick application, try the third type, the invisible zipper with teeth or coil designed to remain on the inside of the garment.

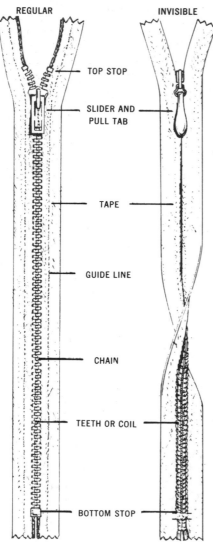

REGULAR   INVISIBLE

TOP STOP

SLIDER AND
PULL TAB

TAPE

GUIDE LINE

CHAIN

TEETH OR COIL

BOTTOM STOP

Know Your Zipper

The zipper has become such a commonplace and essential fastener that we have come to take the ingenuity of its construction pretty much for granted. For your own information and to unravel any difficulties you may have in use or application, you should be able to identify and understand the function of the various parts of your zipper.

TOP STOP is the small metal bracket or thread bar tack at the top of the zipper which prevents the slider from running off the tape and the teeth from pulling apart.

SLIDER AND PULL TAB is the mechanism which enables you to work the zipper. It locks the teeth together to hold the zipper closed, and unlocks the teeth to open it.

TAPE is the fabric strip on which the teeth or coil is fastened and is the part which is sewn to the garment.

GUIDE LINE is a raised line woven into some zipper tapes to act as a stitching guide.

CHAIN is formed by the interlocking teeth when the zipper is closed.

TEETH OR COIL is the locking part of the zipper upon which the slider runs. It may be made of metal, nylon, or polyester.

BOTTOM STOP is the metal bracket or bonded part of the coil at the bottom of the zipper and garment opening. The slider rests here when the zipper is unzipped .

ZIPPER TEETH: Teeth or coils are made of different materials to make the problems of application, wear, and care easier for the woman who sews. Metal teeth come in two different weights, light and heavy, according to the use intended for the zipper and are excellent for heavy duty uses. Synthetic teeth or "coils" of polyester or nylon have been developed which have inherent flexibility and can be dyed to match the zipper tape.

CARE: Take as good care of your zipper as you do of your fine, custom-made garment. Use caution when pressing the zipper area. Always place a pressing cloth between the zipper and your iron. Protect the zipper from excessive strain by closing it before laundering or dry cleaning. If the zipper seems stiff and sticky to operate after laundering or cleaning, run a piece of beeswax or soap over the teeth or coils.

LENGTH: Consider the specific length of the placket area when purchasing a zipper. Zippers come in lengths from 4″ to 36″. The name of the zipper usually implies its use in dressmaking. An additional word of professional advice for those of you using the back of your pattern envelope as a guide to zipper selection: if you make adjustments in your pattern's length through the zipper area, you may need to either purchase a longer or shorter zipper or shorten the one you have as directed on page 327.

A Skirt or Neckline Zipper is designed to open at one end at the edge of a garment and has a bottom stop at the other end to prevent the slider from running into the seam (1). It may have metal teeth or synthetic coil. The skirt type ranges in length from 6″ to 9″; the neckline type runs from 4″ to 36″; and the invisible and covered teeth or coil types come in lengths from 7″ to 24″. It is also available 14″-22″ long in a decorative, heavyweight version with a circular pull tab.

A Dress Zipper opens within a garment seam and has stops at both ends (2). It is available with metal teeth or synthetic coil and in regular and covered teeth types. The lengths run from 10″ to 14″. A skirt or neckline zipper can be substituted by making a top stop as directed on page 327.

A Trouser or Blue Jean Zipper opens at one end, usually at a waistline. It is a heavy-duty variation of the skirt zipper with special bar supports on the slider to withstand frequent pressing and extra wide tapes for double reinforcement stitching (3). It usually has metal teeth and ranges in length from 6″ to 11″.

A Separating or Jacket Zipper opens at both ends (4). It usually has metal teeth. The lightweight type ranges in length from 10″ to 24″, the heavyweight types from 14″ to 24″. The covered teeth type comes 12″ to 22″ in length. It is also available in a reversible version which has a dual-sided slider and comes 16″ to 22″ long.

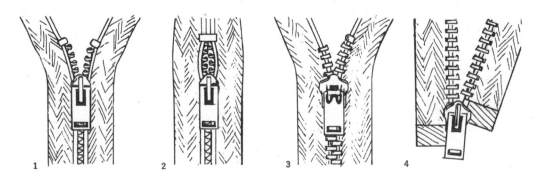

BOOK II

Your
Pattern
Profile

INTRODUCING

...the world's most famous designers of haute couture. Vogue made its first such introduction in 1949, and the enthusiastic reception has only grown over the years. And small wonder; as more and more women have begun sewing the most elegant clothes these high-fashion couturiers could design, sewing has become, for you and millions like you, a creative art form. Through the pages of your Vogue catalogue you are able to attend the greatest collections Europe and America have to offer, for these exciting designs are not mere copies but actual reproductions of the original toiles.

They Design For You

Any discussion of haute couture must begin with Paris, which has always been the well-spring of world fashion. Where the genius of the French designers leads, fashion has invariably followed. And so Vogue introduces to you the style-setters, creators of the fashion fireworks that explode twice yearly in Paris to light the world of fashion. These talented designers are the creators of all the exciting clothes offered in Vogue's famous Paris Original Model patterns. No longer is their genius limited to the elegant apparel of a select few; make it your own with Vogue patterns.

PARIS

Pierre Balmain creates clothes based on classicism and simplicity of line, elegant reflections of his early architectural training.

Marc Bohan of the **House of Dior** has a reputation for flouting convention, innovating trends. His youthful silhouettes are dramatic with color.

Pierre Cardin, known to many as the Master Tailor, faithfully endorses subtle detail and simplified shape. He is a genius of cut and color.

Jules Crahay designs sophisticated clothes exemplified by modest tailoring, soft femininity, and unusual cut and detailing for the **House of Lanvin.**

Molyneux has established his name as a fashion watchword via his streamlined, slim tailoring with marvelous detail and cut.

Givenchy is universally known for his luxurious and dramatic collections. His clientele numbers fashionables from all over the world.

Gerard Pipart of the **House of Nina Ricci** incorporates youth, vitality, and dynamic ideas in his original and energetic designs.

Michel Goma instills a breath of youth to the collections of the **House of Patou.** His beautiful designs combine the seductive and the naive.

Yves Saint Laurent presents a complete fashion format spiced with originality and imagination. Where St. Laurent leads, fashion follows.

Guy Laroche directs his line to the active life, with designs that range from classic to avant garde. His emphasis is on supple, well-designed shaping.

Emanuel Ungaro aims his crisp, mobile designs at a youth-oriented but definitely couture market. His look is modern with sporty detailing.

They Design For You

In recent years, Paris has been joined by the "new couture." Rome, London, Dublin, and Madrid have moved into the fashion world and made it their own, imparting their inimitable personalities and outlook to the fashions they create. Here you will find the Savile-Row tailoring and subtle elegance of the British Isles intermingled with the flair and drama of the Latin countries. Their fresh yet chic approach, so obvious in all their designs, has inestimably widened the world fashion scope. Realizing this, Vogue features selections from these great collections in their International Couturiers patterns—selections made always with you, the truly fashion-conscious woman, in mind.

ENGLAND & IRELAND

Belinda Bellville adds a youthful flair to crisp, well-bred daytime wear and thoroughly romantic evening and wedding dresses.

Jo Mattli has established his own fashion trademark: timeless, mobile, beautifully tailored, and extremely wearable suits.

Michael of London clearly evidences his remarkable sense of proportion in clean, natural lines. He prefers a casual yet urbane look.

Sybil Connolly, with designs characterized by their perfection of detail and proportion, makes interesting use of stitching detail and native Irish tweeds.

ITALY

Fabiani, known for his imaginative, strong architectural tailoring, fashions with meticulous workmanship, dash, and sophistication.

Pucci, a dynamic designer famed for his use of vivid, explosive prints, contrasts fluency of line with intricacy of cut and construction.

Federico Forquet leans toward the classic in his styling, but drama is his forte. He places strong emphasis on color, silhouette, and detail.

Simonetta is a prodigious couturier who creates enchanting sports and cocktail clothes with great inventiveness and ultra-femininity.

Galitzine lends a fresh, youthful, carefree air to designs that clearly look to the future. Her clothes have flair, finesse, femininity.

Valentino, whose hallmark is balance and understated detail, demonstrates inimitable design skill and color sense in clothes known for their simplicity.

SPAIN

Pertegaz develops a superbly tailored look founded on perfection of design, cut, and construction influenced by early training in menswear.

101

They Design For You

American designers no longer have to take a back seat to those in Paris and other international fashion capitals. Brash, young, modern, sparked by originality and excitement, the American collections are as news-making as those anywhere in the world. The casual California way of life and the cosmopolitan atmosphere of New York combine in a fashion melting-pot as versatile and changeable as the nation itself. Vogue continues its tradition of seeking out the best fashion creations from the promising American designers. You will find them presented in the Vogue Americana collection, devoted to bringing you the newest and best America has to offer.

AMERICA

Bill Blass projects a young, cosmopolitan perspective in feminine clothes designed for the sophisticate—classic for day, exotic for evening.

Donald Brooks creates easy, elegant clothes. The Brooks classic is his day dress—all uncluttered line, pure color, and masterful detail.

James Galanos is widely acclaimed for his total fashion outlook and brilliant use of fabric. His theory: silhouette is all-important.

Chuck Howard uses his creativity and originality to design thoroughbred clothes for the active life, immaculately cut and unhampered by gimmicks.

Oscar de La Renta links natural talent with a firm belief in the importance of fit and shape. His clothes: spritely, alluring, full of exuberance.

Teal Traina evolves dramatic fashion trends as an innovator and perfectionist in workmanship and fit. His look is pure, carefree elegance.

Chester Weinberg is known for his crisp, understated cut and contemporary styling. The Weinberg look is one of great purity and individuality.

Pattern Prospectus

Years ago women who sewed at home were forced to struggle with muslins, tissue paper, or vague patterns with mysterious markings. So that you will never have a similar experience, the pattern companies have put an end to that apprehensive feeling frequently felt before starting a project.

The special comfort and security you enjoy when using a Vogue Pattern is not accidental. It is the natural result of extensive surveys and studies made by Vogue Patterns to determine the fashion and technical needs of your particular figure type. At the couture collections, we buy designs with you in mind. We cover the fashion market in order to bring you the most meaningful trends in both apparel and accessories. In addition, we combine the latest procedures with the expertise of fine craftsmen and translate this knowledge through the accuracy of our computer to produce the most technically perfect patterns available. Then, to simplify your selection, we systematically organize all our designs in our catalogue so that all you have to do is turn to a particular section to find an endless array of styles from which to choose. We also back up all our efforts with extensive checking and double-checking to maintain Vogue Pattern's high standards.

You will find sewing is so much easier when you have the sure guidance of an expert. We take great care to have the most realistic illustrations and the finest photography along with detailed instruction sheets to help you every step of the way. We cover every detail, but that doesn't mean you can't branch out to individualize each item you make. In fact, that's probably why you decided to sew with Vogue in the first place. Vogue Patterns has eliminated the guess work and made "fashion, fit, and fun" synonymous with home sewing. We offer you, the creative woman, a source of fashionable, up-to-date patterns to make a wardrobe of exciting, tempting clothes.

Your Body Measurements

Custom fit begins with accurate measurements. You shouldn't begin to buy or alter a pattern without knowing your exact contours, so make up a convenient chart of all your measurements. Be sure to wear appropriate undergarments and shoes when measuring.

Whether you take the measurements or a friend takes them—be honest; make sure the tape is held snug and taut (but not tight) against the body and parallel to the floor for most circumference or width measurements. The illustrated figures and the text on the opposite page will guide you in taking accurate, meaningful body measurements. If you are planning to make pants, see page 157 for the measurement to take.

When your chart is completed, keep it ready for adjustment and alteration comparisons at all times. This is a perfect way to assure yourself of getting the right size every time you buy a pattern. Eventually you may be able to transfer your adjustments and alterations to most patterns automatically without going through the process of discovering the specific fitting adjustments for each and every pattern. Don't forget to note the date on the chart for future use.

To be sure that small figure changes are not creeping up on you unnoticed, take your bust, waist, and hip measurements often to be aware of any possible changes. Even if your weight remains stable, your measurements may shift. It is thus conceivable that you may not only change sizes but figure types as well.

Bust: Measure over the fullest part of the bust and then straight across the back (1).
Chest: Measure around the body, directly under the arms and across top of breasts (2).
Diaphragm: Measure around the body, halfway between the bust and the waist (3).
Waist: Tie a string around the body at thinnest part to establish your waistline and measure circumference at the string (4). (Note: Leave the string in place to facilitate measuring from the waist to points at which measurements 5 through 7, 9, 10, and 16 are **taken.**)
High Hip: Measure 2″ to 4″ below your waist over top of hip bones (5).
Full Hip: Measure at fullest part of hips; mark position with pins on undergarment and measure down from waist to pins to establish hipline, usually 7″ to 9″ from waist (6).
Back Neck to Waist: Measure from prominent neck bone down center back to waist mark (7).

Back Width: Measure from prominent neck bone down center back 4″ to 6″ and mark. Then measure at this point from arm crease to arm crease (8).

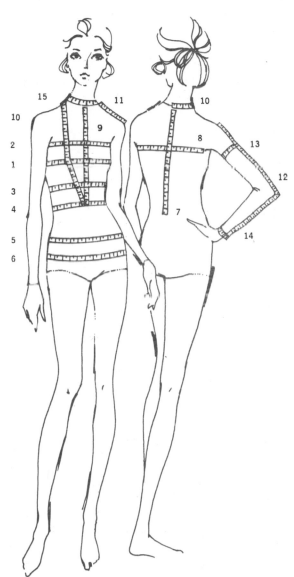

Front Neck to Waist: Measure from hollow between neck bones to center front waistline (9).

Bust Point: To establish position of bust point, measure from prominent back neck bone and over shoulder to bust point, and from bust point to center front at waist. Record both measurements (10).

Shoulder: Measure from base of neck to shoulder bone (hinge) (11).

Arm Length: Measure from shoulder bone to elbow and on to wrist bone with arm slightly bent. Record both lengths (12).

Arm Circumference: Measure around fullest part of arm, generally 1″ below armpit (13), wrist at bone (14).

Neck Circumference: Measure fullest part of neck (15).

Skirt Length: Measure from center back waist to desired point on leg for hem, referring to the back of the envelope and page 337 for a description of lengths. This will help you to estimate any length adjustments necessary on your pattern and any changes from the recommended amount of fabric to purchase.

Choosing the Pattern for You

"Buy the correct pattern size" is never a strong enough statement to infer all the problems which can occur if you do not select the correct pattern size. Of course, choosing the right size eliminates wasted effort and money, but just imagine how many more creations you can turn out if you don't have to spend time needlessly on adjustments which can be eliminated by starting with the proper size. To be sure you are buying the correct pattern size, you should also consider figure changes that may have taken place over the years. How many women do you know who plunge directly into cutting the same size they've worn for the last five years, only to discover that those few pounds added or subtracted make an irreversible difference in fit once the fabric is cut? Even if you have maintained the same weight, it is very possible that certain body areas may have become fuller while others have become more slender. These small body changes may require a careful re-evaluation of the silhouettes that are most becoming on you rather than necessitate the purchase of a larger or smaller pattern size.

There is yet another factor which will affect the size you should purchase. Be aware of how fashion influences the fit of your garments, too. There are years or seasons when the trend is toward a closer, more revealing fit as opposed to a looser, freer line.

Figure Types

Pattern sizes begin with grading or sizing of contemporary average figure types. The National Bureau of Standards and the pattern industry have established standard body measurements which are the basis for body measurements in pattern sizes. Compare your bust, waist, hip, back waist, and height measurements with those of the figure types to see which one corresponds with your own body configuration. There is a wide variety of figure types to choose from to make sure you will not have to compromise. They include Misses, Women's, and Half-Sizes. (Refer to pages 109 to 111 for more specific information.) You may find that you do not conform exactly to these measurements. Very seldom do people's measurements and body contours conform to idealized standards, since two people wearing the same size may differ several inches in height alone. The standards are simply meant to be a generality that you can use as a starting point for size selection and alterations.

Your Correct Size

Compare your body measurement with those for your figure type, and circle those closest to your own. ***Buy most patterns by the bust measurement*** because this area is the hardest to alter. Measurements listed are the actual body sizes; true pattern dimensions have wearing ease built in beyond the actual body sizes in most designs for an attractive fit. These dimensions change, adding further fullness when style ease is needed to obtain a certain silhouette, so be sure to choose your pattern size by listed body measurement. Frequently women fall between two sizes. If this applies to you and you happen to be a thin, small-boned type, choose the smaller of two sizes. Conversely, a large-boned person will require all the ease of the larger size.

Usually your waist measurement is used in selecting skirts, slacks, and shorts unless your hips are larger in proportion to your waist. In that case, we recommend that you use the hip measurement as the deciding factor because the waist is easier to adjust.

Ease...for mobility and fashion

Each Vogue Pattern takes into consideration your need for comfort and mobility by building in *wearing ease* to allow you freedom of movement without restraint. *Style ease* is an integral part of many designs and will have additional dimensions added to the pattern beyond the wearing ease, as dictated by the garment's style lines.

WEARING EASE: Without the built-in "liveability" found in most patterns your garments would not be comfortable—you would not be able to stretch, sit, walk up or down stairs in comfort. To have the garment move as you do, *never* use the wearing ease instead of making adjustments to bring the pattern in line with your body measurements.

"Vogue's Guide to Perfect Fit of Fitted Garments" is the perfect sewing tool to help you overcome fitting problems (see pages 124-153 for detailed information). To help you further understand wearing ease, this chart shows in actual measurements how many inches are given for wearing ease in Vogue Pattern's fitted garment shell beyond the standard body measurements given for each size.

	Misses'	Women's	Half-Size
BUST	3″	3½″	3½″
WAIST (dress)	¾″	1″	¾″
WAIST (skirt)	½″	¾″	½″
FULL HIP	2″	2¾″	2½″

Caution: All Vogue Patterns do not have this exact wearing ease—halter-neck, extremely cut-away armholes and strapless, or "skinny" strapped bodices have minimal wearing ease beyond the standard circumference measurements. Patterns stating "Use only stretchable unbonded knits," "For two-way stretch knits," or "One-way stretchable synthetics" may have little or no wearing ease; the fabric's elasticity allows a comfortable fit.

STYLE EASE: The most significant contributing factor to diversified pattern designs is style ease. This ease (beyond requirement needed for wearing ease) allows the designer to create many silhouettes with varying degrees of style fullness. Working with four basic silhouettes—fitted, semi-fitted, slightly fitted, or loosely fitted—the designer can create a style from any point of view. The variety can be endless when these basic shapes are combined. *Fitted* garments will follow your contour, just touching the body without constraint; wearing ease may also be style ease (1). *Semi-fitted* garments incorporate some style ease at bust, waist and hip; fitting smoothly over the bust, they "skim" the waist and hips (2). *Slightly-fitted* garments have considerable style ease, just following the body shape (3). *Loosely-fitted* garments have considerable style ease; fullness starts above the bust and falls loosely around the body (4). Regardless of current fashion trends, choose a pattern whose silhouette is most flattering—accent good figure points and minimize flaws.

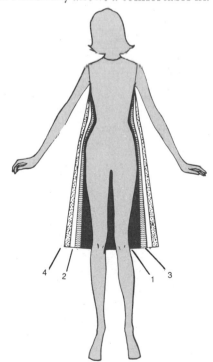

DIVERSIFICATIONS USED BY DESIGNERS: In the fast-moving life styles of today, the pure basic silhouettes would not emphasize some of the beautiful fabrics available—they would become "hum-drum" and uninspiring. A designer may use two or more of the basic shapes in one garment, and then take this same silhouette and modify it to compliment two completely different fabrics.

Throughout the Vogue Patterns counter catalogue or the International Vogue Pattern Book you will find many fashion variations of the four basic shapes. These modifications are usually described in the caption as: high fit, waist fit, hip fit, bias fit, and geometric seaming. These designs offer alternatives to achieve figure-flattering garments.

High fit represents a close fit over the bust and just under it. The remainder of the garment may not be fitted; style ease may start 2" below the bust incorporating a semi-fitted skirt. An empire bodice or a princess-seamed dress are familiar examples.

Waist fit reflects a fitted area through the waist area only in the form of a midriff insert, an extra wide waistband, or a bodice and skirt gathered to fit an inside waist stay. Many combinations of style ease can be found above or below the waist.

Hip fit denotes garments with a close fit through the hip area. Dropped waist seams and fitted hip yokes are easy to spot, but a classic shirt dress with a loosely fitted bodice can be combined with a straight skirt that is hip fitted.

Classic designer favorites are bias cut garments and geometric seaming details. **Bias** garments have minimum seam and darts as the garment will mold smoothly over body curves regardless of style ease. **Geometric** seaming offers the designer spectacular use of lines—horizontally, vertically, or asymmetrical—with curves and corners for more diversity. These details can be found in any basic silhouette or style variation.

With this new-found knowledge, approach your next sewing project with confidence—precise measurement is the first step; selecting correct figure type is the second; understanding ease the third; and the last step is the right silhouette and style lines for the fashion conscious individual!

Figure Types and Sizes

We have described the three Vogue Pattern figure types on the following pages to guide you in your pattern size selection. Once again, we stress that figure type is a matter of measurement, not age. Your pattern is your sewing blueprint, from which you will build your exact dimensions for perfect fit. Choosing the correct size and figure type will therefore minimize alterations and further adjustments, and make sewing easier for you.

You will probably find that your measurements do not correspond exactly with those in any specific size. Do not be alarmed; the woman who is lucky enough to have those standard measurements is indeed difficult — if not impossible — to find. The size you choose should be the one whose measurements correspond most closely to your own.

If, in comparing your measurements to the size ranges, you find that you fall between figure types, take stock of your body structure. Stand in front of the mirror and ponder awhile. Is your body long and slender or shorter and more closely put together? Then refer to the introductions included with each figure type for a general description of the figures. They will give you a clue to your perfect figure type. Now refer back to the figure types and choose the one best for you.

MISSES'

The Misses' size range has been developed to encompass patterns for a well-proportioned and developed figure. You'll find her hip measurement on the chart to be at the 9″ level. Without shoes, she stands about 5′5″ or 5′6″ in height. The Misses' figure is considered the statistically "average" figure.

SIZE	6	8	10	12	14	16	18	20
BODY MEASUREMENTS								
Bust	30½	31½	32½	34	36	38	40	42
Waist	23	24	25	26½	28	30	32	34
Hip	32½	33½	34½	36	38	40	42	44
Back Waist Length	15½	15¾	16	16¼	16½	16¾	17	17¼
PATTERN MEASUREMENTS								
Shoulder Length	4¾	4¾	4⅞	5	5⅛	5¼	5⅜	5½
Back Width	13¾	14	14¼	14⅝	15	15½	16	16½
Sleeve Width	11¾	12⅛	12½	13	13⅜	13⅞	14⅜	14⅞
Sleeve Length	22⅜	22⅝	23	23¼	23⅝	23⅞	24⅛	24⅜
Skirt Length (From Natural Waistline at Back)	22¼	22½	22¾	23	23¼	23½	23¾	24

WOMEN'S

The Women's figure is somewhat larger, longer, and more fully developed than the Misses' figure, but is just as well-proportioned. She stands approximately 5'5" or 5'6" tall without her shoes on. According to the chart, the fullest part of her hips has been measured at 9" below the waistline.

SIZE	38	40	42	44
BODY MEASUREMENTS				
Bust	42	44	46	48
Waist	35	37	39	41½
Hip	44	46	48	50
Back Waist Length	17¼	17⅜	17½	17⅝
PATTERN MEASUREMENTS				
Shoulder Length	5½	5⅝	5⅝	5¾
Back Width	16⅝	17⅛	17⅝	18⅛
Sleeve Width	15	15½	16	16½
Sleeve Length	23⅞	24⅛	24⅜	24⅝
Skirt Length (From Natural Waistline at Back)	24⅜	24½	24⅝	24¾

HALF-SIZE

The woman with a fully-developed figure and short back waist length belongs in this size range. Her waist and hips are larger in proportion to her bust than in the other figure types. The fullest part of her hips is 7" down from her waist. She stands approximately 5'2" or 5'3" without her shoes on.

SIZE	10½	12½	14½	16½	18½	20½	22½	24½
BODY MEASUREMENTS								
Bust	33	35	37	39	41	43	45	47
Waist	27	29	31	33	35	37½	40	40½
Hip	35	37	39	41	43	45½	48	50½
Back Waist Length	15	15¼	15½	15¾	15⅞	16	16⅛	16¼
PATTERN MEASUREMENTS								
Shoulder Length	4⅝	4¾	4⅞	5	5⅛	5¼	5¼	5⅜
Back Width	14⅛	14½	14⅞	15¼	15¾	16⅛	16⅝	17⅛
Sleeve Width	13⅛	13⅝	14⅛	14⅝	15⅛	15⅝	16⅛	16⅝
Sleeve Length	22⅛	22⅜	22⅝	22⅞	23⅛	23⅜	23⅝	23⅞
Skirt Length (From Natural Waistline at Back)	23	23¼	23½	23¾	23⅞	24	24⅛	24¼

Fashion...Envelope Front

Vogue Patterns understands the desire of women—and men—to be beautifully dressed for every mood and occasion. We literally go to the ends of the earth to bring you the most complete selection of designs—from the great European collections, New York City's Seventh Avenue design centers, to our own design rooms. Even a brief look through your Vogue Pattern catalogue will convince you of the abundance of fashion to be found there.

Vogue Paris and *International Design Originals* offer you the height of the European fashion market for both men and women. Paris, the pacesetter for decades, features those famous designers whose individual flair consistently creates excitement and change throughout the fashion world. The International Designers encompass a wider range of European couture. The best designers of Spain, England, Ireland, and Italy all contribute elegant and dramatic fashions, created by the intricate touch and cut of master tailoring that points to haute couture. All of these Designers patterns are featured in large envelopes with a full color photograph on the front.

American fashion is internationally famed for its young, sophisticated, contemporary, and easy-to-wear outlook. The *Vogue American Designer Originals* are fresh, unhampered clothes, for male, female, young, and young-at-heart. These patterns also appear in the large envelope, complete with a color photograph and fashion sketch.

In addition to the best from European and American showrooms, *Vogue Patterns Own Designers* offer a vast selection of the very newest fashion trends with every occasion and need in mind—Dresses (day-time, after-five, and leisurewear), Sportswear (active and spectator), Coats and Suits, Women's and Half-Size, Bridal, Lingerie, and Maternity to round the outstanding designs for women. And for the *men* . . . casual or active sportswear, classic jackets and pants or suits and loungewear.

To complete the broad range of fashion already included in the catalogue, there are several special categories which must not be overlooked. *Very Easy Vogue Patterns* are a dream come true for the fashion enthusiast who has too much taste and too little time, whether a beginner or an experienced seamstress—fabulous style coupled with simple, easy-to-follow construction and a small number of pattern pieces. Very Easy Vogue is a fast and economical way to sew a beautiful wardrobe. The *Classics* category is devoted to the individual who likes understatement, a look that is free and uncluttered, and a style that will continue from season to season. The *Trendsetter* collection is perfectly tailored to the innovator who likes active on-the-go fashion with a flair for individual style. The *designers* show up everywhere in the Vogue Pattern catalogue—dresses, sportswear, women's and half-sizes, coats and suits, and bridal gowns. Another most important section is *Vogue Basic Designs*—classic examples of pure, simple design, outfits to delight the eye and span the years. Each Vogue Basic Design can be created with several style variations. The most important day of your life calls for a very important pattern—*Vogue Bridal Designs* are among the most exquisite available anywhere. Whether your taste runs toward traditional lace, ruffles, beading, and long trains or toward modern elegant simplicity, you will be delighted with the unique and outstandingly beautiful selections offered for the entire bridal party. *Vogue Lingerie Designs* offer the ultimate in at-home fashions and comfortable undergarments. *Vogue Maternity Designs* for the mother-in-waiting give her the very latest in fashion trends.

Last, but not least is *Vogue Patterns for Men* created by American and European designers as well as Vogue's own designers. There are fashions to suit the most discriminating male—suits, latest style trousers, sportswear incorporating the newest trims, robes, caftans, and pajamas. Whether his tastes are classic or innovative, Vogue offers a choice of patterns to reflect his particular needs and preferences.

There is a world of fashion at your finger tips in every Vogue catalogue and a fantastic look in each pattern. Whatever your age, size, life style, or personal taste, there is something there for you. The choice is yours . . . the Vogue choice.

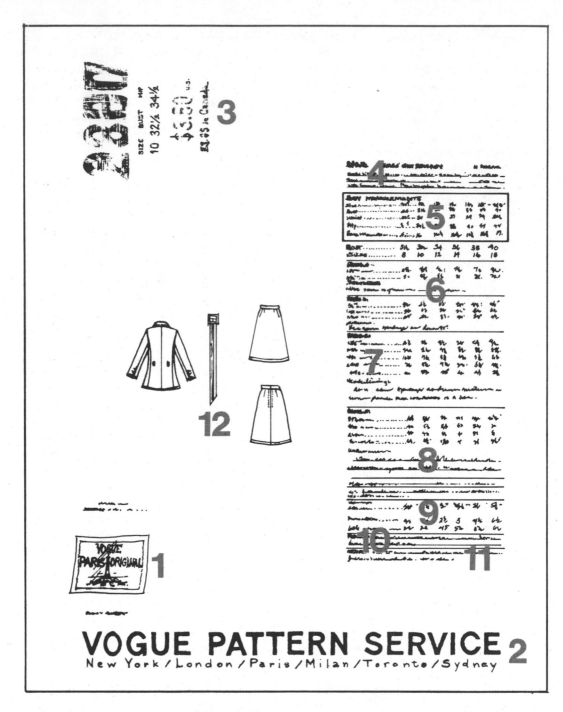

VOGUE PATTERN SERVICE 2
New York / London / Paris / Milan / Toronto / Sydney

1 *Labels:* This is a reminder to ask at the pattern counter for your Vogue Paris Original, International Couturier, or Americana design label.

2 *Vogue Pattern Service:* The truly international aspect of Vogue Patterns is reflected by its representative offices in several countries.

3 *Style Number, Size, and Price:* Buying information is found in the upper left-hand corner of the envelope back. Also stated are bust and hip measurements for quick reference.

4 *Descriptive Caption:* Sizing category, type of garment, and total number of pattern pieces are stated. The detailed explanation will describe the silhouette plus pertinent details not visible in the sketch.

5 *Body Measurements:* Patterns are computed for these measurements. Included in the pattern tissue are wearing ease and style ease as dictated by the design.

6 *Yardage:* Sizes are across the top. Garment type and/or version letter are just above fabric widths, including interfacing, lining, underlining, and trims needed for each version. Fabric widths have nap indications alongside them.

7 *W/WO:* This key indicates whether the yardage shown is for fabrics with or without nap. With nap (W) fabrics have layouts with pattern pieces placed in the same direction. Without nap (WO) layouts do not plan for extra yardage required by directional fabrics; if using these fabrics, you will have to plan layouts and add to the yardage specified for the design.

8 *Fabric Design Suitability:* This important information tells if the pattern is not suitable for stripes, plaids, or diagonal fabrics. It states "No Allowance Made for Matching Stripes and Plaids" when these fabrics are suitable because the additional yardage needed varies with the size of the fabric design.

9 *Width at Lower Edge:* This measurement will tell you the sweep of a skirt or the width of the pant leg.
Finished Back Lengths and Side Lengths: These lengths are used as a starting point for pattern tissue length adjustments.

10 *Fabrics:* Suggestions listed in this area are well-known fabric types suitable for the design to give you a wide choice. The most important quality of desirable fabrics, soft or crisp, is given to help achieve the silhouette intended by the designer.

11 *Notions:* All required and optional notions with recommended sizes for your garment are listed here. They were chosen in the correct proportion to complement the garment design as featured.

12 *Back Views:* These drawings show styling and construction details for all design versions that were not visible in the fashion illustration.

Information...Envelope Back

The envelope front was instrumental in your pattern selection. Now use the envelope back to your advantage. All envelopes contain the complete information you will need to make the proper selection of fabric and notions. In addition, you will find sizing information, pertinent facts about the design features, and concise yardage calculations presented in a logical manner for quick reference.

Metric Conversion Charts

For Body Measurements

To determine your pattern size, compare your body measurements to the body measurements listed below. The chart lists measurements in both inches and centimeters.

MISSES'

Size	6		8		10		12		14		16		18		20	
	in	cm	in	cm	in	cm	in	cm	in	cm	in	cm	in	cm	in	cm
Bust	30½	78	31½	80	32½	83	34	87	36	92	38	97	40	102	42	107
Waist	23	58	24	61	25	64	26½	67	28	71	30	76	32	81	34	87
Hips	32½	83	33½	85	34½	88	36	92	38	97	40	102	42	107	44	112
Back waist length	15½	39,5	15¾	40	16	40,5	16¼	41,5	16½	42	16¾	42,5	17	43	17¼	44

MISS PETITE

Size	6 MP		8 MP		10 MP		12 MP		14 MP		16 MP	
	in	cm	in	cm	in	cm	in	cm	in	cm	in	cm
Bust	30½	78	31½	80	32½	83	34	87	36	92	38	97
Waist	23½	60	24½	62	25½	65	27	69	28½	73	30½	78
Hips	32½	83	33½	85	34½	88	36	92	38	97	40	102
Back waist length	14½	37	14¾	37,5	15	38	15¼	39	15½	39,5	15¾	40

WOMEN'S

Size	38		40		42		44	
	in	cm	in	cm	in	cm	in	cm
Bust	42	107	44	112	46	117	48	122
Waist	35	89	37	94	39	99	41½	105
Hips	44	112	46	117	48	122	50	127
Back waist length	17¼	44	17⅜	44	17½	44,5	17⅝	45

HALF-SIZE

Size	10½		12½		14½		16½		18½		20½		22½		24½	
	in	cm	in	cm	in	cm	in	cm	in	cm	in	cm	in	cm	in	cm
Bust	33	84	35	89	37	94	39	99	41	104	43	109	45	114	47	119
Waist	27	69	29	74	31	79	33	84	35	89	37½	96	40	102	42½	108
Hips	35	89	37	94	39	99	41	104	43	109	45½	116	48	122	50½	128
Back waist length	15	38	15¼	39	15½	39,5	15¾	40	15⅞	40,5	16	40,5	16⅛	41	16¼	41,5

For Fabrics

To convert fabric widths and yardages from inches and yards to centimeters and meters, compare what is listed in each yardage block to the chart below.

FABRIC WIDTHS	in	cm	in	cm	in	cm	in	cm	in	cm	in	cm	in	cm	in	cm
	25	65	27	70	35	90	39	100	42	107	45	115	54	140	60	150
Yardage	Yd	m	Yd	m	Yd	m	Yd	m	Yd	m	Yd	m	Yd	m	Yd	m
	⅛	0.15	¼	0.25	⅜	0.35	½	0.50	⅝	0.60	¾	0.70	⅞	0.80	1	0.95
	1⅛	1.05	1¼	1.15	1⅜	1.30	1½	1.40	1⅝	1.50	1¾	1.60	1⅞	1.75	2	1.85
	2⅛	1.95	2¼	2.10	2⅜	2.20	2½	2.30	2⅝	2.40	2¾	2.55	2⅞	2.65	3	2.75
	3⅛	2.90	3¼	3.00	3⅜	3.10	3½	3.20	3⅝	3.35	3¾	3.45	3⅞	3.55	4	3.70
	4⅛	3.80	4¼	3.90	4⅜	4.00	4½	4.15	4⅝	4.25	4¾	4.35	4⅞	4.50	5	4.60
	5⅛	4.70	5¼	4.80	5⅜	4.95	5½	5.05	5⅝	5.15	5¾	5.30	5⅞	5.40	6	5.50
	6⅛	5.60	6¼	5.75	6⅜	5.85	6½	5.95	6⅝	6.10	6¾	6.20	6⅞	6.30	7	6.40

1 *Cutting Line:* The heavy outer line of the pattern piece is indicated by scissors. It may also be found within the pattern designating a "cut off" for a style variation.

2 *Seamline:* The long, broken line, ⅝" inside the cutting line (unless otherwise specified) and indicated by a presser foot, is where all seams should be stitched for an ample seam allowance.

3 *Buttons and Buttonholes:* These symbols give you the length of buttonhole, size of button, and precise location for each.

4 *Fold Line:* This solid line marks where the garment is to be folded during construction. *Roll Line:* A solid line shows where the pattern piece is to be softly creased to make a soft, rolling fold.

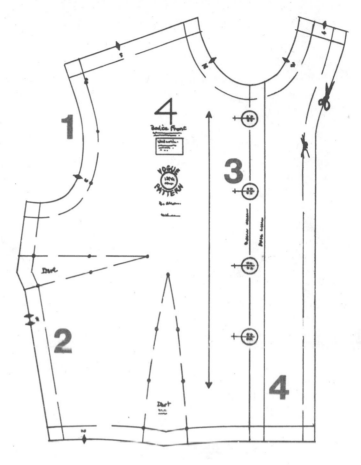

Blueprints...Pattern Pieces

Pattern pieces are like blueprints. The master plans of any dressmaking project, they guide you by including all the construction symbols needed to make your sewing easier and more accurate. Just as no contractor would ever begin building a house without understanding the architect's code or key, you could have disastrous results unless you know the symbols of your craft. Every one of them has been printed on your pattern for a very specific and necessary purpose. Get acquainted with them; learn to recognize the markings on each piece and to understand their uses. Then all you will have to do is follow them faithfully. Mistakes made before you sew because you didn't understand the pattern markings will only be compounded as further construction ensues. A good working knowledge of symbols, notches, 'and lines will allow your project to run smoothly, quickly, and correctly. Remember that to know the meaning of the pattern pieces' characteristic lines and symbols is to be assured of a finely constructed garment, correctly executed according to Vogue Pattern procedures.

1 *Large ●'s and Small ●'s:* These symbols are printed on the tissue pattern for accurate joining of garment sections. They are particularly helpful where even distribution of gathers and ease is required, or when you are matching plaids, stripes, etc.

Triangles (▲) and squares (■) are also construction symbols to aid in matching. You must remember to sew to or through the center of all symbols.

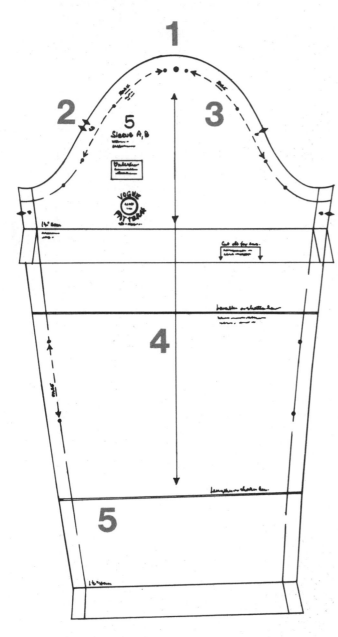

2 *Notches:* Used for accurate joining of seams, notches are numbered in the order in which seamlines are matched.

3 *Easing Line:* When two seamlines are to be joined and one is slightly larger, a single row of short, broken lines with an arrow and small ● at each end is placed along the larger seamline; this is the area to be drawn up with a row of stitching.

Gathering Line: Two rows of short broken lines indicate that a much larger area must be drawn up to fit a smaller area along the seamline. An arrow is placed at each end of lines with small ●'s to help distribute the fullness evenly.

4 *Grain Line:* This heavy solid line with arrows at either end indicates the direction of the grain. Most often it runs parallel to the fabric selvage, along the lengthwise grain. When the pattern is illustrated in border prints, scallop-edged laces, etc., the tissue will state, "place on lengthwise or crosswise grain."

5 *Adjustment Line:* Double lines are printed to indicate areas where lengthening or shortening must be done before cutting, if necessary.

1 **Pattern Piece and Version:** Name and letter identifies pattern piece. The numbers relate to you the order in which each garment section is to be constructed.

Special Cutting Instructions: Any information on the cutting of interfacing, lining, or underlining pertaining to the pattern piece will be found in this enclosed area to highlight its importance. It also states when a piece is to be cut other than twice.

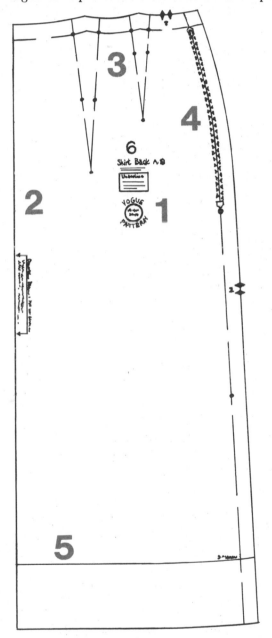

Vogue Pattern Trademark: Your guarantee of fine styling also includes the pattern style number and size. Each is clearly marked to make identification simple.

2 **Center Front or Center Back Lines:** These solid lines indicate where garment is to fall at the center of the body. In many instances a pattern piece is to be placed on the fold of fabric before cutting. When this occurs, brackets will be shown on the line to indicate that it is to be placed on the fold. Always transfer the center front or center back lines to fabric for reference to grain, fit, or buttonhole placement.

3 **Dart:** Corresponding symbols that are to be carefully matched are placed on broken lines that meet at a point to comprise the dart marking.

4 **Zipper Placement:** This symbol indicates the placement of zipper on seamline. Pull tab at top and stop at the bottom indicate the exact length of zipper to be used.

5 **Hemline:** This line indicates the finished edge of the garment. Also included along this line is information concerning the depth of the hem for optimum drape of design and weight of fabric. Generally, the wider the sweep of the hem, the narrower its depth.

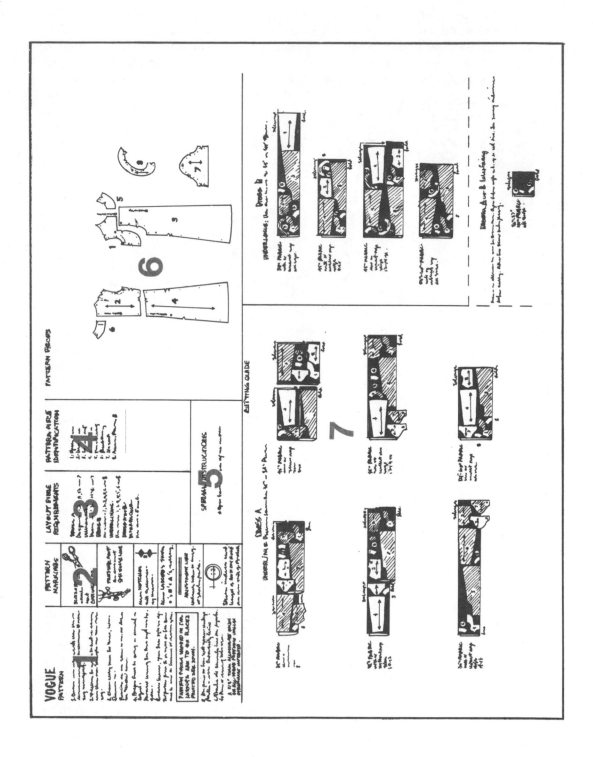

1 *Step-by-Step Procedure:* Helpful hints are given for preparing fabric, arranging fabric for cutting layouts, and for cutting and marking the pattern.

2 *Pattern Markings:* The most important symbols on the pattern tissue are identified and explained. These should be especially reviewed before cutting and marking.

3 *Layout Piece Requirements:* All pattern pieces needed for each version of the garment are listed by number, along with pieces needed for underlining, interfacing, and lining.

4 *Pattern Piece Identification:* Listed numerically are the names of pattern pieces and the versions for which they are used.

5 *Special Instructions:* These instructions are concerned with the cutting of specific pattern pieces, fabrics, or bias pieces which require additional layout preparation.

6 *Pattern Pieces:* Pattern pieces show center fronts and backs, grainlines, piece numbers, cut-off lines, and notches. Recognition of the actual pattern piece is made simpler by noting this section first.

7 *Cutting Guide:* The garment cutting layouts are divided into style versions and then into sizes and fabric widths. Each layout is also marked as to suitability for nap. Underlining, interfacing, and lining layouts are also given in the same manner. Pattern pieces to be placed with the printed side up are shown without shading, while those that are to be placed printed side down are shaded. Carefully follow the illustrations when you fold your fabric. If any pattern pieces extend beyond the fold, they are to be cut on a single thickness after all the other pieces are cut. Circle the layout you are using for easy reference.

Pattern Cutting Guide

In your Vogue pattern envelope you will find a cutting and sewing guide along with the actual pattern pieces which, if followed thoroughly and consistently, can answer almost any question you might have about the general planning, pinning, cutting, and construction of your garment.

The information available in the cutting guide is everything in capsule form that you will need to know before you begin to actually sew. If time is spent studying the correct procedure for preparing the fabric and laying out your pattern, no tears need be shed because you've run out of fabric by not placing your pattern pieces correctly or an equally avoidable mistake.

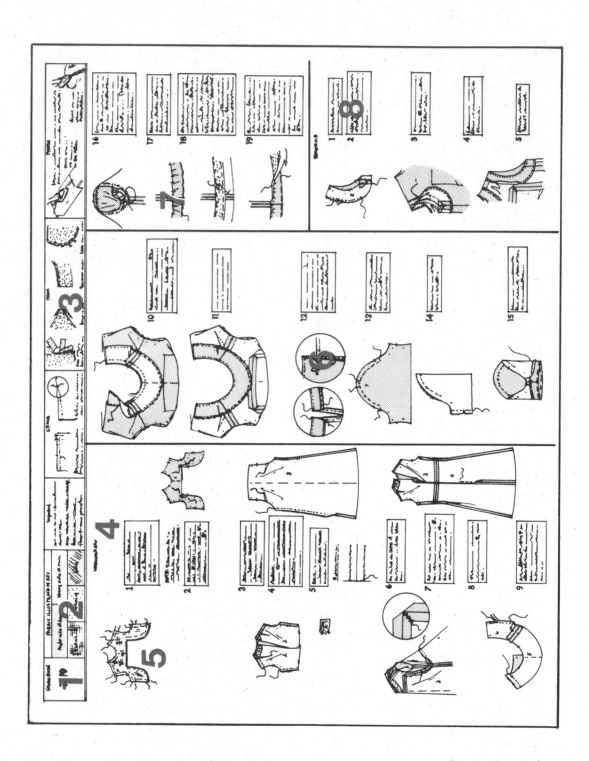

1 *Pattern Identification:* The pattern number is given along with the page number. To give you the benefit of couture construction in designer patterns and comprehensive directions for multi-version styles, you may find several instruction sheets in the envelope. Pages are numbered consecutively as well, stating the amount you will find.

2 *Fabric Illustration Key:* This explains the use of shading and texture in technical sketches: underlining is shown by crosshatching, interfacing by dots, lining with shading lines, right side of fabric by tone. *We follow the same distinctions throughout the illustrations in this book.*

3 *Helpful Hints:* Important points to remember on stitching, trimming, and pressing are shown and explained for your benefit.

4 *Titles:* The construction procedures for different parts of the garment and the individual versions are presented separately. A title in large bold type introduces each section.

5 *Underlining Sketch:* Generally, only one sketch in the sewing guide is used to illustrate the technique used for underlining garment pieces. Each subsequent piece is worked in the same manner. Following sketches illustrate only one layer of fabric, but it is assumed that all pieces are underlined.

6 *Enlarged View:* You will find that details of important and/or difficult construction areas are enlarged and circled to clarify the sewing procedure involved. Be sure to pay special attention to each enlarged view.

7 *Construction Sketches:* Many sewing techniques are easier to understand when they are shown in comprehensive illustrations. They are meant to be used with the written instructions, since some procedures cannot be sketched.

8 *Sewing Directions:* Construction of each garment section is explained individually as it is needed. Every procedure is outlined and numbered consecutively for quick reference.

Pattern Sewing Guide

On the reverse side of the cutting guide you will find a step-by-step sewing guide arranged by garment versions with numbered and outlined instructions for fast reading and comprehension. The large and precise technical sketches that accompany the written instructions are easy to understand and as informative as having a sample of your garment in front of you. Across the top of the sheet are the fabric illustration key and suggestions on stitching, trimming, and pressing which can serve as excellent reminders.

The cutting and sewing guides are indispensable ingredients in achieving the perfect fit and finish to your Vogue pattern. Whether you're a nervous beginner or a highly skilled seamstress, following the instructions diligently to the completion of your garment can only help to make the most professional looking garment possible.

Your Perfect Sewing Tool

Vogue's Guide to Perfect Fit is the foundation for professional sewing workmanship. It allows you to experiment successfully while working toward your ultimate goal—a perfect fit. Fit is what separates an average garment from a truly superior one. Exquisite fabric and couture sewing techniques cannot make up for an ill-fitting garment that sags, pulls, and wrinkles. The difference between sewing a garment together, ignoring balanced fabric grains and fit, and a garment that has been adjusted and altered to your personal contours is beyond comparison.

Probably every seamstress has had the bitter experience of painstakingly constructing a garment only to find her time and effort wasted because her lovely creation doesn't fit. More often, the pleasure of a garment may be blunted by a minor fitting problem—tight hipline or baggy neckline—which keeps it from being as comfortable and attractive as it should be.

Vogue, understanding this frustration, has developed its Guide to Perfect Fit patterns, available in two styles: a basic fitted shell with a waist seam, suitable for determining pattern adjustments for any style; and an A-line basic, developed specifically for A-line fashions. Making the fitted shell with a waist seam and the straight skirt first (rather than the A-line skirt which is also included with your pattern) will help you better understand all your personal fitting needs. You will then be able to relate your own shape and contour more realistically when using the A-line fitting pattern.

This sewing tool is truly the way to achieve a perfectly fitting wardrobe, for it gives you a personally fitted guide to use for everything you sew. It will help you discover exactly what your own fitting problems are and what adjustments must be made to compensate for them. Many adjustments simply cannot be made satisfactorily after cutting and sewing your garment, and your completed muslin will show you how to make them before you ever touch shears to your fabric. Think of the confidence Vogue's Guide to Perfect Fit will give you by taking most of the guesswork out of personal alterations.

For Everything You Sew

Achieving a perfect fit depends on more than just buying the correct pattern size. The standard body measurements compiled by the pattern industry are simply average body measurements of women within a particular size range. Since individuals within that size may vary in any number of ways from the standard measurements, they serve simply as starting points from which you must make adjustments to fit your own dimensions.

All Vogue Patterns, regardless of style, are based on the same standard measurements; thus, once you have determined and made all your adjustments on your muslin fitting shell, they can be transferred directly to any pattern you choose in the same size. If, for example, you need to take in ½" on the shoulder seams of your fitting shell, you will also take in ½" on the shoulder seams of a suit, a coat, a dress, or a blouse. Following these adjustments will ensure a good fit that will not interfere with the built in wearing ease allowed in every pattern. What could be easier?

Elegant styling and superb fit are dependent on these adjustments being made before you cut into your fabric. As you make pattern changes, remember to:

- ☐ Keep grainlines, center front, and center back foldlines straight.
- ☐ Make adjustments with discretion to carefully preserve style lines of design.
- ☐ Maintain wearing ease built into pattern.
- ☐ Use adjustment lines provided for lengthening and shortening.
- ☐ Make corresponding changes on all related pieces—bodice front and back, skirt front and back, facing front and back, lining front and back, etc.

Once you see the value of Vogue's Guide to Perfect Fit Patterns, you will want to care for the perishable tissue pattern as you would any truly important sewing tool. Back the paper pattern with heavy cardboard and you have an easy, handy, and permanent record for achieving perfection each and every time you sew. Try on the muslin shell periodically to see if your measurements have changed at all, and readjust accordingly.

On the following pages are explained all the specific procedures you will need for personal fitting. The changes you will make are divided into two categories. *Adjustments* are minor changes which are made "in the flat" on your pattern tissue before you cut your muslin. *Alterations* are major changes that are made on the muslin fitting shell to ensure they will relate to your body contours.

All the changes are clearly illustrated for you. *Only the front pattern pieces are shown for adjustments, as equal changes are made for the front and back pattern pieces. Alterations, which are more localized, may not require changes on both front and back pieces, and thus only the affected pieces are shown.* So that you may relate your adjustments and alterations to everything you sew, we will also show you how to make them on other basic shapes (princess lines, raglan sleeves, etc.) when applicable.

Flat Pattern Adjustments

Let us help take the mystery out of pattern adjustments. You need not be reluctant to try an original idea to get a better fit as long as you remember this principle: since all patterns and fabric are flat, any change you make must be done in such a manner that the pattern tissue will also remain flat after it is adjusted.

Armed with your personal measurements, note their difference from the body measurements on the envelope back. With the specific variations recorded, you are ready to make the flat pattern adjustments before cutting out the muslin fitting shell.

There are some styles with unusually shaped pattern pieces or complex seaming details that may be more difficult to lengthen or shorten in a flat pattern piece. However, do not let this stop you from experimenting. Make your length adjustments on the pattern pieces as accurately as your common sense leads you to feel is correct. Then cut that portion of your garment from muslin and stitch it together with machine basting. Fit it carefully to your figure, re-stitching as necessary. When satisfied with the fit, rip the muslin apart. Use pressed seams as a guide and transfer the changes to your pattern.

Flat basic pattern pieces are essential tools of the pattern and clothing industries for maintaining consistency in sizing. Use your adjusted fitting patterns the same way to achieve a personalized and perfect fit.

When making the flat pattern adjustments on the following pages, follow these three rules:

- ☐ Follow your pattern's Cutting and Sewing Guide. Always pin first. Make sure you have made your length adjustments the same amount along the entire adjustment line. Also pin and check when adjusting circumference measurements. After the changes are made to your satisfaction, anchor them permanently with transparent tape.
- ☐ When re-drawing printed construction lines which have been interrupted by your adjustments, simply joining the two ends will result in an irregular line. To re-establish a smooth line, you will have to add to one line and subtract from the other equally, thus tapering your new line to the original line.
- ☐ When making circumference adjustments, you must keep in mind that each major pattern piece represents a quarter of your body. Think of your body divided in half horizontally by the waistline and in half vertically by the center front and back lines. Since, as a general rule, only the right half of the pattern is given, the amount of adjustment taken on the front bodice piece, for example, is only one quarter of the total adjustment.

The adjustment and alteration of the pattern pieces on the following pages show the cutting line and dart corrections indicated by **bold lines.** Correct seamlines accordingly.

Remember that only the front pattern pieces will be shown for all flat pattern adjustments. Be sure to make the comparable adjustments on the back pattern piece.

Length Adjustments

While making pattern length adjustments for your figure, you may find yourself an interesting sizing statistic. You may be long-waisted with a shorter than average hipline, or your arm may be longer from shoulder to elbow and average from elbow to wrist; thus you must adjust the pattern lengths to your personal needs.

SHORTENING PATTERN PIECES: There are areas indicated on every Vogue pattern piece where shortening may be needed to adjust the pattern lengths to your personal needs. Two adjustment lines, placed close together, are shown within the body area, and a note is placed at the lower edges of skirts. The hipline may also need to be raised to the correct position. Remember to make equal changes on front and back pieces.

To *shorten bodice and sleeves,* crease pattern between the adjustment lines within the body area and make a fold half the amount needed to be shortened. Secure the change with tape.

To *raise skirt hipline* to meet your needs, crease just above hipline of pattern. Make a fold half the amount needed to bring hipline into position. Secure the change with tape. To make this adjustment on other styles, use your adjusted fitting pattern as a guide to bring hipline into position.

To *further shorten skirt* at lower edge, simply cut away excess pattern tissue, following the shape of pattern.

Correct seamlines, dart lines, and cutting lines as shown on the pattern pieces.

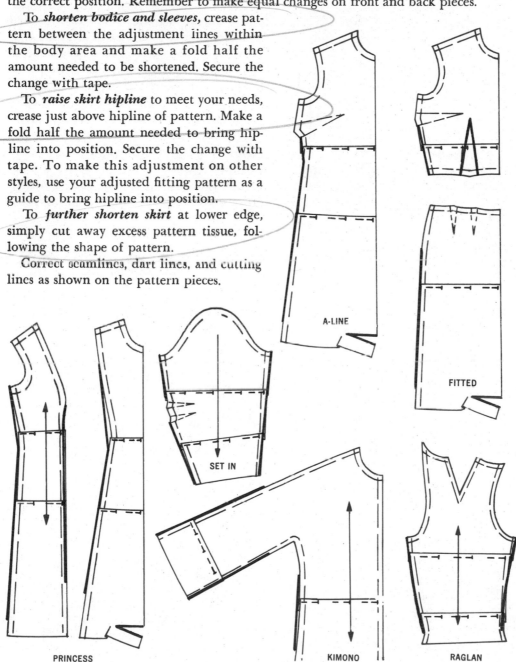

A-LINE

FITTED

SET IN

PRINCESS

KIMONO

RAGLAN

LENGTHENING PATTERN PIECES: On every Vogue pattern piece there are areas indicated where lengthening may be needed to adjust the pattern to your personal needs. Within the body area are shown two adjustment lines, placed close together, and a note is placed at the lower edge of skirts. The hipline may also need to be lowered to the correct position.

To lengthen bodice and sleeves, cut pattern along adjustment lines within the body area. Place tissue paper underneath. Spread the cut pattern edges apart the required amount and secure the changes with tape.

To lower skirt hipline, cut pattern along hipline. Place tissue paper underneath; lower hipline into the correct position and secure the change with tape. To make the hipline adjustment on other styles, place your adjusted fitting pattern underneath the pattern pieces and use it as a guide to bring hipline into position.

To further lengthen skirt at lower edge, extend pattern with tissue paper and fasten with tape. Extend the seamlines and cutting lines at sides, and draw the cutting line across lower edge, retaining original curve.

Correct all necessary seamlines, dart lines, and cutting lines on pattern pieces.

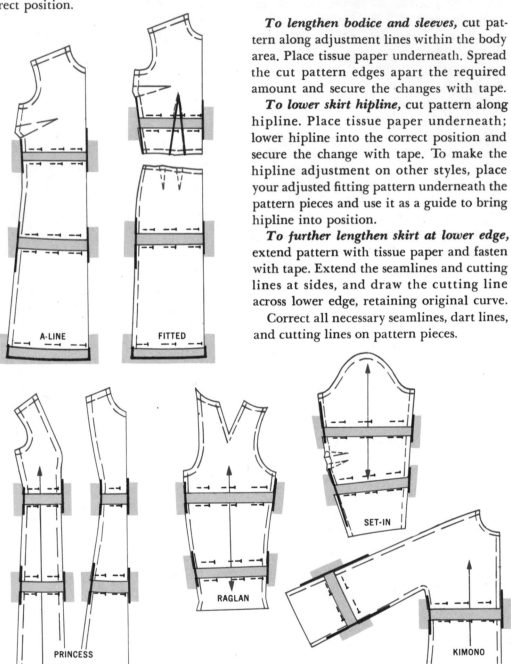

A-LINE

FITTED

PRINCESS

RAGLAN

SET-IN

KIMONO

Circumference Adjustments

Changing the pattern to coincide with your body contours allows you to make the fitting pattern personally yours. You will be amazed how much better your garment will actually flatter your figure when your own curves are really built into the pattern before you ever cut your fabric. Be sure to make equal adjustments on front and back pieces.

REDUCING WAIST AND HIPS: For adjustments *less than 1"*, draw in new seamlines and cutting lines at the sides. First mark ¼ of the amount to be reduced at the waist and hipline and pin the bust dart along the dart lines. Connect markings and draw new seamlines and cutting lines, tapering from waist to bustline. Remove pins and press tissue.

For adjustments *larger than 1"* in the fitted style with a waistline seam, it will be necessary to slash pattern as indicated and lap the edge ¼ of the amount required. Clip the seam allowance where necessary for the pattern to lie flat.

For a princess style, adjust each seam, dividing the amount by the number of seams.

A-line styles should not be reduced more than 1" or the style lines may become distorted.

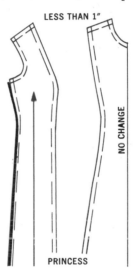

LESS THAN 1"

NO CHANGE

PRINCESS

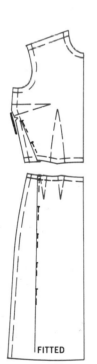

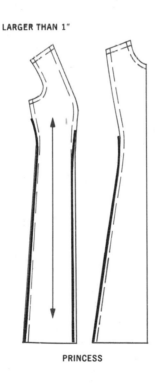

LARGER THAN 1"

FITTED

PRINCESS

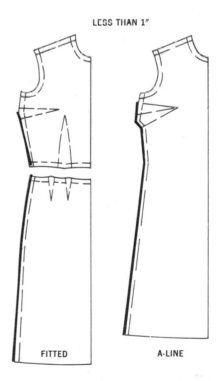

LESS THAN 1"

FITTED

A-LINE

ENLARGING WAIST AND HIPS: For adjustments of *less than 1″* (not shown), mark ¼ the amount needed to be enlarged at waist and hipline and pin bust darts together along the seamline. Connect markings by drawing new cutting lines and seamlines, tapering above waist to bustline.

Correct all necessary seamlines, dart lines, and cutting lines on pattern pieces.

For adjustments *larger than 1″*, slash pattern as indicated. Place tissue paper underneath. Spread slashed pattern edges ¼ of the amount needed at waist and hipline. Secure with tape. For a fitted style, make sure you have slashed enough so the pattern will lay flat. A small pleat will form in the seam allowance or hem area. For princess styles, divide the amount needed by the number of seams and adjust each seam as indicated.

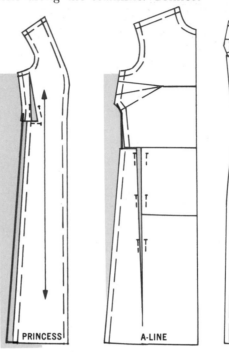

PRINCESS   A-LINE   FITTED

LARGER THAN 1″

REDUCING WAIST WITHOUT ALTERING HIPS: Mark the appropriate pattern pieces ¼ of the amount needed to be reduced at the waist seamline or waist indication. Connect markings by accurately drawing new seamlines and cutting lines. The lines should taper back to the original seamline near the bust dart and just above the hipline. Be sure to adjust any related pattern pieces.

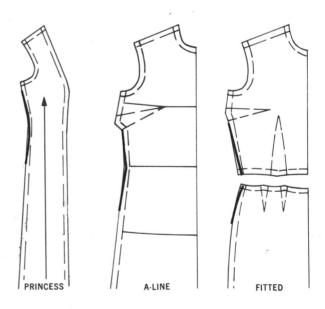

PRINCESS   A-LINE   FITTED

130

ENLARGING HIPS: If adjustment required is *2" or less*, place tissue paper under side edges. Mark ¼ of the amount needed at hipline and hemline. Draw new seamlines and cutting lines, connecting the marks, and taper to the waist.

For adjustments of *more than 2"*, slash pattern parallel to grainline or center fold. For skirts, slash from top to bottom. For A-line styles, slash to hipline and then cut across hipline to side seam. Over tissue paper, spread each piece ¼ of the amount needed at hipline and secure with tape. Taper seamline and cutting line to bust dart or bust area. For princess styles, be sure to divide the amount needed by the number of seams and adjust each seam as indicated.

Take out excess circumference at waist by adding darts near the side seam or reducing pattern along the side edges, retaining hip adjustment.

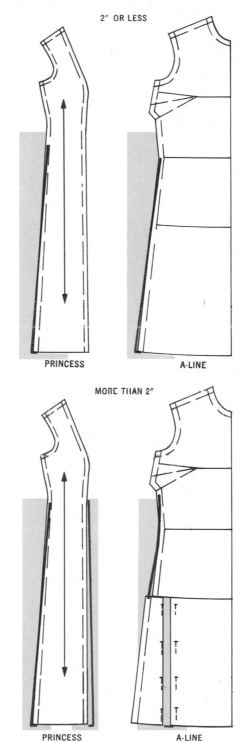

2" OR LESS

PRINCESS   A-LINE

MORE THAN 2"

PRINCESS   A-LINE

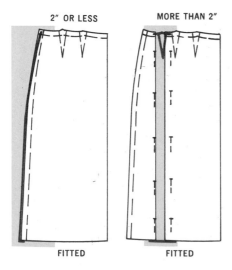

2" OR LESS   MORE THAN 2"

FITTED   FITTED

Plumb Line

With all your flat pattern adjustments made on your personal fitting pattern, you are ready to make your muslin fitting shell. Refer to the instruction sheet for fabric preparation and follow the cutting and sewing guide. For a quick and permanent method of transferring markings to right side of your muslin, mark with tracing wheel and carbon. Try on the shell and use a plumb line to help judge the direction of the grainlines and seams. To make one you will need 5 feet of heavy cord (cording, string, twill tape) with a metal weight (horseshoe magnet, drapery weight, etc.) tied to one end. To simplify its use, you will need approximately 15″ of seam binding and a heavy piece of cardboard or soft wood about 6″ long and 2″ wide with a hole pierced in the center.

To check your center front and center back markings, tie seam binding around neck and attach plumb line. Place line at top of center front thread tracing and then at center back seam. To check side seams, tie plumb line to board and place under your arm. To check sleeve grains, have someone hold the plumb line at the shoulder seam and suspend it down over sleeve. Be concerned about the grain above the elbow only.

Your vertical seams and thread tracings are to hang parallel with the plumb line and the crosswise grain and thread tracings should be at right angles to it. If they are not, mark variance with pin or chalk or have someone do it for you.

Use the instruction sheet and analyze your muslin before straightening grainlines and seams. For minor adjustments, remove stitching from any faulty seams. Smooth fabric into position, using up to ½″ of one seam allowance if necessary. In many instances, the "off grain" condition may indicate that additional alterations are needed to compensate for posture, bone structure, or body contour, necessitating a larger alteration. Turn to the next section for a solution.

Personal Fitting Alterations

Now that you have your muslin fitting shell on, you may find areas that need further altering before they fit properly and the grains and seams are straight. The alterations in this section pin-point areas where you may need further changes to accommodate your body contour or bone structure. Make the necessary alterations as directed, being careful not to over-fit; too precise a fit will tend to accent a figure fault.

When all the alterations are completed, transfer the changes to your pattern pieces, using the same techniques as for flat pattern adjustments. If you find it too difficult to translate any adjustments, take your muslin fitting shell apart to use as a guide. In many cases, all the pattern pieces will not need to be changed, as the alteration can be done on just the front or the back. When you have recorded all necessary alterations, they can be transferred to every pattern you use. If ever in doubt about the accuracy of a pattern adjustment, test it by first constructing the section in muslin. When altering a different basic shape (princess lines, raglan sleeve, etc.) requires a slightly different procedure, we have illustrated it for you. Eliminate time-consuming fitting on each and every garment, and make your pattern do the work for you.

Necklines

The neckline of the muslin fitting shell (called a jewel neckline by our designers) should encircle the body at the base of your neck. All necklines are raised or lowered from this point to give you many variations. For styles other than a jewel neckline, the back pattern piece will have a note stating exactly how much lower or higher it is at the base of neck.

When a neckline pulls, is too large, or does not hug your body in a flattering manner, it will need further alteration. Choose one of the following procedures to help you achieve a perfect fitting neckline

TIGHT NECKLINE: Neckline pulls uncomfortably around neck. To correct, draw a line on the garment at the correct neckline location. Stitch along this line. Clip to the new seamline at ½″ intervals until it is comfortable. Adjust front and back pattern pieces of bodice and facing in equal amounts by drawing in new seamlines and cutting lines.

LARGE NECKLINE: Neckline is too big and does not reach to the base of neck. To correct, fill in neckline to base of neck with folded shaped bias strip of fabric; baste. Adjust front and back pattern pieces of bodice and facing in equal amounts by extending the seamlines and cutting lines as indicated by the strip.

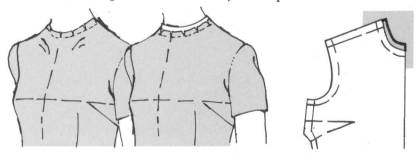

GAPING NECKLINES: This problem is caused by the wrong bust cup size, too small a pattern, a hollow chest, or a pigeon chest. Even though you bought your pattern by bust measurement, the pattern may not allow enough room across the garment front for your bust cup size or body contour. Therefore, the bodice will not drape smoothly over the body contours, causing gaping and distortion of lower necklines.

Cut bodice in muslin. Try on the bodice to find your problem area. Gaping and pulling can be caused in the same neckline. You may need only one of the alterations listed below or a combination of two. The changes will be same for square, V-, or U-necklines.

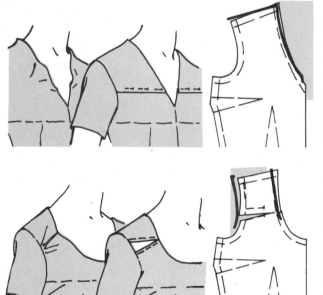

Excess fabric causes neckline to wrinkle above bust and stand away from body. Pin out wrinkles, tapering to armhole seam. Transfer alteration to pattern front by lowering cutting lines and seamlines at shoulder and neck and by shortening the amount needed at center front.

Pulling at the armhole distorts neckline above bust. Slash from neckline to armhole seam. Spread as needed. Insert strips of fabric; baste to cut edges. Transfer alteration by slashing pattern front in same way. Spread as needed and fasten with tape. Correct shoulder, armhole, and neckline seams and cutting lines.

Skimpy bodice front will not have enough fabric circumference over bust, causing distortion and gaping at neckline. Make the bust with large cup alteration, page 145, keeping it within the style line of the bodice front as indicated.

DECOLLETÉ OR LOW NECKLINES: Cut your neck facings in muslin and stitch together. Stitch along neck seamline; turn seam allowance to inside along stitching, clipping at ½" intervals, and baste. Try on facing and see where it rests on your body. Fill in a very low neckline to the desired depth. Transfer alteration to facing and front pattern pieces before you cut your fabric. Correct cutting lines and seamlines.

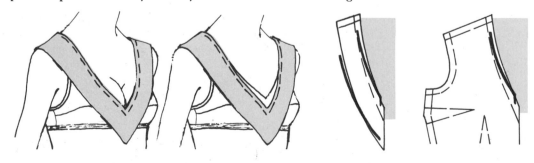

Shoulders

Since your shoulders support the hang of the entire garment, it is essential that they are fitted properly with the fabric smoothly molded over the body. Be sure the shoulder seams rest directly on top of shoulders and that they end at arm hinge and at base of neck.

SLOPING SHOULDERS: Wrinkles appear near the bust dart at armhole and across end of shoulder in back because the shoulder and armhole seams are not placed at the angle needed for your figure. To correct, try shoulder pads. If wrinkles do not disappear, however, remove sleeves. Pin out excess fabric at shoulders, tapering to neckline. Lower armhole seamline the same amount. Transfer alteration to pattern.

For raglan and kimono sleeves, transfer the alteration to pattern pieces as illustrated.

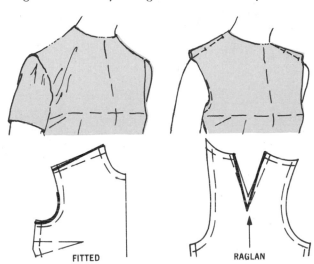

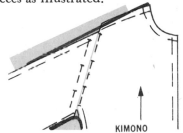

FITTED   RAGLAN   KIMONO

SQUARE SHOULDERS: Pulling around shoulders and armhole creates wrinkles across back and front near neckline because the shoulder area is not wide enough for your bone structure. To correct, remove sleeve. Slash front and back near shoulder seam from armhole edge to neckline. Spread cut edges the amount needed until wrinkles disappear. Insert strips of fabric under cut edges and baste. Transfer alteration to pattern pieces.

For raglan and kimono sleeves, transfer the alteration to pattern pieces as illustrated.

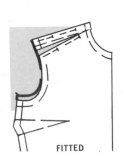

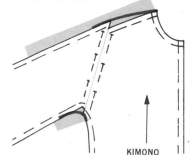

FITTED   RAGLAN   KIMONO

NARROW SHOULDERS: Armhole seams fall beyond the end of the shoulder for set-in sleeves. Other sleeve types wrinkle across upper arm and sometimes pull and restrict movement. To correct muslin garment, pin dart in front and back deep enough to pull armhole seam into place. Adjust bodice pattern pieces the same amount.

The muslin fitting shell covers only the basic style with a normal shoulder seam and a set-in sleeve. To transfer the alteration to style variations, adjust pattern pieces as shown below and test in muslin *before* cutting into fashion fabric.

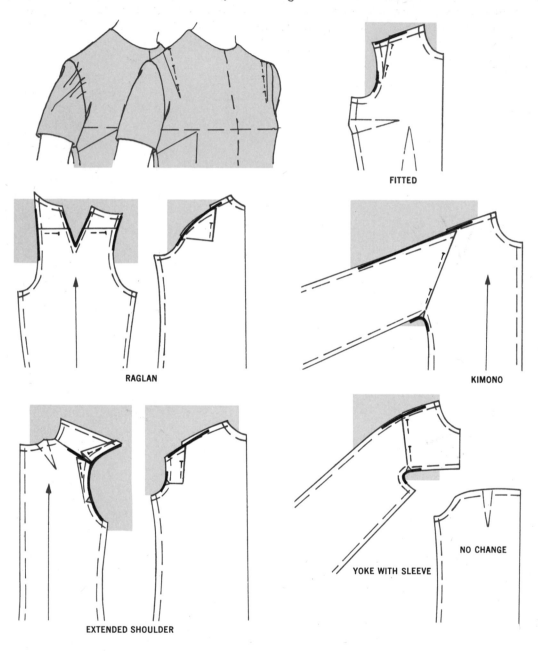

FITTED

RAGLAN

KIMONO

EXTENDED SHOULDER

YOKE WITH SLEEVE

NO CHANGE

BROAD SHOULDERS: Armhole seams draw up over shoulder, causing wrinkles and pulling in a set-in sleeve. Other sleeve types pull and do not have enough ease in the shoulder area for movement. To correct muslin garment, slash front and back from shoulder seam to armhole seam. Spread cut edges amount needed until wrinkles disappear. Insert strips of fabric under cut edges; baste. Adjust bodice pattern pieces the same amount.

The muslin fitting shell covers only the basic style with a normal shoulder seam and a set-in sleeve. To transfer the alteration to other style variations, adjust pattern pieces as shown below and test in muslin *before* cutting your fashion fabric.

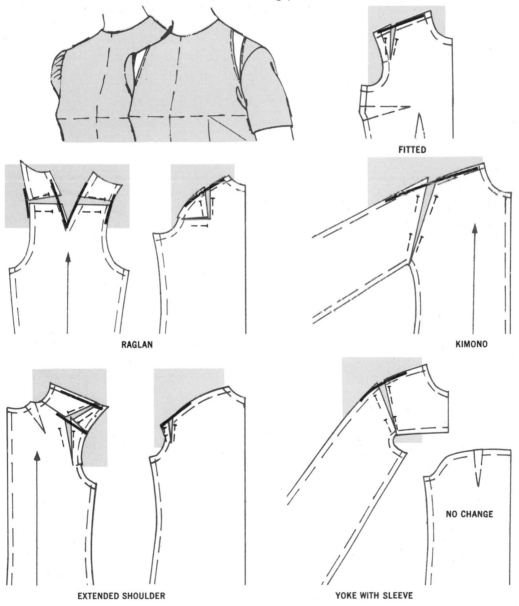

FITTED

RAGLAN

KIMONO

EXTENDED SHOULDER

YOKE WITH SLEEVE

NO CHANGE

Sleeveless Armholes

There is nothing less attractive than an armhole in a sleeveless garment that does not lie correctly on the body. An armhole that is too small will bind and cut. When the armhole is too big it will gap, exposing your undergarments.

TEST SLEEVELESS ARMHOLE: Cut bodice in muslin. Stitch along seamline at armhole. Turn seam allowance to inside along stitching. Clip at ½" to ¾" intervals, baste.

Try on bodice. The underarm portion should be 1" below the armpit and the garment should fit smoothly around armhole. It should not bind, pull, or restrict arm movement.

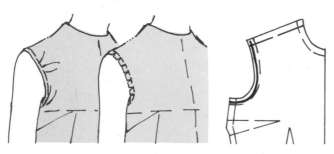

TIGHT ARMHOLE: Draw correct line at armhole. Stitch carefully along the line and clip to the new stitching at ½" intervals until the armhole seam is comfortable. Transfer the alteration to both the bodice and facing pattern pieces.

LARGE ARMHOLE: To correct a large armhole, insert bias strips of fabric to fill in the amount needed around and under the arm. When placed accurately, baste securely and transfer the alteration to bodice and facing pattern pieces.

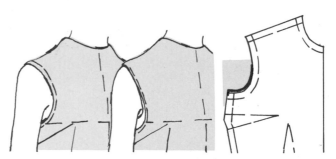

GAPING ARMHOLES: Pin out excess fabric at shoulders to bring armhole into place, tapering to the neck. If alteration is extensive, you may have to raise the underarm further by inserting a bias strip of fabric; baste. Transfer alteration to bodice and facing pattern pieces.

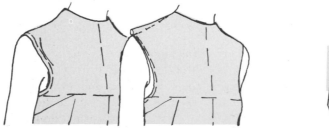 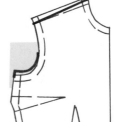

Buying the pattern by bust measurement should give the correct circumference for armhole to fit comfortably. If it still gaps in front or back, pattern is too small at bust or back and you will need to alter the bodice. To eliminate *gaping in front bodice,* make the alteration for a bust with a large cup, page 145; for *gaping in back bodice,* make the rounded back alteration, page 147, or the large back alteration, page 148.

Sleeves

The ease needed in a sleeve cap has traditionally been a stumbling block for many, since the pattern pieces and their markings are designed for the standard figure. Many times the only thing wrong with your sleeve is improper distribution of ease due to your body contour or bone structure. However, these same figure problems can affect the length of the sleeve cap, too.

IMPROPER DISTRIBUTION OF EASE: Diagonal wrinkles will form, starting at the sleeve cap and continuing across the sleeve, and distort the lengthwise grain. When this occurs, remove sleeve cap from armhole between notches. For wrinkles that start at

front of sleeve cap, re-distribute the ease, moving it forward until the wrinkles disappear. For wrinkles that start at the back of the sleeve cap, re-distribute the ease, moving it backward until the wrinkles disappear. Baste sleeve into armhole and check appearance.

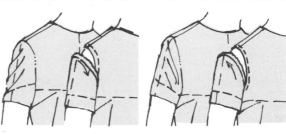

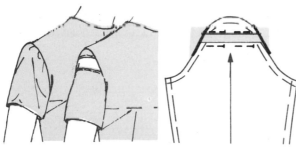

SKIMPY SLEEVE CAP: Sleeve cap pulls and collapses, causing wrinkles. To correct, slash across sleeve between seam. Insert strip of fabric under cut edges. Spread the amount needed to increase ease around upper armhole seam and baste. Adjust sleeve cap area of sleeve pattern the same way.

SLEEVE CAP TOO DEEP: Sleeve cap wrinkles across top of sleeve just below seam. Reduce the amount of ease, by pinning out excess fabric. Adjust the sleeve cap area of sleeve pattern the same way.

EXCESS EASE IN SLEEVE CAP: Sleeve cap wrinkles around armhole seam. To correct, release stitching. Smooth sleeve cap and pin in a shallow vertical dart at top; baste sleeve in place. Slash pattern at shoulder marking 3″ to 4″. Lap edge amount to be decreased (pattern will bubble slightly). Make 1½″ clips at each end of ease so the seam allowances will lie flat. Be sure to maintain the girth across the sleeve cap where the ease ends and shorten the sleeve cap slightly as indicated.

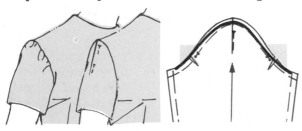

LARGE ARM: The sleeve pulls due to a lack of wearing ease. To correct, slash sleeve along lengthwise grain. Insert strip of fabric under cut edges and spread amount needed, tapering to shoulder seam and sleeve edge. If sleeve cap still pulls, remove stitching, add a piece of fabric to extend cap, and baste. Add ease thread to strip and insert in armhole. Adjust sleeve pattern the same amount, folding pattern so it will lie flat. Re-draw grainlines.

For raglan and kimono sleeves, transfer alteration to pattern pieces as illustrated. Test in muslin *before* cutting fashion fabric.

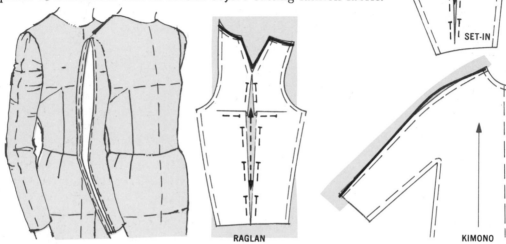

THIN ARM: The sleeve wrinkles and sags. To correct, pin out excess fabric; make a lengthwise fold from sleeve cap to lower edge, tapering fold at lower edge if necessary to provide room for hand to slip through. Adjust sleeve pattern piece in the same way. The sleeve cap will have less ease.

For raglan and kimono sleeves, transfer alteration to pattern pieces as illustrated. Test in muslin *before* cutting fashion fabric.

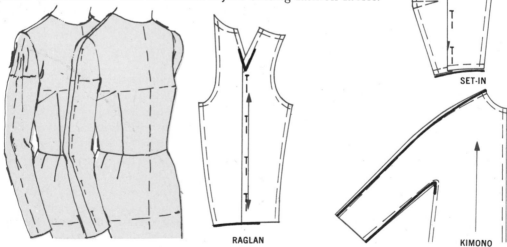

THICK ELBOW: Sleeve pulls from shoulder and is snug around elbow. To correct, remove stitching between notches on sleeve seam. Slash sleeve between darts to lengthwise grain marking and then slash to sleeve cap edge. Insert strips of fabric under cut edges. Spread amount needed and baste. Make an additional dart between existing ones. Re-stitch seam. Adjust sleeve pattern the same way. **Re-draw grainlines.**

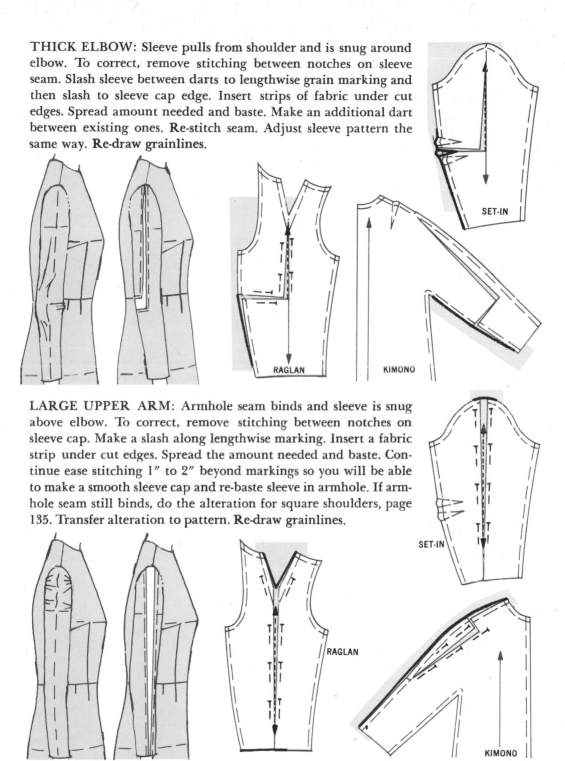

SET-IN

RAGLAN

KIMONO

LARGE UPPER ARM: Armhole seam binds and sleeve is snug above elbow. To correct, remove stitching between notches on sleeve cap. Make a slash along lengthwise marking. Insert a fabric strip under cut edges. Spread the amount needed and baste. Continue ease stitching 1″ to 2″ beyond markings so you will be able to make a smooth sleeve cap and re-baste sleeve in armhole. If armhole seam still binds, do the alteration for square shoulders, page 135. Transfer alteration to pattern. **Re-draw grainlines.**

SET-IN

RAGLAN

KIMONO

To make thick elbow and large upper arm alteration for raglan and kimono sleeves, transfer alteration to pattern pieces. Test in muslin *before* cutting out of fashion fabric.

Bust

Because the bust area is the most difficult portion of the pattern to alter, purchase appropriate patterns according to your bust measurement. This should give you the circumference needed in this area. In some cases, however, the contours of the body or bone structure across the **back** can take away the necessary girth needed and the fabric will not lay smoothly over the bust. For these alterations, see page 148. Sometimes the only alteration needed is the re-positioning or re-shaping of the darts, but frequently other situations, such as a bust with a large cup or a small cup can require detailed alterations to fit the contour of your bust. Once you do them, you will see the difference immediately and be on your way to constructing a better fitting garment.

BUST DART LENGTH: This is the most important feature in creating a smooth, flattering fit over your bosom. The proper dart lengths will vary with every woman, as they are dependent on the shape as well as the size of your breasts. The underarm bust dart should end ½" from the apex and the front darts should end ½" to 1" below the apex so fabric will cup smoothly over bosom. Refer to page 105 to determine the location of the apex of your bust. If, however, lengthening or shortening the dart is not sufficient to accommodate your body contour, refer to the alterations listed on the following pages.

To **shorten underarm dart,** mark muslin with a pin where dart should end. To correct, open side seam and re-stitch dart in proper length. (Do the same for front darts if included in your pattern.) Adjust pattern the same way.

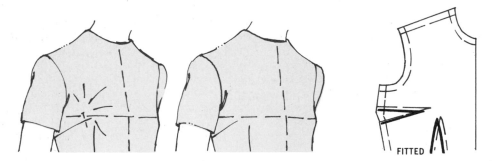

To **lengthen underarm dart,** mark muslin with a pin where dart should end. To correct, open side seam and re-stitch dart in proper length. (Do the same for front darts if they are included in your pattern.) Adjust pattern the same way.

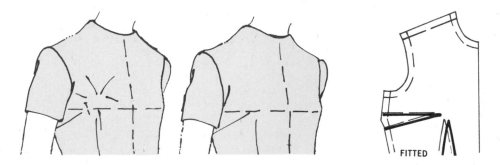

HIGH BUST: Bust darts do not fall in line with the fullest part of the bust and need to be raised. Make a line on muslin where dart should be. To correct, open side seam and re-stitch dart in proper position. Adjust position of dart on pattern as shown. This alteration is applicable to *all* underarm bust darts, regardless of their angle. Lengthen front darts as indicated, if necessary.

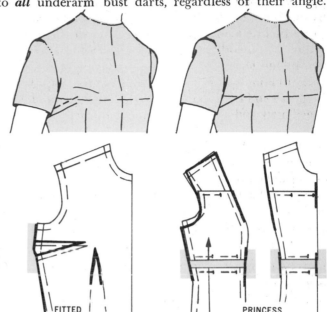

To alter styles that have bust shaping without the use of darts, place your adjusted fitting pattern underneath the pattern pieces to use as a guide. Above the armhole notch, make a fold ½ the amount needed to be raised and secure with tape. Slash through pattern below bust area and spread over tissue paper, adding the amount the bust was raised to maintain your bodice length. Secure with tape. Make new seamlines and cutting lines for armhole below notches.

LOW BUST: Bust darts do not fall in line with fullest part of the bust and need to be lowered. Make a line on muslin where dart should be. To correct, open side seam and re-stitch dart in proper position. Adjust position of dart on pattern as shown. This alteration is applicable to *all* underarm darts, regardless of their angle. Shorten front darts as indicated, if necessary.

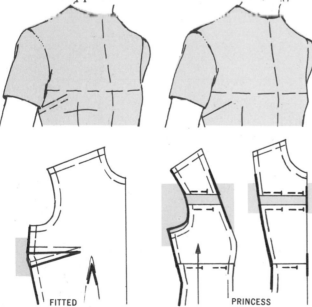

To alter styles that have bust shaping without the use of darts, place your adjusted fitting pattern underneath the pattern pieces to use as a guide. Slash through pattern pieces at armhole notch. Spread over tissue paper, lowering bust shaping area into position. Secure with tape. Make a fold below the bust area ½ the amount the bust was lowered to maintain your bodice length. Secure with tape. Make new seamlines and cutting lines for armhole below the notches.

BUST WITH SMALL CUP: Bodice wrinkles over point of bust. To correct muslin garments, pin out excess fabric; taper horizontal folds to the side seams. Taper vertical folds to the waist seam (lower for A-line style garments). Transfer the alterations to front pattern piece. When the tapering extends into skirt portions, be certain to add the amount taken out to the seams. For A-line styles, slash through the center of the dart to allow these edges to overlap. The darts will become shorter and narrower; adjust their length to your figure. Correct cutting, seam, and dart lines.

To transfer this alteration to garments without darts, place your adjusted fitting pattern underneath the front pieces to use as a guide. Reduce pattern sections for bust as indicated. Test in muslin *before* cutting out of fashion fabric.

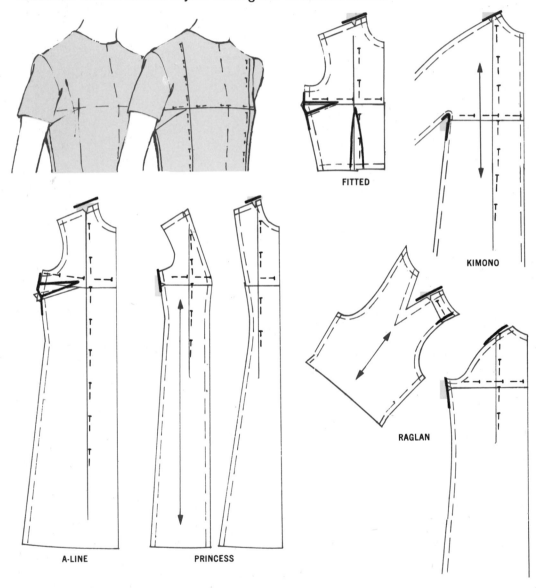

FITTED

KIMONO

A-LINE

PRINCESS

RAGLAN

BUST WITH LARGE CUP: Bodice pulls over bust, flattening bust at apex. To correct muslin garment, slash through bust darts and across front. Slash down front from shoulder to the waist seam (lower for A-line style garments). Spread edges amount needed until bust is not flattened. Insert strips of fabric under cut edges and baste. Transfer alteration to pattern front. When enlargement extends into skirt portion, be certain to take out the amount spread at the seams. Correct cutting, seam, and dart lines. Darts will become deeper; adjust their length to your figure. Trim darts to within ½″ of stitching if necessary to reduce bulk; press cut edges open.

To transfer this alteration to garments without darts, place your adjusted fitting pattern underneath the front pieces to use as a guide. Enlarge pattern section for bust as indicated. Test in muslin *before* cutting out of fashion fabric.

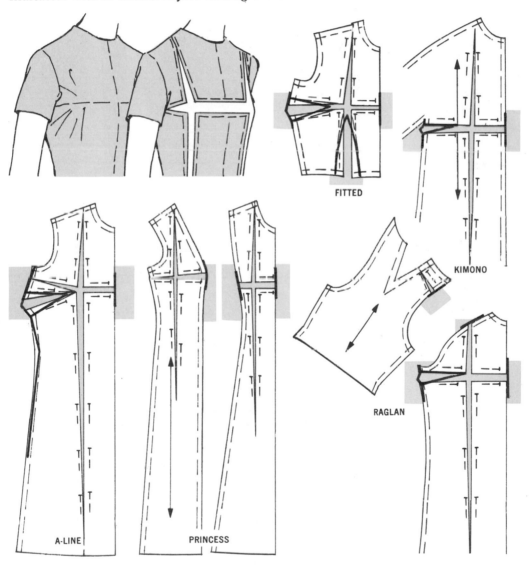

FITTED

KIMONO

A-LINE

PRINCESS

RAGLAN

Chest

The upper portion of the chest above the bust would seem to be an area of little concern when fitting a garment. The bone structure of the rib cage and collar bone controls the bodice length along the center front, however, and may create a need for alterations.

HOLLOW CHEST: Bodice wrinkles above bust and below neckline. To correct muslin garment, pin out wrinkles, tapering to the armhole or shoulder seams. Adjust front pattern at neck and shoulder edges the amount needed.

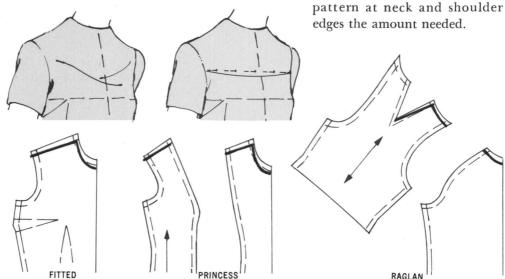

FITTED   PRINCESS   RAGLAN

PIGEON CHEST: Collar and breast bones protrude, causing bodice to pull above bust and distort armhole seam. To correct muslin garment, open armhole seam. Slash across front above bust and up through center of shoulder area to seam. Insert fabric strips under cut edges. Spread amount needed to fit body contour. Baste, keeping slashed edge flat. Re-stitch seams. Transfer alteration to front pattern pieces as indicated.

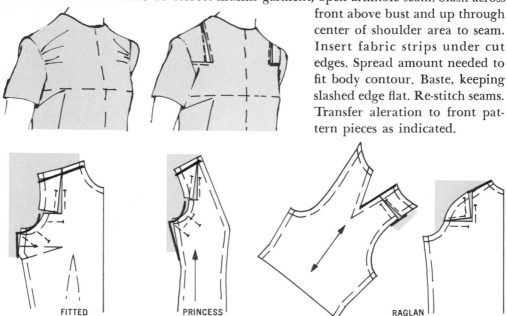

FITTED   PRINCESS   RAGLAN

Back

The entire garment back should mold smoothly over your body contour from the neck to the hem edge. There should be no wrinkles or pulling and the hem must be even. Adjusting the pattern to your measurements will give the girth needed, but the fabric may not drape evenly due to bone structure or posture and will require alteration.

VERY ERECT BACK: Bodice back has parallel wrinkles across back above shoulder blades. To correct, pin out wrinkles, tapering to the armhole or shoulder seams. Adjust bodice pattern the amount needed at neck and shoulder edges.

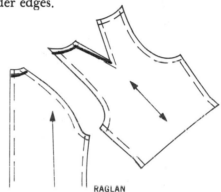

RAGLAN

FITTED   PRINCESS

HIGH, ROUNDED BACK (DOWAGER'S HUMP): Bodice wrinkles and pulls across the shoulders and near the sleeve tops. To correct muslin garment, slash across back between armhole seams. Remove stitching from zipper above slash. Insert strips of fabric under cut edges and spread them the amount needed. Baste, keeping slashed edges flat and allowing for center back opening. Pin darts in neck edge to fit contour. Add strips to extend back edges to center opening. Adjust bodice back pattern piece the same amount, adding dart at neck edge as indicated.

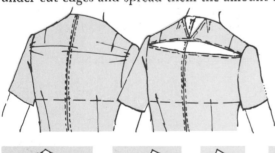

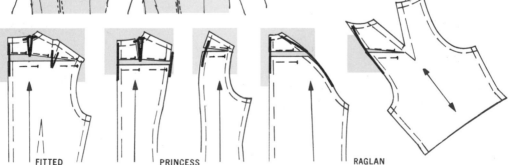

FITTED   PRINCESS   RAGLAN

NARROW BACK: Bodice is loose through shoulder area. Garment with waist seam may have extra fullness above the seam, while A-line garment may be longer in back at the hemline. To correct, pin out excess fabric, joining darts from shoulder to waistline. This will make the back darts continuous from shoulder to waist. Transfer alteration to pattern back as indicated. For princess style, simply take a deeper seam.

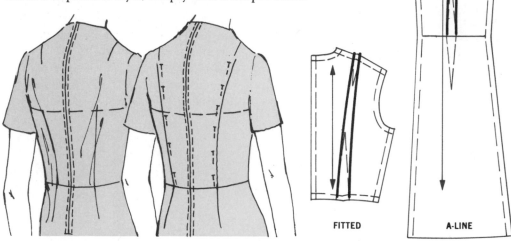

FITTED   A-LINE

LARGE BACK OR PROMINENT SHOULDER BLADES: Bodice wrinkles and pulls across fullest part of back and is tight when raising arms. To correct, remove stitching at shoulder seams, darts, and side seams. Slash across back below armhole and up through center of shoulder dart. Spread edges amount needed. Insert strips of fabric under cut edges and baste. Make existing dart deeper or add a dart to fit contour and then restitch seam. Transfer alteration to pattern back.

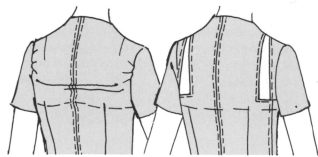

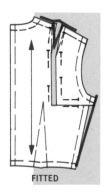

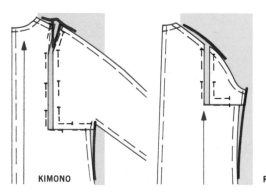

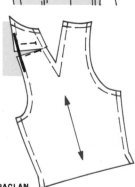

FITTED   KIMONO   RAGLAN

SWAY BACK: Garment wrinkles across back below waistline. To correct muslin garment, pin out wrinkles, tapering to side seam. Transfer alteration to pattern back by removing excess length along center back seam the necessary amount. Darts will become shorter.

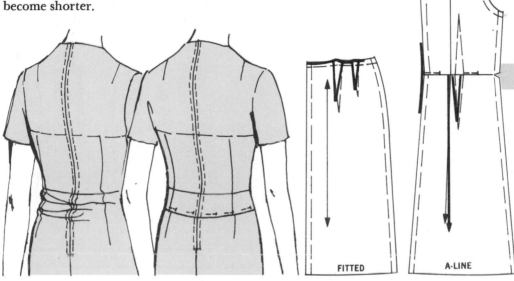

Hips

Since the hip circumference was already taken care of before making the muslin fitting shell, you now must be concerned about the effect your bone structure or posture has on the garment. The fabric should mold smoothly over the buttocks and hip bones without wrinkles or pulling.

PROTRUDING HIP BONES: This is usually noticeable only in fitted garments. Bones protrude, causing pulling across front. To correct, remove stitching from darts and seams. Pin darts to fit contour. If this makes the waistline smaller, add to side seams. Restitch darts and seams. Transfer alteration to pattern front.

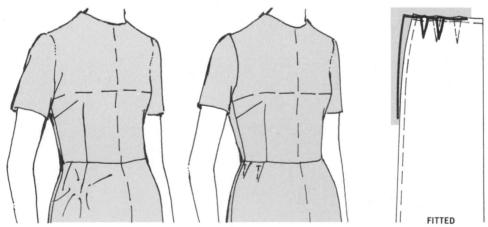

FLAT BUTTOCKS: Skirt area wrinkles and sags at back, causing uneven hemline. For both styles, release darts. Pin darts, making them shorter to fit body contour and narrower to retain the same waist measurement. To correct A-line garment, release zipper below back bustline. Pin out excess fabric at side and center back seams. To correct garments with waist seam, pin out excess fabric across hips. Pin out sag, making hemline even.

Transfer alteration to pattern back as indicated.

A-LINE

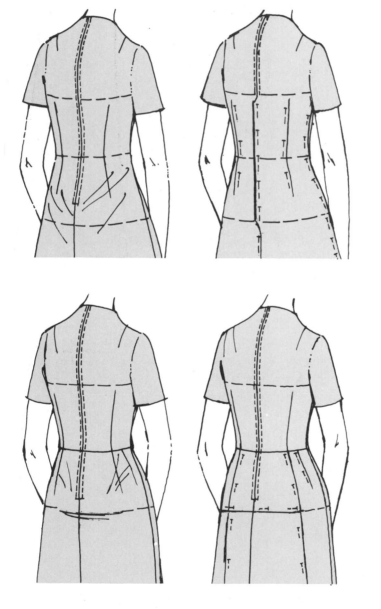

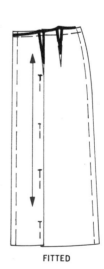

FITTED

LARGE BUTTOCKS OR LARGE BACK AT TOP OF HIPS: Wrinkles form between waist and hipline with pulling that distorts side seams. Hemline is shorter in back. To correct A-line garment, release darts, seams, and zipper below back bustline. Place strips of fabric under center back and side seams. Make equal adjustments at each seam to bring side seams into position; baste. Pin darts to fit contour. To correct garment with waist seam, release darts below waist and remove the stitching from waist seam. Pin darts to fit contour.

Transfer alteration to pattern back as indicated.

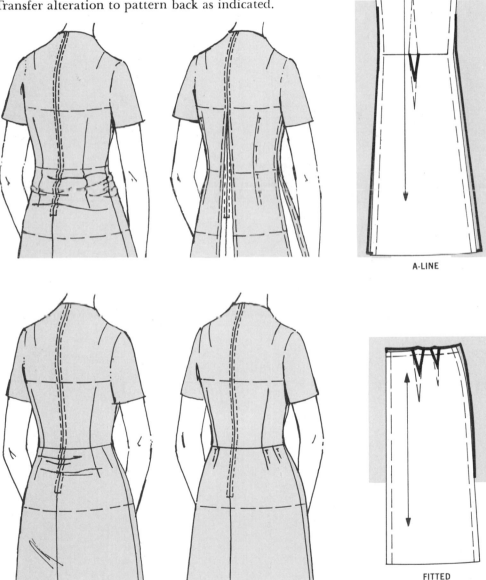

A-LINE

FITTED

ONE LARGE HIP: Skirt pulls up on one side of front and back, causing uneven hemline. Most obvious in fitted garments, it may also show in other garments.

To correct garment with waist seam, remove stitching from shorter side, waist, and darts. Drop skirt until grain and hem are straight. Insert strips of muslin at sides and top; baste. Pin darts to fit contour. Re-stitch seams. For A-line garments, remove stitching from shorter side and darts. Spread edges until grain and hem are straight. Insert muslin strips at sides; baste. Pin back dart to fit contour. Re-stitch seam.

Make a paper pattern for the left half of the skirt and transfer the alteration to the side that needs to be enlarged. You will then have a record of both sides of your skirt. (Shown below are the pattern pieces for the right side only.)

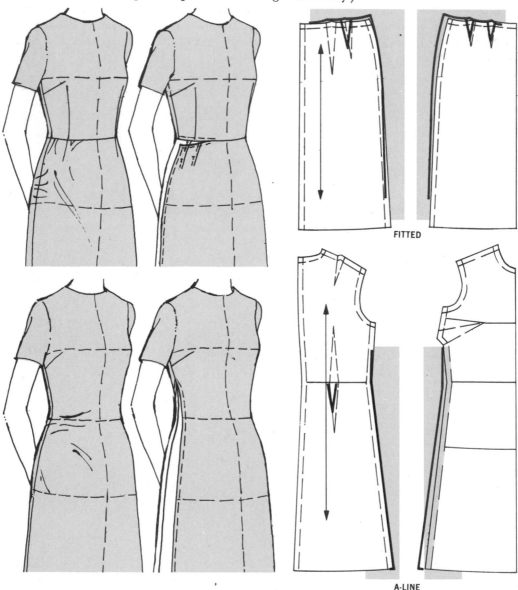

FITTED

A-LINE

Abdomen

The hip circumference measurement allows for the girth of this area, but will not compensate for wrinkles and pulling caused by posture and body contour. As with all figure flaws, fabric molded smoothly over this area will minimize rather than accent it.

LARGE ABDOMEN: Skirt front rides up, pulling side seams forward and causing waist and hipline to pull up. To correct garment with waist seam, release front waist seam and darts. Drop skirt front until it hangs even. Baste fabric strip to top of skirt. Pin darts to fit contour. If this makes the waistline smaller, add to side seams. Re-stitch darts and seams. Transfer alteration to pattern as indicated.

To correct A-line garment, slash front up to bust area. Spread edges amount needed until side seams, waistline, and hipline fall into position. Place strips of fabric under slashed edges and baste. Transfer alteration to pattern front as indicated, slashing through bust dart to make pattern lie flat, and let edges overlap.

FITTED

A-LINE

Combine Two Patterns

How many times have you wished your pattern had longer sleeves or a different neckline than the one shown? Perhaps you've even passed up a pattern style which you loved because it had a design feature that was not flattering on you. With some initiative and practice, you can avoid the necessity for such compromises by using parts of different styles to create a garment which is truly custom-designed for your particular taste and figure. This information is intended to allow you to exercise your designer instincts and to provide some guidelines which will help you combine patterns successfully.

Within each size range of a Vogue Pattern, the structural body relationships of shoulder to neck, bust to waist, etc., never change—a size 12 bodice from one style number will fit a size 12 skirt from another style number if they both have waistlines and the styles are similar, for example. To achieve the preferred silhouette for your needs, it is possible to combine necklines, collars, and other features from two different style numbers if the structural features of the two are the same.

Most people who understand the alterations required for their particular figure flaws will also know what style lines will minimize them. This knowledge can reduce your style selection at times because either the bodice or skirt are not right for you. If in doubt, refer to Your Figure Analysis. But don't let these limitations discourage you.

NECKLINES: The shape of your neckline can either reveal or camouflage your neck and upper body, and you should be aware of which function you wish it to serve. When you have a limited number of flattering necklines to choose from, you must be aware of the bodice style. A bodice with raglan or kimono sleeves requires a different style of draping and shaping to achieve the proper fit than does a bodice with a set-in sleeve, so the necklines of the two styles cannot be interchanged. Empire and low-waisted seaming or dropped shoulders are also very stylized and need careful evaluation of the neckline before you cut into your fashion fabric. Do not be afraid to experiment, however, as long as you test your proposed adaptations in muslin.

COLLARS: Do not make a hasty decision when you decide to substitute one collar for another. Even if two collars look alike, you must check the bodice pattern pieces to make sure they match line for line before substituting them. The shape of the neckline must vary with each different collar style in order to get the proper shaping in the collar. Interchange the collars of different styles only when the bodice pieces match **closely**. Also make sure that the location of the closings is the same.

SLEEVES: While it is obvious that radically different sleeve styles, such as raglan and set-in sleeves, cannot be interchanged, very subtle variations can also make a big difference. The bodice style is the deciding factor in interchanging sleeve versions, for it controls the size of the sleeve cap and the amount of necessary ease. The shoulder seams of the two bodices must be at the same angle and end at the same point where the arm joins the body. The lengths of the armhole curvatures must also be alike. If you wish to stray from these general rules, be very sure to test your experiments in muslin before cutting into your fashion fabric to avoid disappointing results.

Combine Two Sizes

Let's face it! Very few of us have perfect figures. Often it is easier to use two pattern sizes rather than alter a bodice or skirt drastically. The secret to combining these two areas is in making the waistline a transitional area. Assuming that you have chosen your two patterns according to your body measurements, you will have to adjust the measurements of one or both so the waistline corresponds to your measurement.

Note the difference in inches between the waist measurements of the two sizes, referring to the body measurements on the back of your pattern envelope, as the waistline will be the starting point when adjusting the two patterns. If your waist measurement is the same as one pattern size, adjust the waist of the other pattern to correspond. If the waist needs to be adjusted on both patterns, determine how much to enlarge or reduce the waist of each piece, dividing the amount to be changed by the number of seams involved. Adjust each piece accordingly.

Keep center fronts, center backs, and grainlines straight. For fitted styles with a waist seam, adjust the waist area of the bodice and skirt so the waistlines match when joined. Adjust the position of the darts in the skirt so they will meet the bodice darts at the waist, retaining the distance across the centers of the garment between the darts. For A-line styles, cut both patterns apart and join the sections needed with transparent tape. Shown below, in both styles, are the situations that may require two sizes—the smaller size bodice combined with a larger size skirt and the larger size bodice combined with the smaller size skirt. Mark ¼ the amount needed for waist at side seam for both front and back pattern pieces. Draw new side seams from the bust to the hip, simulating original curves as much as possible.

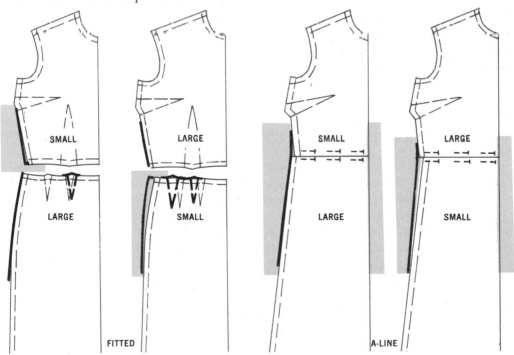

Pants, Pants, Pants

Casual slacks, city pants, pantsuits, pantskirts, or elegant evening pants will always be an important part of the fashion scene. They can be worn from morning to after dark—on the street, out to dinner and the theater, entertaining at home, or for active sports. Not to be forgotten are shorts: they too can be the basis of a smart costume.

The length of your pants or shorts is important to your total look. Full-length pants that are too short can have a skimpy, "outgrown" look, and pants that are too long can be clumsy and troublesome. Make sure your shorts do not end at an unattractive point on your leg; sometimes even an adjustment of ½″ in length can make a world of difference in their attractiveness.

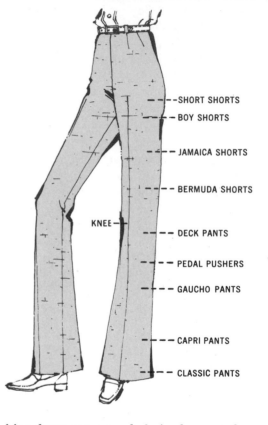

At all times you should strive toward a balanced silhouette. A long jacket, tunic, or top can camouflage those few extra pounds or inches or give a taller illusion to your total look. You may prefer a shorter top with a shorts costume or if you are short-legged. Consider your accessories; the same ones you wear with dresses may not be appropriate or in correct balance with pants.

Select the pattern for your pants carefully, choosing the type of pants which are best for your figure type. If you have prominent hips, a hip hugging style with fitted thighs would not only be hard to fit, but would also be unflattering. If you have heavy thighs, pants that are wider and straight-legged from the hips down are a good choice because they will not cling or accent the thighs. If your figure is very curvy, avoid side zippers.

Choose your pants by waist measurement unless your hip measurement is larger than that shown with the waist size; if so, select your size by hip measurement and adjust the waistline. Purchasing the correct hip size keeps pattern alterations to a minimum.

Pants are not difficult to construct, but can be hard to fit because of the endless variations in body shapes. For accurate fit, check several points: the waist should be comfortably snug, the hips should be roomy enough for ease in sitting, the thigh area should not bind, and the crotch area must not be too tight or too loose.

Pants, of all your garments, demand the most perfect fit. Although such accurate fitting can take a good deal of time and effort, you need do the most major alterations only once if you make a pants fitting muslin. This will require precise measuring, flat pattern adjustments, and detailed fitting; once done with a classic style in muslin, however, you can transfer the alterations to every pair of pants you make in the future, always ensuring perfect fit.

MEASURE YOURSELF: Be sure to wear the proper undergarments with your pants. Some can flatten the contour and give a "stuffed sausage" look. Be sure they do not cause unsightly indentations or bulges over the fullest part of your hips or thighs. Wearing the correct undergarments and shoes, take these measurements:

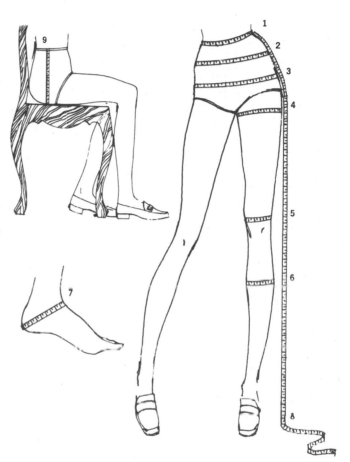

Waist: Tie a string around the body so it settles comfortably at the waistline. Measure your waist at the string (1). (Note: leave string in place to facilitate measuring from waist to points at which measurements 2 through 7 are taken.)

High hip: Measure across top of hip bones 2″ to 4″ below waist (2).

Full hip: Measure the fullest part of your hips. Vogue places this hipline approximately 7″ to 9″ from the waist, depending on size range (3).

Circumference of Leg: Measure fullest part of thigh (4), knee (5), calf (6), and instep (7).

Length: Measure at side from waist to floor or desired length (8).

Crotch Length: Sit on a hard chair and measure from the waist at side to the chair seat (9).

Flat Pattern Adjustments

The most critical step in achieving perfectly fitted pants should be done right now. Adjustments dealing with length and circumference changes should be made on the pattern pieces *before you cut* your muslin. The most important fitting area is the *crotch.* Unless the crotch is in the correct position, no amount of adjustment made later can overcome a poor fit.

Be sure to keep grainlines straight and connect the seamlines and cutting lines in a smooth, gradual line, tapering to the original lines as indicated on the pattern pieces.

CROTCH LENGTH: To help establish the crotch length you need for better fitting pants, draw a line on the *back* pattern piece at the widest part of the pattern crotch. Next, measure from the waist seamline to the crotch line, using measurement 9. The crotch length should be your measurement plus ½″ to ¾″ for sitting ease. If not, it must be adjusted by lengthening or shortening the pattern pieces as explained on the following page. Be sure to make an equal change on the front pattern piece.

To shorten this area, make a fold ½ the amount needed at the adjustment line on each pattern piece. Fasten with tape. *To lengthen,* cut the pattern along the adjustment line, place tissue paper underneath, and spread the amount needed. Fasten with tape.

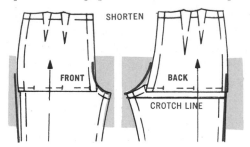

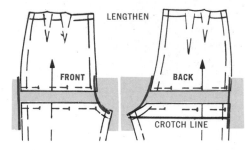

Other information you will need for adjustment and fitting guides should be added to your pattern tissue now. Use the measurements and their locations you established on page 157. Start with the front pattern piece and draw position lines perpendicular to the grainline as measured down from the waistline. Extend the grainline. Then draw lines for high hip (2), full hip (3), and thigh (4). Note your personal measurements on the tissue near each line; this will expedite checking these areas to see if they need adjusting.

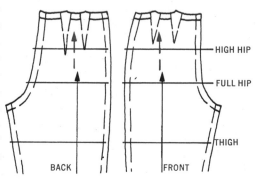

Lay the back pattern over the front; match sides. Indicate the end of each line from the front piece along the side seamline. Draw lines perpendicular to the back grainline from these locations.

PANTS LENGTH: After the crotch alteration is done, check the total length (measurement 8) of the pants along side seamline. If they are *too long,* make a fold ½ the excess amount above hemline across the leg of pattern front and back; fasten with tape. If they are *too short,* slash across the leg above hemline on pattern front and back. Place tissue paper underneath and spread the amount needed. Fasten with tape.

WAIST CIRCUMFERENCE: If your waist (measurement 1) is *smaller,* first determine the amount needed to be decreased. Then take away ⅛ of this amount from the pattern front and back at each center and side seam. If your waist is *larger,* add ⅛ the necessary amount to the pattern front and back at each center and side seam. Be sure to make corresponding adjustments on the waistband or facing pattern pieces.

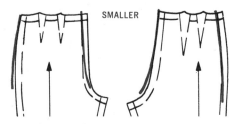

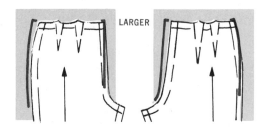

HIP CIRCUMFERENCE. No change should be necessary if your pattern has been purchased by hip measurement. However, to adjust the pattern slightly for your hip measurement, see the treatment for skirts, pages 129-131.

LEG CIRCUMFERENCE: If the pattern measurement is close to that of your thigh (measurement 4) plus one inch for wearing ease, no adjustment is necessary. To make leg *smaller,* slim the pattern the required amount. To make leg *larger,* add to the inner leg seam. Always include the amount necessary for wearing ease (at least one inch). Remember to retain the crotch curve shaping and gradually taper new lines back to meet the original lines.

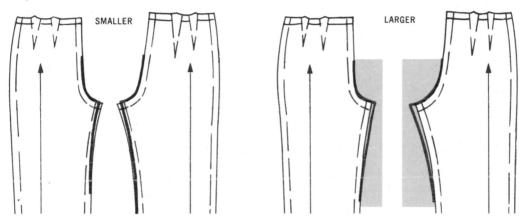

If you are making tapered, slim-fitting pants, it would also be wise to check the knee (measurement 5), calf (measurement 6), and instep (measurement 7). If your measurements (plus at least one inch for wearing ease) are larger or smaller than the pattern measurements, adjust the leg seams accordingly.

Make a Pants-Fitting Muslin

After muslin pants are cut out according to your altered pattern, transfer all seamlines and markings with tracing wheel and dressmaker's carbon. Also trace your hipline (high and full) and your thigh line to the right side of the muslin.

Be sure to follow your pattern's Sewing Guide carefully. All pants are not made in the same way. Generally, the crotch area is sewn after the leg seams so that it will not bunch or bind. Machine baste pants together. Baste a temporary waistband of grosgrain ribbon to the waist seamline to support pants while fitting.

Take a critical look in a full length mirror to spot problems due to bone structure or body contour. The side seams should be perpendicular to the floor (use plumb line, page 132, to check this). The traced lines should be parallel to the floor. If they are pulled or distorted or if wrinkling occurs, you will need further fitting and pattern adjustments to compensate for your figure flaws. Check the areas listed on the next page. If minor adjustments do not correct the problems to your satisfaction, you may need one of the more specialized alterations on the following pages. For comfort and attractiveness, avoid fitting pants too tightly.

Personal Fitting

These fitting alterations can only be accomplished by fitting your muslin and cannot be made after the fashion fabric has been cut. Since the alterations are quite individualized, the same changes are not always required on both the front and back pattern pieces. Therefore, ask yourself these questions:

- ☐ Do the pants wrinkle at the high hipline? To correct, release darts. Pin to fit body contour, lengthening or shortening darts as needed. Re-stitch.
- ☐ Is the crotch too tight or too baggy? To correct, let out or take in inner leg seam slightly as needed at the crotch point.
- ☐ Does the waist pull downward at center front or back when you sit or stand? To correct, set waistband higher at the center seam, tapering to seam at sides.

FOR LARGE ABDOMEN *(Left)*: Release darts. Drop the top of pants until the side seams fall into position. Baste a strip of fabric to the top and add to the front inner leg seam until the pants hang without wrinkles. Pin darts to fit contour. Transfer the changes to your pattern.

PROTRUDING HIP BONES *(Right)*: Release darts and pin to fit contour. This may include widening or shortening the dart. If this makes the waistline smaller, add to side seams, then transfer alteration to pattern.

SWAY-BACK: If you have a sway back, see treatment for sway-back skirts on page 149.

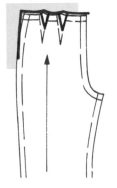

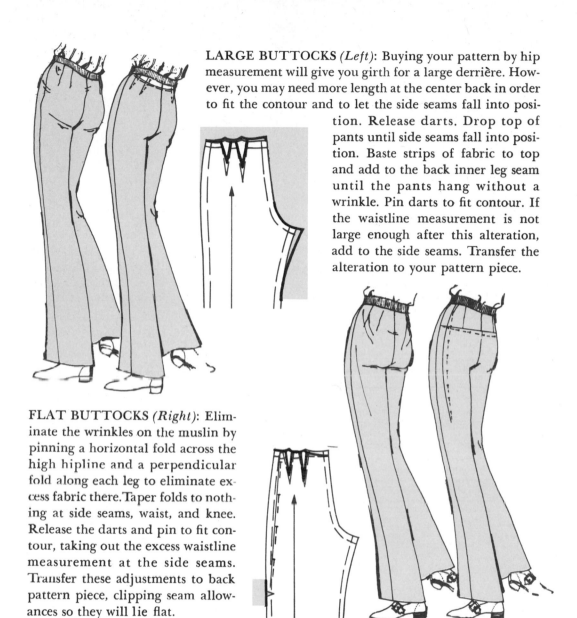

LARGE BUTTOCKS *(Left)*: Buying your pattern by hip measurement will give you girth for a large derrière. However, you may need more length at the center back in order to fit the contour and to let the side seams fall into position. Release darts. Drop top of pants until side seams fall into position. Baste strips of fabric to top and add to the back inner leg seam until the pants hang without a wrinkle. Pin darts to fit contour. If the waistline measurement is not large enough after this alteration, add to the side seams. Transfer the alteration to your pattern piece.

FLAT BUTTOCKS *(Right)*: Eliminate the wrinkles on the muslin by pinning a horizontal fold across the high hipline and a perpendicular fold along each leg to eliminate excess fabric there. Taper folds to nothing at side seams, waist, and knee. Release the darts and pin to fit contour, taking out the excess waistline measurement at the side seams. Transfer these adjustments to back pattern piece, clipping seam allowances so they will lie flat.

FINAL STEPS: When constructing pants, baste and fit to see how your fabric drapes over your body contours, making minor fitting adjustments to compensate for your fabric. Since the crotch area receives considerable strain, use a smaller straight stitch or a very small zigzag stitch when stitching the curve of the crotch seam. Clip seam at top of curve and press open. Add a second row of stitching ¼″ from first row between clips. Then trim and overcast this edge. This portion of the seam remains unpressed.

Armed with the knowledge you have gained by making a fitting muslin, make your pants pattern pieces a permanent sewing tool by mounting them on cardboard. Use them as a guide to alter any style of pants, shorts, culottes, pantskirt, and jumpsuit you plan to make. You will find it is a handy, time-saving device.

BOOK III

Creating Fashion for the Individualist

Your Complete Sewing Handbook

Now you're about to begin your adventure into the actual creation of fashion. Let's suppose that you have already made your fabric selection and chosen your pattern. Thread, bindings, trims, interfacings, all the things you need to shape fabric into fashion are at hand, and you are ready to make your first move. This is the time for you to consult your sewing handbook.

Since your pattern instructions cannot possibly elaborate on every variation of your particular garment, we've designed this handbook to be used along with your pattern instruction sheet. It's a step-by-step guide that will help you to understand *why* certain procedures should be followed, and *how* to put these procedures to use. It will help you to sew creatively with a minimum of effort and a maximum of fun. Turn to it often, and the results you achieve will be worth every minute you invest.

Here you will find a multitude of different sewing techniques that represent the most practical approach to good dressmaking. When a specific explanation is crucial to the quality of your garment, special technical or couture comments will be brought to your attention by this symbol, ✤. And, so that we will always be one step ahead of your thoughts, all material is cross-referenced to make every piece of relevant information easily and readily available.

Since making your sewing quicker and easier is our job, let us point out a time-saving plan that should serve as a guide for every project you sew:

☐ Do all preparatory steps first—cutting, marking, and basting the underlining to your fabric—as these operations definitely require a large, flat, clean surface that may be difficult to find once you've begun sewing.

☐ Complete sewing of small details, such as pocket flaps and buttonholes, on each garment section *before* it is joined to the other sections, as the weight of the entire garment can be extremely cumbersome when you are trying to be so precise.

☐ Make all buttonholes at one work session to assure consistent results.

☐ Organize yourself by attempting to finish a complete stage of construction at each sitting.

☐ Spend your extra moments on those often envied finishing details such as overcasting seams, attaching lingerie straps, etc.

☐ And, as a final word of professional advice, be sure to press seams as you finish each section.

Prepare with Care

You're excited about your new project, and anxious to start sewing immediately. Hang onto your enthusiasm, but don't be so eager to begin cutting that you neglect the all-important preparation. Fabric and pattern may both need attention before you do the final layout, and the success of your finished garment depends on care in these preparatory steps. First we suggest that you recall your fabric terminology.

Grain is the direction in which the threads composing the fabric run. Every woven fabric consists of crosswise threads worked under and over the more sturdy lengthwise threads. The narrow, flat, woven border resulting at both lengthwise sides when the crosswise threads reverse direction is called the *selvage.* The threads composing it are strong and densely woven. This border is a pre-finished edge, and may be used to advantage in center back seams, waistbands, etc. The direction of the lengthwise threads running parallel to the selvage is known as *lengthwise grain,* or sometimes "straight-of-fabric". These threads are very strong and stable, since they must withstand great tension during weaving. For this reason, garments are usually cut with the lengthwise grain running vertically for durability. The direction of the crosswise threads, running from

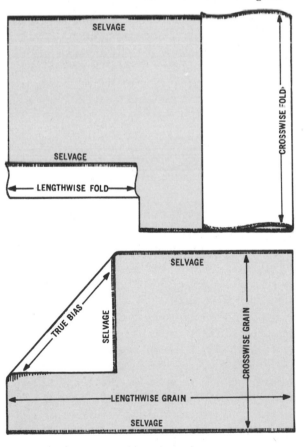

selvage to selvage at right angles across the lengthwise threads, is known as the *crosswise grain.* In most fabrics it has a very slight amount of give.

A third term used to describe direction on woven fabric is *bias.* Bias is any diagonal intersecting the lengthwise and crosswise threads. Fabric cut on the bias grain possesses much greater elasticity than that cut on the crosswise grain. Maximum stretchability occurs on the *true bias,* which is obtained by folding your on-grain fabric diagonally so the crosswise threads are parallel to the selvage. Thus, true bias exists at any 45° angle to any straight edge of a fabric whose lengthwise and crosswise threads are perpendicular.

Fabric as sold in stores is folded or rolled lengthwise on a cardboard or metal form. In this packaged state it is known as a *bolt.* You will find that on the bolt the selvages may be located at the top and bottom of the retainer, or both selvages may be at one end with a fold at the other end. Occasionally the right side of the fabric is not readily discernible from the wrong. The way the fabric is displayed on the bolt can be an excellent clue in distinguishing the right and wrong sides, for you will find that certain fabrics are usually wound on the bolt in a consistent manner. For example, cottons and linens are almost always folded in half with their right sides out, then placed on the bolt. Wools can be packaged either pre-folded with the right side in and wrapped on a rectangular bolt or rolled unfolded on a tube with the right side toward the inside. Many easily marred delicate fabrics and imported fabrics are also rolled with their right side on the inside as protection against damage. Besides indicating the right and wrong sides, such packaging can warn you that special handling is necessary. Fabrics such as vinyls, napped fabrics, and velvets **must** be stored on rolls until the moment you cut them. Folding them may leave permanent marks.

If you've purchased the fabric in a state other than its usual packaging, or forgotten which side is which, try the following procedures to differentiate the right side from the wrong side. Look at the center fold which is parallel to the lengthwise grain or selvages, and refer to the usual packaging procedures mentioned above. Examine the selvages for slubs, nubs, and other irregularities. In general, the selvages will look less finished on the wrong side of the fabric. You can also examine the fabric surface itself to see if the finish used will indicate the right side. The finished side may be shinier, flatter, more brushed, or the weave more pronounced.

As a last resort, pick the side you like best! There is no reason why you cannot use either side of many fabrics. Just be very certain to use the same side consistently when laying out your pattern on the fabric. If you neglect to do so, the slightest variation in shading can destroy the good looks of your garment.

Get Organized

Get your fabric, pattern, and equipment organized. Sort all of your pattern pieces, selecting those for the view you have chosen, as indicated by your Cutting Guide. Among these, group together the pieces for the lining, interfacing, and main garment, and press them with a warm, dry iron. Check the proportion of the garment length to your figure by holding up the pattern to your shoulder or waist, with hems folded up. If a change is indicated, an adjustment in length should be made in the paper pattern at this time. If your muslin basic pattern or your previous experience indicate a consistent difference in a certain area, such changes should also be made in the paper pattern. Compare your measurements with those on the Body Measurement Chart and, especially if you are foregoing a muslin trial copy, allow ample room in the pattern for any measurements which are larger than those given for the pattern size. Remember—when in doubt, leave extra room! Better to have nice, wide seam allowances because you over-estimated than to have to skimp because you didn't leave enough.

Now, turn your attention to your fabric. Carefully steam press it to remove wrinkles and fold lines. If the fabric has been long in the store, this may reveal a soiled mark along the fold, which must be washed out or dry cleaned before you proceed. In some fabrics, such as knits and permanent finish fabrics, the crease may not always be removed by pressing. For these fabrics, avoid layouts where pattern pieces are placed on the fold. If no other layouts are included in your pattern, place the pattern pieces so that the crease will not appear in a conspicuous place on your garment.

Straighten Fabric Ends

Straighten the ends of your fabric to coincide with the crosswise threads by snipping close to the selvage, pulling a crosswise thread until the fabric puckers, then cutting along that puckered line across the entire width. This is the most time-consuming method, but also the most accurate. If a crosswise thread is readily visible, you may omit pulling threads and cut directly. Tearing the fabric is the quickest means, but should be used only with extreme caution. The pulling action may throw the first several inches off grain at both fabric ends, or if the tear is not done swiftly and accurately, the cloth may suddenly split along the lengthwise grain.

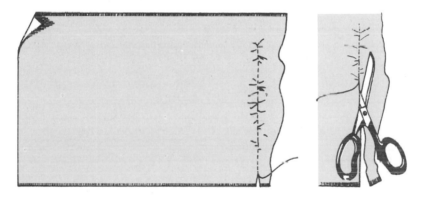

Straighten Grain

We cannot emphasize strongly enough how vital the correct grain is to the final appearance of your garment. Your fabric is on grain when crosswise and lengthwise threads are at perfect right angles to each other. Check the grain after ends have been evened by aligning a large corner of the fabric with the corner of your cutting surface. If the corners do not match, straightening the fabric is not only in order, but is an absolute must. You can choose from several methods of straightening, depending upon how much your fabric is off-grain. We discuss the methods of straightening on the following page.

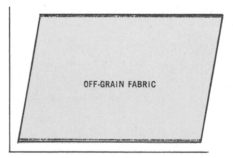

OFF-GRAIN FABRIC

A common situation is to find that the fabric is only slightly off-grain. You may not have noticed this until you've begun to fold the fabric, matching the ends and selvages according to your Cutting Guide. The solution is steam pressing the fabric to urge the threads into proper alignment before you proceed any further. Fold the cloth in half lengthwise and pin every five inches along the selvages and ends. You may need to pin your fabric to the ironing board to keep it square as you press, stroking firmly from the selvages toward the fold. (Fabric is always folded with right sides together.)

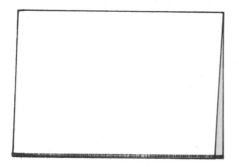 

Fabric which is very much off-grain can be straightened by pulling the fabric in the opposite direction from the way the ends slant until a perfect right angle corner is formed. If a washable fabric is badly off-grain, fold it and put it in warm water for a few minutes. Pull the fabric before it dries completely to obtain an on-grain condition. Then pin a selvage to a taut clothesline every few inches, and allow to dry. Repeat if necessary. In some cases you may have to try a combination of the above techniques for the best results. Note that permanent finish fabrics (such as some knits, some under-linings, and others you'll discover by examining the fabric and reading labels and hangtags), can never be straightened. It is perfectly all right to use them as they are, matching and pinning the selvage only, not the ends. Some printed fabrics may not be off-grain, but the print design does not coincide with the grainline. These fabrics should be avoided. If you should wish to use them, you must allow the print design to dictate the layout, not the grain.

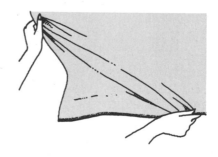

Always Pre-Shrink

Shrink your fabric before cutting if it has not been pre-shrunk by the manufacturer or if it will shrink more than one per cent, according to the label. For pre-shrinking cottons and other washables, follow the method for straightening the grain of washable fabrics, but use hot water. Leave the fabric immersed for thirty minutes to an hour.

Woolens should be shrunk by a dry cleaner if possible. To do it yourself, first straighten fabric ends, snip selvages at intervals, and fold in half lengthwise. Baste across the ends and along the selvages. Place a very damp sheet on a flat surface and lay the fabric on the sheet. Fold carefully, keeping the sheet on the outside. Leave the fabric folded overnight in a tub or basin. Unfold, smooth and stretch the fabric into shape and on grain. Let the fabric dry and press lightly with a steam iron. Then test for grain perfection as previously discussed before cutting.

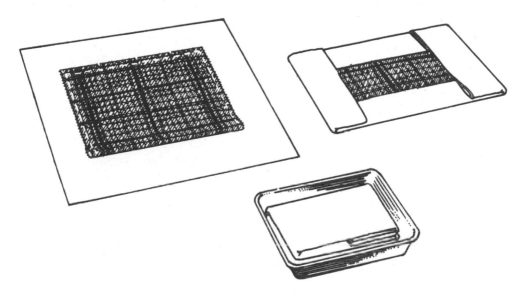

Cutting Layouts

Never treat your Cutting Guide lightly. All pattern layouts have been pre-tested by professionals, in order to provide you with a completely reliable guide for laying out your pattern swiftly and economically. You may wonder why you've been coming out with extra fabric after you've laid out your pattern according to the Cutting Guide. But don't forget that any adjustments in the width and length of your pattern, or minor variations in fabric widths, can mean several inches of difference in the amount of fabric used.

Size standards are set by the pattern industry to accommodate thousands of women, and as you become familiar with your own departures from the average body standards, you will know automatically whether to buy more or less fabric. If you think you can bend the rules by laying some pieces a little off grain to fit, *don't.* A simple maneuver like this can jeopardize all your future efforts on that garment—one side of the skirt may flare more than the other, the entire bodice section might ripple and pull, and facings cut off grain will pucker.

Assuming your pattern alterations are double-checked and your fabric is fully prepared, circle the correct layout for your version, size, and approximate fabric width. Before you begin, read the pertinent information on the general subject of cutting, and refer to any specific sections that apply.

Now you are ready to begin. When double layers are shown on the layout, fold the fabric right sides together. If a particular layout shows single **and** double thicknesses, pin the pattern on the double layer first. Then fold your fabric as shown in the layout and measure from the selvage to the fold in several places to be sure the fold is exactly on grain. Make crosswise or lengthwise folds correspond with crosswise or lengthwise grain on your fabric.

Professional Hints

Here are some ideas used by professionals—useful hints to follow as you lay out and cut your pattern. Follow these suggestions for perfect results every time:

- ☐ Pin fabric every three inches or so on indicated foldline and along all ends and selvages. The selvages may have to be clipped every few inches so that the fabric will lie flat.
- ☐ Extend a short grainline to pattern ends with pencil, and measure often to be sure that the pattern is placed on the correct grain.
- ☐ Double-check all alterations to see that seam and cutting lines are redrawn and all corresponding pieces are altered, including facings.
- ☐ Lay out all pattern pieces before you begin cutting.
- ☐ Place pattern pieces printed side up unless otherwise indicated by the Cutting Guide. Shading of the area on the layout indicates that the piece is placed printed side down.
- ☐ Pin first along lengthwise grainlines and foldlines.
- ☐ Place pins perpendicular to and ¼" inside the cutting line and diagonally at the corners of the pattern, spacing them about every three or four inches apart, or closer for sheer or slippery fabrics.
- ☐ When your layout shows a pattern piece extending beyond the fabric fold, cut the other pieces first, then unfold the fabric, and cut out the remaining pattern piece.
- ☐ To avoid distorting the fabric, cut "directionally" with the grain.
- ☐ Never cut out a pattern with pinking shears. Use them only to finish seams during construction. Use long, bent-handled shears, and cut with steady, even slashes.
- ☐ Never lift the fabric from the table. Keep one hand flat on the pattern piece while cutting.
- ☐ Use the point of the scissors to cut notches outward and groups of notches in continuous blocks for easier matching.
- ☐ Be sure to use each pattern piece the correct number of times. Such pieces as pockets, cuffs, welts, and belt carriers are likely to need more than the usual two pieces.
- ☐ Fold the cut pieces softly and lay them on a flat surface.
- ☐ Save fabric scraps left from cutting. They are often needed for such things as bound buttonholes, sleeve plackets, and other sections not cut from pattern pieces; or for testing tension, stitch length, and pressing techniques.

All About Special Fabric Layouts

If you have been avoiding fabrics that require special layouts, such as napped or pile fabrics, plaids, stripes, and border prints, let us dispel your fears by providing a reassuring supplement to your Cutting Guide. You can usually use the same methods for preparing, pinning, and cutting, but do give more than average attention to laying out your pattern pieces and basting the garment together. Then you can be sure your fabric will be as attractive on you as it was on the bolt. For fabrics with designs large enough to require matching, the single most important goal to aim for is a totally harmonious effect. No one motif should stand out from the rest of the garment, or one part of the fabric distract the eye from the overall garment design. The dominant parts of a fabric design are usually placed at the hemline or centered vertically in the front or back. Fabrics with a direction, such as napped fabrics, uneven plaids, unbalanced stripes, or one-way prints will look right only when the nap or motif runs in the same direction throughout the garment. For example, plaids or stripes with a right or left direction should follow in a regular progression around the garment. When you are matching, always take care to match seamlines, *not* cutting lines. If you haven't had any experience with the special demands of an unusual fabric, arm yourself with our suggestions, and a spirit of adventure. Choose a fairly simple design until experience bolsters your confidence, and sew ahead.

Directional Fabrics

Fabrics with nap, pile, shading, or one-way designs must be cut with all pattern pieces placed in the same direction. If your pattern suggests these fabrics, your Cutting Guide includes a "With Nap" layout. If in doubt as to the direction of your pattern piece, hold the tissue over the portion of the body where it will be worn.

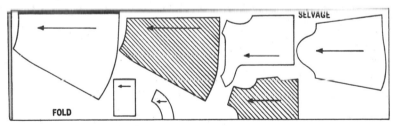

Napped fabrics are those which are brushed after weaving to produce a directional, fuzzy surface on one side (such as fleece). Pile fabrics are actually constructed so some of their component yarns rise at an angle from the woven surface of the fabric (such as velvet). Both give a different impression in color and texture according to the direction of the nap or pile. Cut with nap running down for a lighter, shinier look; with nap running up for a deeper, richer color. The fabric will feel rough when you move your hand against the direction of the nap, and smooth when with the nap. With piles and naps, pin the pattern to the wrong side of the fabric so that the pattern tissue does not shift. The woven or printed designs that appear on one-way fabrics have a definite up-or-down direction. Textured fabrics (such as satin and brocades) also have to be treated as one-way fabrics because of the way light is reflected off their surface, causing a shading effect.

Plaids

Plaids present an additional design dimension in any garment. When sewing with plaids, therefore, the idea is to avoid extremely complicated fashions and let the plaid tell the story. Also keep in mind that the size of the plaid should be in scale with both the garment and the person wearing it if it is to flatter rather than overwhelm. For the best results, plaid garments should be made only in designs recommended for plaids by your pattern catalogue or the back of the pattern envelope. If "Not Suitable for Plaids," it is because they cannot be properly matched at the seams.

There are several things to keep in mind when purchasing a plaid fabric. First, always remember to buy extra yardage for matching. The actual amount will be determined by the size of your pattern, the size of the plaid repeat, and the number of lengths of major pattern pieces required by your Cutting Guide. Secondly, never purchase your plaid from a small sample, as it seldom shows the repeat. A strong vertical or horizontal movement in the fabric, which might easily affect your choice of fabric, can only be noted from looking at a large piece of fabric. Thirdly, if you decide on a printed rather than a woven plaid, check carefully to see that the stripes of the plaid are on grain. If the plaid is printed just slightly off grain, match the plaid since it is more noticeable than the grain in this particular instance. Do not buy an extremely off-grain printed plaid, since it will not drape or mold satisfactorily when made into a garment. The same is true of bonded plaid fabrics.

For the most attractive and professional-looking results, be concerned with the placement of the lines of your plaid, especially the dominant stripe. The lines should always be continuous from front to back and from neck to hem. This also holds true for two-piece dresses and suits; the plaid lines of the jacket or top should match those of the skirt. Horizontally, avoid placing a heavy, dominant stripe at the bustline or waistline. It is generally preferable to place it at the hemline; this means, of course, that you must determine the finished length of your garment and mark it on the pattern tissue before you cut. On an A-line or other curved hem, the horizontal lines will appear to arc slightly downward toward the side seams if the center fold or seam is on the straight grain. In such a case, ignore the traditional rule and place your fabric's least dominant section along the garment's lower edge, thus drawing a minimum amount of attention to the distortion of the plaid design at the hemline. Vertically, place the dominant line of the plaid at center front if possible. Always make all your fitting adjustments on the pattern before you cut out your fabric, or you may destroy all your careful placement and matching efforts.

Since the kind of plaid you buy will determine your layout, you should understand the elements of a plaid design. A plaid is composed of stripes crossing each other at right angles, spaced evenly or unevenly, and repeated in sequence. All manufactured plaids consist of a *repeat* or a four-sided area in which the pattern and color of the design are complete. These units, arranged continuously side by side, form the fabric pattern and determine whether the plaid is even or uneven. In an *even plaid,* the stripe arrangement is the same in both the lengthwise and crosswise directions, creating a perfectly square repeat. When folded in any direction through the center of any repeat, the halves must form a mirror image. In an *uneven plaid,* the design and spacing are different in the lengthwise, crosswise, or both directions.

Plaid Test

To test the plaid, first fold the fabric diagonally through the center of any repeat. (Plaid must be perfectly on grain.) If spaces and colors match, test further by folding the plaid vertically or horizontally through the center of any repeat.

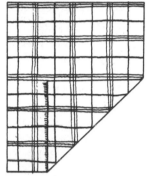 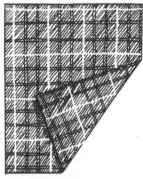 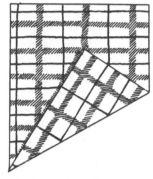

In an even plaid the spaces and colors match in both directions.

In an uneven plaid the spaces and colors do not match in both directions.

Plaids which at first appear even may, in reality, be uneven.

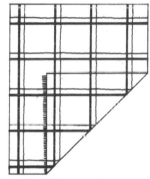 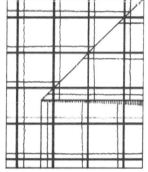

The design in this plaid does form a perfect square when folded diagonally, **but** does not make a mirror image when folded vertically or horizontally through the center of any repeat.

Slip Basting

Slip basting will help to ensure a perfectly matched plaid. To slip baste, work from the right side of the fabric. Crease and turn under the seam allowance along one edge. Lay the folded edge in position on the corresponding piece, matching the plaid at the seamline, and pin. Slip the needle through the upper fold, then through the lower layer using a single long stitch. Continue this stitch for the entire length of the seam. You can now machine stitch the seam in the normal manner from the wrong side.

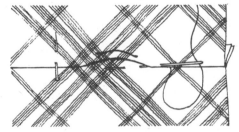

Even Plaids

Even plaids are relatively easy to match. Prepare your fabric according to the cutting layout. Since the fabric is not always folded correctly on the bolt, make sure the fold is at the center of the dominant line or the center of the plaid design. The selvages will not be even when the fabric has to be re-folded. The "Without Nap" layout can be used, but often the shading or coloring makes the "With Nap" layout most effective. The pattern pieces should be placed so the notches and the symbols along the seamline are matched at the side and center of the front and back pieces. Center seams must be placed with the seamline directly in the center of the plaid repeat for a straight seam, while a shaped seam (center or side) should start out in the center of the plaid repeat. When the seams are joined the design will chevron—the angle will depend on the shape of the seam. *Always match the seamlines, not the cutting lines.*

Start by placing the predetermined hemline along the dominant line of the plaid. Plaids should be matched at the front armhole seamline at the notch, but the curve of the sleeve cap may make the plaid impossible to match around the rest of the armhole seam. You will also have difficulty matching diagonals—darts, shoulder seams, etc. The side seams will not match above the bust dart. With two-piece garments, remember that the plaids should be continuous from the top to the bottom when worn. Always match design details such as cuffs and pockets to the plaid portions they cover on the finished garment. Lapel facings should be cut from the same part of the plaid as the bodice. For interesting fashion details, you may wish to cut pockets, yokes, cuffs, and bound buttonhole strips on the bias.

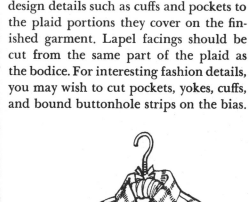

Not a cutting layout—for pattern/plaid position only.

Uneven Plaids

To be realistic, we must admit that sewing with uneven plaids is not for the novice. But it can be a rewarding experience if you remember to choose a pattern with as few construction lines as possible to reduce the number of matching points.

The matching and placement concepts are the same as even plaids with the following exceptions. Uneven plaids cannot be matched in both directions. Pick the stripes of the plaid design that you want to be emphasized, both vertically and horizontally, relative to your figure. Choose desired plaid stripe for the center front. Fold fabric, matching two desired stripes for front sections. Pin at intervals, matching plaid lines of both layers. Next, pin the front pattern pieces to fabric, placing center front on desired line. Match plaid lines for front sections, either vertically or horizontally as the fabric dictates. When front pattern pieces are placed satisfactorily, place back pieces, matching side seamlines to those of the front. You may need to re-fold your fabric. Always use a "with nap" layout. Some plaids and fabric widths necessitate planning and cutting the garment on a single thickness, using the same methods as explained above. Be sure to turn pattern pieces over (printed side down) to cut the left side of garment sections.

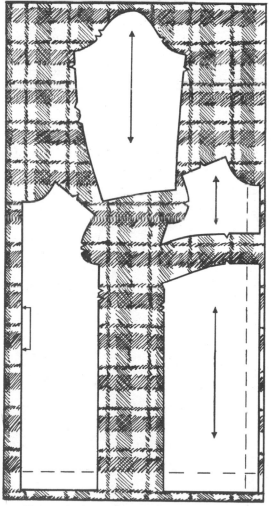

Not a cutting layout—for pattern/plaid position only.

Bias-cut Plaids

Some of the most attractive plaid effects are brought about by cutting the plaid on the bias. The final result is a chevron, which is two sets of stripes meeting at identical angles. The specific angle of the chevron will depend upon the angle of the seams in relation to the lengthwise grainline. When selecting your fabric for a bias-cut garment, choose an even plaid without a pronounced diagonal weave. (Some plaid fabrics are actually printed or woven on the bias; these are cut on the straight grain as for an even plaid and matched as for a bias-cut plaid.)

Unless your pattern is specifically recommended for bias-cut fabrics, you will need to establish a bias grainline on each of the pattern pieces by drawing a long line at a forty-five degree angle to the lengthwise grainline. Lay the pattern out on a single thickness of fabric to make sure that the plaid will chevron properly. Cut the right and left sides individually, turning the pattern pieces over (with the printed side down) for the left side. With each pattern piece, be sure that the plaid design corresponds at the symbols and the notches before cutting the fabric. This will ensure you a perfectly matching plaid once the seams are joined. To prevent the bias seams from stretching, pin strips of tissue paper to the wrong side of the layer that will remain flat while you are slip-basting. Also place the tissue paper under the fabric on the machine bed when stitching the bias seams.

Not a cutting layout—for pattern/plaid position only.

Checks

In matching checks, let the scale of the pattern be the deciding factor. Checks ½" square or larger are usually matched, following the same principles as for even plaids. Smaller checks do not require matching unless they would be visually disturbing in the finished garment if left unmatched.

Stripes

Sewing with stripes should definitely influence your pattern selection. Designs illustrated in stripes are especially suitable; if your pattern is marked "Not Suitable for Stripes," it is because they cannot be matched properly or will distract from the design lines. It would also be wise to read Your Figure Analysis, pages 21-23, to help you decide which stripe and direction—balanced or unbalanced, horizontal or vertical—will be best suited to your figure. The amount of extra fabric required for matching horizontal or unbalanced vertical stripes will depend upon the size of the stripe repeat and the number of pattern lengths in the Cutting Guide. The principles for working with stripes also apply to wide wale corduroy and other obviously wide-ribbed fabrics.

While the methods for laying out stripes are basically the same as for plaids, stripes are easier to match because the design runs in only one direction. Stripes should run in the same direction throughout the garment. Other parts of the garment—cuffs, waistbands, and pockets—must be adjusted to match the body of the garment. Stripes on a notched collar should match those on the lapel. Set-in sleeves should match at the front armhole seamline at the notch. Buttonholes should be aligned with the direction of the stripes and, if the stripes are very large, they should match the color of the stripe.

You will have to discover which stripe is dominant in order to plan your layout. Squint at the fabric to see whether the widest stripe, the stripe at the center of the design, or the stripe with the strongest color is dominant. You may even find that a particular group of stripes, acting as a part of the overall design, becomes dominant and is then treated in the layout the same way as a single dominant stripe. Distinguish between balanced and unbalanced stripes by folding the dominant stripe in half along its length. If the stripes match when a corner of the fabric is folded back, the stripe is balanced.

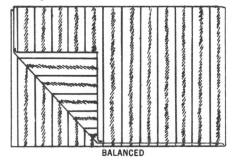
BALANCED

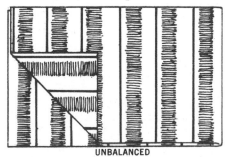
UNBALANCED

Once you've become familiar with the principles involved in stripe layouts, let the stripes suggest creative visual effects. Don't be afraid to use a bias binding, pocket, or cuff, or perhaps a horizontally striped yoke on a vertically striped dress.

Balanced Stripes

HORIZONTAL: Matching a balanced stripe horizontally is the easiest of the stripe layouts. The lengthwise grainline arrow should run perpendicular to the stripe. The general rule is to place the dominant stripe at the hem foldline, so you must predetermine the hemline before you cut. There are two exceptions, however; if you have an obviously curved hemline or if thus placing the dominant stripe will also place it at bustline or hipline, place the hemline at a less dominant location. If you do place the dominant stripe at the hemline, center a portion of it at the hemline in the center front and back of the garment to obtain the proper optical illusion. Match the stripes at center seams and at side seams below the bust dart and make sure they are continuous from neck to hem, especially with two-piece garments such as suits.

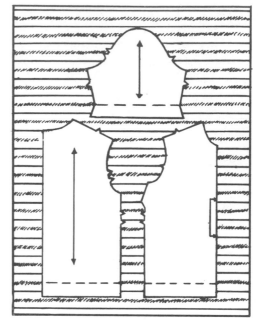

Not a cutting layout—for pattern/stripe position only.

VERTICAL: With the lengthwise grain arrow of your pattern parallel to the stripes, center the dominant stripe at center front and back for the best looking results. For a center fold, simply fold fabric through dominant stripe. If the center is on a seam or opening, pin two dominant stripes together and place center seamline (not cutting line) through the center of the dominant stripe. If the pattern has a straight center front or back seam, you will have to plan carefully to allow for the seam allowances and for matching the stripes. If you are making a two-piece garment, make sure that the dominant stripe is at the centers of both pieces and runs continuously from the top or jacket to the skirt. Place the sleeve so that it matches on the front armhole seamline at the notch.

For an A-line skirt, a chevron will form

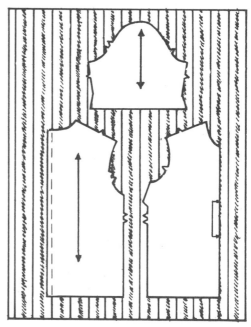

Not a cutting layout—for pattern/stripe position only.

at the side seams, the angle of which will depend on the fullness of the skirt. Note: Do not use styles for striped fabric that state specifically "not suitable for stripes," as this designation was made because you will not be able to match the stripes at the seams.

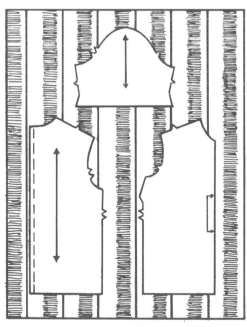

Not a cutting layout—for pattern/stripe position only.

Not a cutting layout—for pattern/stripe position only.

Unbalanced Stripes

HORIZONTAL: To plan for an unbalanced horizontal stripe, place the dominant stripe in the same manner as for a balanced stripe on the previous page. Be sure the lengthwise grainline arrow is perpendicular to the stripe. Predetermine and mark the hem lengths of all the garment sections before you cut your fabric. Then, using a "With Nap" cutting layout, lay all your garment pattern pieces in the same direction. Use the notches and symbols to adjust the layout until the side seams match and the sleeve matches the bodice at the front armhole seamline. Also take care to lay the pieces so that the stripe design will be continuous and running in the same direction from neck to hem, especially with two-piece garments such as suits. For example, the stripe on a jacket hem should be a continuation of the stripe on the skirt.

VERTICAL: To use an unbalanced stripe vertically, the lengthwise grainline arrow should correspond with the stripe. To have the stripes move in same direction around the body, use a "With Nap" layout. Choose the desired stripe for the center front. Next, fold through center of the stripe for a center front fold or pin two matching desired stripes together for a center front seam. Pin pattern to fabric, placing center front on desired stripe. Place back pieces with same stripe at center. Re-fold fabric if necessary. Depending on design repeat, you may be able to plan side seams so stripes are continuous around the garment, but shoulder seams will not match. With shaped seams, sides will not chevron nor is it likely the stripes will match. Some designs may necessitate cutting fabric in a single thickness.

To have both sides of the garment form a mirror image, the center seam must be straight and parallel to the grainline. Place left side pattern pieces in the opposite lengthwise direction as the right side pieces. (This treatment cannot be used with fabrics requiring a "With Nap" layout.)

Prints

BORDER PRINTS: Special layouts are included with patterns illustrated in border prints; for others, you will need additional yardage. For your initial attempt, choose a fabric with the border running along one lengthwise edge and place it where the hem will fall. When the pattern is laid out along the crosswise grain, the garment can only be as long as the width of the fabric unless you seam it at the waist or bodice. Place the predetermined hemline at the border and the lengthwise arrow along the crosswise grain of the fabric. The pattern hem should be perpendicular to the center front and back and as straight as possible; if the hem is not straight, follow the edge of the border to create the best optical illusion. Avoid obviously A-line patterns. Match the motif at the side seams where feasible; if fabric has a dominant motif, place it at the center front and back.

Not a cutting layout—for pattern/print position only.

LARGE-SCALE PRINTS: Carefully place the motifs of a large-scale print. Your goal should be a totally harmonious effect in the finished garment, where nothing stands out as visually disturbing. Large flowers and bold crosswise or lengthwise designs should be placed so that major body curves are avoided. For a pleasing visual balance, it is best to center large-scale designs vertically. You should definitely avoid placing large flowers or circles, etc. directly on the bust or derriere. Some large-scale prints have a definite vertical or horizontal direction, and thus fall into the category of one-way prints. If this is true of your fabric, use the "With Nap" layout, letting your own judgment guide you in deciding whether the motif is prominent enough to require matching. It would be wise to analyze critically the scale of the print in relation to the scale of your figure. Very large prints are most effectively presented in styles with few design lines or in long garments, as evening clothes or loungewear.

Marking by Method

Marking is a wonderful convenience because every notation on your fabric makes sewing that much easier. All those symbols and lines are put on the pattern piece for a reason, each having its separate purpose which ultimately helps to create the shape of your garment. Happily, you will know exactly where to stitch on a curve, where ease should be adjusted, and whether corners will match perfectly.

All markings on pattern pieces should be transferred to the wrong side of the fabric as soon as the garment sections are cut and before pattern tissues are removed. Markings include construction symbols, seamlines, foldlines, darts, center front and center back lines, grainlines, and position marks. Always transfer these markings from your pattern pieces because they serve as continuous reference points for making your garment through all stages—pinning, stitching, fitting, even sewing on buttons. After you've completed marking the wrong side of your fabric, remove your pattern tissue and transfer position marks, foldlines and any other long lines to the right side of your fabric, temporarily, with thread tracing. At this time, thread trace lengthwise and crosswise grainlines on the right side of each of your main pattern pieces, as special guidelines for fitting. If underlining is being used, you may want to mark it instead of your fashion fabric. Pin it to your fabric wrong sides together and then thread trace all necessary markings through both layers of each piece.

The tremendous variety in weights and types of fabric available means that every woman will need to use more than one method of marking. Determine the fastest, most accurate, and most appropriate way to mark your particular fabric from among the following methods.

TRACING WHEEL AND DRESSMAKER'S TRACING PAPER are used with hard-surfaced fabrics and all underlinings. First, test the color that you intend to use on a scrap of fabric. Steam press the scrap to see if the tracings disappear. You may not have realized it, but white is best for white as well as light colors; red, yellow, or blue are better for dark colors. *Never* use vividly contrasting colors unless you know that they will disappear during pressing or cleaning. If your garment is underlined, mark only the underlining, not the fabric. Insert double layers of dressmaker's tracing paper 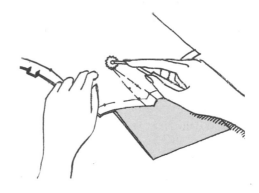 around both layers of underlining, with the carbon side next to the underlining. With the fingers of your left hand holding the layers in place, trace over all markings, using just enough pressure on the tracing wheel to make light lines. If your garment is not underlined, trace markings on the wrong side of your fabric, one piece at a time. The carbon side of the paper should be next to the wrong side of the fabric when you trace.

Use a ruler to guide tracing of straight lines. Trace through the center of any symbols. Indicate small symbols on seamlines with a short line perpendicular to the seamline. Also indicate the ends of darts, the points of slashes and other small symbols which do not cross any seamlines with short horizontal lines; mark large symbols with an X; and so on, until you have developed your own shorthand for delineating the differences between the various construction symbols. Refer to the marking equipment section page 445 if you need information on the types of tracing wheels and tracing paper to buy for your particular fabric.

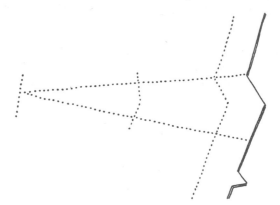

TAILOR'S TACKS are used on delicate fabrics which might be marred by other methods of marking. They are especially necessary for soft-surfaced fabrics, such as velvet or spongy tweeds with napped or nubby faces. The technique is always the same whether you mark the fabric as a single or double layer. Using a long double strand of thread *without* a knot, take a single small running stitch through the tissue and fabric at a bold symbol. Then, sew another stitch crossing over the first, pulling the thread until a large loop is formed. As you go on to the next symbol, leave a loose thread, as shown. Clip the loops and the long threads connecting each tack. Raise the pattern tissue carefully, roll the upper fabric back gently, and cut the threads between the layers, leaving tufts on either side. When you are marking a single layer at a time, the tufts will appear on the right side, the short stitches on the wrong side. Use the fabric as soon as possible or fold it carefully to prevent the clipped threads from slipping out of position.

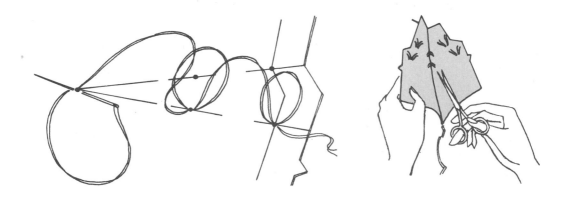

PINS AND CHALK OR CHALK PENCIL are used on soft- or hard-surfaced fabrics. Place pins through the pattern and both layers of fabric at symbols, construction markings, and corners of pattern. Turn the piece over and chalk the wrong side of the fabric at each pin. Turn the piece back to the pattern side. Starting at the edge and working toward the center, hold the pins as you remove the pattern by forcing the pinhead through the tissue, and chalk the fabric. Remove pins as you work. Run thread tracing along the chalk lines if the chalk tends to rub off.

THREAD TRACING is uneven basting for quick marking of grainlines on all garment fabrics and for transferring necessary position marks to the right side of your garment fabric. Using a single thread (do not use knots), begin by taking a small backstitch. The type of uneven basting stitch to use as you thread trace is a mattter of personal choice; it should be one that you find works best for you. With very little practice you will be able to develop a rhythm that makes this procedure a simple routine. Use silk thread on napped fabrics, piles, and light colors to avoid leaving an imprint. After all symbols and construction lines are transferred to the wrong side of your fabric or underlining by one of the previous methods, remove the pattern tissue. Pin underlining to fabric where necessary. Thread trace center front and back lines, foldlines, and grainlines on *one* section at a time.

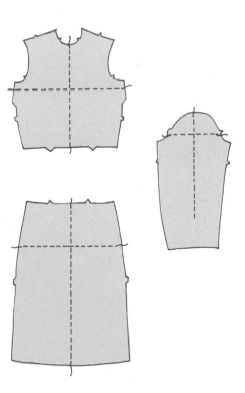

We suggest that you thread trace a lengthwise grainline on sleeves, starting at the shoulder and ending at the elbow, and a crosswise grainline at bust, hip, and sleeve cap. These lines will save you much guesswork in fittings. With one glance in the mirror many needed adjustments will become obvious, as distortions in these long thread tracing lines appear.

For fabric which is to be underlined, work on a large flat surface, and always pre-shrink **both** fabric and underlining before cutting out pattern. Center the marked underlining over the unmarked fabric, checking to be sure that the traced grainlines and center fold lines coincide with the grain of your fabric. Pin together along the traced lines and around the raw edges. Your cut edges will not always be exactly even, but that is to be expected since the two layers were cut separately.

From the underlining side, run a line of thread tracing along all markings through both layers. For all seamlines, baste next to, **not on,** the traced line so the basting threads will be easy to remove later. Take out pins.

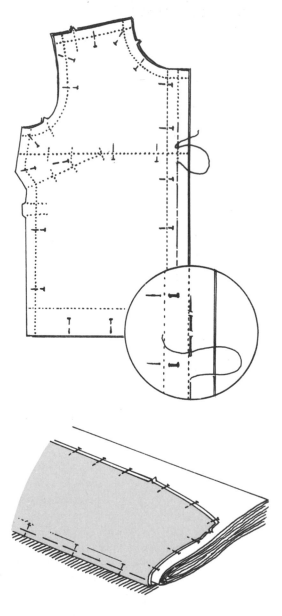

❀ Prior to completing the thread tracing, you might want to check to see if your two fabric layers are working together as desired. Try holding each pinned section over your body to see how the two layers react to its contours. If bubbles or ridges form in either the fabric or underlining, the two fabrics are not molding as one. Remove all pins except those along the center lines and, with your fashion fabric uppermost, fold both layers along this pinned center line. Insert a thick newspaper, large magazine, or cardboard between the folded fabric. Smooth the fashion fabric (with the grain straight or cross) over the underlining and pin where it lies along all raw edges and at all construction lines. Your underlining and fashion fabric are now relating to each other the way they will be when worn. Notice that the underlining extends slightly beyond the edges of the fashion fabric. (The difference between the seam allowances will increase with the thickness of your fashion fabric. If you are using a heavy fabric, try cutting your seams ¾" to compensate for it.)

For fabrics which are not underlined, the fastest way to transfer construction or grain lines is to remove the pattern tissues and thread trace along the previously marked lines. Since the buttonhole markings vary with the method and type of buttonholes you wish to make, see Buttonholes, page 307, for specific ways to mark them. See Special Handling on the following pages for marking techniques to use on fabrics such as leather and vinyl.

Special Handling

Certain fabrics themselves are unique and special in hand and/or appearance. In fashion, they can be used to make a simple design extraordinary, or an extraordinary design even more so, and they should be a vital part of your Vogue Patterns sewing repertoire. The following information will help you develop your sewing abilities and widen the scope of your wardrobe with these special fabrics.

Fabrics With Give

Just arriving on the fabric scene today are *stretch fabrics*—some woven, some knits—to use for comfortable, well-fitted swimwear, lingerie, pants, and jumpsuits. With the proper techniques, sewing with these fabrics can be easy and rewarding. *Knits* are the most versatile of the new fabrics—they make comfortable, packable, easy-care clothes. Jersey, double knit, tricot, jacquard, and rashel knits are available in every weight, texture, color, and fiber.

STRETCH FABRICS: Greater elasticity is the prime feature of stretch fabrics—their basic structure is what gives them an advantage for certain types of garments. These fabrics can be either woven or knitted, with one-way or two-way stretch, in both natural and synthetic fibers. Swimsuits, jumpsuits, and lingerie are "naturals" for stretch fabrics.

When making a garment from a stretch fabric, the best way of utilizing the built-in stretch is to cut your garment so the stretch is horizontal. Change the grainline to achieve maximum stretch as suggested for Knits page 187. Power net, used for lingerie and as a support in swimwear, functions best when its maximum stretch is vertical, so that the crosswise stretch encircles the body. In sewing stretch fabrics, apply construction tips found in Elasticized Edges on pages 188-189. Treat terry, velour, and leather-look fabrics as you would their counterparts in non-stretch fabrics.

KNIT FABRICS: In sewing knits, one of your major concerns will be the degree of stretch which determines both fashion applicability and construction techniques to be used—they differ tremendously from one another in appearance, texture, and hand.

Knits fall into three categories of stretchability: stable, moderately stretchy, and stretchable. Vogue Patterns has developed and tested a Stretch Gauge (see next page) to assist you in determining the stretchability of individual knit fabrics.

Stable knits (type A) are ones which have a limited degree of stretch and retain their original shape well. They can be handled like a woven fabric, but move with the body to a somewhat greater extent, retain their shape, and resist wrinkling.

Moderately stretchy knits (type B) are intermediate and combine some characteristics of both stable and stretchable knits. Whichever of these they most resemble determines the fashion use and construction required.

Stretchable knits (type C) have pronounced stretch and recovery characteristics. These fabrics are used in a stretched condition over body curves and are perfect for the Vogue Patterns which have been created for "stretchable unbonded knits." Be aware of super-stretchable knits—they may be used like stretchable knits for bodysuits, lingerie, and swimwear, but cannot be used with other fabrics that may distort them.

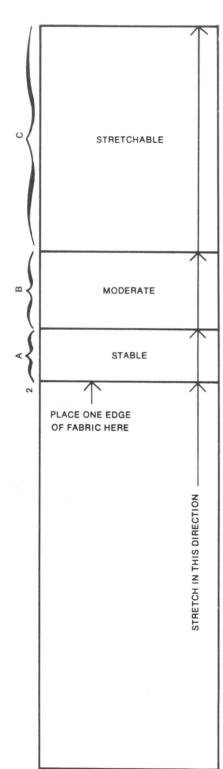

STRETCHABLE

MODERATE

STABLE

PLACE ONE EDGE
OF FABRIC HERE

STRETCH IN THIS DIRECTION

Use the Stretch Gauge to measure a fabric's stretchability. Indicate with pins or cut a 4″ square of fabric on the straight grain, and place it in a relaxed state on the stretch gauge. Align the left corner with point 1, and the right corner with point 2. Holding the left edge in place, gently stretch the fabric to the right; if the fabric design is distorted or the upper edge curls, it is stretched too much.

When the fabric is stretched, note the stretch category into which it falls. Its crosswise stretch category will determine sewing procedures, while its lengthwise stretch category will give additional information on the fabric's behavior.

Now release the fabric end in your right hand to observe its ability to recover. If it springs back immediately, you are assured of a garment whose shape will not change. If the fabric does not recover well, you will have to control the stretch during construction to avoid a misshapen garment.

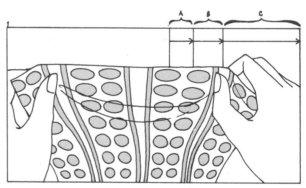

When selecting both pattern and fabric, keep in mind the stretch characteristics inherent in that particular knit. Patterns marked, "Suitable for Knits" require a stable one. Those marked "use only stretchable unbonded knits," have very little wearing ease and require this type of knit. Before combining two fabrics, be sure the knit has a good recovery and will support another fabric (i.e., stretchable knit bodice with a heavier fabric skirt). For a moderately stretchy knit, select a pattern that will look "clingy," or draped, with soft fullness. Coordinate notions, threads, linings, and under fabrics with care, weight, and stretchability of fabric for a beautiful garment.

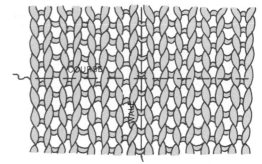

Before Construction: As with woven fabric, knits must be straightened and preshrunk. If tubular, split the fabric on one fold and press out the crease on the other. Chalk or thread-trace along the course (crosswise line of loops); also mark the wale (lengthwise line of loops) next to each long edge of the fabric. Use these indications to determine whether your fabric is on grain. If not, refer to pages 167-168 to straighten it.

To *maximize the stretch characteristics* of your knit, the direction of the greatest stretch should encircle your body horizontally. It may be necessary to change the direction of the grainline on your pattern pieces in order to accomplish this. For example, if your fabric stretches most crosswise, you should have a lengthwise grainline on your pattern pieces, and vice versa. You can draw a new grainline, if necessary, at a right angle to the existing printed grainline, unless this is on the bias. In such a case, draw a new grainline at a 45° angle to the original.

Lay out your pattern pieces on the right side of the fabric to facilitate marking—the cut edges of knits usually roll toward the right side when pulled in direction of greatest stretch. The right side also may be more decorative or textured. Slippery or bulky knits should be cut one layer at a time. Pin with ball point pins, fine sharp silk pins, or needles, and cut with very sharp shears. Allow 1″ seam allowances on vertical seams as a precaution. Support the weight of the fabric on the cutting surface to avoid grain distortion. A "With Nap" layout is recommended as many knits are directional.

Construction Pointers: In the construction of a garment from a knitted fabric, there are some special techniques to remember.

Use ball point or very sharp sewing machine needles in a size appropriate to your fabric. Dull or rough needle tips may cause snags or skipped stitches. Test the tension, stitch length, and pressure on a scrap of your fabric before actually stitching your garment; often, knits call for lighter tension and pressure. A presser foot is now available which employs rollers to gently guide your fabric under the needle. As you stitch, stretch your fabric very slightly as it passes under the presser foot. Plain seams (page 216) are appropriate, or substitute narrow zigzag stitches; an alternative is to straight stitch the seam, then zigzag stitch in the seam allowance, and trim close to the line of zigzagging; press to one side and continue construction in a regular manner.

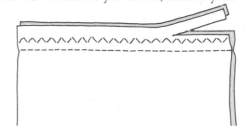

Use regular *pressing* techniques for knits, but be wary of the tendency to over-press, as this causes irreparable stretching and distortion. Always test-press your fabric; many knits are composed of fiber types which may be damaged by heat.

To fit knits, especially stretchable ones, use *stretch basting* rather than regular basting. Working toward the lower edge, baste vertical seams loosely with a double thread; the beginning of this thread must be securely fastened. Near the end of the thread, take a single backstitch and leave about 12″ of thread free. Begin and end these lines of basting as necessary until the entire seam is complete. When you try on the gar- (see next page)

ment you can see seam problems at a glance. Redistribute the fabric along these threads until all wrinkles and pulls have been eliminated and the correct amount of stretch has been incorporated in the seam. After re-basting and checking the fit, you can stitch with confidence. For further information on fitting, refer to pages 348-351.

Although stretch may be desirable in some seams, it must be controlled in others—the shoulder or waist seam—by using the taping technique on page 214. Garment areas where stretch is not desirable should be interfaced, underlined, or lined. Otherwise, linings should be made from stretchable fabrics.

Closures must be handled according to the stretchability of the knits. Zippers, buttons, buttonholes (bound, hand- or machine-worked), or loops all can be used with knits with modifications. Buttonholes can be worked in almost any knit, but should have interfacing for support. If your pattern has none, use lightweight interfacing cut into ovals and catch-stitched or fused in place. Loops are a favorite closure to use with knits as a substitute. The easiest method for bound buttonholes in knits is the Organza Patch Method. Button weight should be considered to avoid fabric distortion from heavy buttons. Remember that buttons may require reinforcement. (Refer to pages 303-314 for complete information on buttons, buttonholes, and loops.) Sturdy stable knits can take most any weight of zipper; supple and lightweight knits are best served with a regular or invisible polyester coil zipper. To apply a zipper in stretchable knits, put on the garment. Pin sides of opening to zipper tape, stretching the fabric gently to fit. The fabric may appear to wrinkle in the zipper area when the garment is not worn, the fabric's stretch is reacting to the zipper tape. Refer to pages 326-333 for standard zipper applications or the exposed zipper (page 403) which can be decorated or simply topstitched.

Elasticized edges are often used as a substitute for casings (see pages 323-325) to finish knits at sleeve, neck, waist, and leg edges for both dress and casual clothes.

To cut elastic, follow the pattern's cutting guide, or cut ½″ to ¾″ wide elastic 3″ to 4″ shorter than body circumference; cut ¼″ to ⅜″ wide elastic 2″ shorter than legs or wrists. Then join elastic in a ½″ seam, reinforcing as shown (1).

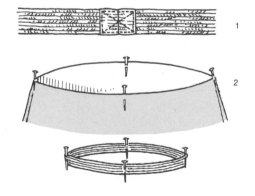

To position, place elastic so seam allowances are away from the body. Then divide both elastic and garment edge into quarters; mark. Reduce the spaces between the marks on the fabric if it is greater than 6″, dividing the elastic accordingly (2). Then pin to garment as suggested for the method on the following page.

Exposed elastic finish: Place elastic on outside of garment with one edge along the seamline; match markings; pin. Stretch elastic and fabric as you stitch inner edge of elastic; use a zigzag or straight stitch. Do not stitch over pins (1). Trim seam allowance to ¼″. Turn elastic to inside favoring garment edge, encasing raw edge of fabric. Stitch both edges of elastic to garment, stretching and removing pins as you sew (2).

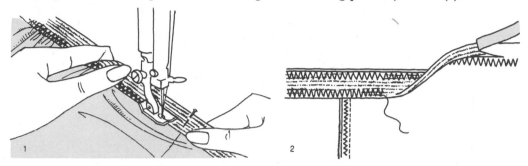

Enclosed elastic finish: Place elastic on inside of garment with one edge along seamline or foldline; match markings and pin. Stretch elastic and fabric as you stitch inner edge of elastic, using a zigzag or straight stitch. Do not stitch over pins (1). Turn garment edge to inside enclosing the elastic, favoring garment edge. Stitch raw edge in place, catching remaining elastic edge and outer garment layer in the stitches (2). Note: illustrations show a ⅝″ seam allowance and ½″ elastic, adapt edges for wider elastic.

Interior casing substitute: Will provide shape and a snug fit within garment areas. Simply place prepared elastic between placement lines; match markings and pin. Stretch both elastic and fabric as you stitch with a zigzag or straight stitch. Do not stitch over pins (3). (Add a second row of stitching for wider elastic.)

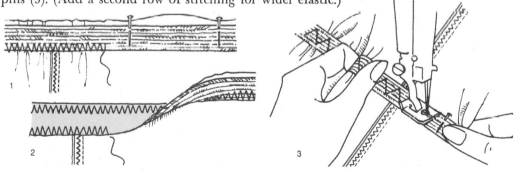

Traditional finishes on knits can be applied in a variety of ways at neck, sleeve, and opening edges or hems. Facings or bands are most often applied (see pages 249-259). Edges can also be bound in either self- or contrasting fabric for a decorative effect. Hems require no special procedures—the type of knit determines how the hem will be finished. Soft knits may look best with an interfaced hem, while more stable knits need no hem support (see pages 337-340 and 383-384). Hem edges that encompass corners can be turned up and mitered for a smooth finish. Pages 242-249 cover mitering and all types of bindings, most of which are suitable for knits. Note: Knits made from synthetic fibers are often full of static electricity even when wearing anti-static undergarments. A spray-on static remover is available—check the label to make sure it will not discolor your fabric.

Fabrics That Flow and Float

Supple, drapable fabrics that glide and glow on your body—sheers, crepe, and laces—deserve special attention. They may be cotton, wool, synthetic, even metallic; they can be firm or loosely constructed, soft or crisp, knits or wovens. Sheers can also have embroidered or flocked surface interests.

Complete your usual pattern adjustments and alterations. If your fabric is soft and fragile, test your pattern in a very soft muslin before you cut your fashion fabric. Crisper fabrics may not need a test muslin. Sheer and lace fabrics should not be fitted tightly, as the tenuous nature of the fabric may not endure stress. Follow the suggestions on pages 166-180 to straighten and pre-shrink fabric.

SHEER FABRICS: Crisp sheers—such as voile, organdy, and dimity—are quite durable and easy to manage. Softer sheers—chiffon, georgette, organza, or batiste—are airy and drapable, requiring greater care when cutting and stitching. Think sheer as you select the pattern; remember that sheers reveal all. If you're in great shape, why not show it. If you have some extra pounds choose a style that will look well with sheer sleeves and underline the rest of the garment.

Sewing sheer fabrics requires extra care. Under fabrics may be necessary for certain parts of your garment, to provide support and to shield the see-through quality. The under fabrics should match sheer in both fiber type and its care. Eliminate interfacing if possible. Self- or underlining fabric is an appropriate substitute if interfacing cannot be entirely avoided. Use a lining only if the garment is entirely underlined. An underdress, underskirt, or camisole made from lining or other suitable fabric is an apt partner to any sheer garment.

Before Construction: If your sheer has a nap, or sheen, use a "With Nap" pattern layout. Net does not have a grain and can be cut in any direction, but bind the edges, though, as it is scratchy. Delicate sheers should be pinned to your cutting board or to a sheet which is fastened to your cutting surface. Use silk or ball point pins, extra-sharp scissors, or scissors especially for lingerie fabric, to prevent the fabric from becoming caught in the blades. Mark carefully using pins, chalk, or tailor's tacks; tracing wheel and/or dressmaker's carbon may permanently damage fabric. Handle gently to prevent stretching cut edges. Underlined garments should be marked on the underlining fabric only.

Construction Pointers: The nature of the soft sheers makes seams hard to stitch. The threads tend to shift, so the crosswise fibers do not always remain perpendicular to the lengthwise fibers. To avoid mangled fabric, stitch seams with fabric between layers of tissue paper. The most appropriate seam finishes for translucent sheers are French Seam, French Whipped Seam with overcast or zigzag finish, Simulated French Seam, or Self-Bound Seam (see pages 218-219). See pages 219-220 for seam finishes for underlined sheers.

Press with care using scraps of your sheer to test the heat, pressure, and steam of the iron. Enclosed seams should be pressed over a press pad or thick towel so no lumps or ridges will come through to the right side. Use a press cloth and press lightly, smoothing the seam flat with your fingers (see pages 341-347).

To finish sheers for a translucent look, omit facings at neck, sleeve, and opening edges, and substitute self- or contrasting single or double binding following procedures on pages 244-249. If you retain facings, trim seam allowances to about ⅛" wide. This holds true of collar seams, etc., without interfacing.

For *closures,* underlined sheers will usually support buttonholes, loops, or buttons. Translucent sheers must be able to support the button weight, with only hand- or

190

machine-worked buttonholes (see pages 303-313). Zippers are usually too heavy for translucent sheers. Substitute a continuous lap (page 318) for loosely fitted sheers (1), using snaps, hooks, and thread eyes. For more fitted sheers, use dress placket (page 319).

For a zipper in a garment with an underlined bodice and an underskirt with a sheer overshirt, turn in the edges of the overskirt along seamline and narrow hem, matching finished edges to the seamline of the underskirt. Insert the zipper in the bodice section by hand or machine. Finish stitching the zipper to the underskirt only, keeping the hemmed edges of the overskirt free (2).

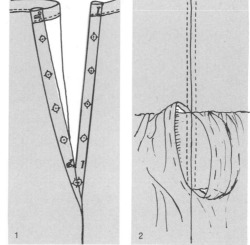

In a *layered sheer* garment, use four or more layers, of one color for a "watered" look or each a different color for a moiré look. Place the layers of fabric on your cutting surface, right sides up; pin together. With very lightweight thread and a sharp needle, "quilt" the layers together with long running stitches 6″ to 12″ apart. Proceed with cutting (1). Treat the bodice layers as one in construction; make and gather skirt layers separately, baste each skirt layer to the bodice in graduated levels. Stagger hems, making the outer layer the correct length and each following layer ¼″ to ½″ shorter (2).

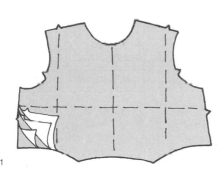

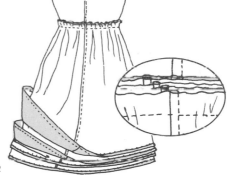

Traditional *hems* are used for underlined sheers, while a translucent sheer that stands alone is best hemmed with a hand-rolled, narrow or horsehair braid hem. See pages 337-340 and pages 383-384 for the wide choice of hems and their finishes.

For a corded hem on firm sheers, using cord with a special foot and a zigzag stitch, consult your sewing machine manual. Another machine finish that adds body but not weight is a wire hem, using thin malleable wire or cloth-covered millinery wire. Secure wire ends by overlapping and wrapping them with thread. Make your hem allowance no more than 1″ wide. Place the wire on the inside, along the hemline, encasing it in the hem allowance. Zigzag in place with very small stitches. Trim the excess hem allowance close to the zigzagging.

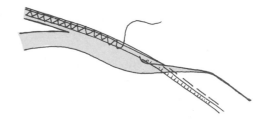

LACE FABRICS are unique because of their intricate nature. Once the product solely of hours of hand work, lace is now made mostly by special machinery. Some laces are strong enough to endure machine washing—others are treated so they can be made into swimwear. Throw away old-fashioned ideas that lace is used for formal or dress-up clothes. They are now constructed so a lace garment can be a caftan, bikini, robe, pants or jumpsuit—anything that is right for you and your life style!

Lace can be used for an entire garment or just a portion such as a bodice, sleeves, or midriff inset, and it works equally well with velvet, sheers, crepe, taffeta, or even gingham. Choose a pattern with simple design lines as there is much beauty and elegance in a lace garment—select a fabric that stands alone, minus under fabrics! A camisole and underskirt or slip of crepe, satin, or taffeta provide modesty and comfort for sheer, or openwork lace. Opaque lace needs no underlining, but can be added if you desire. Should you wish underlining, however, lightweight satin or taffeta, organdy, batiste, crepe, polished cotton, nude marquisette, tricot, or jersey are recommended. Sheer, fragile laces should virtually never be interfaced, but the more substantial opaque, underlined laces may need it. Use interfacing that will suit the weight of your lace.

Check washability when purchasing lace—most laces made from synthetic fibers can withstand even the most tortuous machine washing. Linen and silk laces, however, require either hand washing or dry cleaning.

Before Construction: Most laces are designed with a net background, so no grain straightening is necessary. The main concern is the pattern of the lace and its direction, as lace can usually be cut either crosswise or lengthwise. Look at the lines of your pattern to determine if any lace motif can be used as a decorative edge, without facing or hem. Or if you can use this as a trim. For an all-over lace design you may want to use a contrasting fabric as an accent.

To retain the beauty of sheer or open-work lace, substitute a single or double binding instead of neck facings and hems for sleeve and skirt edges or pants. Cut the bindings

from satin, taffeta, crepe, or any other suitable fabric. Binding made from scraps of a companion slip-dress would be ideal. To make successful binding, follow the directions on pages 244-249. When the facings are retained and the interfacing omitted, trim the seam allowances to about ⅛″ in width. Do the same for other enclosed seams such as collars to preserve the sheerness.

To use the lace design as a finished edge, cut out around the motif as shown to create your own decorative edge.

Use a scalloped or other decorative edge as a finish for *straight edges* such as a V-neckline, and sleeve or skirt hems (see sketch on next page). Position seamline or hemline at the outer edge of motif as shown for a completed garment edge (1).

A *curved edge* as is found on an A-line skirt or bell sleeves requires several steps to achieve a completed garment edge. For an A-line skirt, fold fabric matching the scallops. Position the pattern hemline along the outer edge of the scallop. To raise the edge to conform to the hemline curve, cut along a motif as indicated. Raise strip, overlapping

Fascinating Fabrics

Super fashions—your own originals—begin with fabric flair . . . a simple style becomes
sensational and a silhouette drapes with perfection . . . and your ideas
become a masterpiece! New vitality for the classics—a shirtdress in a stable knit . . .
a sleeky stretched cover-up . . . or a body-hugging maillot swimsuit—
for the smartest, personally-sewn wardrobe.

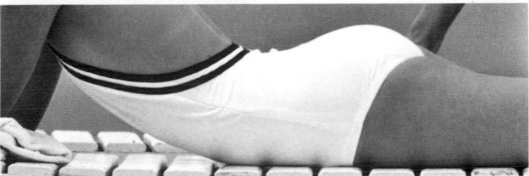

Stand-out crisps, clingy softs, fluid sheers . . . mixed, matched, or alone . . . be creative, be intuitive . . . all are crowd-pleasers.

Take your pick—sensuously ruffled voile . . . gracefully floating chiffon . . . the classic combination—lace with organza and satin . . . or satin in two colors—the secret is opulence plus elegance.

Fabric Happenings

Be adventurous, be daring . . . try your hand at something special . . .
Crimped, coiled, or looped yarns (sometimes laced with shiny metallic fibers)
. . . cut or uncut pile, on a knitted or woven base . . .
glazed or soft-napped surfaces that look like real leather or suede . . . fuzzy
surfaces that look like real fur—It's hard to tell at a quick glance
which is real and which is fake!

Be an experimenter . . . try
a fabric with surface intrigue . . .
choose a fabric you have
never sewn before—shiny ciré
to wear in the rain . . .
a terry sweatsuit for jogging . . .
challenge the unknown.

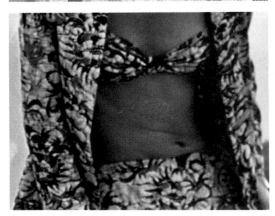

Unusual fabric can be used any
time, anywhere . . . try a washable
brocade for poolside . . . a shimmering metallic for glitter at home,
or on-the-town . . . a silky, sultry
jungle print.

edges until pattern hemline curve is accommodated, making tiny chips between motifs so strip will lie flat, if necessary. Baste strip in position and cut out skirt section. Appliqué strip to skirt by hand or machine as directed below (2). The results—a couture finish.

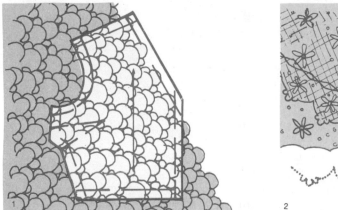

Construction Pointers: Since lace is both sheer and delicate apply the suggestions made for sheer construction and closures pages 190-191 for the translucent and underlined garments. Translucent lace seams may require a self-finish as suggested for sheers.

You may want to applique the seams and darts for an elegant finish. The edges are overlapped, matching motifs, and sewn together by hand or machine. Before *cutting* out the garment sections, match the motifs along the seamlines. Cut one edge with a ⅝″ seam allowance for the underlap (or wider for a larger design) and the other edge along the motif design for the overlapping layer. Match seamlines and design with overlap uppermost; pin, then baste keeping overlap smooth. On the outside, appliqué the motif edges to underlap with tiny whipstitches or machine zigzag stitches (1). On the inside, trim away underlap close to the stitching (2). Finish darts in same manner, determining their depth before overlapping.

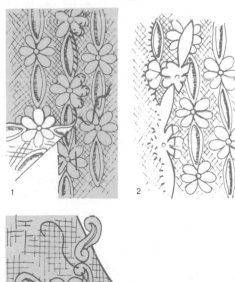

Use *self-trim* instead of a facing to accent a scooped neckline or finish a hem edge. Cut along a line of motifs to form a lace strip. Place strip over garment with one edge along seamline or hemline; baste. Appliqué inner edge to garment same as for the seam above (3). For exceptionally curved edges you may find it necessary to make small clips between the motifs so the strip will lie flat. Overlap the motif edges and sew securely.

Hems are the final touch in a lace garment. Use the same hemming techniques suggested for sheers. To face a hem in lace use a doubled net strip in place of the bias facing suggested on page 339. To retain the beauty on a scalloped edge and still underline the lace garment, attach underlining in either of two ways: Cut the under fabric with a straight edge level to the inner points of the design. Turn up the under fabric and whipstitch in place (1). Trim the under fabric to match the shape of the scallops and staystitch ⅛″ from the trimmed edge. Whipstitch shaped edge of under fabric to the lace (2).

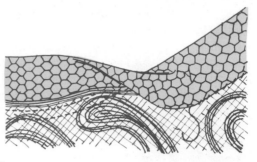

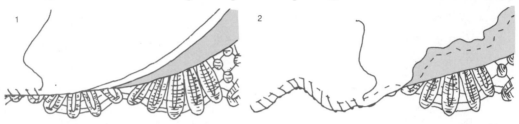

CREPE FABRICS: Choose your crepe according to the pattern style—light and medium weight for draped, flowing designs and heavier, sturdier, or bonded weaves for more tailored or fitted garments. Underlinings, if you use them, should be crepe-compatible, such as soft, uncumbersome batiste or organza. If you underline the crepe, omit interfacing, or substitute it with another layer of underlining. Do not use fusible interfacing.

Use the same cutting and marking techniques for sheers, page 190. Since crepe can stretch, use tissue paper as directed for Stretchy Seams, page 218. Very soft crepes may need the seams taped at stress points (see page 214). When *pressing,* test effect of heat and steam on fabric scraps. Use a press cloth, and press on the wrong side to avoid shine. Crepes can usually support a zipper. Buttons and buttonholes are applicable, too. See the closures section in sheers for more sewing tips (pages 190-191).

Allow your crepe garment to hang at least overnight before completing the hem. Refer to pages 337-340 and pages 383-384 for a choice of hem finishes.

Fabrics With Luster

Satin, metallic, taffeta, and brocade fabrics add dimensions of opulence to your wardrobe. Sewing these fabrics requires a knowledge of their nature rather than special techniques. So go ahead—make yourself something glamorous, from a cover-up to a theater coat, in a glittering, shiny fabric.

For some garments you may want a soft elegant look that can only be achieved with underlining. Choose a weight of organza that will support your fashion fabric as it will be used as a "hanger" for hems, facings, etc., so that no seam of other finishes will leave an impression on the outside of the garment.

Make your normal adjustments and alterations. A test muslin is important if your fabric is fragile and if fitting changes could leave permanent marks in the fabric. Follow the preliminaries before cutting, as explained on pages 164-170.

SATIN FABRICS: There was an era when satin was worn only for formal occasions—now it can go anywhere at any time of the day. Satin may be single faced or double faced, with a crepe or twill weave back that can be used in reverse. It varies from soft and drapable to firm and crisp weight that will hold sculptured design lines. Some weights do not need interfacing, but use it if you are not underlining your garment.

Before Construction: The sheen of satin comes from its weave—the lengthwise threads are caught by the crosswise threads after a longer space than usual, which creates "floats" on the right sides of the fabric. These "floats" reflect light and produce a shiny surface, which requires that satin garments be cut according to a "with nap" layout. Use silk or ball-point pins and pin within the seam allowance only, because pin holes will show on the completed garment. Use very sharp shears to avoid snags; mark with tailor's tacks and silk thread within the seam or dart allowance.

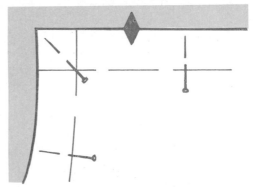

Construction Pointers: Handling the fabric is most important—use polyester or silk thread to avoid puckering. Set your machine for a medium stitch, 14-16 per inch, and hold the fabric taut during stitching to prevent sliding and bubbling. See pages 219-220 for seam finishes.

Test your satin for heat and possible discoloration from steam. *Press* lightly with a press cloth, using brown paper or a seam roll to protect the fabric. See pages 341-347 for extensive instruction on pressing satin correctly.

For *closures*, zippers are suitable for most satins with the exception of the very fragile —for better control insert by hand with a prickstitch, page 209. Any type of button and buttonhole may be used, though buttons with rough edges may mar your fabric.

The final touch is an invisible *hem* from the outside of the garment. Choose any of the standard finishes (see pages 338-340). A speciality for a soft, rolled hem is the padded hem on page 384. Don't overlook the need for a hand-rolled hem, narrow hem, or horsehair as shown on pages 383-384.

METALLIC FABRICS: Metallic fabrics are considered to be any fabric that contains some metallic threads. They range from knits to wovens, soft to crisp, shiny lamé to rich brocades. Metallic knits are everywhere—at the pool, the opera, or at home.

Underlining is optional, but may be necessary to prevent the metallic threads from breaking at the seams. Lining may be mandatory to prevent the fabric from irritating the skin—use a soft but tightly woven fabric. Interfacing is not recommended; use lining fabric in place of self-facing to protect skin.

Before Construction: Follow a "with nap" layout because the shiny threads cause a directional glow. Pin within the seam allowances and cut with old shears, since the metallic threads will dull the blades. Mark with tailor's tacks.

Construction Pointers: Use polyester thread and a fine machine needle which may have to be changed several times, lest it become too dull. If your fabric is sheer, use tissue paper when stitching seams. Test before stitching. Or, if the fabric is heavy, tape the

shoulder, neck, and armhole seams to preserve the lines (see page 214). Seam finishes may be necessary to avoid skin irritation (see pages 219-220).

Pressing requires caution since steam may tarnish and discolor metallic threads, just as an iron that is too hot may melt some synthetic metallics or make them brittle. Press lightly—too much pressure may break the metallic threads. Or, finger press seams open or edges in place, covering your finger with a thimble.

Most standard *closures* are acceptable for metallics. Make sure the threads will not break when creased if you use a zipper. Buttons and buttonholes are also appropriate, but do not make bound buttonholes on fabric that ravels.

The *hemming* methods are the same as for satin, page 195, if the fabric is non-irritating. However, if the fabric irritates, use the bias faced hem, page 329.

TAFFETA FABRICS: Crisp, fresh-looking taffeta garments are a long-time fashion choice for day, evening and lingerie wear. Taffeta is found in many weights and fibers with greater durability due to new synthetic blends. For handling, use the methods suggested for Satin, pages 194-195.

With the return to romantically feminine clothes, the fitted bodice with a full, gathered skirt is a stand-out. With soft taffeta—as well as with satin, brocade, crepe, lace and velvet —you may need a supporting ruffle to give the skirt the correct silhouette. To make, use organdy, crinoline, or other stiffening fabric, depending on the weight of your fashion fabric.

Cut a strip twice the desired width of ruffle and the same circumference as the skirt before gathering; fold in half lengthwise, turning in narrow ends ⅝". Edgestitch ends together and gather raw edges of ruffle. Pin to waist seam allowance only, placing ends so they won't interfere with zipper or other closure. Distribute gathers evenly, then stitch to seam allowance only with two rows of stitching. To make removable, gathered edge may be bound and the ruffle attached with secure hand stitches.

BROCADE FABRIC: At one time these luxurious fabrics were worn for only the most auspicious occasion, but with the advent of synthetics, beautiful vests, jackets, hostess gowns and loungewear are seen everywhere. These fabrics have a flat or raised woven-in design and are reversible; therefore, you have a choice. Use one side to make the entire garment, or make a portion of an ensemble from the reverse side—make pants and jacket from one side with a color coordinated contrasting vest from the other. Some may have metallic threads which require the same techniques as metallic fabrics pages 195-196, plus those required for the surface interest.

Brocades are handled almost identically to satin (pages 194–195) with the exception of pressing. Be sure to pad your ironing board with a towel so the design won't be flattened, and test heat endurance on scraps. Cover loose design threads with a press cloth to avoid accidentally pulling them.

Fabric Futuristically

Exciting new fabrics are available to the home sewer—leather, leather-like, felt, bonded/laminated, and double-faced fabric—present a challenge as they offer all sorts of diversified sewing projects, and are quite stimulating to work with. Many patterns are available that are "just right" for any one of these fabrics which invite you to employ your creative talents to make it a fashion success!

LEATHER AND LEATHER-LIKE FABRICS: One of the newest materials to excite the creative seamstress is leather and its imitators, vinyl and synthetic suede cloth. The vinyls are plastic, some have fused backing of woven or knitted fabric. Famous designers are presenting major portions of their line in these look-a-likes, so take your cue from them. Pick simple design lines and avoid styles that require extensive easing. Styles featuring topstitching are naturals—set-in sleeves are easily adapted by reducing the excess ease (see page 139).

Leather is not sold by the yard, but by the square foot. Think of the pattern shapes as you calculate the footage. It may be necessary to add horizontal seams suggesting a yoke or vertical seams suggesting gores or princess lines—this adds to the individuality of your project. Use this chart to convert the fabric yardage specified for your size into leather square footage. Be aware that this formula does not give measurements of quantity that are as precise as the yardage given: since there are 13 square feet in one yard of 54" fabric, you must multiply the number of yards specified for this width in your size by 13. Allow additional footage for piecing and irregularities in the leather: 0.15 for a large skin or 0.20 for a small skin.

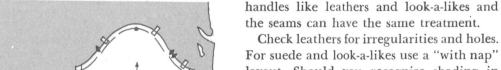

Specified yardage	4
Conversion figure	× 13
Converted yardage (square feet)	52
Piecing percentage (for large skin)	× 0.15
	260
	52
Piecing allowance (square feet)	7.80
Converted yardage (square foot)	+52
Total square feet needed	59.80

Before Construction: These materials crease easily—roll them in a tube until ready for use. Every mark you make is permanent; letting out darts or seams can be disastrous so make a test muslin for the unknown situations. Cotton felt is a perfect solution as it handles like leathers and look-a-likes and the seams can have the same treatment.

Check leathers for irregularities and holes. For suede and look-a-likes use a "with nap" layout. Should you recognize shading in others follow the same rule. Smooth leathers, heavy buckskin types, and vinyl have no nap or bias to consider so a "without nap" layout can be used. Cut a single layer at a time, holding pattern pieces in place with tape or weights. Use very sharp fabric shears, single-edge razor blade or other suitable cutting tool. Mark the wrong side with chalk or a smooth-edged tracing wheel and dressmaker's carbon paper.

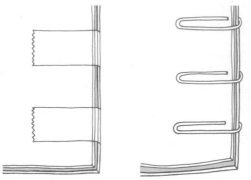

Construction Pointers: Since seams are a focal point, especially on leather, your sewing machine must be clean and set up correctly. For best results, use a leather machine needle in the size appropriate for the weight of the skin or vinyl—a regular needle will work on some. Use 8-10 stitches per inch and test the pressure on the presser foot, protecting the material with tissue paper between the feed-dog and the fabric.

Hold regular seams together with paper clips or tape and stay seams with tape to prevent stretching (see page 214).

Press seams or flatten edges using warm dry iron, with a brown paper serving as a press cloth. Or, use a mallet or a hammer padded with cloth for pressing. Topstitch seams (page 220) or apply rubber cement under each seam allowance to flatten (1). Pound cemented edges in place; when dry, lift seam allowances and peel away the rubber cement (2). Seams will stay open and flat, without leaving an impression on the outside of the garment. Darts are slashed open and flattened the same way as seams.

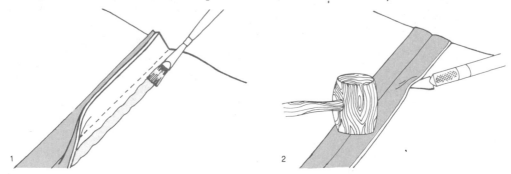

Seam finishes can be modified for leathers, vinyls with backing that does not fray, and synthetic suede (standard seams and hand stitches are explained on pages 207-221). For a flat-felled seam, trim away one seam allowance; lap sections, matching seamlines. Hold in place with a thin line of rubber cement. Topstitch 1/8″ from trimmed edge and again 1/4″ away (1). For a lapped seam, topstitch 1/8″ from trimmed edge (2). For a slot seam, eliminate both seam allowances of sections to be joined, cut strips the length of the seam and twice the desired stitching width from the seam, plus 1/2″. Center trimmed edges over the strip, glue in place. Topstitch each side of the trimmed edges, catching strip in stitching (3). Note: Glue may be hard to remove, do not glue beyond the seamline.

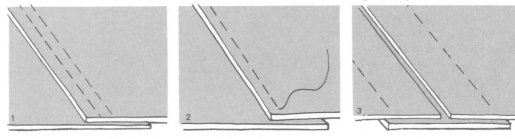

You can be creative too with seams on leather and durable vinyls. These same edges can be held in place with cross stitches (1), overcast stitches (2), zigzag machine stitches (3), using a ¼″ underlap. Laces made of leather strips, heavy cord, etc., will hold edges together. Punch holes and lace as indicated (4), (5), and (6).

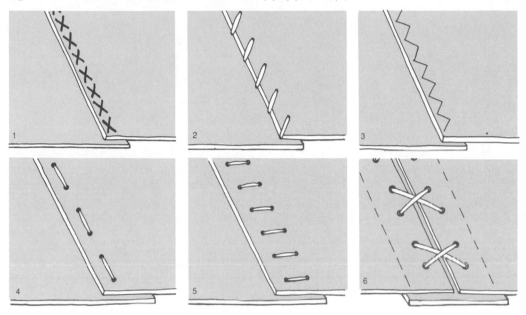

For details like collar, pocket, and facings, eliminate seam allowances from both layers. With wrong sides together, match cut edges; glue. Topstitch ⅛″ from edge to match lapped seams (1) and again ¼″ away to match flat-felled seams (2).

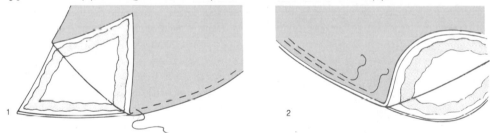

The **buttonhole** method shown here works best on leather and other materials that do not fray, although regular bound buttonholes can be made in some vinyls.

Cut a rectangular opening the length of the buttonhole marking and ⅜″ in width. For each buttonhole cut two strips ½″ longer than rectangle and 1½″ wide. Fold strip lengthwise, grading edges and flatten. Center strips over buttonhole opening, with folded edges meeting. Hold in place with a thin line of rubber cement. Then glue the facing in place smoothly over the buttonhole. On the outside (see sketch on next page), edgestitch

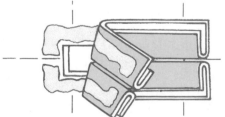

the rectangle through all thicknesses to anchor the buttonhole lips and hold all layers in place (1). To complete the buttonhole trim away facing just inside the stitching (2).

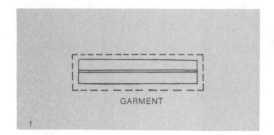

GARMENT

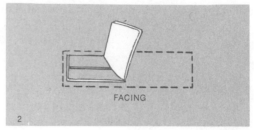

FACING

Zippers are inserted in the supple materials in the same manner as for fabric. Heavier leathers can use another approach when a flat-felled seam is used. Before stitching seam, make a ½″ clip through zipper symbol on the underlapping layer and trim away ½″ to upper edge. Tape zipper in place; edgestitch in place across the clip and along the trimmed edge (1). Lap remaining layer over zipper, matching seamlines; tape. Stitch ¼″ to ½″ from edge; start at top of zipper and stitch to end of seam through all thicknesses.

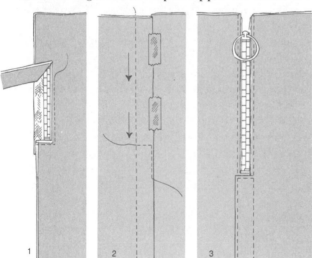

Then stitch across end of zipper and along trimmed edge completing flat-felled seam (2).

For an exposed zipper, trim away just enough of both layers of the leather so the zipper teeth are exposed and the pull tab works easily. Center zipper under trimmed edges; tape. Using a zipper foot edgestitch zipper to garment (3).

Don't overlook toggles, clasps, etc., that work well with leather. Remember too, that grommets and rawhide laces go with the rugged look of leather.

Hems are simple for leathers and vinyls—a 1″ to 2″ deep hem is adequate for most. Apply rubber cement, fold up hem allowance, and flatten as required for the seams. Notch curved hems so they will lie flat. A topstitched hem is also a good finish for leather.

The final touch . . . Some leathers and suedes spot easily so avoid getting them wet. When dirty, send to a professional dry cleaner. Vinyls can be dry cleaned, so sponge with a damp soapy sponge to clean. Use drip-dry linings to avoid water spotting. If you find your garment very warm, insert metal eyelets in underarm area for greater comfort.

FELT FABRICS: The many weights and vibrant colors that are available in this non-woven fabric should inspire you to try a felt garment—or at least use it for appliqué work. Its edges do not ravel and is without grain, allowing you to place the pattern pieces in any direction, resulting in more economical layouts. Further the life of a felt garment with underlining as it is not too durable under the stress of wear. The seam finishes, facings, and collar edges, as suggested for leather pages 198–199, work equally well for felt. Omit the glue as you can pin, and press felt like any other fabric. Machine buttonholes work best, but don't hesitate to make a slit the length required, then stitch a rectangle around it for reinforcement. For a waistband, use a strip of grosgrain ribbon as suggested on page 335 step 2. Hems may be omitted, or stitched in place using a decorative machine stitch or a straight one. For curved hems, cut out wedges to eliminate bulk as suggested on page 384.

BONDED/LAMINATED FABRICS: The outer surfaces or face of these fabrics can be almost anything—lace, jersey, knit, crepe, or tweed—and nearly every day new ones are appearing on the horizon. The technology of fusing two or more layers together force the layers to act as one when handled. The backing is usually tricot or loosely-woven cotton. Bonding can change the hand of the face fabric, stabilize an open weave, reinforce a stretchy or pliable surface, or pre-underline a garment. When purchasing this type of fabric, look for even bonding throughout the length with firmly bonded edges. The face and backing fabrics should be on-grain.

These fabrics make up best in a pattern with simple styling—avoid soft draping or gathers. Do not attempt to straighten the ends and put the face fabric on-grain as this is impossible—simply cut it as is, using the grain on the face fabric. Seams may not need finishing as the bonding will prevent raveling.

Laminated fabrics where the foam is not covered with a fabric layer require special treatment. Adjust the pattern seam allowances before cutting to allow additional ease for foam backing; do not overfit, as foam weakens under strain. Mark with tailor tacks as tracing wheel marks may disappear. Stitch with a fine needle and use tissue paper on both sides of the foam so the fabric will feed through the machine. Welt, flat-fell, and topstitch seams are recommended for flatter seams. Slash dart and press open to eliminate bulk. Interfacing is rarely needed, but you may want to stabilize buttonholes with strips of underlining fabric. Press laminated fabrics from the right side with a steam iron, being careful **never to touch an iron to the foam side**. Hem through the entire fabric as the foam alone will not hold the stitches and line garments to protect foam from wear.

DOUBLE FACED FABRICS: These fabrics combine two fabric layers which are held together with fine threads or bonding—and there is no wrong side—so with the proper finishes the garment can be reversible.

Choose a pattern with simple lines as the seams must be clean-finished so no raw edges are exposed. This fabric is usually too bulky for gathered styles and too firm for soft ones—classic or tailored garments with few details are best.

Before Construction: Allow wider seam allowances for flat-felled seams and only 1" hems for sleeves and lower edges. Omit facing—interfacings are not used either. All markings must be made with tailor tacks and thread tracings.

Construction Pointers: Separate the layers by clipping the threads or pulling them apart. There are three ways to finish the seams: For a flat, plain finish, separate layers to a depth of 1½". Stitch the one layer in the usual ⅝" seam; press open. Trim remaining layer ¼", then turn in edges over the first seam, slipstitching folded edges together.

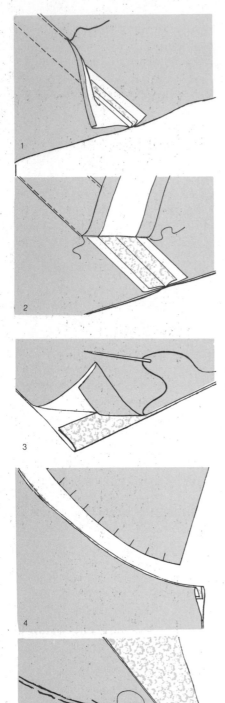

For a flat-felled seam, stitch the sections together along seamline. Separate the seam allowance layers, then trim and grade all but the uppermost layer. Turn in the edge and edge stitch in place (1).

For a strap seam, stitch the sections together along the seamline; press open. Separate the layers, then trim and grade. Cover the entire seam with a trim or a bias strip of the fabric. Separate the two layers so you have a single thickness. Make a bias strip as long as the seam and about 1⅞" wide. Turn in the edges ¼"; press. Position over the seam and edge stitch through all layers (2).

Edges for the hem, neck, and collar edges can be bound or the layers can be turned in and slipstitched together. Separate layers to a depth of 1½", turn in along seamline or hemline, and press lightly. Trim one edge ¼" and slipstitch or edgestitch together (3).

A *curved seam* is accomplished quite easily if all seam allowances fall in the same direction—the collar joining the garment is the most common example. Separate the inner curved edge to a depth of 1½"; staystitch each layer. Clip curves to staystitching as you turn in these edges; baste. Press carefully keeping the curve smooth. On the outer curve section, make clips about ¼" deep (4). Place the outer curved section between the turned in seam allowance of the other section; match seamlines and symbol as you pin and baste. Slipstitch each side separately, or edgestitch close to fold through all layers (5).

Closures do not present a problem—use machine buttonhole and buttons or any decorative closure. Make one set of buttonholes, but sew on two sets of buttons for reversible garments—one in the normal position and the second set on the reverse side of the first. When the garment is reversed the closure will be in the opposite direction.

Zippers can be inserted quite effectively. Separate the layers to a depth of 1½". For a slot zipper in a skirt, turn in the edges of each layer along the seamline; press lightly. Sandwich zipper between folded edges and stitch as usual. For an exposed separating zipper, turn in the edges beyond the seamline enough to clear the zipper teeth and allow the pull tab to move freely. Sandwich zipper tape between folded edges and edgestitch through all layers, catching the zipper tape in the stitching.

Fabrics With Surface Style

Intriguing surface interests make fabric selection even more diversified—favorite pile fabrics are velvet, corduroy, and terry cloth as well as melton and fleece. Fast approaching in the "must-have" category are beaded and sequined fabrics for a glimmering, day-time blouse or shrink-top. Creative seamstresses may prefer woven or knitted rib fabrics and luxury fabrics such as camel's hair to cashmere.

The most important feature to consider when using these fabrics is how they will look on you—will they compliment your figure? The surface depth, the design (crosswise, lengthwise, floral, or geometric), and its brightness may work against you—creating an optical illusion making you appear shorter or taller or thinner or heavier. Be realistic, select the fabric and the pattern that is just right for you. Your sewing project will return double-fold—a figure-flattering fashion with pizzazz.

PILE FABRICS: Plushy, luxurious feeling pile fabrics come with many different faces —velvet, velveteen, corduroy (ribbed or uncut), plush, velour, terry cloth, bouclé, melton, and fleece—all have many common characteristics. The most important is nap—

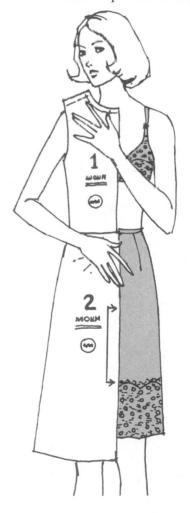

stroke the surface with your hand—the smoother feel is the "run" or the direction of the pile or nap; the rough feel is caused when you brush the pile or nap in the opposite direction. This affects the color and texture of your garment; when the nap or pile runs up, the color is deeper, richer, and the textured surface is more visible. Let the fabric weight determine what pattern is best—knits may need specific techniques (see pages 185-189).

Before Construction: Decide which direction you want to place the nap or pile; use a "with nap" layout (see page 171), placing pattern pieces as they will be worn. Depending on the fabric weight and the pile depth, cut the pattern from either a single or double thickness of fabric.

Mark with tailor tacks and baste denser pile such as velvet with silk thread to prevent slippage. To reduce bulk make facings from lining or other lightweight fabrics. For knitted pile fabrics, apply appropriate cutting and marking methods.

Construction Pointers: Make a test seam to check sewing machine. Use 10-12 stitches per inch, matching needle size and thread to fabric weight; decrease pressure on presser foot as needed; stitch in direction of nap; hold fabric taut while stitching.

Choose the appropriate stitches, seams, and finishes from those listed on pages 206-223. Slash darts and press them open to reduce bulk.

Along with the pressing techniques suggested on pages 341-347, you need a needle board—a wise investment for a professional look. If the pile is crushed it can never be restored. Test-press a fabric scrap before you start. Place fabric, pile down on the needle board; press. When pile is exposed on both sides, use a self-fabric press cloth on the inside of the garment (1). Substitute a self-fabric scrap or a fluffy towel for a needle board. Or, cover your iron with a damp cloth, then hold fabric lightly. Run the inside of the garment across covered iron to press seams open and steam out wrinkles (2).

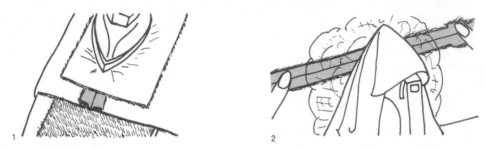

Closures should not present a problem (see pages 303-317 and 326-333). Use a button, zipper, or other closure of the correct weight for your fabric. Choose appropriate button-hole or loop method, or zipper application (invisible or regular).

Hems should be finished according to the weight and depth of the pile. Hemming procedures are found on pages 337-340 and 383-384.

FAKE FUR FABRICS: The long-haired fake furs add a dimension not found in the usual pile fabrics, although there are many fur-like fabrics that can be handled exactly like velvet. Follow the techniques suggested for pile fabrics, plus these additional tips: For long hairs, cut one layer at a time, using a razor blade as suggested for real fur page 375. Baste seams firmly, pushing hairs back as you work. Use a needle to work out hairs caught in the seam (1). Slash darts; press open. Shear hairs from seam allowance and exposed dart edges to reduce bulk (2).

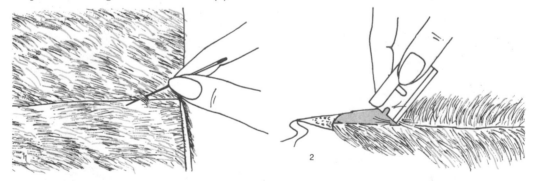

Never press the face of a fur—some are easily melted or the hairs may mat from the steam. Use a dry iron on the inside of the garment. Substitute snaps, hooks, and decorative closures for buttons and buttonholes. If unavoidable, some fabrics adapt to machine or bound buttonholes (substitute leather or other fabrics for the lips). If you want to construct your fake-fur garment like a real fur, turn to pages 375-378.

BEADED AND SEQUINED FABRICS: Found in many forms, beaded and sequined fabrics may have some hidden characteristics—they can be attached with a continuous thread, secured with prongs, or sewn individually to a base of knitted or woven fabric. Beads or sequins may form an all-over design, may be sprinkled in random motifs, or used individually adding glitter to brocades, lace, and other special fabrics.

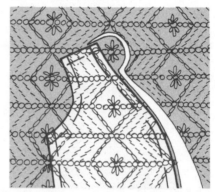

Choose a pattern that will complement your fabric—simple lines without gathers, pleats, or buttonholes, and avoid set-in sleeves if possible. Consider a bodice, sleeves, midriff section, or possible collar and cuffs to add sparkle to another fabric.

Before Construction: Make your usual adjustments and alterations and do make a test muslin if expenditure is great and the silhouette unknown to you. Use an expendable pair of shears for cutting—beads are unavoidable and can easily dull the blades. Cut around beads where it is impossible to cut through, cutting one layer at a time. Cut all facings from lining and be sure to line the garment to protect your skin from the roughness of the fabric. Staystitch seam allowance edges immediately after cutting to prevent losing beads when attached continuously. Tailor tacks usually work best for marking.

Construction Pointers: Use stitch length, tension, and needle size required by the base fabric. Remove beads from seam allowances and dart area, then sew with a zipper foot. Rest foot in seam allowance only, since beads would break under pressure. For beads or sequins attached by a continuous thread fasten by hand or catch them in the seam.

Never use steam for pressing—it may cause the backing to curl and erase the sheen from the beads and sequins. Use a low heat setting as they could melt, then press along the seam or edges with the tip of the iron. When garment is nearly finished, go over it and replace any missing or broken beads near seams or edges. Remove beads from hem allowance to prevent snagged hosiery or use a faced hem, page 339. Some garments may need an interfaced hem page 340, a soft hem page 384, or a double-stitched hem page 340.

RIBBED FABRICS: The most significant features of the ribbed fabrics are their weight and the direction of the rib. Lightweight faille will not create a problem, but a heavy ottoman with crosswise ribs may add girth to both the design and your figure. The fiber content and construction will determine the extent of special handling needed. They can be knitted or woven, soft or crisp, and the ribs can be lengthwise as in corduroys, pique, and bedford cloth or crosswise as in bengaline, broadcloth, ottoman, and faille. Knits now produce body clinging ribbed fabrics in crosswise velours or lengthwise sweater ribs. So like any pronounced striped fabric they require care when selecting them.

Treat your ribbed fabric according to its weight, stretchiness, drapability, and surface depth, choosing the special handling techniques from any of the preceding pages. For a couture touch, do match the ribs if they are 1/4" wide or wider.

LUXURY FABRICS: The ultimate in sewing is to make a luxurious garment that your budget would otherwise prohibit. A camel hair coat, cashmere shirtdress, beaded or brocade silkdress, or a vicuña blazer are all within your reach—choose a Vogue Pattern, a luxury fabric, and sew yourself a treat. Don't skimp on the inner fabrics: interfacings, underlinings, and lining fabrics should match your fashion fabric's quality.

And please, make a test muslin—the time spent is well worth the effort—a personally fitted haute couture garment, without a flaw, can be yours!

Basting

Basting is a ***temporary*** stitch used in the preparatory phase of your sewing. Whether matching plaids, indicating markings, attaching interfacing, or holding fabric pieces together for stitching, the trick is to use the right stitch in the right place and to follow these common-sense principles. Always work on a flat, smooth surface. Pin your garment pieces together before basting, and use contrasting colored thread. Begin with a knot or a backstitch, and always remove basting ***before*** pressing permanent stitching. Silk thread is recommended for fine fabrics or when basting stitches are not to be removed before pressing, as in the case of pleats or hems. Always baste alongside the seamline in the seam allowance for easy removal of your basting threads.

EVEN BASTING is used for basting seams subjected to strain. It is generally used for long seams on any fabric and for areas that demand close control, such as set-in sleeves. Usually done flat on a table, or when one layer of fabric is to be eased to the other, it

is done in the hand, with the eased layer on top. Space stitches evenly, ¼″ long and ¼″ apart, beginning and ending with backstitches rather than a knot. For firm basting, take a backstitch every few inches. Gear length of stitching and type of needle to suit fabric and probable strain.

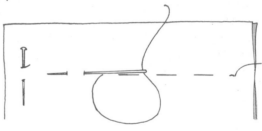

UNEVEN BASTING is used for marking, for attaching underlining and interfacing to fabric at edges, and for holding fabric together only at seams and edges which are not subjected to strain, as in a hem. Take a long stitch on top and a short stitch through the fabric.

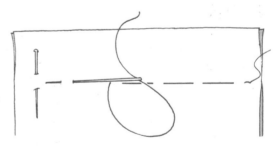

DIAGONAL BASTING or **TAILOR BASTING** is used for holding facings, interfacings, and linings in place during fitting. Take short stitches through the fabric at a right angle to the edge, spacing them evenly. This results in diagonal stitches on the upper side and short horizontal stitches on the underside.

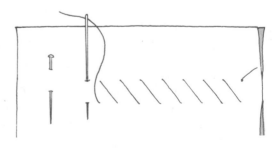

SLIP BASTING is used for matching strips, plaids, and prints; intricate curved sections; and for fitting adjustments made from the right side. Crease and turn under the seam allowance on the edge. Right sides up, lay the folded edge in position on the corresponding piece, matching the fabric design at the seamline; pin. Slip the needle through the upper fold, then through the lower garment section, using a stitch ¼″ in length. The result is a plain seam with basting on the wrong side.

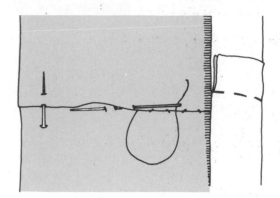

MACHINE BASTING is used for firm fabrics that won't slip or show needle marks. Set your machine for the longest stitch and loosen the upper tension slightly so thread is easily removable. To remove, clip the top thread at intervals and pull out the bottom thread.

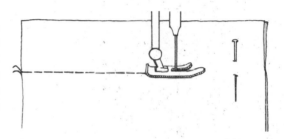

Hand Stitches

With the advent of the sewing machine, the drudgery of making clothes was eliminated and fine hand sewing was elevated to the position it so rightly deserves. Hand sewing plays such an important part in the construction of clothes that no properly made dress can be completed without it. It is the attention paid to the hand sewn details which determines the quality of your finished garment. As hand sewing becomes less of a necessity, it becomes an increasingly desirable luxury. Whether you love hand sewing or regard it as a necessary evil, there are ways you can do it quickly yet precisely enough to pass the closest scrutiny.

Hand sewing means to stitch *permanently* in place by hand. Choose a needle size in accordance with your fabric and thread, consulting the thread and needle chart on pages 92-93. Use a single 18″ to 24″ length of thread, coated with beeswax for added strength and slipperiness. It may seem elementary, but learn to wear a thimble on the second finger of your sewing hand. You'll be able to sew hard-surfaced fabrics quicker and easier and with greater assurance. Keep stitches fairly loose to avoid a puckered, strained look. Work from right to left unless otherwise stated, reversing direction if you are left-handed. To secure the thread in the fabric, start with a few small backstitches or make a knot at the end and conceal it in the wrong side of your fabric. For the latter technique, always knot the same end you put through the eye, as explained on the next page.

Cut thread at an angle, never break, bite, or tear the end; pass cut end through the needle eye, then knot the same end you put through the eye like this: using the left hand, hold the thread between the thumb and first finger. With your right hand, bring the thread over and around the fingertip, crossing it over the thread end, as shown. With your thumb over the crossed threads, and the longer thread taut, gently push the thumb toward the fingertip, causing the thread end to roll around the loop. Slide the loop off the fingertip and, lightly pitching the rolled end between the thumb and second finger, pull the longer thread in the right hand taut to set the knot.

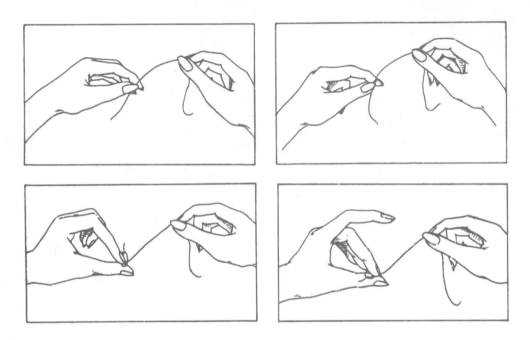

To end your hand stitching, you have the same choices — several backstitches or a knot. Begin the knot by taking a tiny stitch on the wrong side of your fabric, directly over your last stitch. Pull the thread until a small loop remains. Run your needle through the loop, pulling the thread a second time, until another small loop is formed. It is through this second loop that you insert your needle for the last time. Pull the thread taut, forming an inconspicuous knot at the base of your stitches.

RUNNING STITCH is the most basic of stitches. It has many uses—easing, gathering, tucking, mending, and sewing seams that are not subjected to much strain. Take sev-

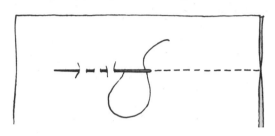

eral small forward stitches, evenly weaving the needle in and out of the fabric before pulling the thread through; pick up as many stitches as your fabric and needle will allow. For permanent seams, use stitches ⅟₁₆″ to ⅛″ long; for easing and gathering, ⅟₁₆″ to ¼″ long.

BACKSTITCHING is one of the strongest hand stitches. It is especially useful for repairing hard to reach seams that have ripped. It has the appearance of a machine stitch on the right side, but the stitches overlap on the wrong side. With right sides together,

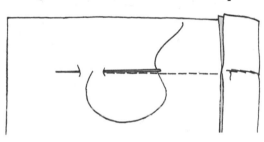

following the seamline, bring the needle through the fabric to the upper side. Take a stitch back about ⅟₁₆″ to ⅛″, bringing the needle out again ⅟₁₆″ to ⅛″ forward on the seamline. Keep inserting the needle in the end of the last stitch and bringing it out one stitch ahead. The stitches on the underside will be twice as long as those on the upper side.

HALF-BACKSTITCH is suitable for any seam. It is also used to understitch finished facings to prevent the edge from rolling toward the outside of the garment. Follow the same method as the backstitch but carry the needle back only half the length of the last stitch while continuing to bring it out one stitch ahead.

PRICKSTITCH, a variation of the backstitch, is often used for inserting zippers. The needle is carried back only one or two threads, forming a tiny surface stitch with a reinforced understitch.

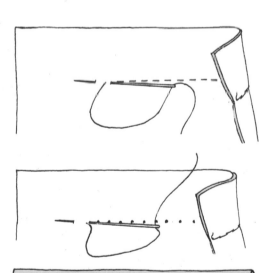

HAND PICKSTITCH is used as a decorative finish and has the same appearance as the prickstitch. The only difference is that the bottom layer of fabric is not caught when backstitching. The thread should not be taut, and should lie bead-like on the fabric surface.

SLIPSTITCH is used to hem, attach linings, hold pockets and trims in place, and provides an almost invisible finish. Slide the needle through the folded edge and at the same point pick up a thread of the under fabric. Continue in this manner, taking stitches ⅛″ to ¼″ apart; space the stitches evenly.

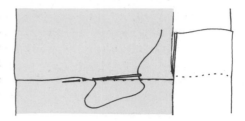

HEMMING STITCH, used for all types of hemming, is most often used for hems finished with seam binding, especially when the garment is not underlined. Take a tiny inconspicuous stitch in the garment, then bring the needle diagonally up through the edge of the seam binding or hem edge. Continue in this manner, spacing stitches about ¼″ apart.

BLINDSTITCH, used for hemming and holding facings in place, is inconspicuous on both sides of the garment. First, finish the raw edge of the hem or facing. Roll this edge back on the garment about ¼″; take a small horizontal stitch through one thread of the garment or underlining fabric, then pick up a thread of the hem or facing diagonally above. Do not pull the stitches tight.

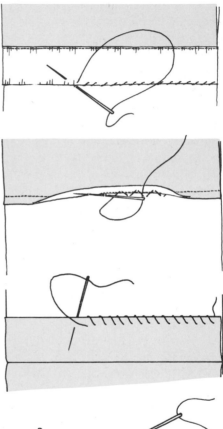

OVERCAST STITCH is the classic stitch used to finish raw edges to prevent them from raveling. Working from either direction, take diagonal stitches over the edge, spacing them evenly apart at a uniform depth.

OVERHAND STITCH holds two finished edges together with tiny, straight, even stitches. It is primarily used to join lace edging or to attach ribbon to a garment. Insert the needle at a diagonal angle from the back edge through to the front edge, picking up only one or two threads each time.

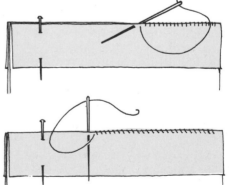

WHIPSTITCH is a variation of the overhand stitch. It may serve the same purpose, differing in that the needle is inserted at a right angle to the edge, resulting in slanted stitches.

CATCHSTITCH is used for holding two layers of fabric together in place while still maintaining a degree of flexibility. Its most common uses include attaching raw edges of facings and interfacings to the wrong side of garment sections, sewing pleats or tucks in linings, and securing hems in stretchy fabrics such as knits. Working from **left** to **right,**

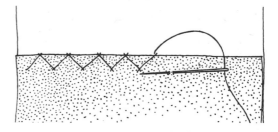

make a small horizontal stitch in the upper layer of fabric a short distance from the edge. Then, barely outside the edge of the upper layer, make another stitch in the lower layer of fabric diagonally across from the first stitch. Alternate stitching along the edge in a zigzag fashion, keeping threads loose.

BLANKET STITCH is used for a wide variety of hand-finished details. Always work from **left** to **right** with the edge of the fabric toward you. Anchor your first stitch at the edge. For the next stitch and each succeeding one, point the needle toward you and insert

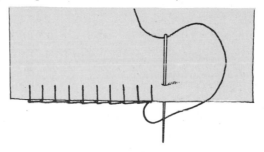

it through the right side of your fabric, approximately ¼″ above the edge and ¼″ over from the preceding stitch. Keep the thread below your work and under the needle, as shown. A variation of the blanket stitch is generally used to form inconspicuous thread eyes, loops, belt carriers, and French and bar tacks. See Loops and Fastenings for instructions.

BUTTONHOLE STITCH—Highly specialized for making buttonholes; find this stitch on page 311.

CHAIN STITCH—A substitute for the blanket stitch; best exemplified in Loops and Fastenings, page 316.

PAD STITCH—An essential stitch in tailoring, where precise shaping and control are necessary; see page 358.

Seams and Seam Finishes

Be it plain or fancy, the mark of professional sewing is a perfect seam—a seam that is never puckered, never stretched, never wobbling, and is finished without a tangle of ravelings or crooked edges. A smooth, sleek appearance is the result of careful seam handling. If you are not satisfied with the way your seam looks, it is easy to remedy. Simply rip the seam out by using a pin, a seam ripper, or small scissors—but never a dangerous razor blade. Correct any unhappy results at an early stage, and you will be rewarded by a professionally finished garment.

You should start now to develop these good habits for every garment you sew. To stitch a perfect seam, always adjust machine tension, pressure, and stitch regulator to suit the fabric texture and weight. See pages 185–205 for additional hints on handling of special fabrics or thread and needle sizes before you begin. The usual seam allowance set by the pattern industry is ⅝″ unless otherwise specified. If your machine doesn't have a seam guide attachment or stitching lines marked on the stitching plate, place a small piece of colored tape ⅝″ from the needle hole as a guide.

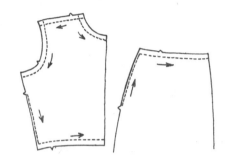

STAYSTITCHING: Prior to pinning, basting, and permanent stitching, curved areas which require extra handling should be staystitched. This will act as a guideline for clipping and joining the curved edge to the other edges, as well as prevent stretching. Staystitch in the direction of the grain ⅛″ away from the seamline in the seam allowance, using the regular machine stitch length suited to your fabric. For zipper openings, stitch ¼″ from cut edge.

DIRECTIONAL STITCHING: To prevent stretching seam areas of your garment, you should stitch seams in the right direction (with the grain) just as you do when staystitching. If it is hard to tell from the cut piece which is the direction of the grain, run your finger along the edge. The threads with the grain should lie smoothly; those against will come loose and the edge will begin to fray. Without testing, you can generally stitch from the widest part to the narrowest part of each pattern piece.

WITH GRAIN   AGAINST GRAIN

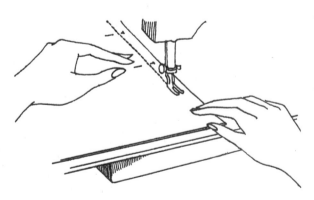

JOINING SEAMLINES: When pinning the edges of your fabric together, place the pins at right angles to the seamline with the heads toward the seam allowance. Your seams will be held in place accurately, and in this position pins can be stitched over by most sewing machines. Basting next to the seamline in the seam allowance is advisable unless you are a very good seamstress.

FINISHING THE ENDS: To finish the ends of the seam, begin to stitch ½″ from the end, backstitch to the end, and stitch forward. Stop stitching just the tiniest bit from the other end of the fabric and backstitch for ½″. The seam may also be stitched from end to end without backstitching and the ends secured by tying a knot. Although in the past a square knot has been the common solution to the problem of a knot which might come undone, there is a faster, more secure way to tie a knot. Hold thread that emerges from the fabric in your left hand. Form a loop (1). With your right hand, bring the thread ends around and through the loop from the back (2). Holding the loop in your left hand, work the intertwined thread down to the base and hold in place with your left thumb (3). With your right hand, begin pulling the thread taut until the loop disappears and forms a knot (4).

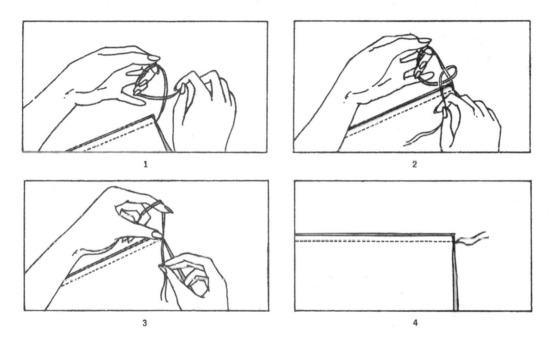

If you must end your stitching before reaching the edge, pull one of the thread ends through to the other side; then tie both thread ends together in the same manner as above. Learn to tie all your knots by these two methods and to automatically clip the threads to ½″ after you finish each knot.

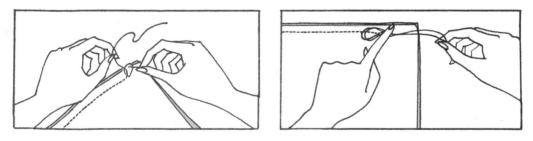

TRIMMING: Seam allowances should be trimmed only where less bulk is desired. In general, enclosed seams call for ¼″ seam allowances, but if the fabric is very light you may want to trim less. Cut diagonal corners from the ends of the seams, especially if they will later cross other seams.

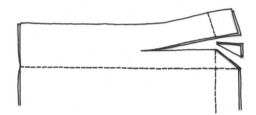

GRADING: When seam allowances are turned together in one direction, they must be graded to avoid making a ridge and to make seams lie flat without bulk. Grading is especially important when the fabric is heavy or if there are more than two layers of fabric. Each layer should be trimmed to a different width. Enclosed seams may be trimmed a little narrower than exposed seams. Generally the garment seam allowance is left widest.

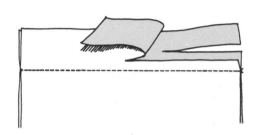

NOTCHING AND CLIPPING: Curves must be graded first and then trimmed in a special way in order to lie flat. On an outward curve, cut small wedges or notches from the seam allowance at even intervals; on an inward curve, clip into the seam allowance at even intervals. These intervals should be about ½″-1″, depending on the sharpness of the curve. Be very careful not to clip past the seamline.

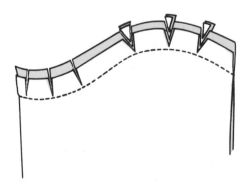

TAPING A SEAM: A seam may be stayed or taped to strengthen and prevent stretching in the finished garment by using twill tape or woven seam binding. This technique is often used at waistline and shoulder seams. The tape should be placed over the seamline of one garment section, with the edge extending ⅛″ into the seam allowance. Baste next to the seamline and sew the tape on permanently as the seam is machine stitched.

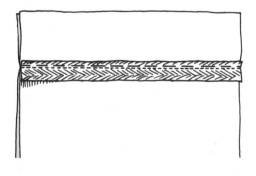

UNDERSTITCHING: When a seamline is pressed to form an edge that encloses the seam allowances, one side should be understitched. This technique is often used for facings to prevent them from rolling to the outside of the garment. Be sure to clip or notch curved edges when necessary. Press both seam allowances toward the facing and grade them. From the right side of the facing, work the half-backstitch or machine stitch close to the seamline and through all the seam allowances. Turn the facing in and press the seamed edge.

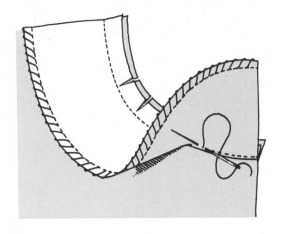

REINFORCING: Whenever you stitch a seam with a corner, use reinforcement stitches to strengthen it at the point. If it is an inward corner that will need to be clipped for easy

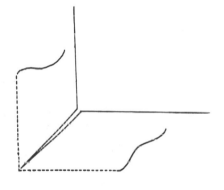

sewing, reinforce it before joining in a seam. Just inside the seamline, stitch for about an inch on either side of the point with *reinforcement* stitches (15 to 20 per inch depending on your fabric). To obtain a sharp outward corner, leave the needle in the fabric at the point and pivot the fabric. When joining two corresponding pieces of fabric, as in a collar, use reinforcement stitches for an inch on either side of the corner. If the corner is at an acute angle, you should take one small stitch *across* the point. Grade the seam allowances and trim the corners, as shown.

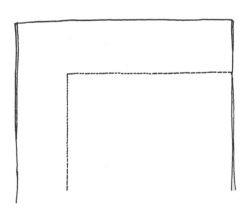

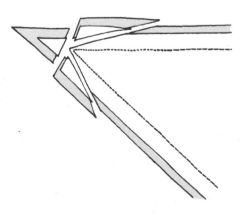

Construction

The main purpose of all seams is to hold your garment sections together. Depending on the various fabrics and design lines, this can be accomplished in many different ways. You will find on this and the next several pages all the principles pertaining to seams you may possibly require.

PLAIN SEAM: Placing right sides together, stitch along the seamline with a ⅝" seam allowance. Keep the cut edges even to serve as a guide. Always press the stitching line flat first to blend the stitches into the fabric; then press the seam open.

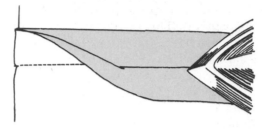

INTERSECTING OR CROSSED SEAMS: Stitch one seam and press open. Stitch the second seam in the same manner. Pin the two seams with right sides together, using a pin point to match the crossed seams exactly at the seamline. Then pin on either side of the seams and stitch. Trim corners diagonally as shown.

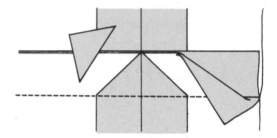

SEAM WITH EASE: To ease, stitch close to the seamline between markings with long machine stitches. Pin the two layers right sides together with the eased side facing up. Pull up the ease thread and distribute the fullness evenly. Anchor the thread ends. Baste carefully to control the extra fabric and stitch.

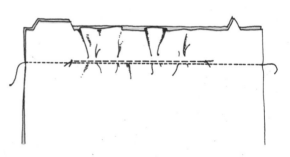

ENCLOSED SEAMS: Collars, cuffs, and pocket flaps, when finished, may have seams that are enclosed within them. After stitching, press the seam open with a point presser so that the seamed edges will be sharp. Grade the seam allowances.

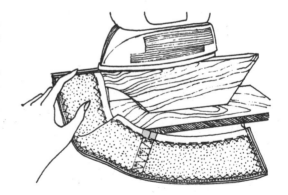

JOINING A GATHERED EDGE TO A STRAIGHT EDGE: See page 228 for techniques to use on gathers.

JOINING AT A CORNER: Before stitching the seam, reinforce the inward corner for an inch on either side with small stitches next to the seamline in the seam allowance. Clip to the point. Pin both sections right sides together with clipped section up and stitch, pivoting at the point (1). This pointed seam may be completed in one of three ways: press the seam open, trim fullness from the outward corner, and catchstitch the trimmed edges together (2); press both seam allowances toward the outward corner, trim fullness from the outward corner, and catchstitch the trimmed edges of both seam allowances together (3); press both seam allowances toward inward corner (4).

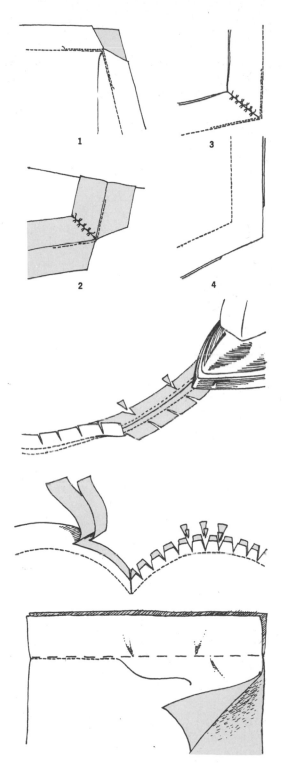

PRINCESS SEAM: Staystitch both curved edges ⅛″ from the seamline on the seam allowance. Clip the inward curved seam allowance to the staystitching so that it will lie smoothly. Stitch the two edges together with the clipped edge uppermost. As you press, notch the outward curving seam allowance so that it lies flat.

SCALLOPS: Stitch the curved scallop seam with small reinforcement stitches (15-20 per inch). Take one stitch across each point to make turning easier later. Now clip into each point being careful not to cut through the stitching. Grade seams and notch all curves.

JOINING NAPPED FABRIC TO UN-NAPPED FABRIC: First pin, then baste closely using small stitches along the seamline. Always stitch in the direction of the nap with the unnapped fabric uppermost. This procedure will help to reduce slippage caused by the nap.

STRETCHY SEAMS: You may have discovered that some fabrics are inclined to stretch or shift during sewing, creating uneven seams. To prevent mishaps, try placing tissue paper on the machine bed under the seams. Stitch through both the fabric and the paper; then tear the paper away. Where "give" in the seams is desirable, use a small zigzag stitch (12-15 stitches per inch) and loosen the tension slightly. Take extreme care not to stretch the fabric.

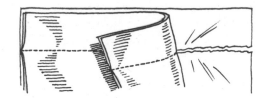

BIAS CUT EDGE: If you are joining a bias edge to a straight edge, pin and baste the bias edge to the straight edge. When stitching, be sure to always keep the bias side up in order to control the stretch of the bias and to avoid puckers. If you are joining two bias edges, stretch the fabric slightly as you stitch over tissue paper so that the finished edge will hang correctly. Otherwise the seam may pucker and the threads will break when the garment is worn.

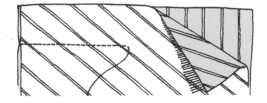

FRENCH SEAM: This seam is well suited to sheer fabrics. It looks like a plain seam on the right side and a small, neat tuck on the wrong side. It is used on straight seams. Pin *wrong* sides together and stitch ⅜″ from the seamline in the seam allowance. Trim to within ⅛″ to ¼″ of stitching. **Right** sides together, crease along the stitched seam; press. Stitch along the seamline encasing the raw edges. (See French Whipped Seam for curves.)

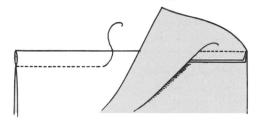

SIMULATED FRENCH SEAM: This seam can be made after first making a plain seam. Do not press it open. Instead, turn both of the seam allowances toward each other ¼″ and press. Now edgestitch the folded edges together.

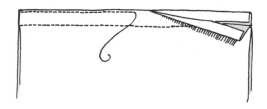

FRENCH WHIPPED SEAM OR DOUBLE-STITCHED SEAM: For lace and embroidered fabrics or curved seams on sheer fabrics, stitch a plain seam, then stitch again ⅛″ away in the seam allowance. Trim to ⅛″ from this stitching and carefully overcast the raw edges by hand or with a fine zigzag stitch.

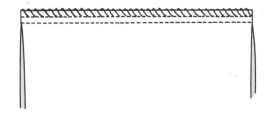

Seam Finishes

Since the inside story is as important to fine couture as the outside, all seams should be finished by the most suitable method if they are not covered by a lining. A seam finish helps the seam allowances to support the garment shape, insures durability, prevents raveling, and contributes to the over-all neatness of the garment.

HAND OVERCAST: This finish is suitable for most fabrics. For a seam pressed open, stitch ¼″ from each raw edge, then trim to ⅛″. (For firm fabrics, stitching and trimming may be omitted.) Overcast the edge by hand, using machine stitching as a guide.

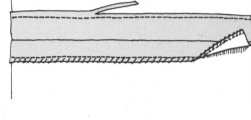

BOUND EDGE: For heavy, bulky, easily frayed fabrics, especially in unlined jackets or coats, encase each raw edge in purchased double-fold bias tape. Place the slightly narrower edge of the tape on top and edgestitch.

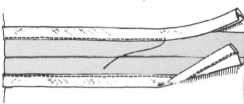

TURNED UNDER: Use this method for lightweight fabrics and plain weave synthetics. It is not suitable for fabrics with bulk. Turn under the raw edges of the seam allowances, press if necessary, and stitch close to the edge.

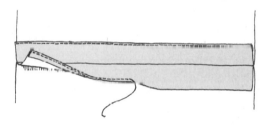

SELF-BOUND SEAM: Trim one seam allowance of a plain seam to ⅛″ or ¼″, depending on your fabric. Turn the edge of the other seam allowance under and slipstitch or machine stitch over the seam, encasing the trimmed seam allowance.

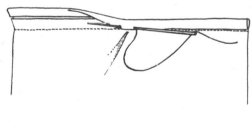

PINKED: If you are working with a firmly woven fabric which does not ravel, pink the edges with pinking or scalloping shears. For an even more secure finish, you may wish to stitch ¼″ from each edge before you begin to pink.

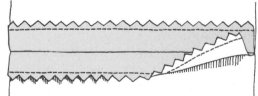

MACHINE ZIGZAG: For fabrics which tend to ravel easily, use a zigzag stitch to reinforce each raw edge. Use a smaller stitch for lightweight fabrics and a larger stitch for heavy, bulky fabrics, pre-testing for the best results.

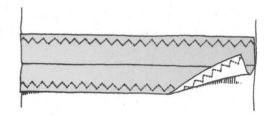

HONG KONG FINISH: For a couture touch, see page 383.

Special Seams

You can be creative in your sewing by letting your seams show. Topstitching on the right side of the fabric adds a special decorative touch. Choose one as a design feature in your garment and be inventive—your finished product will be an original!

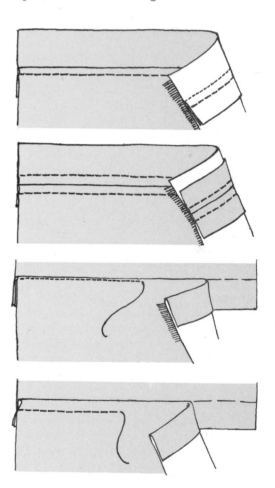

TOPSTITCHED SEAM: Press a plain seam to one side as indicated on the pattern. Topstitch the desired distance from the seam on the right side of the fabric through all thicknesses. See Stitchery, page 395, for further instructions.

DOUBLE TOPSTITCHED SEAM: First press a plain seam open. Topstitch the desired distance from each side of the seam on the right side of the fabric. Be sure your stitches go through both thicknesses of the fabric.

LAPPED SEAM: Turn in the edges of the overlapping section along the seamline and press. Working from the right side, pin the folded edge over the remaining section with the fold along the seamline. Stitch close to the fold through all thicknesses.

TUCKED SEAM: Follow the directions for a lapped seam and slip-baste the fold in place. To form the tuck, stich the desired depth from the fold through all thicknesses, stitching no closer than 1/4″ from the raw edges. Remove the basting.

220

FLAT-FELL SEAM OR FELLED SEAM: Place *wrong* sides together (right sides together for an inside fell), stitch a plain seam, and press it toward one side. Trim the lower seam allowance to ⅛". Turn under the edge of the other seam allowance ¼" and place over the narrow seam allowance. For non-bulky fabrics, machine stitch close to the folded edge; for bulky reversible fabrics, slipstitch the fold in place.

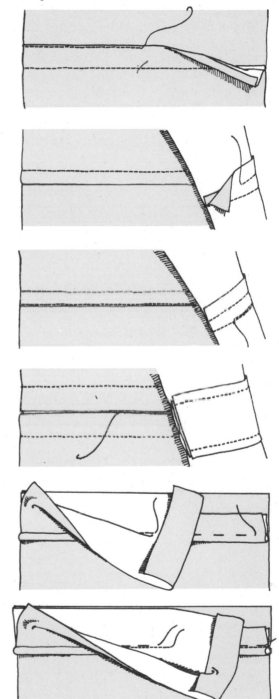

WELT SEAM: Stitch a plain seam and press it toward one side. Trim the lower seam allowance to ¼". Then stitch through only the upper seam allowance and garment close to the trimmed edge, encasing the lower seam allowance.

DOUBLE WELT SEAM: When completed, this seam gives much the same appearance as a flat-fell seam. First construct a welt seam as directed above. Then topstitch close to the seam on the right side of the fabric, as shown.

SLOT SEAM: Machine or hand baste a plain seam; press open. Cut a strip of fabric as long as the seam and slightly wider than both seam allowances. From the right side, topstitch the same distance on each side of the seam. Remove basting threads.

PIPED SEAM: Baste piping to the right side of one of the fabric sections along the seamline. Place the second section over the piping right sides together and baste; then stitch on the seamline through all thicknesses.

CORDED SEAM: Encase the cording in a bias strip, using a cording or a zipper foot. Attach the cording and baste the fabric sections together, like the piped seam. Stitch along the seamline through all thicknesses, using a cording or zipper foot.

Darts

Darts create the difference between the flatness of fabrics and the curving third dimension of the feminine form. They rank highly among the basic sewing concepts which must be understood before you can construct a garment with any degree of fit. Their function is to provide carefully shaped fullness. Although darts are dealt with on pages 142-143, it is always wise to keep a few working axioms in mind. ❊ First, and above all, a low bustline will detract from what otherwise could be a youthful appearance. For this reason, if you have an inkling that a low bustline is the cause of your fitting problems, adjust the straps of your foundation garments before you adjust your patterns or fit your garment. Then make certain that the dart position provides fullness that conforms with the lengthwise and crosswise contours of your figure. The dart should point to the fullest part of the body—to the point of the bust, to the curve over the pelvic bone, and so on. Since the length of the dart has been designed for a person of average height, you may have to adjust the dart length to agree with your own proportions—for a short figure, slightly shorter darts; for a tall figure, slightly longer darts. If the vertical bodice darts require relocating, the skirt darts should be realigned to match.

Marking

Transfer the dart markings to your fabric, using the most suitable method. You may not notice until the dart is folded that the subtle styling of many designs requires concave or convex curves as opposed to straight darts. Use your tracing wheel or tailor's chalk to make short horizontal lines indicating the bold symbols for matching sides, as well as the end of the dart. Always have the darts on the left and right sides of the garment mirror each other in length and placement.

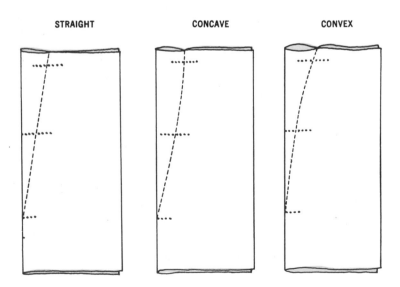

STRAIGHT   CONCAVE   CONVEX

Stitching

Begin sewing all darts at the wide base and taper to nothing at the pointed end. In fact, your last two or three stitches (12-15 stitches per inch) should be directly on the fold. The contour dart, which begins and ends with narrow points, should follow the same principle. Sew the first stitches very slowly to be sure that they are only catching a few threads of the fabric. The thread ends of all darts, particularly at the point, should be secured with a knot rather than by backstitching. Tie the knot, as shown, working it to the end of the dart. Backstitching often results in an unsightly bubble or pucker because the previous line of stitching was not duplicated exactly.

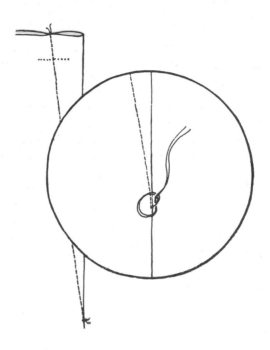

Dart Slash with Pleats or Gathers

Reinforce the point with small machine stitches just outside the seamline and slash to this stitching. Make pleats or gathers as you normally would and baste them to the seamline of the dart. For better control in this particular dart, stitch with the gathered or pleated side facing the machine. You can taper smoothly to a fine point and thereby achieve an even line on the right side. Knot the thread ends; then press the dart upward.

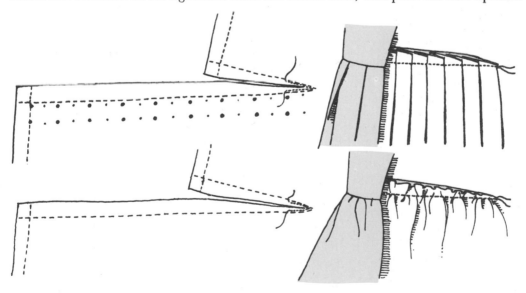

Trimming

Generally, darts require little additional handling other than pressing, but there are some situations which require special techniques.

Deep darts or darts in medium to heavy fabrics should be slashed ½″ to 1″ from the point and pressed open.

Sheers look best when the dart is trimmed. Make a second row of stitching approximately ⅛″ from the first; then trim ⅛″ from this stitching. Overcast the raw edges.

Contour darts are usually found at the waistline. Clip them several times on the fold along the curve to relieve strain, as shown.

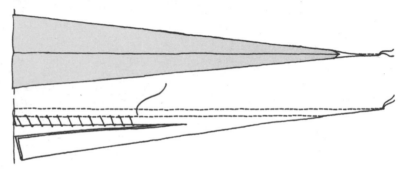

Pressing

Always press darts before the major seams are stitched or before they are intersected by seams. The dart fold and stitching line should be pressed flat first to blend the stitches together. Be careful not to crease the fabric beyond the end point. Next, spread open the garment and press each dart over the curved surface of a tailor's ham or press mitt to maintain the built-in shape. Once you've steamed the dart into its proper position the area around the dart may become slightly wrinkled. Touch up this area while the dart is still on the tailor's ham with a dry iron.

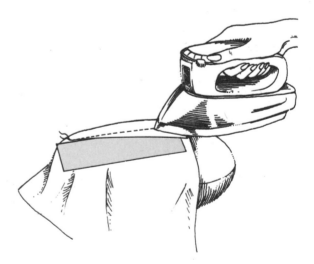

Vertical darts should be pressed toward center front or center back, depending on their location. Horizontal darts are pressed downward unless otherwise specified. Deep darts, however, are pressed open with the point pressed flat. Place brown paper between the dart and garment to prevent ridges if your fabric mars.

The Essential Seam

The structural basis of fashion—seams are the designer's
language, through which a third dimension is given to fabric . . .
They are the linear facts in the image of style . . . Sinuous curves
that emphasize your own or abrupt angles that give meaning
to a silhouette, seams direct the eye in subtle ways . . .

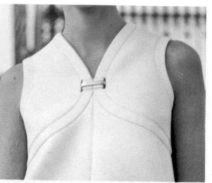

The shape of a lady
is basic, but seams
and darts can be
made to conform to
her curves in an
infinite variety of
ways . . . Artful
seaming is the claim
to fame of many a
successful couturier
. . . An exacting
form of sculpture
with masterful and
wearable results.

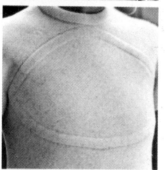

Shapemaking Darts and Tucks

Darts and tucks are fashion shapemakers. A key to
individual fit, the dart's careful control of fullness creates the curvy
third dimension of the feminine form and a tuck
repertoire fulfills a multitude of structural and ornamental
needs while controlling and shaping fullness.

For lady-like detail and subtle shaping, designers add tucks . . . down the front . . . at the shoulder and bustline . . . around the waist . . . the soft touch of tucks is a perfect accent.

One dimensional fabric to three dimensional garment . . . darts create the curves . . . French darts, curved darts, double pointed darts, dart tucks . . . curves that match your own for a fabulous fit.

The Soft Touch

Gathers round a pretty neckline or curving into a nipped waist—
the substance of a hundred silhouettes, and, if deftly used, terrific camouflage . . .
Gathers love the fluid crepes . Whispery knits gather into enthralling folds,
alternately shy and clingy, shaping themselves with motion . . . The classic display for
a beautiful cloth—the rich toga-draping that demands a fine, soft texture and proves
quality . . . Soft swirls of a long gathered skirt draw yards of fabric into
dancing poetry, and make you feel your most curvy and feminine.

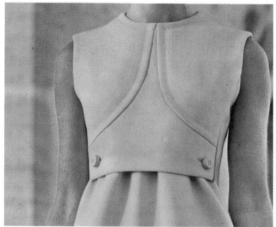

The spirit of gathers is in
the fabric . Test it for gathering
while it's still on the bolt . . .
Crush a length together in
your hand . Is it stiff and bulky
or soft and drapey?
Whether they're at a neckline,
a waistline, or a sleeve,
gathers always reflect the
texture of the fabric
they're made of . . .

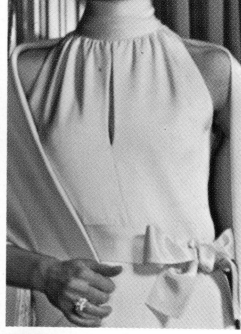

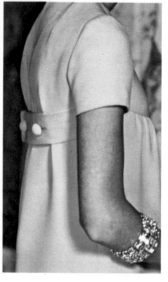

A Ripple of Femininity

The stuff of romance—lace edged white ruffles are sure to melt the hardest masculine heart . . . Try them in surprising textures . . . Use their softness in contrast with the strictness of tailoring, and give them character with a strong-willed fabric—crisp, perky gingham or soft, sensuous crepe.

Ruffles—recalling a more opulent age in a rich, dramatic ruff . . . Softening the sensitive gesture of an expressive hand as the graceful border of a cuff, or spilling elegantly from a 'tweed sleeve . . . Curvy flattery for faces—flirty and a bit shy, modestly hiding the edge of a low-cut neckline.

At hemlines, necklines, cuffs, and closing edges, bringing out the most feminine of your many moods, and the most attentive and protective of his . . .

The Perky Pleat

There's nothing like the snappy swing of pleats to put a lilt in your walk and a gleam
in the eye of a passing gentleman . . . Rippling gracefully as you dance—
recalling the brisk highland fling in a cheerily swirling kilt—reflecting a jaunty tempo . .
Crisp and sharp or soft and rounded, released from a yoke or a handsome hipline,
pleats are chic and versatile, timeless and timely, and well worth the effort.

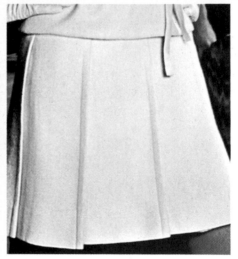

Flippy flapper skirts, ready
for action .. The skinnying vertical
of a single central box pleat . . .
The tidyness of a ladylike
pleated-skirt suit . . . Pleats
set your fashion stride
toward style and comfort . . .

The Elegant Edge

Tailored flattery with a rich custom touch, the sharp,
crisp corner and the handsome accent of a finely-moulded binding
add snap and style . . . Subtle self-binding in smooth bias curves
is smart finishing—and dependable elegance . . . Bright,
contrasting edging enhances your careful seaming and lightens
your mood . . . Careful pre-shaping is the secret.

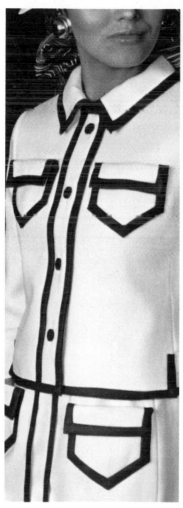

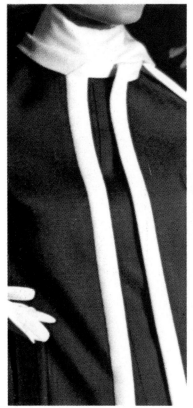

Binding is many
widths and weights,
in supple bias
to conform to curves . . .
Classic middy braid,
and fabric
to match or to contrast,
folded, piped,
or corded,
forms the finish
or the trim for pockets
and sleeves,
collars and hems . . .

The Face Framers

The fashionable neckline is a variety of shapes and an optical illusion to use
to your advantage. Pure and simple jewel necklines beg for adornment and love to
play clever scarf tricks. V-necks were born for ascots, and alone they're a
grand face-lengthener... Halters flatter the bold and beautiful shoulder...
While the many others exercise the designer's imagination...

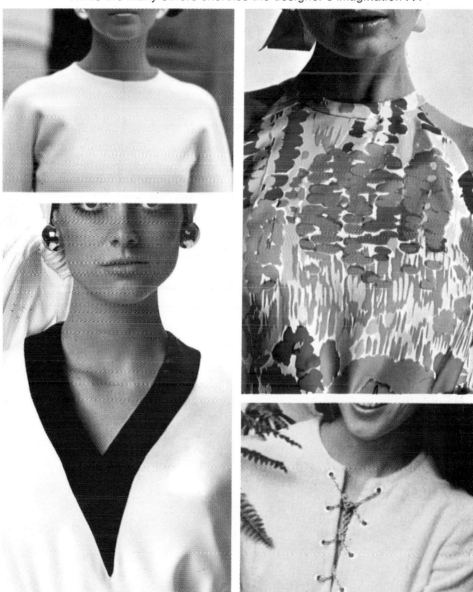

The come-hither decolleté is a
devastating tactic for evening
drama . . . and sewing gives you
the option of just how much to bare
. . . Round or square, bateau or
keyhole, U-shaped or scooped.
Many necklines to suit the
many styles, moods, and
occasions in your varied life.

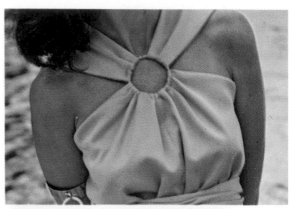

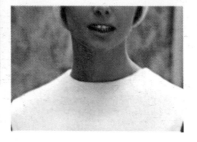

The Collar Collage

Myriad collars vary the fashion landscape and show off your
sewing proficiency. Choose them with the principles of line in mind,
according to your most flattering silhouette, and learn the
tricks that will help you create them. . . . The classic lines
of a notched lapel reward patience and care with
handsome distinction. . . .

Long, unbroken curves
make the shawl collar a
perfect figure lengthener,
while the neat mandarin
and bias rolled collar
flatter a swan-like neck. . . .
The innocent round-shaped
collars grace a pretty
face with charming
symmetry and poise.

Collars on stands are a handsome
hint of masculine swagger with a
feminine air . . . perk up a low
mood with a tie collar in a
voluptuous pussy-cat bow.

Tucks

The tuck is a versatile element in the designer's repertoire and fulfills a multitude of structural and ornamental needs. Each tuck is a slender fold of fabric that can be stitched along all or part of its length. Tucks are usually folded on straight grain, and, if chosen for decoration, the fold is generally formed on the outside of the fabric.

When tucks are used to control fullness and shape the contour of the design, the fold is formed on the inside, stitched to a designated point, and then released. They may be stitched on or off grain and either straight or contoured, like darts. Or they may be just small pleats of fabric secured by a seam. These released tucks, or dart tucks as they are sometimes called, are found at the shoulder line and waistline of a bodice or skirt, and should point toward the fullest part of the body in those areas.

Decorative tucks, stitched on the right side of the fabric, require very careful selection of needles and thread to coordinate with the fabric. Generally you should try to match your thread to your fabric. However, you may achieve interesting effects by using thread just one shade lighter or darker than the fabric.

If you are planning to add tucks to a garment, choose a design with few style lines and be sure to have the placement, width, and spacing of the tucks relate to your figure. The three commonly known types of tucks are: BLIND TUCKS, where each tuck touches or overlaps the next, SPACED TUCKS, where there is a predetermined space between each tuck, and PIN TUCKS, which are very narrow spaced tucks.

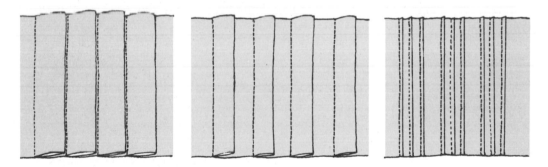

The Picture of Uniformity

If you would like decorative tucks on a garment, and the pattern does not call for them, tuck the fabric before cutting the pattern piece, using a gauge to ensure accuracy.   You will undoubtedly need more fabric than is required by the pattern piece. To determine the amount of additional width, decide first on the width and spacing of the tucks by making a small sample. Next, estimate how many tucks will fit in the intended garment section. Multiply the width of the tuck by two to allow for both thicknesses. Then multiply this figure by the number of tucks to find out how much wider your fabric will need to be for tucking purposes. You may need approximately as much additional fabric as the length of one pattern piece, depending on the size of your tucks, because the extra width required may interfere with your original pattern layout.

Quick Ways to Make Tucks

Tucks are usually made on the straight grain. Do be sure to make the fold of the tucks parallel to the threads in the fabric. Marking your tucks will be unnecessary if you make a cardboard measurement gauge, cutting a notch for the depth of the tuck and a second notch to indicate the space from fold to fold. Working from right to left and sliding your gauge as you sew, baste all your tucks in place. Some fabrics may be measured by pulling a thread where the fold of the tuck will be, then proceeding to baste as above. When you have finished basting the tucks in place, stitch them. Be very sure to stitch from the side that will be seen so that you can control the finished look and the evenness of the stitching as much as possible. Tucking may be pieced, if necessary, by carefully lapping, then stitching the tucks.

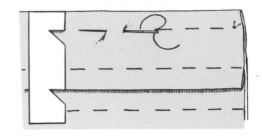

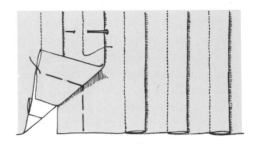

Press tucks as you stitch each one, or directly after stitching the series. First press the crease in the tuck from the right side of your fabric but on the underneath side of the fold. This step makes the final pressing much easier. Press the entire tucked area from the wrong side. Use very little steam to prevent puckering or the tuck fold from making unwanted indentions in the fabric. To prevent the latter problem in some fabrics, you may have to use strips of brown paper under the fold of each tuck as you press. Touch up the right side of the tucks as necessary. Tucks may be made with the aid of a machine attachment called a tucker.

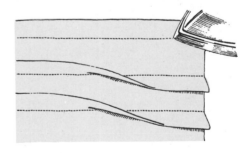

CROSS TUCKS are done before the fabric is cut into pattern sections. Measure, baste, and stitch the base rows first. Press carefully before dealing with the crossing tucks.

Again measure, baste, and sew with these new tucks at right angles to the earlier set. The earlier rows of tucks should lay with the folds facing downward as you stitch. Press all the tucks in the proper direction. Lay your pattern piece with the tucked area in the desired position and the folds of the tucks parallel to the straight grain arrow on the tissue pattern. Cut out the garment as you would normally. You may find that a line of staystitching around the seam allowances of the tucked area helps to keep the tucks in place and lying in the right direction.

CORDED TUCKS begin with accurate measuring and marking. To determine how much fabric will be required for each tuck, pin a piece of fabric around the cording, remove, and measure from pin to pin. Remember to include the fabric between tucks. Then mark the right side of your fabric accordingly with thread tracing. Place the wrong side of the fabric over the cord, pin and baste each tuck, enclosing the cording. Using a cording foot or zipper foot, stitch close to the cord.

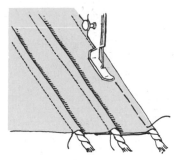

SHELL OR SCALLOPED TUCKS should be made after you have determined the depth of your tucks and the distance between them. Mark their foldlines on the right side using a gauge. You will find that 1/4" tucks are generally the most suitable. Baste each tuck and then form the scallop by hand, sewing as follows:

Lightly mark every 1/2" with small dots along the length of the tucks. For a hand sewn tuck, sew tiny running stitches between dots and, at the same time, sew over each tuck at the designated intervals using two overhand stitches. Draw the thread taut before making the next set of running stitches. If you prefer a quicker and more sturdy method, you may stitch along the tucks by machine. If you have either a quilting foot or edge stitcher attachment for your machine, use it to keep the stitching an even distance from the edge. Then hand sew two tight overhand stitches at the marked 1/2" intervals, running the needle and thread inside the tuck between scallops.

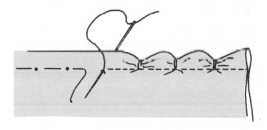

RELEASED TUCKS OR DART TUCKS may have fullness released at one or both ends of the tuck. Construction techniques will vary greatly according to where the tuck is located on the garment. Regardless of construction, the most significant factor to remember about all released tucks is that the released fullness below the stitched fold should *never* be pressed flat. The stitching line at the point of releasing fullness can be backstitched, or the thread ends tied securely. When the tucks are pressed to one side, stitch across to the fold and backstitch or knot the thread ends.

Gathering and Shirring

Softness and femininity will always be associated with the graceful fullness produced by gathering and shirring. Gathers are small, soft folds made by drawing fabric up on a line of hand or machine stitching. Shirring is formed by numerous rows of gathers and is both decorative and functional. It can be used to achieve varied surface effects such as smocking and may be used at waistline, yokes, and sleeves.

In order to have small, even folds when stitching for gathering and shirring, do not use a longer stitch than necessary. First, try approximately 8 stitches per inch. A heavy duty bobbin thread such as nylon or silk makes it easier to pull up gathers without breaking the threads. The bobbin thread can be pulled more easily by loosening the upper tension. If the fabric still does not gather easily, lengthen the stitch accordingly. Normally, thick and closely-woven fabrics need longer stitches than lightweight and sheer fabrics.

How to Gather

With the right side of the fabric up, stitch along the seamline and again ¼″ away in the seam allowance. To form the gathers, pin the edge to be gathered to the corresponding edge at notches, centers, and all remaining markings. Draw up the bobbin threads at one end until almost half of the gathered edge fits the adjoining straight edge. Fasten gathers by winding threads around a pin in a figure-eight fashion. Draw up the remaining half and again fasten the threads. Adjust gathers evenly between pins; then stitch on the seamline with the gathered side up. Press the seam, taking care not to flatten the gathers, and then lightly press in the desired direction.

When you are using a gathering stitch on heavy, bulky fabrics, try to avoid stitching across your seam allowances. When applying your gathering stitch, stitch up to the seamline and stop; then begin on the other side of the seamline.

If you have a zigzag machine, you may gather by using a large zigzag stitch over fine strong string. Gathering by hand is done with small, even running stitches, the same length on both sides of the fabric. Sew at least two rows. For hand gathering it is best to work on an individual fabric piece *before* the pieces are joined to each other. To stay gathers, seam binding may be stitched or hand sewn along the seamline.

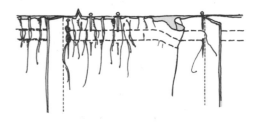

GAUGING is a hand sewing variation of gathering used to hold a large amount of fabric in a small place. Take a short stitch on the right side of your fabric and a long stitch on the wrong side, keeping the stitches in each row directly in line with those of the row above. You will need at least two rows of gauging to control the fullness.

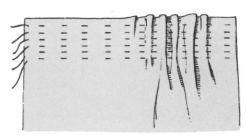

228

Shirring

Shirring is formed by several rows of gathering, requiring ***absolute accuracy*** for best results. Make as many rows as you desire, using only soft or very lightweight fabric that has been steam pressed to eliminate any stiffness of fabric and to soften the finish. Gather on the bias or crosswise grain for the most satisfying effect. Never press directly

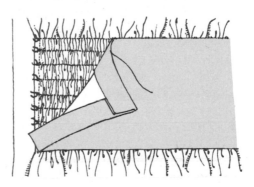

on the shirred area, but work the point of the iron into the area below the shirring. When using more than two rows of shirring, secure each row separately with a knot. If rows of stitching are not secured by a seam, fold fabric on the wrong side and stitch narrow pin tucks over knotted ends.

Stay shirring by placing a strip of self fabric over the wrong side of the shirred area; turn in the raw edges of the strip and sew it in place with small stitches.

CORDED SHIRRING is made by encasing cording in a fabric tuck. See page 227 for corded tucks. Draw up the cording until the desired fullness is reached. To make the shirring flexible as would be required for a waistline area, use rounded elastic instead of

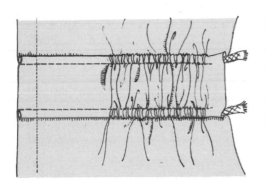

cord. If you are not treating the cording as a drawstring, anchoring will be a necessity. The type of anchoring to use is dependent upon the width of the cord or string. Thick cording should be secured by stitching it in place with several reinforcement stitches. Trim the cording close to the stitches to eliminate bulk. Stitch the seam after anchoring the cording. Secure fine string or cording by knotting it and stitching over the knot in a seam or, if no seam exists, make a narrow pin tuck enclosing the knots.

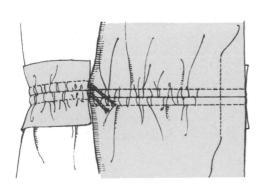

SHIRRING WITH A SELF-FACING requires a plain seam that is pressed open. Stitch about ⅛″ to ¼″ from either side of the seamline to form a casing. Draw fine strong string or button and carpet thread through the casing between the seam and each row of stitching, and then adjust your shirring to the desired fullness. Knot the ends and then stitch over them in a seam or enclose them with a narrow pin tuck.

ELASTICIZED SHIRRING is used to snug fabric into place comfortably and prettily. It consists of multiple rows of flexible gathering stitches. Wind elastic thread on the bobbin by hand, stretching it slightly and winding it firmly until the bobbin is almost full. Then set your machine for a long stitch (about 7 stitches per inch) and use a scrap of your garment fabric to test the tension, which might have to be loosened. Mark the location of the shirring with thread tracing or tailor's chalk clearly visible on the right side of your fabric. Now stitch from the right side, holding the fabric taut as you stitch. Continue to stretch the elasticized fabric in each of the preceding rows as you sew so that the shirring will be evenly distributed. You may use the previously stitched row as a guide along with your markings to keep the lines straight. Be sure to knot all the thread ends and, in addition, stitch over the knots in a seam or encase them in a narrow pin tuck, as explained on the previous page.

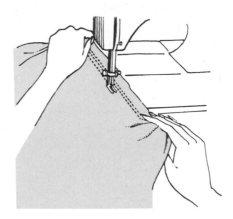

Ruffles

Whether they are of eyelet, organdy, or self-fabric, gathered or circular ruffles always lend a feminine touch. Let them frame your face, border your hem, or become the perfect ending to a graceful sleeve. The effect can be soft or pert; the mood, sophisticated elegance or little-girl freshness. However you choose to use the ruffle, let your fabric and your mood inspire this softer, more romantic look in fashion.

If you do not have a pattern piece for your ruffle or if you want to estimate its fullness, remember that you will need a fabric strip three times the length of the edge to which it will be joined for a very full ruffle; a fabric strip twice the finished edge length for minimum fullness. Wide ruffles should have more fullness than narrow ones to keep them from looking skimpy. The sheerer your fabric is, the fuller the ruffle should be. You should realize inward corners will require less fullness and outward corners more fullness than the rest of the ruffle. Always keep in mind the proportions of the ruffle and the garment so that neither overwhelms the other.

For gathering a ruffle, it is wise to use a strong bobbin thread such as nylon or silk. These slide through the fabric easily for even distribution, and have less tendency to break under tension. Always make a double row of stitching—one on the seamline and the other 1/4" away in the seam allowance. The two rows will help to distribute the fullness evenly and will protect each other, should one break during the ruffling process. When you have attached the ruffle, remove any gathering stitches that might show.

All Kinds of Ruffles

CIRCULAR RUFFLE: A circular ruffle can be added to any edge—cuffs, V-neckline, rounded neckline—wherever you wish. It is cut from several circles which are first slashed and then joined along the straight grain. This method produces a maximum amount of fullness. Exert great caution when laying out, pinning, and cutting the ruffle sections. You will find that exact location and maintenance of the grainline is most important if the circular ruffle is to drape correctly.

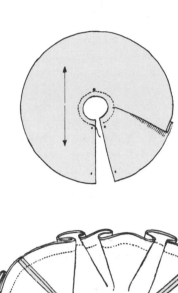

The edge of this particular ruffle may be faced with self–fabric or it may have a narrow hemmed edge. You may staystitch each ruffle section ⅛″ from the inner seamline in the seam allowance before joining.

Should a narrow hem be the required finish, join circles and complete hem before basting the ruffle to its proper edge. If your ruffle has a facing of corresponding circles, stitch the seamed facing and ruffle sections together along the outer edges. Trim seam allowance to ¼″. Turn the ruffle and press. Baste the raw edges of the ruffle and facing together for handling ease.

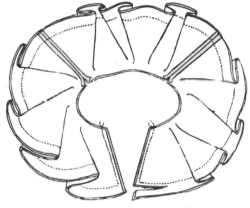

If you are applying ruffles to a neckline or any other curved edge, first stay the seamline so that its shape will not be distorted by the weight of the ruffle. Whether the ruffle is cut single or is faced, the inner circle should be staystitched and then clipped where necessary as you pin the ruffle to the garment in order to fit smoothly on the seamline. As a rule, deep curves require a clip at almost every ½″ up to the line of staystitching; shallow curves will, of course, require fewer clips. If the ruffle still does not lie flat, do not cut through the staystitching; merely clip more frequently. Then baste the ruffle in place. Finish the ruffle application with a shaped facing, as directed on page 251.

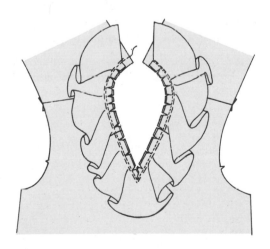

STRAIGHT RUFFLE: A straight ruffle is gathered and constructed from a continuous strip of material. It may be folded in half lengthwise with wrong sides together for a self-faced ruffle, or may be constructed of a single layer of fabric with a narrow hem at the lower edge. It can be cut either on the straight grain or on the bias. If the ruffle must be seamed, the seam should be made on the straight grain. Bias ruffles applied to a small area, such as a sleeve, are the exception—in this case, make the seam of the ruffle on the bias to match the seam of the garment. To gather, simply stitch two rows of long machine stitches. Draw the gathers to the proper length. When adjusting gathers over a short distance, secure both threads at one end and gather from the opposite end. For longer distances, begin gathering from one end, secure the threads, and then gather from the other end.

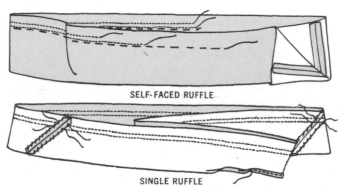

SELF-FACED RUFFLE

SINGLE RUFFLE

Pin the ruffle to the garment edge, matching seamlines. Adjust the gathers until they are evenly distributed and baste in place. To make machine stitching and turning easier, press the basted seam allowances flat, holding the tip of your iron parallel to the seam, not on the ruffles. Finish the application with a bias facing as directed on page 233.

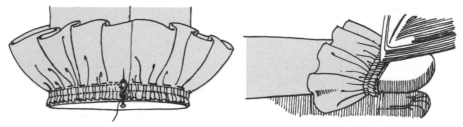

RUFFLE WITH A HEADING: A ruffle with a heading, sometimes called a double ruffle, is ruffled on both sides of the gathers. It does not need to be finished with a facing and can easily be applied. A variation of the straight ruffle, it is cut in the same manner. Cut a strip the desired length and width, including extra width for a hem on both edges. Mark the gathering line with thread tracing and make a narrow hem on both raw edges. Stitch two lines of long machine stitches, each 1/8" from the gathering line.

If the ends of the ruffle are to be joined, join them with a seam; trim and overcast. If the ends are left hanging free, finish with a narrow hem. To apply the double ruffle to a raw edge, trim garment seam allowances to 1/4". Pin wrong sides together with the ruffle side up. The bottom row of gathering stitches should be even with the seamline of the garment. Baste, adjusting the gathers and stitch close to the bottom of gathers.

232

Press the garment away from the ruffle. Baste the ruffle to the right side of the garment, enclosing the raw edge; stitch close to the top row of gathers. Remove basting and thread tracing.

To apply the ruffle to a finished edge, pin it wrong side down on the right side of the garment. Baste, adjusting the gathers. Top-stitch twice, stitching close to both rows of gathering stitches.

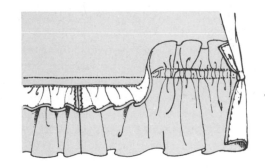

Finish with Flair

SHAPED FACING: For ruffles contained by a facing, choose your ruffle and baste it to the garment edge along the seamline. Pin the facing to the garment edge over your basted ruffle. The ruffle is now sandwiched between the two layers, right sides together. Stitch along the seamline. Trim, grade, and clip the seam allowance so that the facing will lie flat when turned. Turn the facing to expose the finished ruffle. Press, being careful not to press over the ruffle. Understitch the facing by hand through all thicknesses to prevent it from rolling to the outside. If you are using a zipper, insert your zipper and slipstitch the facing along the zipper tape. Blindstitch the facing to the garment or underlining.

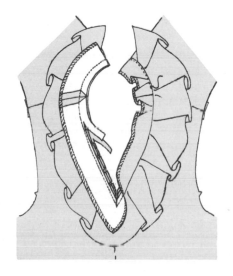

BIAS FACING: Ruffles on hemlines generally do not require a shaped facing. Simply cut 1¼″ wide bias strips. ✤ For better control and a finer finish, you may wish to cut your bias 2″ to 2½″ wide. This wider strip will help your garment control the fall of the ruffle. Now, with the raw edges even, pin the bias strip over the basted ruffle. Stitch a ¼″ seam at the ends. Then stitch a ⅝″ seam through all thicknesses, trim and, if necessary, grade the seam allowances. Turn the bias to the inside and press. Turn the raw edge under ¼″ and slipstitch it to the garment or underlining.

Pleats

Pleats are always in style, adding a special feminine swing to your fashions whether they're crisp, sharp pleats in a tailored skirt or supple, rolled pleats in a soft dress. Pleats are, quite simply, folds of fabric which provide controlled fullness where you want it. The time and patience required to make them perfect will seem well worthwhile as soon as you see yourself in your new pleated creation.

All pleats should be shaped with precision. Complete mastery depends on transferring the pleat markings accurately, basting pleats to keep them in place during preparation, fitting with care, and pressing correctly.

The proper pattern size for a pleated skirt should be determined by your hip measurement, because the waistline is easier to adjust. Whether the pleats are pressed or hang freely, they look best when executed in firm, resilient fabrics such as synthetics (except rayon), blends, wools, and heavy silks. Some of these can be more crisply pleated than others. If you want a sharp edge on permanent-press fabrics or other fabrics that have been treated with a crease-resistant finish, try edgestitching both the front and back edges of the pleats. Crisp pleats in underlined garments are difficult to maintain, so special care should be taken to attach the underlining to the garment along all foldlines. Your pattern usually will not recommend underlining a multiple-pleated garment.

Although there are many variations, basically pleats are of just two types: folds in the fabric made by doubling the fabric over on itself, and folds with an underlay or separate piece stitched to the pleat extensions on the underside of the garment. There are four well known variations, used either singly or in series: KNIFE or SIDE PLEATS with all folds turned to one side; BOX PLEATS with two folds turned away from each other and underfolds meeting at the center; INVERTED PLEATS, box pleats in reverse, with folds turned toward each other and meeting; and ACCORDION PLEATS, always pressed along the entire length with folds resembling the bellows of an accordion.

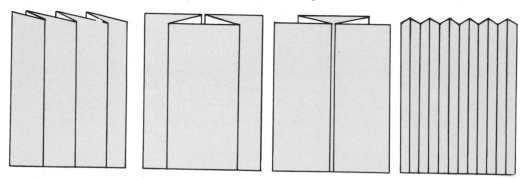

Marking

Before you begin, it is important to be aware of and understand the three "line" indications in pleat patterns. The *roll line* used in unpressed pleats is meant to alert you to the fact that the pleats will form soft rolling folds, not creases, while the *foldline* used for pressed pleats indicates a sharply creased fold that can be edgestitched. The *placement line* indicates that the rolled edges or folded edges are brought to this line. Begin by transferring these lines and all other markings to the wrong side of your fabric. If you are making the pleats from the right side, thread trace all marked lines to the right side. Use different colors of thread to key the various "line" indications.

Straight Pleats

It's best to do pleating on a surface large enough to hold the entire pleated garment. Choose a desired length from another garment, taking whichever measurement is longest —the side seam, center front, or center back. Transfer this measurement, plus a waistline seam allowance and hem allowance, to your pattern before cutting fabric.

Join all but one seam and hem the garment to within 8" of either end. (In making multiple pleats, the hem should be completed before making the pleat folds.) Join the remaining seam, leaving an opening for inserting the zipper, and complete hem. Your length can then be adjusted from the waistline after the pleats are formed. For treatment of hems in pleats, see page 340.

Your pleats can be made either from the right or wrong side, depending upon the designer's intended appearance of the garment and the method that works best for you. Pressed or unpressed pleats are both made the same way; pressing makes the difference.
FROM THE WRONG SIDE: Bring the indicated markings for each pleat together and baste. Press or turn pleats in the direction indicated for your type of pleat. Baste pleats in place along waistline edge.
FROM THE RIGHT SIDE: Following your markings, turn the fabric in along foldline or roll line. Bring the edge to the placement line and pin. Starting at the hem edge and working upward, baste each pleat in place through all thicknesses. Baste pleats in place along waistline edge.

Try on the pleated garment section, referring to Fitting, page 237, for any adjustments.

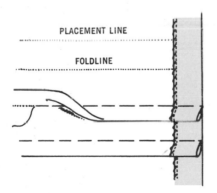

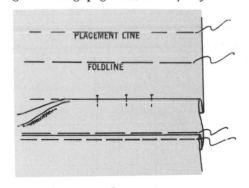

For pressed pleats, make certain the pleats are accurately measured, marked, and basted. Pin them to the ironing board at their edge and steam them on both sides just enough to set them. Use a press cloth on the right side to avoid shine.

Support overhanging fabric by a chair or table to prevent the weight of the fabric from pulling the pleats out of shape.

Shaped and Stitched Pleats

These pleats are most frequently used to reduce bulk in the hip area. The removal of bulk is achieved by trimming away the upper portion of the pleat, leaving a ⅝″ seam allowance along the stitched seamline. To form shaped and stitched pleats, join all skirt sections together. Start pleats 6″ to 8″ from the lower edge (to allow for hemming later), and bring the indicated pleat and/or seamlines together following markings; baste. Before stitching, try the garment on to see if adjustments are needed. If so, refer to Fitting on the following page. When the necessary adjustments are completed, stitch along the indicated seamlines from bottom upward. Complete the hem and baste remainder of pleats into place before pressing. You may wish to refer to the hem section, page 340, for ways to handle hems in pleats.

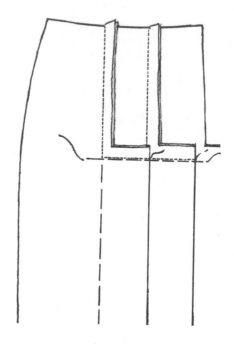

With this type of construction, a stay of lining fabric will be needed to support the upper edge of the pleats. On the straight grain, shape a stay to fit into the desired area. Baste the upper edge to the pleated area at the waistline; then turn under and slipstitch the lower edge of the stay over the upper edge of the pleats along the seamlines. On inverted box pleats, a self-stay can be formed by trimming away only half of the top of the pleat, leaving a seam allowance of ⅝″. The remaining pleat fabric can then be basted across the upper edge for support.

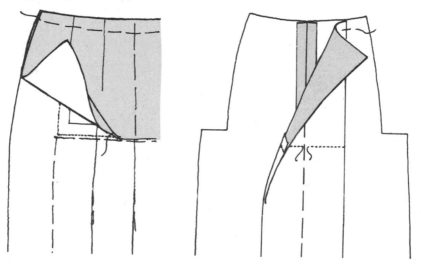

Pleats with a Separate Underlay

Pleats having an underlay are made from the inside and are often used singly. Bring the co-ordinating markings together and baste. Open out the pleat extensions. Stitch the pleat underlay to the pleat extensions and baste in place across the upper edge.

Press the seam allowances away from the underlay. Check the fit for necessary adjustments, following the instructions for fitting below. Then join all seams and prepare your hem. For ways to handle hems on pleats, see page 340.

Fitting

After basting the pleats in place, and before trying on your garment, baste a temporary belt of grosgrain ribbon at the waistline on the inside to ensure that the pleats will be supported and hang properly as you fit your garment.

When fitting, you may find that the waistline is too large or too small if you have adjusted your pattern to accommodate your hip measurement. Distributing the change evenly between the pleats, make a hairline adjustment on the placement line of each pleat at the waistline. The tiny dotted lines on each side of the placement line indicate the small change needed to make the difference in fit. On straight pleats it is very important to maintain the straight grainline on the outside fold of each pleat by carefully controlled tapering of the placement line. If you adjust the waistline area, be sure to retain ½″ to 1″ extra for ease.

After pleats and hems are completed, retain only the basting at the upper edge and baste grosgrain ribbon to the skirt again. Try it on before attaching to the garment or waistband. If your pleats do not fall straight to the hem but tend to open up, raise the skirt at the waist until the hem is even, using a larger waistline seam allowance. However, if the pleats overlap, drop the waist until the hem is even, using a small waistline seam allowance.

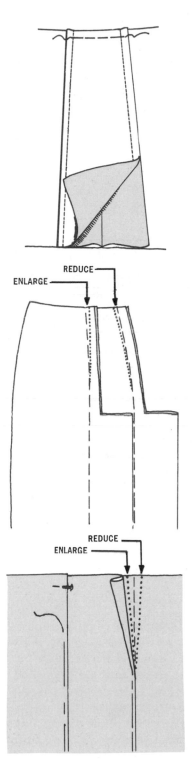

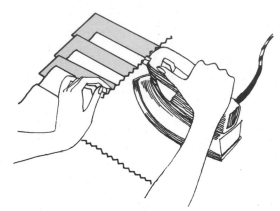

Pressing

If you discover that light pressing creates an unattractive ridge or line on your fabric, insert strips of brown paper under the fold of the pleat before you press. To assure yourself of a sharp, lasting press, iron on both sides of the pleats. Unpressed pleats may require a very slight steaming just to set the shape and fall of the pleat as the designer intended. This can be done most effectively as the garment hangs on your dress form.

Edgestitching

When you are certain that your pleats fit and hang properly, are well pressed, and are hemmed evenly, the folds can be edgestitched to keep creases sharp. This should be done before the skirt is permanently attached to the garment or waistband.

SKIRTS WITH SHAPED AND STITCHED PLEATS: Release the stitching for about 1″ at the hipline of each pleat. Edgestitch the creased edge of each pleat on the outside from the hem to the hipline. Connecting stitches, topstitch along the seam through all thicknesses from the hipline to the waistline. Then pull the thread ends to the inside and tie.

SKIRTS WITH STRAIGHT PLEATS: Stitch close to the outside creased edge of each pleat from the hem up toward the waistline. You may also want to stitch the inside folds on the wrong side.

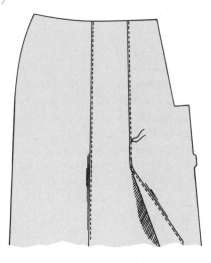

Zipper Applications

A zipper is the easiest and most secure way to close a pleated garment. For knife pleated skirts, see Zippers, page 333. For shaped and seamed pleats, use an invisible zipper application, found on page 328.

For box or inverted pleats and pleats with an underlay, the zipper is usually placed at the left side or center back seam, where the folds of the pleats meet. In this case, either the centered application or the invisible zipper will work successfully. It is wise under all circumstances to follow your pattern recommendations. However, if you have gone out on a creative limb and your garment does not lend itself to a zipper, try binding the edges or using a continuous lapped placket as on page 318.

Commercial Pleating

To find a firm doing commercial pleating, refer to your Yellow Pages, check fashion magazines, or inquire at the notions counter of a department store in your city. Before you take your fabric, ask the pleater exactly how large the piece must be and what you must do to prepare it.

ACCORDION OR SUNBURST PLEATS: These pleats can only be successfully made by a commercial pleater. They are usually pleated into sections; the sections are then joined together along the long straight edges, and the zipper is inserted. Easestitch along the waist seamline, then enclose in a seam or waistband. If you have relatively large accordion pleats (an inch or so), lap one over the other occasionally as you easestitch to fit the pleats into the desired area. Use a rolled or narrow hem to finish the lower edge.

KNIFE PLEATS: These are often made more expediently by commercial methods. Prepare the fabric by stitching all the seams, except the one that will contain the opening, and complete the hem. After the garment has been pleated, locate the remaining seam at an inside fold of a pleat. Remove stitches from hem for about 3″ and stitch the last seam, leaving an opening. Finish the opening with placket or zipper and complete hem. A faster method would be to stitch the last seam through the hem and overcast the raw edges of the hem together, and then finish the opening. For additional information on handling hems in pleats, see page 340.

Godets

A godet can be used to add flounce to a sleeve or swing to a skirt. It can be a pie-shaped, semi-circular, rectangular, or pleated piece of fabric set into a seam, dart, cut-out, or slash to give extra width to a hem. The godet lends great mobility and comfort, and it can be an exciting and lively fashion detail as well.

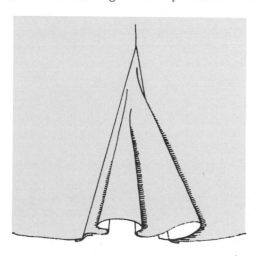 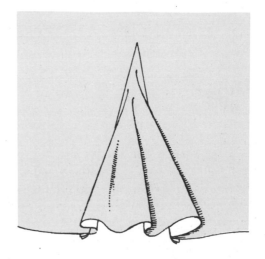

Inserting the Godet

A pie-shaped godet (the most common one) is usually cut with straight grain down the center of the piece of fabric, leaving bias edges on the sides. When fabric is particularly heavy or stretchy, ribbon seam binding should be centered over the seamlines and basted to the wrong side of the main garment pieces for support. With heavy or loosely-woven fabrics, stitch the godet to the garment for only a few inches on either side of the point and let the remainder of the godet hang free for at least 24 hours to allow the bias to set. Pin or baste the free seam allowances of the godet to the garment where they fall; then complete stitching. This is an exception to the rule of always stitching with the grain. Cut away any extra fabric at the bottom of the godet.

IN A SLASH: This treatment presents two problems—stitching a perfect point at the end of the slash and adjusting the bias edge of the godet to the straighter edges of the slash. Reinforce and stay the stitching lines of the slash by sewing just inside the seamlines in the seam allowance, using small stitches (15-20 per inch) on both sides of the point and pivoting at the point. Where fabric is especially fragile, a patch of underlining fabric should be used for reinforcement, as in Gussets, page 293. At the point, clip exactly to the stitching (1). Pin the godet to the slash, turning the patch inside and matching the godet marking to the clipped point first. Baste and stitch, slashed side up, on either side of the point. Hang to let bias set; then baste and stitch from point to hem (2).

IN A SEAM OR DART: First stitch the seam or dart to the marking; pull threads through and tie securely. Pin godet to garment, matching seamlines and markings. Baste, stitch, hang to set bias, and complete same as in a slash (3).

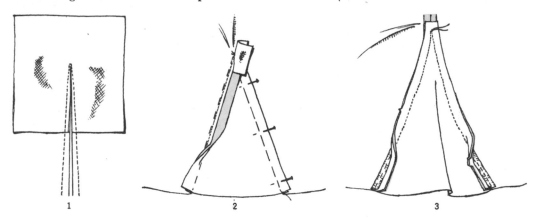

1   2   3

Finishing

PRESSING: When a godet is set into a seam or dart it may be pressed open as follows. For a dart, slash within ½″ to 1″ of the point and press open with the point flat. Clip the seam allowance of the godet 1″ below the point. Press seam allowances open below the clip, toward the garment above the clip, and press seam allowances open above the godet (1). When set into a slash, a godet is usually most effective if all seam allowances are pressed entirely toward the garment (2). If the godet seam is to remain unpressed, the hem must be treated as the hem of a seamed pleat, page 340.

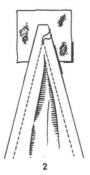

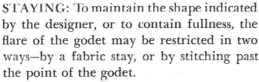

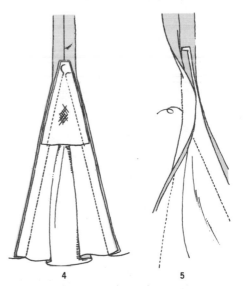

3

TOPSTITCHING: This can be a particularly attractive finishing detail on a casual garment with a godet. It may be added to any type of godet insertion and is usually done on the garment rather than the godet. Press all seam allowances toward the garment and topstitch through all layers (3).

STAYING: To maintain the shape indicated by the designer, or to contain fullness, the flare of the godet may be restricted in two ways—by a fabric stay, or by stitching past the point of the godet.

A fabric stay is used to slightly release the flare toward the outside. Try on the garment and experiment with the hang of the godet to determine the size of the stay. Then measure and cut an underlining triangle to the desired width and length. Stitch it into the godet seams, stitching next to the seamline in the seam allowance (4).

You may prefer to have the godet held in a sharp point to the outside. Stitch the finished seam again past the point of the godet, with the godet toward the outside (5).

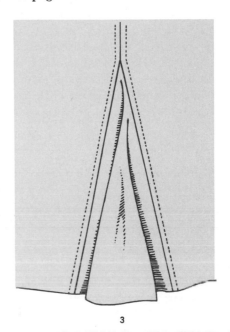

4   5

HEM: Allow garment to hang 24 hours before hemming. Often small, flat lead weights attached to the garment hem adjoining the godet or a stiffening of horsehair braid help achieve the intended effect of the godet. For the various hemming techniques, see Hems, pages 337-340 and 383-384.

Mitering

Like the use of wine in cooking, mitering is a subtle art. When successful, it merely enhances the total effect; it is noticeable only when incorrect. Mitering is a neat and easy means of eliminating bulk at corners. Since your goal is to achieve a flat, neat looking miter, you must concentrate on trimming at just the right moment in your mitering plan. Also remember that most miters involve folds, either at right angles or 45° angles to the seam or strip being mitered. The method you use to miter depends on many factors—whether you are working with garment areas, binding, or continuous strips of trim, and whether the miter is made as you attach the trim or before application.

Continuous Strips

If your band or trim has seam allowances, press them to the inside before you begin mitering. To miter the band before it is applied, pin the band to the garment for an accurate measurement of where the miter should be made. Measure to the outermost point where the corner will be formed, and mark with a pin.

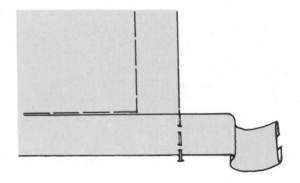

Remove band and fold it with right sides together at marked point (1). Turn the fold diagonally to meet the turned-back edges of band, as shown, and press (2). Open the diagonal fold and stitch along the pressed crease. ❖ Since it is important that the knots do not show once the miter is finished, pull the thread ends to one side of the band and knot. Trim to ⅛″ and press the seam open (3). Then attach the strip (4).

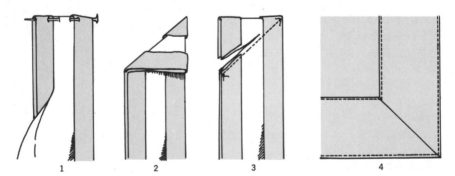

To miter while you are attaching the trim, as shown on the next page, use trim with a finished edge such as ribbon or braid. Pin trim in position, then edgestitch or hand sew the inner edge (1). Fold the band back on itself, then diagonally to the side, making a right angle; press.

Again fold the band back on itself and stitch on the diagonal crease—through the band and garment.   Since it is important that the knots are invisible once the miter is finished, pull the thread ends to one side of the band, as shown, and knot (2). If trim is bulky, you may trim the small corner close to the stitching. Press flat from the right side, miter remaining corners, and edgestitch or hand sew outer edge in a continuous motion (3).

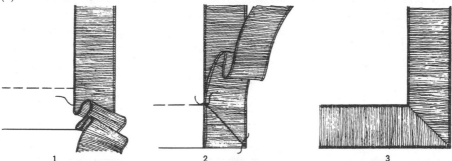

Square Corners

Pockets, appliqués, or any other applied areas requiring square corners, need to be mitered so the excess fullness can be easily trimmed away. Pressing is the key feature. Turn all seam allowances to inside and press (1). At the corners, open the seam allowances and turn them to the inside diagonally across the point, as shown, and press. Trim corner to ⅜″ from the pressed diagonal crease (2). Slipstitch to fasten miter (3).

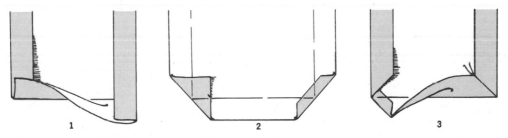

For a quick sturdier method, make a diagonal fold in the turned-back seam allowances at the corners and press. Stitch along the pressed diagonal crease (1). Trim the seam to ⅜″ or less for bulkier fabrics, as shown.   Press diagonal seam open (2), then turn the corners to the inside (3). Press.

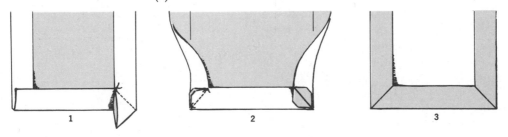

Bindings

The versatile bias binding was designed to enclose raw edges, thus providing a finish that both conceals and strengthens them. A binding can be beautiful as decorative trim around closure edges—whether you use self-fabric or a contrasting fabric. It can be helpful around a neckline or armhole when used in place of facings. One of the greater satisfactions of sewing is a bias binding that turns smoothly and evenly over an edge with nary a twist, a pull, or a ripple to mar its flat surface. To achieve a perfect binding, cut strips of fabric evenly on the true bias, join them on the grain, and press and shape them before application.

Cut Bias Strips

The ideal bias strip is cut from one piece of fabric long enough to fit the desired area. However, this is not always the most economical usage of the fabric, so piecing becomes a necessity. This can be done in one of two ways—by continuous pieced strips or by individual pieced strips.

For either method, take a rectangular piece of fabric cut on the straight grain. Fold it diagonally at one end, as shown, to find the true bias. Using the bias fold as a guide, mark fabric with parallel lines the desired width of the bias strips, marking as many strips as needed, allowing for ¼″ seams. Make a diagonal fold along last line of markings and cut along both folds, discarding the triangular ends. Mark a ¼″ seamline on both ends as shown (1). See binding application methods, pages 246-249.

CONTINUOUS PIECED STRIPS: Continuous pieced strips are easy to make. On the marked piece of fabric, join the shorter ends, right sides together, with one strip width extending beyond the edge at each side. Stitch in a ¼″ seam and press it open. Begin cutting on the marked line at one end and continue in circular fashion (2).

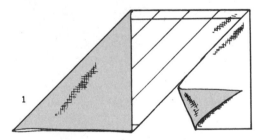

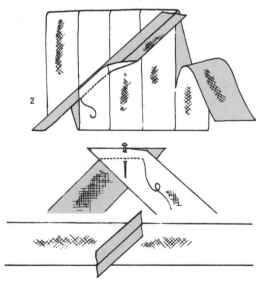

INDIVIDUAL PIECED STRIPS: Individually pieced strips are more time consuming. Cut along the markings for the bias strips. The short ends, previously cut on the grain, will appear diagonal. Mark a seamline ¼″ from each end. With right sides of the strip together, match the seamlines (not the cut edges), pin, and stitch. Press the seam open.

Commercial Binding

You can purchase bias strips ready-made in a variety of colors and a choice of several widths. Whether single or double-fold, the edges are usually pressed under for your convenience. Depending upon your needs, the folds can be pressed open and the full width of the bias made available. The techniques used for applying or piecing the commercial bias strips are the same as those suggested for bias cut strips you have made yourself. No matter which type of binding you are using, it should be pre-shaped to conform to the area where it will be stitched. Look below for the best method of pre-shaping.

Pre-Shape the Binding

First, the bias should be pressed to pre-shape the strip and to take out the extra slack by steaming and stretching it gently (1). You will then have a slightly narrower taut strip to work with, eliminating the problem of a wobbling seamline. Fold the strip in half lengthwise, wrong sides together, and press again lightly (2). Then for single binding, open, fold cut edges toward the center, and press lightly (3). Lastly, shape the tape into curves that correspond to those on the garment (4). Since one folded edge of the finished binding will be even with the seamline of the garment, you must always trim the seam allowance from the edge to be bound. When applying the bias strips to the garment, try to place the piecing seamlines at inconspicuous locations wherever possible. Also, leave 2″ extra on the bias strip free at the beginning of any application for finishing. Note: Commercial binding can be shaped, but the slack has already been removed by the manufacturer.

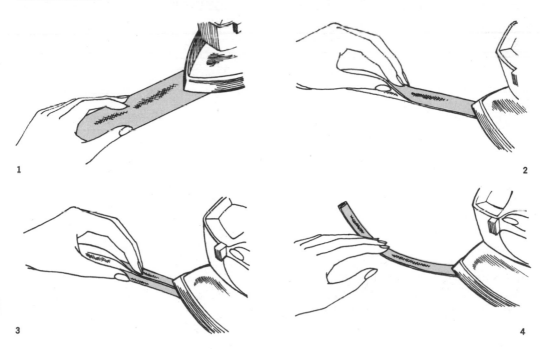

1

2

3

4

Single Binding

Trim the seam allowance from the garment edges to be bound. Cut bias strips four times the desired finished width plus ¼" to ⅜", depending on your fabric. This will give you ample width for stretching and turning. Pre-shape your bias strip with a steam iron, as shown earlier, to match the curves of the garment edge. Open out the bias strip and, with right sides together and the raw edge of the strip even with the raw edge of the garment, pin it to the garment. Baste the strip at a distance from the edge slightly less than the width of the finished binding. Stitch next to but not on the basting, so that the basting threads can be easily removed (1). Turn bias over the seam allowance. Pin and slipstitch over the seamline (2).

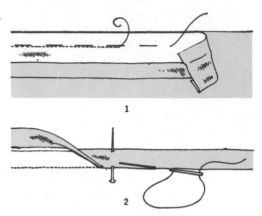

Double Binding or French Binding

This method makes an attractive finish for sheers. Trim the garment seam allowances. Cut bias strips six times the desired finished width plus ¼" to ⅜" to allow for stretching and turning. Fold the strip in half lengthwise with wrong sides together, and press lightly. Pre-shape the bias to match the garment edge. Trim raw edges so entire strip can be folded equally. Divide it into equal thirds and press again. Open out the folded edge of the strip. With raw edges of strip and garment even, pin the strip to the right side. Baste the strip at a distance from the edge slightly less than the width of the finished binding; stitch next to the basting (1). Turn the strip over the seam allowances and slipstitch in place (2).

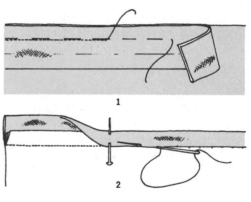

Machine Applied Binding

This is a speedy, one-step method in which success depends upon careful pressing. Pre-shape the bias strip as mentioned previously, with one very notable exception. Instead

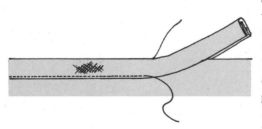

of folding the tape equally in half lengthwise, fold the bottom half slightly wider than the top half, as shown. This overlap on the bottom half will ensure its being caught by the machine stitching. With the wider edge on the wrong side, encase the trimmed garment edge with the folded bias strip. Edgestitch through all layers, as shown, and your binding is completed.

Corners

When bias bindings are used as trim, they will often have to be applied around corners. This can be the most difficult operation when you are using a binding.

OUTWARD CORNERS: Open out one pre-folded edge of your bias strip; then pin or baste it in place as for Single or double binding. Stitch from one end to the corner and backstitch for reinforcement (1). Fold the strip diagonally, as shown, to bring it around the corner. Pin or baste, then stitch the adjoining edge through the corner from one end to the other end (2). Fold to form a miter at the corner on the right side and turn the bias over the seam (3). To finish the wrong side, form a miter (with the fold of the miter in the opposite direction from the one formed on the right side, so that the bulk of the miter will be evenly distributed). Turn, pin, and slipstitch the binding over the seamline, fastening the miter at the corner, if desired (4).

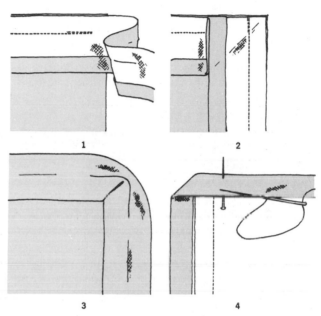

INWARD CORNERS: Reinforce the corner along your planned seamline, as instructed on page 215 (1). Open out one pre-folded edge of your bias strip; then pin and baste it to the garment, pulling the corners so the binding remains straight. Stitch from the wrong side of the garment, keeping the binding straight (2). Form a miter on the right side (3). Pull the fold of the miter to the wrong side through the clip, and form a miter on the wrong side in the reverse direction from the one on the right side (4). Turn, pin, and slipstitch the binding over the seamline, fastening the fold of the miter at the corner, if desired (5).

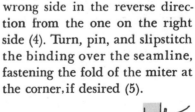

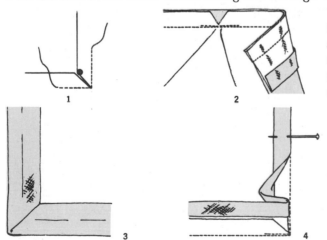

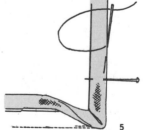

When making machine finished binding for an outward or inward corner, pin and baste the bias strip to the edge as for single or double binding. Form a miter at the corner, as on the preceding page. For machine stitching, follow the directions for machine applied binding, page 246, remembering to pivot at the corner. If desired, fasten the fold of the miter with slipstitches.

Joinings

A joining is often required where the binding is applied to a long or continuous edge, such as a front closure or hem. Try to locate the joining at an inconspicuous place.

A binding applied as described in Single or Double Binding is joined by stopping your stitching slightly before reaching the area of the joining. Open out the strip and fold the garment so the strip ends are at right angles as they are for piecing, page 244. Stitch the ends close to the garment, but without catching the garment in the stitching. Trim the seam allowances to ¼″ and press open. Complete stitching the strip to the garment across the joining. Now you may finish by slipstitching the binding over the seam.

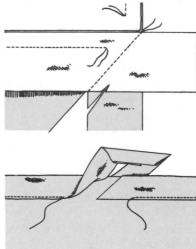

To lap a machine applied binding, edgestitch to within 2″ of the starting point, leaving extra binding on both ends. Fold one end to the inside on straight grain and trim to ¼″. Trim the other end as shown, also on the straight grain. Pin or baste and continue stitching across the joining. Slipstitch the joining if desired.

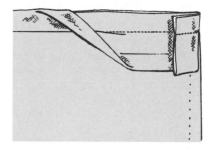

Endings

Binding an edge which ends at a seam or opening requires a special finishing technique. In any of the following cases, the facings should be completed and the seam allowances turned under or the zipper inserted before the binding is applied.

To finish a single or double binding, pin, baste, and stitch the binding to the garment through all layers and to the ends of the bias, which extend about 1″ past the garment opening edge on both ends. Trim the bias ends to ¼″ beyond the garment edge. Then trim the garment seam allowance on a diagonal at the corner and fold the extending bias ends back. Turn the strip over the seam allowance, matching the folded edge with the line of machine stitching. Slipstitch the open ends; then pin and slipstitch the folded edge to the garment.

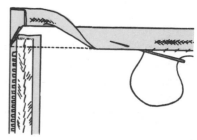

A machine finished binding, since it is applied and stitched in one step, requires care in trimming and stitching the ends to achieve a tidy finish. Fold in about ½″ at one end on the bias grain and trim, as shown. To encase the raw edge of the garment with binding, make sure the under edge is deeper than the top edge and that the ends are even. Starting at one end, edgestitch in place through all layers to about three inches from the other end. Measure and cut off the binding ½″ past the garment fold. Trim; fold in binding end. Complete stitching; finish the open ends with slipstitching.

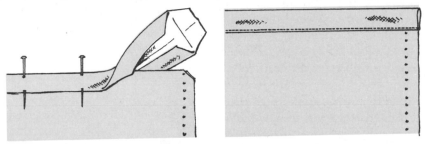

Facings

A well applied facing does much for the look and comfort of your new garment, regardless of where it is used. The purpose of a facing is to neatly finish and conceal a raw edge by turning it to the wrong side of your garment. Your facing will always perform this task beautifully if you consistently strive for a smooth, flat appearance.

Although the shape and actual construction of facings vary stylistically, they fall into three basic categories—a shaped facing, an extended facing, or a bias facing. Let your fabric and the edge to be faced determine the most suitable method.

There are some construction procedures that can be used on all types of facings to produce the best results, as well as to simplify the work at hand. The garment edge is usually stabilized or reinforced in some manner, either by small stitches, interfacing, or ribbon seam binding. Except for the bias facing, one edge of most facings must be finished since it will be exposed on the inside of the garment. A sturdy way of finishing many facings is to stitch ¼″ from the unnotched edge, trim to ⅛″ and overcast; or zigzag.

For a more attractively finished appearance with added fashion interest, you may try enclosing the edges with bias binding, stretch lace, or other lightweight, flexible trims. When the facing is attached, press the seam or foldlines carefully before you turn and tack the facings to the inside of the garment. To prevent any shaped facing or variation of it, such as the combination facing, from rolling to the outside, open out the facing and understitch it to the seam allowances. If the facing edge is at a visible area, you can *favor* the garment slightly along the seamline so that the facing does not show. You should, however, use caution or you may destroy the clean line of the edge. Always tack the facing to the inside of the garment to keep it in place. Blindstitch the facing to the underlining only, or if the garment is not underlined, sew it to the inner seam allowances. Tack loosely; many short, tight stitches will give your garment a strained or puckered appearance. When making adjustments and alterations on your garment, don't forget the facings! They must be changed to conform to the new lines of the garment.

Extended Facing

An extended facing is cut in one piece with the garment, and folded to the inside. It is used mainly for finishing edges where seams are not necessary because the edge to be finished is cut on a straight line and can simply be extended. Extended facings can finish many areas of a garment which have a fold at the edge rather than a seam.

Because extended facing edges are usually overlapped, be sure to transfer position lines with thread tracing. Interface for reinforcement, especially if a buttonhole closing is intended. Your pattern will usually include a tissue for the interfacing.

Use long running stitches to attach the interfacing to the garment or underlining along the foldline. Catchstitch the remaining edges. For a finer finish or if you are using a bulky fabric, trim the underlining from the facing ¼" from the interfacing edge (1).

Turn facing to the right side along the foldline. Seam binding or twill tape may be applied as a stay, if necessary. Pin seam binding to the interfacing seam allowance which extends beyond the foldline. Hand or machine stitch close to the edge of the seam binding.

If your pattern doesn't include an interfacing piece, cut the interfacing from the facing portion of the garment pattern, plus a ⅝" extension at the foldline. Trim ⅜" from the edge opposite the foldline and ⅝" from the shoulder and neck edges. Then attach the interfacing as above.

If additional facing sections are to be joined to the extended facing, attach these sections before stitching the facing to the garment. Trim, grade, and clip the seam allowances (2). Turn the facing to the inside and press. Understitch close to the neckline seam through the facing and the seam allowances just as you would a shaped facing. Finish the raw edge and anchor the facing (3).

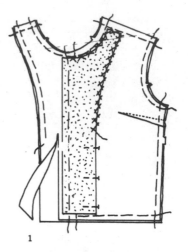

1

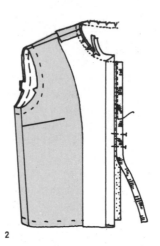

2

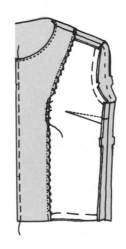

3

Shaped Facing

A shaped or fitted facing is the most commonly selected method used to finish necklines and sleeveless armholes. It is a separate piece provided with your pattern and cut to match the shape of the area to which it will be applied. You will often find it desirable not to underline these facings in order to reduce unnecessary bulk.

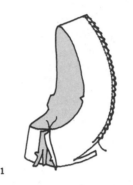

Prepare the facing by stitching, trimming, and pressing the seams. One edge of the facing must be finished since it will be exposed on the inside of the garment. Stitch $1/4$" from the unnotched edge, trim to $1/8$", and overcast (1); or zigzag stitch the raw edges.

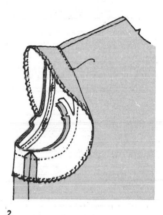

1

To prevent stretching of a curved or bias area, reinforce with stretched bias binding before attaching the facing. Center, then baste the bias binding over the seamline on the inside of garment—not on facing, which must be able to mold to the garment edge. Reinforce corners, such as those on a V-neckline or square armhole, with small stitches on the seamline for an inch on either side of the point.

2

Pin and baste, matching seams and markings. Then with the facing side up, stitch the facing to the garment. Trim, grade, and clip the seam allowances. Press the seam allowances toward the facing.

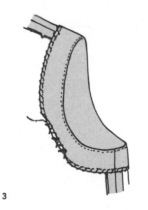

To keep the facing from rolling to the outside, open out the facing and understitch it to the seam allowances pulling it taut as you stitch (2). Understitch by hand on custom clothes, using small backstitches close to the seam through the seam allowances and facing. On casual clothes which must be durable enough to withstand repeated machine washings, this same operation can be successfully accomplished by machine stitching. Turn the facing to the inside and press. Blindstitch the free edge to the underlining (3). If your garment is not underlined, tack the facing to the inner seams.

3

Combination Facings

This is a variation of the shaped facing in which the neckline and armhole facings are cut and applied as one piece. It is often used on garments with narrow shoulder seams, as a dress with cut-away armholes. You will find it quite simple to apply if you remember one rule; do not sew the shoulder seams of either the garment or the facing until after the facing is stitched to the garment.

❋ Prior to pinning the facing to the garment, pin a minute tuck in both garment shoulders, as shown. This ensures that the seams and facing will not show on the right side once the facing is turned (1).

Join the garment sections at the side seams, leaving the shoulder seams open, and press. Join the facing sections together in the same manner and press. Then, finish the un-notched edge as desired.

Pin the facing to the garment, right sides together. Since the raw edges will not be even, follow the seamline of the facing. Stitch to within ⅝" from shoulder edges and backstitch. Grade; clip seam allowances (2).

Release the tuck in the garment shoulders. Turn the facing to the inside and press. To prevent the facing from rolling to the outside, understitch it to the seam allowances close to the seam. Fold the facing seam allowances back and stitch the garment shoulder seams, carefully keeping the facing free (3).

Do not tie threads at the seam edge. Bring both threads to one side and tie so the knots will not show when the facing is completed.

You may wish to reinforce a curved neckline with ribbon seam binding, or a square neckline with small stitches at the corners.

Trim and press open the garment seams. Turn in the facing edges and slipstitch them together over the garment seam (4). On bulky fabric you may wish to trim the facing seam allowance to ¼" before turning them in.

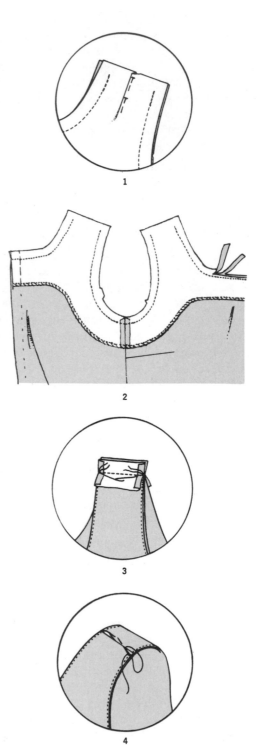

1

2

3

4

Bias Facing

Ease of handling and versatility make a bias facing a suitable replacement for your regular shaped facing. It is particularly useful when you do not want to use your garment fabric (if it is scratchy or bulky) or where a wide facing may be objectionable (as in sheers).

Cut a bias strip from your lining or underlining fabric four times the desired width plus $\frac{1}{4}$" to $\frac{3}{8}$" to allow for shaping (or use double-fold bias tape with folds pressed open) and the length of the garment edge plus 2" to allow for finishing the ends.

Fold the strip in half lengthwise. Press the strip lightly, steaming and stretching it into curves corresponding to those of the garment edge. As the bias takes shape, its width will become distorted. Equalize the width of the bias facing by measuring from the folded edge the desired facing width plus a $\frac{1}{4}$" seam allowance, marking the strip as you work. Trim away excess fabric along markings.

Your closure should be completed before you apply your bias facing. If you have a zipper, trim the zipper tape away below the seamline. Trim the garment seam allowance to $\frac{1}{4}$". With raw edges even, place the folded strip on the right side of the garment with 1" extending beyond the closing edges. Pin, baste, and stitch directionally with grain continuing to the ends of the bias strip (1).

Clip the seam allowances, and trim the two extending bias ends to $\frac{1}{4}$". Turn the bias strip to the inside, *favoring* the garment edge slightly so that the binding is inconspicuous. Turn the bias ends in (2). Pin the bias strip in position and slipstitch the folded edge to the underlining (3). Finally, fasten the closing edges with a hook and eye.

If the facing ends meet, as on an armhole, fold in the ends $\frac{1}{4}$". Trim the excess length and slipstitch free ends together to finish.

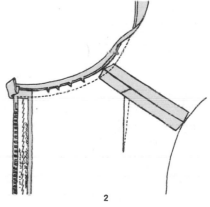

1

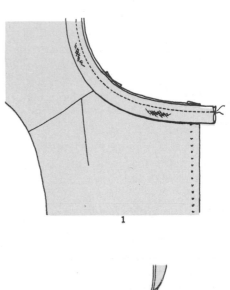

2

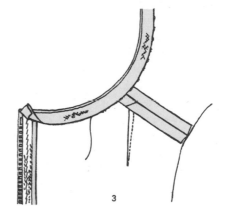

3

Neckline Finishes

If you covet that custom-made look, you must aim for a flat, smooth line at the neck. Never take shortcuts on the neckline or, no matter how much loving attention you have given to other details, you may sacrifice the appearance of the entire garment.

Should you be working with soft or loosely woven fabrics which tend to stretch, stabilize the neck area with interfacing or ribbon seam binding. Attach either reinforcement to the wrong side of the neckline before you begin the neckline finish.

Pin your neckline finish to the garment, carefully matching seams, markings, notches, and centers. All neckline finishes require your thorough understanding of trimming, grading, and understitching. Trim and grade every seam after stitching. Always clip or notch corners and curves to avoid unsightly puckers. Understitch the facing close to the seam so it won't roll to the outside. Then complete the neckline by attaching handwork only to the underlining so that the stitches won't show.

Shaped or Fitted Facing

A shaped facing is the most common type of neckline finish and its uses are almost inexhaustible, ranging from round to square to V-shaped necklines. Although we illustrate a V-neckline because its extreme shape tends to create problems, our instructions will supply you with all the basic techniques needed to construct a variety of perfectly flat, smooth necklines—neatly finished with corresponding shaped facings.

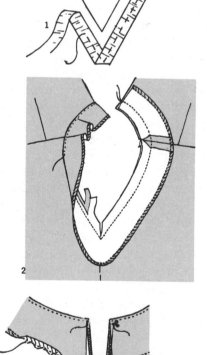

Stitch the facing pieces together; trim and press. Then finish the unnotched facing edge. Because many necklines are cut on the bias grain, they must be reinforced with ribbon seam binding to prevent stretching. On the wrong side of your garment, center and baste ribbon seam binding over the seamline, folding out fullness at any points or corners (1). Pin and baste the facing to the neck edge. Stitch, pivoting at any points or corners. Grade and clip the seam allowances. Press the seam toward the facing and understitch (2). Turn the facing to the inside and press. If your pattern requires a zipper, insert it. Turn the facing ends under to clear the zipper teeth and slipstitch the ends in place. Blindstitch facing edge to underlining and fasten with a hook and eye (3).

Slashed Opening

Shaped facings are used in conjunction with slash necklines. They are usually combined with high round necklines. Interface the neckline and opening so that the opening will lie flat without drooping. If your pattern doesn't include an interfacing tissue, make your own. Cut the interfacing the same as the facing. Trim all seam allowances away, including the opening edges and ⅜″ from the inner edges of the interfacing sections. Pin the corresponding interfacing sections to the front and back garment pieces and catchstitch them to the underlining along the seamline (1). Stitch the back of the garment to the front at the shoulders and press open. Join the facing back and front in the same manner. Trim the facing shoulder seam allowances. Finish the unnotched edge as desired.

Pin and baste the facing to the garment along the stitching lines of the opening and neck edge. Stitch the opening to within 2″ of the point. Then change to smaller stitches (15-20 per inch according to your fabric) for 2″ on either side of the point and take one stitch across the point. Stitch remainder of opening and neck edge, pivoting at corners. Slash opening to machine stitching, being careful not to cut through it. Trim opening edges if necessary for firmly woven or heavy fabrics. Trim, grade, and clip the neck seam so that the garment seam allowance is left widest (2).

Turn and press the facing to the inside. To keep the facing from rolling to the outside, understitch it to the seam allowances. Anchor the facing to the underlining or tack it to the shoulder seam allowances (3).

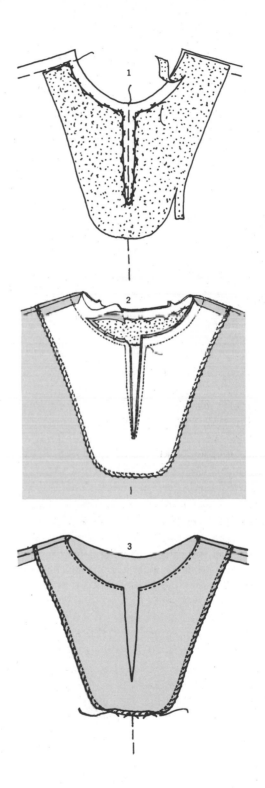

Bound Neckline

Bound necklines share the versatility of shaped facings and can be used to finish virtually any type of neckline. Its bias qualities make binding particularly suited for curved edges. Refer to Bindings, page 244, for instructions in preparation and application.

Corded or Piped Neckline

This finish can be added to any neckline. The distinction between piping and cording refers to the size of the filler used: piping is thin; cording is thick. First cut a bias strip (the size of the filler) plus ¼″ to ⅜″ and two ⅝″ seam allowances. Allow at least ⅝″ for finishing the ends. Bring the bias strip around the filler, matching the raw edges. With your zipper foot and using 8-10 stitches per inch, stitch close to, but not on, the filler. Baste the corded or piped strip to the right side of the garment, matching seamlines.

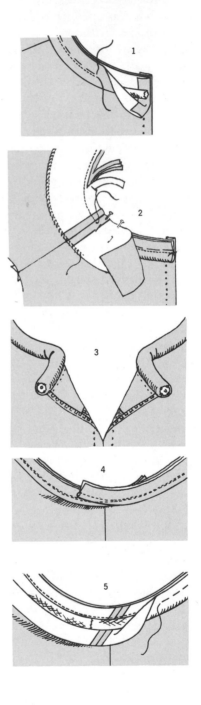

Finish the raw ends according to the nature of the neckline and the filler thickness. To finish ends at a closing, pull the bias back, removing stitches for 1½″, exposing the filler. Cut the filler off just inside the end of the opening, leaving the empty bias strip. Fold in the bias ends (1). Slipstitch the ends and restitch the bias, enclosing the filler. Using a zipper foot, apply a shaped facing (2). For thick cording, apply snaps to the ends (3). Narrow cording or piping requires a regular hook and eye closure on the garment.

On a neck edge without a closing, place the joining at the shoulder seam or other inconspicuous location. For narrow piping, pull the bias back, removing a few stitches from the bias so you can cut the filler off where the ends cross. Overlap the two empty bias ends, easing the ends of the bias slightly toward the seam (4). For thick cording, do not enclose the filler with bias until you have stitched one edge of the bias to the garment and pieced it. Then, using the proper length of filler for the neckline, enclose it in the bias, using a zipper foot (5). Apply a shaped facing over all piping or cording with a zipper foot.

Applied Band

An applied band can take many shapes, such as square, round, keyhole, or V-necklines. It is often used as a decorative device.

Carefully mark all construction symbols. Staystitch the neck edge of the garment directionally and insert the zipper. Interface one band section, trimming away the interfacing seam allowances and catchstitching the interfacing to the band along seamlines. (If the band sections have seams, stitch them before you join the band to its facing.) Then pin and baste the band sections together, leaving the notched edge open. Stitch; then trim, grade, and clip the seam allowances, leaving the interfaced band seam allowance widest (1). To make the final pressing easier, press the neckline seams open. Then turn the band and press it flat.

Pin and baste the edge of the interfaced band section to the garment, matching markings at shoulder seams and clipping the garment seam allowance. Stitch from the band side for the best control, then trim and grade the seam, leaving the garment seam allowance the widest (2). Notch the band seam allowances to eliminate extra fullness so that all seam allowances can be pressed toward the band. Turn the band, rolling the neckline seam just slightly to the inside to prevent it from being seen on the finished garment; pin.

Depending on whether you desire a pronounced band or a flat finish, there are two ways to complete an applied band. For a pronounced band, turn the remaining free edge under where it falls over the stitching and baste close to the edge. Trim away any excess seam allowance close to the basting. Slipstitch the band over the seamline (3). When a flat finish is desirable, finish the free edge with a stitch and overcast or zigzag treatment. Do not turn the edge under, however. Just blindstitch the free edge where it falls, covering the band seam completely (4). Fasten the band with hooks and thread eyes.

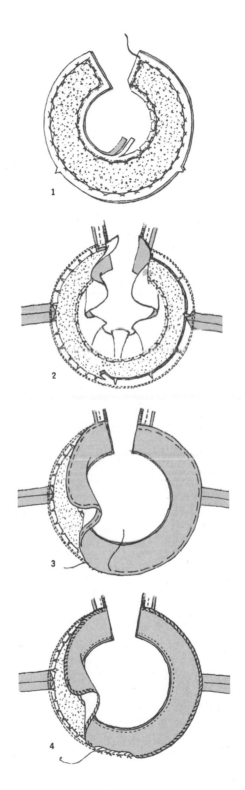

Neckline Placket

A neckline placket is a variation of the applied band. Reinforce the front opening corners with small stitches on the seamline, pivoting at corner. Clip to corners. Stitch shoulder seams, then staystitch the neck and front edges of garment (1). Insert your zipper.

To prevent stretching, staystitch the notched edge of the neckband sections. Interface and construct each band as for the applied band, page 257, stitching along the curved unnotched edges and center back. Leave the lower ends free. Trim and grade the seam allowances, clipping and notching where necessary to allow the bands to lie flat (2). For easier turning, press the seam open first. Then turn the bands and press them flat.

Leaving the lower end free, baste the interfaced edge of the left neckband to the left half of the garment, clipping where necessary. Stitch with the neckband up. Trim, grade, notch, and press the curved seam allowances toward the band. Turn the free edge of the band under and baste close to the fold, clipping as necessary for the band to lie flat; slipstitch (3). (Or, for bulky fabrics, use the optional method described in Applied Bands, illustration #4.) Do not turn the band under at the lower edge. Just stitch across the end through garment and band (4). Press the lower end toward the garment.

Apply the right neckband to the right half of the garment as above, ending stitching at the right front corner (5). Finish the lower end by turning in and grading the seam allowances and slipstitching them together (6).

Lap the right band over the left band, matching centers. Slipstitch the lower edge in place along the seamline. Sew buttons or invisibly tack the bands together at the markings.

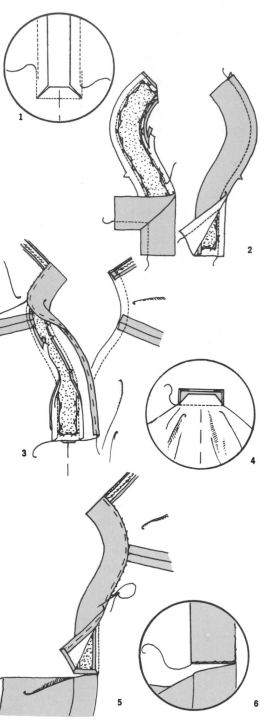

Cowl Neckline

A cowl usually consists of a yoke cut on the bias for draping ability and a stay cut on straight grain for reinforcement so that the cowl will drape as the designer intended. The stay is usually cut from lining fabric. In this neckline, pattern markings are especially important.

Join the underlined yoke sections at the shoulders. Press the seams open and clip. Center and baste ribbon seam binding over the back seamlines of the yoke between markings.

Prepare a narrow shaped facing, finishing the inner unnotched edge as desired. Being sure to match markings, pin, baste and stitch the facing to the yoke; stretch the yoke to fit. Trim and grade the seam, press it open and clip where necessary. **Roll** the facing to the inside (1).

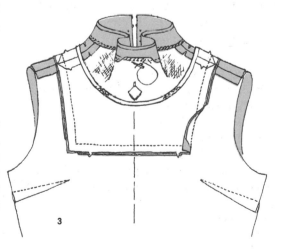

To press, hold the iron over the rolled edge. Steam, never resting the iron on the fabric, and pat lightly with a clapper. If you do not have a clapper, use a ruler.

Stitch the darts in the back stay and press them toward center back. Stitch the back and front stay at the shoulders. Press the seams open. To finish the stay neck line, use double-fold bias tape pressed open, or a 2″ wide bias strip of lining fabric, applied as a bias facing. Place the right side of the stay on the wrong side of the yoke. Baste the raw edges together, stretching the lower yoke edge to fit (2).

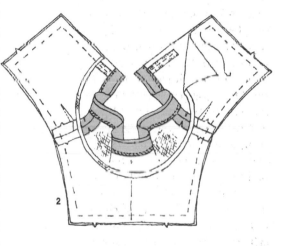

Baste and stitch the yoke to the garment. For pressing and finishing corners, refer to Seams and Seam Finishes, page 211. Insert your zipper and blindstitch the facing to the underlining. If your fabric needs a weight in order to drape properly, cover a flat weight (see page 381) and attach it to the cowl underlining with a French tack (3). Experiment with the placement of the weight to determine its most functional position.

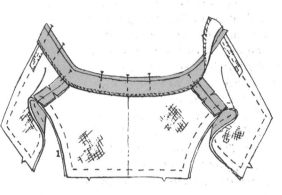

Collars

A visible mark of quality workmanship on a garment is its collar. Regardless of style, the collar is a detail that requires careful handling in every stage of construction in order to retain its quality appearance. When you're browsing through a fashion magazine or pattern catalogue, you'll find the variation in collars can be quite staggering. But however exotic the collar shape may seem, three basic shapes—flat, standing, and rolled—are the starting point for all variations.

The deeper the curve on the collar neck edge, the flatter your collar will lie, especially as the curve corresponds more closely to that of your garment neck edge. A flat collar is almost identical to the garment in the shape of its neck edge; while the opposite extreme, the standing collar, will have a straight or very slightly curved neck edge. The neck edge of a rolled collar can vary in shape from straight to a curve opposite that of the garment; how close it comes to the neck, and the depth of the roll, are determined by the shape of the collar neck edge. This collar gently rises from the neck seam and turns down to create a rolled edge around the neck. The line along which the collar is turned is called the **roll line** or **roll.**

Any rolled collar should be characterized by a smooth roll with the neck seam completely covered. We cannot overemphasize the importance of establishing the proper roll of your collar. The pattern piece for the upper collar is usually larger than that for the undercollar. This ease allows the collar to roll and accommodates the depth of your fabric. However, only an average roll depth can be allowed on most pattern pieces, so you may have to add as much as ¼″ to ⅜″ to the upper collar to allow for very bulky or heavy fabric. Then be sure to ease or stretch the collar sections to each other when you stitch them together.

The very best way to ensure that your collar will look right is to fit it before you permanently attach it to the garment. Baste the collar to the neck edge, **lapping** the seams for easier fitting rather than matching them right sides together. Then try the garment on or put it on a dress form and check the features mentioned above, as well as those mentioned for your particular collar type on the following pages.

Here are some rules which any woman can use as a standard to determine whether a collar is well made. All collars with corners and center front or back openings should be symmetrical—with identically shaped curves or points, and the inside edge smoothly encircling the neck without straining or rippling. The underside, or **undercollar,** should never show, nor should seams at the finished edge. If these details check, your collar should hug the garment closely without the corners flipping up or the neck seams showing unintentionally at the back or front of the garment.

The necessary body and shape of the collar are maintained by interfacing, which is usually cut from your collar pattern. The seam allowances are trimmed away, then the interfacing is catchstitched to the undercollar. You will often find that cutting the interfacing on bias grain will help you achieve a more perfect roll. For this situation, you will have to use your own judgment depending on the type of fabric used.

The technique of applying the interfacing, as always, must be determined by a combination of factors—the weight of your fabric, the collar type, and the mood of the garment, whether soft or tailored. Note that a collar meant to be softly rolled, made of a soft or sheer fabric, or part of a very soft style (as in many blouses), may not require interfacing. For those of you who have queries about interfacing selection, detailed suggestions on the subject are part of "The Undercover Story," pages 75–85. If you feel that your fabric or garment requires tailoring techniques (as will many loosely-woven or very firm wools, heavy or bulky fabrics, and suits or coats), refer to the tailoring section.

For a More Perfect Collar

There are some professional tricks we want to highlight because they contribute so much to the finished product if consistently applied to every collar made. Always stitch the collar sections together directionally, stitching with the collar grain. Start stitching at the center first, then stitch toward one end. Repeat for the other half, overlapping stitches ½". At corners use 15-20 stitches per inch and one stitch across the point when the point is very sharp.

The importance of trimming to reduce bulk cannot be stressed enough. This technique is most often overlooked and can be the single contributing factor to an unattractive collar. Trim the seams, grading the ones to be enclosed so that the seam allowance of the upper collar is left the widest. Trim the corners diagonally as closely as possible without cutting into your stitching to ensure that the corner seams will miter once the collar is turned, as for Enclosed Seams, page 216. You should not trim ravelly fabrics closer than ¼" from the seamline. Notch or clip curves so that the seam allowances will lie flat without pulls or bumps when the collar is turned.

❀ There is a professional way to turn and press a collar swiftly and accurately. Pre-press the collar *before* you turn it to the right side and you will not only obtain a more finished appearance, but eliminate problems with "shine" and handling of the fabric on the right side as well. Press the collar seam allowances open over a point presser or a tailor board. Then press the seam allowances toward the undercollar side. Holding the seam allowances together at one corner, turn the collar corner by pulling the upper collar over your hand. Repeat for the other corner. If necessary, use a needle or pin from the right side to pull the corners to a point. *Never* use the point of a scissors to poke corners out because you can easily poke a hole in your fabric.

Press the outer edge, using a press cloth. Carefully *favor* the upper collar edge by rolling the outer seam just slightly to the underside of the collar. This ensures that the seam will not be visible at the edge of the completed collar. For thick or resilient fabrics, flatten and smooth the outer edge with a pounding block.

When you attach the collar, take special care to align the markings of the collar with those on the garment at the shoulders, front, and back. To help ensure a perfectly symmetrical collar, stitch the neck edge directionally also.

Buttonhole placement and the neck seam of the collar are interrelated. Although applying interfacing and bound buttonholes to a flat section of your garment may seem speedier, *do not* complete this operation until you have fitted your garment with its collar. If the neck seams need to be adjusted, re-space buttonhole placements accordingly.

Let us entice you to attempt all kinds of collars without fear. We have attempted to simplify the difficulties of the collar construction by including simple but detailed instructions for the traditional types of collars on the following pages.

Shaped Collar

The shaped collar is unquestionably the easiest collar to make. It is a flat collar with curved edges and angular or curved corners. This collar, often known as a Peter Pan collar, has very little roll because it is cut on straight grain with a neck edge curved like the garment neck edge. Both the upper and undercollar sections are cut from the same pattern piece. The collar itself may be one or two-piece, with or without a front or back opening.

First trim the interfacing and catchstitch it along the seamlines to the section that will be your undercollar. Stitch the collar sections together, leaving the neck edge open. Trim, grade, and notch the seams (1). Then turn and press the collar, favoring the outer edge seam of the section that is to be your upper collar.

Even collars with very little roll need some help from you if they are to be set correctly on the garment. With the upper collar on top, work your collar into the shape shown on the pattern envelope. Roll the neck edge, as shown; then pin along the roll and just above the neck seam (2). To make attaching the collar easier, baste the neck edges as they fall together along the seamline of the undercollar. If your collar is made in two sections, baste the sections together at the center front neckline.

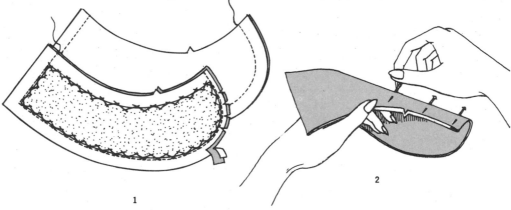

For either a front or back opening, prepare a buttonhole closure by checking the buttonhole placement, then attaching your interfacing to the garment and making the necessary buttonholes. If using a zipper, you may insert it now or after attaching your collar.

With the interfaced section of the collar next to the garment, pin the collar in place, matching markings, and baste (3). The upper collar will bubble slightly, but that is as it should be, since you've shaped the collar over your hand.

If you are finishing the collar seam with a shaped facing, prepare the facing and finish the unnotched edge. Pin or baste the facing to the neck edge over the collar; again match markings, and stitch. Trim, grade, and clip the seams. Turn the facing to the inside and press. Understitch the facing to the neckline seam allowance (4).

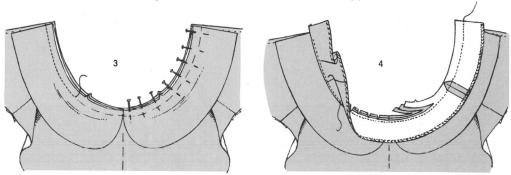

For a zipper closing, turn under the ends of the facing to clear the zipper after it has been turned to the inside. Anchor the facing and fasten the closing with a hook and eye. For a buttonhole closing, turn the facing to the inside, anchor the facing, and complete the back of the buttonholes.

There are other means of finishing the collar and garment seam. You can also use a standard bias facing application (found on page 253) when you wish to reduce bulk in a heavy fabric. Or, for one-piece collars, you may stitch the undercollar to the garment neck edge, keeping the upper collar free to be turned in and slipstitched over the seam.

Rolled Collar

Any molded collar with curved or angled corners and a pronounced roll around the neck is considered a rolled collar. It is usually cut with a two-piece bias undercollar and a slightly larger one-piece upper collar cut on crosswise grain. The center back seam brings the collar close to the neck, giving excellent control and fit. The standaway version of the rolled collar is cut in one piece on bias grain and folded at the outer edge. Careful molding and handling of the roll also shape the collar.

Although your upper collar is generally larger than the undercollar, heavy fabrics may require an additional ⅛″ to ¼″ added to the upper collar to allow for the roll.

First stitch and press the undercollar's center back seam. To reduce bulk, trim away interfacing seam allowances. With center back edges meeting, place ribbon seam binding over them and stitch. Catchstitch interfacing to undercollar. (For one-piece collars folded at the outer edge, use long running stitches to sew interfacing to collar at the foldline.)

Stitch collar sections together, stretching the undercollar to fit and using small stitches at the points. Trim corners carefully so the points will be sharp when turned (1). Turn and press the collar, favoring the upper collar at its outer edges so that the seam is on the undercollar side.

Now establish the *roll line.* Shape your collar until it looks like the pattern illustration, continuing to favor the outer edge of the upper collar. Baste raw edges together from the undercollar side as they fall, and thread trace the roll line (2).

Lap collar over garment, matching neck seamlines; baste (3). Try the garment on or put it on a dress form to check the collar set and roll. The collar should lie as close to the neck as the illustration shows without riding low or high. The roll should be smooth, even, and unbroken from front to back. Be sure that both points lie symmetrically against the garment when closed. Check buttonhole positions and general fit of your garment (4). The finished edge of the collar should cover the back neck seam. Adjust the collar at the neck seamline until all of these features are correct. When satisfied with the appearance of your collar, transfer any adjustment lines and remove the collar (5). If you have not already done so, attach your garment interfacing and make your buttonholes. For a zipper closing, insert the zipper.

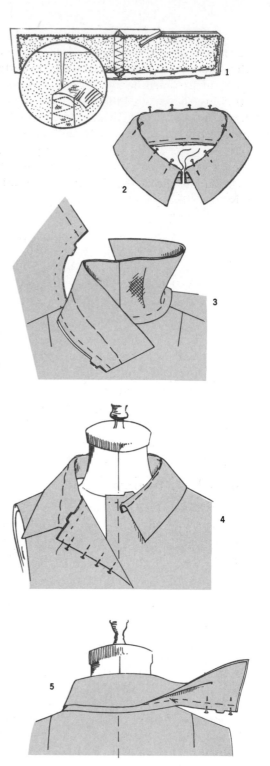

Staystitch the neck edge of the garment and the self-facing. Baste the collar to the garment, clipping the garment neck edge only where necessary and stretching or easing the collar to fit as indicated on your pattern. The upper collar will bubble along the roll when opened out (6). Complete the facing, finishing the unnotched edge and staystitching the neck edge. Baste the facing over the collar, matching markings. Clip the facing neck edge only where necessary. Stitch from the garment side. Then trim, grade, and continue clipping the seam through all thicknesses. Turn the facing to the inside, baste close to the folded edges, and press. Understitch the facing to the seam allowance close to the neckline seam and to within one inch of the opening edges (7).

Complete the facing side of the buttonholes. Then anchor the facing in place. If you wish, the rolled collar seam can be finished with a bias facing for a back opening.

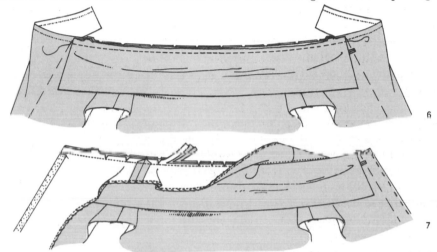

Notched Collar

This collar always has a front opening, usually with one edge lapped over the other. You may recognize it as a convertible collar. If this collar seems formidable, we point out that it is really a rolled collar with lapels added. The lapel undersections are created by an extension of the garment front edge.

Proper treatment of the notch area can be tricky, so we have chosen a method which reduces the difficulties. For the best results, this collar should be constructed following the shaping techniques in the tailoring section, page 362, especially if your fabric is very resilient or the slightest bit bulky.

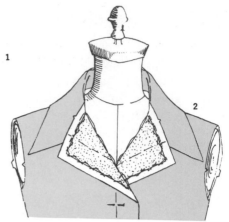

Construct collar section as for rolled collar, page 263, ending stitching ⅝″ from neck edge (1). Also press and shape as for rolled collar and baste the collar neck edges together.

Staystitch garment neck edge directionally. Interface lapel area, trimming and catchstitching interfacing to garment seamlines. Lap and baste collar to garment neck edge. (Turn any extended facing back at foldline and baste along neck edge before basting collar.)

Begin rolling the lapel at the top buttonhole marking. Check the fit of your collar and garment, as for a rolled collar. Make any necessary adjustments at the neckline seam until the collar sits close to the back of the neck, rolls smoothly, covers the back neck seam, and falls symmetrically. When you are satisfied with the collar, mark the roll line and transfer adjustment lines before removing it from the garment (2). Make buttonholes.

Baste the undercollar to the garment, clipping the garment neck edge; stitch between the markings (3). Prepare the facing and staystitch the neck edge. Baste the upper collar to the facing, clipping the facing. Stitch together between markings. Stitching from the garment side to eliminate bubbles that sometimes occur when the collar meets the lapel, join the facing to the garment. Start where it meets the collar, reinforce the corner, and continue around the facing. Trim, grade, and clip the seams (4).

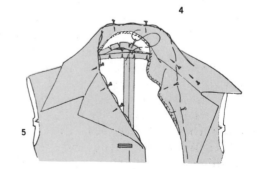

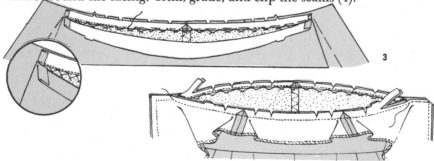

Press collar and garment neck seams open. Turn the facing inside and press. Try on the garment to check the roll of the lapels. Favoring the outer edge of the upper collar and the garment edge below the top buttonhole, pin along the roll and again above the neck seam. Loosely blindstitch both neck seams together as they fall (5). Complete the facing side of buttonholes and anchor facings.

266

Collar with Stand

Many man-tailored shirts have collars with stands. Such a collar has practically no roll; it turns down at the top of the stand and nearly always has a front closure.

Prepare the collar the same as you would for a shaped collar, page 262. For the band, trim the interfacing seam allowances and catchstitch the interfacing to one band section along the seamline.

Pin the interfaced band to the undercollar and the remaining band to the upper collar, right sides together, and baste. Stitch the ends and upper edge to within ⅝" of the neck edges. Trim, grade, clip, and notch the seam allowances (1). Then turn the band and press. The collar is now encased in the band.

Complete the garment front opening, interfacing where required. Staystitch the garment neck edge. Pin or baste the interfaced band to the garment neck edge, clipping the garment as necessary. Check buttonhole placement of the band and front opening. Stitch, trim, and grade seams, leaving the garment seam allowance widest (2). Press the seam toward the band. On the remaining free edge of the band, trim and turn the seam allowance under and baste close to the fold. Slipstitch the folded edge over the seam (3). Topstitch if desired. Make machine-worked buttonholes.

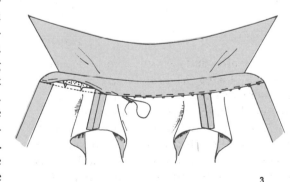

1

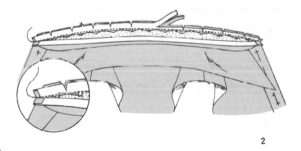

2

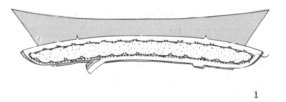

3

Bias Turnover Collar

A bias turnover collar, which is commonly known as a turtleneck collar and sometimes misnamed a rolled collar, is really a one-piece standing collar, rolled or folded over to cover the neck seam. A smooth turnover is made possible by cutting the collar on the bias. When worn high without rolling over on itself, it may be called a funnel collar.

Before you begin working with the collar, complete the following procedures on the garment. Staystitch the bodice neck edge directionally. Interface the necessary garment areas and insert your zipper or otherwise prepare the closing. Apply facings where they are needed. Now you should turn your attention to the collar.

Cut interfacing on the bias to extend ⅝″ beyond the foldline of the collar and trim away the seam allowances. Catchstitch interfacing to the collar along the seamlines. Sew it along the foldline with long running stitches (1). Fold the collar and stitch the ends to within ⅝″ of the neck edge. Trim and grade the seams. Turn and then press the ends only; do not press the foldline.

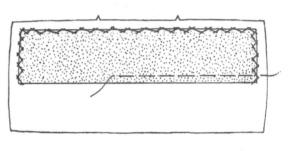

1

Baste the interfaced collar edge to the garment, clipping the garment neck edge where necessary and stretching or easing the collar to fit. Be sure to match markings. Then stitch and trim. To avoid unsightly ridges in the finished collar, grade all the seam allowances, leaving the garment seam allowance widest (2).

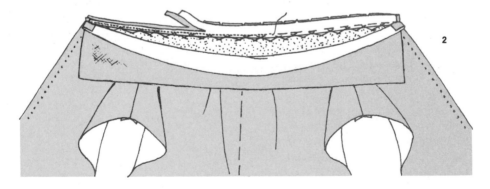

2

Press the stitched seam allowances toward the collar. Lap the remaining raw edge in place at the seamline and baste loosely. To check the fit, try on the garment or use a dress form. To establish the roll on the garment, turn the finished edge of the collar down to just cover the neck seam. Stretch the finished edge gently until it fits the contour and slightly covers the neck seam. Thread trace the roll line through all layers. Remove basting, trim, and turn in remaining edge as it falls over seam; slipstitch (3). (For bulky fabrics, finish remaining collar edge with a stitch and overcast treatment and blindstitch in place.) Turn the collar over and fasten the ends with hooks and eyes (4).

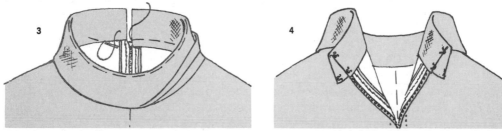

Shawl Collar

If the upper collar and lapels are cut as one piece and the collar has a roll, it is usually called a shawl collar. A shawl collar can vary greatly in shape, having a curved, scalloped, or notched edge. Traditionally found on wrap coats and robes, the shawl collar is usually wrapped in the front and held with a sash rather than buttons and buttonholes.

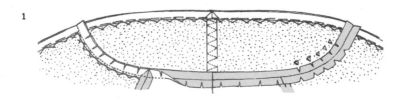

To begin, stitch and press open the center back seam of the undercollar. Trim away the interfacing seam allowances, and bring the center back edges together. Center ribbon seam binding over them and catchstitch or zigzag it in place. Catchstitch interfacing to the undercollar along the seamlines. Catchstitch interfacing to the garment front and neck edges in the same manner. Stitch the undercollar to the garment, stretching the collar to fit and clipping the garment neck edge as necessary. Notch the undercollar seam allowance to make it lie flat and press the seam open (1).

Try on the garment or put it on a dress form to check the fit. Check the buttonhole placement and make the buttonholes if your pattern includes them.

Before joining the collar/facing section to the garment, reinforce the inner corner with small stitches along the seamline, pivoting at the marking. Clip to the corner (2).

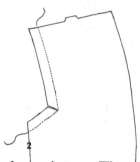

Stitch the center back seam of the collar/facing and press it open. Then pin it to the back facing along the neck and shoulder edges, clipping the back neck facing where necessary. Stitch, pivoting at corners. Press the seam open. Trim excess fullness at corners and catchstitch. Finish the unnotched edge of the facing. Stitch the collar/facing unit to the garment and undercollar, stretching the undercollar to fit. Trim and grade seams, leaving the garment seam allowance widest; notch curves (3). Turn the collar/facing to the right side and press. Favor the outer edge of the collar so that the seam is on the undercollar side. Below the place where the collar begins to roll, favor the front edge of the garment so that the seam is on the facing side.

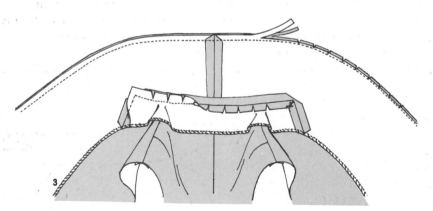

Try the garment on again or put it on a dress form to set the roll of the collar. The roll should be smooth and unbroken and the collar should lie close to the back of the neck. When you have achieved the desired effect with the collar/facing in its proper position, pin the facing in place. Continue to favor the collar and garment edges as mentioned previously. Blindstitch the facing seam allowances, as they fall, to the garment seam allowances at the neck edge. Also blindstitch the facing edges in place (4). Complete the underside of any buttonholes.

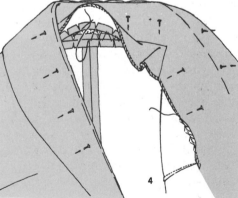

Standing Collar

Generally known as the Mandarin or band collar, this basically uncomplicated collar is able to take on many exciting forms. It can be a stiff and close military collar or a soft loose band, and it can be cut in one or two sections depending on whether the finished edge is straight or curved. The depth of the collar and how closely it is fitted to the neck greatly affect the overall design of your garment. This collar will always work and look better if you cut your interfacing on the bias. It will curve around your neck smoothly—without stiff cracks or breaks that mar a fine appearance.

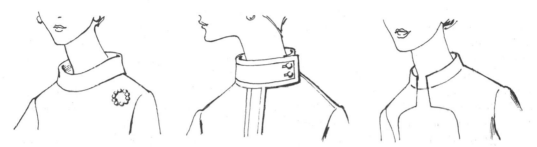

Cut a bias strip of interfacing to fit between the seamlines, or seamline and foldline, and catchstitch it to the collar. Fold the collar and stitch the ends to within ⅝" of the neckline edge. Trim, grading the seam allowances (1). Turn and press the ends only, *not* the foldline, or you may have an undesirable crease in the finished collar.

For either a front or back opening, insert your zipper or prepare a buttonhole closure by attaching your interfacing to the garment and making the necessary buttonholes. Attach and turn closure facings to the garment as needed, finishing the unnotched edge.

Baste and stitch the interfaced side of the collar to the garment neck edge, matching all markings and clipping the garment where necessary. Trim and grade the seams, leaving the garment seam allowance widest (2). Press the seam toward the collar. Trim and turn in the remaining edge of the collar and slipstitch over the seam. For hard to handle fabrics, you may want to baste close to the fold of the turned under edge before slipstitching the edge in place (3). Fasten the collar ends with hooks and thread eyes. Complete buttonholes and anchor the facing in place as required.

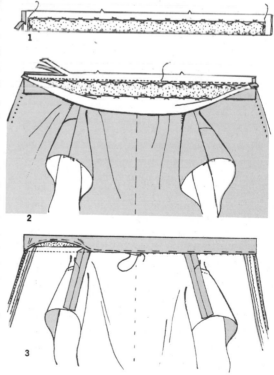

Tie Collar

This collar, basically a turnover or standing collar ending in a tie, adds a delightfully feminine touch to any garment. The difference between the two collar styles is only a matter of dimension; the tie will generally be wider on the turnover collar.

Trim interfacing seam allowances away and catchstitch the interfacing to the collar seamlines. Sew along the foldline with long running stitches. Do not interface ties: added bulk would cause difficulty when tying. Reinforce the seamline at the point where collar and tie meet; clip to the seamline. Fold the collar; stitch the tie along the ends and to its termination points. (For a back opening, you have two collar sections. Stitch the back opening ends; then, stitch the tie ends to their termination points.) Trim and grade seams and corners (1). Turn the collar and tie ends; press the seams lightly.

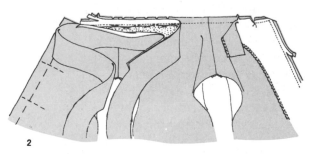

Staystitch garment neck edge. Attach garment interfacing and make buttonholes. Finish unnotched edges of the facing. Stitch facing to the garment, stopping where the collar begins. Clip to the end of the stitching. Trim and grade the seam allowances. Turn and press. Baste facing and garment neck edges together and anchor the facing at the shoulders.

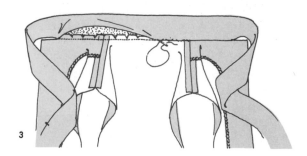

Baste one edge of collar to garment, clipping the garment neck edge where necessary. A space has been allowed between the termination point of the collar and center marking in order to knot the tie. Stitch, trim, grade, and clip the seam (2). Press the seam toward the collar. Turn in the remaining edge and slipstitch over the seam (3). Complete buttonholes. For a back closing, fasten the collar with hooks and eyes.

Detachable Collar

This category includes two types of collars—the first lies on top of an existing collar; the second fits inside a collarless neckline. When you are using this collar to provide a removable, washable trim on a garment which requires dry cleaning, it may be wise to omit the interfacing.

The most familiar type of detachable collar forms a decorative overlay to your garment's original collar. It must be longer and wider in order to cover the existing collar. Unless your pattern is designed for a detachable collar, you will probably have to adjust its dimensions so that the decorative collar has the same shape and size as the garment collar when it is worn. Determine how much to add to the pattern by comparing the weight and depth of your garment fabric with the fabric for your detachable collar.

Construct the desired collar and stitch its neck edges together ⅛" from the seamline in the seam allowance. Clip the seam allowances to the stitching every ½" so the detachable collar neckline can spread to fit the garment neckline smoothly (1).

Extend the collar neck edge with bias binding to allow for fastening it to the garment. For a ½" finished binding, cut a bias strip 1¾" wide and the length of the neckline plus 1". Then apply the bias as a single binding to the collar neck edge, shaping the binding and clipped edge of the collar so it will fit the garment neck edge as you work (2). Grade seam allowances if necessary. Pin the collar to the neck edge of the garment, matching seamlines, and slip-baste the binding to the neck facing (3).

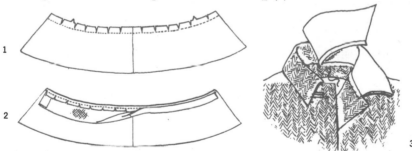

If you don't have a pattern for the second type of detachable collar, it is possible to use a collar from another pattern with the same neckline. Construct the collar and finish the edges with bias binding in the same manner as described above. Then attach it to your garment with snaps or slip-basting. If the closure on your collar does not correspond to that of the garment, fasten the collar in place with snaps rather than slip-basting.

If you wish to add matching detachable cuffs to complement your detachable collar, refer to Cuffs, page 290, for detailed instructions.

Sleeves

A sleeve should be a thing of beauty and comfort. It should look handsome, conforming to the shape of your arm without signs of pull or strain. Since the arm is probably the most active part of the body, the sleeve should perform well in motion without causing discomfort or distorting fit. These qualities are relatively easy to achieve, yet we must honestly admit that the prospect of inserting a sleeve often causes consternation—but unjustly so, since no special sewing skills are needed for this operation. What is really necessary is a working knowledge of preliminary fitting and pressing techniques.

The comfort of a sleeve is determined mostly by the fit and ease of the two points of action—the upper arm and elbow. The sleeve cap must be neither too tight nor too loose, and in any long or three-quarter sleeve there must be room for the elbow to bend. When the arm is at ease, the sleeve should hang evenly and gracefully in a curve that corresponds to the natural curve of your arm. Any extraneous folds will indicate that the sleeve is improperly set. A gentle reminder, too, is that the fit of the sleeve is extremely dependent upon a well-fitting shoulder; the shoulder seam must sit exactly at the top of the shoulder and divide the body approximately in half from front to back.

A profusion of sleeves is at your disposal, in lengths and shapes to suit every whim—dolman sleeves, pleated sleeves, leg-o-mutton and peasant sleeves, bell, bishop, and lantern sleeves. Variations of these have changed the shape of fashion. Most of them fall into three basic types. The first type is the SET-IN SLEEVE which joins the garment in a seam that encircles the arm over the shoulder. The area of the sleeve at the end of the shoulder or upper arm, called the *sleeve cap,* must be shaped and eased to curve smoothly into the armhole (or *armscye*). The second type, the RAGLAN SLEEVE, joins the bodice in a diagonal seam extending to the neckline area, providing a smooth, round silhouette and a great degree of comfort. It tends to be a good choice for hard-to-fit shoulders, since the diagonal seam can be readily adjusted to accommodate differences in the individual figure. Shoulder shaping is achieved by a curved seam or a shaped dart. The third type, the KIMONO SLEEVE, is cut in one with the garment or a part of it, such as a yoke. If it is loose-fitting or short, it may simply be reinforced in the underarm seam, but tighter versions frequently call for gussets or further refinements designed to combine greater comfort with a finer degree of fit.

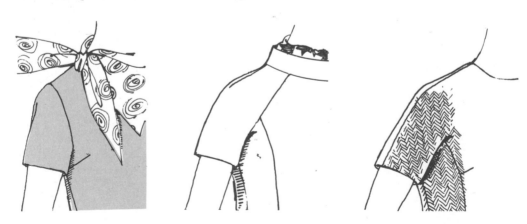

Set-in Sleeve

The one-piece set-in sleeve is the most classic and most popular of these sleeves, and allows for many variations in style. Slightly more refined in fit, the two-piece set-in sleeve is inserted in exactly the same manner, but often calls for the fairly sophisticated sleeve finishes explained in the tailoring section. ❀ If you are using heavy or bulky fabrics, or fabrics such as permanent press or velveteen which cannot be eased, see page 139 as a guide to adjusting the pattern tissue.

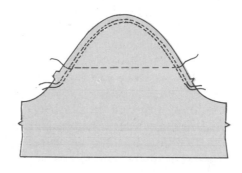

To begin your sleeve, run a line of thread tracing, as shown, along the crosswise grain of the sleeve cap. Easestitch on the right side of the sleeve cap (about 8-10 stitches per inch) just inside the seamline in the seam allowance between markings, as shown. An additional row of easestitching ¼" from the first row in the seam allowance will give you more control over the fullness and simplify the process of easing.

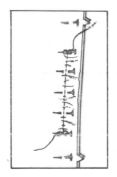 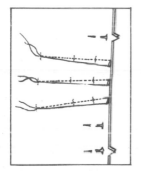

If the sleeve is long or three-quarter length and snug, elbow shaping is needed for comfortable movement, either by easing or using darts. To ease, stitch with large stitches along the seamline on the back edge of the sleeve between markings. Pin the sleeve seam, matching notches and markings; adjust ease. Where darts are indicated, stitch and press downward. Match markings; pin and stitch the sleeve seam.

With the garment wrong side out, place sleeve in the armhole, right sides together. Pin together at the notches, markings, and underarm seam, being sure to use the stitching line at the underarm for the sleeve when indicated on your pattern. Pull the easing threads up until the sleeve fits the armhole; secure thread ends around a pin in a figure eight fashion. Adjust the fullness and pin about every ½". If not indicated by markings, be sure to leave one inch of flat area at the shoulder seam where the grain will not permit easing. Baste firmly along the seamline.

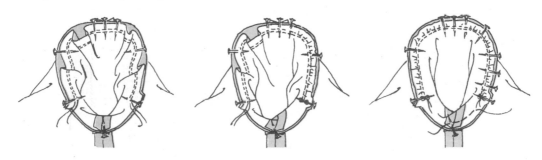

Now try on the garment. First check the line of thread tracing. If it is not perfectly parallel to the floor, you have an obvious indication that a slight adjustment is in order. If the grainline slants or ripples, you will find a quick referral to Sleeves, page 139, extremely helpful. Then check the length, allowing for the anticipated finish (hem, cuff, etc.) and any blousing in a full sleeve. Finally, be sure that the ease is located where it is needed, adjusting it for your particular upper arm shape and shoulder curve.

After fitting, tie the ease thread ends securely and remove the sleeve from the armhole. Holding the curve of the sleeve cap over a press mitt, shrink the fullness by using a steam iron. Begin by steaming the seam allowance to shape the sleeve cap, being careful not to press beyond the stitches (1).

Hold the sleeve in your hands and turn in the seam allowance along the ease thread. You should have a smooth rolling sleeve cap without puckers or pulling. If dimples remain on the roll near the seamline, slide fullness along the threads until your problem has been eliminated and steam again. Do not be overly alarmed if your unattached sleeve still retains some puckering, as some fabrics do not respond well to shrinking and may need additional handling when the sleeve is being placed into the armhole for permanent stitching (2).

Before you permanently set in the sleeve, complete the sleeve finish. The separate piece will be easier to maneuver than the entire garment. Replace the sleeve in the armhole, pinning and basting it in place. Try it on, checking the shoulder and arm shaping and the sleeve finish.

For a problem sleeve, place the garment on a dress form. Turn in the sleeve seam allowance along ease thread and, from the right side, pin into armhole. Pin and slipbaste in place, working with the sleeve cap until you have a smooth rolling shape (3).

When the sleeve is set in to your satisfaction, start at the underarm and stitch the armhole seam with the sleeve side up, controlling the fullness as you work (4).

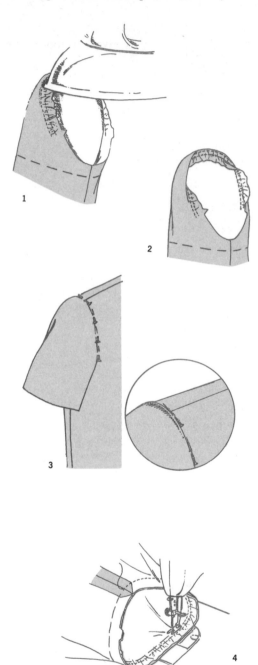

Stitch again in the seam allowance ¼″ from first row of stitching. To reduce bulk, trim close to this second row. If the garment is unlined, overcast or zigzag the seam allowances to prevent ravelling (5). Never press sleeve cap seam after the sleeve is set in. Simply turn the seam allowances toward the sleeve to give a smooth line to the seam and support to the sleeve cap.

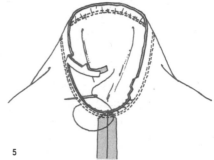

5

There are a few extreme instances when the sleeve cap seam is still not perfectly smooth and rounded—such as lightweight or limp fabrics, fabrics which do not ease, certain designs, and certain figure irregularities. These situations can prove difficult and may call for lambswool padding. We must stress that it is not a remedy for a poorly set-in sleeve. For detailed instructions on how to insert sleeve padding, put lining in a sleeve, or set in a two-piece sleeve, refer to the tailoring section.

Raglan Sleeve

This sleeve is well liked for its comfortable fit and relatively easy construction. Its diagonal seamline can lead into another seam or form part of a neckline. It can be cut on the straight or bias grain, with a one- or two-piece construction. The shoulder curve is part of the sleeve shape, and is created by a dart, a seam, or gathers.

First stitch the dart or shoulder seam and the sleeve seam. Press the seams open. Pin and baste the sleeve into the armhole, matching notches, symbols, and underarm seams. Try on the garment.

The curve of the dart or seam should conform to your own shoulder and upper arm shape, with the sharpest part of the curve neither above nor below the point of your shoulder. Test it, standing in a normal position with your arms down. Then swing your arms, making sure there is enough room for comfortable movement. Adjust if necessary, referring to the hints in the adjustment section.

Stitch, then stitch again ¼″ away in the underarm seam allowance between the notches. Clip at ends of the second row of stitching, trim close to this stitching, and overcast or zigzag the edge. Press the seam open above the clips.

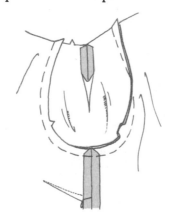
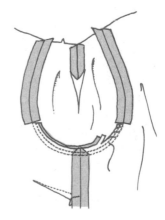

Kimono Sleeve

The classic kimono sleeve is a gem of simplicity. The T-shaped garment that every little girl has made for her doll is a perfect example. However, arms are seldom at right angles to the body; when they are in a relaxed position, the T-shape creates folds. This draped effect can be a graceful design feature in a kimono sleeve with a large opening; however, as the arm opening becomes smaller and shaping adjustments are made to eliminate folds, further sewing refinements are necessary for comfort and strength.

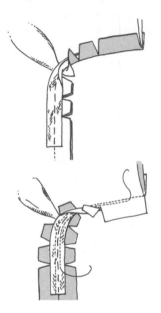

INVISIBLE REINFORCEMENTS: If the sleeve is cut as an extension of the bodice, the main thing to remember is that the underarm area must be adequately reinforced, since it undergoes considerable strain with arm movements. Pin the back to the front at shoulders and sides. Center a piece of stretched bias tape over the seamline at the underarm. Baste both seams, then clip the curve, being careful not to cut the tape. Fit your garment, then stitch the seam, using a smaller stitch (15-20 per inch according to your fabric) on the curves. Press the seam open.

An alternative method is to stitch the underarm seam, using smaller stitches on the curve. Clip the curve; press the seam open. Center a piece of stretched bias tape over the open seam and baste through the seamline. Stitch on both sides of the seamline as you spread the clips, catching only the tape and seam allowances.

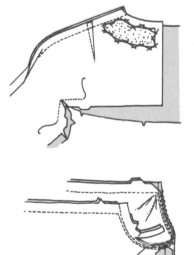

KIMONO SLEEVE CUT WITH YOKE: When the kimono sleeve is cut in one with a yoke, you will get a closer fit without the additional construction of a gusset. The seaming detail allows for easier shaping and fitting adjustments. Reinforce the inner corners at the point where the yoke ends and the sleeve begins; clip to markings. Stitch the yoke/sleeve front and yoke/sleeve back sections together along the shoulder and sleeve seams. Press the seams open.

With the yoke/sleeve section dropped into the dress section, place right sides together. Pin and baste the yoke/sleeve section to the dress along the bottom of the yoke and underarm, matching markings. Stitch from the yoke/sleeve side, pivoting at corners. At the underarm, stitch again ¼" away. Trim close to the second row of stitching and overcast. Press the garment seam toward the yoke. The underarm seam remains unpressed.

Sleeve Finishes

Let every gesture of the arm display a perfectly polished sleeve finish—tastefully suited to the overall design, neatly pressed, and flawlessly completed. Feel free to adapt the finish in accordance with the pattern design and your fabric.

The style description on your pattern envelope includes mention of the sleeve length preferred by the designer. Check the length of your sleeve when it is pinned into the armhole, referring to the diagram below for an explanation of the designer's length. If a cuff is a part of the design, be sure to take its depth into account in the total sleeve length. Also allow for blousing in a full sleeve.

Here are the suggested lengths which should be used for reference when you are adjusting your pattern or fitting your garment:

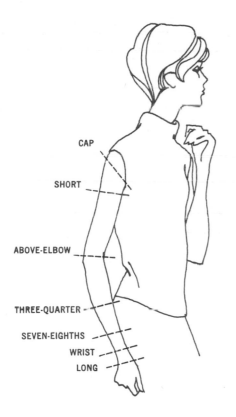

CAP: A very, very short sleeve, actually an extension of the shoulder and not usually continued under the arm.

SHORT: The typical short sleeve lies with its lower edge relatively straight across the upper arm.

ABOVE-ELBOW: As the name suggests, the arm above the elbow is completely covered by the sleeve.

THREE-QUARTER: This sleeve is three-fourths the length of the arm. It ends halfway between the elbow and the wrist bone.

SEVEN-EIGHTHS: A sleeve which terminates approximately 2″ above the wrist bone or halfway between the three-quarter and the long sleeve.

WRIST LENGTH: This sleeve grazes the wrist just at the prominent wrist bone.

LONG OR FULL LENGTH: Falls 1″ below the wrist bone at a comfortable length before reaching the hand.

Keep in mind that the "correct" sleeve length for you is one which is in proportion to your figure. Sleeves influence the total silhouette of your garment. Their shape, length, and finish can exaggerate a figure flaw or lead the eyes away from it. Select a length and type which becomes you and choose your finish from those on the following pages.

Finish a Sleeve with Finesse

A well-made finish enhances the sleeve and handsomely sets off the completed garment. Be precise—avoid sloppy plackets, uneven hems, and mis-matched closures with half-sewn snaps. Consider the mood of your garment when choosing a sleeve finish, because varying the finish can give your sleeve an entirely different appearance. A sturdy zipper closing is perfect for durable casual clothes, while a fragile thread loop and button closing would be more suitable for dressy or couture garments.

Try on the sleeve. For any of the lapped closings, check to see that the lap will open properly when finished. It should be in back of the sleeve (above the little finger) and open toward the body. Be doubly sure that the right and left sleeves open in opposite directions so that your careful work won't result in two left openings. Establish the location of any buttons or fastenings. Remember that a long sleeve without a closing needs to have an opening big enough for the hand to pass through, while the sleeve with a closing can have a smaller opening circumference. Allow ½″ to one inch for ease between the circumference of the arm and the opening when the sleeve is fastened.

Fit the sleeve, then remove it from the garment for easier handling when you apply your sleeve finish. Use interfacing for a precise, well-shaped look that lasts through the rigors of wearing and cleaning. Careful matching, stitching, and trimming are natural steps toward achieving a sleeve finish with savoir-faire.

STRAIGHT HEM: Although it is the most basic and easiest of all sleeve finishes, the straight hem can be quite elegant as it gracefully circles the arm in a smooth curve. Careful construction and an appropriate interfacing are necessary for a hem that is to hold its curved line without "breaking." The interfacing you use should be determined by your fabric for the desired effect—whether it be a creased edge or a rolled edge. Lamb's wool will give a very soft rolled edge; other interfacing fabrics add more body, and the edge can be softly rolled or creased. Cut the interfacing in bias strips equal in length to the circumference of the finished sleeve plus ½″ and equal in width to the depth of the hem.

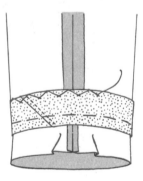

Stitch the underarm seam of the sleeve. Place the lower edge of interfacing ⅝″ below the hemline; overlap ends ½″ and sew, as shown. Sew the interfacing to the garment or underlining along the hemline with long running stitches and along the upper edge of the interfacing with long catchstitches. Turn up the hem to cover the interfacing. Baste close to the fold. Check to see that the hem is an even depth all around, and trim if necessary. Finish the raw edge of your hem with a stitch and overcast or zigzag finish. Blind hem the edge to the underlining or your garment fabric.

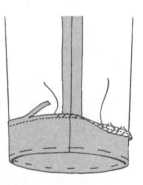

The Mobile Sleeve

Short and snappy or long and skinny, trim and efficient or flowing
generously from a gathered wrist, sleeves are a wealth
of design potential and a matter of proportion . . . Their shape coordinates
a look, and sets a fashion tone . . . Perfect shoulders
distinguish a well-set sleeve, and form the focus of a kimono
or raglan, molding a smooth curve . . .

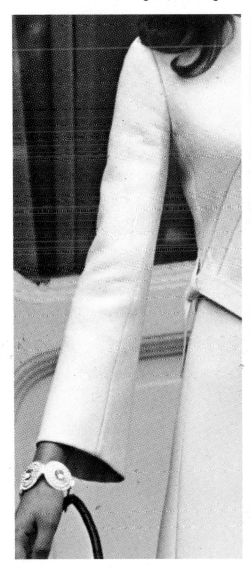

The feminine of handsome
is a trimly tailored suit sleeve,
vented and buttoned, with
a lace edge peeking out . . .
Misty sheer sleeves, demure and
alluring, or crisp cap sleeves
with proper finesse . . .

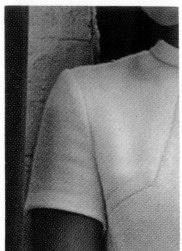

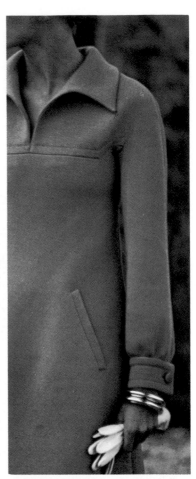

The dramatic softness
of a gathered
crepe sleeve is given
to expansive gestures—
and female moods . . .

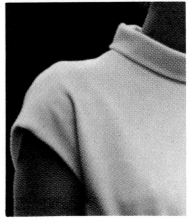

The Clever Cuff

The neatest trick up fashion's sleeve, a cuff polishes off a put-together appearance. . . . That half-inch edge beneath a suit sleeve that finishes the look of distinction, or the smooth band encircling the gathers of a full sleeve, cuffs are a pretty accent for a pretty hand. . . . Let the chaste white of detachable cuffs— dew-fresh and ladylike— complement your basic black with incomparable chic. Showcase for a handsome cufflink, the French cuff is a smart tailored touch.

In many styles and varieties, cuffs may be unassuming finishing details or eye-catching design features. Matching or contrasting, turned back or extending from sleeves of any length and shape, they often sport the extra emphasis of a row of beautiful buttons.

The Indispensable Pocket

Those practical carry-alls on a little boy's blue jeans turn into fashion
in hundreds of ways—conveniences that are as varied as they are versatile . . . Such
ladylike accessories as gloves and handkerchiefs would be lost
without them . . . From shy pockets hiding in seams to brazen contrasting patches,
pockets present many fashion fronts, and many personalities. . . .

Pockets slip easily into
vertical seams and behind pleats
to play multi-purpose
design tricks . . . Applied patch
pockets are visual diversion, and
especially effective in
a perfectly matched plaid . . .

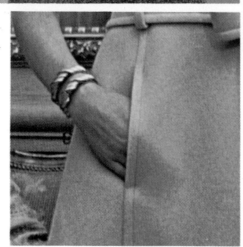

Pockets with flaps—
pockets high or low, vertical
or diagonal, serving
fashion more for the eyes
than for the hands.

The Classic Closure

Buttonholes are a tiny detail, but their perfection is a
point of pride in the art of sewing . . . Knowing what technique is
right for a garment's weight and style demonstrates the
judgement of a fine seamstress, and making them exact and
uniform proves your sewing skill . . . Whether buttons are a focus or
a convenience, let them show off faultless buttonholes.

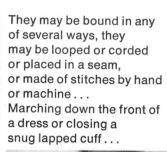

They may be bound in any
of several ways, they
may be looped or corded
or placed in a seam,
or made of stitches by hand
or machine . . .
Marching down the front of
a dress or closing a
snug lapped cuff . . .

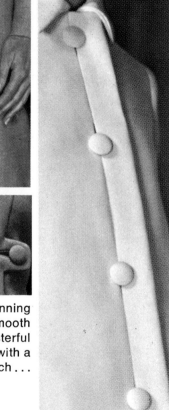

Care in planning
and marking will smooth
your path to masterful
buttonholes with a
professional touch . . .

Waistline Wizardry

As fashions vary, waistlines may be high, low, or natural, but wherever
they span the silhouette, a handsome belt defines them in style . . . Snug or loose,
their effect is a clear horizontal that attracts the eye, and earns
fashion attention in many ways . . . Snappy showcase for a gorgeous trim or a
beautiful buckle, and an obvious advantage for the wasp-waisted.

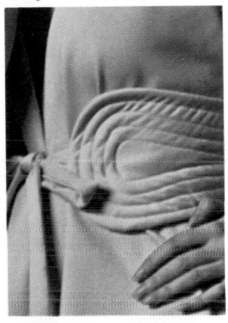

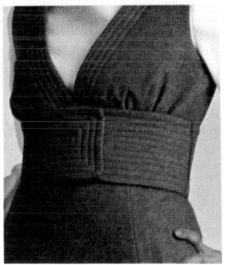

The matter of proportion
depends on your
fashion type . . . A belt
that knows its place
flatters your figure—
and your ego. . . .

A broad shaped belt,
topstitched for emphasis—
a skinny bias-covered rope,
knotted or bowed—A soft cloth
tie securing a wrapped
coat, or a crushed or pleated
cummerbund . . . Each makes
a different statement of style,
to accent or accessorize
your proud creation. . . .

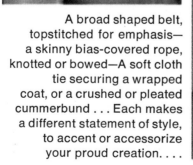

The Versatile Zipper

Those mechanical marvels that dismiss the chores of dressing
with a song . . . Hiding inconspicuously in a supple seam, hand-sewn with
precision, or serving bolder purposes as the topstitched feature
of a sporty design . . . Sophisticated dressmaker detailing conceals zippers
within handsome slot seams, a clever combination of form and function . . .

Chunky brass zippers
are fashion fun in improbable
places like pockets and
shoulder seams . . . There's a
new zipper type—ingenious
and invisible . . .

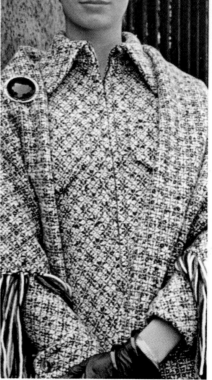

Zip-front jumpsuits
are good sense
and great fashion—
borrowed from a practical
man's world . . .
Handy zippers are
precious time-savers in
your busy life . . .

SNAP CLOSING: Stitch the sleeve seam above the marking. Clip the back seam allowance ½″ above the opening. Press the seam open above the clip, and the front edge to the inside along seamline. Turn up the lower edge of the sleeve along the seamline or hemline and baste close to the fold. Finish the raw edge with ribbon seam binding, easing if necessary. Sew the hem in place. To finish opening edges, place ribbon seam binding ⅛″ over the raw edges, turning under the top ends as shown and leaving ½″ extending past the hem fold. Stitch close to the edge of the seam binding, continuing to the end of the seam binding. Turn in the seam binding ends. Turn the front edge inside along the seamline; turn the back edge inside along the seam binding edge, as shown. Press. Slipstitch the lower ends and long edges of the seam binding in place. On the inside, lap the back seam allowance over the front below the clip, matching seamlines. Slipstitch the upper edge in place, taking care not to sew through to the right side. Fasten with snaps.

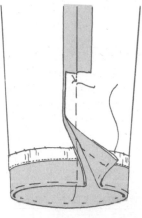

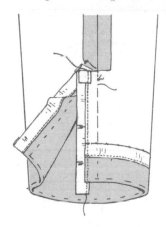
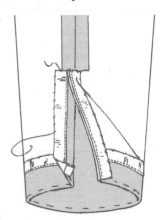
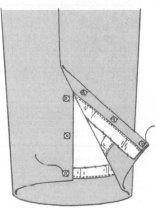

THREAD LOOP AND BUTTON CLOSING: This finish is perfect for the row of tiny buttons that is such an elegant touch on a sleeve. It eliminates the bulk of fabric loops, enabling you to use many small buttons spaced closely together. Finish the lower and opening edges of the sleeve with ribbon seam binding, as described above for the snap closing. Lap the opening and align the buttons on the undersection with the edge of the overlap. Space the loop markings evenly. Make the loops as instructed in Thread Closures and Fastenings, page 315. The loops should be uniform in size and shape and just large enough for the buttons to pass through. Secure each end of the loops on the wrong side.

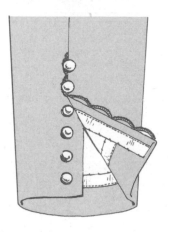

FABRIC LOOP AND BUTTON CLOSING: On the back edge only, clip the seam allowance ½″ above the opening. Turn up the lower edge of the sleeve along the hemline and baste close to the fold. Finish the raw edge with ribbon seam binding, easing if necessary. Sew the hem in place. Make fabric loops according to the instructions in Loops and Fastenings, page 314. Machine baste them along the seamline of the overlap, as shown, and check to see that they are just large enough for the buttons to pass through.

Press seam open above clip. Place ribbon seam binding along the seamline over the loop ends and ⅛″ over the back raw edge, leaving extra seam binding at both ends. Stitch close to seam binding edge. Turn front edge to the inside along the seamline and back edge to the inside along the seam binding, turning under seam binding ends. Slipstitch upper and lower ends in place and hem long edges to underlining or garment.

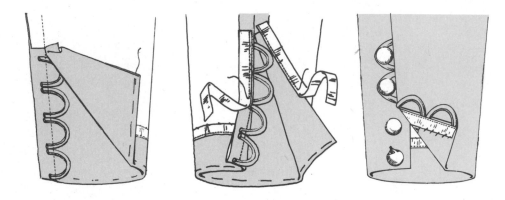

ZIPPER CLOSING: Stitch and press open the sleeve seam above the marking. Mark the hemline. Finish the hem edge with a stitch and overcast method or zigzag stitch. Then baste and press open the remainder of the seam, clipping at the hemline. On the inside, center the closed zipper face down over the basted seam with the zipper tab just above the hemline; baste. Trim the zipper tape away below the hemline to eliminate bulk. On the outside, prickstitch the zipper in place along the sides and across the upper end.

Turn and pin the hem and baste close to the fold, turning in the ends to clear the zipper teeth. Slipstitch the ends to the zipper tape. Blind hem free edge in place.

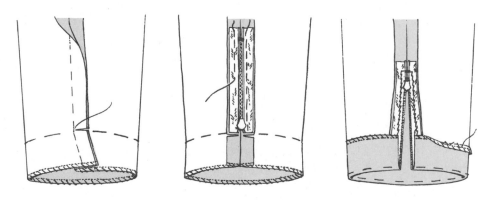

SLASHED OPENING: For the opening facing, cut a 2½"
wide strip of self-fabric the length of the opening plus
one inch. Finish the raw edge on the sides and one end of
the facing with the stitch and overcast method or zigzag
stitch. Right sides together, center it over the slash markings with the raw edge at the bottom. Stitch along the
stitching lines, using small stitches, and take one stitch
across the point. Slash carefully to the point, without cutting through the stitching. Turn the facing inside and
press. This finish may be completed with a binding, cuff,
or hem. The facing should be blindstitched to the underlining or the garment after the finish is completed.

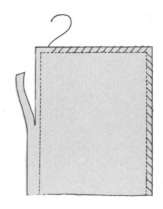

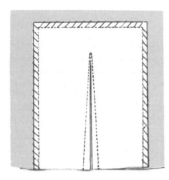 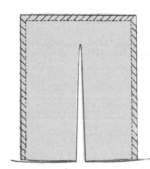 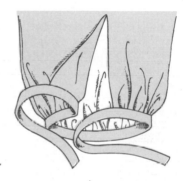

LAPPED CLOSING WITH ROLLED HEM: Generally used with a buttoned cuff, this
closing allows for a cuff opening without the necessity of making a sleeve placket. Reinforce the area to be hemmed, using small stitches along the seamline through the markings; clip to the markings. Trim the seam allowance between the clips to ⅜"; trim any
underlining up to the stitching. Turn raw edge along stitching to form a rolled hem and
slipstitch. Whipstitch the ends. Stitch underarm seam, add gathers, and apply cuff.

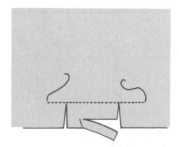 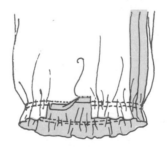 

CONTINUOUS LAPPED PLACKET: An extremely durable and simple opening for
sleeves, and for other areas of the garment as well, is the continuous lapped placket. For
the construction techniques, refer to pages 318 and 319.

SHIRT SLEEVE PLACKET: This sporty finish designed for a man-tailored shirt requires precision and care in its making for a fine professional look. First reinforce the sleeve opening by stitching along the seamlines, using small stitches. Slash between the stitches and carefully clip to the corners.

Stitch the right side of the underlap piece to the wrong side of the back edge of the sleeve (the edge nearer the underarm seam). Trim and press the seam allowances toward the underlap. Then turn under the remaining long edge of the underlap ¼" and press. Place the pressed edge over the seam allowances and edgestitch through all thicknesses.

Stitch the right side of the overlap piece to the wrong side of the remaining slashed edge. Trim the seam and press it toward the overlap. Stitch the base of the triangular end of the slash to the end of the overlap. Press the stitched end of the overlap up. Turn in the overlap at the seam allowances and along the foldlines; press and baste. Pin the overlap in place along the folded edges.

Keeping the underlap free, stitch the outside fold of the overlap to the top of the opening. Tie thread ends securely on the wrong side. Stitching through all layers, stitch across the placket, securing both the point of the slash and the top of the underlap in the stitches; pivot and stitch along the remaining edges of the overlap. Tie ends securely on the wrong side.

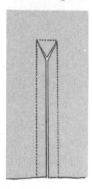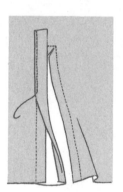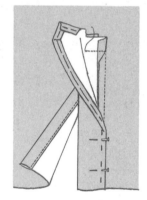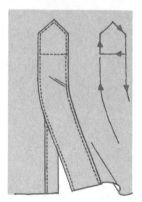

SELF-FACING WITH SLIT: This finish continues partway up the vertical seam and usually includes mitered corners. Interface the opening and hem before you stitch the sleeve seam. If you do not have an interfacing pattern piece, use your sleeve pattern as a guide, and cut the interfacing on the bias equal in width to the depth of the hem and equal in length to the circumference of the sleeve plus 1¼". Position the interfacing so that it extends ⅝" past the hemline and slit foldlines, as shown. Sew the interfacing to the underlining with long running stitches along the hemline and slit foldlines and with long catchstitches along the upper edges.

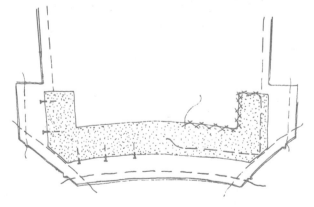

Miter the corners of your sleeve by turning the edges to the outside along the hemline and foldlines; then stitch to the corners. Trim and press the seams open. Stitch the long sleeve seam to the appropriate marking. Turn the corners and the facing to the inside along the foldlines and hemline; press. Baste close to the fold. To finish the raw edges, stitch ¼" from the edge, trim to ⅛", and overcast. You may prefer to zigzag stitch the raw edge. Blind hem the free edges to the sleeve or underlining. Reinforce the end of the slit with a bar tack on the inside sleeve.

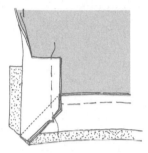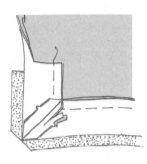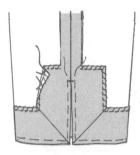

BIAS FACING: Cut a 1½" wide bias strip in a length equal to the circumference of the sleeve plus 2". With raw edges even, pin the bias strip to the sleeve, right sides together. Join the ends on straight grain in a diagonal seam; trim to ¼" and press open. Then stitch the bias to the sleeve; trim and grade the seam allowances. Turn the bias inside, favoring the right side of the sleeve, and press. Turn the raw edge under ¼" and slipstitch to the sleeve or underlining.

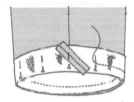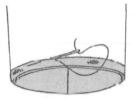

SHAPED FACING: Use the stitch and overcast method to finish the unnotched edge of the sleeve facing. Stitch the facing ends together. Trim the seam allowances to ¼" and press open. Stitch the facing to the sleeve; then trim and grade the seam. Turn the facing to the inside, favoring the outside of the sleeve, and press. Blindstitch the free edge to the garment or underlining.

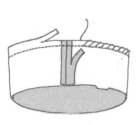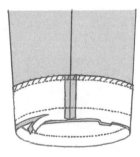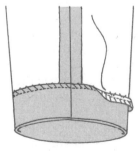

Cuffs

The cuff is one design detail that constantly changes, but never goes out of style. Of the two main categories, the primary function of the EXTENDED CUFF is to add length to the sleeve, whereas the TURNBACK CUFF rolls back to cover the base of the sleeve and often serves solely as a decorative feature. Both may control fullness. They can be straight bands folded in half, or may be shaped from separate fabric pieces. If a sleeve opening is used, a cuff should fasten closely around the wrist; but without an opening, a cuff must be big enough for the hand to pass through. Remember that trimming and grading of all seams is essential to a well-made cuff. Generally, seams should be pressed toward the cuff. For pressing tips, refer to Seams, page 342 and 343.

INTERFACING: The outer layer of the cuff should be interfaced. Use the cuff pattern piece, but cut it on the bias for greater resiliency. Then trim the seam allowances away and catchstitch the interfacing along the seamlines on the wrong side of the cuff. For a cuff cut in sections, trim away all seam allowances from the interfacing and sew it to the wrong side of the outer cuff section. For the cuff made from one piece, cut the interfacing to extend ⅝" past the foldline (to help maintain a smoothly rolled edge) and sew it along the foldline with long running stitches. If this cuff is to be topstitched, however, trim the interfacing along the foldline.

BUTTONHOLES: If buttonholes will be used, transfer the placement markings to the right side of the cuff with thread tracing before applying interfacing. For bound buttonholes, apply interfacing and make buttonholes before stitching the cuff sections together. Machine or hand-worked buttonholes are made after the cuff is completed.

Extended Cuffs

BAND CUFF: This cuff is the simplest of all cuffs to make. Stitch the cuff ends together and press open. Stitch the gathered sleeve to the interfaced half of the cuff, right sides together. Trim and grade the seam (1). Press the seam allowances toward the cuff. Turn the cuff inside along the foldline, wrong sides together, and baste close to the fold. Trim and turn in the raw edge along the seamline; slipstitch it in place over the seam (2).

❧ You may find it easier to attach a thickly gathered sleeve to a band cuff *before* you close the sleeve or cuff seams. Stitch the gathered edge of the sleeve to the open cuff, matching markings. Trim and press the seam allowances toward cuff. Then stitch the long underarm sleeve seam and cuff seam at the same time.

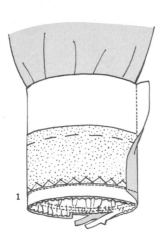
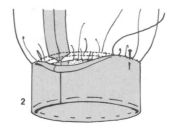
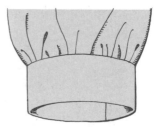

LAPPED CUFF WITH AN OPENING: A buttoned cuff is most often used on full-length, gathered or pleated sleeves with a continuous lapped placket (see page 318). Make your bound buttonholes. Fold the cuff lengthwise, and stitch the ends from the fold to within ⅝" of the long edge. Trim, grading seams (1). Turn and press. Fold under the front lap of the sleeve placket so that the folded edge is even with the cuff edge. Place the back lap of the sleeve on the cuff at the marking. Stitch the gathered sleeve to interfaced half of cuff (2). Press, trim, and turn the cuff the same as a band cuff. Baste close to the fold. Trim and turn in the raw edge along the seamline and slipstitch it over the seam and extension end (3). Complete with a button and buttonhole closure (4).

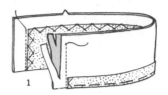

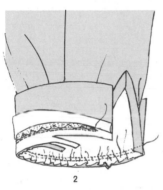

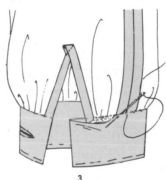

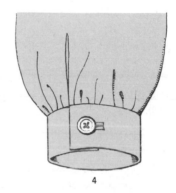

2

3

4

LAPPED CUFF WITHOUT OPENING: You will probably want to put a button trim on this cuff. Fold the cuff lengthwise. To form a finished extension, start stitching at the fold, pivot at the corner, and stitch as far as the marking. On the other end, stitch from the fold to within ⅝" of long edge. Clip the seam allowance to marking on the long notched edge. Trim and grade the seam. Turn to the right side and press (1). Stitch the gathered sleeve to interfaced half of the cuff. The end of the cuff section will meet the extension marking at the clip, as shown. Clip the sleeve seam allowance at the marking (2). Press, trim, and turn the cuff the same as for a band cuff. Baste close to the fold. Trim and turn in the raw edge along the seamline; slipstitch (3). Fasten extension in place on the right side, as desired (4).

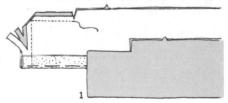

1

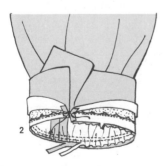

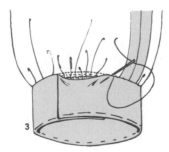

2

3

4

SHIRT SLEEVE CUFF: A shirt sleeve cuff is used with a shirt sleeve placket and is usually topstitched. Stitch the cuff sections together, ending 5⁄8″ from the long notched edge. Trim, turn, and press (1). Stitch the *wrong side* of the gathered sleeve to the *non-interfaced* section of the cuff, placing the placket edges even with the cuff edges. Trim and grade the seam (2). Press the seam toward the cuff. On the outside, turn in the remaining edge where it falls over the seam and baste in place. Topstitch close to all edges of the cuff and again 1⁄4″ away from the first line of stitching. Fasten with a machine-made or hand-worked buttonhole and button (3).

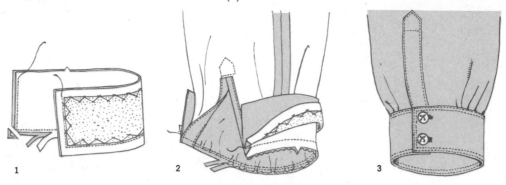

FRENCH CUFF OR BUTTON LINK CUFF: These cuffs are worn with the ends extending rather than lapping. The French cuff is folded back on itself and fastened by cuff links passing through four buttonholes. Bound buttonholes should be made on the outermost cuff only, after inserting the interfacing. The two buttonholes which do not show are machine-worked to prevent bulk. The button link cuff is constructed the same way, but is not folded back and has only two buttonholes for the link buttons.

For a French cuff, the inside layer of the cuff will be on the outside when turned back; therefore, catchstitch the interfacing to the inside cuff section and sew it along the foldline with long running stitches. Stitch the cuff sections together, ending 5⁄8″ from the long notched edge; trim, grade, turn, and press (1). Matching markings, stitch the gathered sleeve to the non-interfaced side of the cuff. Trim and grade the seam (2). Press the seam toward the cuff. Turn the raw edge under on the inside and slipstitch over the seam. Slipstitch the extended ends when applicable. Make any remaining buttonholes by hand or machine. Turn the lower edge to the outside along the roll line so that the buttonholes meet; press lightly. Fasten with link buttons or cuff links (3).

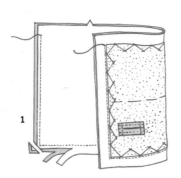
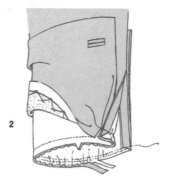
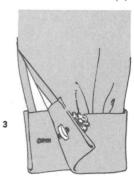

Turnback Cuffs

We have illustrated only the most classic examples of straight and shaped cuffs. Their variations are unlimited, including scalloped, slashed, and sculptured design edges that may circle the sleeve in a continuous seam or stop at multi-shaped finished ends. They can be attached to the sleeve in many ways as well, and often serve a dual role as extended cuffs by simply not folding them back.

SHAPED CUFF: Made from two fabric pieces, this cuff has many variations. Catchstitch interfacing to one fabric piece along all seamlines. Then stitch the cuff sections together, leaving the notched edge open; then trim and grade the seam allowances (1). Turn and press the cuff. Then baste and stitch the cuff to the right side of the sleeve through all thicknesses (2). Finish the notched edges with a bias or shaped facing (page 285), stitching through all layers. Roll the cuff to the outside along the seam, favoring the cuff so the seam is on the inside (3).

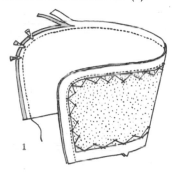

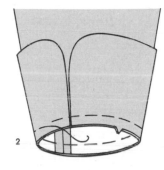

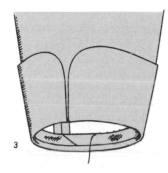

STRAIGHT CUFFS: Usually a single rectangle cut on the bias or straight grain, a straight cuff can also be two fabric sections. This cuff should be slightly larger in circumference at its foldline than the sleeve to which it is attached so that it can turn back easily. Apply interfacing to one half of the cuff, catchstitching it to seamlines; extend ⅝″ beyond foldline and secure with long running stitches. Stitch the ends of the cuff together. Trim the seam allowances to the foldline and press them open. Stitch the non-interfaced side of the cuff to the sleeve, right sides together; trim (1). Press the seam open. Then turn the cuff inside along the foldline, wrong sides together; baste close to the folded edge. Apply lace or seam binding to the raw edge. Blind hem to the sleeve or underlining (2). Roll the cuff to the outside over the sleeve (3). Steam, pounding lightly with a clapper or a ruler where necessary.

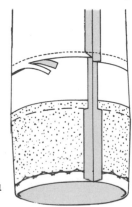

CUT IN ONE WITH THE SLEEVE: These cuffs should taper out slightly to be somewhat larger than the sleeve at the finished edge; this will ensure that the sleeve will not pucker when the cuff is turned back.

After you have determined the finished length of your sleeve, add twice the desired width of the cuff plus 1″ for a hem to the finished length of the sleeve; be sure to taper the cuff out from the hemline to the cuff foldline. Interface the cuff area before stitching the seams. Cut the interfacing equal in length to the circumference of the cuff and in width to the depth of the cuff plus two ⅝″ seam allowances. Sew to the cuff at foldlines and roll lines with running stitches. Stitch the sleeve seam and press it open (1).

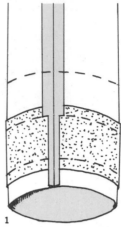

To form the rolled cuff, finish the raw edge with the stitch and overcast method. Turn the cuff inside along the foldline. Baste close to the fold (2). Roll the folded edge to the outside, forming the cuff. Baste through all thicknesses to hold the roll in place (3). On the inside, blindstitch hem edge to the sleeve (4).

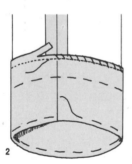
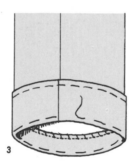
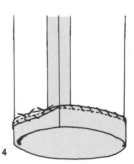

VARIATION WITH A SLIT: Prepare your cuff as in step #1, above. Finish the raw edge, then turn the interfaced side to the outside along the foldline. Mark the position of the slit and stitch along the markings, taking a stitch across the point. Clip the slit close to the stitching, and, using a sleeve board, press just the slit area. Turn the cuff to the inside and finish, as above.

Detachable Cuffs

There are few fashion accents more elegant and lady-like than the crisp, trim appearance of detachable cuffs. They can be straight or shaped. You can make them in a continuous band, open, or partially open with a slit or a slash. They may be designed to turn back over a sleeve or an existing cuff, or they can simulate a shirt cuff by extending below the hem of a jacket sleeve.

Detachable cuffs that are designed to turn back over a sleeve or an existing cuff will require some special handling in order to fit smoothly over the thickness of the sleeve or the existing cuff underneath it. You will have to shape the cuff piece, tapering it so that the finished edge which fits over the sleeve will be somewhat wider than the inside edge which slips inside the sleeve. Cuffs that are meant to extend below the sleeve without turning back will have to be made to fit just the inside measurement of the sleeve to which they will be applied.

Detachable cuffs are often used to provide a removable, washable trim on a garment which requires drycleaning. In such an instance, it may be wise to omit interfacing in the cuffs to ensure washability.

BAND CUFF: This is usually made by stitching the ends of the cuff together and pressing the seam open. Fold along the foldline with wrong sides together. Turn in the remaining raw edges along the seamline and slipstitch (1). From the right side, lap the sleeve over the cuff the desired depth and pin. Turn to the wrong side and slipstitch or snap the cuff in place (2).

 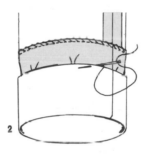 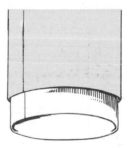

CUFF WITH A SLIT: Fold cuff right sides together and stitch each end. Grade seams, turn, and press. Join cuff by slipstitching ends together, leaving a slit. Baste raw edges together. Then encase them in a bias strip (self-fabric or commercial binding) cut to fit the inner circumference of the sleeve. Simply edgestitch the binding to the raw edges, overlapping the ends (1). From the right side, lap the sleeve over the cuff the desired depth and pin. Turn to the wrong side and slipstitch or snap the cuff in place (2). Roll the folded edge to the outside, forming the cuff, and anchor the corners with a bar tack if desired (3).

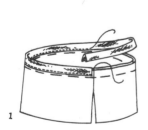 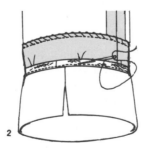 

Gussets

Just the mere mention of the word "gussets" can cause panic if you aren't accustomed to sewing them. But don't despair—you can attain foolproof results with even the trickiest of gussets by using appropriate reinforcement and *very careful* stitching.

A gusset is a triangular or diamond-shaped piece of fabric set into a garment at a slash. Most commonly it will be found at the underarm curve of a kimono sleeve, set in a slash which cuts across the garment from front to back. It makes possible a longer, slimmer kimono sleeve with an armhole closer to the body — in general, a more sophisticated fit than the kimono sleeve without a gusset. Another by-product of the gusset is added comfort through increased flexibility of the sleeve. Because the area under the arm receives a maximum amount of strain and needs ease for movement, the gusset should always be cut on the bias.

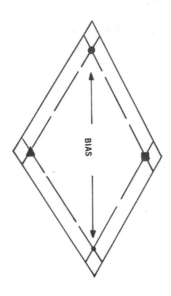

The gusset can be of one or two-piece construction—with a dart at the underarm or a seam joining the two sections. Frequently the gusset is combined with a portion of the garment, such as the underarm section of the sleeve or a side panel of the bodice, and it is then known as a combination gusset.

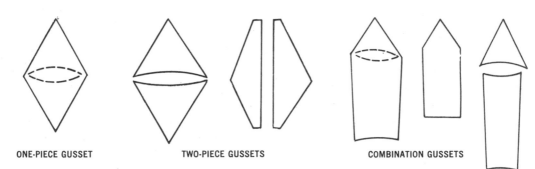

ONE-PIECE GUSSET   TWO-PIECE GUSSETS   COMBINATION GUSSETS

If you haven't had much experience with gussets, you should check the fit of a gusset by making a muslin of the sleeve and shoulder area for one side of the bodice front and back. Once you have slashed into the fabric, it is far too late to do anything about the fit, and impossible to repair the slashed fabric. Since body shapes and the way the arm joins the body vary with each woman, we can only cautiously recommend one general rule concerning the fit of gussets: the slash point of the gusset in the front and back should start exactly where the arm begins to separate from the body as you stand with your arms at your sides.

292

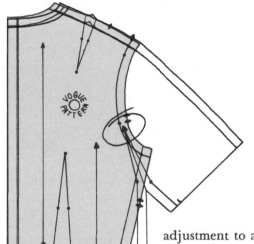

If you have a basic pattern with a regular armhole which fits you well, and assuming that the pattern you are about to use is perfect in every way but the fit of the gusset, you may wish to check the gusset fit this way: align the bodice pieces of your basic pattern over the bodice pieces with the gusset, matching center fronts, center backs, waistlines, and shoulders as evenly as possible. If the slash point corresponds with the lowest armhole marking (opposite the notches), then the gusset should be at a comfortable height. If there is a difference, mark the pattern tissue where the point should be. Keep the adjustment to a maximum of ½". Follow suggestions below before cutting the slash lines. The gusset has ample seam allowances to make this alteration. Note that the armhole marking and slash point will not match if the sleeve is loose-fitting or if it is outerwear, such as a coat. The slash point on a coat is lower than that for a dress to provide ease in wearing coat over other garments.

The level of the gusset dart or seam from front slash point to back slash point is important. It should approximately coincide with the position of the underarm seam for a regular set-in sleeve. The height of this curve in relation to your underarm may vary slightly, depending upon the style and proportion of the garment. When you are checking your gusset, concentrate on maintaining the ease for movement that was built into the pattern when it was designed. This is one time when you cannot just measure the garment or the pattern and add a couple of inches for ease, because the ease in a bodice with a gusset may be quite different from that of a bodice with a set-in sleeve. To eliminate problems in this area, always buy your pattern by your body measurements.

A Gusset Needs A Little Help

Before you slash the garment, it must be very carefully reinforced. Cut 2" bias squares of underlining or 4" long pieces of ribbon seam binding for each slash point. Center them over the slash points and stitching lines on the right side of both front and back

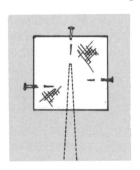 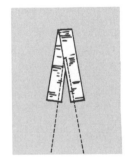

sections. Or, for fabrics that ravel easily, *very lightweight* iron-on interfacing or iron-on mending tape is a good method of stabilizing the fabric. Center it on the wrong side of your fabric at the slash point *before* you underline. For all reinforcements, stitch along the stitching lines, using short stitches (15-20 per inch) and taking one stitch across the slash point.

293

Test Fitting

So that you can work with the garment without undue strain on the points, make a preparatory slash to within ¼″ of the point between the stitching lines. Baste seams required to join the front and back sections before inserting the gusset. Prepare the gusset by basting any seams or darts.

From the right side, lap the garment over the gusset, placing stitching lines of the garment on the seamlines of the gusset; baste. The reinforcement square or seam binding should remain on the right side until the gusset is fitted. Try your garment on and check the fit of both the gusset and garment. When you are satisfied with the fit, mark any adjustment lines on your gusset and your garment; then remove the gusset.

For all gusset types, complete slashing, cutting between stitching lines right up to the point. Be sure to press the reinforcement squares or seam binding away from the garment so they can be treated as a seam allowance while you are pinning and stitching.

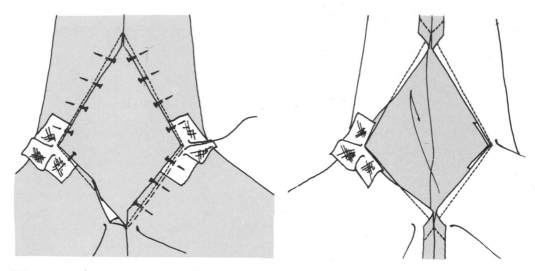

How to Insert your Gusset

There is very little difference between the insertion of one or two-piece gussets. Most diamond gussets include a contour dart which shapes the gusset, eliminating bulk under the arm. In the two-piece diamond gusset, a shaped seam is used for the same purpose and joins both parts of the gusset or the gusset to a part of the garment. The other variation, a triangular gusset, is quite simple to construct because the gusset and the garment side seams are continuous.

DIAMOND GUSSETS: Begin by reinforcing the gusset areas of the garment as mentioned previously. If you are satisfied with the test fitting of your gusset, stitch all bodice seams, ending the stitching at the markings as shown on your pattern and leaving the gusset area open. Press all the seams open. Prepare the gusset by stitching any dart or shaped seam, if necessary. Stitch ¼″ from previous line of stitching and trim close to this second stitching; overcast. Pin or baste the gusset to the garment, right sides together, placing the stitching line of the garment along the seamlines of the gusset.

294

From the garment side, stitch the gusset to the garment. Use small stitches and stitch on the garment alongside the previous stitching, beginning at the seams or markings and pivoting carefully at the point, treating the reinforcement patch or seam binding as seam allowances. End stitching at seams or markings so that the side seam allowances of the garment are not caught in the stitching. (For the combination gusset, also stitch all garment seams, ending at appropriate markings and leaving gusset area open. Insert this gusset the same as above.) Press all

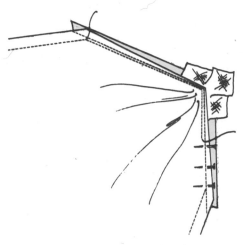

gusset seams toward the garment, pressing any seams of the combination gusset as instructed by your pattern. Clip where necessary to press the required seams open.

TRIANGULAR GUSSETS: Begin by reinforcing the gusset areas, as previously directed. Following a test fitting, stitch the shoulder seam only and press it open. Then complete slashing to the points. Right sides together, pin or baste the gusset pieces into their corresponding garment slashes, placing the stitching lines of the garment along the seamlines of the gusset. Stitch gussets in place the same as for the Diamond Gusset, being very careful at the slash points. Press the gusset seams toward the garment. Matching the gusset seamlines of the garment front and back, stitch the underarm seam of the bodice and sleeve in a continuous seam. Press the side seam open, clipping where needed.

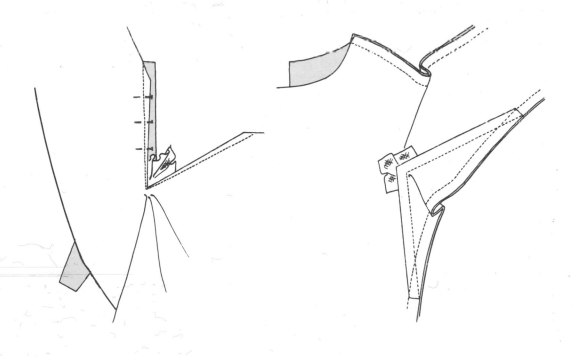

THE FINISH: If you use squares of underlining for reinforcement, trim the square of fabric to ⅜". Press the gusset seam toward the garment. On some combination gussets, you may want to press all the seams open. To further strengthen the gusset on sporty or casual clothes, topstitch close to the gusset seam on the outside, as shown.

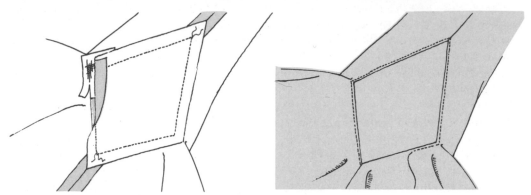

Pockets

If you are a novice at the art of sewing, or even if you've acquired a great amount of skill, you probably will be confused at the seemingly endless variations in pocket types and names. To help clear your mind, just remember that pockets branch out from two basic constructions—pockets of self-fabric applied to the garment, and pockets of lining pushed to the inside through a seam or slash, and sometimes covered by a flap or a welt.

Often the pocket type will be the main style-setting feature of a garment. With subtle manipulations in size, decoration, and number, a patch pocket can run the gamut from tailored to softly feminine. Flap, welt, and buttonhole pockets are the natural selection for a crisp, neat, and precise look, creating an essentially tailored appearance.

Pockets are important; they can beautifully accent a professional seam or they can blatantly expose a poor construction job. A few simple but vital rules will bring about very successful results: thread trace all pocket markings to the right side of all pocket and garment parts; pull pockets through openings very gently; keep all corners true; use interfacing for body; strive for even, balanced welts or flaps; and anchor the side edges of flaps and welts *invisibly* to the garment.

One excellent rule for positioning pockets below the waist is that they should be located at a level where your hands can slip into them naturally and comfortably. If placed too near the hem, they will look and feel awkward. However, there are instances when the rules are meant to be flexed a little. Pockets above the waist, and patch pockets anywhere, are so often meant to be strictly decorative that you should concentrate on whether their position is flattering, regardless of how accessible the pocket may be.

When adjusting your pattern, don't overlook the pockets. They may require relocating. If you happen to shorten the hem a major amount without moving the pockets, you run the risk of having pockets which are either too shallow or are at an awkward and unattractive location. If you are adjusting your pattern along the lengthen or shorten lines, don't forget to check the pocket placement lines as well.

All types of pockets made in lightweight or loosely woven fabrics need to be interfaced. Interfacing provides added strength, reinforces the opening, and preserves the pocket line. A lightweight interfacing such as muslin, placed on the underside of the garment directly behind the opening, contains just enough body to give the finished pocket a crisp look and feel. Welts and flaps should be interfaced if their shape and resiliency are to be preserved. The interfacing is generally cut on bias grain to extend ⅝" past the foldline. Patch pockets usually need no interfacing, but are often lined for a custom finish.

As a decoration or means of emphasizing a design line, topstitching is superb. As a method of applying your pocket, however, topstitching is not generally recommended. The patch pocket in particular will have a neater appearance if the topstitching is done before the pocket and garment are joined. It will then be easier to topstitch a straighter, more even line than when you are trying to concentrate on connecting the pocket and the garment. The topstitched pocket is then sewn to the garment by hand from the wrong side. It is possible to topstitch your pocket in place on lightweight, closely woven fabrics, but stitching over many thicknesses of bulky fabric or napped fabric can become a problem, even if you topstitch very carefully.

Patch Pocket

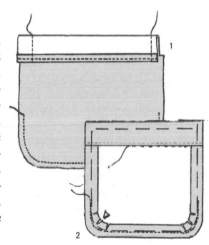

UNLINED: Turn under the top edge ¼" and stitch. Then turn the upper edge of the pocket to the outside along the foldline. Stitch ends and trim, as shown. If yours is a rounded pocket, ease-stitch the rounded area ¼" away from the seamline on the seam allowance to ensure a flat finish (1). Turn both the hem and seam allowance to the inside. On a rounded pocket, pull in the ease-stitches. If the pocket is square or rectangular, miter all corners (if you need mitering instructions, refer to page 243). Baste around the edges, notching away the excess fullness. Slipstitch the hem to the pocket (2).

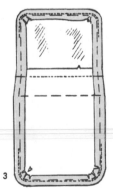

LINED: Stitch the pocket lining to the pocket self-facing. Press the seam toward the lining. For rounded pockets, easestitch the rounded areas ¼" away from the seamline on the seam allowance. Turn in the edges of the pocket along the seamlines, drawing up the ease thread where necessary. Starting at the foldline, your pocket should taper in from the pocket to the lining so the lining will fall ⅛" inside the finished pocket edge. Baste close to the edge (3). Turn the lining and self-facing to the inside along the pocket foldline. Slipstitch the lining (4).

SELF-LINED: Cut the desired pocket shape twice the length of the pocket plus seam allowances on all sides. Simply fold your pocket right sides together and stitch both sides and a portion of the bottom. Leave an opening for turning. Trim and grade the seam allowances (1). Turn the pocket, press it, and slipstitch the opening shut (2).

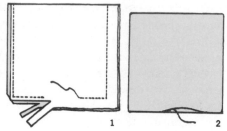

ATTACHED: When topstitching is desired, do it before you attach the pocket. From the right side, pin and baste the pocket in place. If the pocket is to be applied to a curved area of your garment, such as the front hip, place the garment over a curved surface in order to pin the pocket in place. From the wrong side, work a small backstitch through garment and pocket. Be sure the stitches do not show on the right side.

Pocket Flaps and Welts

Just about any type of pocket can be covered or set off by a flap or welt. Both may also appear by themselves as decorative fakes. The major distinction between a flap and a welt is that a flap hangs downward freely while a welt generally points upward and is securely attached along its sides.

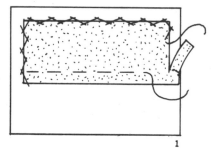

The example shown is a decorative flap, but the same construction principles apply to any flap or wide welt. Interface one half of the flap so that the interfacing extends ⅝″ past the foldline. Trim away interfacing seam allowances and catch-stitch to the flap along the seamlines. Sew along the foldline with long running stitches (1). With right sides together, fold and stitch the flap ends to ⅝″ from the flap base. Trim and grade the seam; clipping or notching will be necessary for a shaped flap (2). Turn and press.

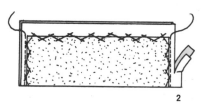

When the direction of the seam allowance coincides with the direction of the finished flap or welt, you must establish the roll of the flap at the seamline so that it will lie flat. Turn the seam allowances of the flap down over your hand to establish the roll line, adjusting the flap or welt if more upper fabric is required (3). Pin and baste along the new seamline of the upper portion through both layers. Remember this treatment will be necessary only when the flap or welt turns over its own seam allowance.

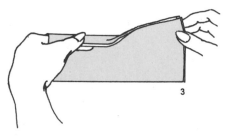

To attach the flap, place the new seamline along the placement lines on your garment and stitch through all thicknesses. Turn back the upper seam allowance and trim the lower one close to the stitching. Turn in ¼″ on the long edge of the upper seam allowance, folding the ends in diagonally, and turn it down over the trimmed edge (4). Then edgestitch. Fold the flap down and press, being careful not to overpress or unsightly ridges from the flap edges will appear on the garment. To secure upper sides of corners, slipstitch to the garment from right side, or backstitch heavy fabrics from the wrong side (5).

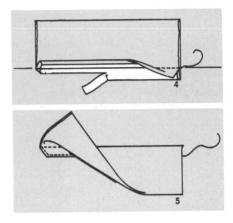

One-Piece Welt Pocket

For this pocket the welt is pressed upward over the opening of a lining pocket. If your fabric needs more body, interface the welt in the usual way. Construct and press the welt. It will be easier to work with if you baste the raw edges together on the seamline and trim them to ¼″ from the seamline. Always do any required topstitching before you attach the welt. Then pin the welt to the garment, placing the seamline of the welt over the lower stitching line on the right side of the garment; baste. Now pin and baste the lining pocket over the welt with the deeper portion above the welt. Stitch along the stitching lines, backstitching or using small knots at the ends (1). Slash between your stitching to within ½″ of both ends; clip diagonally to the corners. Turn the pocket to the inside, turning the welt up. Overcast the raw edges of both narrow seam allowances (2). Press. Positioning the pocket and garment as shown, carefully stitch around the pocket edges, being very sure to catch the base of the small triangular ends in your sewing. Trim and overcast the pocket edges. The final step takes place on the outside; just slipstitch the ends of the welt in place (3).

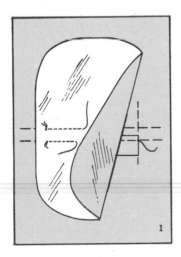
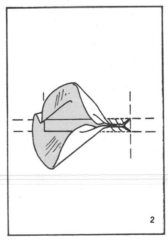
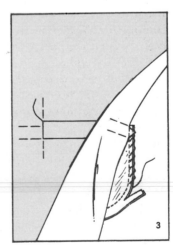

Buttonhole or Double Welt Pocket

This pocket opening looks like a large bound buttonhole. It has two very narrow welts that face each other and is the exception to the rule that welts point upward. Fold both long edges of the welt, wrong sides together, to meet at the center; press. With cut edges up, center folded welt over the pocket markings; baste. Slash through center of welt; do not cut the garment (1). Baste garment fabric section of pocket in place along upper stitching line over welt, matching markings. Baste lining section in place along lower stitching line in same manner. Stitch through all thicknesses along the indicated lines; backstitch or knot the ends (2). From the wrong side, slash through the center for pocket opening. Clip diagonally to ends of stitching, making triangular ends ½" deep. Pull pocket parts to inside through slash (3).

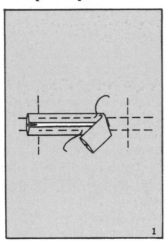
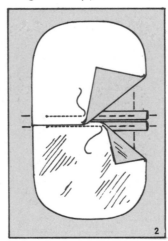
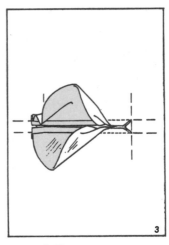

Press welts to meet in center of opening and whipstitch together loosely. Matching pocket edges and starting at the top, stitch side and lower edges together, catching base of the small triangular ends in stitches (4). Trim and overcast edges. To support weight of pocket, catchstitch upper edge to underlining (5).

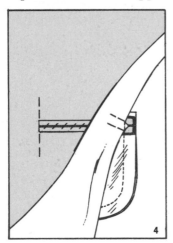
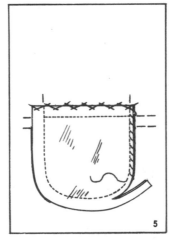

Self-Welt Pocket with Flap

In this instance, the flap and a narrow welt are combined for a very tailored, precise appearance. Make flap according to directions on page 298, steps 1 and 2. Baste raw edges along seamline. To make welt, fold wrong sides together and baste along seamline on long raw edge. Trim basted seams of both flap and welt to ¼". On the outside of the garment, baste the flap to the upper stitching line and the welt to the lower stitching line; the long raw edges will meet (1). Matching markings, baste larger pocket section over flap and smaller section over welt. Stitch through all thicknesses along the indicated lines; backstitch or knot ends (2). From the wrong side, slash through the center to within ½" of end of stitching for pocket opening. Then clip diagonally to the ends of the stitching without cutting the flap or welt. Pull all pocket parts to inside (3).

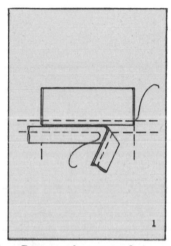
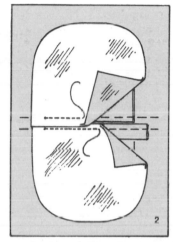
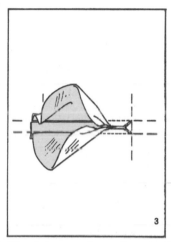

Press welt upward (over opening) and flap downward. Matching pocket edges and starting at the top, stitch side and lower edges together, catching the base of the triangular ends in your stitches (4). Trim and overcast these raw pocket edges. To support the weight of the pocket, catchstitch the upper edge to the underlining (5).

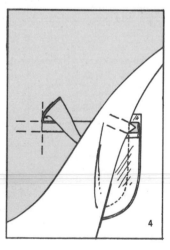
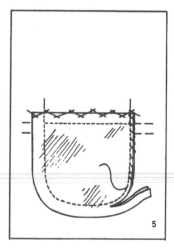
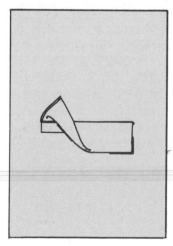

Seam Pocket

This inconspicuous variety of pocket is concealed in side or front seams. The pocket top may be controlled from the inside by a waistline seam. A seam pocket is generally made of lining fabric and faced at its edge with garment fabric. First sew the pocket pieces to the garment sections; press the seams toward the pocket (1). For bias garment seams or very stretchy fabric, use running stitches to sew ribbon seam binding to the underlining over the foldline between the pocket opening markings. Baste the garment sections together at the seam and across the openings; also baste the pocket pieces together. Start stitching from the lower edge and continue around the pocket, pivoting at corners. Use reinforcement stitches at all pivot points (2). Turn the pocket toward the front along the foldline or roll line. Clip the back seam allowance above and below the facing extension so you can press the seam open above and below the pocket. Press lightly for a fold or steam and pound gently for a soft roll. Catchstitch the seam allowances of the pocket top to the underlining to keep it in place (3).

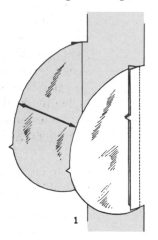

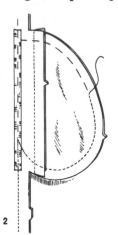

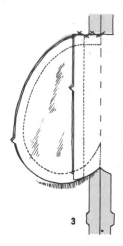

1   2   3

How to Add a Seam Pocket

You can add this type of pocket in self-fabric to your garment. The dimensions are given in scale. Seam allowances should be added to all edges. Cut two for each pocket (4). The pocket with a straight upper edge is the style suitable for waistline seams. Just align the pocket opening edge with the seamline on your garment, being sure that the pocket is at the correct level for your hands. If desired, pocket and garment can be cut in one piece, eliminating the seam at the pocket opening. Then construct and press the pocket, as described above. If your fabric is not wide enough to accommodate the pocket, you will have to make a separate pocket of lining or self-fabric and add facing extensions to the pocket area.

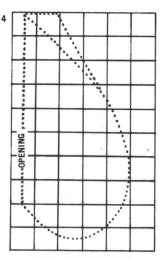

EACH SQUARE EQUALS 1″

Buttons

Buttons are an important finishing touch not only in their more practical sense as fasteners, but also as adornments and essential parts of the garment design. Gone are the days when buttons simply closed the front or back opening and cuffs of a garment. Today you will see them everywhere—perching on shoulders, outlining seams, closing skirts and pants, fastening waistbands, attaching belts, ending sleeve vents. Buttons can be of any material—plastic, metal, leather, wood. They can match, contrast, or complement; give a tailored, casual, or dressy look.

Think of the many different ways you can use them to close a garment—with buttonholes, loops, frogs, or a short chain between two buttons. Adding buttons not called for by your pattern can often add impact as well. Perhaps you would like extra buttons (a row of small ones instead of a few larger ones) or fewer buttons (adding covered snaps on the inside between them to prevent gapping). You might care to group your buttons in clusters or space them irregularly. Even if the button placements are essential to the look of your garment, you can still change the mood of your garment by a simple change of buttons.

However you use buttons, remember that they must relate to the fabric, the design of the garment, and especially to the wearer. Spacing and proportion are the keys to expert selection and placement. For example, a petite figure calls for many small buttons or a few larger ones. It is best to remain with the button size recommended by the designer. If you prefer to experiment, the best way to find the correct size for your button is to pin on different sizes and see how they look *before* stitching your buttonholes. Refer to the button chart on page 88 to determine correct button sizes.

If you've lengthened or shortened your garment, you may need to adjust the number of buttons and the buttonhole placement accordingly. Be sure that there are buttons located at all points of stress. Place a button at the waist of a fitted jacket or coat to prevent gapping unless you have a belt. If you are using a belt or sash, place your buttons sufficiently above and below the belt so they won't interfere. It is also wise to have a button at the fullest part of the bustline for a large-bosomed figure. If your garment still gaps between buttons, close these spaces with covered snaps. Exactly which placement you choose will depend upon your button size and your own taste.

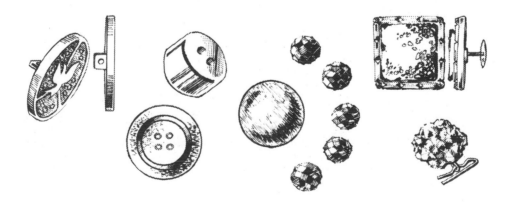

BUTTON PLACEMENT: The time it takes to see that your buttons are placed correctly is well spent, for it ensures that your garment will close in a straight line and lie

flat. Pin the garment closed, matching center basting lines. For a horizontal buttonhole, push a pin through the end of the buttonhole near the finished edge of the garment. The center of the button should be sewn at this point and directly on the center front or center back line. Vertical buttonholes have the button placed ⅛" below the top of the buttonhole and on the center front or center back line. Place each button directly in line with the button above.

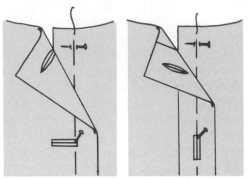

THREAD: To sew on the button, use buttonhole twist, button and carpet thread, heavy duty thread, or a double strand of cotton thread which has been drawn through beeswax. You will find that the beeswax prevents knots from forming in the thread while sewing. For easy handling, your thread should not be much longer than 18". Secure your thread with a couple of small backstitches on the right side under the button, rather than with a knot, for a neater application.

SEW-THROUGH BUTTONS: These should have a thread shank to allow the buttoned fabric to lie smoothly and not pull around the buttons. The length of the shank should equal the thickness of the garment at the buttonhole plus ⅛" for movement. Always begin sewing on the right side. Place a pin, matchstick, toothpick, or other object over

the button and sew over the object when sewing on the button. Remove the object, raise the button to the top of the stitches, and wind the thread tightly under the button to form the thread shank. Backstitch several times into the shank for a secure finish. Buttons used for trim will not need a shank; however, delicate fabric may need a reinforcement of ribbon seam binding (see reinforced button at right).

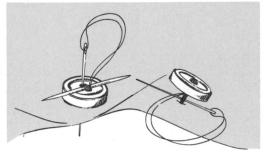

SHANK BUTTONS: Attach the button with small stitches sewn through the shank. If your garment fabric is very thick and bulky, a thread shank must be made as with the sew-through button. Remember that the direction of the shank should always be aligned with that of the buttonhole. To make your shank buttons detachable, insert them through eyelets and secure with toggles. Stud buttons are simply inserted through eyelets.

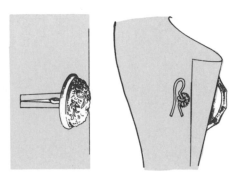

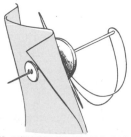

REINFORCED BUTTON: For coats and suits, reinforced buttons are advisable. Place a small flat button on the back of the garment under the larger button. Sew directly through from one to the other for added stability. Use a small folded square of ribbon seam binding in place of the reinforcement button for delicate fabrics. Place it inside the garment directly beneath the holes where it cannot be seen when worn.

LINK BUTTONS: Link buttons are most commonly used with cuffs, but may also be used to close vests or capes. You may use either purchased or covered buttons. Run heavy thread through two buttons, leaving the thread long enough to form the link and to pass through the joined garment edges. Work over the thread with a blanketstitch (see page 315). Fasten thread securely. Buttons can also be sewn to the ends of a narrow turned fabric strip.

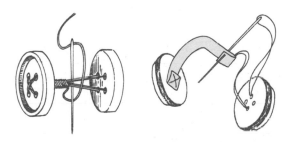

COVERED BUTTONS: If you want your buttons to be inconspicuous or if your fabric is hard to match, buttons covered with self-fabric may be your answer. Use a commercially prepared kit available in many sizes and shapes or make your own with bone rings.

For a covered ring button, select a bone ring the size of the button you need. Cut a circle of fabric slightly less than twice the diameter of the ring. Gather the edge of the fabric with a small running stitch. Insert the ring, pull up the gathering thread, and secure. Add a special touch by sewing a small running stitch just inside the ring through all layers with buttonhole twist. Attach with a shank. If you should desire a finishing technique for the back of your button, refer to page 382.

Another type of self-fabric button, Chinese ball button, is described on page 315.

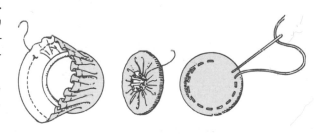

JEWELED BUTTONS: Here is a suggestion for those times when you wish to use jeweled or rough-edged buttons on fabrics which might snag or, pull. Sew your button directly to the buttonhole, using covered snaps underneath to secure the opening. Using this technique will give you the look of a buttonhole closing without the possible mishaps. See page 316 for information about the placement and sewing of snaps.

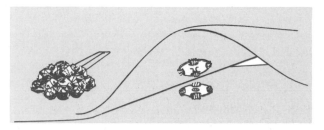

Buttonholes

Let the design and the fabric determine your choice of buttonhole. Couturiers use bound buttonholes for a tailored professional look on all garments, hand-worked buttonholes for soft or delicate fabrics, and machine-worked buttonholes for man-tailored and casual garments. Your pattern markings include exact placement and size of buttons and buttonholes as recommended by the designer.

There are some general rules for determining button placement. The top buttonhole on a center closing is generally placed below the neckline edge at least half the width of the button plus ¼″. The last buttonhole on a dress should be 3″ to 4″ from the bottom, **never through the hem;** omit the last buttonhole if necessary. Buttonholes are not usually placed closer than ⅝″ from a closing edge. For a large button, the extension from the end of the buttonhole to the closing edge should be a very minimum of half the button's width plus ¼″.

Any changes from the designer's intended placement or size should be carefully planned. If you have adjusted the length of the pattern tissue, adjust the buttonholes by evenly spacing them between the top and bottom buttonholes. If you are adding buttonholes, the most important consideration in the placement is the size of your button. Remember that large buttons are placed further apart than small ones. With this in mind, read the introduction to Buttons, page 303, before you buy your buttons and make your buttonholes. If your button is larger than recommended, do not move the buttonhole away from the edge, as this will change your center line; rather, extend the closing edge to accommodate the button. (Make this adjustment on the pattern **before** you cut your fabric so the underlap on the left side will be as wide as the overlap on the right side.)

Always test the buttonhole on a scrap of your fabric with the appropriate underlining and interfacing to discover any problems you might encounter. If you are making a bound buttonhole, ravelling and fraying corners may be alleviated by using the organza patch method; lightweight, sheer, or very difficult fabrics may require hand-worked buttonholes. Refer to Pressing, page 345, for tips on pressing your buttonholes.

BUTTONHOLE SIZE: The size of the buttonhole should always be determined by the button. Minimum buttonhole length is equal to the diameter plus the thickness of the button. Add ⅛″ to allow for the shank and slight size reduction due to fabric thickness.

To find the buttonhole length needed for a thick or ball button, wrap a ¼″ wide strip of paper around the button and mark with a pin where the ends meet. Then fold the paper strip flat and measure between the pin and the fold to determine the correct buttonhole size. Add the ⅛″ mentioned above.

In general, attractive buttonholes are slim, about ¼″ wide with each lip ⅛″ wide. They may be slightly narrower for lightweight fabrics and·a little wider for bulky fabrics, but total width should not exceed ⅜″.

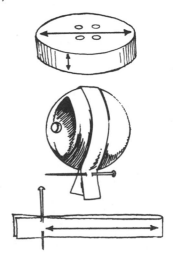

PLACEMENT MARKING: Make your buttonhole markings on the right side to make certain that the finished buttonhole will follow the fabric grainlines. First mark the position and length of your buttonhole with pins or chalk, then thread trace for precise markings.

Begin all *horizontal buttonholes* ⅛″ to the side of the buttons nearest the closing edge to allow for the natural tendency of the garment to "pull" away from the closing. This "pull" is downward for *vertical buttonholes:* begin them ⅛″ above the actual button placement and directly on the lengthwise placement line. Vertical buttonholes, which tend to hold buttons less securely, are generally used in non-functioning positions or on narrow plackets, as on a man-tailored shirt.

The reference point in placing your buttonholes is always the garment center line; center lines must meet when your closing is fastened. (Do not try to alter your garment simply by moving the buttons or buttonholes, as this changes your center line and distorts the shape and fit of your garment.) Thus the center line should always be the first line marked when marking your buttonhole placement. Next mark the short horizontal lines for the position of the buttonholes and, lastly, the long continuous vertical lines to indicate their length.

For a center closing, the buttons are positioned on the underlap center line, the buttonholes in corresponding positions on the overlap center line (1). For a double-breasted closing with functional buttonholes, place each row of buttons an equal distance on each side from the underlap center line, and buttonholes in corresponding positions from the overlap center line. Remember the *buttons* are placed equal distances from the center line, not the buttonholes, and make certain both rows of buttonholes extend in the same direction from the buttons (2). For an asymmetrical closing, first make sure center lines match. Mark the short placement markings perpendicular to the edge and the long length lines parallel to the edge (3).

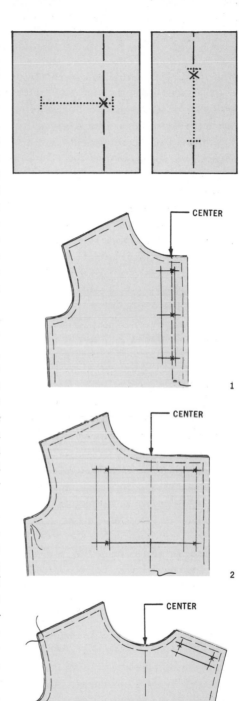

1

2

3

INTERFACING: If you are using lightweight interfacing, make the buttonholes through it so they will be reinforced and supported (1). For interfacing made of heavyweight material which is too stiff or bulky to be sewn with the buttonhole, make the buttonholes through just the fabric and underlining before attaching interfacing. Then cut openings in the interfacing slightly larger than the buttonhole opening. Place interfacing on the fabric, pull buttonholes through, and sew the edges of the buttonhole to the interfacing (2). Finish attaching interfacing to garment. To interface the buttonhole area in fabrics or garment areas that may not need interfacing, cut a rectangle of interfacing 1″ wider and longer than the buttonhole. Center it over the buttonhole markings and catchstitch it to the underlining before making the buttonhole (3).

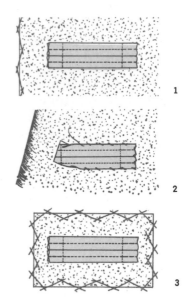

Bound Buttonholes

Make bound buttonholes before attaching the facing. They are made from strips of fabric cut on either straight or bias grain. Strips cut on the bias provide extra ease for buttoning and unbuttoning; take away strain from the corners, where there is a probability of the fabric pulling out of the seam; and can add an interesting design feature in plaid or striped fabrics. Carefully stitch, using small stitches corresponding to the garment's fabric weight and finish (15-20 per inch depending on your fabric).

SLASHING OPENING: After stitching, there are two methods of slashing your bound buttonhole. After securing your thread ends, cut through garment at the center of the buttonhole, cutting between stitching lines from the wrong side with small sharp scissors. Then slash along the center of the stitching, stopping ¼″ from each end, and clip diagonally to the ends of the stitching or into the corners, being careful not to cut the stitching. Or, you may cut diagonally through the center of the buttonhole, slashing directly to the ends of the stitching or corners.

SECURING CORNERS: You must carefully secure the ends of your buttonholes if they are not to pull out or ravel when worn. With the garment placed right side up, fold garment back at each end of the buttonhole to reveal the strip ends with the fabric triangle on top. Then stitch back and forth across the base of each triangle several times with small stitches to square the corners and strengthen the ends. Trim ends to ¼″ and catchstitch them to the underlining.

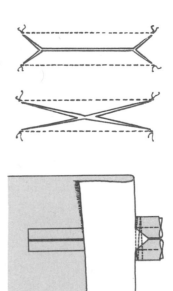

ONE-PIECE FOLDED METHOD: This is a simple method which requires only one fabric strip per buttonhole. Cut a strip of self-fabric 1″ to 1⅛″ wide and 1″ longer than the buttonhole. Mark a center line along the length of the strip. With wrong sides together, fold edges so they meet at the markings; press lightly (1). With the cut edges up, baste the center of the strip over the buttonhole markings, extending the ends ½″ beyond the end markings. Stitch with small stitches ⅛″ from each side of the center, starting at the middle of the side and going across the ends. Carefully count the stitches on the ends for accuracy. Overlap stitches where you began (2). Slash, being careful not to cut through the stitching. Turn strip to the inside and press (3). If you wish to cord your buttonhole, refer to page 313. Fold back the garment and finish the corners as in Securing Corners, page 308.

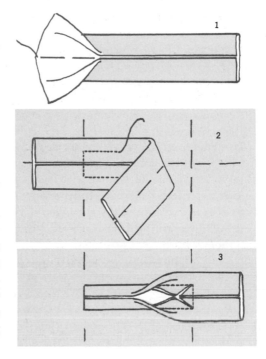

TWO-PIECE METHOD: This method is fast and easy for firm fabrics. Cut a strip of self-fabric 1″ wide and long enough for all the buttonholes. For the length of this strip, multiply the length of each buttonhole plus 1″ by twice the number of buttonholes. Wrong sides together, fold strip in half lengthwise and press lightly. Machine baste ⅛″ from folded edge. Cut the strip into sections the length of the buttonhole plus 1″ and trim the cut edge to a scant ⅛″ from the stitching (4).

Baste one strip to the right side, placing the cut edge along the thread traced position line. Using small stitches, stitch the length of the buttonhole through all thicknesses directly over the stitching on the strip. Leave the thread ends long enough to tie. Repeat for the second strip on the opposite side of the thread traced line so that the cut edges meet (5). Pull the thread ends through to the wrong side and tie. Slash, being careful not to cut through the strips. Turn the strips to inside and press (6). If you care to cord your buttonholes, refer to Corded Buttonholes, page 313. Finish the corners as in Securing Corners, page 308.

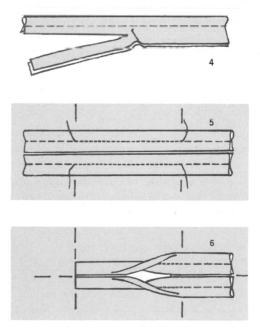

ORGANZA PATCH METHOD: This method is almost foolproof, and is especially suitable for fabrics that ravel easily or are bulky. Eliminate another problem with these fabrics by applying the interfacing *after* making buttonholes, rather than making them through all layers. Turn to page 308 for directions.

For your patch, always use a crisp, sheer fabric with the same qualities as organza. Cut patch 1″ bigger than the buttonhole. Center the patch over the buttonhole marking on the right side of the garment; pin. If you find the markings difficult to see, emphasize them with tailor's chalk. Stitch ⅛″ from each side of marking, using small stitches. Start at middle of the marking, pivot at corners, and carefully count the stitches at ends for accuracy. Overlap stitches where you began. Slash, being careful not to cut stitching (1). Turn patch through slash to the wrong side of garment. Press seam allowances away from opening. You now have a neatly finished hole in your garment the exact size of your finished buttonhole (2).

Cut two strips of your fashion fabric 1½″ longer and wider than the buttonhole. Baste the two strips right sides together along the center, forming a seam. Press the basted seam open (3). Then accurately place the strips on the wrong side of the opening with the basted seam at the center. This forms the two even lips for your buttonhole. Pin the strips in place close to each end (4). Turn the garment to the wrong side. Pin and stitch the long seam allowances to the strips to hold the lips in place, stitching on the garment (outside the buttonhole) alongside the previous stitching so the organza does not show on the outside. Extend the stitching lines ½″ on both ends of the seam through the organza and strips (5). To cord your buttonhole at this time, refer to page 313. Secure corners, as on page 308. Apply interfacing. Trim excess fabric from patch and strip, rounding out corners, and press.

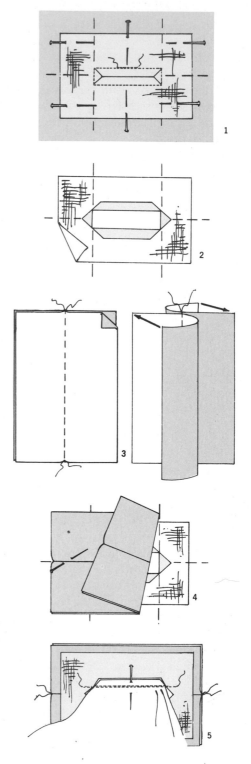

TO COMPLETE BOUND BUTTONHOLES: For a quick and easy finish, pin or baste facing to garment through all thicknesses. Hold buttonhole lips together with diagonal basting for hard-to-handle fabrics. Stick a pin from the outside through each end of the buttonhole opening. Be sure that the pins are in line with the grain of the facing. Slash the facing between the pins and turn in the raw edges. Hem around the buttonhole, as shown, taking a few stitches at each end for reinforcement.

To make a better-looking finish on garments to be worn open, establish the length of the buttonhole on the facing with pins. Then cut to within ¼″ of each end and clip diagonally into the corners. Turn in the raw edges and hem around the buttonhole, reinforcing the corners. An additional finish for a thoroughly professional look, or for extremely difficult fabrics, is presented in the couture section, page 382.

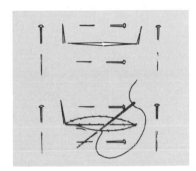 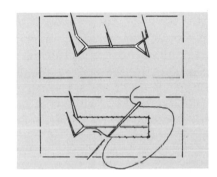

Hand-Worked Buttonholes

These buttonholes are sewn through all layers after the facing is applied. Machine stitch a scant ⅛″ on either side and across both ends of buttonhole marking. Carefully slash along the length marking.

Take an 18″ length of buttonhole twist and insert the needle at one end, anchoring the thread with backstitches on the wrong side. Work the buttonhole stitch by inserting the needle through the slash from the right side and bringing it out just outside the stitching line. Keep thread under eye and point of needle as shown (1). Draw up the needle so a purl (knot) is formed at the buttonhole edge (2). Repeat, keeping stitches even and each purl exactly on the edge of the slash. Fan stitches at the end closest to the finished edge as shown (3). Place a bar tack at the remaining end.

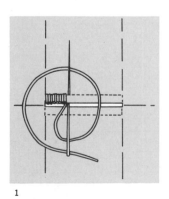 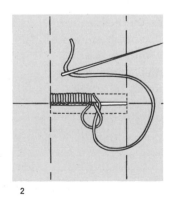 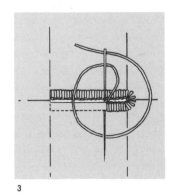

1   2   3

BAR TACK: Finish both ends of the buttonhole with a bar tack. First take 3 or 4 long stitches across the width at each end of the buttonhole. Then work the blanket stitch over the core threads, catching the fabric underneath.

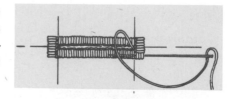

KEYHOLE: If you prefer a keyhole buttonhole on man-tailored clothes, follow instructions for hand-worked buttonholes, with one exception: make a hole with an awl at end nearest opening edge to form keyhole. Then work buttonhole stitches around hole and slash; finish remaining end with a bar tack.

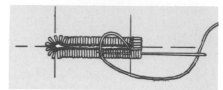

EYELETS: This is a special type of buttonhole used with studs and cufflinks, drawstrings and belts. Sew around placement marking with small running stitches. Cut an opening the desired size or punch a hole with an awl. Bring needle up through fabric from the wrong side a scant $\frac{1}{8}''$ from the edge of the hole. Leave 1″ of thread on the wrong side and work around the hole with buttonhole stitches. Fasten threads securely on the wrong side.

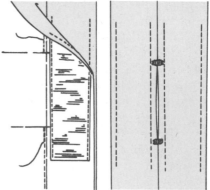

Machine-Worked Buttonholes

These buttonholes are particularly suited to casual and man-tailored clothes or clothes that require frequent laundering. Attach facing before making buttonholes. Use interfacing in a color close to your fabric, for it may show at the edges. Thread trace buttonhole markings through all layers. Make buttonholes with a buttonhole attachment or zigzag machine. For a stronger buttonhole, stitch over buttonhole a second time.

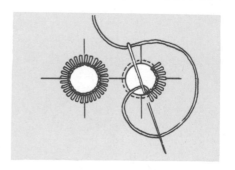

Seam Buttonholes

These buttonholes are actually small openings in a seam. Mark buttonhole placement; pin and baste seam. Cut two strips of ribbon seam binding for each buttonhole 1″ longer than opening. On one seam allowance, place strip next to seamline along markings and stitch close to each edge. Repeat on other seam allowance. Then stitch garment seam, ending stitching at markings; backstitch. Press seam open. Remove basting from opening. Add bar tacks at ends on wrong side.

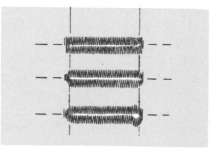

Corded Buttonholes

Cording buttonholes reduces their elasticity, but adds additional body, strength, and durability. Their raised appearance also provides a finer finish.

There are two methods for cording bound buttonholes. For the one-piece or patch method, draw a strand or two of string or yarn through lips just before stitching triangular ends (1). For the two-piece method, fold strip, wrong sides together, around cable cord or twine; machine-baste with a conventional or invisible zipper foot (2).

For hand-worked buttonholes, work the buttonhole stitch over buttonhole twist secured at one end with a pin. Add a bar tack to the end and clip the cord (3).

For machine-worked buttonholes, your machine may have a special foot for cording; refer to your manual for specific information.

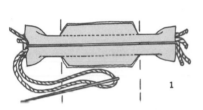 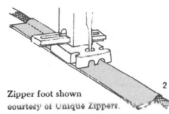 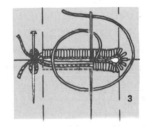

1

Zipper foot shown courtesy of Unique Zippers.

2

3

Loops and Fastenings

Some details, no matter how time-consuming, are those little touches that add greatly to the pleasure of wearing a garment you have made. Loops and fastenings are perfect examples and with careful planning and accurate marking they can be fun.

Fabric Closures

Loops, Chinese ball buttons, and frogs—all can add an impressive touch to a simple style whether used singly, in combinations, or with purchased buttons. They can be made of self-filled or corded bias tubing, in contrasting or self-fabric; purchased braid; or other tubular material that complements your garment fabric.

SELF-FILLED TUBING: Cut a bias strip the desired length and the finished width plus enough seam allowance to fill the tubing. The additional seam allowance depends upon your fabric—the bulkier the fabric, the narrower the seam allowances. Experiment to determine the correct width for your particular fabric. Remember also that the strip will become somewhat narrower as it is stretched during stitching. Right sides together, fold bias in half lengthwise and stitch, stretching bias as you sew. At end, slant the stitching diagonally, making the tube wider. To turn, pass a heavy thread and a tapestry needle, eye first, through the bias. For a narrow tubing, turn in the raw edges, roll bias between your finger, and sew edges together, eliminating turning process.

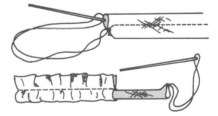

CORDED TUBING: Cut a bias strip of fabric the desired length and wide enough to fit around the cord plus ½" for seam allowances and stretching. If necessary, piece the bias as directed on page 245. Cut a piece of cable cord **twice** the length of the bias; the extra cord will facilitate stitching and turning. Fold the bias over the cord with right sides together and edges even. Place one end of the bias ¼" beyond the center of the cording.

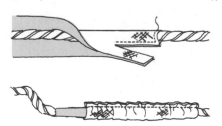

Using a zipper foot, stitch across the end at the center of the cording. Then stretch the bias slightly while stitching the long edge close to the cording. Trim the seam allowance. To turn right side out, slowly draw the enclosed cord out of the tubing; the free cord will be pulled into the tubing automatically. Cut off the stitched end and the excess cording.

PAPER GUIDE: Fabric loops can be applied singly or in a continuous row, depending on the fabric weight and spacing desired. Mark the seamline the length of the closure area on a strip of lightweight paper. Make a line for the distance that the loops are to extend (approximately half the diameter of the button, plus the thickness of the cording). Make spread of each loop equal to button diameter plus twice the cord thickness.

SINGLE LOOPS: Cut each loop the correct length to fit within the markings plus two seam allowances. Form each loop with the seamed side up and the loop pointing away from the edge, keeping the edges of the paper guide and the loops even. Use narrow masking tape to hold them in place. Using large stitches, stitch on the paper close to the seamline within the seam allowance. Then remove the masking tape. Pin paper guide to the appropriate garment edge on the right side of the fabric, matching seamlines. Stitch close to seamline near first stitching. Tear away paper and apply facing.

CONTINUOUS LOOPS: With a long strip of bias tubing, form a continuous row of loops on the paper guide within the markings, extending them ½" into the seam allowance. Tape and stitch them to the paper and then apply them to the garment in the same manner as single loops. The short looped ends in the seam allowance may be trimmed to ¼" to reduce any unnecessary bulk before applying facing.

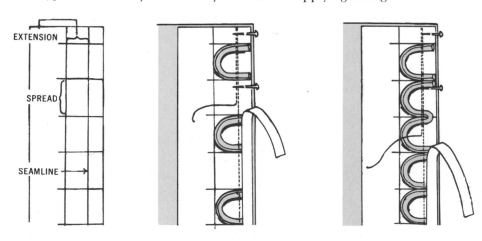

CHINESE BALL BUTTONS: These can be made of purchased braid or either self-filled or corded tubing. Cut a piece of tubing 16″ long and follow the diagram for the loop formations. Keep tubing seamline on top and loops open while shaping the button. Then draw the ends to pull the loops closer together, easing and shaping the loops to form your button. Clip off any excess tubing and fasten the ends securely to the button.

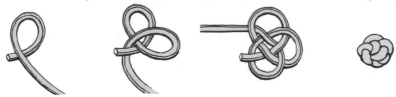

FROGS: Follow the diagram, using soutache braid, round braid, or self-filled or corded tubing. Keep tubing seamline on top while forming the frogs. Use small hand stitches to tack each successive loop as it is formed and tiny invisible stitches to attach the finished frog. You can vary the shape by changing the size of the loops, but remember to keep one loop large enough to extend beyond the garment edge and pass over the button. For intricate shapes, form the frog on paper with masking tape and basting before stitching.

Thread Closures and Fastenings

The blanket stitch is the classic stitch used for most thread loops and fastenings. Use matching double thread or single buttonhole twist. Take 2 or 3 foundation stitches the desired length and depth of your loop, securing the ends with small backstitches. These stitches form the core of your loop, and it is essential that they are the correct size; if you are using a belt, button, or hook with your loop, make sure the loop size accommodates them and allows for ease. Then, with the same thread, work blanket stitches closely over the entire length of the foundation threads.

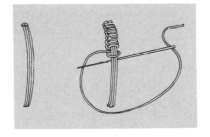

Although the same stitch is used to form thread loops or fastenings, their names vary according to their location and purpose.

THREAD LOOP is usually placed at the corner of a neck opening and fastens to a small button. It is also often used in place of a metal eye on delicate fabrics or in conspicuous locations. Its length should be equal to the diameter plus the thickness of the button. A longer loop is used to form a **BELT CARRIER**. Usually placed at the side seams, it should be just large enough to let the belt slip through. A **THREAD EYE** is often used with a metal hook. Relatively taut, it is the same length as the metal eye it replaces.

The BAR TACK is used to reinforce places of strain, such as the end of a buttonhole or a slit. A FRENCH TACK or SWING TACK holds two parts of a garment together, such as the two hems of a lined garment, and is usually placed at seams on the wrong side.

THREAD CHAIN: If you prefer, a thread loop or fastening made with the chain stitch can be substituted for the French tack, thread loops, belt carriers, and lingerie strap holders. Use a double thread or single strand of buttonhole twist securely fastened to the garment with one or two small overlapping stitches (1). Form a loop on the right side by taking another short stitch. Slip the thumb and first two fingers of your left hand through the loop while holding the needle and thread end in your right hand (2). Using the second finger of your left hand, pick up a new loop and pull it through the first loop, tightening as you proceed (3). Continue to work the chain to the desired length. Place the needle through the last loop to form a knot and end the chain (4). Secure the free end with several small stitches.

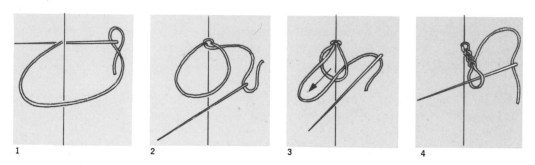

Commercial Fasteners

There are many commercial fasteners available. The key is to select the one most suited to your individual needs. These fasteners, to be truly functional, should be chosen in a size appropriate to the fabric weight, the amount of strain the closure will receive, and the type of cleaning and care the garment will require. Choose a fastening that will also be inconspicuous while the garment is being worn. To simplify matters, we have divided the commercial fasteners into three basic categories—snaps, hooks and eyes, and nylon tape fasteners.

SNAPS: These fasteners are used on overlapping edges which receive a minimum of strain. The ball half of the snap is sewn on the under side of the overlap. The socket is sewn on the upper side of the garment section closest to your body. Sew the ball on first. Take several small stitches close together through each hole, picking up a thread of the garment with each stitch. Carry the thread under the snap from hole to hole. To mark the location for the socket, rub tailor's chalk onto the ball and position the garment as when fastened, or use a pin through the ball section.

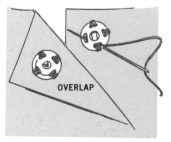

See page 382 for covering snaps, and for using snaps on edges which just meet, and page 89 for types and sizes.

HOOKS AND EYES: Hooks and eyes are most frequently found at neck edges or waistbands. To attach the hook, work stitches around the circular holes, picking up a garment thread with each stitch. Secure the thread, but do not clip. Slip the needle through the fabric, surfacing to sew the hook end to the garment to hold it flat.

To fasten straight or curved metal eyes, work stitches around the circular holes as for the hook. For curved metal eyes, continue to sew a few stitches on either side of the eye to hold it flat. If you prefer, a taut thread eye may also be used.

If the closing edges just meet, such as a neckline, sew a hook and a curved metal eye on the wrong side of the garment. Place and sew the hook $\frac{1}{16}$" from one edge. The curved eye should be placed with the loop extending slightly beyond the other edge.

If the edges overlap, sew the hook even with the overlapping edge on the inside. Then sew a straight metal or thread eye on the outside of your garment on the underlap.

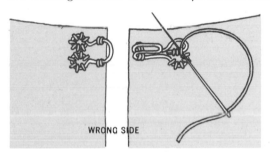
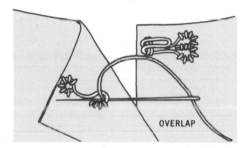

WRONG SIDE

OVERLAP

Large or heavy duty hooks and eyes are used on areas which receive excessive strain, such as waistbands. Position them as you would regular hooks and eyes and sew them on through the holes. In addition to the slide type shown here, large covered hooks and eyes are available for closures on heavyweight garments, such as furs and coats.

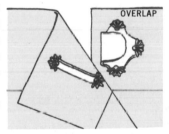

OVERLAP

For a couture finish, cover your hooks and eyes as on page 382. See page 89 for specific sizes and types.

NYLON TAPE FASTENERS: This fastener operates on the same principle as hooks and eyes. One strip is faced with tiny hooks, the other with a pile fabric serving as minute eyes. When pressed together, the two strips fuse until pulled apart. They are excellent on loose-fitting garments such as jacket fronts, belt overlaps, etc., but are not suitable in place of a zipper, on tight-fitting garments, on very lightweight fabrics, or whenever extra bulk is not desirable.

There are several effective methods of application. You may machine stitch the lower strip in place through all layers and the upper strip through just one layer where it cannot be seen. This application must be done during the construction process. Another method is to apply the upper strip by hand, using a sturdy slipstitch through just one layer of fabric, and the lower strip by machine through all layers. Topstitching both strips through all garment layers is also popular as a design detail on casual clothes.

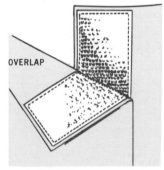

OVERLAP

Concealed Plackets

The fine, custom-made look of your garment can be enhanced by a well-made closing. Unless it is a featured fashion detail, make it as inconspicuous as possible. A placket is a lightweight finish which provides a secure closing. The most common types of plackets are the continuous lap and the dress placket. Hide the placket anywhere you need it; the possibilities are unlimited.

Continuous Lap

Inserted in a slash or a seam, the continuous lap can be an extremely durable closure if properly made. It is adaptable to many situations: most often used in a sleeve, you can use it on a skirt when a small opening is needed, or as a neckline opening on a casual garment.

IN A SLASH: Reinforce the area to be slashed with small stitches along the stitching line, taking a stitch across the point. Slash to the point. Cut a straight strip of self-fabric 1½″ wide and twice the length of the slash. Spread slash open and, right sides together, place its stitching line ¼″ from one long edge of strip. Stitch with small stitches on garment beside previous stitching. From the right side, press lap away from garment. Turn the free edge in ¼″ and slipstitch over the seam.

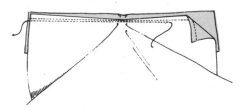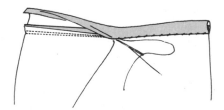

IN A SEAM: Stitch the seam, leaving an opening for the placket. Backstitch at the end of the seam for reinforcement. Press the seam open, leaving the placket seam allowances unpressed. Clip the seam allowances at end of opening and trim the opening edges to ¼″. Cut a straight strip of self-fabric 1½″ wide and twice the length of the opening. Spread the seam open and, right sides together, stitch the strip to the opening edge with small stitches in a ¼″ seam. Grade the seam. Turn the free edge in ¼″ and slipstitch over the seam.

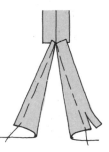

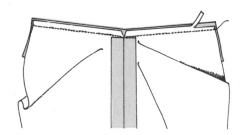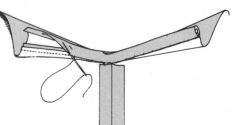

FINISHING: Bulk may be decreased by cutting 1¼″ wide strip on a selvage. Use the raw edge for the first seam; then slipstitch the selvage over the seam allowance without turning it under. When a more durable finish is desired, substitute topstitching for slipstitching. All continuous lap plackets should be finished by turning them inside and stitching a diagonal line at the top of the fold. This will keep the lap from turning to the outside.

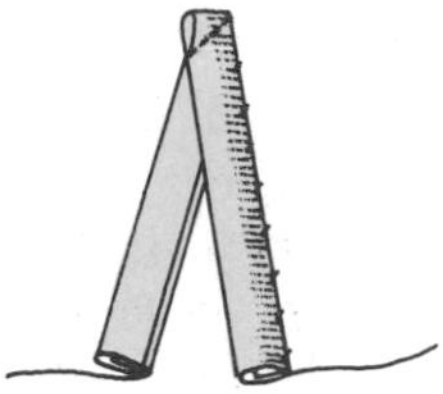

Dress Placket

This type of placket is usually placed in a side seam and centered at the waistline. It is an effective closing for lightweight, sheer, or lace fabrics, where a zipper tape would be unsightly. The following example is applicable when the standard ⅝″ seam allowance is used on the garment. If you use a narrower seam allowance, the width of your placket should also be narrower to make it as inconspicuous as possible.

Stitch the seam and press it open, leaving an opening between markings for the placket. Use two straight strips of self-fabric two inches longer than the opening for the placket. Cut front strip 1¼″ wide and back strip 1¾″ wide. Finish one edge of each strip as you plan to finish your garment seams. With raw edges matching and right sides together, center front strip between markings and stitch to opening edges along seamline. Trim and grade seam allowances, leaving garment seam allowances widest. Fold strip to inside along the seam; press (1).

Clip the garment back seam allowance ½″ beyond each end of the opening. Right sides together, center and stitch the back strip to the opening seam allowance ¼″ from the edge. Press small seam open. Lap back strip over front so that folded and finished edges cover garment seam allowances (2).

Stitch both strips to the front seam allowance at the upper and lower ends of the placket opening, keeping the garment free. Blindstitch long free edges in place on front and back placket. Catchstitch raw edges to garment seam allowances (3).

Fasten opening with snaps; place a hook and eye at waistline. ✻ When pressing, do not let the iron rest on the placket.

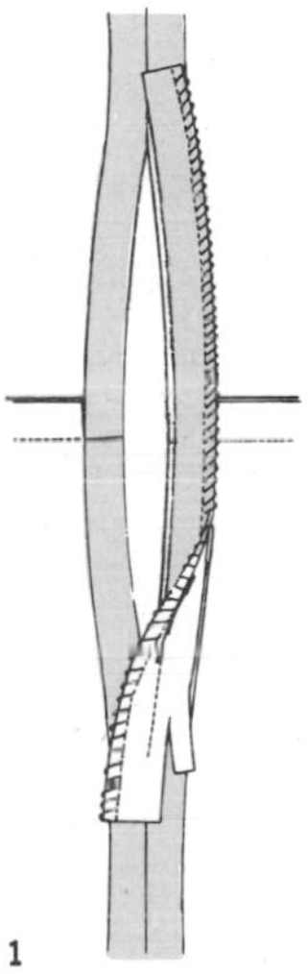

1

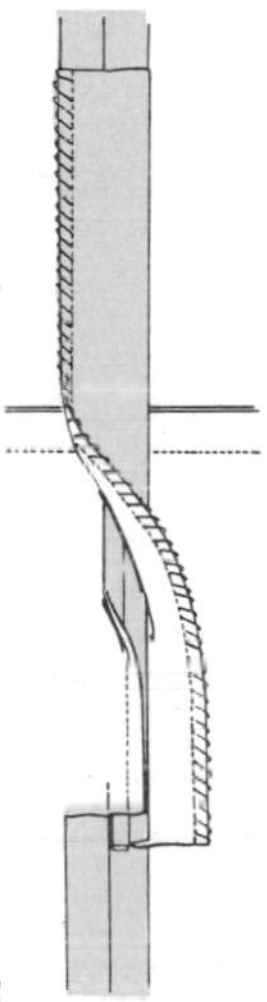

2

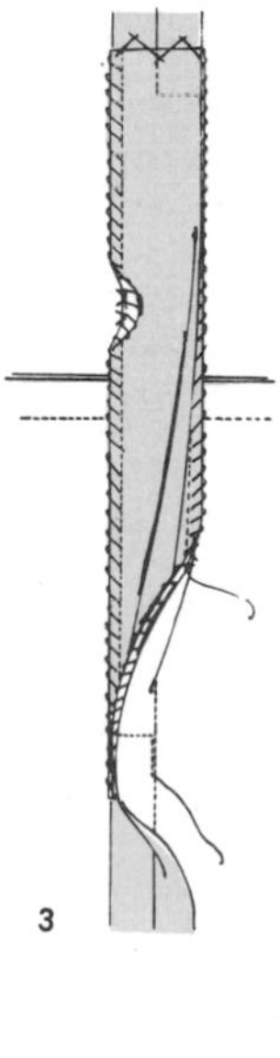

3

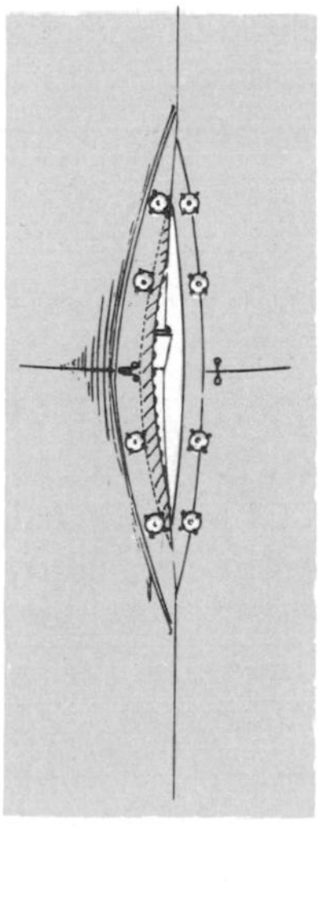

Belts and Carriers

Since ancient Grecian times, belts and belt carriers have been moving up and down fashion's silhouette in an amazing variety of shapes and widths. Modern belt-making techniques can best be exemplified by the basic types shown below.

If you are adding a belt and your pattern doesn't include one, you must plan the belt carefully. To find the proper length, encircle your body where the belt will be worn with belting or interfacing in the desired width; add 7″ to this measurement for finishing your belt. ❋ Wider belts extending above your waistline require additional length.

STRAIGHT BELT WITH INTERFACING: On the lengthwise grain, cut two strips of fabric the required length and width of the finished belt, adding ⅝″ seam allowances on all edges. Shape one end as desired. If your fabric is stretchy or loosely woven, stay-stitch the long edges ⅜″ from the raw edge (1). Cut two interfacing strips the finished width and length. Stitch the interfacing sections together in rows at ¼″ intervals, or substitute one strip of grosgrain belting for the interfacing (2).

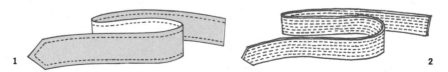

Center the interfacing over the wrong side of the belt and pin. Turn the belt seam allowances over the interfacing. Notch pointed end where necessary to make the fabric lie flat. With long running stitches, sew the seam allowances to the interfacing only (3). Staystitch the belt facing ½″ from the raw edge. Turn in the edges of the facing ¾″ and baste, notching pointed end as necessary; trim to ⅜″ (4). Center and pin the facing over the belt, then slipstitch in place (5).

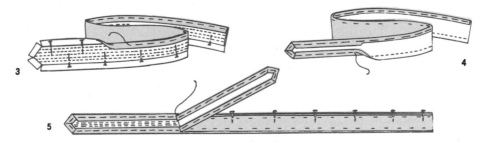

STRAIGHT BELT WITH COMMERCIAL BELTING: Follow manufacturer's directions, or cut one fabric strip on the lengthwise grain the required length and twice the width of the belting plus seam allowances. Shape one end of the belting as desired. Fold belt strip right sides together over the belting, and stitch with a zipper foot close to the belting. Do not catch belting in stitches. Trim seam allowances to ¼″ (1). Slide the seam around to the center of belting, and press seam open with the point of your iron. Stitch the shaped end and trim (2). Remove belting and turn; do not press. Slip the belting into the belt, shaped end first, cupping slightly for easier insertion (3). See next page.

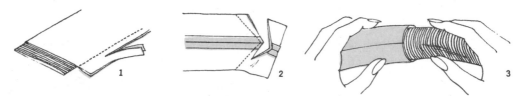

CONTOUR BELT: Follow the instructions for cutting the straight belt. Easestitch the shaped ends and outer curved edges. The interfacing will require some special handling. Pin two layers of interfacing together and trace an outline of your contour belt on them. Stitch the layers together within the outline at ¼" intervals along the lengthwise grain. Cut out belt along traced outline. For a stay, baste a strip of stretched bias tape to the inner curved edge of the interfacing and stitch in place directionally. Then construct the belt as you would a straight belt, adjusting the ease threads as necessary.

Fastening Belts

There are several ways to fasten a belt—with a prong and eyelet buckle, a clasp buckle, hooks and eyes, or snaps. Try on your finished belt. Mark the center front position on both ends for all fastenings but the clasp buckle. Trim the unfinished straight end to measure 2" from the center front line. Stitch ¼" from the trimmed end and overcast.

PRONG AND EYELETS: Pierce a hole for the buckle prong at the center front marking nearest the overcast end. Overcast the raw edges of the hole (1). Slip the buckle prong through the hole; turn back the end and sew securely in place (2). For a half buckle, make a fabric loop (see Carriers, page 323); slide it over belt close to the buckle and secure.

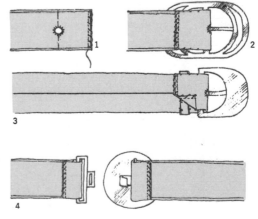

Then secure the belt end (3). On the finished end of your belt, make one eyelet at the center front marking and one or more on both sides for adjustments. You may use commercial eyelets, which come in a variety of colors, or make your own hand-worked eyelets as instructed on page 312.

CLASP BUCKLE: Slip the ends of the belt through the buckle and bar fastener, folding the ends back along the bars, and try it on. Trim excess at ends to 1". Stitch ¼" from each end and overcast. Slip the ends through the bars; turn back and attach securely (4).

HOOKS AND EYES OR SNAPS: Slip the buckle over the overcast end of the belt; turn the end back at the center front marking and securely sew it in place. Match your center fronts and mark the position for the fastenings on both ends. Sew the hooks and eyes or snaps securely to belt, placing them just far enough from the end so they do not show (5). Snaps will do very nicely for the many loose belt styles; hooks and flat eyes are more suitable for closely fitting belts which are subject to greater strain. You may wish to combine both fastenings on the same belt. Secure the belt with hooks and eyes while using snaps to hold the loose end.

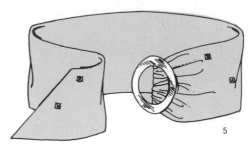

Some Variations on the Theme

TIE BELT OR SASH: Your personal preference will determine the type—narrow or wide, bias or straight grain. Cut fabric twice the finished width and the desired length (long enough to tie) plus seam allowances. Piece where necessary, then fold the sash in half lengthwise. Stitch the ends and the long edge, leaving an opening, as shown. Trim corners and grade seams. Turn and press the sash. Slipstitch the opening.

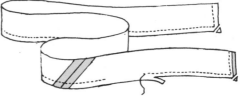

CORDED BELT: Use purchased cord or make your own, page 314. Finish ends with a simple knot, or allow extra fabric for a Chinese Ball Button as on page 315.

TRIMMED BELT: Make a straight belt as directed and fasten it with hooks and eyes or snaps. Attach your favorite pin, a jeweled button, or a self-fabric bow at the closing.

CUMMERBUND: Cut a bias rectangle the measurement of your rib cage plus ½″ and at least 9″ wide. Stitch ¼″ from the long edges and overcast. Turn in long edges 1″; press lightly. Make a row of gathering stitches ¼″ from each end for a back opening and two rows ¼″ apart for gathers at sides of belt. Pull gathers to the desired depth and fasten threads on the inside. Check fit, respacing gathers if necessary to make it snug.

Cut four pieces of feather boning ¼″ to ½″ shorter than the depth of the belt; remove casing. For sides, cover boning with seam binding, center over gathers, and sew in place. For back opening edges, stitch ½″ wide grosgrain ribbon along gathering stitches, extending ends ½″. Catchstitch boning over gathers. Turn in ends, folding ribbon to wrong side; favor cummerbund. Sew ribbon securely to underside of gathers. Fasten with hooks and eyes so ends meet. Make and attach grosgrain or self-fabric underlap.

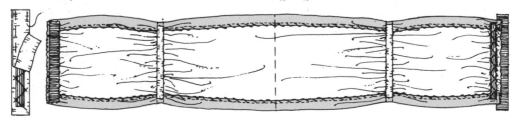

Carriers

If you are adding a belt and your pattern doesn't include markings, first establish the belt position on your garment. Make placement marks at desired intervals, and be sure to mark the width of the belt for your carriers.

FABRIC CARRIERS OR BELT LOOPS: The loops should be long enough to accommodate the belt width plus ¼″ (possibly a little extra if your fabric is very thick). Cut a straight strip from a selvage edge three times the desired width, and make two folds with the selvage edge on top. Slip-stitch the selvage in place (1). Bring ends together and whip-stitch. Place the carrier over the markings and sew to the garment at both ends (2). For other methods of making loops, see Loops and Fastenings, page 313.

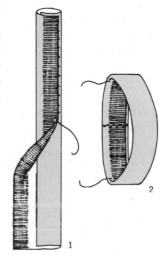

THREAD CARRIERS: There are two kinds of thread carriers. One is made of a core of long threads reinforced with blanketstitches, and the other is a thread chain. Fabric carriers or loops are often design features, but thread carriers should be nearly invisible. Use thread that matches your belt. See Thread Closures and Fastenings, pages 315–316.

Casings

Casings, which often go unnoticed, are significant in that they enable fabric to be snugged into place with elastic or pulled into graceful folds with a drawstring. Most important, they provide comfort while adapting to the body shape. One essential principle to be remembered is that a casing must always be wide enough to allow the elastic or drawstring to be pulled comfortably. It should be equal in width to the elastic or drawstring, allowing ⅛″ to ¼″ for their thicknesses plus ½″ for seam allowances. It should be equal in length to the area to which it is to be applied plus ½″.

Elastic

Using elastic in a casing will ensure regularity in fit. Unlike the drawstring tie, an elastic pull is not adjustable. It will breathe and move with you, but will not change from the specific measurement you give it. Elastic is used most commonly in sleeves and waistlines. The opening for its insertion is inside the garment. The length of elastic depends upon its stretchability and should be slightly less than the measurement of the body at the casing position, plus ½″ for lapping. Usually, the narrower the elastic, the shorter it will have to be. Pull elastic through casing with a bodkin or a safety pin, being careful not to twist it. Lap the ends ½″ and stitch securely (1).

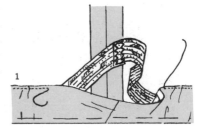

The elastic should have enough tension to prevent drooping when the elastic relaxes. Close the opening at the edge of the casing, stretching the elastic as you stitch (2). For an opening across the casing, slipstitch the opening edges together securely (3).

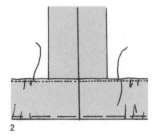 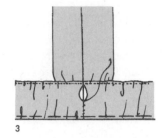

Drawstring

Cord or tubing knotted at the ends, braid, leather strips, ribbon—anything that captures your fancy can be used as a drawstring. Its length should be equal to the measurement of your body at the casing position plus an extra amount to allow for tying a knot or bow. Often quite decorative, the openings for the drawstrings are usually made on the right side of the garment before you make the casing.

There are two types of casing openings for drawstrings. The first, the eyelet or buttonhole type, is made in the outer fabric between the casing placement lines before the casing is applied. From the wrong side, stitch casing in place. When the casing is completed, pull drawstring through the casing with a bodkin or safety pin. The second type of opening is in a seam. Stitch seam, leaving an opening the width of the drawstring; reinforce each end.

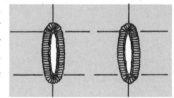 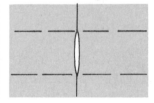

Applied and Self-Casings

A self-casing is formed by an extension of the garment that has been folded to the inside (forming a hem) and edgestitched. An applied casing is a separate strip of fabric cut on the straight or bias grain or like a shaped facing. You may use pre-packaged bias tape for a quick applied casing. Trim garment seam allowances to ¼″ wherever casing is to be applied. For the self-casing, allow an extra ¼″ seam allowance on the long edge, and ¼″ seam allowances on all edges for an applied casing. Either type can be used on a finished edge, such as the lower edge of a sleeve; at the waistline, to create a blouson effect; or with a heading, which extends beyond the casing to form a ruffle.

AT FINISHED EDGE: For a self-casing, mark and then turn in the fabric along the foldline; baste. Turn in raw edge ¼″ and edgestitch to the garment, leaving the desired opening (1). Self-casings used on a slightly curved edge must be extremely narrow. The stitched fold may need to be stretched or gently eased while stitching. For an applied casing, cut the casing as indicated above. Right sides together, pin one edge of the strip to the garment, turning ends to inside. Stitch in ¼″ seam, turn to inside, and press. Finish as self-casing (2).

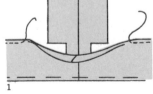 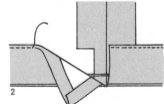

WITH A HEADING: The extension for a heading requires extra fabric. For a self-casing, extend the garment edge, twice the desired width of the heading, plus the casing and a ¼″ seam allowance. Mark heading foldline. Turn fabric to inside and baste close to fold. Mark casing seamlines. Stitch, leaving desired opening (3). For an applied casing, extend the garment edge twice the width of the heading plus a ¼″ seam allowance. Mark heading foldline. Turn fabric to inside; baste along foldline. Cut casing as instructed in introduction. Turn all edges under ¼″ and press. From the wrong side, baste casing in place, matching raw edge of casing with raw edge of heading. Edgestitch bottom and top edges of casing to garment, leaving desired opening (4).

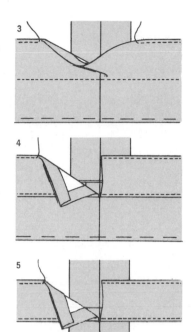

AT THE WAISTLINE: Cut the casing. Turn in both edges ¼″ and press gently. Mark the garment waistline and prepare an opening if drawstring is to be used. From wrong side, place the bottom edge of casing along waistline markings. Stitch along both edges. Insert elastic or drawstring and finish as required (5).

Shaped Casing

The shaped casing forms a channel for a sash or scarf that will be tied loosely at neckline or waistline. Leave opening in the garment seams at the desired location; reinforce with catchstitches and bar tacks. The finished casing should be ¼″ to ½″ wider than the finished opening. Attach casing to garment as you would a shaped facing. Understitch seam allowances to casing and finish free edge. Then blindstitch this edge to the garment or underlining.

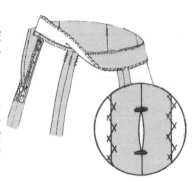

Zipper Openings

For a casing with a drawstring, measure and complete drawstring, then cut into two equal lengths. For a casing with elastic, the elastic need not be split. For slot seam zippers, end casing at seamline. Sew raw edges of elastic or drawstring securely to casing at each end, keeping garment free (1). For invisible zippers, extend casing and raw edge of drawstring or elastic ¼″ beyond seamline into seam allowance (2). After either type zipper is applied, whipstitch seam allowances securely to casing and elastic or drawstring.

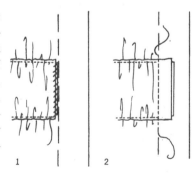

Zippers

Zippers are those mechanical wonders used to close an amazing variety of fashion features. They provide a fast, readily accessible means of getting in and out of your clothes, an asset so valuable in our busy, time-conscious days. Since their invention, zippers have grown lighter, less obvious, and more supple. The culmination of this progressive movement is the completely invisible zipper. It can be installed in almost any seam without interrupting a single design line. The invisible zipper most certainly appears to be the closure of the future, yet is available now. Whether you prefer the invisible zipper's versatility or the more familiar regular zipper, complete instructions for all of the major methods of zipper insertion are offered here.

There are several things to consider before you make your final selection. Concern yourself with the drape of the garment, the care of the fabric, and the closure location. The length and specific type required, if any, will be indicated on the back of your pattern envelope. Most important, you will find that zippers won't be the least bit tricky if you follow the directions carefully and rely on these basic application tips:

- ☐ Close the zipper and press out creases before application. When pressing on the right side of the garment, use a press cloth and a dry iron to prevent any unsightly shine, puckers, or impressions.
- ☐ Press nylon zippers cautiously. If the temperature is too high or the teeth are not properly protected, the zipper may lose the coating which enables the slider to move with ease.
- ☐ Always close the zipper before laundering or drycleaning.
- ☐ Pre-shrink the zipper if it will be applied in a washable garment.
- ☐ Staystitch the zipper opening edges directionally in seam allowance.
- ☐ Extend seam allowances of the zipper opening with ribbon seam binding if they are less than ⅝" wide.
- ☐ Always pin the zipper from the top downward.
- ☐ Remember that plaids or stripes should match at the zipper closing as well as at other seams. For a regular zipper, baste the closing shut, matching the pattern of the fabric; for an invisible zipper, mark the zipper tape with lines corresponding to the pattern of the fabric.
- ☐ A zipper foot is essential for machine stitching and, if it is adjustable, permits stitching on either side of the zipper without turning the fabric.
- ☐ For straight stitching by hand or machine, learn to use the sewing guideline that is woven into some of the regular zipper tapes.
- ☐ Always sew both sides of your zipper in the same direction.
- ☐ To stitch past the slider, pull the tab up and turn the slider on its side, or leave the needle in the fabric, raise the foot, and move the slider down.
- ☐ For an easier and a truly custom-tailored way to apply a zipper, use the prickstitch as directed on page 209.
- ☐ Bias seams or stretchy fabric may require a stay before inserting the zipper. Cut two strips of seam binding the length of opening, and baste to the wrong side along the seamline in the seam allowance.

For zipper types and lengths available, see notions section in Book I, pages 94 and 95.

Hand Application

Applying a zipper by hand is a custom technique. It is especially desirable on pile, delicate, or stretch fabrics. Follow the directions given for zipper placement in either the lapped or slot applications. Then use a tiny prickstitch (page 209) to complete the final stitching. Always sew with a fine needle and use a double strand of regular thread coated with beeswax for normal use, silk thread to match fabrics with sheen, or buttonhole twist for added durability. Use the prickstitch for the entire length of the zipper. There will be a space between the top stitches, but the understitches will be long and overlap to

The invisible zipper should also be applied by hand for the best results on hard-to-handle fabrics. Follow the basic instructions for exact placement, but insert it with a sturdy prickstitch very close to the zipper teeth.

Zipper Underlap

To protect your skin and undergarments, place a piece of grosgrain ribbon (at least one inch longer than the opening) over the teeth. Hem the upper edge of the ribbon, ending the ribbon at the slider. Sew the long edge to one seam allowance of the opening with a backstitch. Catch-stitch the lower end to the seam allowances. Fasten with a tiny snap.

Shortening Zippers

Some garments may require a zipper length that cannot be purchased. In such a case, purchase a longer zipper and shorten it. Choose the method that applies to your particular needs from those shown below.

AT BOTTOM: For any type of zipper, baste or stitch zipper to the garment, then take several whipstitches over the teeth ¼" below end of opening to keep zipper teeth together (1). Next sew a large straight metal eye above the whipstitches to act as a new bottom stop. Cut off the excess zipper ½" below the metal eye (2). Complete your zipper application if you haven't already done so.

AT TOP: If your zipper must be shortened from the top, first baste zipper to within one inch of point where zipper teeth should end. Open zipper to basting and remove extra teeth. To make new stops, bend straight eyes in half and slip over the zipper tape above the teeth; sew securely. Close zipper, turn down tape ends, trim away excess tape, and sew ends securely in place (3). Complete your zipper application.

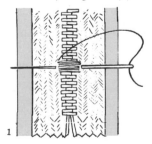

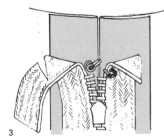

Invisible Zipper

The invisible zipper is suitable for almost any garment or fabric. Its fast application does away with the older methods by replacing them with a quick, neat "seam-like" installation. You will never be stymied by a difficult color match; insertion renders the zipper invisible, therefore eliminating the need for an exact color match. In order to insert your invisible zipper, a special foot must be added to your sewing machine; it can be purchased wherever invisible zippers are sold.

Unlike the other zippers, the invisible zipper is applied to the opening edges before the remainder of the seam is stitched. This enables you to work with a flat, flexible area instead of the entire garment. The facings are usually applied after the zipper is installed, taking steps before the zipper is inserted to maintain a flat seamlike appearance at the facing ends. If your garment requires special construction, you may insert an invisible zipper at the same point you would a regular zipper. Simply end seam stitching 2″ below marking for the opening. Then insert as directed below.

FACING: Reinforce the neck seamline for 2″ from the opening edges, using small stitches. Clip seam allowance to the stitching 1″ from the opening edges on both the right and left sides of your garment. Fold down and press (1). Insert your zipper as directed below. Turn back both facing ends 1″ from the opening edges. Trim to ⅝″. Then join the facing to garment. Trim and grade the seam (2). Turn, understitch the facing to the seam allowances and press. Fold down zipper tape as you turn the facing. Close zipper and slipstitch facing ends to the zipper tape (3).

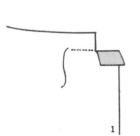
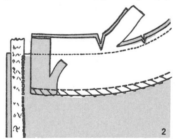
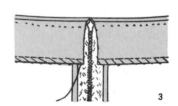

APPLICATION: Open the zipper and place it face down on the right side of the fabric. Have the teeth lying on the seamline and the tape in the seam allowance, parallel to the edge of your fabric. (To align teeth of a polyester invisible zipper on the seamline, use your finger to open out the pre-set fold.) Before stitching, you may wish to pin or baste the zipper in place (1).

Align the notch at the center of the hole on the special zipper foot with the needle. Lower the foot over the teeth, as shown, and stitch from upper edge to pull tab (2). Keep stitches as close to the teeth as possible.

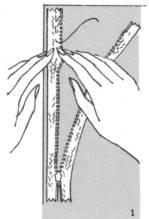
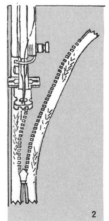

Now close the zipper to position the other side on the opposite seam allowance. Pin or baste as desired. Open the zipper and stitch as shown earlier (3). Close the zipper.

To finish the seam below the zipper, slide the zipper foot to the left so that the needle is in line with the edge of the zipper foot. Keeping the zipper tape ends free, lower the needle, then the zipper foot. Stitch slowly, connecting previous stitching (4). A regular zipper foot may also be used to stitch seam. For some fabrics it may be necessary to connect stitches by hand after seam has been stitched. To complete the application, stitch each end of the zipper tape to the seam allowances, keeping garment free and repositioning foot for each side (5).

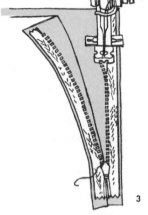

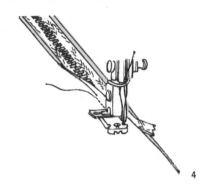

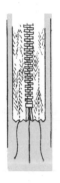

3   4   5

Application shown courtesy of Unique Zippers

Slot or Centered Application

This application is the one most frequently used. Attach the facing before installing the zipper. Trim and grade the seam; understitch the facing to the seam allowances. Then turn and press the facing. Waistbands, etc., are applied after zipper is inserted.

Open out facings. Machine baste opening edges together along seamlines, and press seam open. Face down, place closed zipper on opened seam allowances with zipper teeth centered over the seamline and baste (1). Locate the pull tab ¼″ below neck seamline.

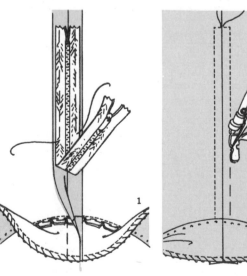

On outside, stitch by machine or hand across lower end and continue along sides, ¼″ from basted seam (2).

Completing the facing is both quick and easy. Simply turn the facings to the inside, folding in the ends to clear the zipper teeth. Slipstitch the ends in place. Anchor the remaining facing edge. Fasten the neck edge with a hook and eye on the inside of your garment (3).

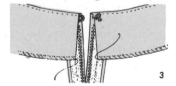

1   2   3

Lapped Application

This sturdy, easy method neatly conceals your zipper, making it particularly suited for zippers that do not match perfectly with the color of your fabric.

When the garment edge is faced, the facing should be attached before the zipper is inserted into the opening. Because the facing may have a tendency to catch in the teeth of the closure and provide excess bulk over the zipper pull tab, we recommend a technique calling for special manipulation of the facing *before* it is stitched to the garment.

FACING: As you are pinning the facing in place, turn back 1″ on the end of the over-lapping side and trim to ⅝″. Then stitch the facing to the garment, continuing to the very end of the opening. Trim, grade, and clip all seam allowances, stopping just short of the unfaced portion of the seam allowance (1). Understitch the facing to the neckline seam allowances, then turn and press (2).

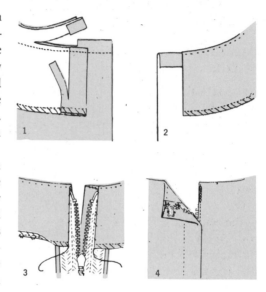

Insert your zipper as directed below. Turn the facing and zipper tape to the inside. The overlapping facing end will automatically clear the zipper teeth. Turn in the other end to clear the zipper. Slipstitch the facing ends in place and the upper neckline edges together. Anchor the remaining facing edge (3). Complete the lapped application with a hook sewn on the inside and an eye sewn to the outside of your garment (4).

APPLICATION: Complete steps 1 and 2 if you are applying your zipper to a faced garment edge. Then mark the seamline on the underlapped opening edge with thread tracing. Turn in the edge ⅛″ from the traced seamline in the seam allowance; baste and press. A tiny fold will appear in the seam allowance at the lower edge. Then turn in the full seam allowance on the other opening edge; baste and press (5).

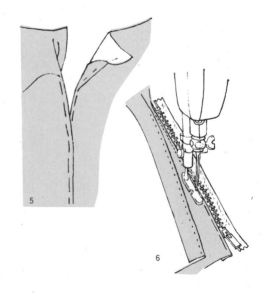

Place the underlapped edge over the zipper tape with the bottom stop of the zipper even with the end of the garment opening. Baste close to the zipper teeth, leaving enough room for the pull tab to slide easily. Stitch close to edge by hand or machine (6).

Position the overlapping edge to just cover the stitching on opposite side of opening. Baste remaining zipper tape in place to be sure it does not shift during stitching. Now stitch by machine or hand across the lower end, pivoting at corner and continuing along the side ⅜″ from the edge (7).

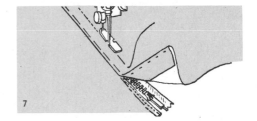

Separating Zipper

FACING: Begin by treating both sides of the facing as shown for the overlapping side of the facing in the lapped application. Follow steps 1 and 2 on the previous page.

APPLICATION: Machine baste the opening edges together along their seamlines, keeping the facing and hem free; press open. Face down, center the closed zipper on the opened seam allowances with the zipper stop at the bottom of the opening. Turn down the tape ends at the top on each side of the pull tab; tack securely. Baste the zipper in place (1).

On the outside, stitch ¼″ from each side of the center front by hand or by machine as you would a slot application, still keeping the facing and hem free.

On the inside, turn the facing and hem ends in to clear the zipper teeth; slipstitch. Catchstitch the remaining facing and hem edges in place. Turn in any lining seam allowances, making sure the long edges clear the zipper teeth; baste close to the edge. Slipstitch in place (2).

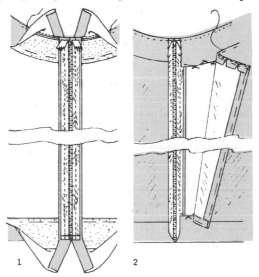

Separating zippers with two pull tabs for reversible garments are available. The zipper area inside the reversible garment is finished so that it is identical in appearance to the outside. Baste zipper in place as above, keeping the long edges of the opening free on the inside. From the inside, turn under the seam allowances so the edges meet over the center of the zipper; baste. From the right side, sew along basting through all thicknesses.

Side Zipper Opening

The regulation dress zipper has a top stop in addition to the standard bottom stop. You may purchase this zipper, or convert the regular or invisible types. To make a top stop, simply whipstitch the upper edges of the tape together or place a metal eye at the top of the teeth (as on page 327) once you have decided on the correct length for the opening. Trim any excess. The zipper is then inserted in a seam that is closed at both ends.

Before inserting zipper, be sure the opening length is equal to the zipper length, with the bottom stop barely concealed. If the zipper is too long, shorten it as on page 327.

Insert your zipper the same as lapped, slot or centered, or invisible application, ignoring facing instructions. As you complete the zipper, sew the ends and the long edge by hand, or stitch by machine.

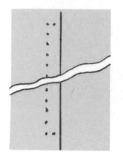
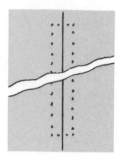

Fly Front Placket

Most commonly found on trousers, the fly placket may be used occasionally on jackets and coats. You can purchase a specially designed trouser zipper or use a regular zipper; the choice depends on the care required by your garment and the weight of your fabric. We recommend that you use the fly placket only when your pattern is specifically designed for it. This type of application nearly always requires shortening the zipper due to the variation in length among different sizes. When the zipper application has been completed, the waistband is attached.

Turn in both front extensions along the foldlines and baste close to the folds. Pin or baste the closed zipper under the left front, with the teeth close to the basted edge and the bottom stop at the bottom of the opening. (Note: the zipper may extend above the opening edges.) Lap the right front extension over the zipper, even with the center front marking on the left front, and baste it in place (1).

With the right front extension opened out, baste the zipper tape to it, being careful not to catch the front of the garment. Stitch the zipper in place close to the teeth and again ¼″ away on the tape (2).

Then turn the extension back and baste it to the garment. On the outside, stitch along the stitching line through all thicknesses (3). Pull the thread to the inside and tie.

Stitch the fly and lining inserts together. Trim, turn, and press the seam. Baste the raw edges together. On the wrong side, baste the fly insert to the left front extension over the zipper. Make sure the raw edges are even and the lining faces the inside (4).

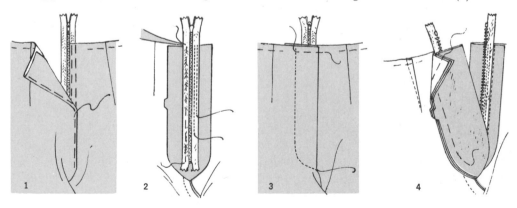

Open the zipper. Keeping the right front free, stitch on the outside through all thicknesses; place your stitches near the zipper teeth and close to the folded edge of the left front. Machine baste along the seamline across zipper tapes so the pull tab will not slide off the end. Now trim the ends of zipper even with the upper edge if necessary (5).

Because the base of the opening is subject to strain, secure with a bar tack (6).

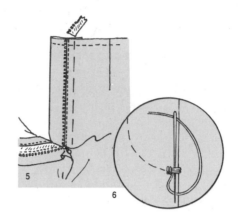

Knife Pleated Skirt

The placket opening is usually located at the center back or the left side and is the last seam to be stitched. Stitch this last seam, leaving an opening for the placket. (Your last pleat is made **after** this seam is stitched.) Be sure to have the seam at an inside fold so that it will not show. Use a regular skirt zipper and make sure that the under fold of the pleat will be deep enough to accommodate your zipper. To make your last pleat, turn the overlapping section to the inside along the pleat foldline and baste. Clip the seam allowance of the undersection at the placket marking, as shown. Turn the seam allowance of the undersection to the inside ⅝″ and baste (1). Place the edge of the undersection over the zipper tape with the bottom stop even with the end of the opening. Have the edge close to the teeth with just enough room for the pull tab to slide easily. Baste carefully, then stitch the undersection to the zipper tape near the zipper teeth (2).

Place the remaining side of the zipper face down on the underlay of the overlapping section. The zipper teeth will extend beyond the seamline. Baste the zipper to the underlay, keeping the rest of the skirt free. Then stitch ⅛″ away from the zipper teeth, continuing across the end of the zipper below the stop; backstitch (3). Attach the waistband and close it securely with hooks and eyes as shown on page 317.

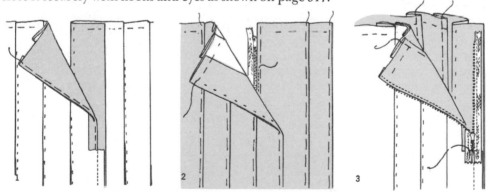

Zippers used with box, accordion, or inverted pleats that hang free from the waistline can be inserted by the invisible or slot application.

For creating your own decorative zippers, turn to the Trims section, page 403.

Waistbands

A properly sewn and fitted waistband is a joy to wear. It never stretches, wrinkles, or folds over as some waistbands have a way of doing, nor does it bind you or slip down on your hips. To attain this ideal combination of fit, good looks, and comfort, you must know a few general facts about waistbands.

Your preference and garment style determine waistband width. Most waistbands need the reinforcement and body of interfacing or ribbon seam binding to prevent stretching —particularly loosely-woven fabrics and wide or contour waistbands. With knits, use elastic in the waistband to ensure the proper stretch and fit. Unless the garment is gathered, the skirt is usually eased to the waistband to accommodate the curve of your body directly below the waistband. For this reason, your garment should be ½″ to 1″ bigger at the waistline than the finished waistline measurement. If the ends of the waistband overlap, the overlapping edge faces toward the left or the back. Side closings are on the left side. The underneath section usually extends at least 1¼″ for the underlap. Put in the zipper before you apply the waistband, unless directed otherwise by the pattern.

Straight Waistband

This waistband is cut on the lengthwise grain for the least amount of stretch, and can be constructed in many ways. Base your construction on the type of fabric, the style of the garment, and the wear that it will receive. First construct the garment leaving the appropriate seam open for the zipper. Then apply your zipper, leaving ⅛″ plus the seam allowance between the zipper stop and the raw edge of the waistline area.

Interface the notched edge of the waistband as required by your fabric. Then turn waistband, right sides together, along foldline. Stitch ends to within ⅝″ of the edge. Grade seams and trim corners (1). Turn and press, using a pounding block or clapper on heavy or bulky fabric.

Pin and baste the waistband to the garment, matching markings. Ease the garment to fit the waistband; stitch. Trim and grade seams, leaving garment seam allowance widest. Press seam toward waistband. Turn in the remaining raw edge and slipstitch over the seam, continuing across the underlap (2).

Fasten with hooks and eyes, placing larger hooks at the point of greatest strain (3).

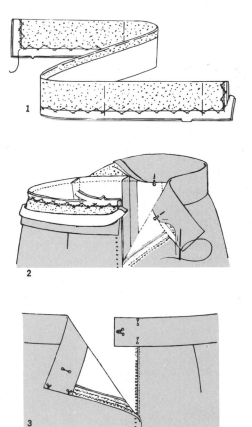

Variations on a Straight Waistband

If your fabric is fairly heavy or bulky, you may wish to use one of the following methods to eliminate bulk and make a flat, smooth waistband.

First, to reduce the ridge caused when all seam allowances at the waistline are turned in same direction, lay the waistband pattern piece with *seamline* of the unnotched edge even with selvage. The selvage acts as a finished edge and is not turned under (1).

The second variation produces a thinner, less bulky appearance. Cut the waistband from your fabric equal to its finished width plus two seam allowances. Lap grosgrain ribbon (purchased in the same width as the finished waistband) over the upper seam allowance, even with the seamline; stitch ribbon close to edge (2).

Finish both waistbands by folding them right sides together along the upper seamline. Stitch across both ends. Trim corners and grade seam allowances. Turn and press. Attach them to the garment as usual. Slipstitch the selvage of the fabric or the edge of the grosgrain ribbon over the seam, continuing across the underlap. Be sure that the ribbon does not show on the outside.

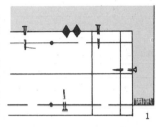
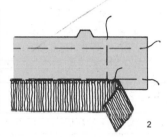

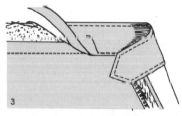

The last variation is a quick, sturdy way to finish a waistband on a casual or sporty garment. Stitch the right side of the waistband to the wrong side of the garment. Press seam toward the waistband. Turn in the remaining edge and baste it over the seam on the right side of garment. From the right side, edgestitch around the entire waistband through all thicknesses (3).

Contour Waistband

A wide contour waistband should be interfaced for stiffness and reinforced along the long edges of one waistband section with stretched bias tape. Trim away the interfacing seam allowances. Center, then catchstitch the interfacing between the seamlines of one waistband section. Stay the upper and lower seamlines by basting a stretched bias tape $\frac{1}{8}''$ over seamlines. Pin waistband sections together along the upper edge and ends. Baste, then stitch the upper edges and both ends to within $\frac{5}{8}''$ of the edge. Trim corners and grade the seam allowances. Turn and press (1).

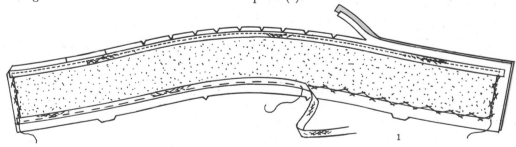

Pin the waistband to the garment with the right sides together, matching all markings. Adjust the ease; baste and stitch (2). Trim and grade seam; press toward the waistband. Turn in the remaining edge and slipstitch over the seam, continuing across the underlap. Fasten the end of the waistband with hooks and eyes (3). Be sure to keep hooks aligned with the edge of the waistband and the eyes directly above the zipper opening.

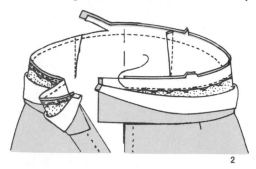

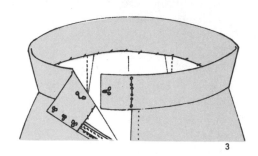

Faced Waistline

Skirts or pants without visible waistbands are usually finished with a facing made from lining, lightweight fabric, or ribbon to reduce bulk.

FABRIC: Cut and prepare facing. Stay facing waist seamline with ribbon seam binding or twill tape, placing one edge ⅛″ over the seamline; baste. Pin the facing to the garment, easing garment to fit. Stitch, trim, and grade seams. Understitch facing to keep it from rolling to the outside(1). Turn and press. Turn in ends; sew to zipper tape. Tack facing to garment at seams and darts. Add a hook and eye at top of closing (2).

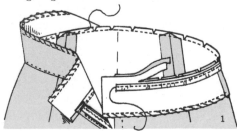

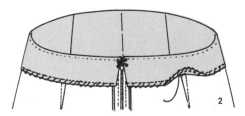

RIBBON: Shape a ¾″-1″ wide strip of grosgrain ribbon by steaming it into curves corresponding to those of the waistline edge. Be sure to stretch the edge that is to be left free; if you shrink the edge to be joined to the garment, it will stretch during wear. Fit ribbon to your body, allowing 1″ for ends. Trim garment seam allowance to ¼″. Place grosgrain over raw edge of garment with one edge along seamline and ends extending ½″. Because you are joining two opposing curves, pin or baste carefully, easing the garment to fit. Stitch close to edge of ribbon and complete as for a fabric facing above.

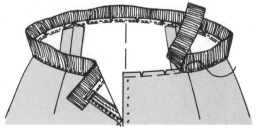

Hems

One of the most important fashion aspects of any garment is its hemline. Although the real purpose of the hem is to help your garment hang well by adding weight to the edge, variations in hem lengths will also change the silhouette and proportion of your garment. To be really complete, your wardrobe should include several different hemlines and the accompanying illustration will show you the ten principal lengths.

The point from which hemlines fluctuate up or down is mid-knee, or knee length. Going upward we have short, just above the knee; mini, mid-thigh; and micro-mini, high-thigh. Going downward are the longuette lengths: above calf, just below the knee; mid-calf, halfway between knee and ankle; midi, between mid-calf and ankle; and maxi or ankle length, even with the ankle bone. Even longer are evening length, one inch above the floor, and floor length, touching the floor.

We wish to emphasize the fact that there is no standard hem length that is correct for every woman. Always let the lengths most becoming to *you* influence your choice of hem levels.

The fabric and the style of your garment determine the depth of your hem. You'll need a wider hem for lightweight or gauzy fabrics and straight skirts. Stretchy fabrics, such as knits, or flared skirts dictate narrower hems. Narrow rolled hems or very deep hems are suitable for sheers.

Measure the hem during the last fitting, after all the changes have been made that might affect the hang of the hem. Turn to Fitting, page 351, for the correct methods to use when marking a hem. If your hem is bias or circular, let the garment hang 24 hours to set the bias before marking.

Pin the hem in place with the pins at right angles to the hemline. ***Regardless of measurements, the hem should look right.*** Minor corrections may have to be made to allow for optical illusions, especially with plaids, stripes, or pleats.

A well-made hem is always the least noticeable hem. Eliminate bulk, reduce extra fullness, press carefully to prevent ridges, and never pull the stitches tightly as you sew.

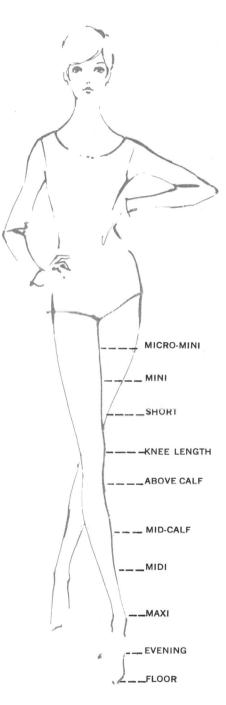

MICRO-MINI
MINI
SHORT
KNEE LENGTH
ABOVE CALF
MID-CALF
MIDI
MAXI
EVENING
FLOOR

PLAIN HEM: This hem, the simplest and most basic of all the hems, has little or no fullness. The operations used to complete it are the preliminary steps for most hems.

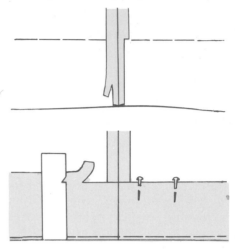

After determining the length, trim any seam allowances below the hemline to ¼", eliminating bulk that could cause ridges when the hem is pressed. Then baste close to the fold of the hem, measure the hem depth, and trim evenly. Press the hem with brown paper between the hem and the garment, steaming out any fullness. Finish the raw edge in the manner best suited to the style and fabric. Sew the hem in place with a slip-stitch or hemming stitch for turned-under or seam binding finishes and a blindstitch for pinked or overcast finishes. Then use the pressing techniques applicable to the hem edge desired, as described on page 347.

EASED HEM: When your hem has excess fullness which must be adjusted, an eased hem should be used. To ease, stitch ¼" from the raw edge, using long stitches. Pull up the ease thread every few inches, then shrink out the fullness with a steam iron. Refer to Pressing, page 347, for detailed information on how to shrink hems. Finish the raw edge and sew as suggested for the plain hem above.

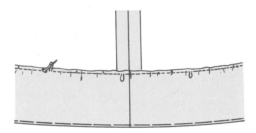
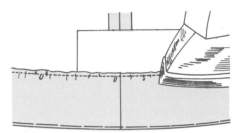

CIRCULAR HEM: This hem should be about one inch in depth to eliminate bulk and excess fullness. Let the garment hang for 24 hours before marking. Then mark and complete hem, following the steps for the eased hem above.

NARROW HEM: For blouses, lingerie, and accessories, use a narrow hem. Folding in the raw edge ¼", turn up a narrow hem. Stitch by machine through all thicknesses for casual clothes, or slipstitch to complete the hem.

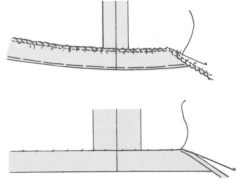

Silks and sheers require the couture touch of a hand-rolled hem; refer to page 384.

Hem Finishes

SEAM BINDING: This finish is best for loosely-woven fabrics which tend to ravel and for machine washable garments. Pre-shrink binding for fabrics you intend to wash. Use ribbon seam binding for straight hems and bias tape or stretch lace for eased and circular hems. (For fabrics which are pressed with a hot iron, use binding that can withstand the heat.) Stitch tape or seam binding ¼" from the raw edge of the fabric. For bias tape, easestitch the hem, adjust fullness, and machine stitch the tape to the raw edge. Then complete the hem.

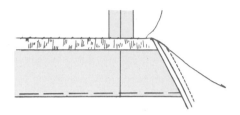

STITCHED AND OVERCAST: This method creates a very fine finish. The completed hem is inconspicuous from the outside after pressing and the raw edges are finished securely without bulk. Stitch ¼" from raw edge, using a large stitch if your hem will be eased. Overcast edge, using this stitching as a guide. To ensure an invisible hem, turn the edge back ¼" and blind hem.

STITCHED AND PINKED: Here is a quick and effective finish for fabrics which ravel slightly. Stitch ¼" from the free raw edge; use a large stitch for an eased hem. Then pink or scallop the edge and hemstitch.

TURNED-UNDER: Use this finish for light and medium weight washable fabrics, for sheers, and for limp hems. Turn in the raw edge ¼" and stitch close to the fold. (Omit this stitching for sheers.) Then complete hem.

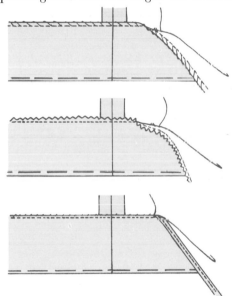

Special Hems

BIAS FACED HEM: A facing constructed of a lightweight fabric will provide a smooth finish for garments with inadequate hem allowances, very full skirts, or very bulky fabrics. You may use either commercial bias facing or your own bias strip cut from a lightweight material the desired width plus ¼" seam allowances for upper and lower edges.

Mark your hemline, leaving at least ½" additional fabric at the bottom edge. For a very curved hemline, shape the bias to the garment. Match raw edges and stitch in a ¼" seam, joining the ends of the facing as on page 248. Press seam open. Turn in raw edge ¼", turn facing up, and slipstitch.

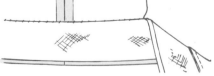

HEMS WITH PLEATS: Press open the seam within the hem area where it crosses the hem at the edge of a pleat fold. Finish the raw edge of the hem, then measure up from the hemline the width of the hem and clip the seam. Both seam allowances above the hem will face in one direction, helping to keep the pleat fold flat.

An effective way to ensure that any pleated hem stays creased is to edgestitch the fold of the pleat. Stitch through all thicknesses of the hem on the inside.

To handle fullness effectively in a pleated hem, re-stitch the seam below the hemline at a slant opposite that of the garment seam above the hemline. Remove previous stitching and trim the seam below the hemline to ¼". Complete a hem without fullness as for a plain hem; otherwise complete as for an eased hem.

DOUBLE-STITCHED HEM: This hem is ideal for unlined heavy fabrics and knits. Stitch and overcast the raw edge. Mark the hemline with thread tracing; shrink and adjust any ease. Baste along the center of the hem. Fold back the hem along the basting and catchstitch the hem to the underlining. This line of stitching is for support only; do not pull the stitches too tightly. Turn up the top edge of the hem and sew it with a second line of loose catchstitching.

INTERFACED HEM: Your garment style or fabric may require the control of an interfaced hem to create a smooth, unbroken line. Mark the hemline with thread tracing. Use regular interfacing fabrics for body or lamb's wool for a softer effect. Then cut a bias strip the width of your hem and long enough to lap the ends ½". Piece if necessary and pre-shape the interfacing to correspond with the curve of your hem. Place strip over hemline with one edge extending ⅝" below the thread tracing. Sew to underlining with long running stitches along the hemline and long catchstitches along the upper edge. Then turn the hem up and baste close to the fold. Stitch and overcast the raw edge. Blindstitch hem to underlining, easing fullness if necessary. To press, steam the hem, never resting your iron on the fabric. Refer to Pressing, page 347, for additional information.

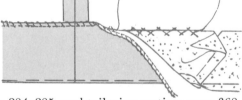

For hems at corners, see Sleeve Finishes, pages 284–285, and tailoring section, page 368.

For couture hem finishes, see page 383 for the Hong Kong and horsehair braid finishes; page 384 for soft and extremely curved hems.

For an explanation of pressing techniques and equipment to use on hems, see page 347.

Pressing

That finely finished look every woman strives for is as much a product of good pressing as it is of careful construction. Do not ignore pressing directions in your haste and zeal. If you postpone your pressing until the garment is completed, it will be too late to accomplish well-defined edges and sculptured contours. Set up your pressing equipment near your sewing machine and use it faithfully.

The most important idea to remember is that pressing is *not* ironing. Pressing is the process of lifting the iron and setting it down again in the proper position. You can use pressing to accomplish feats not possible with a needle and thread.

Specifically, pressing techniques depend on the particular fabric and garment construction, but there are some basic rules which should always be followed:

- ☐ Have an assortment of equipment available so that you can place the fabric in the most practical position for the area being pressed.
- ☐ Always test an odd scrap or an inconspicuous area to determine the best technique for your fabric. Test a piece large enough to allow a comparison between the pressed portion and the unpressed portion.
- ☐ Check your fabric's reaction to *steam* and *moisture.* Both should be used sparingly, or water marks, puckering, and dulling may result.
- ☐ Press with the grain of your fabric whenever possible; be very careful not to stretch edges or curves by pulling the fabric.
- ☐ Whenever possible, press on the wrong side of your fabric. If you must press on the right side, use a press cloth.
- ☐ Use brown paper strips to prevent impressions of seam allowances, darts, or pleats from appearing on the right side of your fabric. Cut strips at least 2″ wider than the area to be pressed.
- ☐ Always press seams and darts before they are crossed with other seams to eliminate any extra bulk.
- ☐ Never press any sharp creases until the fit of your garment has been double-checked.
- ☐ Try to use only the tip of your iron and work in the same direction as you stitched.
- ☐ To avoid marring fabric, do not press over basting threads or pins.
- ☐ Above all, know your fabric and *do not overpress.*

Press Cloth

To prevent shine and protect your fabric from the heat of the iron and its impression, use an appropriate press cloth between the fabric and the iron. Press cloths are made of a variety of fabrics. The one you use depends upon the nature of your garment fabric. Select one of a weight similar to the weight of your fabric and use a size approximately 12″ by 18″. An extra scrap of your fabric makes an excellent press cloth. In general, a wool press cloth is best for preserving the spongy texture of woolens, while firm cotton is ideal for most flat-surfaced cottons and medium weight blends. Cheese cloth, used singly or folded several times, will readily adapt to most of your needs because it is supple and you can see through it for pressing details.

You may use a dry press cloth with either a dry or steam iron. A uniformly damp press cloth may be necessary. If so, moisten it with a sponge, or immerse, wring, and press it until the proper dampness is achieved. To avoid shrinkage, **never** place a really wet cloth on your fabric and don't have the iron so hot that the cloth dries immediately. Keep in mind that there are several very suitable commercial press cloths in addition to making your own. For a listing of types available see the equipment section, page 448.

Steam

The moisture of steam provides the slight amount of dampness needed to get truly flat seams or edges. Curved or softly draped sections of your garment may be "set" to hang correctly by steaming them into position. Steam is of special value for collars and lapels. They will always roll correctly if carefully steamed in position on a dress form or a rolled towel during construction.

Use a press cloth if you apply the iron directly. If the iron is held about 3″ from the fabric, no cloth is needed. Let the steam do most of the work. Steam, then mold the fabric with your fingers while it is still damp. Allow the steam to dissipate and the fabric to dry before you resume working.

Seams

Initially, all seams are treated alike. Press along the stitching line in the same direction as the seam was sewn to merge stitches with fabric. Open the seam flat with the tip of your iron. Then let the shape of the seam dictate further handling.

FLAT SEAMS often leave ridges in the right side of your garment. Steam press with the garment over a seam roll or with brown paper under the seam allowances. To get some seams truly flat, you may have to steam the surface and use short quick movements with a pounding block on the seamline only.

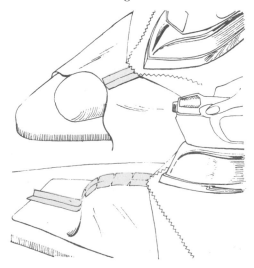

CURVED OR ROUNDED SEAMS pose different problems. The seamline should be pressed flat, but the seam area should maintain its built-in roundness. Employ the techniques used for a flat seam, but vary the equipment. Use a tailor's ham, press mitt, or dressmaker's cushion, alone or with a sleeve board, as your pressing surface.

SEAMS AT FINISHED EDGES with allowances completely enclosed within parts of your garment (such as facings, cuffs, pocket flaps, and collars) should be pressed before turning. Due to the confined area, narrow seam allowances, and the necessity of precise pressing, you will find it easier to work without a press cloth. After stitching, place the seam over the edge of a point presser or tailor board and open it with the tip of your iron to facilitate turning and ensure a flat seam which will not roll (1). Then lay the section flat on the ironing board with the underside up. Turn pressed seam allowances toward the section until the stitching line shows and press very lightly to make turning and favoring the outer edge easier (2). Turn right side out and press with a cloth from the underside; keep the seam on the underside (3).

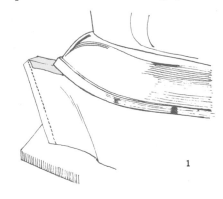

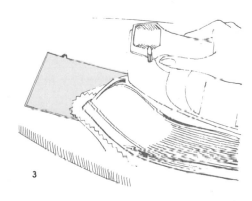

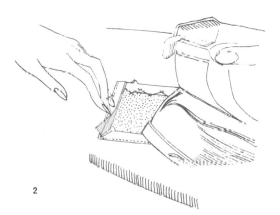

Darts

Darts require a subtly rounded pressing surface such as a tailor's ham, dressmaker's cushion, or press mitt. First press the dart flat, as it was stitched, being careful not to let your iron stray past the pointed end. Then open the garment and press the dart in the proper direction, working from the wider end toward the point. Do not give the dart a sharp crease until the garment has been fitted. In general, vertical darts are pressed toward center back or front and horizontal darts are pressed downward. Press contour or double pointed darts like single pointed darts, one half of the dart at a time, working from the middle to the pointed ends. Slash darts in heavy fabrics along the fold to within ½″ to 1″ of the point. Over a rounded surface, open the dart edges with the tip of your iron. Using a press cloth, press darts completely open. After pressing the dart, press the surrounding garment area.

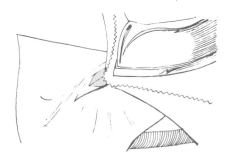

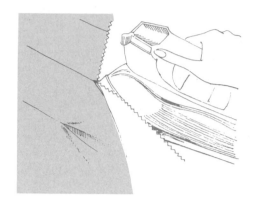

Tucks

First press tucks from underneath side of fold. To retain the soft fold of a released tuck, never press past stitching line. Be cautious with steam; too much may cause puckering. Press the fold of released tucks toward center front or back from wrong side. Tucks made on right side are pressed from stitching line toward folds; put brown paper under folds of wide tucks. Use a press cloth when pressing from right side.

Gathering and Shirring

Press from the wrong side wherever possible. Hold the gathering along the stitching as you work. Move your iron from the flat, ungathered area toward the rows of stitching. Use the tip of your iron to get between the folds of fabric. Repeat the procedure until no sharp creases remain. Press gathered seam allowances flat before stitching.

Pleats

When you are sure of fit, baste the length of each pleat; then press on both sides of the pleat, using a press cloth and very little steam. Press just enough to *set* the pleat. If the pleats fall correctly, press again to within 8″ of the lower edge, setting the creases permanently; use strips of brown paper under the folds. Hem and set remainder of pleat creases. (Press the full length if the hem is already completed.) ❖ To prevent overhanging fabric from distorting the pleats, support with a chair or table.

Soft or unpressed pleats should be steamed to fall gently into folds rather than sharp creases. Place the garment on a dress form so the folds fall naturally and steam thoroughly with your iron. If a dress form is not available, pin the pleats in place on your ironing board cover and steam them, holding the iron 2″ to 3″ from the fabric. Let the fabric dry completely before removing the garment from the board.

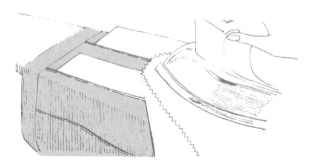

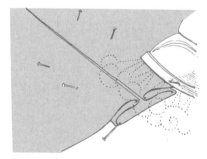

Plackets and Zippers

Because these features can be found in curved or flat areas, let the shape of the garment area determine the appropriate equipment to use. Position your placket right side down on a press pad, thick woolen scrap, or a heavy towel placed on your ironing board or a tailor's ham. The padding will prevent unwanted ridges from appearing as you press. Work from the wrong side; use a press cloth and limited moisture since excess dampness may create puckers. Do not press directly on zipper teeth, hooks and eyes, or snaps to avoid marring them or the sole plate of your iron. Should you need to touch up the right side of your fabric, place brown paper between the placket lap and the fabric underneath and press, protecting the fabric with a press cloth. Again be especially sparing in your use of steam and moisture.

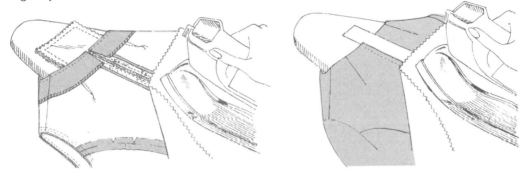

Buttonholes

Since buttonholes call for detailed construction techniques, you'll find that careful pressing applied at the appropriate times will greatly simplify the entire procedure. After stitching the buttonhole to garment, use a press cloth and brown paper under the strip edges to press the buttonhole from the right side, merging fabric and threads. Then use a sleeve board, placing the wrong side of the buttonhole area on the larger side of the board to prevent the surrounding garment area from becoming wrinkled. Lift up the strips and touch up portions of the garment between the buttonholes, if necessary. Then lay garment flat on ironing board and press the surrounding garment area.

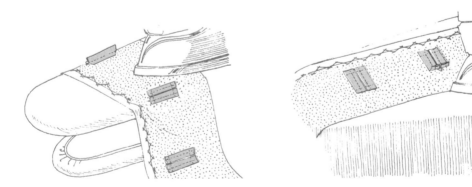

Pockets

The procedure for pressing pockets is quite similar to that of buttonholes. After stitching the pocket to the garment, press from the right side, using a press cloth. For welt or flap pockets, first put brown paper between the garment and the welt or flap. Then turn to the wrong side and press along seamlines, using a press pad. Then lift up the pocket and touch up the garment area underneath the pocket, using the moisture appropriate to your fabric.

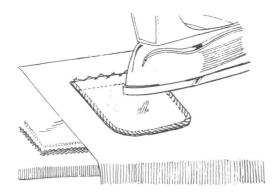 

Sleeves

Start by pressing the sleeve seam open over a sleeve board. After easing and fitting the sleeve cap, remove the sleeve from the garment and place it on a press mitt slipped over your hand or the narrow end of a sleeve board. Then use the tip and side of your iron to shrink the fullness from the seam allowance only. Be very careful not to press beyond the stitching line or flatten the sleeve cap. Some fabrics, such as permanent press and velvet, do not respond well to shrinking. If your fabric and sleeve cap need additional handling, see Set-in Sleeves, page 275. After the sleeve has been stitched into the garment, press along the seam over a tailor's ham to blend the stitches into your fabric. Avoid extending the iron into the sleeve cap and use steam sparingly.

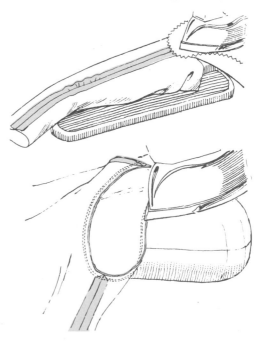

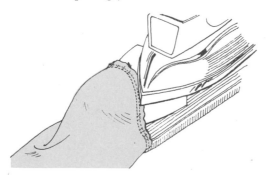

Hems

After marking, baste hems near the fold. Place brown paper between hem and garment and steam out any excess fullness. Avoid pressing over basting threads. For a great amount of fullness, easestitch along upper edge as directed on page 338. Then, holding iron above hem, steam it, shrinking as much fullness as possible. Once hem has been sewn in place, remove basting. Steam again. Use a pounding block if crisp edge is desired.

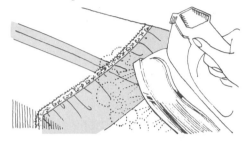

SOFT HEMS with a gently rolled edge may be preferred in place of a sharp crease. To achieve this finish, simply hold the iron 2"-3" from interfaced hem, steaming the fabric thoroughly. Never rest the iron directly on the fabric. Pat *lightly* with a pounding block or ruler to mold the hem. Let the garment dry thoroughly before wearing.

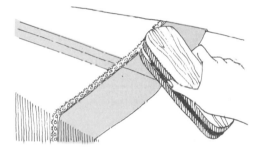

PLEATED HEMS with seams at the fold must be pressed carefully before hemming. First clip the pleat seam at the top of the turned up hem after the raw edge is finished. Press seam allowances open below clip. Grade the seam allowances of bulky fabric. Press a sharp crease in the underfold with the edge of your iron. If the folds still do not lie flat, stitch close to the edge of the fold.

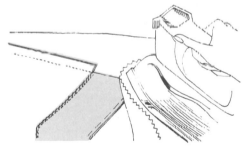

Final Pressing

The last pressing operation should just be a mere touch-up job, never a cure-all for haphazard pressing during construction. Soft pleats, godets, collars, and other areas that need "setting" should be pressed with garment on a dress form or a hanger. Just steam and pat into position without touching iron to fabric. You may use tissue paper padding under collars, inside sleeve caps, and in other areas to hold them in place while fabric dries. Do not remove garment from dress form until fabric is completely dry.

Certain fabrics (satin, crepe, metallics, velvet, silk, synthetics) and trims (paillettes, sequins, beads, trapunto) will require special pressing techniques and equipment; see Special Handling, pages 185–205 and Trims, pages 385–403.

Fitting

As you sew, you should always try on your garment after completing each unit of construction to check the fit. But what exactly is good fit? Clothes which fit well are clothes which allow enough ease for comfort and freedom of movement, hang smoothly without wrinkles or bulges, and flatter the figure. If a garment does not conform attractively to your contours, all your efforts at fine construction will have been wasted.

There might seem to be a fine line between fitting and alterations. In reality, however, alterations or adjustments are those *significant* changes which should be made on the pattern tissue before you even reach for the fabric, while fitting involves those *minor* changes necessary to perfect and finalize the garment. Tissue pattern alterations alone may not guarantee a flawless fit, since paper, by its very nature, will behave differently than your fabric.

Before you attempt to fit any garment, wear the undergarments, shoes, and belt intended for that garment, and work before a full length mirror in a well-lighted room.

First Fitting

This fitting should tell you how your fabric will mold into the style you have chosen. It should include only the garment areas that constitute the basic outer layer; omit the collar, cuffs, facings, sleeves, and any other details such as pockets. Baste darts and press lightly with fingers. Pin or baste the major seams at shoulders, sides, and waistline along the seamlines. Pin shut any openings where zipper, buttons, or plackets will later be placed. For the best fit, the garment should always be tried on as it will be worn, with the right side out.

Stand naturally and look into the mirror. Make sure the garment provides enough ease for comfort. Sit, bend, walk, and move your arms. The garment should look balanced, with adequate length from the neck to the waist and from the waist to the hem. Keep in mind that most figures are not perfectly symmetrical. Do not allow yourself to fit so closely that figure flaws such as a high hip or low shoulder become noticeable. Check the placement of closures and fastenings, the number of buttons, and so on to be sure that the closings will not gap. Don't become alarmed by high necklines and armholes; they will be smaller during the first fitting stages because the seam allowances are not turned in the proper direction until these edges are finished.

CONCENTRATE ON THE FABRIC: Learn to use your hands to lightly smooth the wrinkles, easing the fabric into the correct position. Grainlines and remaining wrinkles will tell you how the fabric is reacting to your figure. Check the placement of darts, necklines, armholes, and seams for any indication that the basic structure of the garment does not agree with the basic structure of your body.

SEAMLINES—GRAINLINES—WRINKLES: All lines are very important guides in fitting. Note the positions of your seamlines and grainlines. They should divide the body as intended by the designer. Grainlines should be parallel to the floor if they are crosswise and perpendicular to the floor if vertical (unless a section has been cut on bias grain as part of the design). Thread trace the grainlines on the fabric, indicating crosswise and lengthwise grainlines on each of your main garment pieces.

Wrinkles are the tell-tale signs of a grain distortion or of areas which are too tight or loose. If a vertical seam or grainline is not perpendicular to the floor or does not hang as your pattern envelope illustrates, look at the adjoining horizontal (or approximately horizontal) seams to see whether reducing or increasing their depth will sufficiently correct grainline and seam positions. Use a plumb line as an aid as directed on page 132. Changes may have to be distributed between both the horizontal and vertical seams to bring the fabric into position. For these changes, you may open and re-pin seams on your figure, but it is faster to pin or chalk mark new seamlines and then make the change after you remove the garment. Fitting problems should be solved by the least complicated changes possible to avoid unnecessary work and unintentional disruptions of the design.

Be aware that moving seamlines will mean that corresponding changes will have to be made in the adjoining garment sections.

Horizontal straining—stress at seams—indicates that a garment is too snug. Even after pattern alterations have been done, heavy or tightly woven fabric may require more wearing ease. Release all your seams slightly in even amounts to produce the needed ease.

DARTS: If the point ends in an unattractive location, remove the basting and adjust length of your dart. Relocate the point end first. You can adjust the depth of the dart to compensate for the thickness of your fabric.

NECKLINES: Necklines often require minor corrections. To remedy tight or high necklines, deepen the neck seamline an even amount around entire neckline to avoid distorting the line. If your neckline is a little large, slightly increase the shoulder seam or the center back seam at the neckline, tapering to the shoulder. Remember, straining at the neckline may be caused by the seam allowance that has not yet been turned under.

TO COMPLETE FITTING: Baste garment sections together along the new seamlines established during the first fitting, stitching any darts or seams that did not require fitting changes, and press. Press basted seams open with fingertips. Try on the garment again, testing the fit before stitching these areas together permanently.

Second Fitting

The second fitting takes place after sewing the darts and major seams, attaching the facings, and basting the sleeves or armhole facings into position. Test a jacket over a blouse, or a coat over a dress or jacket for really precise fit. Turn up the proposed hem. Review the appearance of your garment critically in the mirror. Side, back, and front seams should be straight and perpendicular to the floor by now. Diagonal wrinkles are often the result of fabric slippage as you sew. Smooth fabric perpendicular to the wrinkles to discover where to open and re-stitch the seam. Then check the new seamline. ❖ It is important to machine stitch directionally, generally sewing up from the hemline and down from the neckline. If you are letting out seams in fabric which frays easily, extend seam allowances with ribbon seam binding to ensure durability.

CLOSINGS: Pin the closings in position, matching center markings. *Asymmetrical closings* by their very nature need additional care and handling to prevent stretching any bias edges. Center markings should be anchored securely before you proceed with the fitting, or the additional weight of the closing details may distort grainlines and seams.

SLEEVES: The fit of the sleeve affects the entire garment. Raise your arms; freedom of movement is vital. Alterations should be handled during the tissue stage as in pattern adjustment section. For set-in sleeves, review page 275. Kimono sleeves (page 278) and gussets (page 292) can only withstand very minor fitting adjustments.

Make sure that the fabric grainlines on the set-in sleeve cap are at right angles to prevent rippling toward the front or back of armhole. Minor fitting adjustments can be done at the upper portion of the armhole. Remove basting between notches. Raise or lower sleeve cap until it is positioned correctly, taking a deeper or narrower seam allowance on the bodice at shoulder; do not change the sleeve seam allowance.

The underarm seam below the notches will be trimmed after the sleeve has been permanently set in. About 1″ below the armpit is ample room for movement. Contrary to what may seem logical, the lower the underarm part of the armhole, the more the sleeve or armhole facing may resist movement, causing pulling and straining. Remove the basting across the underarm. Raise or lower the sleeve, taking a deeper or narrower seam allowance on the bodice at the underarm as needed.

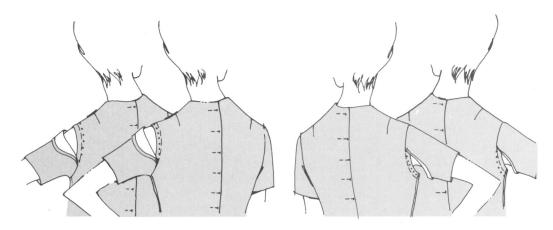

Final Fitting

After the garment has been completely sewn and pressed (except for the hem), try it on to determine the length. Review the final pressing to be sure that your seams are flat.

In the second fitting, the hem is pinned up to establish the most flattering length. Experiment with the estimated hem length. Once a length has been chosen, the actual measurement with a pin or chalk hem-marker can take place in the final fitting.

Essentially, fashion dictates hem lengths; but the type of garment, the nature of the fabric, and the height of the wearer determine the depth of the hem. Usually the hem allowance is 3″, which adds weight and therefore influences the drape of the garment. Of course, if the hem is for a very full skirt or a sheer fabric, the depth will vary—1″ for a circular skirt and as narrow as ⅛″ or as wide as six inches for a chiffon overskirt.

HEMS: When preparing a hem, there are several fundamental steps to follow. As with any other phase of fitting, the proper undergarments and shoes must be worn when measuring the hem. If you plan to accessorize with a belt, sash, or jacket, wear it while you are measuring. It will be a factor in determining the hem length in proportion to the total garment design and will affect the garment length considerably when worn.

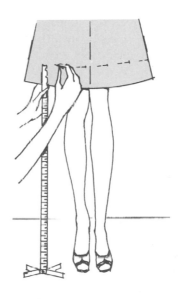

For absolute accuracy, always have someone mark your hem for you. To avoid discrepancies, stand stationary and have the person doing the marking move around you. Pins should be placed every 3″ for a straight skirt and every 2″ for a flared skirt. If your garment has a bias or circular hem, let it hang for 24 hours before measuring, allowing the bias to set and preventing hemline sag.

After the hemline has been marked, pin up the hem to see if it looks good. Insert the pins at right angles to the hemline, letting it fall in a natural manner. Regardless of length, the hem should look right. It should be parallel to the floor, but occasionally a perfectly straight hem will appear uneven, especially in garments with pleats, plaids, or that are bias-cut. If such a situation occurs, the hem must be changed to adapt to the optical illusion. Make the correction, using a carefully controlled, gradual change in the hem depth; then try the garment on again to see if the hemline appears to be even. Once the best hemline has been accurately established, turn to page 339 for the ideal hem finish to select for your individual fabric and design.

Your honest, objective, critical awareness is vital if you want to improve your sewing with each item you make. We hope that these suggestions have encouraged you to try to solve your individual fitting enigmas undaunted. If the most orthodox solutions don't work for you, don't be afraid to invent others. Be intuitive, flexible, and creative and you'll see how effortlessly you can accomplish a more perfect fit.

The
<u>Simple</u> Truth
About
Impeccable Tailoring

If you want to make a tailored garment, be prepared to spend a reasonable amount of time and effort. *Tailoring* by its very nature is synonymous with difficulty to some people —enough so that they are fearful of trying it themselves. Actually, tailoring is simply the additional pressing and hand sewing techniques required to shape and stabilize the fabric to retain the precise look intended by the designer.

A tailored garment is molded and shaped by pressing and sewing with the aid of supporting inner fabrics and specialized hand stitches. The *simple truth* is that tailoring is not difficult once you realize there are no short cuts to a professional finish. Develop good habits now and they will remain with you to polish every succeeding project.

Choose a style whose construction is consistent with your previous sewing experience, but also try to select one which will give you a real appreciation of what tailoring techniques actually add to a garment. Attempt to make yours a learning experience as well as an enjoyable challenge. If you already have some experience in the fine art of tailoring, treat any familiar information as a refresher course to recall important basic methods.

Creative Tailoring

Tailoring can be divided into two categories by the degree of tailoring required. First there are tailored wool suits or coats that require special pressing and shaping techniques and special handling of the underlining, interfacing, and seams. The second category consists of garments which require tailoring techniques in certain areas, such as the collar and lapels of a soft dress, and of fabrics which require tailoring to achieve the proper molded look, such as limp, loosely-woven, dressy, or washable fabrics. To be creatively tailored, garments of either type should have all these identifying characteristics:

- ☐ Pattern and fabric have been chosen to compliment your figure.
- ☐ Garment has smooth lines without wrinkles or sagging, and is molded to retain its shape without being stiff and uncomfortable.
- ☐ Buttons, flaps, pockets, and cuffs are positioned properly and are in the right proportion for the wearer.
- ☐ Collar rolls smoothly and evenly without seams showing at the outer edge and sits softly on garment without curling.
- ☐ All edges are pressed into soft or crisp edges as planned by the designer with seams at facing edges invisible.
- ☐ Hems are invisible with just the right amount of pressing.
- ☐ Lining does not pull or interfere with the hang of garment.

Tailoring will require some special equipment in addition to that needed for dressmaking. These tools, most of them pressing aids, will help to give you a better looking garment: tailor's ham or cushion, seam or sleeve roll, point presser or tailor board, pounding block or clapper, pressing mitt, pressing pad, pressing cloths, sleeve board, pointer and creaser, needleboard, and silk thread for basting.

Shop Wisely

When you approach tailoring, your preliminary decisions are the most important —style and fabric. For your first tailoring project, choose a style with basic lines that are flattering to your figure. Consult the suggestions given in Your Fashion Templates, pages 24-27, in addition to following the current trends. To show off your skill, your garment should show fashion awareness as well as a long life.

All Vogue patterns clearly state on the back of the pattern envelope what type of fabric may be used for each design along with all pertinent buying information. Purchase all notions and findings, as suggested, to expedite your tailoring project once it is started. Choose a fabric that can withstand standard wearing and cleaning. All your materials, inside and out, should help maintain the built-in shaping of tailoring.

Vital Preparation

First prepare your fabric. Pre-shrink all underlining, interfacing, tape, and other notions that will be used in your tailored garment, as the great amount of steam used in tailoring will affect all fabrics and findings.

Test your garment by making the jacket or coat shell in muslin. Refer to the recommendations shown in Your Perfect Sewing Tool, page 124, for any figure problems. Jacket patterns allow an additional amount of wearing ease at the circumference of the bust, waist, and hip, plus style ease when needed. This will provide ample room for your jacket to move easily over a dress or blouse and skirt. Coats also have an additional amount of wearing ease so you have ample room to wear a suit underneath. Coat sleeves are made large enough to be worn over a jacket. ❦ Two notes of caution, however: first, do not confuse the top of a two-piece garment with a jacket, as these tops are made with the same measurements and ease as a one-piece dress; and second, you cannot wear a coat over a jacket that is a cut-off version of the same pattern.

Now turn your attention to cutting the pattern pieces. Always cut your fashion fabric first and *cut seam allowances wider*. They should be at least 1" wide on all edges that may require fitting over the bust, waist, and hip area of the garment, and on sleeve underarm seams, outer edges of upper collar, and lapel facings. Transfer all center markings before removing the pattern tissue.

Next, cut your underlining fabric, making the seam allowances wider as for your fashion fabric. Transfer all seamlines, construction lines, grainlines, and symbols to your underlining with a tracing wheel and dressmaker's tracing paper.

Refer to Interfacing, page 356, before cutting your interfacing. Cut out the given lining pieces, using wider seam allowances as for your fashion fabric. Also refer to skirt lining, page 355, if your pattern does not include one. With your cutting completed and all fabric pieces stored on a flat surface, you are ready to do your first sewing.

Thread trace seamlines to the undercollar; for this garment section only, follow the thread tracing as a sewing guide in place of the marking on the underlining. Then pin the underlining to all of the fabric pieces, matching center lines and grainlines; review the marking section, page 184, and baste.

Some garment areas will require special attention as you baste to maintain their proper contour. Shape the undercollar, placing the underlining uppermost (1). The fashion fabric should be uppermost while you are shaping the upper collar (2) and sleeves (3). Turn jacket lapels along roll line as you baste, keeping the underlining uppermost (4). If your garment piece contains pleats, fold them, basting as you do to insure smooth layering. Baste along foldline and roll lines, then turn fashion fabric along these markings in the direction they will fall.

Finally, baste along your traced seamlines. You will refer to these seamlines constantly during fitting. Then thread trace along the lengthwise and crosswise grain of your fashion fabric on all major pieces. These markings will also be used as fitting guides.

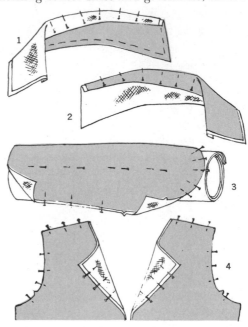

First Stage: The Skirt

Since all tailored garments must be fit to move easily over one another, the skirt is the first unit to be constructed. Before you begin the actual construction, make a waistline stay to support the fabric during fitting. Cut a strip of 1″ wide grosgrain ribbon your waist measurement plus 2″. Position it around your waist, allowing ½″ wearing ease; pin. Mark closing and centers.

You should prepare the skirt for fitting by first attaching the underlining as in (3) above; then, basting darts and pleats; flatten with fingertips. Baste seams or pin closely along the seamlines. Sew ease or gathering threads by hand. Lap skirt over waistline stay, matching centers, and adjust the ease or gathers. Pin and baste the waistline seam of the skirt along the edge of the stay (1).

Important fitting checkpoint: Try on skirt and position correctly on body. Fit skirt according to First Fitting, page 348. Transfer any new seamlines, dartlines, etc. to underlining with tailor's chalk. Re-baste any adjustments. Remove waistline stay. Stitch any seams or darts that were not changed; press open. Try on again to check fit. Stitch together permanently; press. Insert zipper.

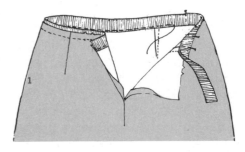

SKIRT LINING: The lining is constructed very much like the skirt. Most patterns do not include separate pattern pieces for a skirt lining; therefore, cut your lining from the skirt pattern pieces, allowing the same width seam allowances. To reduce bulk in a gathered or pleated skirt, cut your lining from a straight or A-line skirt pattern. Then baste the lining together as for the skirt, following the same alterations and leaving the appropriate seam open for the zipper. Pin lining to the skirt at the upper edge, wrong sides together; ease skirt to fit lining if necessary. Pin and baste attached skirt and lining to the waistline stay as before (2).

Important fitting checkpoint: Try on skirt and lining, positioning them correctly. Lining should hang free of skirt without bubbles or wrinkles in lining or binding or pulling in skirt. As with all circumferences, the outer layer (skirt) should be slightly larger than the inner layer (lining) for both layers to work together. Make any alterations by changing each seam minutely. A real problem will occur if the lining is considerably smaller than the skirt; it will be uncomfortable, the lining will wear out before the skirt due to strain, and you will not be able to complete the lining satisfactorily. When you have eliminated all fitting problems, stitch lining sections together.

Determine at this time whether you will hem your skirt and lining together or separately. If you are using a soft lining fabric, the two should be hemmed together; if you are using a crisp lining, they may be hemmed either way. The seam allowances will need to be finished only if your fabric is exceptionally ravelly or the hems are done separately.

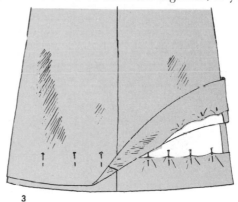

Pin the skirt and lining together along the upper edge, slipstitch lining to zipper tape, and baste upper edges together. Pin hems to an approximate length, making the lining ½" shorter than skirt (3).

The skirt hems should not be completed until you are prepared to sew the hem of the jacket or coat. The two hems must be in proportion to one another if you wish to achieve the most attractive results.

WAISTBAND: The final step is to attach the waistband. This permanently joins the skirt and lining at the waist. Use the waistband construction most suitable to your fabric (pages 334–335) adjusting it to your measurement. For a thick or bulky fabric, you may have to allow up to ½" more in the circumference of the waistband. Attach waistband and fasten with hooks and eyes (4).

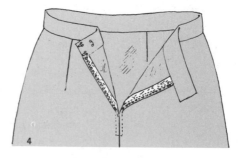

Tailoring Challenge: Jacket or Coat

The construction of a jacket or coat is the same in most cases; exceptions will be noted as they occur. The first step is to construct and fit the *shell* of your garment, which consists of the front and back pieces only. Follow same procedure as for the skirt: prepare and attach underlining, baste and press darts, add ease or gathering threads by hand, and pin or baste sections together. Flatten seams with fingertips or creaser.

Important fitting checkpoint: Try on garment shell over the skirt. Match the center front markings and pin. Position it correctly on your body. After fitting, transfer any new seamlines, dart lines, etc., to underlining. Stitch and press any darts and seams that were not changed. Baste along any new construction lines and flatten seams. Try garment shell on again with the skirt to check adjustments (1). ❖ Remember to allow enough room in a jacket for movement over a blouse or dress, and enough in a coat for over a jacket.

Stitch the shell together permanently, using your pattern's sewing guide for basic construction procedures. Press any remaining darts and seams.

Interfacing for Shaping

The degree of built-in shaping that highlights the tailored garment is dependent upon the proper use of interfacing. It must support the shape and withstand numerous wearings and cleanings without overwhelming the fabric's draping qualities. Interfacing also protects your fashion fabric from ridges being formed at seam allowances and darts during cleaning and pressing. If you are in doubt as to the appropriate weight and type of interfacing for your fabric, refer to The Undercover Story and chart on pages 82 and 83.

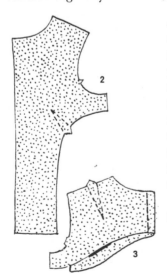

ADAPTING PIECES: Interfacing is necessary for support around the neck, shoulder, front, and armhole edges. If interfacing pattern pieces are not available, you will need to adapt your existing pattern pieces. Except for armholes, eliminate all seam allowances, including style seaming details. Pin all front pattern pieces together to act as a unit. To draw your interfacing pattern, use a piece of tissue paper large enough to cover the desired interfaced area. (For a facing seamed to front edge, eliminate seam allowance; for an extended facing, make the interfacing extend ⅝" beyond foldline.) Make the inner shaped edge ⅝" smaller than the width of the front facing and draw a curved line from it across front, ending 2" below armhole seamline (2). For the back section, pin the pattern pieces together. Place tissue paper over them and draw pattern, starting 2" below armhole and making it about 5" deep in the center back (3).

DARTS: There are three ways to make darts in interfacing. The first two are to be used when darts do not correspond exactly to the garment darts. (They can also be used for lightweight interfacing when darts do correspond.) The third is best suited for darts that do correspond to those of the garment.

First method: trim along dart lines (1). Bring cut edges together, center a strip of underlining or ribbon seam binding over the edges, and stitch securely (2).

Second method: slash through the center of dart lines (3). Lap edges, matching dart lines, and stitch together; securely reinforce the point with additional stitches (4).

Third method: simply trim darts away along dart lines (5). Pin interfacing to garment and pull garment dart through cut edges; catchstitch edges to underlining (6).

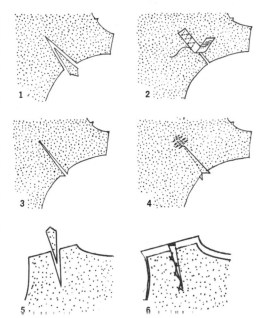

ATTACHING INTERFACING: You must first make sure the interfacing and garment shell will relate well to one another. Pin the two layers together, placing front, neck, and side edges along seamlines, and match armhole seamlines. For extended facings, place interfacing edge $\frac{5}{8}$" beyond foldline. Pin the interfacing to the garment and then baste shell along the center markings or seams only.

Important fitting checkpoint: Try on garment shell. If bubbles or ridges form in either interfacing or shell, they are not molding as one. If so, remove pins. With the right side of your shell uppermost, place both layers over a rounded surface similar to your body contour. Smooth the shell over the interfacing (with the grain as you did for the underlining), and pin where it falls inside the seamlines. Re-pin along foldlines and raw edges. Also make sure your lapels will roll smoothly; turn interfacing to outside along proposed roll, and pin along roll line and edges of interfacing as it falls in place (7). The interfacing should now relate to your garment shell and your body contour.

After any necessary adjustments and re-pinning, pin the interfacing securely on the inside. Examine interfacing edges along the seamline. They should be a scant $\frac{1}{8}$" short of the seamline. If necessary, trim interfacing so it will not bubble when seams are pressed open or encased.

Now baste interfacing to front along all edges. Sew it to the underlining along hemlines and any foldlines with long running stitches, and along the inner curved edge with catchstitches (8). For bulky fabrics, leave the interfacing free in the buttonhole area until after bound buttonholes are made.

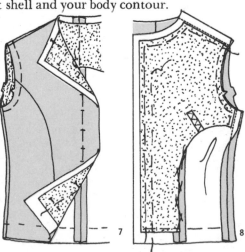

For back interfacing, cut away shoulder darts along the stitching lines. Pull garment dart through cut edges; catchstitch edges to underlining along dart seamline. Baste neck, shoulder, and side edges in place and baste armhole edges together, retaining the garment's shape as you work. Catchstitch sides (1).

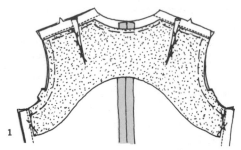

Now attach the front and back interfacing to your underlining with diagonal tacking (shown below), leaving the interfacing free over your buttonhole markings on the right front. If you are not using underlining, sew the interfacing edges to the seamlines with catchstitching and along the foldlines and hemlines with long running stitches.

HAND STITCHES FOR TAILORED GARMENTS: In order to ensure that all layers of fabric will be stabilized, you will need to master two hand stitches. The firmness built in by these stitches will enable the layers to move as one through repeated wearing and dry cleaning. Both are variations of diagonal basting. Use a sharp needle and matching thread, coating a single unknotted thread with beeswax to eliminate possible snarls. Secure the thread end at the edge of the interfacing with backstitches, and work in the direction of the grain.

Diagonal Tacking is used to attach interfacing to the underlining only. Take a tiny horizontal stitch through interfacing, catching a thread or two of underlining; repeat directly below, placing stitches approximately ¾"-1½" apart and forming a diagonal stitch on the interfacing side. Keep stitches long and loose and do not catch the fashion fabric as you sew (2). Cover surface of interfacing, shaping fabric as you sew to retain the garment contour. If you have not used underlining, omit this stitch and catchstitch edges of interfacing to garment along seamlines.

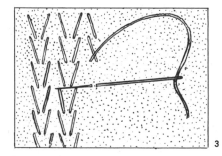

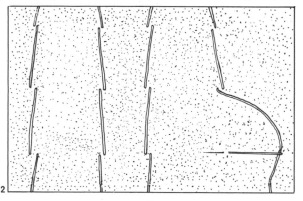

Pad Stitching is used to mold and control undercollars and lapels (whether underlined or not) by actually sewing in the shape. It is done exactly like diagonal tacking except that you sew through all layers, catching only a thread or two of the fashion fabric and holding the fabric in the desired position as you sew. Make stitches ¼"-½" apart (3). It would be wise to practice first on scraps of your fabric layers to get the feel of manipulating your fabric.

Important fitting checkpoint: Try on your garment shell and evaluate your work so far. If you notice a slight droop around the back of the armhole between the seam and shoulder blade or a slight indentation on the front between the armhole seamline and the apex of the bust, you need padding to get that impeccably tailored look.

TAILOR'S PADDING: Cut another layer of interfacing the width of the shoulder seamline less ½″, using armhole shape on one edge and a curved shape on the remaining edges to extend to ½″ beyond the end of the problem area. Then cut a piece of lamb's wool or heavy cotton flannel ½″ less than the interfacing piece on all edges. To attach padding to garment back, sew lamb's wool to interfacing with long running stitches along all edges. Use diagonal tacking to hold the center area in place. Now place the additional interfacing layer over the lamb's wool and attach it to the main interfacing in same way (1). Attach the padding to the garment front section in the same manner (2).

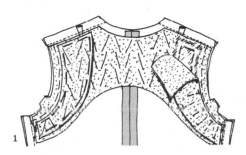

Undercollar and Lapels

Since many collar styles can be used on a tailored garment, turn to the collar section and review the introduction and the construction most closely related to your garment.

INTERFACING: To prepare interfacing for collar, trim away all seam allowances except the center back seam, if applicable (3). The interfacing sections can be joined in two ways for the center back seam. For the first method, you can lap the ends, matching seamlines, and stitch; trim both seam allowances close to stitching (4). For the second method, trim away center back seam allowances. Match edges, place a strip of underlining or seam binding over them, and stitch securely (5).

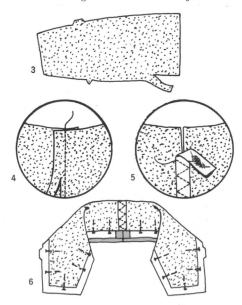

Then center the interfacing over the undercollar between the outer seamlines. Pin in place *along the neck seamline.* Shape the pieces as they will be worn. Make sure the interfacing is a scant ⅛″ short of the seamline. If not, trim the interfacing so it will not bubble later when seams are pressed open or encased (6). Catchstitch the edges to the undercollar. Staystitch the neck edge if you haven't already done so.

FIT AND SHAPE: Lap and pin undercollar neck edge over garment neck edge; match seamlines and markings. (If extended facings are to be used, they should be turned back at foldline, wrong sides together, and basted along neck edge at this time.) Baste collar in place, clipping the neck edge where necessary to lay flat.

Important fitting checkpoint: Try on garment or put it on a dress form to establish roll on collar and lapels. Lap and pin right front over left, matching centers and buttonhole markings. Check position of buttonhole markings to make sure they are correct for your figure. Begin rolling lapels at top buttonhole markings. The collar should lay as close to the neck as shown on the pattern illustration without riding high or low. The roll should be smooth, even, and unbroken from front to back. Be sure points of collar and lapels lay symmetrically against the garment.

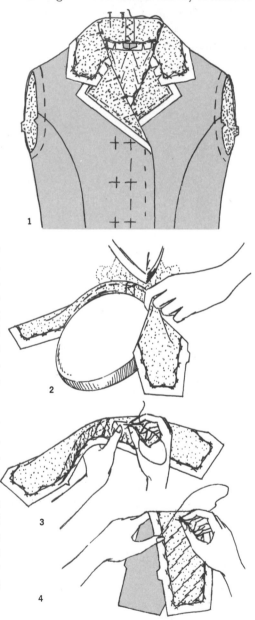

❉ The outer seamline of the collar should cover the back neck seamline. Adjust collar at the neck seamline until all features are correct. Transfer any seamline adjustments to both collar and lapels. Pin along roll line on both collar and lapels. This roll is very important in determining the finished shape. Thread trace roll lines on collar and lapels and remove collar (1).

STABILIZE THE ROLL: Pin the undercollar to a tailor's ham. Using steam, hold iron over roll, never resting it on the fabric. Work from center back to center front, shaping each half separately but identically along your established roll. Never press the roll into a crease; use your finger to shape the roll (2). Allow undercollar to dry thoroughly. Now shape lapels in the same manner and allow to dry.

PAD STITCH UNDERCOLLAR: The area between the neck seamline and the roll line (called the **stand**) must have small pad stitches placed close together—¼″ or less—to stabilize the stand. Hold the undercollar over your finger in the shaped position. Pad stitch heavily from the neck edge to the thread traced roll line; work along either the straight or crosswise grain (3). When you have completed the stand area, use larger stitches (about ¾″ apart) to pad stitch the remainder of the undercollar (4).

To blend the pad stitches into the under-collar, it must be pressed carefully. With the fashion fabric side up, press the outer curved area, placing a damp pressing cloth over the fabric. Press to the roll only (1). Do the same along the stand, always retaining the roll, and allow to dry thoroughly.

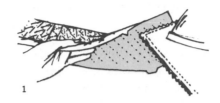

BOUND BUTTONHOLES: Before you can pad stitch the lapels you must complete your bound buttonholes. To select the type of buttonhole you prefer, refer to the button-hole section, pages 306-313, and read thoroughly. Re-space buttonhole markings evenly if you have made any alterations. If you are working with heavy or bulky fabrics, attach interfacing to garment after buttonholes are made as directed on page 308. For man-tailored garments, you may wish to make corded keyhole buttonholes just before completing the garment. After completing bound buttonholes, finish tacking the re-mainder of right front interfacing to under-lining with diagonal tacking.

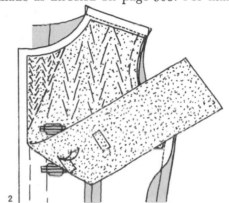

PAD STITCH LAPELS: After completing bound buttonholes, pad stitch the lapels. Start at roll line and fill in area between thread tracing and seamlines, spacing stitches about ½″ apart (2). Press the lapel area as for the undercollar and allow to dry.

Taping for Stability

According to traditional tailoring techniques, you should tape edges which will re-ceive strain during wear and cleaning. Tape is especially needed along the front edge of your garment, around the neck seam, and on lapels because these areas have a tendency to pull or stretch out of shape. You may wish to tape other areas that might "give" with wear, such as shoulder or armhole seams, and foldlines of a seam pocket or vent openings.

Ribbon seam binding lends itself well to taping: it is thin, firmly woven, and usually pre-shrunk. Cotton twill tape, ¼″ wide, is often used; be sure it has been pre-shrunk.

To apply seam binding, place it ⅛″ over seamline (or foldline for an extended facing) with the larger portion within the garment area. This automatically grades the binding when the seam is completed. Baste the edge which will be caught in the seam and sew the inner edge to the interfacing with diagonal tacking. Make the stitches about ½″ apart and catch a few threads of the interfacing with each stitch (3). If you wish to use twill tape, it is applied in the same manner. Place one edge over the seamline just enough to be caught in the seam (4).

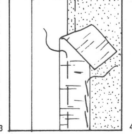
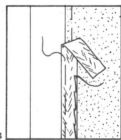

Begin by placing the tape along the front shoulder edge, extending it slightly beyond neck and armhole seamlines. Sew it to the seam along stitching with catchstitches. Sew the inner edge to the interfacing with diagonal tacking. Then tape front edges, extending tape slightly beyond the neck seamline and hemline. For lapel area, the tape must be placed from the shoulder seamlines to the point where the lapel begins to roll; placing tape just along roll line of lapel will not give enough support. Secure both edges to interfacing with diagonal tacking.

To tape foldlines, position tape the same as for a seamline; secure both edges by sewing it to interfacing along foldline with long running stitches and along the remaining edge with diagonal tacking.

To tape curved edges such as neck and armholes, seam binding is the best choice. Twill tape will add bulk to the seam, as it tends to roll when stitched in a curved seam. Make scant ¼" clips at even intervals, place unclipped edge ⅛" over seamline, and baste. Sew clipped edges to interfacing with long diagonal tacking stitches, placing the long stitch over the clipped edges (1). After mastering the techniques of taping, you may want to try a quicker method. ❊ If you are sure that your garment fits well, you may eliminate some handwork by machine stitching tape to the interfacing before it is attached to your garment. Make sure the tape extends a generous ⅛" beyond the trimmed edge of the interfacing so the interfacing will not catch in the seam.

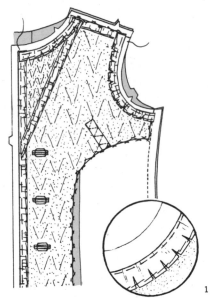

1

Collar and Facings

When you have completed taping, return to your collar. First pin undercollar to garment once again and check for all small, last-minute adjustments that may be needed.

PREPARE UPPER COLLAR: The upper collar will need additional handling to make sure it is large enough to hide the outer seam when the collar is completed. ❊ Make a minute tuck at the center of upper collar neck seamline, letting it taper to nothing at other edge. When released, it will automatically allow just enough fabric for you to favor the outer edge easily so any seams will fall on the undercollar side. Then pin upper collar to undercollar along neck edge, matching seamlines(2). Now shape collar as it will be worn with upper collar on top. Pin outer edges in place as they fall. To baste upper and undercollar together, follow seamline you thread traced on the undercollar previously (page 360). This maneuver will result in narrower seam allowances on your upper collar (3).

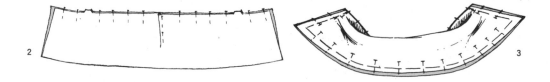

2   3

Stitch the collar sections together from the undercollar side, stitching along the thread traced seamline. Use small stitches at points and end stitching ⅝" from neck edge. Trim, grade, and notch or clip seams as needed. Press seams open on point presser for easier turning. See Seams at

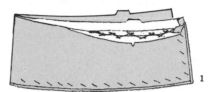

Finished Edges on page 343 of the pressing section. Turn the collar and tailor baste along the outer edges, using silk thread. Favor the upper collar at its outer edges so that the seam is on the undercollar side as you baste (1).

Press, using a damp pressing cloth to create a lot of steam. Then use a pounder or clapper to shape the edge to the desired effect (crisp or slightly rolled, depending on the style of your garment). Work with your fingers and the pounder to avoid shine or overpressing and allow to dry thoroughly. Staystitch the neck edges of the garment and facing pieces if you haven't already done so.

ATTACH COLLAR AND FACING: Pin undercollar to garment between markings (where collar ends and lapels begin). Baste, clipping garment seam allowance as necessary, and then stitch. Stitch neck and front facings together; press. Clipping facing seam allowance as necessary, pin, baste, and stitch upper collar to facing between markings (2).

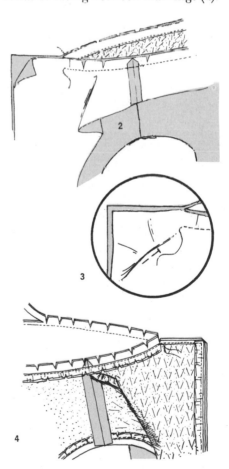

Make a minute pin tuck on lapel/facing, so you will have enough fabric to favor the lapel seam when garment is turned to right side (raw edges will not be even at the point). Pin the facing to the garment (3).

Baste facing to garment, following garment seam lines. Start stitching from the garment side where garment meets collar in order to eliminate bubbles that sometimes occur where the collar meets the lapels. (For bulky or heavy fabrics you may not be able to start exactly at the markings; leave thread ends long enough that you can complete that area by hand later.) Reinforce points and continue around lapel/facing. Clip seam at end of collar to stitching. Trim and grade lapel facing seams as needed. Trim only upper collar and facing neck seam, leaving the garment and undercollar seam ⅝". Clip both neck seams (4).

Press facing seams and both collar neck seams open on a point presser. Turn facing. Using silk thread, tailor baste facing edges for pressing to within 5"-6" of lower edge. Favor the lapels at the outer edge so the seam is on the undercollar and garment side; below the point where the lapel begins to roll, favor the garment so the seam is on the facing side. Press these edges with a damp pressing cloth, using a pounder to achieve the desired effect. Retain basting.

Try on jacket and re-establish roll. Remove jacket and pin about ¾″ above the neck seam to hold the layers in place. Lift up facing and sew the neck seams together with long, loose stitches in a zigzag pattern, being very careful *not to force the seams together* if they don't meet. This holds the upper

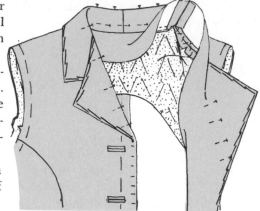

collar in place so it will not twist or pull during wearing or cleaning. Retain pins in facing.

At this time you should decide how to finish the underside of the bound buttonholes. The couture method, page 382, must be done at this time. The conventional methods, page 311, can be done before the buttons are attached.

Sew inner edge of facing in place with long running stitches to within 4″-6″ of lower edge.

Pockets, Flaps, and Welts

Your most important consideration will be placement. Remember to reposition any pocket, flap, or welt placement lines if you have altered your pattern. There is nothing more frustrating than to end up with a beautifully made pocket that is too close to the jacket hem to be usable because the hem had to be sewn over it.

Pockets can be classified into two groups—utilitarian and decorative. Utilitarian pockets should be at a comfortable height for use, while decorative pockets should be placed as featured in the design. Both should add a balanced look to the total silhouette. To make sure that the pocket, flap, or welt placement is right for your garment, take the exposed portion and turn in the seam allowances along the seamline to simulate the finished item. Pin up garment hem along proposed hemline, then pin pockets, flaps, or welts to garment at placement lines. Try on garment (include skirt with jacket) and check position.

Experiment with the placement and size until you achieve the desired effect. Carefully analyze the position of the pockets, flaps, or welts in relation to the center front marking, and be sure they end an equal distance from the center marking and the lower edge of garment. Transfer any necessary adjustments to the garment and individual pieces. You are then ready to construct and apply your pockets, flaps, or welts; refer to the instructions on pages 296–302 and choose the method that best suits your needs.

Sleeves

Tailored sleeves are basically the same as any other sleeve. The two-piece set-in sleeve is considered the classic tailored sleeve when its hem is interfaced appropriately and the seams are taped to ensure that they will retain their shape.

Since a poorly executed set-in sleeve will mar the appearance of a tailored garment, it would be wise to take the time right now to review all sections that will help you get a perfectly fitting sleeve. Then you will be able to insert your sleeve quickly, neatly, and easily. Turn to pages 132, 139–141, 274–279, 292–296, and 350.

Since the major alterations have already been done, your problem now will be adapting the fabric to your needs. Add the sleeve cap ease threads, using the stitch length appropriate for the fabric, and break the stitching at the seams. ✣For extremely heavy fabric, add the ease threads by hand. Pull up ease threads the desired amount and secure them for fitting. Do not shrink the sleeve cap at this time. Baste the sleeve seams along the seamline, right sides together, and press seams open with finger tips or lightly with an iron so you do not leave an impression. Then baste the sleeve in the armhole.

Important fitting checkpoint: Try on garment with skirt to evaluate the sleeve lengths with the sleeve hems pinned in place. Allow enough room in a jacket sleeve to move freely over a long dress sleeve. Coat sleeves should be full enough to fit over a jacket sleeve. Place shoulder pads on shoulders if the sleeve needs support. Check sleeve lengths again. Stylized sleeve hems require careful planning *before* cutting so you will have only minute adjustments.

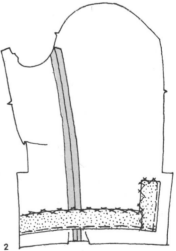

Use a plumb line to check grainlines (1). Make any necessary adjustments and mark fabric. Remove sleeve. Apply tape to seams before stitching to support heavy fabrics or to help retain the shape for loosely-woven fabrics. If sleeve has a plain hem, stitch seams; press open, using sleeve board. If the sleeve has a vent opening or other stylized hem, stitch the seams necessary to complete hem.

SLEEVE HEMS: Choose an appropriate interfacing that will hold the curved line of the sleeve hem without "breaking." Lamb's wool or cotton flannel will give a very soft rolled edge; regular interfacing fabrics add more body and the edge can be rolled or creased. Use only interfacing fabric, however, to stabilize any buttonholes on the sleeve.

Cut bias strips of interfacing equal in length to the circumference of the hem (allow additional fabric for lapping ends on a continuous sleeve hem) and equal in width to the depth of hem plus 1⅜". For a vent opening, cut a strip of straight grain interfacing the length of opening plus ⅝" to extend beyond hemline, and wide enough to extend ½" beyond the end of the buttonhole on one side and ⅝" beyond foldline on the other.

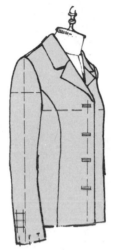

Place interfacing over vent buttonhole markings with one edge and end extending over foldline and hemline. Sew it to underlining along foldline and hemline with long running stitches and along upper end and edge with long catchstitches. Make bound buttonholes. (Make buttonholes through only the lightest weight interfacing; otherwise, apply interfacing after buttonholes are made.)

To interface the sleeve along the hemline of any style, place one edge of interfacing ⅝" below hemline in hem area with the greater portion on the garment side; pin.

For heavy or bulky fabrics, slash through interfacing along seamlines and tuck ends under seam allowances. Sew interfacing to underlining along hemline with long running stitches and along the upper edge and ends with long catchstitches (2).

For hems that will be topstitched, cut interfacing ¾″ wider than the hem depth and place one edge along the hemline. Vent openings should be interfaced only to foldline. Baste hemline and foldline edges in place; catchstitch all other edges.

If you are not using underlining, the interfacing should still be attached in the same manner, being careful to catch only a thread of your fashion fabric so the stitches will not show on the right side of the fabric.

Interfacing applied correctly will protect your fabric so the imprints of hem and seam allowances will not show through to the outside during wearing, cleaning, or pressing. When interfacing is completed, pin hem in place and baste close to fold. (For a vent opening, the layers need to be graded to avoid ridges where the edges of several will fall in the same place.) Trim away ⅝″ from hem allowance edge of vent facing, ending at foldline. Sew hem to interfacing with long running stitches (1). For heavy or bulky fabric, blindstitch the hem in place. Stitch any remaining seams as directed in sewing guide; press. Do the same for the vent opening (2). Press hem over a sleeve board, using pounder or clapper and steam to get the desired edge.

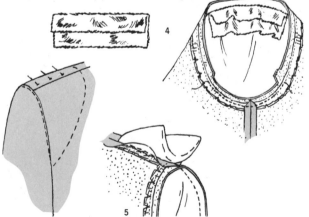

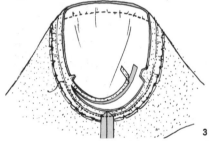

INSERT SLEEVE: Pin sleeve to garment. Adjust ease and baste. *Important fitting checkpoint:* Check position of armhole seam and ease distribution. Remove sleeve and shrink out fullness. Re-baste sleeve into armhole and then stitch. Between notches, add a second row of stitching over the first for reinforcement. Trim seam allowance to ¼″ between notches (3).

SLEEVE PADDING: This is used to support the weight of the sleeve cap fabric so it will not collapse. For padding, cut one bias rectangle of lamb's wool or heavy flannel 3″ wide and 4″ to 6″ long for each armhole. Make a 1″ fold on one long edge. Slipstitch folded edge of padding along seam at cap of sleeve (4).

SHOULDER PADS: Use these to help maintain the shape of the shoulder line if needed. Be careful not to use too thick a pad, or it will distort the natural shape of the garment. Strive for a soft, fluid line rather than a rigid, raised shoulder. Try on jacket for exact pad placement. Pin pad securely on one side of the seam from the outside. Open out any facings at shoulders to avoid unnecessary bulk and sew pads to seam allowances (5).

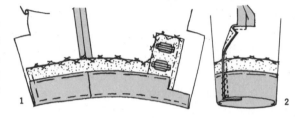

Final Fitting

Now it is time to determine the hem lengths for all the pieces of your tailored garment to ensure they are in proportion to one another. For help when measuring the hems, refer to Final Fitting, page 351.

Important fitting checkpoint: Try on garment and skirt with the hems pinned in place. Wear the appropriate undergarments, shoes, and accessories. Lap fronts, matching centers, and pin. Be sure garments drape naturally and comfortably. Mark any necessary hem adjustments with thread tracing.

The right front must lap over the left front, concealing its lower edge. The inner folds of pleats should not show, nor should the underlap of a vent. Check your button placement markings once more for accuracy. Do you need a strategically placed snap, hook, or inner button to support the left front? Adjust any area that may need a final pinch of fabric removed or let out a bit. It is now the time to complete your hems.

Hems, Vents, and Pleats

You have already hemmed your sleeve successfully, so you are well on the way to finishing all of your hemming details. Work with the bulk of your garment on a table to avoid unnecessary wrinkles as you hem. Since you have already chosen the interfacing fabric for the sleeve hem, you should use the same type for the jacket hem.

Cut bias strips for the circumference of the hem and 1⅜″ wider than the hem. Open out facings. Pin interfacing to garment with one edge ⅝″ below hemline and lap ends over front interfacing. Trim and catchstitch ends to front interfacing. Then attach to garment hem as for sleeves (1).

❊For heavy or bulky fabrics, slash strip where it falls over seams and tuck edges under seam allowances. For a shaped or eased hem, pre-shape interfacing to fit contour of garment before applying.

Turn up garment along hemline and baste close to the fold; use silk thread (2). If necessary, add ease thread to hem edge before pinning it to interfacing.

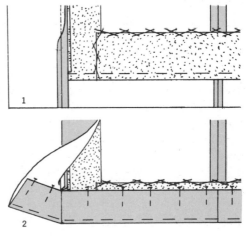

CORNER QUANDARY: We will suggest several ways to handle corners; select the one best suited for your fabric, design, and individual needs. The first, while probably the quickest and most popular method because the garment hem **can be lengthened** at a later time if necessary, does not give the best results for bulky fabrics. Prepare the hem as on previous page. The facing should taper slightly so it will not show on the outside. Trim ⅝″ away from end of hem between top and basting. Then trim ⅝″ from top of hem to seam or foldline. Sew the hem to the interfacing with long running stitches or blind hem in place for bulky fabrics (1). Press the hem, using steam and pounder or clapper to get the desired edge.

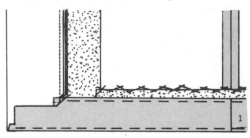

The completion of this type of corner depends upon your fabric. For lightweight fabrics, make a ¼″ clip at the top of the hem and turn it in below the clip; pin. Slipstitch the facing below the clip and across the lower edge (2). For heavier fabrics, turn back the facing at the lower edge; blindstitch loosely to hem. Sew the raw edge of the facing securely to hem with hemming stitches (3). For both, sew remainder of facing in place above hem. Press, being careful to avoid shine on your fabric.

This alternate method will give you a flatter hem for bulky fabrics, but the hem **cannot be lengthened** later. Prepare hem as on previous page. Mark where facing edge will fall on hem. Open out facing. This method requires staggered trimming. First trim facing hem to ⅝″, ending at seam or foldline. Then measure ½″ from the marking toward the facing, and slash hem at this point to within 1″ of hemline. From this point, trim across hem to seam or foldline. Clip alongside seam to first trimming line. Secure the trimmed edges with long, loose catchstitches (4). Sew hem in place and press, using steam and pounder or clapper to get desired edge. Turn facing to inside; press. Slipstitch lower edge together (5). Finish raw edge of facing with hemming stitch; press (6).

Excess fabric or extremely curved hems may be a problem also. Some openings work well with mitered corners, page 243. For handling an extremely curved hem, see page 384 of the couture technique section.

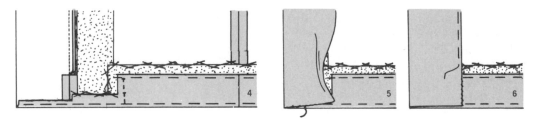

VENT OR PLEAT OPENINGS: Jacket and coat vents or pleats differ only in length from those found in a sleeve hem. End the interfacing at the seamlines or extend it ⅝″ beyond the foldlines, interfacing the outer layer the same as you would the hem. Be sure to support the foldlines with tape to stay the fabric (1). Use your sewing guide for the basic construction. Choose the corner finish appropriate for your fabric from the opposite page.

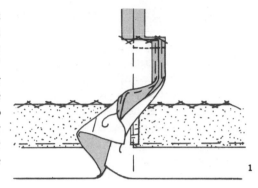

MAKE SKIRT HEM NOW: If you are making a skirt as part of an ensemble, complete the hem at this time so you can follow through and make the hem for the lining at the same time as the jacket.

An Ultimate Pressing

Place the garment on a dress form or a well-padded hanger suspended from a wire so you can work around it. Look your garment over well—front, back, sleeves, collar, and pockets. Are there any creases or wrinkles that may need to be eliminated? Remember, once you have attached the lining there is little you can do to press some areas well. Use your pressing mitt and pressing cloth, or use the dress form as a pressing aid. Allow your garment to dry thoroughly on the dress form or hanger with the garment hanging free and the openings pinned in the proper position. Pad sleeves, collars, or other areas with tissue paper to help retain their shape.

Lining as a Finale

Lining a garment is the final construction step in tailoring. Lining fabric should complement fashion fabric in weight, wearability, and cleaning requirements. Be sure interior construction does not show through the lining. A smooth fitting lining is absolutely essential for professional results and will greatly influence the total look.

The lining is the last layer to be applied. It demands the same careful attention to construction and detail as your actual garment shell. A lined garment must slide easily over another garment. Pleats and wearing ease should be placed where the garment must give with body movement at center back, above and below waistline, bust area, hem edges of sleeves, and hem of garment. Center back pleat should be ½″ to 1″ deep from neck to hem. Adjust the pattern before cutting to allow for pleats or wearing ease if necessary. If warmth is a factor in the garment you are making, refer to Interlining, page 373, before you stitch the lining together.

CONSTRUCTION: Baste darts and seams together. Make the same seam adjustments as you did for your garment. Press seams, darts, and pleats with fingers or creaser. Lining will mar easily, so do not use an iron.

Slip lining into garment, wrong sides together. Lap lining over facings and pin or baste, matching seamlines around front, shoulder, neck, and armholes. *Important fitting checkpoint:* Try on and test lining to make sure it does not interfere with the garment. Look for excessive wrinkles. The inner circumference of your lining should be just like the inner measurements of a cylinder, smooth and slightly smaller than the outside. Adjust lining, fitting as necessary. Mark any adjustments. Stitch only underarm bust darts. All waistline or shoulder darts, pleats, and tucks should be basted first, then anchored in place from right side of fabric with cross stitches through all thicknesses. Place cross stitches at neck, waist, and lower edges of back pleats. Stitch all major seams except shoulder seams. Press, using steam sparingly. Staystitch front, back shoulder, and neck edges, and across underarm between the notches. Turn in front, back shoulder, and neck edges along seamline. Baste, clipping or notching seam allowances so they will lay flat. Do not press edges (1).

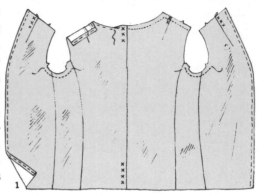

INSERTION: Work from center back to front opening edges. Pin lining to garment, matching center back. Then, matching any back seams first, sew the seam allowances together loosely by hand with long running stitches, ending the sewing 6″ from lower edge. Sew any side or side front seam allowances together in the same manner. Now pin armhole, front shoulder, and front edges of lining in place. Sew front shoulders to back seam allowance with long running stitches (2). Slipstitch front turned-in edge to facing, ending 4″ to 6″ from lower edge. Place stitches about ⅛″ apart and secure with backstitches at 3″ to 4″ intervals. Next, pin back shoulder and neck edges in place and slipstitch them to front lining at shoulders and to the back neck facing. Baste armhole edges together alongside seamline in seam allowance. Clip underarm of lining between notches every ½″ (3). For vent openings, attach lining as directed on sewing guide.

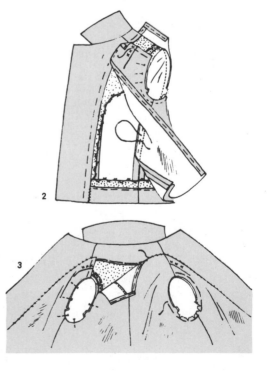

❧ In man-tailored garments, the garment sleeves may not be sewn into the armholes until after this phase of the lining is completed. Then sleeve is sewn into armhole through all thicknesses. The sleeve lining is completed in the regular way.

Lining Hem

Now that the lining shell has been carefully sewn in place along facing and shoulder edges, you have only the lining hem to do. If you follow carefully the methods of handling your lining hem, you will have a better fitting garment and the lining will not overwhelm the fashion fabric, causing pulling or distortion at the hem edges.

ANCHOR LINING: Work with garment on a dress form or on a padded hanger attached to a wire suspended from ceiling so you can work around the garment. This way the lining will drape well with the garment. From the outside, pin the lining to the garment 4″ to 8″ above hem, placing pins at right angles and at 2″ to 3″ intervals (1).

ATTACHED HEM: Begin by trimming the lining even with garment edge (2). Then add an ease thread ¼″ from raw edge of the lining if the hem requires it. On the outside, make a ¼″ wide tuck across the lining below the pin line, placing the pins parallel to the fold. Now turn in the raw edge ¼″ and pin to hem where it falls (3). Slipstitch entire lower edge of lining to garment hem. ⚜ Should you wish to use a chain weight on your jacket, adjust width of exposed jacket hem by turning in the raw edge of the lining deeper until you have established the desired width. If necessary, trim away excess lining fabric before slipstitching.

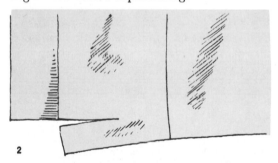

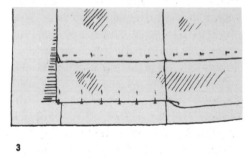

Remove pins from tuck. The lining will now smoothly fall down over the hem, forming a soft fold (4). Steam and pat into place with pounder. This fold allows for body movement and stretching during wearing without putting strain on garment hem. Slipstitch remaining turned-in edges of lining to facings or any vent opening, continuing to the edge of the fold (5).

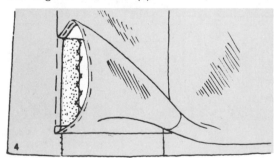

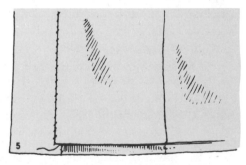

FREE HANGING HEM: Pin lower edges of garment and lining together as shown in illustration #1 on previous page. Then turn up lining hem so the lining is ½″ shorter than the garment and baste close to the fold. Now measure the depth of the lining hem and trim evenly if necessary. Use appropriate finish and method to complete lining hem. Press lightly (1). Slipstitch remaining turned-in lining edges to facing and hem or any vent openings (2). Sew lining hem to garment hem with 1″ French tacks at seams (3).

Some garments will require a combination of these two methods of hemming a lining, such as a coat with a full pleat in the back. The front of the lining would be attached and the back would hang free to allow the pleat to drape naturally.

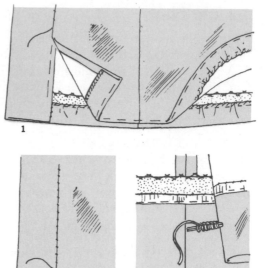

Sleeve Lining

This step will require additional molding. Baste seams and darts and adjust ease if necessary. Finger press seams. Wrong sides together, baste lining sleeves into armhole of garment lining along seamline, lapping edges and adjusting sleeve cap ease.
Important fitting checkpoint: Try on garment. Check fit of sleeve lining. Examine garment sleeve for wrinkles or bubbles. Shape sleeve cap lining inside garment. Mark adjustments on cap and seams; baste.

Stitch basted sleeve lining sections together and press seams open. Add new ease threads if sleeve cap was adjusted. Shrink out excess ease now, since this will be the last time you should press this part of the garment. Staystitch underarm between notches. Turn in along seamline and baste; clip to stitching if needed so underarm seam allowance will lie flat.

With wrong sides together, sew lining seam allowances to garment seam allowances with long, loose running stitches, starting and ending 4″ from each end (4). Turn lining back over garment sleeve (5).

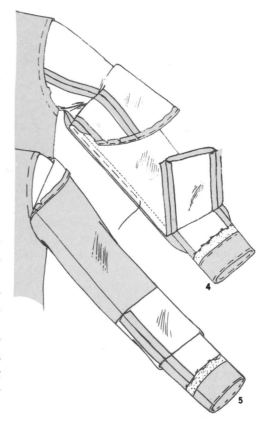

Now it is time to pin sleeve in armhole, matching seamlines and markings. Adjust ease and slipstitch, placing stitches ⅛" apart and backstitching at 1" intervals (1).

With garment on dress form or padded hanger, complete sleeve lining hem. Anchor hem first with pins as you did for the garment and then complete, using the attached hem method on page 371. You need the fold at the lower edge of the lining hem for movement and strain the same as you do in a garment hem (2).

Press all lining edges, using a light touch. Steam front and neck edges, patting lightly. Do the same for the fold formed at lower edge of an attached lining.

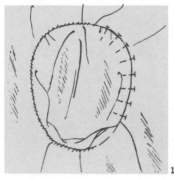

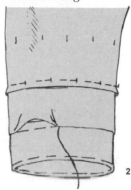

Interlining

You may wish to add a fourth layer of fabric to your garment for warmth. It is called interlining; one of the most common types is known as lamb's wool. For additional information about types and selection of other interlinings, see The Undercover Story, page 75. Be sure to take interlining into consideration when fitting your garment, as it will use up needed wearing ease.

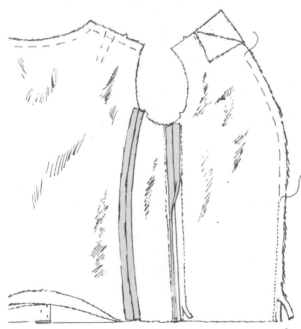

The easiest way to interline is to sew it as one with the lining. Cut interlining from lining pieces, omitting the back pleat. Cross stitch the lining back pleat in place. Then baste the interlining and lining pieces together, maintaining the proper contour as you did for the underlining and fashion fabric on page 354. Stitch darts and seams; slash darts and press open, trimming interlining close to stitching. After staystitching front, shoulder, and neck edges, trim away interlining close to stitching. Do the same for all seams (3). Now attach the lining in the usual manner.

Final Touches

Now is the time to put all the small finishing touches on your garment. In your haste to finish your garment, don't let yourself resort to sloppy or haphazard work. Give all your finishing details the same painstaking attention you gave the rest of your garment. If you haven't already done so, finish the back of your bound buttonholes or add your machine or hand-worked buttonholes. Attach your buttons, referring to pages 304-305 for the correct technique for your garment.

Important fitting checkpoint: Try on garment. Look at the nearly finished results. Does the front opening need a little support? Perhaps you will need a covered snap to hold the left front of a double-breasted garment in place (1) or one strategically placed at waist or bust to prevent gaping due to posture. Check your convertible collar in both positions. Do you need something to hold the lapel closed on a cold day? A perfect finishing solution is a tiny thread eye on one lapel edge and a nearly invisible covered hook under the collar (2).

You may wish to personalize your garment with those little custom touches that mark your tailored garment as truly haute couture. Perhaps you would care to add an elegant lace along front and neck edges where lining meets facing, or a gold chain weight to aid the drape of your jacket. See the couture techniques beginning on page 379.

At last you have finished all the construction of a tailored garment. But this is no time to relax in your vigorous striving for perfection. Try on your garment once again; while you are admiring the product of all your efforts in the mirror, also give the entire garment a detailed examination to double-check your workmanship. Did you miss a basting thread peeking out from a seam? If so, remove it with tweezers. Does the back pleat of your coat need a little help to drape properly, or does your jacket need some weight across the back to hold it in position?

When your discriminating eye is satisfied, you can consider your beautifully-made garment finally complete. You now have a garment which will retain the image you so carefully created through many cleanings and wearings, so you need never fear that all your efforts will be wasted. You will also find that as you become more experienced, many of the procedures emphasized in this chapter will become almost second nature to you. Some steps along the way can even be eliminated; once you know what changes needed to be made to fit your first tailored item, these changes can be transferred to each succeeding garment. Congratulations are definitely in order, for you have created a one-of-a-kind, impeccably tailored garment. Not only will you always be able to wear it with pleasure and pride, but you need never again be afraid to tailor any garment.

The Added Elegance of Fur

From time to time, the experienced sewer needs a project that challenges her capability. Making a fur garment not only tests your skill, but also furnishes its own reward. Whether you choose to purchase new fur or remodel an old favorite, you can't go wrong if you follow the directions below closely.

You will need the following equipment for sewing with fur: single-edged razor blades, chalk pencil, safety pins, thumb tacks or push pins, heavy duty needles (size 7 glover's needles are perfect), large board for blocking fur, button and carpet or heavy duty waxed thread, ½" twill tape, interfacing, and heavyweight muslin for a test pattern.

Preparing Fur

Choose your pattern carefully. A style with simple lines is best. Consider one with few pattern pieces, seams, or darts, and front opening edges that can be converted to extended facings. Make a test garment in muslin and try on as it will be worn; try on coats over another garment. Make any changes in muslin, then transfer changes to pattern. Since fur is sewn edge to edge, trim pattern away along seamlines and dart lines.

When working with old fur, pinch the skin side to test for suppleness and pliability. Wet a sample on the skin side and stretch it to test the skin's strength. Bend the fur hairs to be sure they are not too dry or brittle. To revive the fur side, dampen slightly, then gently brush it with the grain. Fluff against the grain and allow it to dry overnight before working with it.

Find the best parts of the pelts by placing your pattern pieces on the fur side first. To ensure similarity throughout the garment place pattern pieces with respect to shading, spotting, and color of adjoining pelts. Outline pattern pieces with a sufficient number of safety pins so you will know where to place them on skin side of pelt. ✳ You may need to join pelts to get a fur area large enough to cut out a pattern piece.

CUTTING FUR: Use a razor blade. Cut from the skin side and raise the pelt to avoid cutting the hairs. Cut over a board. Place the pelts edge to edge, skin side up, or cut area needed to complete a section (1).

JOINING PELTS: Using strong waxed thread and an overhand stitch, sew through the skin only. Work out any hair from the seam with the point of a needle. Reinforce by sewing twill tape over the seam with running stitches along the taped edges (2).

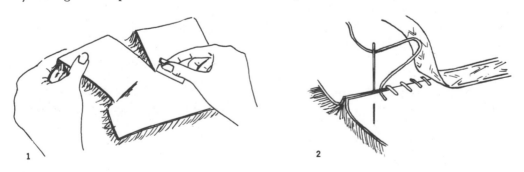

1

2

REPAIR WORN SPOTS: If there are worn spots in any of the pelts, mark them on the fur side with safety pins; place the pins in a triangle with one point toward the top of the garment (1).

From the skin side, mark the triangle with tailor's chalk, drawing lines from pin to pin (2).

Cut out the triangle and use it as a pattern for a replacement piece cut from leftover pieces. Match texture, color, and grain of the fur carefully *before* you cut out the triangular replacement piece (3).

Use a small overhand stitch to sew the replacement piece (4).

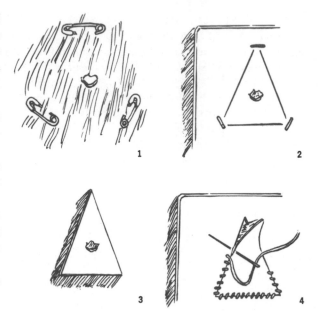

Wet Fur for Cutting

With your pelts atop the work board, place pattern pieces on the skin side and tack in place with thumb tacks or push pins. For jackets and coats with collars, eliminate neck facings to reduce bulk. Chalk mark pattern outlines and darts. Cut out pieces with razor blade without cutting fur. *Do not* cut out darts at this time.

Mark the outline of all the pattern pieces on the board. Using a brush, wet the skin side of each pelt, and place it fur side down over the pattern outline. Carefully matching the outline, tack each pelt in place and allow to dry thoroughly (at least 24 hours). This makes the skin easier to work with.

Remove the tacks when the pelts are dry. Pin the pattern pieces to the skins, check for stretching, and re-draw the outline with a fine chalk pencil if necessary. Cut along the corrected outline and cut out the darts. Mark the notches but do not cut them. Also mark center fronts, foldlines, and hemlines.

Construction Techniques

SEAMS: Sew twill tape to edges to be sewn in seams or darts with a hand zigzag stitch, keeping edge of tape flush with edge of skin. Work with one skin side toward you and fur sides together. Keep edges even and push hairs away. Join seams and darts with a close overhand stitch. Since tape is necessary for reinforcement, be sure to catch it in the seam. Smooth seams with warm dry iron, being sure point of iron touches only taped edges, not the skin.

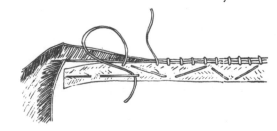

FINISHING EDGES: Hems or other edges that will become a finished edge of your garment must be finished with tape. The tape is then used to anchor linings. These edges are prepared after the seams and darts are sewn. Place the tape on the fur side and sew with small overhand stitches, mitering any corners (1). Finish all edges, then turn the tape to the skin side and sew it in place with long running stitches (2).

INTERFACING: Extended facings are interfaced to give the finished edge a soft rolled effect. Cut a strip of interfacing the length of the facing and twice its width. Place it ¼″ from the facing edge on the skin side and sew along both long edges with running stitches. Attach hook for closure at this time (see hooks and eyes on next page). Turn facing to inside along foldline; sew the two layers of interfacing together halfway between the raw edges of the interfacing and the foldline (3). Then sew the same layers together close to the edge (4). For garments lined to the edge, slide one edge of interfacing under taped edge and sew both long edges in place.

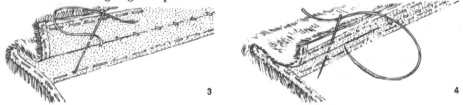

COLLARS: For a detachable collar, back skin with flannel and lightweight interfacing. Sew both layers to the skin ¼″ from edge with long running stitches. Prepare collar edges as you would finished edges (5). Make lining to fit; slipstitch to collar. Sew to garment (6).

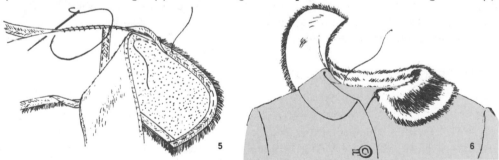

To make your fur collar easily removable as a separate accessory, simply sew a hook and eye to the ends before attaching the lining so they will meet at the neckline.

For a fur garment with a collar, finish edge of upper and under collar as for seams. Sew them together. Then sew undercollar to garment. Shape the roll of the collar, then tack it loosely to the neck seam. This edge will later be finished with the garment lining.

BUTTONS AND BUTTONHOLES: Using button and carpet thread, sew the button through the fur and interfacing, reinforcing the underside with a flat 1″ button. Be sure to make the thread shank long enough to accommodate the thickness of the fur.

From skin side, make a slit the buttonhole size in facing and garment with razor blade. Finish edges with tape on skin side as instructed for seams. On fur side, place additional tape as described for finished edges (1). Turn tape on fur side through to skin side and sew together with running stitches (2). Join facing to garment, working overhand stitches around buttonhole openings.

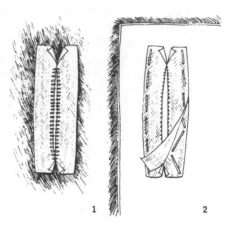

POCKETS: The two types of pockets usually made in fur are seam pockets (page 302) and buttonhole pockets. For the latter type, follow the buttonhole instructions above, cutting the slit long enough for a pocket. Make pocket sections out of lining fabric and stitch together. Sew securely to twill tape on inside of garment.

HOOKS AND EYES: Use large hooks and eyes especially made for fur. For an opening edge with an extended facing, mark placement of hooks and eyes on skin side with chalk. Make a tiny hole through the interfacing and skin at the foldline to allow the bill of the hooks to extend from the fur side. Sew the remainder of the hook to the interfacing and skin (1). Work bill to fur side (2). On opposite side of opening, sew the ring eye (3). For other closures, sew the hooks and eyes to twill tape before attaching the lining.

LINING: For fur garments without neck facings, you will need to extend the lining up to the neck edge. Add neck facings to the lining pattern piece, overlapping seams and allowing for a back pleat before cutting. Cut and sew the lining with seam allowances according to pattern instructions. Slipstitch to the fur, covering taped edges.

Now that you have the basic information, why not get involved in a fur project? Start small, perhaps adding a collar to a cloth coat. Work your way up to sewing with new skins to make a vest or skirt. ❧ Test these techniques by sewing a custom-made coat in one of the exciting fake furs available before you move on to the real thing.

The
Custom Touch
Couture
Techniques

What transforms a dress into The Dress, immediately marks it with true quality and exquisite taste? Fashion is truly a splendid example of the axiom, "little things make a difference," for it is the little but far from insignificant finishing techniques known and followed by the world's most famous designers that will make the transformation work for you. This collection of couture techniques has been gathered for you from the greatest European and American houses of haute couture. They are dedicated to you, the Vogue woman, who delights in making and wearing clothes finished with the infinite touches of a couturier. They are the simple yet irresistible means of putting your signature on everything you sew.

Hidden Details

Most of these techniques are for the inside of the garment and may never be seen by others. Don't, however, let yourself be beguiled into believing that makes them in any way unworthy of the extra time and effort involved. There is nothing mysterious or awesome about any of these methods; without exception, they are actually quite simple and easy to do. And always remember that it is often the hidden details that are the true mark of quality. You cannot help but feel a personal sense of pride each time you see the inside of your professionally finished garment. And, of course, wearing lovely things next to your skin is like wearing exquisite lingerie; it envelops you with a priceless feeling of luxury.

In addition to giving your garments the fine finishing and beautiful detail that are the mark of a couturier, these "extra somethings" above and beyond the actual construction also increase comfort, convenience, fit, and wearability. Using these techniques, you will always know that your garment will close neatly and easily; that everything you sew will hang and drape beautifully; that your garments will retain their precisely controlled shape; that you never need be embarrassed by the appearance of an open jacket or a dress on a hanger; and that you will be as proud of your creation on the tenth wearing as you were on the first.

Create your garments with the elegant expertise admired by all who appreciate the beauty and quality of the very finest couture. Then you will find that your wardrobe will help to give you the poise and assurance that comes with always being fashion-right.

The Inside Story

Lining and underlining are the hidden components of fine dressmaking that, although not immediately visible, are always reflected in the finished effect of your garment. Not only do they assist in creating and retaining the shape of your creations, but also give them a more luxurious look and feel. They are a "must" in all couture garments, and should be in yours as well.

UNDERLINING: If you intend to construct a garment in the manner of the fine designers, follow their example by *mounting* or underlining your garment to give it beautifully controlled shape and body. As an added bonus, underlining will prevent over-handling by keeping your handwork and markings from showing on the right side. Remember, however, that each and every construction mark must be transferred to the underlining, especially the seamlines and grainlines. This extra effort will provide you with a more faithful representation of the design lines and an accurate reference line for any necessary alterations. Underlining just one garment will make you wonder how you ever managed without all its advantages. See pages 183 and 184 for further information and specific instructions.

LINING: Jackets and coats naturally require a lining to conceal their exposed inner construction, and your pattern instructions provide all the necessary guidance for these garments. But what about those other garments whose construction does not call for lining? This simple addition increases the comfort, durability, and aesthetic appeal of any garment and is really quite easy to do.

Cut lining from major garment pattern pieces and construct in same manner as garment, leaving appropriate seams open for closures. (For gathered or pleated skirts, cut your lining from a straight or A-line skirt pattern to reduce bulk.)

Baste the lining to the garment along the seamlines of the raw edges, treating the two layers as one. Turn under and slipstitch the lining edge to zipper tape. Apply either the facings (for dresses) or waistband (for pants or skirts). Blindstitch the facing edges to the lining. Refer to the tailoring section for further information.

Consider "show" value when lining your creations. Rather than discarding scarves that have already seen service in your wardrobe, use them to line a jacket. Use a large designer scarf with the famous signature at the lower front edge, then line the back and sleeves with color-matched crepe. You can also add impact to a lining by using a print, plaid, or contrasting color—perhaps lightweight remnants left over from a previous garment. There is no rule, written or unwritten, which says linings must be drab or inconspicuous. (Of course, this holds true only for underlined garments; you don't want your lining to show through your garment fabric.)

The Shapekeepers

Here are some additional couture touches to help you master the art of controlled shape. Use them to achieve that air of confidence that comes from the assurance that your garment is always hanging straight, draping beautifully, and not in constant need of adjusting to keep it from shifting or your lingerie straps from showing.

WEIGHTS: Weights are used to preserve the design lines of a garment and to prevent it from shifting during wear. They are normally used to ensure the proper drape of a cowl neckline or to make a hem fall evenly. Select type and size by your fabric and desired use.

Flat Circular Weights, used in necklines and pleats, are enclosed in a pouch. Cut an underlining strip long enough to fold around weight, or allow extra fabric for a hanging mount. Stitch ¼″ seams, turn, and insert weight. Pin in place and try on garment. Attach pouch with a French tack, or whipstitch through the extra fabric.

Lead Weight Strips consist of lead pellets enclosed in a fabric casing. Place them inside the hem of your garment as it is being pinned into position so they will fall directly into the fold of the hemline. Begin and end the strip at the edge of your front facings, and tack the casing to the underlining with long running stitches. Never let the iron rest on your hem, as the weights will leave a noticeable impression.

Chain Weights are most frequently used in tailoring. They add the necessary weight to a coat or jacket hem and provide an attractive finish as well. Tack the chain directly below your lining, tucking the ends of the chain under the facing.

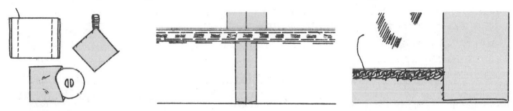

LINGERIE STRAP GUARDS: To prevent shoulder seams from shifting and keep lingerie straps from showing, use about 1½″ of seam binding or a thread chain (page 316). Sew one end to shoulder seam near armhole. Sew a ball snap to free end of guard and a socket snap toward neck edge of garment.

INSIDE WAIST STAY: This stay is suggested for stretchy fabrics, sheath or princess styles, or when skirt is heavier than bodice. Cut strip of ½″-1 inch wide grosgrain ribbon to fit waist, adding 1″ for finishing ends. Turn ends back and stitch. Sew hooks and eyes to ends, extending loops over edge. Tack stay at seams and darts, leaving at least 2″ free on sides of zipper.

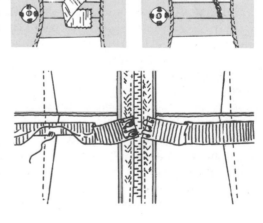

The Finest Fastenings

The master seamstress leaves nothing to chance. She will not let the metallic glint of a snap or hook mar the look of her exquisitely finished garment, or an open jacket reveal any but the most perfect buttons and buttonholes. Follow these tips to make your closures as functional and yet unobtrusive as possible.

COVERED SNAPS: For inconspicuous snaps, cover them with underlining or lining fabric. Cut two fabric circles about two times the diameter of the snap. Take a running stitch around edge of each circle. Place a snap section face down on each. Work ball of snap through center of fabric circle, snapping both sections several times to spread fabric apart. Draw up threads and fasten each section securely.

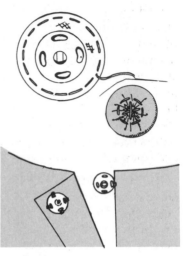

EXTENDED SNAPS: To fasten a collar or stand-up neckline with snaps, sew the ball section in position on the inside of the neckline or collar. Secure the socket section on the opposite side through only one hole, extending it from the edge as would a hook. If your snaps might show, cover them as described above.

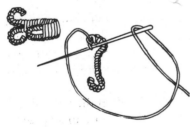

COVERED HOOK AND EYE: Make your hooks and eyes blend visually into your garment by covering them with a double strand of matching thread. Work from right to left, placing blanket stitches (page 211) very close together until the metal is completely covered. For larger hooks, use buttonhole twist for quick and sturdy coverage.

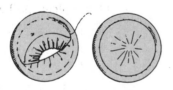

FINISHING BUTTONS: If you wish to cover the wrong side of a covered ring button (page 305), cut a circle of fabric the size of the inner diameter of the ring plus ¼". Sew a gathering line around edge and adjust the gathers. Slipstitch to back of button.

BOUND BUTTONHOLES: Long recognized as a couturier exclusive, beautifully worked buttonholes should become part of your own sewing repertoire. In the buttonhole section we gave you the construction methods. To complete the buttonhole as the great designers suggest, transfer the buttonhole markings to the facing and cleanly finish the facing with an organza patch as directed for the garment in the organza patch method, page 310. Slipstitch facing to finished buttonhole for a professionally executed buttonhole.

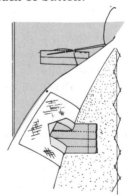

The Finishing Touch

The first things to catch your eye when you look at the inside of a couture garment are the beautifully finished seams and hems. It takes very little extra effort to impart this same custom touch and fine workmanship to your own garments.

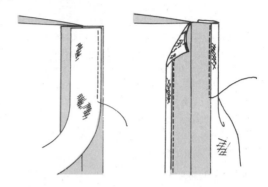

HONG KONG FINISH: This classic finish is used on underlined garments and is actually quite easy to do. Use 1″ wide bias strips of your underlining or lining fabric, or press open double-fold bias tape. Matching edges and using small stitches, stitch the bias strip to the garment raw edge in a ¼″ seam. Turn bias to inside over seam. Stitch along line where binding and garment meet on the right side to catch bottom edge of binding and completely enclose the raw edge.

LACE AND TRIMS: Lace can be an attractive and sturdy substitute for seam binding on your hems and facing edges, or you may wish to tack it on coats or jackets along the edge where the lining meets the facings. Select narrow, flexible lace for curves, and stretch lace for stretchy fabrics. Other trims (such as ribbon, braid, or rackrack) can also be very effective as long as they are relatively lightweight and flexible.

HORSEHAIR BRAID: This hem finish is most often used on full-length gowns, where extra stiffness is required in the hem without extra weight. Carefully mark the hemline. Steam braid to eliminate creases. The cut ends of the braid are very prickly and will require special treatment. To join them, lap ends ¾″ and enclose both sides of braid with a fabric strip applied with a double line of stitching around all edges.

For a narrow braid, trim the hem allowance to ½″. Place the braid on the right side of your fabric and match the edges. Stitch the braid and the hem allowance in a ¼″ seam. Turn the braid up along the hemline. Baste close to the fold and complete the hem.

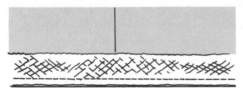

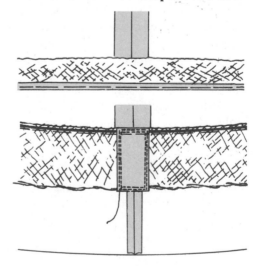

Wide braid usually has one pre-threaded edge for easing; if not, run a gathering stitch along one edge. Place unthreaded edge along hemline; baste. Turn up and baste hem to check hemline. Sew basted edge of braid to underlining with long hemming stitch. Draw gathering thread to ease fullness on free edge. Sew this edge to underlining with long running stitches. Turn and complete hem.

SOFT HEM: A couturier rarely intends that the hem of a garment be pressed knife-sharp. The molded look of a soft hem is achieved by inserting padding along the hemline. The most common method is to simply interface the hem as directed on page 340.

Another method, used especially in very soft fabrics, is to insert additional padding. First apply the interfacing; then, before completing the hem, place a 1″ wide strip of lamb's wool, cotton flannel, or soft cable cord on top of the interfacing at the hemline. Place approximately ⅓ of the strip below the hemline and ⅔ above it so that all the edges will be graded when the hem is turned. Sew to interfacing along hemline; use long running stitches for strips or long loose catchstitches for cable cord.

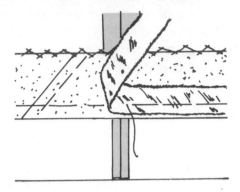

EXTREMELY CURVED HEMS: Some garments are so designed that the hem may have excess fabric or the hem edge circumference is not as wide as that of the garment. In such instances, the hem must be slashed at evenly spaced intervals, no deeper than 1″ from the fold. As you adapt the hem, keep the garment free while sewing. To eliminate excess fabric, cut out narrow wedges and bring cut edges together. Hemstitch them shut. To add width to hem, insert small wedges of fabric and hemstitch them into place.

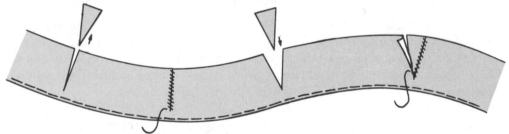

HAND-ROLLED NARROW HEMS: Use this hem to finish sheers, scarves, and lingerie. There are two popular methods, both time-consuming but well worth the effort. For the first technique, machine stitch ¼″ from raw edge; trim close to stitching. Roll approximately ⅛″ of edge between thumb and forefinger, concealing stitching. Stabilize roll with third and fourth finger and slipstitch, taking a single thread at each stitch.

For the second method, stitch and trim as above. Turn edge about ⅛″ and crease sharply. Pick up a thread along crease and carry thread over to raw edge diagonally and pick up a thread alongside the raw edge. Work in a zigzag pattern, making stitches ¼″ apart. Repeat process for about 1″, then pull thread to tighten stitches to create the roll.

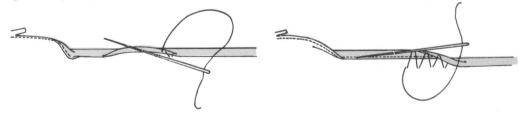

Trims
The Mark of the Creative Seamstress

Trims can add a new and exciting dimension to everything you sew. Apply them always with a tasteful hand, but don't let yourself be inhibited by traditional ideas. Bring rickrack out of the children's wardrobe and into your own; try for example, several rows of jumbo wool rickrack to bring out the subtle colorings of a rich plaid. Use quilting to transform a large-scale print into the perfect fabric for a gala hostess skirt. Go on a fringe binge, mixing and matching types and layers for a lush fashion finish. Or see how funwear can make the city scene with the simple addition of elegant passementerie.

Don't, however, allow your trimming ideas to smother the design of the garment. Your trims should always be an integral part of your garment, coordinating with your design and fabric. Lavish beading, for example, would not only be inappropriate on a casual or tailored garment, but could possibly distract from an ornate brocade gown as well. A fashion rule of thumb is to coordinate elaborate trims with simple garments, simple trims with elaborate garments. Follow the lines of your garment or add lines to a simple style, but do not let your trimming destroy the balance of your garment by markedly interfering with the basic design. Permit your trims to enhance aesthetically and yet relate structurally by realizing their role in a total design concept.

And, as with everything you sew, relate the trim to yourself and your needs. If you love the rich look of quilting but fear the extra bulk on your frame, why not use it on just a collar or pockets? If you want your new creation for both daytime and evening wear, lace may be a better choice than beading.

If you can't find the perfect trimming in your fabric or notions departments, turn to the upholstery, drapery, or interior decorating departments. They often carry some stunning trims intended for use on furniture or draperies. Don't let this discourage you; they will work beautifully on your garments as well.

Even though there is a bewildering variety of trims, generally only two procedures are used for their application. They are either incorporated during the actual construction, or they are applied after the garment is completed. Always keep the method of application in mind while selecting your trim; don't wait until your garment is finished to discover that the trim should have been inserted during construction.

Armed with your good style sense, let your fancy lead the way. Change the look of last season's creation, give impact to a simple garment, or add the perfect finishing touch to a new dress—with trims, the mark of the creative seamstress.

Braid and Bands

If it's variety you're looking for, take a long glance at braid and bands, which range from simple rickrack to gala beaded bands. Included in the galaxy of trims are embroidered bands, braid, lace, sequin bands, purchased fringe, and ribbon—all of them banded trims, in spite of their seeming diversity. Add the many possibilities in use and placement, and the variety totals great fashion excitement.

Whatever type of band you are using, be sure to mark accurately and measure frequently. Select an inconspicuous location to begin and end your application. Machine application, which produces a more casual appearance, is a rapid means of applying trim and may be necessary if the garment requires a very sturdy finish. Hand application with tiny invisible slipstitches will be strong enough to withstand the usual wear and cleaning and will allow increased control, a greater degree of manipulation, and a finer finish.

There are two basic methods of applying braid and bands. The most common method, direct application, is generally done after your garment is completed. Simply pin or baste the trim in place and apply by machine or hand. The second method, inset application, encloses one or both raw edges by sandwiching the trim between two fabric layers (such as the garment and a shaped or bias facing) and must be done during construction.

FLAT BRAID: Generally used as a border effect, use flat braid to outline a jacket front, band a neckline, or frame a pocket. Let braid add a touch of fashion or splash of color anywhere, from neckline to hemline. It is available in a wide range of colors, materials, weaves, and widths, making possible any number of effects. Do not always limit yourself to only one row or one shade; braids are often best in combination.

Pin or baste to the garment and apply by hand or machine. Stitch along both edges; do not pull the threads too tight or puckers will appear. Turn the ends in ¼″ before sewing, overcasting them first if they tend to ravel.

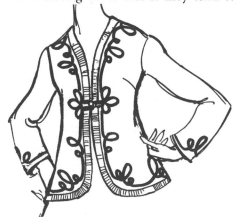

SOUTACHE OR NARROW BIAS BRAID: Use this popular trim to outline a design with tracery or to emphasize an overall silhouette within a garment. Soutache is often used for a Spanish look on a middy blouse or dress. You may wish to combine it with matching frog and button closings.

Mark the design with chalk or thread tracing and pin the soutache in place. Ease the braid around corners; they will be slightly rounded, as soutache does not lend itself to sharp corners. Apply by hand with small, invisible stitches or, to apply by machine, baste in position and use a zipper foot.

PRE-FOLDED BRAID: Designed to trim garment edges, pre-folded braid can also be utilitarian when used to finish raw edges such as a neckline. Purchase pre-folded braid, or fold flat braid or fabric as directed on page 246 for single or double Binding.

For smooth application, shape the braid with a steam iron to achieve curves similar to those of your garment edge. Most braids are folded slightly off center, with the top side slightly narrower than the other to ensure catching the underside when stitching. For better control and a finer finish, apply the braid by hand. However, if you need an especially durable application, turn to page 246 for applying the braid by machine.

For a machine method with a minimum of visible stitching, first sew the upper half of the braid by hand. Then stitch on the right side of the garment with a zipper foot, as close as possible to the braid, to catch the bottom half. Baste the bottom half first if necessary to maintain control.

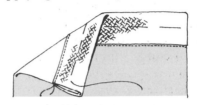

RICKRACK: There is such a large variety of sizes and materials available in rickrack that you need not be traditional nor limited in your applications. For example, imagine the revitalization a double row of jumbo wool or angora rickrack would give a simple wool skirt, or the excitement metallic rickrack might lend to evening clothes.

The zigzag shape makes rickrack very flexible for use around curves and corners. If you are using it on a corner, arrange the trim so an outside point is at the most conspicuous corner. Rickrack is often used at garment edges, exposing only the points after stitching; apply the trim by the inset method or machine stitch along the edge of your garment with matching thread to secure the trim. Apply it within garment lines with a single line of machine stitching down the center or tiny hand-stitches at each point.

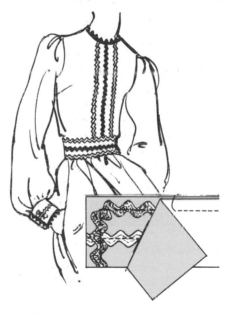

OTHER BANDED TRIMS: Embroidered bands and ribbons are available in any number of colors, patterns, and widths. Combine them with ruffles for ultra-feminine appeal, or use the provincial patterns for a charming Tyrolean look. For a touch of opulence, try tapestry or metallic embroidered bands on evening clothes. Try a new fashion approach with ribbon—perhaps a bold racing stripe of bright grosgrain, that all-time, all-purpose favorite. Combine ribbon with other trims, or team it with a matching bow. Apply these trims in the same manner as you would any banded trim. You will find special hints on beaded or sequinned bands, purchased fringe, and flat lace are given on the following pages.

Fringe

Whatever the current trend, fringe and its related trims will always be present on the fashion scene. Purchased or made in a variety of materials and lengths, fringe has almost limitless uses for everything from clothes to home furnishings. Add rayon fringe to a shiny fabric for a slinky effect, or several rows of wool fringe in various shades to accent the subtle colorings of a tweed. Mix fringe and tassels; combine different shades or outright contrasting colors. And remember that two rows—or three or four—are usually better than one. Easy to make or apply, fringe can create a multitude of effects.

KNOTTED FRINGE: Give your garments a mobile finish with knotted fringe. You may make it in any color and in a variety of yarns —wool, rayon, metallic threads. It works beautifully on the finished edge of any medium to loosely-woven fabric. Experiment to determine the most appealing look; try several lengths, adjust the number of strands of yarn, change the distance between the groups, add more sets of knots. Generally, the fuller your fringe, the richer it will look.

Cut a cardboard strip the depth of the intended finished fringe plus ½″ for each knot. Use the cardboard as a base and wrap your yarn around it. Cut through several strands at one end. With a stiletto or fine knitting needle, make a small hole about ½″ from the finished edge of your garment and insert a crochet hook into the hole from the wrong side. Center the strands over the hook and pull them partially back through the hole. This will form a loop on the wrong side. Next, work the ends through the loop formed by the hook and pull the ends to tighten. Continue this process along the entire length of the edge. A second set of knots may be made by joining two halves of adjacent tassels with a single loop knot as shown. If you have made your strands long enough, several sets of knots may be made for an even more intricate, lacy appearance.

PURCHASED FRINGE: Available in a vast assortment of materials, colors, and styles, all varieties of purchased fringe have a flexible braid heading for attaching the fringe. Just sew this heading to your fabric. Apply with an inset application or with a direct application using either a single row of matching stitching or invisible hand stitches.

SELF-FRINGE: This is a quick, easy trim that is a perfect match every time. It is particularly suited for soft, thick, heavy, or nubby fabrics. Do not feel you must limit your fringing to woolens, however, as most woven fabrics can be fringed with success; experiment first with a small scrap.

First straighten your fabric ends by cutting across the width along the grainline. Determine the desired depth of your fringe and pull out a crosswise thread from within the fabric to act as a guide. With small stitches, make a line of machine stitching along the pulled thread to anchor the fringe. Then remove all the threads beneath the stitching one at a time, always pulling them in the same direction.

TASSELS: These are made in a manner similar to knotted fringe. Again cut a strip of cardboard the desired depth of the tassel to use as a base. Thread a needle with a double strand of your yarn and place strands at top of cardboard with the needle hanging at side. Wind your yarn around the cardboard and the strand of yarn until the proper fullness of the tassel has been achieved. Then tie your threaded strands very securely at the top and remove the cardboard. Wind the strand about ½" from top around the upper end several times; slip needle underneath the wound portion and bring out at top of tassel. Cut the lower loops and attach the tassel to your garment.

POMPONS: The same operations are required for pompons and tassels except that pompons should be very, very full and have less depth. First cut a strip of cardboard the desired depth. Then, using the cardboard as a base, put a separate strand at the top and wind the yarn around the cardboard. Securely tie the separate strand and cut across the other end. Remove the cardboard. Shake pompon gently to make a soft fluffy ball. To make a really full and lush pompon, repeat winding process. Then slip one wound cluster inside the other and tie the two together at the center, forming a cross. Cut all the ends and spread the strands to form a ball. For both methods, trim the strands of your pompons into perfect spheres.

Lace and Ruffles

So romantic, so fanciful, nothing can be more eye-catching than the perfect lace trim. Imagine the wistful beauty of delicate Val edging for a ruffled collar and cuffs, or, if you are more daring than demure, envision the effect of heavy Cluny lace for a bare midriff insertion. Add lace to a velvet pantsuit for a choir-boy or Edwardian look. Combine laces with each other or with other trims—just think of all the possibilities!

Many charming varieties of lace trims have been produced commercially. Cotton, nylon, acetate, and wool are used, singly or in blends, to make flat lace or pleated, gathered, and ruffled versions. Many lace trims are re-embroidered, giving them an added dimension. The inherent fragility of lace calls for handling its open constructions with special care. Let the fiber content and the openness of the lace guide you in deciding between hand or machine application plus any necessary ironing and washing procedures.

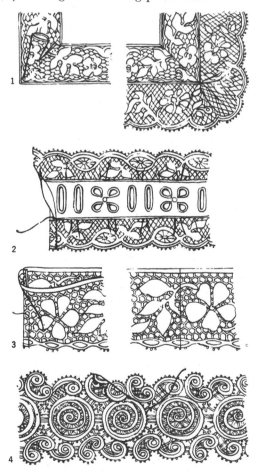

Here are a few techniques you will find helpful in working with lace. If you apply your lace trim by machine, you may find an edge stitcher or hemmer foot attachment useful. To miter corners, pin the lace around the corner, folding it to form a miter. Whipstitch or zigzag along the fold and cut away excess. If you plan to attach one trim to another at a corner, gather the outside band at the corner so it will lie flat (1). (See Mitering, page 242, for additional information.)

If the ends will be left hanging free, finish them by making a narrow rolled hem (2).

When the ends are to be joined, make a French seam. First stitch the ends of the lace wrong sides together in a scant ⅛″ seam. Then crease along the seam, bringing right sides together, and stitch ⅛″ from the seam, encasing the raw edges (3).

The couturier method of joining lace ends is to appliqué along a motif. To appliqué by hand, lap the ends and trim around a motif on the upper layer. Whipstitch around the motif to join it to the under layer (4). Trim away the excess lace on the under layer. To appliqué by machine, lap the ends, sew around the motif with a fine zigzag stitch, and trim the excess lace on both layers close to the stitching.

FLAT LACE: A type of banded trim, flat lace is applied basically as directed in the introduction to Braid and Bands on page 386. While the inset method is exactly the same, there are a few differences in the direct method due to the unique qualities of lace.

There are several methods for a direct application. To apply to a finished edge, whipstitch through both garment and lace (1). If the edge is raw, trim garment seam allowance to ¼″ and make a rolled hem. Whipstitch lace to edge of hem (2). To apply lace within the garment lines, stitch straight edges by machine or hand. Scalloped edges are preferably sewn by hand with small invisible stitches or appliquéd to the garment as directed for joining ends (3).

Another method, insertion, is particularly suited to the open nature of lace, as the fabric beneath is trimmed away. For lace with straight edges, baste in place and cut through fabric halfway between basting lines. Trim fabric to ¼″, overcast, and press toward garment; topstitch from right side through all layers (4). Another method is to topstitch along edges, trim closely, and overcast as shown (5). For randomly scalloped lace, baste in place and hem closely round motif along edges. Trim fabric closely and overcast raw edges.

Another variety of insertion that produces delightful results, but can be rather time consuming, is joining lace to fabric or other lace bands (much like a Mexican wedding dress). Press under edges of fabric strips, then stitch as above.

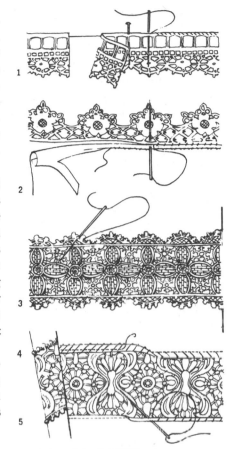

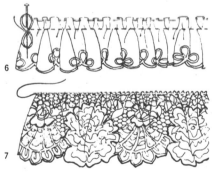

GATHERED LACE OR RUFFLES: You may purchase lace trims pre-ruffled or gather your own. To make a lace ruffle, you will need a piece of lace 2 to 3 times the finished length, depending on the desired fullness. Gather the lace by hand or machine by taking long stitches close to the straight edge of the lace, and distribute gathers evenly. Use two rows of stitching if lace is 3″ or wider (6). With Val lace, just draw up the heavy thread running along the straight edge to gather (7).

You may inset your ruffle or apply it with a direct application as you would for flat lace. Your gathering should be matched to the garment seamline when joining it to a raw edge, with or without a facing. Baste in place and stitch by hand or machine.

Don't overlook the wide variety of ruffles made in other fabrics. Ready-made ruffling can be purchased in a variety of fabrics, widths, and types. You can also make your own ruffles out of fabric. These ruffles are treated in the same manner as lace ruffles. See Ruffles, page 230-233, for further information.

Refer to page 403 for making lace-covered buttons to complement your trim.

Feathers and Fur

Trimming with feathers or fur is a glamorous finale to any garment. Each has been adorning clothes for centuries, yet over the years neither one has lost its lush hypnotic appeal. Add a fur collar to a tweed coat and see how beautifully it frames your face. Perhaps the soft look of a fur halo encircling the neckline and cuffs of a supple dress appeals to you. A full flourish of feathers at your hemline or an unexpected burst at the edge of a sleeve or neckline can be sensational. Don't be skimpy—use rows and rows for a lavish effect. Whatever you do with feathers and fur, don't overlook them!

FEATHERS: Feathers are usually purchased in strips. The most common application is to sew an overhand stitch through the fabric edge and over the cord-like base of the trim. Keep the stitches fairly loose and far apart, but firm enough to support the trim. Conceal the threads and refresh the feathers by using a large blunt needle to work out each vane from underneath stitches.

To facilitate the removal of the feathers for cleaning, attach small thread loops to your garment edge. They should be several inches apart and large enough to accommodate the width of the trim. Then you can simply pass the feather strip through the loops as you would a belt. Close the ends of the strip with whipstitches and work out each vane from underneath the loops.

FUR: These trims are available in a variety of furs and in many widths and lengths. Usually in straight strips, some are already shaped for you to use on collars or lapels. The majority of fur trims are already neatly backed with lining fabric or grosgrain fabric. Therefore, joining the fur to your garment edge is just a simple matter of sewing the backing to the garment with firm but unnoticeable running stitches.

For cleaning ease, however, you may prefer to apply your trim by attaching large covered snaps to both the garment and the fur. Space the snaps according to the weight and width of the trim. Then you can merely snap the fur on and off at your own convenience.

For further information on the handling of fur, turn to pages 375-378.

The Magic Touch of Trims

Edgings

Beading

Galloons

Insertion

Braid & Bands

Ribbons & Braid

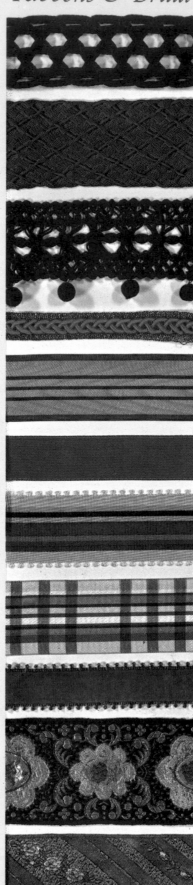

Edgings & Ropes

Rickrack & Braid Fringe & Pompons Braid & Bands

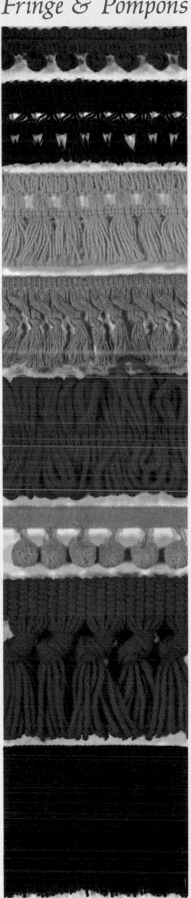

Edgings

Ropes & Rickrack

Bandings

Strands & Braids

Openwork

Beading

What can be more glamourous than a dress shimmering with the glitter of beading? The jeweled look is one you can always count on, for its appeal is perennial. Is last year's gown still hanging in your closet? Make it glow again with beading. Top off your gown or cocktail dress with a matching jacket outlined with beaded tracery or, for the ultimate in luxury, wrap your shoulders with a lavishly encrusted evening stole. If you think the opulence of beads belongs only to wedding gowns and evening bags, think again!

Beading is often a painstaking procedure, but one in which your patience is sure to be greatly rewarded. Following are some suggestions that will make your beading proceed faster and easier. You will, naturally, need a design. Outline a design in a printed fabric, trace one from another source, or create your own. When you have decided upon a design, transfer it to your garment with chalk and thread tracing.

Although beading is usually applied to a completed garment, you may wish to add an overall beading design in the process of construction. Cut out the garment section and back with a lightweight underlining. Mark all construction lines and transfer your beading pattern. Make sure that any fitting adjustments have already been made so that the beading will not interfere during construction. Stitch all seams with a zipper foot.

Use an embroidery hoop to hold the fabric taut for small motifs, and select a fine or special beading needle that will slip easily through the holes of the beads. Use matching thread coated with beeswax or transparent nylon thread. Keep your thread relatively short; a longer thread will tend to get tangled or knotted. Don't pull your stitches too tight or your fabric will pucker. Be careful when pressing; placing a hot iron on your beading may melt, scratch, or dull the beads. To press the garment around the beading, use a pressing cloth on the wrong side and press over a pressing pad or turkish towel; avoid touching the beading .

BEADS: You can attach your beads singly, in groups, or in a long strand. If you desire scattered beads, you will need to sew them individually. Start from the wrong side and use a backstitch. For a straight line of several beads, take several beads on the thread at a time and use a modified running stitch from cluster to cluster. The number of beads you will be able to string at one time depends primarily on the size and weight of the bead; experiment on a scrap first to find out how many you can string without the cluster drooping. For curves, you will have to reduce the number of beads on each stitch, perhaps even sewing them individually on a sharp curve or with large beads. Use a double thread coated with beeswax or nylon thread when sewing beads in clusters. If you are applying pre-strung beads, sew over the threads between beads at intervals.

Bead Loops or Fringe dripping from a garment edge or within the garment lines for a scalloped effect is a look that is always elegant. Use nylon or a double strand of cotton thread to prevent breaking. Count number of beads on each strand to maintain uniformity.

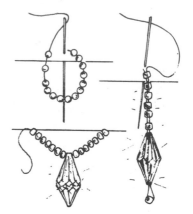

For loops, pull the needle through from the wrong side, string several beads, and return the needle to the wrong side. Secure each loop singly for added security.

Do not pull the loops too tightly or they will appear stiff and rigid. For fringe, string smaller beads, a large bead, and an anchor bead, if necessary; return needle through the same or another series of small beads.

Pre-Beaded Bands and Appliqué are basted and then sewn. Ease the trim around curves as you baste. Sew with invisible slipstitches through the backing. To finish the ends, remove several beads from the backing, turn it under, and slipstitch securely in place. Be sure to firmly secure the last bead to prevent losing beads.

SEQUINS: Sequins can also be applied several ways. Apply single sequins with a backstitch from center hole to edge. For a finer finish, apply with a small coordinated bead. Bring the needle up through the hole, string a bead, and return through the hole. For sequin rows, bring needle through hole and take a backstitch over to edge. Bring needle forward in position for the next one, which will overlap the last and conceal the thread. Pre-strung sequins are applied in the same manner as pre-strung beads.

Paillettes, while larger than sequins, are applied in basically the same manner. The hole is located at the edge rather than in the middle. They may be applied with a backstitch from hole to edge, or with a bead. Rows are applied like sequin rows or individually if they are very large.

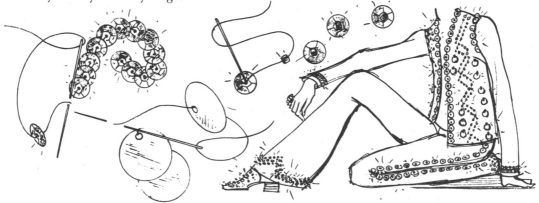

Sequinned Bands and Appliqué can also be purchased. These trims generally have a series of thread chains or an elastic backing to act as a flexible foundation. Invisibly tack these strands to your garment. If you are using clusters, snip away the threads between the motifs and anchor the thread ends with a knot, clear nail polish, or glue to prevent raveling. ❖ Fold transparent tape over the cut ends to avoid unnecessary loss of sequins.

Refer to page 403 for making your own beaded buttons to complement your trim.

Stitchery

The efficiency of the sewing machine has taken away the drudgery of hand sewing, but don't let it take away the enjoyable decorative role of hand sewing as well. Who would care to do without the marvelous custom effect of saddlestitching, or the richly seamed look of its machine-sewn version, topstitching? Decorative tacks can certainly add to a finely tailored appearance. If you have been limiting embroidery to tablecloths and pillowcases, you've been overlooking some great fashion ideas. A bold monogram can always add distinction to any garment. Just think of the wonderful fashion effects you can gain with a needle and thread and a small amount of time!

Embroidery floss, buttonhole twist, and yarn can be used to sew your finishing details with added excitement. Many of the very common hand stitches take on a special flavor when sewn with them. Saddle stitching should always be done with a heavy thread or yarn. And, of course, use lustrous buttonhole twist for your topstitching.

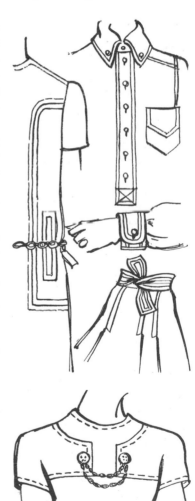

TOPSTITCHING: The most popular form of fashion stitchery, topstitching emphasizes the structural lines of your garment while working to keep the seams and edges flat and crisp. Although done by machine, it gives the same detailed look as fine hand sewing. Don't forget that it is often a construction procedure as well in such features as pockets, pleats, and man-tailored shirts.

The stitching can be done after the garment is completed, but it is often necessary or easier to stitch individual or large areas during construction. Make any fitting adjustments *before* you topstitch seams.

Use silk buttonhole twist in both the needle and bobbin, a size 16 needle, and 6 to 8 stitches per inch. You will probably have to adjust your machine tension before stitching; experiment first on scrap layers of your fabric and underlining. Stitch carefully, using a guide, such as quilting foot, magnet, tape, etc. Be particularly cautious at curves and pivot the fabric at corners; mark these tricky areas with thread tracing before stitching. Stitch two lines very close together on heavy fabrics. Leave thread ends long enough to be worked to the wrong side with a needle and tied.

SADDLE STITCH: This is a trimming stitch which, used with discretion, can be a charming subtle touch. The simplest of all stitchery techniques, it is usually added to a completed garment. Use buttonhole twist, embroidery floss, or yarn—preferably in a contrasting color—and simply make continuous running stitches, evenly spaced and at least ¼" long.

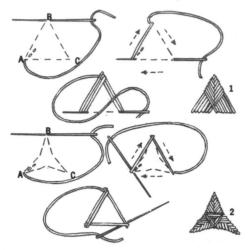

DECORATIVE TACKS: These are used on pockets and pleats on tailored clothes. First mark triangular shape. Secure thread for tack with small backstitches.

For the *Arrowhead Tack,* bring needle out at A and take a small horizontal stitch at B. Insert the needle at C and bring it out again just inside A. Continue until the entire tack is filled in (1).

For the *Crow's Foot Tack,* bring needle out at A and take a small horizontal stitch at B. Then make a small diagonal stitch at C and then across base to A. Continue until the entire tack is filled in (2).

EMBROIDERY: Once confined to home furnishings, embroidery has become an indispensable addition to many good-looking clothes. Mark your design with thread tracing or chalk, and use three or six strands of embroidery floss, yarn, or one of the heavier decorative threads, depending on desired effect. Several designs can be sewn with zigzag machine or special attachments; refer to your manual for instructions.

The *Outline Stitch,* a slanting backstitch, is worked from the left to the right in a single line. Each stitch is followed by a short backstitch back to the right side very close to the previous stitch.

For the *Satin Stitch,* work close parallel stitches over an area padded first with tiny running stitches. For straight lines, the stitch is done on a slant; for curved lines, place the threads closer together on the inside of a curve, further apart on the outside.

For the *Cross Stitch,* bring needle out at 1, cross over and take a stitch from 2 to 3, and then cross over and take a stitch from 4 to 5. Continue these diagonal stitches in same direction. Next, working in opposite direction, cross each stitch, keeping the points together.

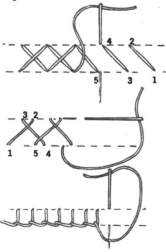

For the *Herringbone Stitch,* bring the needle out at 1, cross over and take a stitch from 2 to 3. Cross over again, taking a stitch from 4 to 5. Repeat to finish row.

For the *Blanket Stitch,* work from left to right between two lines. Bring needle up on lower line and hold thread down, insert needle a little to right on upper line, and bring up directly below on lower line. Draw needle through the loop formed and pull thread taut.

The **Feather Stitch** is a variation of the blanket stitch. The pattern depends upon the location of each consecutive stitch. For an alternating design, draw two guide lines. Make individual stitches ¼" from each other diagonally, holding thread to left. For a single line, make each slanted stitch ¼" directly from preceding one.

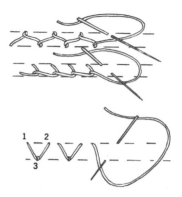

The **Fly Stitch** is another type of blanket stitch. Bring thread out at 1 and work from left to right. Hold the thread down and stitch from 2 to 3. Take a small stitch at 3 to secure the loop. Return to higher point for next V.

To make the **Chain Stitch,** bring the needle to the right side, holding thread down while taking next stitch. As needle crosses over thread, it will form a loop.

The **Lazy Daisy Stitch** is an elongated, detached version of the chain stitch, grouped to form a daisy. Begin at the center of your flower, and return the needle to the pivot point after taking each stitch.

The **French Knot** is made by twisting thread around a needle. Bring needle to right side, hold thread taut, and twist needle so thread loops around it three or four times. Return needle to wrong side, very close to the point where it emerged, and pull thread through loops and fabric until a small knot remains.

MONOGRAMS: A monogram is a simple embroidered way to personalize almost anything you make. Stamp your initials and even your name in all kinds of expected or unexpected places. You may purchase an iron-on transfer pattern or find your own. Unusual letters in magazines or newspapers might appeal to you. Or, most personal of all, use your own handwriting as a guide. Don't limit yourself to capital letters; small letters will often combine to make very attractive and unusual monograms.

Cut out your pattern in paper and pin it to your garment to determine placement. *Lightly* trace around it with chalk or pencil and outline the design with thread tracing. Follow manufacturer's guide for iron-on transfers.

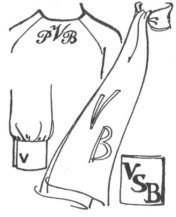

Use an embroidery hoop to hold your fabric taut. If your fabric is soft or loosely woven, apply a backing of a lightweight fabric under the design before stitching; trim excess when completed. The satin stitch is the traditional monogramming stitch, but you may use other embroidery stitches as well. Monogram by hand, or refer to your sewing machine manual for machine embroidery.

Refer to page 403 for making buttons to complement your stitchery designs.

Bows and Tying

The ever feminine bow is always ready to add charm to any garment—what more could you ask of a trim? Bows can be made from ribbon, braid, lace, embroidered bands, self-fabric, or scarves. They can be an integral part of the design of your garment, serve an essential function as a fastening, or simply act as an added adornment. Perch bows made of self-fabric or glittery bands on the shoulders of an evening dress. Replace a worn belt buckle with a tailored bow, with snaps or hooks and eyes underneath. Add self-tied bows anywhere on a garment. If your garment has a sash, ties, or a scarf, you can tie them to produce several different effects. Bows are definitely a timeless fashion highlight.

TAILORED BOWS: Bows can be made from ribbon-like trims or from self- or contrasting fabric. For a bow made of trim, you will need a strip twice the length of the finished bow plus enough to go around the bow for the knot. If you are constructing the strip, add two ⅝" seam allowances to the length; for the width, allow twice the finished width plus two seam allowances. Fold the fabric in half lengthwise with right sides together. Stitch long edges, leaving an opening for turning; trim. Press seam open with point of iron. Bring seam to center of strip. Stitch across ends and trim. Turn through opening and slipstitch shut. Press lightly. To make the knot, cut a rectangle twice the desired width plus seam allowances and the necessary length plus ¼". Fold in half lengthwise, right sides together, and stitch. Press seam open. Turn and press with seam at center.

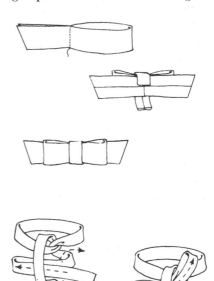

To form the bow, fold your ribbon or fabric in half as shown. Then stitch across the width slightly less than halfway from ends, backstitching to secure. Bring the stitching line to meet the centerfold and tack securely. Press lightly.

To create the knot, wrap the smaller strip around the bow at the center. On the underside, lap one end over the other and whipstitch in place. Tack knot invisibly to the bow.

STANDARD BOW: Here is the way to tie a perfect bow. Begin by making a single knot with two ends even. Use the lower section to make the first loop. Then bring the upper section down and around your first loop to form a knot. Holding the first loop in place with one hand, form a second loop and pull it through the knot. Finally, pull both loops tight so they are even in size and the ends are equal in length. Puff out the bow and the ends. For a neat appearance, the knot should be relatively square and flat.

SQUARE KNOT: You should begin this classic knot with both ends of your tie even and directly in front of you. Then put one end over the other end and tie. Still working with the same end, tie it around the other a second time. Then gently pull the ends to make them even in length; spread the ends apart and straighten the knot.

ASCOT TIE: To make this very simple tie, all you do is loop one end under and over the other end. You can have both of the ends even or you may have the one on top shorter than the one below. When you have completed the loop, carefully spread the folds apart above the loop to expose several inches of fabric for a full, luxurious appearance.

NECKTIE: Let one end fall longer than the other. Holding the shorter end taut, loosely wrap the other end around it twice. Bring this longer end up from behind and pass it down through the circle of fabric formed by the last wrap, as shown. Tighten the underside section until the knot is at the most attractive level.

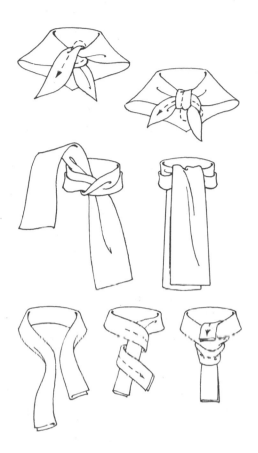

Fabric Trims

Are you wondering what to do with all those left-over pieces of fabric that are too small for a garment but too lovely to throw away? Here is your answer, and a way to embellish your other garments as well. Use those scraps, or newly purchased fabric if you wish, to create appliqués or patchwork. Appliqué can add great charm to a simple garment. It can create any fashion mood you wish—gay when in bright print on a solid or contrasting print, elegant when in antique satin on brocade, and so on. And don't overlook the great variety of purchased appliqués. As for patchwork, imagine the admiring looks you would attract in an evening skirt done in a patchwork of shimmering fabrics, or a pert vest made in squares of brilliant prints. Virtually any fabric can be used for either appliqué or patchwork, so the possible combinations are almost endless.

PATCHWORK: You can make your patchwork out of any fabric which will not ravel easily or is excessively bulky. All the fabric patches should preferably be of relatively equal weight. Decide what shape you want your patches. Make a pattern out of heavy paper the size of the finished patch plus seam allowances of ½" to ⅝". Cut patches on the straight grain and in substantial numbers before stitching any together.

Arrange a number of patches (enough for two or three horizontal rows) on a flat surface until you achieve an attractive combination. Pin together in strips. Stitch, using allotted seam allowances. Stitch the patches together in horizontal rows the width of the pattern piece. Press all seams open on each strip before joining to another strip. Then stitch the horizontal rows together with long seams. Repeat this procedure for the desired length of the pattern piece. When the patchwork is large enough to accommodate your pattern pieces, pin and cut them as with regular fabric.

APPLIQUÉ: This trim consists of a separate piece of fabric applied as a decoration to a larger background. You may purchase the appliqué or make your own by cutting out a motif in your fabric or creating your own design. Avoid fabrics which ravel easily. Prints, contrasting solids, or fabrics with a definite texture lend themselves to appliqué.

For **Hand Appliqué,** transfer design to appliqué fabric and stitch close to outline. Trim excess ⅛″ outside stitching. Baste to garment. Attach with a small blanket stitch around edges, using matching or contrasting thread. If you prefer, turn and press the raw edges to wrong side along machine stitching and sew to garment with invisible slip-stitches.

If fabric does not ravel, such as felt, eliminate stitching and cut directly on the design outline; sew with hemming or blanket stitches.

For **Machine Appliqué,** cut appliqué with a 1″ seam allowance. Back with a lightweight yet stiff backing (such as organdy), then pin to garment and baste. Match thread to appliqué and attach with a close zigzag stitch, stitching slowly. If several appliqués are overlapped, do not stitch portions that will be covered; previous stitching lines may show through or cause your sewing machine to jam. Trim away any excess fabric, keeping the fabric flat on the table and the scissor blades close to the stitching line.

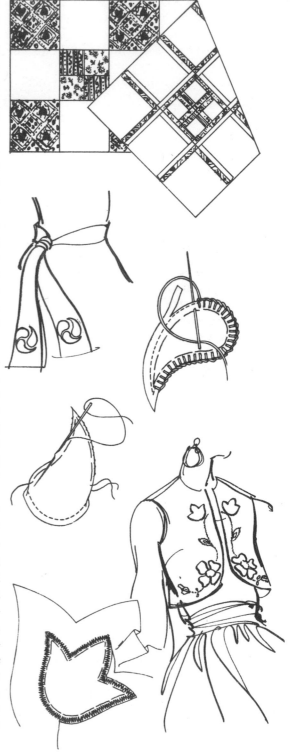

Decorative Surfaces

You can use quilting or smocking to add surface interest to any garment. Let your fabric become its own trim! Both quilting and smocking are probably familiar to you, but remember that in fashion the trick to turning heads is to use the familiar in an unusual way. Take your hint from that, and try working with silk, wool, velvet, crepe, or brilliant prints. Add them wherever your fashion instincts may lead you. Instead of over-all quilting, add it to just the cuffs and lapels of a suit, the collar of a simple dress, along the hems of a pants and tunic combination. Don't limit the soft touch of smocking to bodices; let it make a fluid statement on the hip yoke of a swing skirt, for example.

SMOCKING: The softness of smocking is achieved by accordion-like folds created by stitches taken on the right side of the fabric. Use six strands of embroidery floss, following either small dots transferred to your fabric or the checks in a gingham plaid as a stitching guide. If you would like the look of smocking on areas which require considerable "give," refer to Elasticized Shirring, page 230.

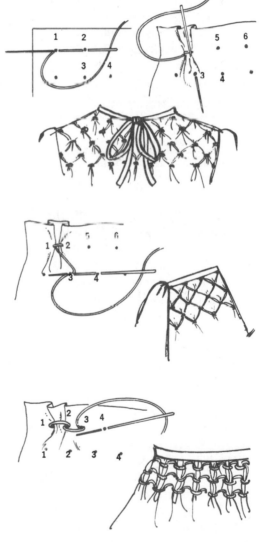

Honeycomb or Seed Stitch Smocking is the most popular smocking pattern. Bring your needle to the right side at 1. Take a small stitch at 2 and another at 1. Pull the thread taut. Re-insert the needle through the fabric at 2 and bring the needle up at 3. Repeat earlier procedure at 3 and 4 and again at 5 and 6. Continue until design is completed.

Diamond or Chevron Smocking is similar to the honeycomb, but the thread is on top of the fabric from row to row rather than underneath. Bring the needle to the right side at 1. With the thread above the needle, take a small stitch at 2 and another at 1. Draw stitches together tightly, and take stitch at 3. With thread below the needle, take a stitch at 4 and again pull tight. Take a stitch at 5 and with thread above the needle, take a stitch at 6. Draw the two together tightly. Continue, alternating from row to row.

Cable Stitch Smocking is yet another variation. Bring the needle to right side at 1, placing the thread above the needle. Now insert the needle through the fabric under 2 and draw up the thread. Hold the thread below the needle and make a second stitch at 3. Again reverse the position of the thread by holding it above the needle for a stitch at 4. Draw up the thread. Complete the row and continue in this manner.

QUILTING: The richly textured look of quilting is created by stitching through two or more layers of fabric in a design or pattern. You may purchase pre-quilted fabrics or make your own for a custom look. A layer of light padding—outing flannel, cotton wadding, or very thin foam rubber—is joined to your fabric to produce the raised effect. Back wadding or foam rubber with batiste or voile before quilting to increase durability. Use your underlining fabric for a backing on unlined garments or for an even more durable finish. Experiment on a sample of your fabric layers to determine the proper tension, pressure, and stitch length. Use matching or contrasting thread, or buttonhole twist for a pronounced stitching line. A quilting attachment is very useful. Complete your quilting before cutting out garment sections, as quilting will reduce the size of the fabric.

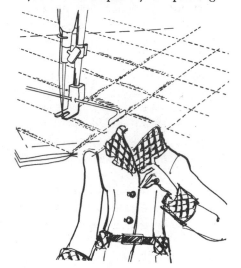

Pin the padding (and backing if used) to your fabric, wrong sides together; baste around the edges and along the lengthwise grain at 2" intervals to prevent shifting. Transfer quilting lines to the right side with chalk and/or thread tracing. Mark all lines for irregular design, or one line to follow with quilting foot for diamond design. If quilting a design in the print of your fabric, use that as your stitching guide. Then carefully stitch along markings on right side. When quilting is completed, cut out your garment sections. To reduce bulk in seams, pull or trim away padding from fabric in seam allowances. Do the same to darts, or slash and press open.

TRAPUNTO: A form of quilting in which the background is left unpadded and only the design stands out in relief, trapunto is done after garment section is cut out. The design is backed with a soft fabric (such as organdy) and padded with strands of yarn. Choose a design, determine its placement and transfer it to the right side of your fabric with chalk or thread tracing. Baste the backing to the wrong side in the desired location. On right side, stitch along pattern with small stitches; tie thread ends on wrong side.

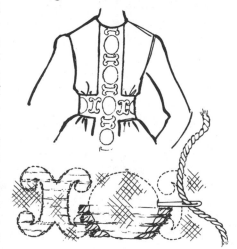

To pad design, thread strands of matching yarn through blunt needle. Insert needle through backing, and carry yarn between fabric and backing from one stitching line to the other. Clip ends of yarn close to stitching. Pass needle as far as possible before bringing up, and do not pull tightly. For large areas or angles and sharp curves, bring needle out and back through backing. When changing directions, leave some slack to fill out angle. Continue until entire area is padded. Slightly stretch fabric around each section of pattern to make the tiny yarn ends recede into backing. Press lightly on wrong side over turkish towel or pressing pad.

Fashion Fastenings

Zippers and buttons are simple fastenings, merely functional and best made inconspicuous—unless you use your creativity to make them delightful design features. Use trims to give your fastenings a new flair. Use them to add color and charm to a garment otherwise free of decoration, or to complement a trim used on other garment areas.

ZIPPERS: Outline your zipper with a favorite trim—braid, ribbon, lace ruffles, fringe, beads, embroidery. Or purchase jumbo zippers with shiny brass or brightly colored teeth and pulls, or with gayly colored tapes definitely meant for show. Don't limit them to a dress or jacket center closing, as charming as they can be; try them on a skirt side seam, sleeve vents, patch pockets, or even on an outside pants seam.

Such trimming will require a somewhat different zipper application, however, which may be slashed into almost any location. (The measurements that are given below are for conventional zippers; you will need to allow for a larger opening for jumbo zippers.)

Position the zipper and mark the garment with thread tracing. Reinforce by stitching ¼" from the position markings, pivoting at corners to stitch along the end markings. Slash along the marking line to within ½" of the ends and then clip diagonally to corners. Turn the edges in ¼"; baste and press. Center the opening over the zipper and baste in place. Edgestitch from the garment side through all layers.

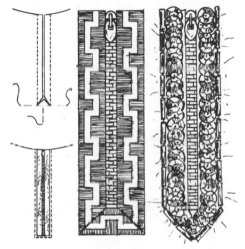

To border with trim, baste it around the zipper and stitch edges by hand or machine. Miter trim to make a squared or pointed end. To decorate the zipper pull as well, glue a small piece of jewelry or beads to the pull, or dangle them from the pull with a small link. Another suggestion is to attach a tassel or pompon (page 389).

BUTTONS: Individually decorated buttons can be truly unusual. They are especially lovely when they complement other trims or your fabric. Here are just a few suggestions, to which you can undoubtedly add many others of your own. First cover buttons with contrasting or matching fabric and then stitch a simple motif directly on the face of the button. Why not pick up a detail from the fabric itself, or try initials like the great designers? Try making sparkling buttons by stitching small beads to them. If you are using a small-scale print, center a motif on your button, perhaps even outlining the motif with embroidery. Another idea to try: cover your button with two layers of fabric, placing sheer lace or eyelet over your garment fabric.

See page 305 for covered buttons, page 315 for frogs and Chinese ball buttons.

A Man's Approach to Fashion

Creating Fashion for Men

Home sewing is joining the menswear revolution. One of the most satisfying as well as one of the most creative endeavors, men's fashions today are vibrantly entwined with style and design. Fashion individuality almost demands custom-made clothes, and sewing them yourself is one of the best and most personal means of acquisition.

Here in Book IV, the tailoring and fitting of men's clothing will be discussed only as the techniques involved differ from those used in constructing women's garments. These variations occur simply because men and women are built differently, and their clothes must be, too. There are no special tricks in making men's clothes—just adaptations of dressmaking methods. You will see that some tailoring of a man's jacket is similar to that of a woman's. Put aside your fears, and involve yourself in creating men's clothes—the rewards will be worth it!

The Dynamics of Men's Fashion

Patterns and fabrics for men's wardrobes are continually expanding, as are the numbers of people who sew menswear. Fabrics which are suitable for shirts, casual wear, classic suits are becoming accessible to the home sewer as well as the professional tailor. With a little imagination, you can produce beautifully tapered shirts in unique fabrics, then combine them with smartly tailored suits in non-conventional or classic fabrics to put your creation in the winner's circle. Apply the same creativity for sports clothes and leisure wear, using perennially favorite fabrics, or the newly popular ones.

The variety of available pattern styles includes the tastes of every male when combined with the expansive array of fabrics on the market. The fashion statement made by sewing menswear can express everything for today's man through his manner of dress—whether exciting or subdued, colorful or quiet. The choice and the satisfaction of creative sewing make menswear great and rewarding fun.

Couture For Men

To compliment the great new swing toward sewing for men, Vogue Patterns offers top fashions for men created by some of today's foremost designers. These patterns afford many possibilities for a man's individual fashion preferences, as they are both versatile and classic. Each pattern brings you the best in contemporary men's fashion.

Bill Blass, an American whose first designs were for women, carries his characteristic clean lines into his designs for men—magnificently tailored garments are emphasized with the trim lines. Pierre Cardin, also originally a women's designer, offers elegantly styled menswear patterns. His French haute couture background is revealed in the superb cut of his clothes and the craft in his workmanship. While style lines or details may appear more complex in these designer patterns, their construction really only involves combinations of the sewing techniques used in all Vogue Patterns.

You will find that the designer patterns are no more difficult to construct than other patterns. What makes the designer patterns special is their unique styling, not their construction techniques. As in all your other sewing, you can adapt your own sewing methods and simplify procedures in making men's designer fashion. The results, however, will be no ordinary garment, but the ultimate in quality design and appearance.

Vogue Patterns' Own Designers

Rounding out Vogue Patterns' menswear collection are our own designs for men. Vogue Patterns' designers have created a series of well-styled garments to complete the range of men's fashions available in patterns. Sport clothes, suits, leisurewear, and sleepwear patterns make it possible to sew a complete wardrobe for a man. Along with the varied styles, the patterns are adaptable, too; a suit can be made in wool flannel or double knit for office wear, then in velvet for evening wear. The shirt and tie have developed new personalities—the shirt collar now takes many shapes to accent the wide ties, complement a perky bow tie, or hug an ascot. Sportswear patterns allow for a great deal of creativity with separates—shirts, pants, tennis outfits, etc.—sometimes incorporating the newest trim ideas such as rib knit bands or colorful zippers. Or a robe can be made in brocade for lounging and in terry cloth for after-shower. Vogue Patterns cover every fashion need—our designers keep abreast of the new trends appearing on the fashion horizon and create timely new designs, incorporating new fabrics, notions and trims—utilizing familiar construction techniques.

PATTERNS FOR SPECIAL FABRICS: The trend toward diversified fabrics for home sewing creates fantastic alternatives for a man's well-planned wardrobe. With this knowledge, special Vogue Patterns for men have been created in these special fabrics. Patterns marked "Use only stretchable unbonded knits" were so designed to meet the demands for a sleek body fit. The elasticity of the fabric itself allows the pattern to have less wearing ease (see page 107) as the fabric gives with body movement. Other patterns are recommended as "suitable for knits," each envelope listing what type of knits is appropriate. Leather and leather-like fabrics are mentioned as workable for several jacket and pants combinations. The directions taken by today's Vogue Patterns with contemporary fashion and fabric are great!

Fabric For The Fastidious

The right fabric is what really "makes" your menswear project. In choosing fabric, follow the suggestions on the pattern envelope back, but don't hesitate to make your own substitutions. Refer to pages 32-49 for a discussion of fabric structure and properties if you need some guidance. Then, take some time to organize your thoughts so you know what you *do not* want and what your budget limitations are—your trip to buy fabric is assured of success rather than confusion.

What's Suitable

The final fabric choice is yours: select problem-free fabrics, or accept the challenge of special fabrics with surface interests. Match fabric to your tastes, life style, and the pattern design and you are well on the road to success. Be aware of the superior knits now available for menswear. For patterns marked "Designed for Knit Fabrics Only, use stretchable unbonded knits," test stretchability using the stretch gauge page 186. These patterns have less wearing ease and require the give of knit fabrics.

A CHIC SHIRT in crisp cotton blends or body-hugging synthetics can be made of many fabrics—knits, broadcloth, muslin, voile, gingham, lightweight corduroy or wool flannel. Then add intrigue with geometrics, prints, plaids, and stripes and you are creating an individualistic shirt. For the man who asks more of fashion make a leather shirt or a luxurious shirt in silk, satin, or crepe for a custom touch.

PANTS fabric should have body so that it wears well and will retain its shape. Test the fabric before you buy—crush it in your hands to see if it springs back into form. Many traditional fabrics like chino, sailcloth, twills, denim, and poplin are now treated with a wrinkle-resistant finish to keep them fresh-looking. A printed or plain pinwale corduroy can be both fashionable and durable. Double knits are extremely comfortable, and can be solid-colored or have multi-color jacquard design. Lightweight or medium weight wools such as flannel and gabardine are both warm and attractive—a fine tartan plaid can look sensational. Experimenters may wish to make pants from leather or the new synthetic suede.

SUITS FOR EVERY OCCASION tell a different fabric story. A tailored jacket should be made from a malleable fabric which has enough body to keep its shape—a fabric that is pliant, yet sturdy. For these requirements, wool is the best material; it is the easiest to shape for tailor-perfect collar and lapels, it drapes well, and it is always in fashion. However, if you prefer an easy-care fabric for suits, double knits are recommended, and are available in subtle plaids and stripes especially designed for menswear. A tailored jacket is not meant to be washed, however; if this is desirable, remember to modify the inner construction and to use washable and pre-shrunk fabric, interfacings and lining.

Other possible suit fabrics include denim, corduroy, seersucker, and linen, in prints, solids, stripes, plaids. Avoid sheer, soft fabrics because you will not be able to build in the foundation that jackets require.

For something truly special, a velvet suit in a deep, rich color with a satin cummerbund would be ideal, or a jacket in brocade with lapels and pants in velvet. For sportswear, try trimming a wool jacket with a leather upper collar, pocket flaps, and elbow patches; and adding leather piping, pocket welts, or belt loops to the pants. Pick out a zingy Madras plaid to accent a spectacular weekend wardrobe.

PAJAMAS AND ROBES are easy, practical garments to sew. For pajamas, fabrics should be soft, washable materials such as surah, broadcloth, pima, or lightweight stable knits in any attractive color or print. Fabric for a robe can be almost anything, depending on when and how a robe will be worn. An after-shower or swim robe would be ideal in terrycloth. For lounging, try lightweight wools, or double knits. For leisure in luxury, think in terms of velvet, brocade, or heavy silk.

VESTS, TIES, ASCOTS are accessories that stylize and individualize a man's appearance, and should be coordinated with his taste and wardrobe. Use an interesting fabric to complement a favorite outfit—wool, corduroy, linen, velvet, brocade, and double knits are possibilities for vests. Ties and ascots can be made in any fabric that is not extremely bulky, heavyweight, or rigid.

SPORTS AND LEISURE WEAR fabrics for swimsuits, tennis outfits, and lightweight jackets are generally cottons, and synthetics —either knitted or woven. Sports jackets can be made from duck, sailcloth, canvas, and denim. Use quilted synthetic fabric for a ski jacket, and lightweight to medium weight washable wools for attractive battle or bush jackets or baseball jackets.

Measuring Men

Accurate measurements are needed for a tailor-perfect fit. The stance of the man being measured should be natural; keep away from mirrors which inspire the assumption of an ideal figure—one that is too erect, and with taut rather than relaxed muscles—will cause the garment to fit improperly with normal stance. Follow the guidelines as illustrated, applying the appropriate measurements to your particular sewing project.

Purchasing the Pattern

Shirt patterns with classic collars are sold by neck size; other shirt patterns are purchased by chest size, or in small, medium, large, etc. Jacket and suit patterns are sold by chest size only. Pants patterns are purchased by waist and seat size.

Neckband: Measure around the full neck for neckband size, plus ½″ for wearing ease (1).

Chest: Place the tape under the arms around the fullest part of the chest (2).

Waist: While a man usually has a definite waist, he must indicate where he likes to wear his pants, which is where the waist measurement should be taken. Tie a string around this established point for the waist (even though this measurement is essentially one of personal preference). Measure body at string (3).

Seat (Hip): Position the tape around the fullest part of the seat (4).

Shirt Sleeve Length: Bend arm up; place tape measure at base of neck. Run tape from center back to elbow, across elbow crook and up over the wrist bone (5).

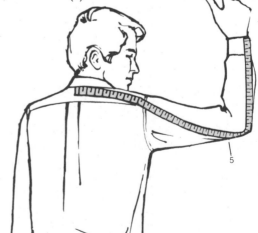

Measuring for Custom Fit

After you have purchased a pattern in the correct size, a few more localized measurements are needed for precision fit. Vogue Patterns are designed for a man of average height, 5′10″ corresponding to a "regular" in ready-to-wear.

Several measurements are needed to customize a shirt—the correct sleeve length for a classic shirt (see opposite page), arm circumference and length measurements for fitted sleeves. Waist, chest, and length measurements must be considered for both types. Pants may need to be adjusted for the correct crotch depth and leg length.

Jackets are fitted according to the shoulder area (vs. the bust area for women); therefore the neck, shoulder, and arm measurements are necessary. The center lengths and the back width are also important for jackets.

High Hip: Measure at the top of hip bones (6).

Thigh: Just under the crotch, measure the fullest part of the thigh (7).

Knee: Measure around the leg at the knee (8).

Outseam (side length): Measure from the waist (see measurement #3) to the top of the shoe heel (9).

Inseam: Take measurement over pants; position crotch correctly on body. Measure along inseam between crotch seam and shoe heel top (10).

Neck: Measure at base of neck (11)

Shoulder: Measure from the base of neck to top of the arm hinge (12).

Center Front Length: Measure from base of neck down the center of the chest to established waist (13).

Arm Length: Measure from arm hinge to elbow, and then from the elbow to wrist bone. Record both measurements (14).

Arm Circumference: Measure bicep at the fullest part (15), and wrist at the bone (16).

Center Back: Measure from the base of neck down center back to the established waist (17).

Back Width: Measure straight across the back, over the shoulder blades, from arm hinge to arm hinge (18).

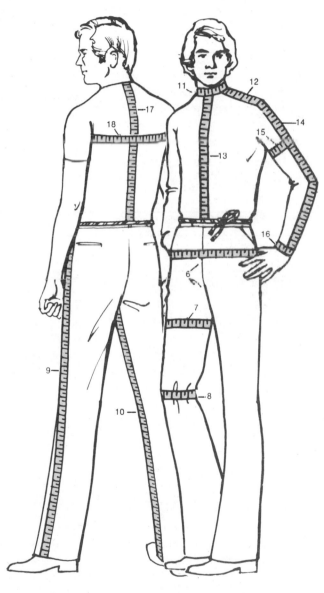

Pattern Know-It-All

The pattern envelope should be read carefully, for it is your pattern measurement and purchasing guide—it has all the vital information concerning standard measurements, required yardage, notions, and findings.

EASE REQUIREMENTS: Menswear may have two kinds of ease—*wearing ease* for body movement and additional fullness called *style ease,* for a certain look (see pages 107-108). Classic shirt patterns have both wearing and style ease; body fitting shirts have only wearing ease. Pant patterns have only wearing ease through waist and seat area; however, some styles with pleats and wider legs may have style ease too. Patterns stating "Use only stretchable unbonded knits," will be nearly exact body measurements. Jackets may have both wearing and style ease and are designed to fit over a shirt and vest.

CHOOSE CORRECT PATTERN SIZE: Now that you have exact body measurements you must select the correct pattern size. *Classic shirts* are purchased by neckband size.

When purchasing a *shirt* or *jacket* by chest measurement, those who fall between two sizes must consider their build. A thin, small-boned physique should choose the smaller size, while a large-boned ample physique will require the larger size. *Pants* have accommodations for this situation—a wider center back seam allowance—so the pants can be fitted for the in-between size.

Men's patterns are sized for men of average build about 5'10" without shoes.

SIZES	34	36	38	40	42	44	46	48
CHEST	34	36	38	40	42	44	46	48
WAIST	28	30	32	34	36	39	42	44
HIP (SEAT)	35	37	39	41	43	45	47	49
NECKBAND	14	14½	15	15½	16	16½	17	17½
SHIRT SLEEVE	32	32	33	33	34	34	35	35

Build Fit Into Each Pattern

Superbly fitted menswear does not "just happen"—it is an art practiced by every tailor of world-wide repute. These craftsmen work with a pattern and a muslin garment before touching shears to fashion fabrics. Tailor-perfect fit should be your goal in creating menswear fashion. If figure flaws cause wrinkles and pulls of excess fabric in ready-to-wear garments, the same thing will happen with a garment sewn from a pattern that has not been adjusted to match statistical pattern measurements with the actual body measurements. These pattern changes are easy to make—review pages 124-161—many mens' figure needs create the same fitting problems as for women.

Adjustments Help Produce a Better Fit

To determine whether you need flat pattern adjustments, compare the standard body measurements given above and those found on the back of the pattern envelope with the personal measurements you established on pages 410-411. Review Flat Pattern Adjustments pages 126-131, on how to adjust pattern lengths and circumferences.

LENGTH ADJUSTMENTS must be made according to the figure—they bring the vertical length of the pattern in line with your measurements. These simple adjustments are often the difference between a comfortable or an ill-fitting garment. There are many combinations that may be required—a tall man may have short arms and a high waist, while a short man may have long legs with a low waist—few people match the pattern's statistical measurements exactly. Build length into pattern before cutting your fashion fabric to achieve a better fit.

Shirts: Properly adjusted sleeve length is most important for any shirt (see pages 410-411, measurements #5 and #14). A loose sleeve with a cuff has a single set of adjustment lines while a more fitted sleeve has two, one above and one below the elbow. The shirt body has only one set of adjustment lines so decide where the shirt tail should end. Be sure to adjust the length of any bands, facings, or other related pieces.

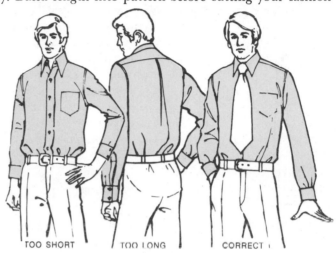

TOO SHORT   TOO LONG   CORRECT

Jackets: Proportion is most important—a classic jacket should cover the seat, ending where the legs join the buttocks—the jacket waist should fall at established waist (measurement #3, page 410). The lapel length is crucial (use measurement #13, page 411, to correct). Usually a tall man will need length in this area while a short man may need the length reduced. Even a regular height (5'10") may need adjustments to bring the pattern in line with his body. Lengthen or shorten the jacket above and/or below the waist as needed. If you do not find adjustment lines on the pattern where you need them (i.e., about 2" above the top buttonhole for a lapel adjustment), draw a line at right angle to grainline; adjust the length accordingly. If necessary, shift pocket placement lines to compliment the proportions after adjusting length below waist. Make same changes in lining, interfacing and facing pieces.

TOO SHORT   TOO LONG   CORRECT

Pants: Your actual measurements for the outseam (measurement #9) and the inseam (measurement #10), when taken as directed on page 411, are used for pants length adjustments. The inseam indicates the length of the leg while the outseam indicates rise (called crotch length in women's pants).

413

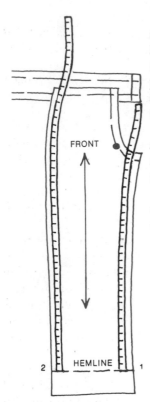

For length adjustment, first measure the *front pattern piece* along the inseam seamline between the crotch seamline and the hemline (1). Then measure the pattern along the outseam from the top seamline of the waistband to the hemline; include any pocket pieces that may affect the outseam length and exclude seam allowances (2). Note: Men's classic pants are worn with top of the waistband at his established waist.

Lengthen or shorten the pant leg as needed, until the *inseam* is the correct length. (This adjustment is not shown.) If an adjustment line is not given, draw a line perpendicular to the grainline in the knee area.

Now, any difference between the pattern measurement indicates that the *pants rise* needs adjusting. Lengthen or shorten the rise as indicated, until the *outseam* is the correct length.

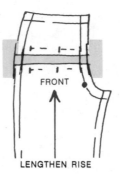

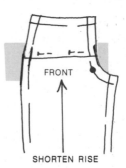

Caution: Make sure front pattern piece adjustment lines are placed above the fly symbol—to adjust below may distort fit or make opening unusable. For pattern pieces without adjustment lines, draw them in at right angles to grainline well above the fly symbol. If adjustments interfere with a pocket, reposition symbols or adjust extensions maintaining the original opening length. Make equal changes in *back pattern piece.*

CIRCUMFERENCE ADJUSTMENTS: To establish a need for circumference adjustment, analyze each garment: for a *shirt* or *jacket* the waist circumference is usually the only flat adjustment needed. See pages 129-131 for reducing and enlarging waist and hip. *Pants* patterns usually give a wider center back seam allowance allowing you to adjust the waist and seat when fitting. If it is not included, see page 158 for the waist circumference adjustment. Other fitting problems should be worked out in muslin.

REMINDER: Flat pattern adjustments for length and circumference do not automatically insure a perfect fit. If this is your first venture into sewing menswear, *take the time to make a muslin fitting garment* to ensure a custom fit *before* cutting the fashion fabric. Select classic styles: the traditional shirt with collar, neckband, and yoke; straight legged pants with regular width waistband and an inseam side pocket; a two-buttoned jacket with moderate lapels and natural shoulders. Choose a good quality muslin—lightweight for a shirt and medium to heavyweight for pants or jacket. If balancing the grain is part of the fitting problem, use a cotton with a woven stripe. *Never* use permanent press

414

fabrics as the grain cannot be straightened.

Be sure fabric is grain perfect (see pages 166-169) before cutting, and use your **adjusted pattern**. For shirt cut all pieces, except pockets; for pants, eliminate pockets if possible; for jackets eliminate pockets, facings, and upper collar.

Use tracing wheel and dressmakers carbon; trace all seamlines and symbols so changes will be obvious. Mark lengthwise and crosswise grains on the right side of the fabric. Sew with machine basting for easier fitting changes. Pin-baste hem.

Test for wearing ease while sitting, moving, stretching, and bending. The garment should balance on the body; lengthwise seams and grain markings should hang straight and perpendicular to the floor. Crosswise grain markings and seams should be parallel to the floor and perpendicular to lengthwise markings.

Shirts: Neckband should be comfortable, neither binding nor loose. Sleeves should have ample length when cuff is closed. Shirt tail should stay securely tucked into the trousers, with adequate wearing ease over waist and hip.

Pants: The top of the waistband should fall on the established waist; the crotch seam should not bind or hang too low. The legs and seat should be wrinkle free.

Jackets should not wrinkle or pull. The shoulder seam should lie straight, directly on top of the shoulder, and extend from the base of the neck to the top of the shoulder bone. The shoulder area and sleeve should fit and mold smoothly with the elbow at the center of the sleeve's fullness. The undercollar should hug the neck in back and the outer edge should just cover the neck seam. The notch area of the lapels should be symmetrical on the body; the lapels should roll smoothly from the top buttonhole. The waist area should be smooth; vents should hang straight without spreading or overlapping.

IMPORTANT ANALYSIS: As you analyze your muslin fitting garment you may still see areas that need to be changed for a tailor-perfect fit. This is the time to fit the muslin to add the necessary ease, or eliminate excess fabric for your personal needs.

Alterations for a Custom Fit

While flat pattern adjustments allowed you to make the pattern statistically accurate for your fitting needs, they cannot accommodate figure flaws due to posture, excess weight, or bone structure. These significant personal alterations **must** be worked out in a fitting muslin as suggested above, and should not be confused with minor fitting changes (see pages 348-351). The problem of an excessively large or small garment must be eliminated in muslin, with the same amount of change made in every garment you sew.

SHIRTS AND JACKETS: Figure flaws and personal preference will allow you to try your hand at custom fitting. Should you need to alter a shirt, make the same amount of change in a jacket. The classic collar and neckband are not usually altered, but for extremely disproportionate neck circumferences it may be necessary (see page 133). For shoulder problems, apply the techniques found on pages 135-137. Chest and back flaws will be apparent in body fitting clothes (see pages 146-148). A fitted sleeve may need altering (see pages 140-141) though classic sleeves usually do not.

PANTS: Tailor-fitting pants depend on personal preference, body contours, and stance. Men often have fitting problems due to posture and excess weight. Refer to page 149 (fitted skirt) to correct for a sway back, page 161 (flat buttocks) for a flat seat.

There are four figure flaws that seem to be unique to men that require alterations not covered on pages 132-161. The first two are caused by excess weight and cause fitting problems in shirts, pants, and jackets. Adjustments made before cutting will not give you girth in the right place to fit correctly. The **bay window** is created by excess flesh through the midriff area. This protrusion will cause the shirt or jacket front to ride up, pull side seams, and strain buttoned closures. In pants, it forces the waistband down across the front as the center front length is too short to cover the extra flesh. Outseams pull forward and the inseams are strained and wrinkled. The **bulging hips** are created by fleshy pads settling on the side hips making the body very broad at this area. These pads cause the shirt or jacket to ride up over hips resulting in pulling, straining, and an uneven hem. In pants, wrinkles and straining are evident through hip area, pulling the outseams, while the inseams are strained causing wrinkles.

The other two are caused by posture or bone structure and create a significant problem when fitting pants. The **forward hip stance** is evident when the abdomen and hip are thrown forward causing a sway back and the chest to appear sunken. "Horseshoe" wrinkles form under the buttocks and pants hit back of legs below knees. The **backward hip stance** is apparent when the hips are thrown high and toward the back. This pulls the pants front down causing wrinkles as the center back length is too short, thus straining the inseam. The pants cling to the legs below the knees.

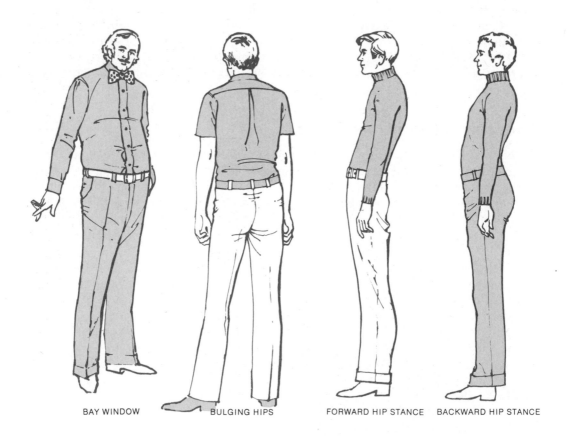

BAY WINDOW   BULGING HIPS   FORWARD HIP STANCE   BACKWARD HIP STANCE

416

Man-spirited Favorites

Today's man has up-dated his wardrobe to meet the demands of his individual
life-style . . . Sunday best is passé . . . comfortable, easy-care suits . . .
mix and match separates . . . classic-tailored suits—
all must be coordinated to fit the occasion and suit the man . . . the young executive,
the man about town, the spectator sportsman, the outdoorsman—
trim and neat around the clock is the order of the day.

Sew up any handsome look—a
jacket in a subtle plaid . . . a plushy
pile—velvet or corduroy . . .
add pants in a complimentary fabric.
Hand-tailor the jacket—or use the
machine . . . indulge in a sumptuous
fabric or a handsome rough
or rugged looking one.

Care-free Casuals

Be a part of the sweeping changes in menswear . . . wear something with individual flair and timeless comfort . . . try new vibrant colors . . . be a standout! Sew up shirts and tops . . . in bright plaids and stripes . . . clingy stretchable knits, in strong solid colors, and unusual textures. Make jean-style pants in rugged fabrics . . . active sportswear trousers in bold plaids . . .   comfortable double-knits.

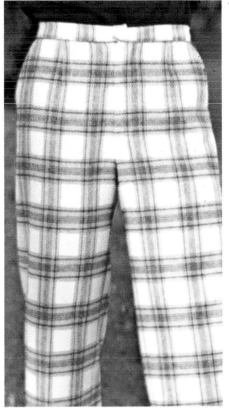

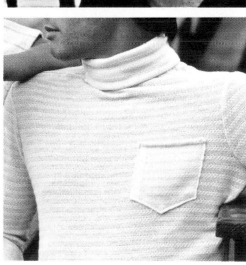

Use a large measure of imagination, and create a smashing, carefree casual wardrobe . . .
Put together a great jacket . . .
plain or fancy—mix fake suedes
with denim, sturdy sail cloth
with knitted band trim . . .
assert your individuality in
something dashing!

Be active—or idle in style . . .
the ultimate in tennis togs is pure
white with a touch of color . . .
for lounging, a plushy robe and silk
pj's . . . your own personal statement for *your* life style!

CAUTION: Correct your fitting muslin as indicated by the pattern pieces to test these alterations before cutting into your fashion fabric. Jacket pattern pieces are not shown; make the same amount of change needed for a shirt.

BAY WINDOW: To correct *shirt* when 2″ or less is needed, slash front to point opposite armhole and spread amount needed. Form a pleat from slash to side edge. For more than 2″, also add to the side seam of front and back.

To correct *pants,* increase the center front length and add to the front inseam until the pants hang straight. Re-shape any darts or pleats to fit contour.

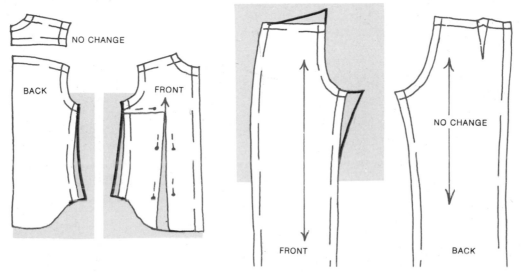

BULGING HIPS: To correct *shirt,* slash front and back to a point just below the armhole and near the side seams. Spread as needed, making equal changes on front and back.

To correct *pants,* increase outseam length and add to the side edges of the front and back until you have the necessary girth. Then add to the inseams until pants hang straight. Shape darts to fit contour, adding darts if necessary.

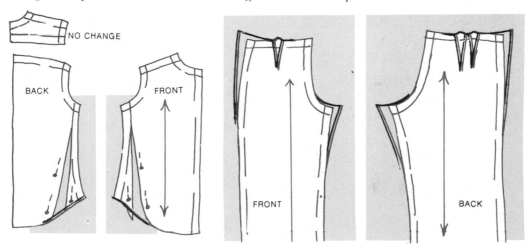

Pants should be wrinkle free—contrary to popular belief, you do not need excess fabric between the seat and the knee for sitting. Work out these wrinkles in a muslin—once mastered you can transfer this knowledge to every pants you make. Be aware of overfitting—this will make it virtually impossible to have them wrinkle-free. Make a horizontal tuck across the back of the leg, just under the seat to remove excess fabric, continuing the tuck across the front, tapering to nothing at the inseam. Re-stitch the inseam in your muslin pants, stretching the back inseam edge to fit.

Transfer alterations to pattern pieces as shown in the two alterations—forward hip stance and backward hip stance.

Correct grainline and shape as indicated. This may be the only alteration you need for a tailor-perfect fit, or it may be needed with the bay window or bulging hips on page 417.

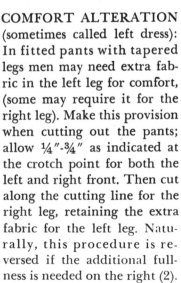

FORWARD HIP STANCE: To correct, decrease the center back length, the width at the seat curve, and the inseam until the pants hang straight (see sketches above).

For more extreme wrinkles between seat and knee, make a horizontal tuck as explained above and shown on the accompanying illustrations. Test in muslin *before* cutting into your fashion fabric.

BACKWARD HIP STANCE: To correct, increase the center back length, the width at the seat curve, and the inseam until the pants hang straight (1).

For more extreme wrinkling between seat and knee, make a horizontal tuck as explained above and shown on the accompanying illustrations. Test in muslin *before* cutting into your fashion fabric.

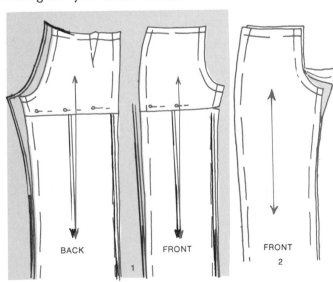

COMFORT ALTERATION (sometimes called left dress): In fitted pants with tapered legs men may need extra fabric in the left leg for comfort, (some may require it for the right leg). Make this provision when cutting out the pants; allow ¼"-¾" as indicated at the crotch point for both the left and right front. Then cut along the cutting line for the right leg, retaining the extra fabric for the left leg. Naturally, this procedure is reversed if the additional fullness is needed on the right (2).

418

Menswear Sewing: Pure & Simple

The keen interest in sewing menswear today is due to the dynamic fashions available—no longer is each man a near carbon copy of the other, they can have individuality in the creation of their wardrobe by sewing at home—Vogue Patterns has answered this need with styles that can be sewn in the newest fabrics. Some are easy to sew and quick to complete. Others will require more time to achieve professional results. The actual construction methods for menswear are basically the same ones used in women's garments. However, the difference between the two is *where* and in *what order* certain construction techniques are employed. Throughout history, the tailor has always plied his trade with care and, we may add, some secrecy. Therefore, an exhausting search into menswear sewing techniques has been made to present here what are the most important facets of sewing men's garments. Also, in certain cases the techniques were modified to make them more understandable and applicable to home sewing.

Adapt Your Knowledge

If you can sew, you can sew menswear. Use your basic know-how to widen your sewing experience by making a man's garment. Couple your pattern's instruction sheet with the ideas given here to create, without difficulty, a beautiful garment. Little sewing tricks, such as how to match plaids and how to press, are just as vital for menswear as they are for sewing any garment. Your repertoire of sewing techniques will be valuable.

Shirts, jackets, and pants are discussed with the purpose of augmenting your pattern sewing guide. The direction given here should aid you in taking your garments one step farther as you consider your fabric choice. The new synthetics (woven or knitted) do not always "shrink" as well as the traditional ones when making a seam with ease (page 216), and some permanent press fabrics look puckered and wrinkled after laundering when top-stitching is used for seam finishes (pages 220-221) and as trim for pockets, bands, or cuffs (page 395). The special tips suggested in the chapter will aid you to make well-tailored garments. Other men's clothes—robes, vests, ties, and ascots utilize sewing methods already presented in other chapters, so they need no further enlightenment here. Your pattern sewing guide supplies basic construction techniques which, for these garments, are methods universally used in both men's and women's wear.

Organize!

Think about your garment before you start to sew. Review the instruction sheet in conjunction with this chapter to see how you will proceed—try to get a clear picture of how the garment goes together before you start. This will aid you in understanding why certain particulars of construction are present, as well as enabling you to substitute other ways of construction. The chart on the following page should give you an over-all view of the specific techniques most often used. Also, it should enable you to organize your project so you can select the most appropriate methods for your fabric or allow you to be more creative. There are no secrets here, so proceed!

Menswear: What to use and where

Legend:
- ✓ Very Common
- ✗ Common
- ● Sometimes Found

		Shirts	Ties & Neckwear	Tops	Vests	Jeans	Pants	Shorts	Jumpsuits	Hand-Tailored Jackets	Machine-Tailored Jackets	Sport Jackets	Robes	Pajamas
SEAMS	Plain	✓	✓	✗	✗	●	✓	✓	✓	✓	●	●	●	●
	Stitch and Zigzag	✓		✓	●		●	●	●		●	●	●	●
	Zigzag (for Knits)	●		●	●		●	●	●		●	●	●	●
	Flat-fell	✓		✗	●	✓	●	●	●		✗	✗	✗	✗
	Slot	✓		●			●	●						
	Lapped	✓		●								●	●	●
	Topstitched	✓		✓	✗	●	●	●	●	●	✓	✓	✗	✗
	Tucked	●		●						●	●	●	●	●
	Welt	●		●		●	●	●		●	●	●	●	●
	Piped or Corded	✓		✓	●					●			✓	✓
STITCHES	Backstitch		●	●	●		●			✗				
	Catch Stitch		✗	✗	●		●	●	●	✓			●	
	Pad Stitch		●							✓				
	Felling Stitch									✓				
	Slipstitch	✗	✓	●	✓	●	●	●	●	✓	●	●	●	●
	Hemming Stitch	✓	●	✗	✗		✗	✗	✗		●	●	●	
	Blindstitch	✗	●	✗	✗		●	●	●	✓			●	
	Hand Pickstitch	●		●	●					●				
DECORATIVE	Topstitching	✓		✗	●	✓	●	●	●	●	✓	✓	✗	✓
	Saddle Stitch	●			●	●	●	●	●	●			●	
	Decorative Tacks	●			●		●	●	●	●	●			
	Monograms	✗	●	●					●			●	●	●
	Braids and Bands	●		●	●		●	●	●			✗	✗	●
	Binding	●		●	●		●	●	●	●	●	●	●	●

420

Make A Shirt!

When making a shirt, think first of the fabric and its care; then the interfacing. Choose the construction method that is most appropriate for your fabric—some permanent press fabrics with topstitched bands and flat-felled seams look wrinkled after laundering. If your fabric needs support, use lightweight, pre-shrunk interfacing.

Customized Techniques

Concentrate on these special construction touches to make a beautifully tailored shirt —choose one that is just right for you . . . and your fabric!

OPENINGS: The familiar band opening is most often used with traditional fabrics and a self-faced opening is usually found on permanent press and knit fabrics. However, today men's shirts employ many opening variations and a wide range of closures. When you start sewing, remember, men's shirt closures lap *left over right.*

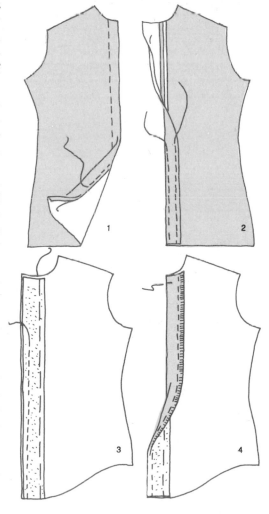

Band: To make, turn in the **right** front along the foldline; press. Turn in the raw edge ¼″ and edgestitch inner fold through all thicknesses (1). For the **left** front, interface if desired; then place the right side of the band to the wrong side of the shirt; stitch in a ¼″ seam and press open. Fold in remaining raw edge on seam line; turn band to outside (over the seam) along the foldline; baste and press. Topstitch ¼″ from both long folded edges (2).

Extended Facing: If possible, cut the front edge on a selvage to eliminate finishing. If fabric needs support, cut interfacing the facing width. Place it on the facing and baste along the foldline; secure outer edge by stitching ¼″ from the selvage or clean-finish the raw edges together (3). Next, turn in front edges along foldline; press. Baste in place at neck and hem edges (4). When interfacing is used, the buttonholes and buttons will hold it in place adequately.

Men's shirts now have many stylized openings—design variations once used exclusively for women are used to create liberated fashions. Just put your creativity to work— use a slashed opening (page 255) with grommets and laces; an exposed zipper (page 403) in a body-hugging knit shirt; and inset band (page 258); or any of the other methods covered in Book III.

BACK FULLNESS: To add pleats or gathers in the shirt back, simply lay the "place on fold line" 1″ to 1½″ from the fabric fold when laying out the pattern. The fullness added can be an inverted (1) or box pleat (2) at center back; a box or single pleat over the shoulder blade (3); or gathers (4).

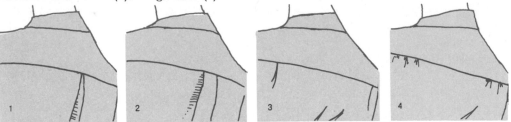

YOKE CONSTRUCTION: Light and medium weight fashion fabrics can be self-faced. Heavyweight fabrics may cause bulk so face the yoke with a durable, lightweight fabric. Stretchy fabrics may need the support of interfacing.

Pin one yoke section to shirt; baste. Use the remaining yoke section (self- or lining fabrics) as a facing, pinning the right side of the facing to the wrong side of the shirt back. Stitch seam through all three layers; trim and grade seam. Press yoke and facing over seam; edgestitch through all thicknesses (1). Next, pin and stitch right side of the yoke facing to wrong side of shirt fronts; trim and grade seam and press. Pin yoke in place over seam and edgestitch through all thicknesses (2). Staystitch neck edge.

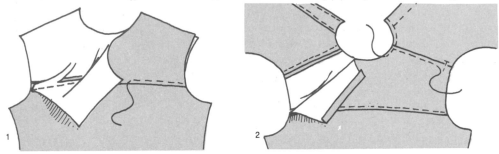

COLLAR CONSTRUCTION: The shape and style should be flattering. If you cannot find the desired shape, experiment, making a *test collar* first before cutting your fashion fabric.

If the fabric is heavy or bulky, shape collar as shown in step 2 of the rolled collar, pages 263-265, before attaching it. When the collar is joined to the shirt and facings in separate seams, such as the notched collar, pages 265-266, it too, needs shaping. *Collar Stays* give support to the collar points and can be easily removable. Make a buttonhole (slightly wider than the stay width) on the undercollar before it is interfaced (1). Then baste interfacing in place and make a pocket for the stay between the layers with two long rows of stitching and short one above the buttonhole (2). Prepare collar and attach. Insert stay when shirt is completed (3).

Classic Shirt Collar: Complete step 1 for collar with stand, page 267. To attach men's shirt collars, which are applied entirely by machine, stitch non-interfaced band to the inside of the shirt, clipping shirt neck edge if necessary (1). Trim, grade, and clip seam allowances. Pull collar and band up, then press seam toward band. Turn in remaining free edge of the band and pin over the seam. Edgestitch through all thicknesses (2).

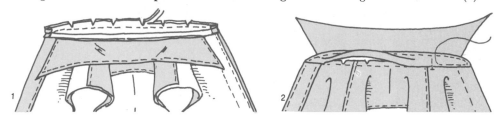

THE MASCULINE SLEEVE: Use flat-felled seams for traditional fabrics and a clean-finished plain seam for permanent press and knit fabrics. For a flat-felled seam in a heavy fabric cut wider seam allowances on one edge. If there is too much fullness in the sleeve cap, remove excess ease following instructions on page 139.

Complete ***sleeve plackets*** before the sleeve is set in. Be sure that one sleeve opens on the ***right*** and the other on the ***left.*** Use the classic men's shirt sleeve placket, page 284, or substitute the slashed opening, page 283 or the continuous lap in a slash, page 318.
Flat-Fell Insertion: Flat-fell seams, page 221, can be made from the ***outside*** or the ***inside.*** The method shown is made from the outside. Narrow hem the shirt tails first. Pin sleeve to shirt, wrong sides together, matching markings; adjust ease; complete the flat-fell seam (1). Join sleeve edges and shirt sides in a continuous seam (2).

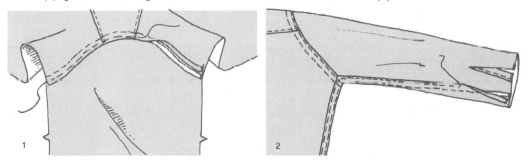

Clean-Finish Insertion: With right sides together, pin the sleeve in the armhole; adjust ease. Stitch in a plain seam; stitch again $1/4''$ away using a straight or zigzag stitch. Trim close to stitching (1). With a straight stitch overcast raw edge. Stitch the sleeve and side seam in one continuous seam and clean-finish same as armhole (2).

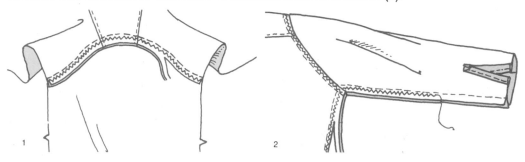

SLEEVE FINISHES: The classic shirt sleeve cuff or the French cuff, page 288, are still the most widely used cuff. A plain hem may require interfacing, page 280, or you may want to use a bias or shaped facing, page 285, as a sleeve finish.

Try a *self-finishing hem* that looks like a stitched band. Allow ½" extra to the sleeve hemline when cutting. Make hem before sleeve is completed—fold hem allowance up along hemline and press. Now turn the folded edge up to enclose the raw hem edge and press. From the outside, stitch ¼" from the last fold through all thicknesses; press hem down and tuck up. Insert sleeve following procedures on page 423.

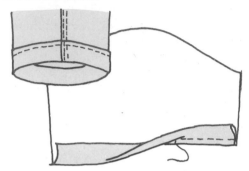

POCKET: Both decorative and functional pockets are easy to construct. See pages 296-302 for the various techniques. Pin pockets in place to check the position—they should be straight and parallel to the center front.

SHIRT TAIL HEMS AND FINISHES: A smooth hem, well-made buttonholes, and correctly positioned buttons are marks of a beautifully tailored shirt.

Shirt Tail Hems: Narrow hems (page 338) are the most common, but vents and wider hems in the shirt tail may be used. Machine stitched hems are the most practical finish for shirts—use matching thread and 10-12 stitches to the inch.

Buttonholes and Buttons: Machine-worked or hand-worked buttonholes (pages 311-312) are the last item made. They are placed vertically on the front opening (with the exception of the neckband) and evenly spaced to accommodate points of strain. Mark and make the neckband buttonhole and button carefully to avoid gaping. See pages 303-313 for tips on buttons and buttonholes. For a button-down collar, anchor it with button and buttonhole at center back (horizontal) and on each point where it falls on the shirt front (vertical). For two-button cuffs, make horizontal buttonholes, moving the lower one in about ¼" for a better fit. For French cuffs, make four horizontal buttonholes.

Tailoring Tips for Pants

A quality pair of pants must combine perfect fit and durability—follow these construction tips from the best tailors to achieve your goal. Pants are one of the easiest garments to sew, but are the hardest to fit. Work out your fitting needs in a muslin, see pages 414-415 for basic information. The few hours used to make a muslin will return double-fold—your sewing time will be cut considerably and every pair of pants will fit perfectly.

Basic Construction Procedures

Take some of the frustration out of pants and construction by working as much on the flat as possible. These pointers suggested will allow you to proceed faster. Be sure to use strong, tightly-woven cotton poplin or blend for pockets and waistband facing—avoid traditional lining fabrics as they may not withstand the rigorous use.

POCKETS: Add pockets to pants back and front; then stitch the outseam (inserting any pocket). Follow your pattern's sewing guide for pocket placement and basic construction.

Instead of French seamed pocket edges, you can stitch pockets right sides together along the ⅝″ seamline then zigzag ¼″ away. Trim close to the zigzagging (1). Or, trim seam allowance to ¼″; bind the raw edge with double fold bias binding or bias hem tape (2). Remember, pockets must be sturdy and last the life of the garment.

FLY AND WAISTBAND: These are sewn to the pants in conjunction with one another—the fly can be more easily inserted with flat construction. Therefore, *do not* stitch inseam or crotch seam at this time.

Fly: Turn under right front seam allowance ⅜″ clipping to fold at symbol; baste and press. For leg reinforcements, cut two sections of pocket fabric as indicated, using pants front as a guide. Baste in place and overcast the raw edges together (3). Interface left fly, if desired, and clean-finish outer edge; stitch to the left front, ending at symbol. Clip pants to symbol; press seam toward facing; and understitch (4). Turn to inside; press.

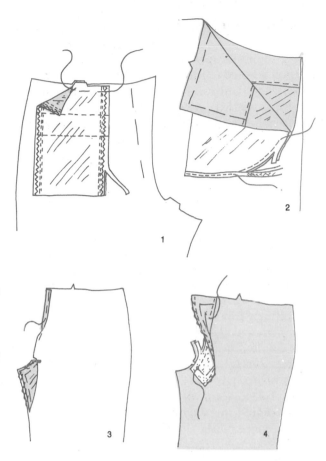

Place closed zipper face up along the turned-in edge with zipper stop ¼″ above symbol; baste. Bring left front over zipper, matching centers; baste (5). (Note: zipper may extend above opening.) On inside, open out left fly; baste zipper in place, keeping garment free. Stitch zipper to left fly, close to teeth and again at tape edge (6). Release basting. Interface right fly, if desired. On inside, place fly over zipper, with raw edges even; pin. On outside, open zipper, baste through all thicknesses, keeping right front free (7).

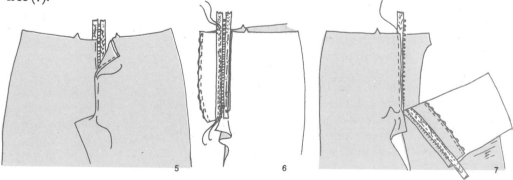

Waistband: Follow these instructions for a professionally made 1½″ wide waistband (a purchased waistband facing may be used). To adapt waistband, extend left front about 2½″ beyond the center front seamline; for a self-faced waistband, make a ⅝″ seam allowance beyond the foldline on the unnotched edges. To make facing, fold fabric on the true bias. Cut one 1½″wide folded bias strip the length of each waistband, plus 2″ for a pleat, and two single layer bias strips 1⅝″ wide and the length of each waistband.

Stitch waistband to pants right and left half matching symbols, opening out left facing. Trim seam to ⅜″; press open. Cut off excess zipper tape (1).

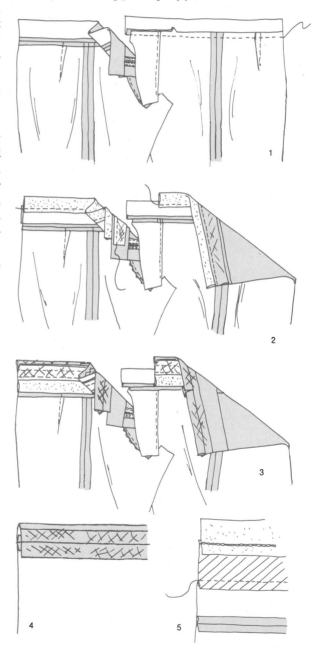

Pin two single bias layers to each waistband section, ending facing at *right* waistband center front and 1″ beyond zipper seam on *left* waistband. Baste in place using a ¼″ seam. Then cut a straight grain strip of interfacing 3½″ wide and the waistband length. Fold in half lengthwise; press. Place interfacing over the basted seam, with one end at center front and back edges even, with raw edges extending ¼″ over the basted seam. Stitch facing strips and interfacing to waistband sections through all thicknesses along the basted seam (2).

Keeping interfacing free, pin the raw edges of the folded bias strip to the facing strips already attached, forming 1″ deep pleats over each outseam; stitch in a ⅝″ seam (3). Turn waistband to inside ⅜″ from seam; turn facing and interfacing down. Press first facing seam allowances down; the second seam allowances up (4). Facing is anchored when belt loops are added.

To apply purchased facing, adapt waistband pieces and face each section between the areas suggested above. Keeping interfacing free, pin facing to the waistband sections, using a ¼″ seam allowance on the waistband (5). Reposition interfacing; turn waistband to inside ⅜″ above the seam, and facing down. Press. To complete waistband and fly see next page.

Complete fly and waistband: If necessary, adapt *right* fly facing or lining, adding the width of the waistband plus ⅝″ to the upper edge and a 2″-3″ long extension, about 1¼″ wide to the lower edge for crotch reinforcement. Cut from pocket fabric, making it double; fold in half lengthwise or stitch the long edges together. Keeping the raw edges even, stitch the lining to the right fly across the top of the waistband, continuing down the side edge to the symbol. Trim and grade seam (1). Turn to the inside; press. Stitch inseam, and then crotch seam between facing edge and front symbols (not shown). On the outside, position extension over front crotch curve, turning in the end ½″ at the inseam; baste free edges in place. From outside, stitch zipper in place, permanently catching lining in stitching; start at waistband seam and end at crotch seam (2). On the inside, stitch edges of crotch reinforcement to seam allowances only; keep pants free (3).

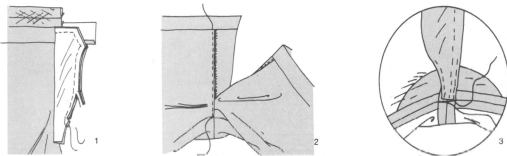

Press center back seam open for about 10″ and turn in ends of facing diagonally; press. Turn facing to the inside and tack facing to back seam. Turn left fly and waistband to inside; slipstitch waistband edges together (4). On the outside stitch along stitching line to hold left fly facing in place, forming a triangle at the end for reinforcement (5).

Prepare belt loops, page 323, substituting two rows of machine stitching for slipstitching. Add the belt loops by machine as shown (6). Fasten opening with appropriate closures.

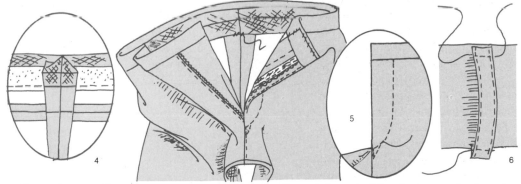

Smooth, even ***hems*** on pants are the result of careful work. Match the method to the fabric; for example, knits and lightweight fabrics may need interfaced hems. Refer to pages 338-340 and choose the hemming procedure most suitable.

Pants with flat, sharp-looking ***cuffs*** look especially well tailored. If your pattern does not have cuffs, establish the outseam length (page 414), then allow twice the desired cuff width, retaining a 1″ hem. The trick for perfect cuffs is to make the upper edge a bit wider than pants leg, so the pants legs do not wrinkle. Interface cuffs in fabrics such as knits to prevent them from collapsing. Cut bias strips the cuff width plus 1¼″; center strips over the outer cuff layer and baste. Machine stitch interfacing in place a scant ⅛″

above the foldline and below the hemline. Stitch the leg seam; taper from the knee to the hemline reducing the circumference of the lower edge. Then taper stitching back to the seamline at the cuff foldline. Continue the seams below the foldline to match the pant leg. Press seams open, clipping if necessary (1). Complete cuff same as for the cut in one with the sleeve, page 290, steps 2, 3, and 4. A zigzag finish may be sustituted for the clean finish suggested.

Press carefully, forming crease. Then secure the cuffs to the pants with French tacks at the seams (2) or stitch on the outside directly in the seams (3).

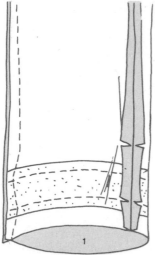

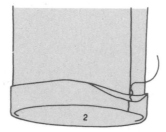

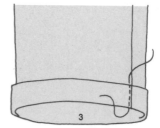

Making a Man's Jacket

Your good sewing techniques will set the stage for a great-looking man's jacket. Review Tailoring, pages 352-373 and make a muslin fitting garment as reputable tailors do—refer to pages 413-415 for suggestions when working out fitting problems. First we will consider a hand-tailored jacket with modifications, then on pages 432-434 you will find machine techniques for fully washable jackets.

A Hand-Tailored Jacket

A tailor-perfect jacket starts with the shell and the inner materials—the built-in support of interfacing, tape, shoulder pads, and tailor padding. Remember, jackets with this construction are meant to be dry-cleaned only. There are several interfacing kits available for men's jackets, but to understand their uses, we suggest you make your first jacket as suggested below.

INTERFACING: Match the interfacing's weight and care to the fashion fabric. Interface jacket front as indicated by your pattern—make any darts in the interfacing (page 357). *Important Fitting Checkpoint:* Baste darts and seams in jacket front and finger-press. Pin interfacing in place; baste along center front and lapel roll line. Baste the jacket shell together. Try on with shoulder pads; make sure interfacing and fabric are molding as one (page 357). Mark any droop across the chest near the armholes. Check pocket position; mark changes. Release basting to separate the back and front.

Next, add *tailor padding* to the front interfacing (see page 359); do not cover breast pocket markings. Then, stitch and press seams or darts in jacket front. Working over a tailor's ham with the fashion fabric uppermost, tailor baste (page 206) interfacing to jacket front, starting at the shoulder edge (see sketch 1 on next page).

428

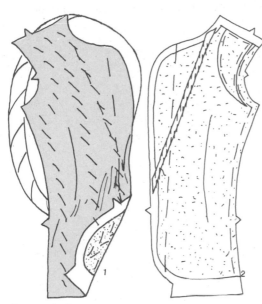

TAPING: Twill tape is used in men's tailoring—½" wide for lapels and straight edges, and ¼" wide for armholes and neck curves. Be sure to pre-shrink twill tape. Ribbon seam binding is a good substitute. See pages 361-362 for taping.

The tape on the lapel roll line is called the **bridle.** Cut tape the length of the line on pattern, marking where tape falls on seamlines. Pin front edge securely; now make bridle ⅜" shorter between seamlines; pin securely, distributing fullness evenly—this will hold lapel closer to the body and prevent stretching. Diagonal tack (page 358) both edges of bridle to interfacing (2). Now padstitch lapel; press to set padstitches as explained for undercollar, page 361.

Next, tape shoulder and front edges. When taping front edges, make the tape ⅜" shorter below the waist and ease jacket to tape (jacket will lie closer to the body). Interfacing should not be caught in the seam.

Make all *pockets* (pages 298-302) in jacket front before joining the back sections. *Stitch jacket shell together,* with any fitting changes. If vents need extra support, see page 367. Staystitch neck edge through lapel markings; then tape neck and armhole edge.

PREPARE UNDERCOLLAR: The steps for the undercollar will depend on the type of fabric—tailors use a French melton. If it is not available, use your fashion fabric. Fuse a scrap of underlining to stabilize an area of loosely-woven or knitted fashion fabric before cutting out the undercollar. Stitch, trim, and press any center back seam; join interfacing at center back (page 359). Pin interfacing to the undercollar along neck edges. Backstitch interfacing to the undercollar along roll line to prevent stretching. Over a tailor's ham, form a sharp crease along the roll line; a pounder and steam may be used (1).

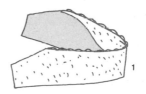

Padstitch the stand from neck edge to roll line (see page 360), but *do not* padstitch remainder of undercollar as instructed for women. Instead, start at the center back and work rows from the roll line to the outer edge, fanning the rows to the points (2). Trim away interfacing if it is seen from the outside. Press undercollar to set padstitches. Allow to dry.

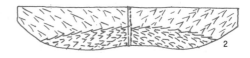

Felling Stitch: This is a hand stitch used by tailors to ensure a flat seam when using a raw edge. Make a vertical stitch over the raw edge inserting the needle at the angle indicated to start the next stitch. Make stitches about 3/16″ long and 1/8″ apart (1).

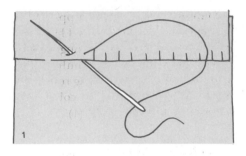

ATTACH UNDERCOLLAR: Baste undercollar to jacket matching symbols, placing neck edge along jacket neck seamline or as indicated by pattern. Sew undercollar to jacket with felling stitch, clipping jacket neck edge to staystitching if necessary (2).

Important Fitting Checkpoint: Try on jacket matching centers and button markings; lap *left* over right and pin. The collar should be high in the back; the outer edge of the undercollar should cover the neck seam and hug the shirt collar smoothly. To make undercollar and lapels lie correctly, stretch the outer edge of the undercollar, working each side from the center back to the corner as shown (3). Crease lapel roll for about 1″ where it meets the undercollar roll. This will help you set the perfect foundation for upper collar and lapels. *Do not* proceed until you have a perfectly set undercollar and lapels, with smooth, unbroken roll and symmetrical notch placement. Make any changes needed.

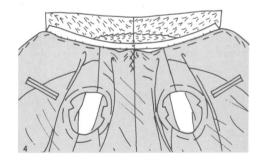

LAPEL AND UPPER COLLAR: First, stitch *front facings to front lining sections,* ending at symbol near hem edge (or about 4″ above hem); add the inside pocket before continuing. Then assemble the remainder of the lining, with the exception of the sleeves; staystitch lining neck edges. Next, join the facing and lining unit to the jacket front, making a minute pin tuck in the lapel area as explained on page 363, step 3, before stitching the seam. Press seam open over point presser, then trim, grade, clip, and notch seam allowances. Turn facing and lining right sides out, tailor baste, and press the finished edges only.

Now, shape the facing over the lapels and pin near seamline. Turn in the neck edge where it falls and turn in lining along seamline, clipping where necessary. Baste and pin folded edge in place (4).

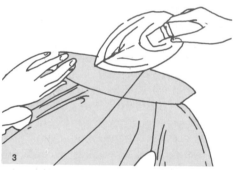

Reinforce neck edge of upper collar through shoulder markings. Then place it over the undercollar, wrong sides together, matching neck seamline; pin. Smooth stand and pin along roll, tailor baste. Now shape upper collar over outer area; pin and baste (1).

For *loose* or *thin* fabrics, enclose raw edges of undercollar with seam allowances of upper collar; baste close to fold. Miter corners and trim to reduce bulk, and trim edges evenly; baste and press. Secure with felling stitch (2).

For *thick* or *firm* fabrics, or French melton, turn in outer edges and ends so they extend a scant $\frac{1}{8}''$ beyond the undercollar; baste close to fold. Remove upper collar, press edges; miter and trim corners to reduce bulk. Repin upper collar into position; baste along stand and the outer edges. Sew collars together with felling stitches (3).

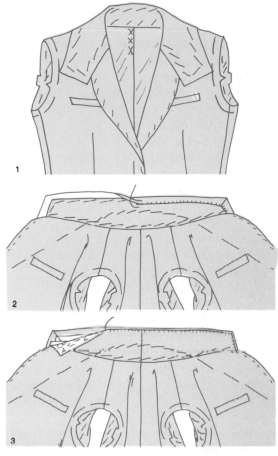

For both methods, the next step is to complete the *gorgeline* (the seam where the upper collar meets the lapels). Turn collar in to meet edge of lapel; pin, then baste.

Important Fitting Checkpoint: Try on jacket to check gorgeline; collar and lapels should lie smoothly without wrinkles or bubbles. Make necessary changes and mark folds of collar and lapel where they meet. Trim lapel seam allowance to $\frac{1}{4}''$; turn in and baste. Next clip upper collar neck edge to shoulder marking and blindstitch back neck edge to jacket. Then trim collar seam allowance to $\frac{1}{4}''$ (1). Now form the gorgeline carefully, turning under the collar seam allowance so it meets exactly the folded edge of the lapel; sew the gorgeline together with a backstitch (2). Slipstitch neck edge of lining in place.

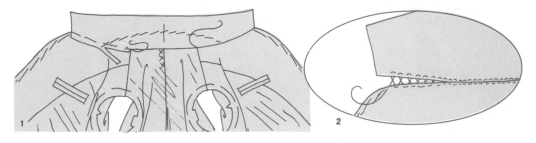

HEMS AND SLEEVES: Make jacket and lining *hems* following pattern on pages 367-369. Review pages 364-366 for pointers on sleeve finishes. Before inserting complete *sleeve,* make and attach sleeve lining as indicated on page 372, sketch 4 and 373, sketch 2.

Important Fitting Checkpoint: Baste sleeve into armhole and fit before inserting permanently, as instructed on page 366. Insert sleeve padding and try on jacket, positioning shoulder pads correctly; the edge of the shoulder pad should line up with the armhole seam allowance edges. Pin pad in place from the outside (see page 366). *Never* trim shoulder pads to conform with the seam allowance edges. Catchstitch shoulder pad to front interfacing and sew the armhole edge securely to the seam allowances. Then baste lining in armhole forming a pleat at each side of the shoulder seam to eliminate excess fabric. Insert sleeve lining as shown on page 373, sketch 1.

FINISHING: Make keyhole buttonholes (pages 312) on the *left jacket front,* cording them (page 313) for a tailored touch. Sew on buttons (page 304-305).

As a couture touch you may want to put decorative tacks (page 396) at the ends of the pockets or work a row of saddle stitching (page 395) along the front edges and collar.

A Machine Tailored Jacket

The following tips will help create a durable, washable jacket. This *unstructured* construction will save time—shaping materials are handled differently to withstand laundering; machine methods are substituted for hand-sewing wherever possible—and can be used for fabrics that require dry cleaning, too. Remember that every item—notions, interfacings, lining—must be washable and require the same care as your fashion fabric.

CONSTRUCTION TIPS: Any jacket pattern can be adapted to this easier way of construction. For speed, fuse interfacing to the *jacket front* with one of the fusible agents, or use an iron-on interfacing (see charts pages 80-85). If you want to catch the interfacing in the seams, *add ⅝″ seam allowance* to the front and neck edges of the front interfacing if they were eliminated in the pattern—it will be held down by the buttonholes and buttons.

Before attaching interfacing, tape the front edges (page 429) using a straight or zigzag stitch. If tailor padding (page 359) is needed, zigzag or straight stitch in place by machine. High-loft non-woven interfacing is great for this and can replace shoulder pads. When interfacing is positioned, attach the bridle (page 429); omit diagonal tacking and substitute a row of machine stitching through all thicknesses along edge next to roll line.

The interior can be *lined* or *unlined.* Consider the time spent constructing a lining against clean-finishing each exposed seam, or facing and hem edges. For *lining,* stitch front facing and front lining section together to within 4″-6″ of lower edge. Add a patch pocket; if desired, then complete lining. Stitch back pleat for 2″ at neck and waist; insert sleeve by machine. For an *unlined* jacket, purchase extra fabric. Cut two additional fronts, instead of using the front facing piece, to cover the front interfacing and shoulder pads; make a self-fabric cover for the back of the shoulder pads. Finish the exposed seam allowances, facing and hem edges using seam finishes on pages 219-221. Self-finishing seams are the flat-fell or welt seam (page 221). The simulated French (page 218) or the seam for knits (page 187) are good for permanent press fabrics. Many firmly woven or knitted fabrics may need only topstitched seams (page 220) for a durable finish.

COLLAR AND LAPELS: This technique works equally well on all fabric weights, but *you must add a ⅝″ seam allowance to all edges of the undercollar* if it has been eliminated for hand-tailoring by the pattern. To stabilize the undercollar and interfacing, substitute a row of machine stitches for the back stitches along the roll line, page 429, then shape as directed. Replace padstitching with machine stitches ending stitches at seamlines as shown (1). A tailoring technique used by manufacturers—eliminate padstitching on the lapels; when the facing is completed, fuse the facing to the jacket between the bridle and the outer edges.

To begin this type of collar, first staystitch the jacket neck edge. Then pin the undercollar to the jacket, clipping jacket neck edge as needed. Stitch neck seam between the symbols. Trim seam allowances to ¼″; press open (2). Now stitch the upper collar to the facing/lining unit or facing unit in the same manner as for the undercollar. Do not trim seam: press it open (3).

With right sides together, pin the facing/collar unit to the jacket matching neck seamlines; baste neck edges together. Now fit the jacket *wrong side out* so the upper collar is on top and the front facing edges are next to the body. Shape upper collar and lapel facing over the undercollar and jacket lapels, maintaining shape of undercollar and lapel roll. Pin collar, lapel, and front edges together as they fall; the undercollar and garment lapel edges may extend beyond upper collar and lapel edges (4).

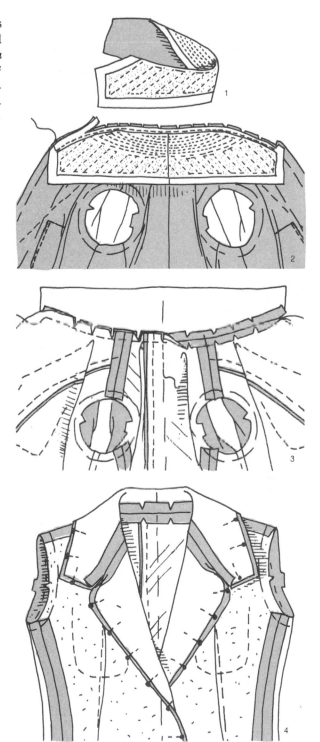

433

Stitch collar edges together between markings along undercollar seamline, stretching or easing (keep neck seam allowances free). Now stitch facing to garment between marking using garment seamlines. Trim, grade, clip, or notch seam (1). Remove neck basting and turn garment right side out. Press edges favoring upper collar; lapel to end of roll; then favor jacket below. Topstitch ¼″ from front, lapel, and collar edges to hold them in place.

Complete *sleeves* including the hem. For the unlined jacket, some lightweight fabrics look well with a machine stitched hem. To insert sleeves and place shoulder pads, see page 366. Sew shoulder pads securely to the front interfacing and the armhole seam allowances.

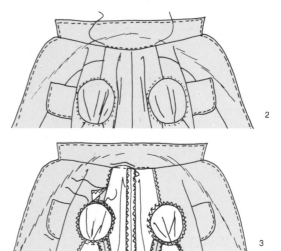

For a lined jacket, match neck seams and stitch in seam between shoulders. Anchor shoulder pads securely to front interfacing and hold the armholes in place with a prickstitch (page 209) making tiny stitches about ½″ apart in the seam (2).

For an unlined jacket, turn in neck edges ⅝″ and sew to jacket by hand or machine. Anchor shoulder and side edges of front facing to the back seam allowances *only* by hand or machine. Then clean-finish armhole seam (3).

Note: There are other collar methods that will work equally well for an unstructured jacket that will look well after laundering. The rolled collar pages 263-265 works well for thin, lightweight fabrics. But do not use it for heavier or bulky fabrics as the collar will be sandwiched between jacket and facing, forcing the seam allowances in one direction. This may cause an unsightly ridge on the gorgeline. The notched collar pages 265-266 may be used for any fabric weight. The tailored collar techniques pages 362-364 are especially good for medium, heavyweight, or bulky fabrics.

FINISHING: Complete the jacket hems, finishing corners as suggested on pages 367-368. Complete lining hem by the free hanging method pages 371-372 for easier pressing.

Make hand- or machine-worked keyhole buttonholes (pages 311-312) in the *left front* and sew buttons (pages 304-305) securely to the *right front.*

Now a final pressing is in order—see page 347. With your jacket completed in record time, you should be happy—the jacket will be able to withstand rigorous wear and give you many hours of pleasure—why not make another in a different fabric!

Custom Fitting Menswear

For a sleek, trim fit, men have had their ready-to-wear shirts and pants "tailored" by the experts. Now you can do the same—make the provisions on the pattern before cutting out your fashion or do it at the fitting stage.

Tapering a Shirt

A natty look starts with a body-fitting shirt—do not over-fit. To remove excess fabric, add double-pointed contour darts (page 224) in front and back. At seams, decrease waist and hips. Divide the amount to be reduced evenly between darts and seams. Transfer fitting needs to pattern pieces as shown.

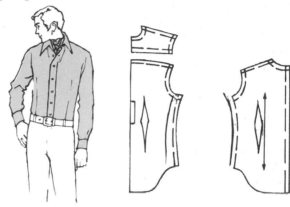

Custom-Fitting Pants

Since the revolution in men's clothing is upon us, pants can be worn exactly as the man decrees—for a trim fit there are two ways to remove the unwanted excess fabric.

BACK-FITTED CONTOURING: This technique creates ultra-tight fitting pants—do not over-fit. Turn the back crease into a fitted seam from waist to hem. Baste, keeping fold on straight grain if possible and test; seam will vary in depth. Transfer to pattern price.

TAPERED PANT LEGS: Turn straight-legged pants into slim-fitting ones—do not over-fit. First, mark the knee level on each leg, then divide the amount to be reduced evenly between the inseam and the outseam. Decrease as indicated above and below the knee. For bell bottoms, taper gradually from the knee to the original width at the hem. Transfer fitting needs to front and back pattern pieces as shown for the back.

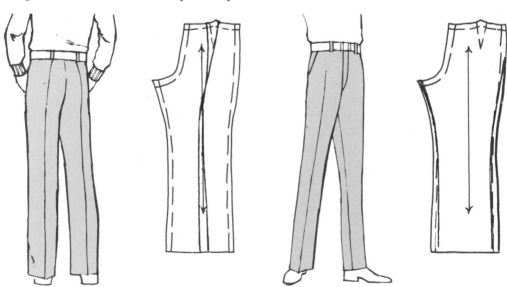

BOOK V

Niceties
and
Necessities

Planning
A Creative Environment

Certainly you have dreamed of a sewing room, a place where those unfinished projects can lie undisturbed until the time arises to pick them up again. Of course, not everyone is able to furnish an entire room to satisfy her sewing whims; small apartments, growing families, and budget requirements constitute the main stumbling blocks. Don't despair! Rise to action and claim a space somewhere for your very own. Nothing sparks your creativity as much as a special place to sew with carefully organized sewing equipment stored within easy reach. Sewing will suddenly become more fun as the annoying, time-consuming task of finding a place to sew is eliminated.

Choose an area with several considerations in mind. Especially important is accessibility to electrical outlets and adequate lighting. Also, think about the noise factor; will the sound of your machine distract others? And, try to find a place where you can locate yourself without interfering with the activities of the other members of the household.

Once that "where shall I sew" decision has been made, the exact arrangements can be completed. Even if you have the luxury of a large area, try not to waste a single inch with superfluous or ill-arranged equipment. Plan carefully so that everything fits away as neatly as the pieces of a jigsaw puzzle. In addition, examine your sewing habits to determine the most efficient arrangement of your tools. We show just three sewing areas, but remember that the possibilities for providing creative sewing space are unlimited once you have thoughtfully evaluated your specific needs and available space.

SEWING NOOK may be the ideal solution if your only available space is a blank wall or a bare corner. Simply apply a little handiwork to create a versatile sewing arrangement. Place a small table against the wall and suspend a pegboard above. Stash sewing equipment which can't be hung on the board in a small chest. Locate it next to your table to provide greater working surface. For additional storage, purchase a variety of rattan baskets and chests to hold your fabrics and other bulky items. Find space in a nearby closet for your unfinished garments, ironing board, and portable sewing machine. Once the materials have been organized, coordinate the décor with the rest of the room for an attractive addition to your home.

A CLOSET *(right)* may provide a perfect opportunity to create a sewing haven. Inside, place shelving for your sewing equipment. Hinge one end of a large board to the lower shelf and use a chest the appropriate height mounted on wheels to support the opposite end. It will serve as storage space for your sewing machine and roll neatly into the lower portion of the closet when the board is folded up and the door is closed. Voilà! You now possess a convenient and compact sewing area.

SHARING A ROOM *(below)* with your husband's hobby or with guest accommodations may be the closest you will come to having a sewing hideaway of your own. Take advantage of the space to build storage cabinets and handy conveniences directly into the structure of the room, such as the bookcase/divider shown. Half of the case serves the needs of the den, while the other portion provides necessary space for your books, patterns, additional small tools, etc. Easy accessibility to all your equipment is an absolute must and the shelves placed against the wall are a beautiful solution. Use them for your bulkier items and avoid dust with colorful roll-up shades. Add decorative touches to make your work more enjoyable.

Have the suggestions on the previous pages inspired any great ideas of your own? We haven't given detailed information, just intriguing thoughts to set your mind in motion. Hopefully, you now realize that despite limited space there is always a way to make accommodations for your creative adventures. First conscientiously examine your work habits to devise ways of saving steps, time, and space. Try to keep your ironing board readily accessible, a full length mirror only a glance away, and your small tools within arms-length. Think of the other tasks which may be performed there so you can plan accordingly—perhaps your personal correspondence. With a little thought you will be surprised at all the truly practical methods you can imagine to make your area fulfill all your sewing requirements, be it an entire room or a nook in your bedroom.

To simplify the planning of your sewing area and to stimulate your own ingenuity, here are some necessities for optimum sewing conditions:

- [ ] Be sure to have good lighting, both natural and artificial. You should include an overhead light for general lighting and a high-intensity lamp for a direct beam to make small detail work easier.
- [ ] Convenient outlets for all your electrical equipment are obvious necessities. An extension cord should also be available when needed for electric scissors, steam pressing on dress form, etc.
- [ ] You will also need a cutting table. The ideal table should be accessible from all 4 sides, hard-surfaced, and high enough to avoid stooping or bending while cutting.
- [ ] Your sewing machine area should be at least wide enough to enable free movement of your fabric and room to place your tools.
- [ ] To provide proper support during either hand or machine stitching, select a comfortable chair with a straight back.
- [ ] Organize a carefully planned system of roll-out drawers, see-through storage boxes and cases for threads, trims, etc., to avoid wasting valuable time in search for a needed item.
- [ ] A totable box to move equipment from one work area to another can be another real time-saver.
- [ ] You will also need a large storage area in which large pieces of fabric or incompleted projects can be laid flat.
- [ ] A pressing area near your machine and storage space is a must.
- [ ] Provide closet space for hanging nearly finished projects and clothes requiring repair.
- [ ] Have a full-length mirror near adequate lighting for admiring your handiwork. The 3-way variety is ideal, especially for fitting.
- [ ] Choose a soft color and bright accents for a cheerful atmosphere. Strive for easy cleanability.
- [ ] Ample waste facilities under the machine area and near the cutting table will keep your lovely area neat.

Try to consolidate your wishes with the suggestions given above to create your very own sewing world. Even if its just a corner of a room, your ingenuity can make it a warm haven for producing dozens of fashionable masterpieces. Don't limit your shopping to the sewing notions counters, but browse in every department to complete your dream of a sewing sanctuary. After all, anything to which you devote so much of yourself certainly deserves to have special consideration.

The Ultimate Luxury

Exercise your cherished decorating fancies to create a sewing room
you will love to be in—a private haven that will restore your spirits and spark
your initiative . . . Fill it with your favorite colors, your prettiest
things—a special chair, a treasured needlepoint picture, an imaginative vase . . .
A cheerful studio will be a background for your most creative moments.

Photos courtesy of House and Garden Magazine

Whether you sew for artistic expression, for fun, or for a gala event the day after tomorrow, you must have dreamed of the ultimate luxury—a place away from the rest of the house, thoughtfully planned for your sole convenience. This sewing studio, designed for a space of 12 by 15 feet — the size of an average bedroom — has all the features that make sewing easier and more enjoyable: plentiful and well directed lighting, abundant space, large flat table, counter surfaces, and practical, carefully planned storage. It is equipped for everything from the initial cutting to the final pressing —your dream realized.

Arranged to accommodate all your spare-time diversions beautifully and efficiently, this ideal offers many practical suggestions . . . Closet space harbors all your sewing essentials . . . a spacious cutting table is designed for comfort and marked off in a handy 6-inch grid.

Plastic drawers unclutter your sewing paraphernalia, and the doors on a convenient counter enclose your sewing machine and neatly secure all its attachments . . . Full-length mirrors reflect your handiwork . . .

How to Build the Cutting Table

Here is the cutting table shown on the preceding pages. The ideal example of a cutting surface, it is designed a generous 3 by 6 feet, made a comfortable 36 inches high, and mounted on lockable casters. Note the handy drop-leaf shelf at each end that holds yardage as you lay and cut out. The cutting table can be wheeled back under the special projects shelf where it will extend only one foot into the sewing studio shown previously.

Anyone with some experience in woodworking and a reasonably good supply of tools should be able to make this cutting table without difficulty. The key to success is precision in measuring. You may find it difficult to come closer than 1/8" to a 15/16" dimension, but try. Remember, just the width of a pencil line may be important.

Step-by-step Instructions

1. From ¾ inch birch plywood (ask for "good one-side" grade) cut out bottom shelf and cutting top to exact dimensions.

2. Cut four legs and notch tops as indicated in sketch.

3. Screw bottom shelf to legs and hold rigid with clamps, if necessary, during assembly.

4. Screw edges to bottom shelf. All screws and nails should be counter-sunk.

5. Place cutting top on top of legs and attach with screws.

6. For the cutting top, screw four pieces of the edging to the top.

7. Attach fold-out shelves with swing-out metal arms (you will need four).

8. Turn table on side and attach four lockable casters.

9. Turn table upright and paint two coats of semigloss.

10. Glue 12-by-12 inch vinyl tiles to top. If you should find the tiles a fraction of an inch undersized, adjust space so you don't end up with a wide crack at one end.

11. Score 6-inch grid with felt-tipped pen.

12. Add numbers: paint with stencil or apply press type numbers from a kit and cover with clear lacquer.

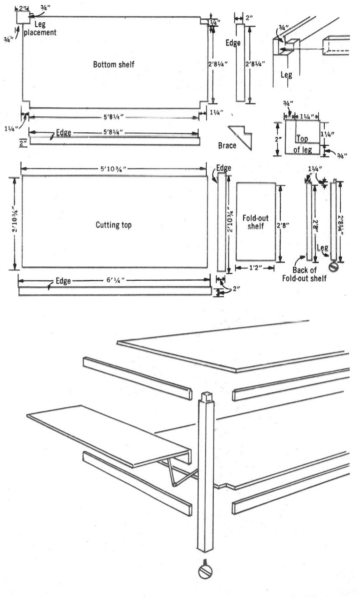

Tools
to Satisfy
Every Sewing Need

A vast assortment of tools and gadgets have been manufactured to serve the woman who sews. Each one has been carefully designed to save time and simplify construction. You should begin by acquiring tools according to your immediate needs (shears, steam iron, etc.) and then start to purchase those extra handy time savers that are constantly appearing on the market. The more basic items will be your only expenditure in the very beginning, while the more complicated tools will become necessary as your skill and interest increases. Thus, your purchases will be spread out as you go along.

Because your equipment is essential to your sewing success, it must be of good quality and always kept in the peak of working order. Experiment with various types of equipment and see which one is best for you. If possible, it is wise to test the tool before you purchase it to be sure the parts are working smoothly. Most importantly, give each tool the same scrupulous attention you would give any other household appliance and there will be no need to buy replacements.

To save yourself time and confusion, have your equipment stored systematically in categories, making each item readily accessible at all times. Keep together all your marking equipment, your fastenings, your thread, and so on. Having them handy will accelerate your work and increase your accuracy. If you follow this advice, it will be easy to get into the habit of using the right tool at the proper time.

Use the following guide as a reference when purchasing your equipment. We have carefully sorted through the extensive variety of tools sold, creating a list of those you should have to sew correctly without needing to improvise. Turn to the following pages to find each item individually described in detail. The illustration on each page is designed to present a fairly complete cross section of all the equipment available.

Bent Handle Shears	Thimble
Scissors	Dressmaker's Silk Pins
Tapemeasure	Pin Cushion
Ruler	Steam Iron
Yardstick	Ironing Board
Tracing Wheel	Press Cloths
Dressmaker's Tracing Paper	Tailor's Ham or Press Mitt
Tailor's Chalk	Full Length Mirror
Seam Gauge	Needles
Assortment of Thread	Extension Cord
Sewing Machine	Waste Container

Measuring

Measuring tools are among the most important items in your sewing box. Good quality equipment and correct usage will assure you of a better fitting garment. Be sure you have a variety available to avoid the temptation to guess or the need to substitute. The key to success is to measure often and accurately.

Tapemeasures are indispensable. They should be 60″ long with metal tips and made of a material that will not stretch, preferably fiberglass. It will be most helpful if the numbers, in inches or centimeters, are clearly printed on both sides. Look to see that the smaller denominations are noted on the tape. Bi-coloring is another helpful feature.

Rulers are necessary for all your sewing projects. You must have at least one 12″ to 18″ long and one 5″ to 6″ long. They can be found in a variety of materials. If you select wood, keep in mind that it may warp. It should have a metal edge for accuracy. The plastic see-through type easily retains its straight edges, is well suited for buttonholes, pleats, etc., and can readily serve all your needs. The numbers should be clearly indicated.

Yardsticks are invaluable for general marking purposes. They should be made of shellacked hard wood or metal. Those made of metal are the most sturdy.

Sewing Gauge is a small 6″ metal or plastic ruler with a sliding indicator. It is ideal for quick, accurate measurment of hems, buttonholes, and pleats.

Dressmaker's Gauge is another small handy marking tool. One side is straight for marking tucks and pleats, the other is scalloped for marking scallops, etc.

Hem Aid is an all-purpose hemming gauge. It is generally made of lightweight metal with one gradually curved edge designed to accommodate the shape of your hems. The different hem depths are clearly indicated on its surface. The straight edges are also marked in inches to provide yet another measuring tool.

T-Squares can be made of either clear plastic or metal. The most practical for the home sewer extends 9″ with a 4″ T-span. Use the T-square for straightening grain, locating opposite grains, altering your pattern tissue, or for other marking tasks.

Skirt Marker is the quickest, easiest, and most accurate way to mark hems. There are several types: pin, chalk, and a combination of both. The pin marker is more precise but does require the assistance of another person, which is not necessary for the chalk variety with a blower on a tube. A skirt marker that combines pin and chalk allows you to have the best qualities of both. Be sure the base is heavy and steady and that the marker extends high enough to be suitable for all your fashion lengths.

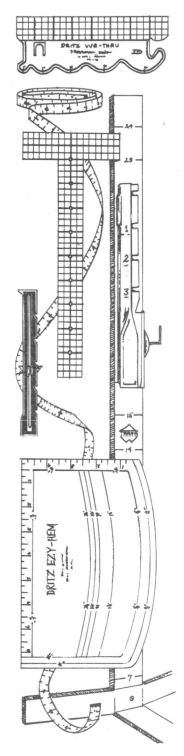

Cutting

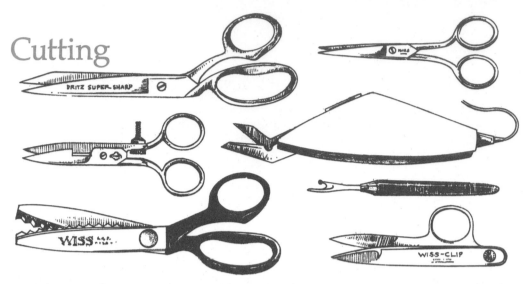

We cannot stress enough how vital it is to be accurate when cutting out the individual pieces of your garment. An even edge, an obvious notch, and a true curve will make sewing much simpler. Remember as you cut that an eighth- or quarter-inch slip can endanger a potentially sleek fit.

When purchasing shears or scissors, look for hot drop-forged steel or extra strong molybdenum which has been coated with nickel for protection and chrome plated to prevent rusting. Test the mechanism to be sure the scissors work smoothly and cut sharply from the back of the blades to the point. Quality shears are put together with an adjustable screw to allow the user to adjust the "run" of the shears to her particular feel.

You will find that your cutting equipment requires a certain amount of attention to maintain its high quality. Shears and scissors should be lubricated and periodically sharpened. Oil the screw portion with sewing machine oil and wipe with a soft cloth. You may sharpen them at home or send them back to the manufacturer for any necessary repairs.

Keep in mind that cutting paper heavier than tissue will dull the blades.

Dressmaking Shears are bent-handle shears with 7" or 8" blades hinged with a screw. The two differently shaped handles accommodate more fingers and yield better control. The bent handles are preferred because the fabric can rest flat on the table when being cut. Left-handed shears are also available.

Scissors have small round handles and are used for more delicate cutting and trimming. Have one pair 5" to 6" long and a second pair 3½" to 4" for buttonholes and small detail work.

Pinking or Scalloping Shears are used to finish raw edges of fabrics which do not ravel easily. Select 7½" to 9" blades with a ball bearing pivot. The blades are not easily sharpened; therefore, cut with caution.

Cutting Area should be a large flat area preferably about 38" high, at least 36" wide, and 6' to 8' long. Ideally the area should be accessible from four sides to facilitate layout and cutting.

Electric Scissors are available with or without a cord for fast, comfortable cutting on light and medium weight fabrics. Be sure they are small enough to hold comfortably.

Seam Ripper is a simple and safe pen-like device that allows careful ripping of adjustments and mistakes. Never, never use a razor blade as a substitute.

Thread Clips are a scissor variation with short blades and an inner spring mechanism to keep them apart. They fit neatly into your hand and are used with a clipping motion to cut stray threads quickly and easily.

Buttonhole Scissors are constructed to allow you to begin cutting within the body of the fabric. A screw and nut arrangement makes it possible to set the blades to cut only a prescribed length.

Marking

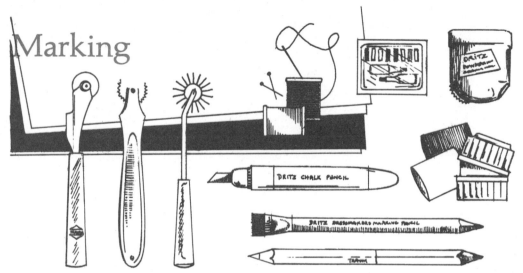

Marking plays an important role in the construction process. Haphazard stitching of seams and darts or arbitrary placement of collars, pockets, etc., caused by incorrect markings will unquestionably yield unfavorable results. The pattern tissue has specific construction lines and symbols printed on its surface for you to transfer to your garment pieces. If you have been accurate in marking these guidelines, construction will be greatly simplified and errors kept to a minimum.

Since you will be working with many varieties of fabric, from lush woolens to transparent voiles, you should have on hand the accompanying types of marking equipment.

Tracing Wheels come in several types. A dull serrated edge is best for most fabrics. Delicate or smooth fabrics require a plain, unserrated edge and may be marked by impression without using tracing paper. For heavy fabrics with smooth textures, a needlepoint wheel makes a more definite mark. Plushy and transparent surfaces call for tailor's tacks.

Dressmaker's Tracing Paper is a form of carbon paper. It is used in conjunction with a tracing wheel to transfer construction markings. Don't use contrasting colors on light fabrics. Choose a color close to that of your fabric, yet still discernible. Always use white on white fabric. Test color you selected before marking to be sure it is removable, and always mark on the wrong side of your fabric. The double-faced variety is a time-saver when marking two layers of fabric.

Thread for marking should be matched to your fabric and purpose. Glazed mercerized cotton is most widely used for thread tracing, general basting, and tailor's tacks. Silk thread is recommended for fine fabrics and when basting stitches are not to be removed before pressing.

Choose thread in a slightly contrasting color to aid removal.

Tailor's Chalk, found in several colored squares, is ideal for many marking tasks. The type with refillable holder and built-in sharpener is most convenient. Since it may be made of either French chalk or wax, test first to see which type is easiest to remove. Do not use wax chalk on hard-surfaced fabrics because it will be difficult to remove by any method.

Dressmaker's Marking Pencil is practical for most hard-surfaced fabrics. Do have at least one with a brush for erasing the markings. Wax pencils may be used, providing the wax either disappears when you press or is removable by dry cleaning.

Pins should be rustproof stainless steel or brass dressmaker's silk pins. To keep them sharp and rust-free, store them separately from your general household pins. For easily marred, special, or delicate fabrics use a slightly finer size 17 pin. Pins with round, colorful plastic heads are especially easy to see and remove. ✸ Remember that using pins is a fast, accurate, but impermanent method.

Hand Tools

You have probably discovered that a beautiful garment is the natural result of good taste and fine workmanship. This workmanship is not possible without having the proper tools available. Listed are all the tools which will make concentrating on the finest detail a pleasure. Here you will find those needed for hand sewing as well as the specific pieces of equipment which will enable you to perform your hand tasks quicker and easier.

Needles of high quality are necessary for all your hand sewing. Avoid those with blunted points or rough spots. The needles most commonly used for hand sewing come in sizes 1-10, ranging from #1 for coarse work to #10 for fine sewing. Sharps are a commonly used medium length, all-purpose needle. For very fine hand sewing on heavyweight fabrics, use the short, round-eye betweens. Milliner's or straw needles are best for basting and millinery. Buy embroidery or crewel needles for embroidery or other sewing requiring a long eye for easy threading. There are also self-threading needles in an assortment of sizes.

Thread should be selected in a matching shade or one shade darker than your fabric. An assortment of sizes and colors is a must for any sewing kit. Color and size numbers are printed on the spool. Greater numbers denote finer thread, using #50 as a midpoint. Buy mercerized cotton thread for most sewing tasks; button and carpet thread for extremely durable sewing; silk thread for fine fabrics and basting; silk buttonhole twist for decorative stitches and hand-worked buttonholes; and nylon or cotton-covered dacron threads for permanent press and man-made fabrics. Buy the specialty threads as you need them, such as elastic thread or embroidery floss. See the needle and thread chart, pages 92 and 93, and the notions section, page 91, for more specific information.

Pins should include fine rustproof dressmaker's brass or stainless steel silk pins for most of your sewing needs. There are other sizes available for very heavy fabrics or household tasks. Glass head pins have brightly colored plastic heads which are easy to see.

Magnet can be very handy to help you find those pins you dropped as you were working.

Thimble will be needed for painless hand sewing. It should fit snugly on your middle finger. They are available in a range of sizes 6 to 11 for both small and large hands.

Pin Cushions are convenient tools. We suggest having two: the large type for the bulk of your pins with an attached emery bag for sharpening and removing rust from pins and needles; and the wrist variety for quick service while sewing and fitting.

Beeswax should be kept handy in a holder to coat your hand sewing threads. It strengthens the thread and reduces tangling, knotting, and breaking.

Transparent Tape is a boon to the home sewer, as it can serve a multitude of purposes. Use it as a topstitching guide, to mend a torn pattern, or to secure your pattern adjustments.

Loop Turner is a specially designed tool with a latch-hook device at one end. It is used to turn tubing or bias cording to the right side.

Bodkin is used to draw elastic, belting, and cording through casings. The safety pin closing simplifies this task. The ball point bodkin is recommended for turning tubing with a closed end.

Awl or Stiletto is used for making eyelets, keyhole buttonholes, or any other necessary holes. It should have a snug fitting cover for your protection.

Tissue Paper should always be on hand. Use it when stitching those fabrics that may need special treatment to go through the feed dog and presser foot of your machine. The tissue is also used when lengthening your pattern tissue, making alterations, or transferring monograms and designs.

Needle Threader is a little device to help you through those frustrating days when you can't thread your needle.

Pointer and Creaser is a flat wooden tool approximately 4" long. One end is pointed, the other is rounded. The pointed end is for pushing out small corners; the rounded end is used in conjunction with an iron to flatten seamlines or to assist finger pressing.

Tweezers are used to remove tailor's tacks, gathering threads, and basting threads. They are particularly helpful when tiny thread ends remain after ripping out incorrect machine stitching.

Lap Board is used if you wish to work in your chair rather than at a table. It is placed over the arms of the chair. The inner edge next to your body is contoured for your comfort. Frequently a leg device is attached at the outer edge which extends to the floor and supports any pressure you may exert on the lap board.

Embroidery Hoop is a two-part frame. One hoop fits snugly over another to hold a section of fabric taut for embroidery or beading. It can be purchased in both metal or wood and in a variety of sizes and shapes. The wood hoops are intended for crewel work. Select a hoop with a spring mechanism which permits adjustment for various weights of fabric. A cork-lined outer hoop will hold the fabric more securely.

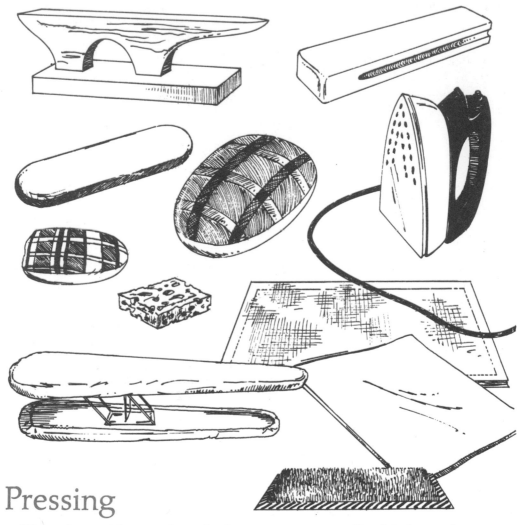

Pressing

The real secret of success in sewing is to press as you sew. Careful, thorough treatment during each stage of construction will result in a good-looking garment that requires only a light touch-up when completed. However, a thorough pressing after the garment is finished will never make up for the step-by-step process you should have done earlier.

You will find that it is quicker and easier to press in units as you sew. For example, stitch and press all darts or all pocket flaps, and so on. Thus, if you have not already made correct pressing a habit, this method of organization will help you begin.

Listed on these two pages are the basic tools you will need to achieve all your pressing goals. Even occasional bursts of sewing require varied pieces of equipment for the different areas of your garment or at least your own substitutes made at home.

Iron you will need for home sewing should combine the characteristics of both a steam iron and a dry iron. The steam vents should be located at the head of the soleplate to provide concentrated steam when it is needed. Be sure the iron has a wide temperature range for the best care of all your fashion fabrics. A controlled spray mechanism can also be helpful.

Ironing Board should be sturdy, level, and adjustable to different heights. Pad the board with cotton batting or purchased padding already cut to fit. Place a silicone treated cover over the surface to prevent scorching or sticking. Keep the cover smooth and soil free so as not to press wrinkles or stains into your fabric.

Press Cloths should be selected in relation to the weight of your fabric. They should be similar in weight for best results. Have at least two on hand: a transparent variety for seeing details, and a two-part wool and cotton type for most general pressing needs. For pressing on the right side, use a scrap of the garment fabric as a press cloth. Keep cheesecloth available for ready use as a press cloth. See Pressing, page 341, for more detailed information.

Tailor's Ham is an oblong, firmly stuffed cushion with subtly rounded curves. It is designed for pressing the curved areas of your garment such as darts, sleeve caps, princess seams, or any place that requires a rounded, curved shape pressed in. There are no substitutes for this item as it simulates actual body curves. Hams come in different sizes and should be covered in half cotton and half wool.

Press Mitt is similar to a tailor's ham, but small enough to fit over your hand. It has pockets on either side to protect your hand. The mitt is good for small hard-to-reach areas or it may be slipped over the end of a sleeve board for sleeve caps. It also may be covered on one side with wool and on the other with cotton.

Sleeve Board is actually two small ironing boards attached one on top of the other. They are designed for pressing small or slim areas, such as sleeves or necklines, that do not fit over your regular board. The sleeve board should also have a silicone cover and padding.

Seam Roll is a long, tubular, firmly stuffed cushion that is rounded at each end. It is used to press small curved areas and long seams in hard-to-reach areas such as sleeves. Because the roll is round, you press only the seam and not the surrounding fabric. This prevents ridges from forming on the right side. Again, one side should be covered with wool and the other side with cotton. To make a seam roll, cover a tightly rolled magazine with scraps of fabric.

Point Presser or Pressing Board is an important pressing aid. It is made of wood and provides many different shaped surfaces for pressing points, curves, and straight edges. The different sizes of curves and narrow straight edges allow you to press seams flat and open without wrinkling the surrounding area. The board can be used as it is for firm fabrics and sharp edges, or covered with a contoured pad for softer edges.

Pressing Pad is three or four thicknesses of soft fabric stitched together to make a padded surface for pressing monograms, buttonholes, sequinned fabric, and other raised surfaces. Place the raised surface face down on the pad and press on the wrong side. The pad prevents puckers and flattening of the decoration. A heavy turkish towel may be substituted.

Pounding Block or Clapper is a block of wood used with steam to flatten seam edges. It was originally designed to be used on hard-finished woolens and linens but it may be used to form soft rolled hems. It is a must for tailoring. First make as much steam as possible with steam iron and damp press cloth. Remove iron and cloth and pound firmly, regulating your pressure and slapping motion to suit the desired edge.

Needleboard is a bed of needles mounted on a flat surface that is placed between your fabric and the ironing board. It prevents flattening pile fabrics. When the fabric is placed face down on the board, the pile falls in between the needles. It is essential for pressing velvet and other high-piled fabrics and very useful when pressing easily marred woolens.

Sponge is a must for any type of pressing. It serves to moisten the press cloth and to mop up any unfortunate spills.

Brown Paper is an essential item to have on hand along with your other pressing tools. Strips should be placed under the folds of darts or the edges of pleats, etc., to avoid unsightly ridges from appearing on the right side.

Clothes Brush should always be available when pressing. Use it to raise the nap of the fabric after pressing to give it a fresh appearance or as a remedy when you have slightly overpressed. Of course, its greatest value is to remove stray threads and lint as you are applying the finishing touches to your garment.

Dress Form

Have you ever had to compromise on fit because you could not reach that puckered seam or extra back fullness? Such compromises could lead to disappointing results; as every fine seamstress knows, an accurate fit is as vital as good workmanship to the lovely look of a finished garment. The perfect solution to these and other tricky fitting problems is a dress form, which duplicates your figure and allows you to fit and alter from all angles.

There are a great variety of dress forms available to the woman who sews at home. The wire mesh variety is adjustable, but does not have a smooth contour or pinning surfaces. The classic fabric-covered cotton batting type is realistically and smoothly shaped, takes pins, and is ideal for working with very heavy fabrics or garments. However, it can be adjusted only by adding padding to the outside of the form (shoulder pads are good for this purpose, especially for adding to the bust shaping). The newest dress form on the sewing scene is the foam form covered with a fabric shell which can be individually fitted to your contours; it is adjustable, realistic, and will not be harmed by pinning fabric to its surface.

Whichever type you choose, it should have a heavy sturdy base and be adjustable for figure changes, different heights, and convenient storage. Compressible shoulders are also a definite plus, as they allow you to slip your garment on and off the form easily.

The most accurate dress form will be one which requires fitting the outer covering to your own individual body contours. Once it is identically matched to your shape, mark all important medians, curves, and joinings of your body (waistline, bustline, etc.) with indelible ink or twill tape basted to the covering. See pages 104 and 105 as well as the sketch on this page for the exact manner in which to locate and measure these areas. In addition to these basic measurements, you may also wish to add other personal measurements that you refer to often when sewing, such as your ideal jacket length or neckline curve. Remember to check your measurements occasionally to make sure your dress form is still accurate, and adjust accordingly if necessary.

Once you begin using a dress form as a part of your sewing equipment, you will be happily surprised at the many uses and convenience it provides. Fitting, of course, will be quicker, easier, and more accurate. You will also be able to see and understand more completely the reasoning behind darts, structured seams, and built-in ease. It will help you check such details as the fall of a hem or the roll of a collar before it is too late to easily make any necessary adjustments. You can steam press directly on the dress form to perfectly set design lines. Most importantly, you can stand away from your garment and see it as others will, giving you greater objectivity and a three-dimensional view you can't get in a mirror.

Sewing Machine

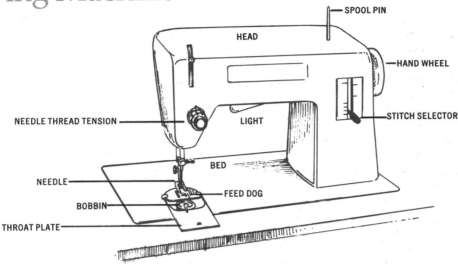

The sewing machine as we know it today has come a long way from the first rudimentary atempts to "stitch by machine." Now, anyone desiring a sewing machine is confronted with the results of an industrial evolution that has yielded an amazing variety of makes, models, and prices. The manufacturers, keeping pace with changing life styles, new fabrics, and the upsurge of fashion sewing, have reached a point where they can offer the public sewing machines to fit everyone's needs and skills. There are three basic types of sewing machines, categorized by the stitch performed:

Straight stitch machines can only stitch forward or backward. A zigzag attachment can be added to move the fabric from side to side.

Zigzag stitch machines, in addition to straight stitching, can stitch from side to side. Decorative variations must be manually arranged.

Automatic stitch machines automatically perform straight, stretch, chain, zigzag, and decorative stitches with built-in discs (pattern cams). Additional discs may be inserted for other variations.

When buying a sewing machine, you must first decide which type is best for your particular needs. Do some comparison shopping and ask for a demonstration of those that interest you. Try them out yourself for ease of handling and personal comfort. Find out what accessories are included with your model and be sure all parts are easily replaceable and that a repairman's services are available if necessary.

Once you have selected your sewing machine you should become familiar with certain elementary principles. First, you must know how the basic working parts operate: the light switch, stitch selector, take-up lever, reverse mechanism, etc. Most importantly, learn how to thread your machine, replace the needle correctly, and wind the bobbin. Refer to your sewing machine manual for this very specific information.

No matter what make or model you may own, there is one very important feature which is characteristic of all sewing machines—*the thread tension.* The strength of your seams depends upon using the correct thread tension. Before stitching any garment, you should test the tension and determine the correct stitch size on a fabric scrap as shown on the next page. Stitch about 3″ on the bias of both lengthwise and crosswise grains. It will be helpful to use a different color for the upper thread and the bobbin thread.

The upper tension controls the thread that goes through the needle. If it is too loose, the thread on the underside of your stitching will appear to lay flat on the surface of the fabric (1). Should the thread appear to lay flat on the upperside of your fabric, the upper tension is too tight (2). The ideal stitch is when the thread tensions are in balance and both threads are drawn equally into the fabric (3). To test further, hold the fabric at both ends of the stitching line and pull sharply until one of the threads breaks. The color of the broken thread will usually indicate which tension is too tight. If both threads require more force to break and break evenly, the tension is balanced. No matter which tension is wrong, the correction should always be made by adjusting the upper thread tension. *Do not* adjust the bobbin tension until you have exhausted all other methods possible.

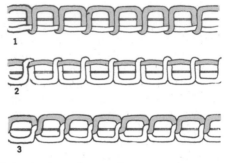

Machine Equipment

Needles can be found in sizes ranging from 9 (for delicate fabrics) to 18 (for heavyweight fabrics). Refer to the needle chart, pages 92-93, for the specific needle size recommended for your fabric. There are a variety of specialty needles available for specific sewing tasks: double or triple needle is mounted on a single base and is used for pattern stitching, ball-point needles are designed for sewing lingerie and elastic, cutting needles make sewing leather easier, and wing needles produce a hemstitch effect. Self-threading or slotted needles can also be purchased to make threading your needle easier.

Bobbins are made of either metal or plastic. Keep several wound with the basic colors you use most frequently. Have additional bobbins available to avoid winding one color thread over another. There are several types of bobbins, so consult your sewing machine's manual before purchasing them.

Tools to keep your machine in the best possible condition are vital. An assortment usually comes with your machine. The most important ones are a brush for removal of lint from the working parts, a small screw driver to open areas for easier cleaning, and sewing machine oil to keep the parts moving freely without friction and wear.

Special Feet

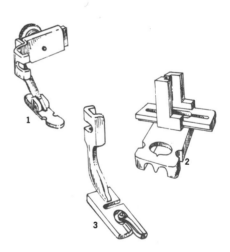

Zipper Foot is designed to stitch very close to a raised edge during straight stitching and can be adjusted to the right or left side of the needle. Used most often for zipper insertion, it can also be used for covering and applying cording in seams (1).

Invisible Zipper Foot consists of several plastic parts. They are assembled according to the style of invisible zipper as well as the make and model of your sewing machine (2).

Hemming Foot turns a narrow hem and stitches it in one operation with either straight or decorative stitches. It may be used to attach ruffles and lace and works best on lightweight fabrics (3).

Gathering Foot locks fullness into every stitch. It is used for both shirring and gathering (4).

Roller Foot is the answer to feeding hard-to-handle fabrics such as nylon, Dacron, or vinyl between the throat plate and the needle. The grid on the foot's round, rolling-pin type construction prevents fabric from slipping while stitching (5).

Button Foot will hold any two-hole or four-hole button securely for zigzag or automatic stitching. It should have a groove to hold a needle over which a thread shank can be formed (6).

Binder Foot applies packaged bias binding or self-fabric bias to an unfinished edge. It ensures a uniform binding without pinning and basting. Use it with either a straight or zigzag stitch (7).

Special Purpose Attachments

Straight Stitch Throat Plate should come with your machine. It has a small hole to prevent soft fabrics from being pulled down into the machine and puckering during stitching (not shown).

General Purpose Throat Plate is a must for zigzag and automatic stitching. It has a wider hole to accommodate the sideways motion of the needle (8).

Seam Guide attaches to the machine bed for accurate stitching of straight, curved, and topstitched seams. Some machines have markings on the throat plate for the same purpose (9).

Ruffler can make uniform gathered or pleated ruffles on light to medium-weight fabrics. Some make and attach them in one operation (10).

Buttonholer makes durable, strong, attractive buttonholes quickly and easily on all fabrics. All models come with templates to make different sizes ($5/16''$ to $1\frac{1}{2}''$) and types of buttonholes (11).

Tucker makes perfectly spaced tucks from $1/8''$ to $1''$ with straight or decorative stitch settings. It enables you to always sew tucks equal in width from beginning to end (12).

Edge Stitcher is used exclusively with straight stitching. It has slots that serve as guides for placement of stitching a specific distance from the edge, usually as close to the edge as possible (13).

Quilter consists of a short open foot and an adjustable space guide for accurately following curved lines and keeping stitching rows evenly parallel. Especially adaptable for lightly padded fabrics, it guides the placement of straight stitching on block, floral, or scroll designs (14).

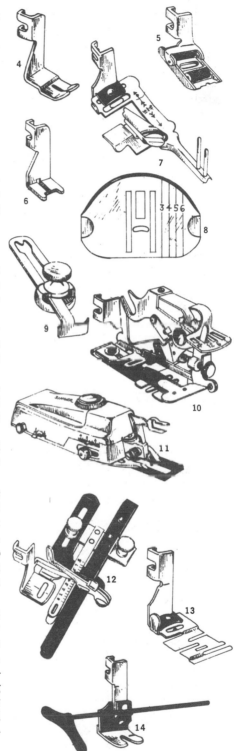

The Vocabulary of Fashion

This list of fashion terminology was collected to give you a firm grasp of the language used by designers and fashionable women everywhere. It includes terms commonly used to describe the silhouettes, styles, and details of clothing design as well as fabric qualities, notions, and construction procedures. We have also included a listing of French terms that have become part of our fashion vocabulary. A knowledgeable and conversational use of the words listed here will certainly increase your fashion confidence.

A-line Dress or skirt resembling shape of an A.

accessories Articles of apparel that complete a costume, shoes, jewelry, etc.

armscye Armhole; opening for a sleeve.

ascot Broad neckscarf; tied so that one end falls over the other.

asymmetrical One-sided, not geometrically balanced.

Backing Fabric joined to wrong side of garment or garment area, typically for reinforcement.

balmacaan Loose overcoat.

band Strip used to hold, ornament, or complete any part of garment or accessory.

bateau Neckline following curve of collar bone.

bell sleeve Full sleeve, flaring at lower edge like a bell.

bias Diagonal direction of fabric. *True bias* is at a 45° angle to grainlines.

binding Strip encasing edges as finish or trim.

bishop sleeve Sleeve that is full in the lower part, either loose or held by band at wrist.

blind hem Sewing hem invisibly with hand stitches.

blouson Bloused effect of fullness gathered in at and falling over a seam, typically bodice over skirt.

bodice Portion of garment above the waist.

bodkin Blunt needle used to pull fabric through narrow enclosed space, such as casing.

bolero Short jacket that ends above waist: Spanish origin.

bolt Unit in which fabric is packaged and sold by manufacturer. Usually contains 12-20 yards.

boning Flexible strips used to stiffen seams or edges.

Caftan Long, coat-like garment fastened with long sash, having extra long sleeves.

camisole Short, sleeveless underbodice; often joined to skirt and worn under jacket.

cap sleeve Short sleeve just covering the shoulder and not continued under the arm.

cape Sleeveless outer garment hanging loosely from shoulders, covering back and arms.

cardigan Close fitting collarless jacket, sweater, or bodice with center front closing.

cartridge pleat Rounded pleat which extends out rather than lying flat.

chesterfield Plain coat usually having velvet notched collar.

chevron V-shaped stripes.

clip Cut in fabric to allow ease on curves or corners.

closure That which opens or closes a garment (buttons, etc.), or area on which they are placed.

coatdress Dress with coatlike lines and front closing.

colorfast Refers to fabric which will not fade or run during cleaning or laundering.

contrasting Opposing; showing off differences of color, fabric, shading, etc.

convertible Notched collar which can be worn either buttoned at neck or open with lapels.

cowl Soft drape of fabric at neckline.

cravat Necktie folded or tied at front with ends tucked inside garment.

crew Round neckline that hugs the throat.

culotte Trouser-like garment with flaring leg portions to simulate a skirt.

cut-in-one Two or more sections cut in one piece, such as sleeve and bodice.

Dickey Detachable shirt front.

dirndl Garment with full gathered skirt.

dolman Sleeve set into a deep armhole so as to resemble a kimono sleeve.

double-breasted Front closing that overlaps enough to allow two rows of buttons.

dressmaking Sewing technique involving fine hand details.

drum lining Lining not sewn into garment seams.

Edgestitch Topstitching placed very close to finished edge.

edwardian Style of 1901-1910. Edward VII was king of England.

empire Style of French empire period; high waistline, décolleté, loose, straight skirt.

enclosed seams Concealed by two garment layers.

ensemble The entire costume. Usually, dress and coat.

epaulet Shoulder trimming, usually band secured with button.

epaulet sleeve Sleeve with square-cut shoulder section extending into neck in form of yoke. Strap sleeve.

eyelet Small, round finished hole in garment or fabric.

Face To finish an edge by applying a fitted piece of fabric, binding, etc. Also, the right side of the fabric.

fancy work Hand embroidery and needlework.

favoring Rolling one garment section slightly over another at the edge to conceal the seam.

feathering Removing stains by rubbing lightly in a circular motion from the outside edge of the stain to its center.

finger press Pressing small area by creasing with fingers.

finish Any means of completing raw garment edge.

flap Shaped garment piece attached by only one edge.

flare Portion of garment that spreads out or widens.

fly Fabric used as lap to conceal opening in garment.

full-fashioned Garments knitted flat and shaped by dropping stitches, in contrast to circular knits which are shaped by seams.

funnel collar Flaring outward at the top.

Godet Triangular piece of cloth set into a garment for fullness or decoration.

gore Tapered section of garment; wider at lower edge.

grommet Large metal eyelet.

grosgrain Fabric or, most commonly, ribbon having heavy crosswise ribs.

gusset Fabric piece inserted at underarm to give ease in sleeve area.

Halter Neckline having band around neck, attached at front to backless bodice.

harem pants Garment with legs softly draped and gathered to narrow lining.

Inset Fabric section or trim inserted within garment for fit or decoration.

interlining Layer of fabric between lining and underlining for warmth.

Jabot Ruffle worn down front of bodice and fastened at neck.

jerkin Short jacket, coat, or vest; usually sleeveless pullover.

jewel Simple, round neckline at base of neck.

jumper One-piece garment with low cut bodice attached to skirt.

jumpsuit Pants and bodice joined in one garment.

Keyhole Round neckline with inverted wedge-shaped opening at front.

kick pleat Pleat used for ease in a narrow skirt; may be a knife, inverted, or box pleat.

kilt Short pleated skirt.

kimono Loose, wide-sleeved robe, fastened at waist with obi; also used to describe style of sleeve.

Lantern sleeve Bell sleeve with wrist section joining at bottom, creating a shape resembling a lantern.

lap Any edge which extends over another edge, as on a placket.

lapels Part of garment that turns back, especially front neckline fold.

layout Cutting chart on instruction sheet showing placement of pattern pieces.

line Style, outline, or effect given by the cut and construction of the garment.

lingerie Women's lightweight underclothing.

longuette Style derived from below-knee hem lengths.

Macramé Bulky, knotted lace woven in geometrical patterns.

mandarin Small standing collar that hugs neck.

marking Transfer of construction symbols from paper pattern to fabric.

martingale A half belt or strap, generally placed on back of garment.

maxi Hem length falling between mid-calf and ankle.

middy Slip-on blouse with typical sailor collar.

midi Hem length falling at mid-calf.

mini Hem length falling at mid-thigh.

miter Diagonal seaming at a corner.

motif Unit of design; used as decoration or pattern.

mounting Term sometimes used for underlining. Two layers of fabric are basted together and sewn as one.

Nap Soft surface with fibers which lie smoothly in one direction.

negligée Decorative dressing gown, worn indoors by women.

notch v, Cutting wedges from seam allowances. n, Pattern symbol transferred to fabrics to indicate matching points.

notions Items other than fabric or pattern required to complete garment.

Obi Broad Japanese sash.

opening Synonymous with closure; also, fashion showing of apparel for season.

overblouse Blouse not tucked in at waistline.

overskirt Decorative skirt worn over another garment.

Pants suit Women's suit consisting of jacket with pants instead of skirt.

peasant sleeve Full sleeve set into dropped shoulder and usually gathered into wristband.

peignoir Originally, a robe of terrycloth worn instead of a towel; now, a robe that matches a nightgown.

pelt Skin of animal with fur intact.

peplum Small flounce or extension of garment around hips, usually from bodice.

peter pan Flat shaped collar, with round corners.

piece Specified length of goods as rolled from loom.

piece goods Fabric sold in pieces of fixed length or by the yard.

pin basting Pinning seams before stitching.

pinafore Sleeveless apron-like fashion worn over another garment.

pinking Cutting raw edge with pinking or scalloping shears to retard raveling.

pivot Stitching around corner by leaving needle in fabric, raising presser foot, and turning fabric in new direction.

placket Garment opening fastened with zipper, snaps, or buttons.

plunge Neckline cut so low as to reveal curve of breasts.

pre-fold Folding and pressing garment section or binding before applying to garment.

pre-shape Shaping fabric into curves like those of area to which it will be applied; done with steam before stitching to garment.

pre-shrink Contracting fabric before construction.

princess line Garment fitted with seams instead of darts.

purl Stitch made by bringing needle out across thread so as to hold it; also looped edge of embroidery, lace.

Raw edge Unfinished edge of fabric.

remnant Unsold end of piece goods, leftover piece of cloth.

right side Finished side of fabric, outside of garment.

rip Removing stitches improperly placed; also, tearing fabric along straight grain.

roll Desired curve and fold (commonly on a collar); shaping established by pressing, pad stitching, etc.

Sash Ornamental band or scarf worn around the body.

scalloped Cut into semi-circles at edge or border.

scoop Deep neckline cut to shape of U.

seam allowance Width of fabric beyond seamline, not including garment area.

seam binding Ribbon-like tape used to finish edges.

secure Fasten permanently by means of knot, backstitching, etc.

self Of same material as rest of garment.

selvage Lengthwise finished edges on all woven fabrics.

semi-fitted Fitted to conform partly, but not too closely, to shape of figure.

shank Link between button and fabric to allow for thickness of overlapping fabric.

shawl Triangular piece of fabric worn around shoulders.

sheath Close-fitting dress with straight skirt.

sheer Transparent fabric; comes in varying weights.

shift Loose-fitting dress.

shirtwaist Dress with bodice details similar to shirt.

shrinking Contracting fabric with steam or water to eliminate excess in specific area.

silhouette Outline or contour of figure or garment.

single-breasted Center front closing with enough flap to allow one row of buttons.

slash Cut taken in fabric to facilitate construction.

slit Long, narrow opening; also, to cut lengthwise.

soft suit Dressy suit with a minimum of inner construction, also *dressmaker suit*.

sportswear Garments meant for informal or casual wear.

stay Means of maintaining shape of garment area.

stiletto Pointed instrument for punching holes in fabric; smaller version called *awl*.

stole Long scarf wrapped around shoulders.

Tab Small flap or loop attached at one end.

tack Joining two garment layers with small, loose hand-stitches or thread loop.

tailoring Construction technique requiring special hand sewing and pressing to mold fabric into finished garment.

taper Cutting or stitching at slight diagonal, generally to make gradually smaller.

tension Amount of pull on thread or fabric during construction.

thread count Number of threads in one square inch of fabric.

topstitching Line of machine stitching parallel to seam or edge, done from right side of garment.

train Extended part of garment, usually wedding dress, which trails at back.

transfer pattern Commercial pattern having design stamped on paper, usually transferred to fabric by iron.

trim To cut away excess fabric.

trimming Feature added to garment for ornamentation.

tunic Long top, worn over garment.

turnover A garment section, usually collar or cuff, which folds back upon itself.

turtleneck High turnover collar that hugs throat.

twill tape Firmly woven tape.

Underlining Fabric joined in garment seams to give inner shape or support.

V-neck Neckline shaped in front like the letter V.

vane Web or flat extended part of a feather.

vent Faced or lined slash in garment for ease.

vest Short, close-fitting garment without sleeves, similar to man's waistcoat.

Welt Strip of material stitched to seam, border, or edge.

wrap-around Garment or part of a garment wrapped around person, as cape or skirt.

wrong side Side of fabric on inside of garment.

Yardage block Guide on back of pattern envelope; includes garment description, measurement, yardage, notions, etc.

yoke Fitted portion of garment, usually at shoulders or hips, designed to support rest of garment hanging from it.

French Fashion Terms

Aiguille (e-gwee-y) Needle.

allonger (a-*lohn*-zhay) To lengthen, to give a longer appearance.

amincir (a-*men*-seer) To make thin; to give a slender look.

appliqué (a-plee-kay) Motif applied to cloth or garment.

atelier (a-te-lyay) Dressmaking establishment; work room or studio.

au courant (oh-koo-*rahn*) Up to the moment; to know all about it.

avant-garde (a-*vahn*-gard) Ahead of fashion; of trend.

Bon goût (bohn-*goo*) Good taste.

border (bawr-day) To finish an edge with self–fabric or commercial trimming.

boutique (boo-teek) A small retail store in which accessories and miscellaneous fashion items are sold. Often part of a couture house.

boutonnière (boo-tow-nyer) Buttonhole.

broder (braw-day) To embroider, embellish.

Chemise (shmeez) Blouse or style with manshirt details.

chez (shay) At home, shop of; as chez Dior, Lanvin, etc.

chic (sheek) Originality and style in dress.

collection (kaw-lek-*syohn*) All apparel exhibited at fashion showing. Spring and fall are the two major periods each year when collections are shown to trade and clientèle (customers).

confection (*kohn*-fek-*syohn*) Ready to wear.

corsage (kawr-sazh) Dress bodice.

coudre (koodr) To sew, to stitch.

cousu main (koo-zü-*men*) Hand stitched.

couture (koo-tür) Sewing or needle work. Product of a seamstress; seam.

couturier (koo-tü-ryay) Male dressmaker; designer; head of dressmaking house.

couturière (koo-tü-ryare) Woman dressmaker; designer.

Dé (day) Thimble.

décolleté (day-kawl-tay) Cut low at neckline, exposing neck and back or cleavage of bosom as in formal evening dress.

démodé (day-maw-day) Old fashioned, out-of-style, unfashionable.

denteler (*dahn*-tlay) To notch, to serrate.

dernier cri (dern-yay-kree) The latest fashion; the last word.

Elegance (ay-lay-gahns) Quality of being elegant; tasteful luxury.

étoffe (ay-tawf) Fabric, cloth, goods, material; also quality, worth.

Façon (fa-*shon*) Make, shape, fashion cut.

fermeture (fer-me-tur) Closing, clasp, fastener.

feston (fes-*tohn*) Buttonhole stitch, especially as used on decorated or scalloped edge.

fleur de lis (fler-de -lee) Lily flower; heraldic emblem of former French royalty. Used as design in fabric, embroidery, jewelry, etc.

fourreau (foo-roh) Fitted or semi-fitted, sheath-like dress.

froncer (fro*hn*-say) To gather or pucker.

Garni (gar-nee) Trimmed, garnished.

garniture (gar-nee-tur) Ornamental trimming.

gaufré (go-fray) Fluted.

Haute couture (oh-koo-tur) High fashion, creative fashion design. Couturier houses as a group.

Idée flèche (ee-day-flesh) Idea that gets ahead, leads.

Jupe (zhup) Skirt.

Maison de couture (me-*zohn*-de-koo-tur) Dressmaking establishment.

manchette (ma*hn*-shet) Cuff or waistband. (Bouton de manchette—cuff link) .

mannequin (man-*ken*) Dressmaker form, dummy. Person wearing new clothes to present at fashion show or collection.

matelasser (ma-tla-say) To pad or cushion.

mode (mawd) Fashion, manner, vogue.

modèle (maw-del) Model to be copied, style of dress.

modelliste (maw-de-leest) A dress designer attached to a fashion house; one whose designs are shown under the name of the house.

Ouvrage à l'aiguille (oo-vrazh-a-lay-gwee-y) Needlework, hand sewing.

Passementerie (pahs-*mahn*-tree) Trimming, particularly heavy embroideries or edgings.

patte (pat) Flap, tab, or strap both decorative and functional.

patron (pa-*trohn*) Male boss; dress pattern.

plissé (pleesay) Pleated cotton with puckered stripes or pattern.

première (pre-myay) Experienced dressmaker in charge of the seamstresses of a dressmaking establishment.

prêt à porter (pre-ah-portay) Ready to wear; more current than "confection."

Répertoire (rep-e-twar) Collection of works by a designer.

Soigné (swa-nyay) Well-groomed, highly finished, carefully done.

soutache (soo-tash) Narrow braid trim.

Taille (tie-y) Size, waist.

tissu (tee-su) Textile, fabric; texture.

toile (twahl) Linen or cotton cloth. Muslin copy of a design, purchased by firms who wish to copy original models. Sometimes made by dressmakers to show customers garments that they are prepared to copy.

Velours (ve-loor) Velvet; velveteen. Fabric raised on surface in finishing to have close, erect, and even nap providing soft, lush look. (Veau-velours — calfskin worked as to resemble velvet).

vendeuse (vahn-doos) Saleswoman. In Paris dressmaking houses, the saleswoman is an important staff member.

volant (vaw-*lahn*) Flounce.

Index

List of Color Plates